CONTEMPORARY STRATEGY ANALYSIS

To Sue

SIXTH EDITION

CONTEMPORARY STRATEGY ANALYSIS

ROBERT M. GRANT

Blackwell
Publishing

© 1991, 1995, 1998, 2002, 2005, 2008 by Robert M. Grant

BLACKWELL PUBLISHING
350 Main Street, Malden, MA 02148-5020, USA
9600 Garsington Road, Oxford OX4 2DQ, UK
550 Swanston Street, Carlton, Victoria 3053, Australia

First edition published 1991
Second edition published 1995
Third edition published 1998
Fourth edition published 2002
Fifth edition published 2005
Sixth edition published 2008 by Blackwell Publishing Ltd

1   2008

Library of Congress Cataloging-in-Publication Data

Grant, Robert M., 1948–
    Contemporary strategy analysis / Robert M. Grant.—6th ed.
        p. cm.
    Includes bibliographical references and index.
    ISBN 978-1-4051-6308-8 (hardcover : alk. paper)—ISBN 978-1-4051-6309-5 (pbk. : alk. paper)
1. Strategic planning.   I. Title.

    HD30.28.G72 2008
    658.4′012—dc22

                                                                                                2007003858

A catalogue record for this title is available from the British Library.

Set in 10/12pt Classical Garamond
by Graphicraft Limited, Hong Kong
Printed and bound in the United Kingdom
by TJ International, Padstow, Cornwall

The publisher's policy is to use permanent paper from mills that operate a sustainable forestry policy, and which has been manufactured from pulp processed using acid-free and elementary chlorine-free practices. Furthermore, the publisher ensures that the text paper and cover board used have met acceptable environmental accreditation standards.

For further information on
Blackwell Publishing, visit our website:
www.blackwellpublishing.com

BRIEF CONTENTS

CONTENTS

PREFACE

The purpose of *Contemporary Strategy Analysis* is to equip managers and students of management with the core concepts, frameworks, and techniques of strategic management that will allow them to make better decisions both for their companies and themselves. To achieve this I have written a book that endeavors to be both rigorous and relevant.

The approach is analytical. If strategic management is all about managing to achieve outstanding success, then the essential tasks of strategy are to identify the sources of superior business performance and to formulate and implement a strategy that exploits these sources of superior performance. The result is a book that is simultaneously theoretical and practical. It is theoretical to the extent that it concentrates on the fundamental drivers of business success. It is practical to the extent that acquiring deep insight into the determinants of business success is the basis for developing strategies that work.

The sixth edition of the book reflects the changing thinking about business strategy and the forces reshaping today's business environment during this first tumultuous decade of the 21st century.

At the most fundamental level has been the debate over the underlying purpose of business enterprises. The excesses of 1998 to 2002 did much to discredit shareholder value maximization as the fundamental goal of the firm and encourage a greater emphasis on corporate social responsibility. For the purposes of strategy analysis, my book focuses resolutely on the pursuit of long-run profitability. Hence, strategy analysis is concerned with identifying and exploiting the sources of profit. At the same time, I acknowledge that making money is not necessarily the primary *purpose* of a business and recognize that long-run profitability and survival require that the business reconciles itself with the social, political, and cultural forces that have an impact upon it.

In terms of the business environment, two key features of this decade are competition and turbulence. Innovation, entrepreneurship, and the dissolution of national and industry boundaries all increase the intensity of competition. As a result, the quest for competitive advantage becomes critical for survival. My primary goal for the sixth edition has been to sharpen and develop the analysis of competitive advantage through a stronger focus on the need to identify, develop, and exploit the resources and capabilities of the enterprise.

As the rate of change of the business environment continues to accelerate – driven by technology, deregulation, changing customer preferences, and volatile exchange rates and commodity prices – the implications for strategic management are far reaching. At the most basic level, strategy making extends beyond questions of resource deployment and market positioning to address fundamental questions such as: What is our business? What are we trying to achieve? What is our identity as an organization? Managing under conditions of rapid change also requires new approaches to strategy analysis. We shall explore the analysis of real options, patterns of industry evolution, the sources of strategic innovation, and the implications of complexity theory.

The harsh realities of this first decade of the 21st century have dispelled the hubris and "irrational exuberance" that characterized the end of the 1990s and punctured optimistic notions of the "New Economy" and the potential for technology and new business models to rewrite the rules of business. The outcome has been a reaffirmation of the fundamental principles of strategy, notably the need to base business strategies on understanding customer needs, competition, and the internal strengths and weaknesses of firms.

Finally, this new edition of *Contemporary Strategy Analysis* reaffirms the codependence of strategy formulation and strategy implementation. Unlike some other strategy texts, I do not split the book into separate sections for strategy formulation and strategy implementation. I offer an integrated approach to strategy formulation and implementation in the belief that these cannot be treated in isolation from one another. A strategy that is formulated without regard to its implementation is likely to be fatally flawed. At the same time, it is through their implementation that strategies adapt and emerge. Hence, I introduce organizational design as part of the basic toolkit of strategy analysis (Part II of the book). Subsequent chapters that explore different types of strategy and different business contexts provide an integrated treatment of strategy formulation and strategy implementation. At the same time, I set limits on how far down the path of strategy implementation it is sensible to travel. Ultimately, strategy implementation takes us into the functional areas of the business – finance, marketing, operations, human resource management, and information systems. I leave these functions to their own specialists.

There is very little in this book that is original – I have plundered mercilessly the ideas, theories, and evidence of fellow scholars. My greatest debts are to my colleagues and students at the business schools where this book has been developed and tested – Georgetown University, City University, UCLA, California Polytechnic, University of British Columbia, and Bocconi University. This edition has also benefitted from feedback and suggestions from professors and students in other schools where *Contemporary Strategy Analysis* is used. I am grateful to all of you. I continue to learn and look forward to sharing that learning with you.

Robert M. Grant
Washington DC
March 2007

I

INTRODUCTION

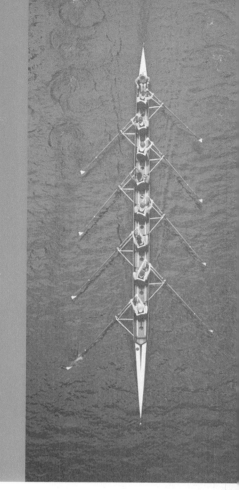

1

The Concept of Strategy

Strategy is the great work of the organization. In situations of life or death, it is the Tao of survival or extinction. Its study cannot be neglected.

—SUN TZU, THE ART OF WAR

OUTLINE

- Introduction and Objectives

- The Role of Strategy in Success

- The Basic Framework for Strategy Analysis
  What's Wrong With SWOT?
  Strategic Fit

- A Brief History of Business Strategy
  Origins and Military Antecedents
  From Corporate Planning to Strategic Management

- Strategic Management Today
  What Is Strategy?
  Corporate and Business Strategy
  Describing a Firm's Strategy
  How Is Strategy Made? Design vs.
      Emergence
  Multiple Roles of Strategy

- The Role of Analysis in Strategy Formulation

- Summary

- Self-Study Questions

- Notes

Introduction and Objectives

Strategy is about winning. This chapter explains what strategy is and why it is important to success – both for organizations and individuals. We will distinguish strategy from planning. Strategy is not a detailed plan or program of instructions; it is a unifying theme that gives coherence and direction to the actions and decisions of an individual or an organization.

The principal task of this chapter will be to introduce the basic framework for strategy analysis that underlies this book. I will introduce the two basic components of strategy analysis: analysis of the external environment of the firm (mainly industry analysis) and the analysis of the internal environment (primarily analysis of the firm's resources and capabilities).

By the time you have completed this chapter, you will be able to:

- Appreciate the contribution that strategy can make to successful performance, both for individuals and for organizations.

- Recognize the key characteristics of an effective strategy.

- Understand the basic framework of strategy analysis that underlies this book and that we shall use both for appraising a firm's current strategy and making recommendations for future strategy.

- Understand the major trends in the development of business strategy over recent decades.

- Understand how strategy is made within organizations and the role played by strategic planning systems.

Since the purpose of strategy is to help us to win, we start by looking at the role of strategy in success.

The Role of Strategy in Success

Strategy Capsules 1.1, 1.2, and 1.3 outline examples of success in three very different arenas: Madonna in popular entertainment, General Giap and the North Vietnamese armed forces in warfare, and Lance Armstrong in cycling. Can the success of these diverse individuals and the organizations they led be attributed to any common factors?

For none of these three examples can success be attributed to overwhelmingly superior resources:

- Madonna possesses vitality, intelligence, and magnetism, but lacks outstanding talents as a vocalist, musician or actress.
- The military, human, and economic resources of the Vietnamese communists were dwarfed by those of the United States and South Vietnam. Yet, with the US evacuation from Saigon in 1975, the world's most powerful nation was humiliated by one of the world's poorest.
- Lance Armstrong possessed a powerful combination of physical and psychological attributes. Yet these endowments were not markedly superior to other top-class cyclists – especially after Armstrong's near-death encounter with cancer.

Nor can their success be attributed either exclusively or primarily to luck. For all three, lucky breaks provided opportunities at critical junctures. None, however, was the beneficiary of a consistent run of good fortune. More important than luck was the ability to recognize opportunities when they appeared and to have the clarity of direction and the flexibility necessary to exploit these chances.

My contention is that the key common ingredient in all three success stories was the presence of a soundly formulated and effectively implemented *strategy*. These strategies did not exist as a plan; in most the strategy was not even made explicit. Yet, in all three, we can observe a consistency of direction based on a clear understanding of the "game" being played and a keen awareness of how to maneuver into a position of advantage.

1 Underpinning Madonna's many years as a superstar has been a strategy built on dedication, opportunism, periodic reinvention of image and product offerings, and a well-coordinated multimarket presence.

2 The victory of the Vietnamese communist forces over the French and then the Americans is a classic example of how a sound strategy pursued with total commitment over a long period can succeed against vastly superior resources. The key was Giap's strategy of a protracted war of limited engagement. With American forces constrained by domestic and international opinion from using their full military might, the strategy was unbeatable once it began to sap the willingness of the US government to persevere with a costly, unpopular foreign war.

3 Lance Armstrong's domination of the Tour de France from 1999 to 2005 was because he and his team did the most effective job of analyzing the requirements for success in the race, developing a strategy around those requirements, and executing it almost faultlessly.

STRATEGY CAPSULE 1.1

Madonna

August 2006 saw the 48th birthday of Madonna Louise Veronica Ciccone but no slowdown in her hectic career. Her world concert tour was in its European leg. *Confessions on a Dancefloor*, upon which the show was based, had reached number 1 position in 40 countries. Together with her earnings from film, video, books, record production, and managing other artists, it looked as though Madonna would be the world's highest earning female entertainer for yet another year and still the best-known woman on earth.

In the summer of 1978, aged 19, Madonna arrived in New York with $35 to her name. After five years of struggle, she landed a recording contract. *Madonna* (1983) ultimately sold 10 million copies worldwide, while *Like a Virgin* (1984) topped 12 million copies. Between 1985 and 1990, six further albums, three world tours, and five movie roles had established Madonna with an image and persona that transcended any single field of entertainment: she was rock singer, actor, author, and pinup. Yet, she was more than this – as her website proclaims, she is "icon, artist, provocateur, diva, and mogul." She has also made a great deal of money.

What is the basis of Madonna's incredible and lasting success? Certainly not outstanding natural talent. As a vocalist, musician, dancer, songwriter, or actress, Madonna's talents seem modest. Few would regard her as an outstanding beauty.

She possesses relentless drive. Her wide range of activities – records, concerts, music videos, movies, books, and charity events – belies a remarkable dedication to a single goal: the quest for superstar status. For close to 30 years, Madonna has worked incessantly to establish, maintain, and renew her popular appeal. She is widely regarded as a workaholic who survives on little sleep and rarely takes vacations: "I am a very disciplined person. I sleep a certain number of hours each night, then I like to get up and get on with it. All that means that I am in charge of everything that comes out."

She has drawn heavily on the talents of others: writers, musicians, choreographers, and designers. Many of her personal relationships have been stepping stones to career transitions. Her transition from dance to music was assisted by relationships, first, with musician Steve Bray, then with disc jockey John Benitex. Her entry into Hollywood was accompanied by marriage to Sean Penn and an affair with Warren Beatty. Most striking has been her continuous reinvention of her image. From street-kid look of the early 1980s, to hard-core sexuality of the 90s, and spiritual image that accompanied motherhood, Madonna's fans have been treated with multiple reincarnations. As Jeff Katzenberg of Dreamworks observed: "She has always had a vision of exactly who she is, whether performer or businesswoman, and she has been strong enough to balance it all. Every time she comes up with a new look it is successful. When it happens once, OK, maybe it's luck, but twice is a coincidence, and three times it's got to be a remarkable talent. And Madonna's on her fifth or sixth time."

She was quick to learn the ropes both in Tin Pan Alley and in Hollywood. Like Evita Perón, whom Madonna portrayed in *Evita*, Madonna has combined determination, ambition, social acumen, and mastery of the strategic use of sex. As a self-publicist she is without equal. In using sex as a marketing tool, she has courted controversy through nudity, pornographic imagery, suggestions of sexual deviance, and the juxta-position of sexual and religious themes. But she is also astute at walking the fine line between the shocking and the unacceptable. In recent years Madonna has devoted increasing time to nurturing the talents of others, mainly through her recording, film production, and management company, Maverick Inc., a joint venture with Time Warner. Her protégés included Mirwais, William Orbit, Donna De Lory, and the Deftones, and the comedian Ali G: "I've met these people along the way in my career and I want to take them everywhere I go. I want to incorporate them into my little factory of ideas. I also come into contact with a lot of young talent that I feel entrepreneurial about."

We can go further. What do these examples tell us about the characteristics of a strategy that are conducive to success? In all three stories, four common factors stand out (see Figure 1.1):

1 *Goals that are simple, consistent, and long term.* All three individuals displayed a single-minded commitment to a clearly recognized goal that was pursued steadfastly over a substantial part of their lifetime.

- Madonna's career featured a relentless drive for stardom in which other dimensions of her life were either subordinated to or absorbed within her career goals.
- North Vietnamese efforts were unified and focused on the ultimate goal of reuniting Vietnam under communist rule and expelling a foreign army from Vietnamese soil. By contrast, US efforts in Vietnam were bedeviled by confused objectives. Was the United States supporting an ally, stabilizing Southeast Asia, engaging in a proxy war against the Soviet Union, or pursuing an ideological struggle against world communism?
- On his return to professional cycling in 1998, Lance Armstrong committed to a single goal: winning the Tour de France.

FIGURE 1.1 Common elements in successful strategies

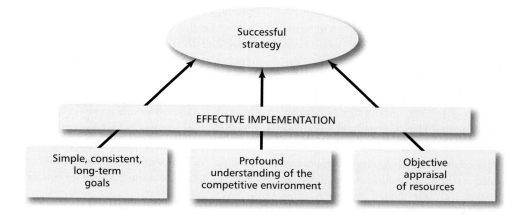

STRATEGY CAPSULE 1.2

General Giap and the Vietnam Wars, 1948–75

As far as logistics and tactics were concerned, we succeeded in everything we set out to do. At the height of the war the army was able to move almost a million soldiers a year in and out of Vietnam, feed them, clothe them, house them, supply them with arms and ammunition and generally sustain them better than any army had ever been sustained in the field . . . On the battlefield itself, the army was unbeatable. In engagement after engagement the forces of the Vietcong and the North Vietnamese Army were thrown back with terrible losses. Yet, in the end, it was North Vietnam, not the United States that emerged victorious. How could we have succeeded so well yet failed so miserably?[1]

Despite having the largest army in Southeast Asia, North Vietnam was no match for South Vietnam so long as the South was backed by the world's most powerful military and industrial nation. South Vietnam and its United States ally were defeated not by superior resources but by a superior strategy. North Vietnam achieved what Sun Tzu claimed was the highest form of victory: the enemy gave up.

The prime mover in the formulation of North Vietnam's military strategy was General Vo Nguyen Giap. In 1944, Giap became head of the Vietminh guerrilla forces. He was commander-in-chief of the North Vietnamese Army until 1974 and Minister of Defense until 1980. Giap's strategy was based on Mao Tse Tung's three-phase theory of revolutionary war: first, passive resistance during which political support is mobilized; second, guerrilla warfare aimed at

weakening the enemy and building military strength; finally, general counteroffensive. In 1954, Giap's brilliant victory over the French at Dien Bien Phu fully vindicated the strategy. Against South Vietnam and its US ally, the approach was similar.

Our strategy was . . . to wage a long-lasting battle . . . Only a long-term war could enable us to utilize to the maximum our political trump cards, to overcome our material handicap, and to transform our weakness into strength. To maintain and increase our forces was the principle to which we adhered, contenting ourselves with attacking when success was certain, refusing to give battle likely to incur losses.[2]

The strategy built on the one resource where the communists had overwhelming superiority: their will to fight. As Prime Minister Pham Van Dong explained: "The United States is the most powerful nation on earth. But Americans do not like long, inconclusive wars . . . We can outlast them and we can win in the end."[3] Limited military engagement and the charade of the Paris peace talks helped the North Vietnamese prolong the conflict, while diplomatic efforts to isolate the United States from its Western allies and to sustain the US peace movement accelerated the crumbling of American will to win.

The effectiveness of the US military response was limited by two key uncertainties: what were the objectives and who was the enemy? Was the US role one of supporting the South Vietnamese regime, fighting Vietcong terrorism, inflicting a military defeat on North Vietnam, or combating world communism? Lack of unanimity over goals translated into confusion as to who was the enemy and whether the war was military or political in scope. Diversity of opinion and a shifting balance of political and public opinion were fatal for establishing a consistent long-term strategy.

The consistency and strength of North Vietnam's strategy allowed it to survive errors in implementation. Giap was premature in launching his general offensive. Both the 1968 Tet Offensive and 1972 Easter Offensive were beaten back with heavy losses. By 1974, Giap recognized that the Watergate scandal had so weakened the US presidency that an effective American response to a new communist offensive was unlikely. On April 29, 1975, Operation Frequent Wind began evacuating all remaining Americans from South Vietnam, and the next morning North Vietnamese troops entered the Presidential Palace in Saigon.

Sources: [1] Col. Harry G. Summers Jr., *On Strategy* (Novato, CA: Presidio Press, 1982): 1; [2] Vo Nguyen Giap, *Selected Writings* (Hanoi: Foreign Language Publishing House, 1977); [3] J. Cameron, *Here Is Your Enemy* (New York: Holt, Rinehart, Winston, 1966).

2 *Profound understanding of the competitive environment.* All three individuals designed their strategies around a deep and insightful appreciation of the arena in which they were competing.

- Fundamental to Madonna's continuing success has been a shrewd understanding of the ingredients of stardom and the basis of popular appeal. This extends from the basic marketing principle that "sex sells" to recognition of the need to manage gatekeepers of the critical media distribution channels. Her periodic reincarnations reflect an acute awareness of changing attitudes, styles, and social norms.
- Giap understood his enemy and the battlefield conditions where he would engage them. Most important was appreciation of the political predicament of US presidents in their need for popular support in waging a foreign war.
- Lance Armstrong and team director Johan Bruyneel took analysis of the requirements for success in the Tour de France to unprecedented levels of detail and sophistication.

3 *Objective appraisal of resources.* All three strategies were effective in exploiting internal strengths, while protecting areas of weakness.

- By positioning herself as a "star," Madonna exploited her abilities to develop and project her image, to self-promote, and to exploit emerging trends, while avoiding being judged simply as a rock singer or an actress. Her live performances rely heavily on a large team of highly qualified dancers, musicians, vocalists, choreographers, and technicians, thus compensating for any weaknesses in her own performing capabilities.
- Giap's strategy was carefully designed to protect against his army's deficiencies in arms and equipment, while exploiting the commitment and loyalty of his troops.
- Armstrong's campaign to win the Tour de France was based on two key strengths: unmatched determination to win and superior team building capability.

STRATEGY CAPSULE 1.3
Lance Armstrong and the Tour de France

On July 24, 2005, Lance Armstrong became the first person ever to win the Tour de France seven times. Armstrong's unprecedented achievement was all the more remarkable for the fact that in 1996 Armstrong was treated for testicular cancer that had spread to his lungs and brain.

Even without cancer, Lance Armstrong was not an obvious candidate for title of the greatest cyclist ever. Despite certain natural advantages – notably a heart 30% larger than normal with an abnormally slow beat rate (32 times per minute while at rest) – Armstrong's aerobic rate was less than that of cycling greats such as Miguel Indurain and Greg LeMond. For most of his career, Armstrong was not the world's preeminent cyclist. He won the world championship just once (1993) and his Olympic best was a bronze medal in the 2000 Sydney games.

Armstrong's seven-year dominance of the Tour de France resulted from a combination of factors, not least of which was his single-minded focus, not just on cycling, but on a single race. Between his 1999 and 2005 Tour de France victories, Armstrong was overall winner in only five other cycle races.

Armstrong raised planning for the Tour to a new level of sophistication. His meticulous preparations included: ". . . computer calculations that balanced my body weight and my equipment weight with the potential velocity of my bike," and "careful computer graphs of my training rides, calibrating the distances, wattages, and thresholds." Armstrong's abilities were well-suited to the Tour – as well as all-round strengths as a cyclist, he developed mastery of bluff and psychological warfare. His feigning exhaustion at critical junctures before devastating his rivals with a powerful breakaway has been deemed "worthy of a Hollywood Oscar." However, it was in team planning and coordination where the major differences between Armstrong and his competitors were most evident.

While the principal prize in the Tour de France is for the individual who achieves the fastest overall time, cyclists compete within teams. The team coordination and the willingness of the other team members (*domestiques*) to sacrifice themselves for the team leader is critical to individual success. Armstrong's US Postal Service team (which became the Discovery Channel team for the 2005 Tour) was remarkable not just for the quality of other team members, but the willingness of these world class cyclists to serve their leader. Olympic gold medal winner Viatcheslav Ekimov – "The Russian Power House" – was critical to pulling Armstrong through the flatter stages of the Tour. Roberto Heras and Jose Asevedo were Armstrong's main support in the mountains – shielding him from the wind and supporting him during breakaways. George Hinkapie rode in all seven of Armstrong's Tour victories as a versatile all-rounder. Why did the team show a unique degree of loyalty to their team leader? Part was Armstrong's infectious commitment, part was his willingness to pay bonuses out of his own pocket to other riders, but also important was reciprocity – while team members gave total support to Armstrong on the Tour de France, in other competitions the roles were reversed and Armstrong served as a *domestique* to other team members.

The team's strategy genius was director, Johan Bruyneel, whose unrivaled knowledge of the Tour spanned sports physiology, game theory, psychology, and tactics. As well as selecting team members, assigning roles, designing overall strategy and planning tactics for individual stages, Bruyneel managed a network of secret agreements with other teams. In return for financial support, other teams agreed to support Armstrong should he find himself split from his own team members. In addition to the conventional roles as team decision maker, enforcer of team discipline, preparation and planning, Bruyneel gave continuous attention to team dynamics: he was a careful listener, encouraged discussion, and welcomed new ideas. Together, Armstrong and Bruyneel recognized a critical ingredient for success: in a sport of independently minded individualists where only the team leader is recognized as the winner, team commitment and loyalty are critical and fragile. A unique feature of the USPS/Discovery team was Armstrong and Bruyneel's fostering of camaraderie, joint ambition, mutual support, and shared emotions.

4   *Effective implementation*. Without effective implementation, the best-laid strategies are of little use. Critical to the success of Madonna, Giap, and Armstong was their effectiveness as leaders in terms of capacity to reach decisions, energy in implementing them, and ability to foster loyalty and commitment among subordinates. All three built organizations that allowed effective marshaling of resources and capabilities, and quick responses to changes in the competitive environment.

These observations about the role of strategy in success can be made in relation to most fields of human endeavor. Whether we look at warfare, chess, politics, sport, or business, the success of individuals and organizations is seldom the outcome of a purely random process. Nor is superiority in initial endowments of skills and resources typically the determining factor. Strategies that build on the basic four elements almost always play an influential role.

Look at the "high achievers" in any competitive area. Whether we review the world's political leaders, the CEOs of the Fortune 500, or our own circles of friends and acquaintances, those who have achieved outstanding success in their careers are seldom those who possessed the greatest innate abilities. Success has gone to those who managed their careers most effectively – typically by combining the four strategic factors mentioned above. They are goal focused; their career goals have taken primacy over the multitude of life's other goals – friendship, love, leisure, knowledge, spiritual fulfillment – which the majority of us spend most of our lives juggling and reconciling. They know the environments within which they play and tend to be fast learners in terms of understanding the keys to advancement. They know themselves in terms of both strengths and weaknesses. And they implement their career strategies with commitment, consistency, and determination. As the late Peter Drucker observed: "we must learn how to be the CEO of our own careers."[1]

There is a downside, however. Focus on a single goal may lead to outstanding success, but may be matched by dismal failure in other areas of life. Many people who have reached the pinnacles of their careers have led lives scarred by poor relationships with friends and families and stunted personal development. These include Howard Hughes and Jean Paul Getty in business, Richard Nixon and Joseph Stalin in politics, Marilyn Monroe and Elvis Presley in entertainment, Joe Louis and O. J. Simpson in sport, and Bobby Fischer in chess. Fulfillment in our personal lives is likely to require broad-based lifetime strategies.[2]

These same ingredients of successful strategies – clear goals, understanding the competitive environment, resource appraisal, and effective implementation – form the key components of our analysis of business strategy.

The Basic Framework for Strategy Analysis

Figure 1.2 shows the basic framework for strategy analysis that we shall use throughout the book. The four elements of a successful strategy shown in Figure 1.1 are recast into two groups – the firm and the industry environment – with strategy forming a link between the two. The firm embodies three sets of these elements: goals and values ("simple, consistent, long-term goals"), resources and capabilities ("objective appraisal of resources"), and structure and systems ("effective implementation").

The industry environment ("profound understanding of the competitive environment") represents the core of the firm's external environment and is defined by the firm's relationships with customers, competitors, and suppliers. Hence, we view strategy as forming a link between the firm and its external environment.

The task of business strategy, then, is to determine how the firm will deploy its resources within its environment and so satisfy its long-term goals, and how to organize itself to implement that strategy.

What's Wrong With SWOT?

Distinguishing between the external and the internal environment of the firm is common to most approaches to strategy analysis. The best known and most widely used of these approaches is the "SWOT" framework, which classifies the various influences on a firm's strategy into four categories: Strengths, Weaknesses, Opportunities, and Threats. The first two – strengths and weaknesses – relate to the internal environment; the last two – opportunities and threats – relate to the external environment.[3]

Which is better, a two-way distinction between internal and external influences or the four-way SWOT taxonomy? The key issue is whether it is sensible and worthwhile to classify internal factors into strengths and weaknesses and external factors into opportunities and threats. In practice, such distinctions are difficult:

FIGURE 1.2 The basic framework: strategy as a link between the firm and its environment

- Is BMW's German home base a strength or a weakness for BMW? Its German origins are fundamental for its reputation for engineering excellence and the skills of its German-based engineers and technicians are essential to its claim to be the "world's ultimate driving machine." At the same time, Germany is a high-cost country with an inflexible labor market and is subject to a plethora of European Union regulations. Hence, BMW's German home base is both a strength and a weakness.

- Is global warming a threat or an opportunity to the world's automobile producers? Global warming may encourage governments to raise taxes on motor fuels and support public transport, thereby threatening the demand for private motoring. At the same time, these circumstances create an opportunity for developing new, fuel-efficient cars that may encourage consumers to scrap their gas-guzzlers.

The lesson here is that an arbitrary classification of external factors into opportunities and threats, and internal factors into strengths and weaknesses, is less important than a careful identification of these external and internal factors followed by an appraisal of their implications. My approach to strategy analysis favors a simple two-way classification of *internal* and *external* factors. What will characterize our strategic appraisal will be the rigor and depth of our analysis of these factors, rather than a superficial categorization into strengths or weaknesses, and opportunities or threats.

Strategic Fit

Fundamental to this view of strategy as a link between the firm and its external environment is the notion of *strategic fit*. For a strategy to be successful, it must be consistent with the firm's external environment, and with its internal environment – its goals and values, resources and capabilities, and structure and systems. As we shall see, the failure of many companies is caused by lack of consistency with either the internal or external environment. During 2006, Vodafone – the world's leading supplier of cellphone services – suffered declining profits and asset write-downs. The problem was a growth-oriented, acquisition-based strategy that emphasized superior content. This strategy no longer fitted the commoditizing market for cellphone services, where there were few advantages from global spread. In other cases, many companies have failed to align their strategies to their internal resources and capabilities. A critical issue for Nintendo in the coming years will be whether it possesses the financial and technological resources to continue to compete head-to-head with Sony and Microsoft in the market for video game consoles.

A Brief History of Business Strategy

Origins and Military Antecedents

Enterprises need business strategies for much the same reasons that armies need military strategies – to give direction and purpose, to deploy resources in the most effective manner, and to coordinate the decisions made by different individuals. Indeed, the concepts and theories of business strategy have their antecedents in military strategy. The term *strategy* derives from the Greek word *strategia*, meaning "generalship." However, the concept of strategy did not originate with the Greeks. Sun Tzu's classic *The Art of War*, written about 500 BC, is regarded as the first treatise on strategy.[4]

Military strategy and business strategy share a number of common concepts and principles, the most basic being the distinction between strategy and tactics. *Strategy* is the overall plan for deploying resources to establish a favorable position; a *tactic* is a scheme for a specific action. Whereas tactics are concerned with the maneuvers necessary to win battles, strategy is concerned with winning the war. Strategic decisions, whether in military or business spheres, share three common characteristics:

- They are important.
- They involve a significant commitment of resources.
- They are not easily reversible.

Many of the principles of military strategy have been applied to business situations. These include the relative strengths of offensive and defensive strategies; the merits of outflanking over frontal assault; the roles of graduated responses to aggressive initiatives; the benefits of surprise; and the potential for deception, envelopment, escalation, and attrition.[5] At the same time, the differences between business competition and military conflict must be recognized. The objective of war is (usually) to defeat the enemy. The purpose of business rivalry is seldom so aggressive: most business enterprises limit their competitive ambitions, seeking coexistence rather than the destruction of competitors.

The tendency for the principles of military and business strategy to develop along separate paths indicates the absence of a general theory of strategy. The publication of Von Neumann and Morgenstern's *Theory of Games* in 1944 gave rise to the hope that a general theory of competitive behavior would emerge. During the subsequent six decades, game theory has revolutionized the study of competitive interaction, not just in business but in politics, military conflict, and international relations as well.[6] Yet, as we shall see in Chapter 4, game theory has achieved only limited success as a practical and broadly applicable general theory of strategy.[7]

From Corporate Planning to Strategic Management

The evolution of business strategy has been driven more by the practical needs of business than by the development of theory. During the 1950s and 1960s, senior executives were experiencing increasing difficulty in coordinating decisions and maintaining control in companies that were growing in size and complexity. Financial budgeting provided the basic framework for annual financial planning, while discounted cash flow (DCF) approaches to capital budgeting provided a new approach to appraising individual investment projects. Corporate planning was devised as a framework for coordinating individual capital investment decisions and planning the long-term development of the firm. Macroeconomic forecasts provided the foundation for the new corporate planning. The typical format was a five-year corporate planning document that set goals and objectives, forecast key economic trends (including market demand, the company's market share, revenue, costs, and margins), established priorities for different products and business areas of the firm, and allocated capital expenditures. The diffusion of corporate planning was accelerated by

STRATEGY CAPSULE 1.4

Corporate Planning in a Large US Steel Company, 1965

The first step in developing long-range plans was to forecast the product demand for future years. After calculating the tonnage needed in each sales district to provide the "target" fraction of the total forecast demand, the optimal production level for each area was determined. A computer program that incorporated the projected demand, existing production capacity, freight costs etc., was used for this purpose.

When the optimum production rate in each area was found, the additional facilities needed to produce the desired tonnage were specified. Then the capital costs for the necessary equipment, buildings, and layout were estimated by the Chief Engineer of the corporation and various district engineers. Alternative plans for achieving company goals were also developed for some areas, and investment proposals were formulated after considering the amount of available capital and the company debt policy. The Vice President who was responsible for long-range planning recommended certain plans to the President, and after the top executives and the Board of Directors reviewed alternative plans, they made the necessary decisions about future activities.

Source: Harold W. Henry, *Long Range Planning Processes in 45 Industrial Companies* (Englewood Cliffs, NJ: Prentice-Hall, 1967): 65.

a flood of articles and books addressing this new science.[8] By 1963, most large US companies had set up corporate planning departments. Strategy Capsule 1.4 provides an example of such formalized corporate planning.

During the 1960s and early 1970s, diversification became the major emphasis of corporate planning for many large companies. Igor Ansoff, one of the founding figures of the new discipline of corporate strategy, claimed that: "Strategic decisions are primarily concerned . . . with the selection of the product-mix that the firm will produce and the markets to which it will sell."[9]

During the 1970s and early 1980s, confidence in corporate planning and infatuation with scientific approaches to management were severely shaken. Not only did diversification fail to deliver the anticipated synergies, but the oil shocks of 1974 and 1979 ushered in a new era of macroeconomic instability, combined with increased international competition from resurgent Japanese, European, and Southeast Asian firms. Faced with a more turbulent business environment, firms could no longer plan their investments, new product introductions, and personnel requirements three to five years ahead, simply because they couldn't forecast that far into the future.

The result was a shift in emphasis from *planning* to *strategy making*, where the focus was less on the detailed management of companies' growth paths than on positioning the company in markets and in relation to competitors in order to maximize the potential for profit. This transition from *corporate planning* to what became termed *strategic management* was associated with increasing focus on competition as the central characteristic of the business environment and competitive advantage as the primary goal of strategy.

This emphasis on strategy as a quest for performance directed attention to the sources of profitability. During the late 1970s and into the 1980s, attention focused on sources of profit within the industry environment. Michael Porter of Harvard Business School pioneered the application of industrial organization economics to analyzing industry profitability.[10] Other researchers focused on how profits were distributed between the different firms in an industry. The Boston Consulting Group pioneered a series of studies into the impact of market share and learning upon costs and profits.[11] These two lines of inquiry – the determinants of industry profitability and determinants of profitability differences within industries – provided the basis of the empirical analysis undertaken by the Strategic Planning Institute's PIMS (Profit Impact of Market Strategy) project.[12]

During the 1990s, the focus of strategy analysis shifted from the sources of profit in the external environment to the sources of profit within the firm. Increasingly the resources and capabilities of the firm became regarded as the main source of competitive advantage and the primary basis for formulating strategy.[13] This emphasis on what has been called the *resource-based view of the firm* represented a substantial shift in thinking about strategy. Rather than firms pursuing similar strategies, as in seeking attractive markets and favorable competitive positions, emphasis on internal resources and capabilities has encouraged firms to identify how they are different from their competitors and design strategies that exploit these differences. Michael Porter, answering the question "What is strategy?", makes the point: "Competitive strategy is about being different. It means deliberately choosing a different set of activities to deliver a unique mix of value."[14]

The technology boom of the late 1990s – fueled by digitization, mobile telephony, and the internet – ushered in a wave of new thinking about business strategy. The new knowledge-based, post-industrial economy was seen to offer unprecedented entrepreneurial opportunities and compelled established firms to "reinvent" themselves – or else succumb to "disruptive technologies."[15] Tom Peters urged companies toward the imperative of "strategic innovation" while Gary Hamel summoned executives to "join the revolution."[16] Fundamental to strategic innovation was the quest for new business models – new approaches to the creation and exploitation of value. E-commerce offered unparalleled opportunity for devising new business models: eBay in person-to-person auctions, E-Trade in online stock broking, WebVan and Peapod in grocery retailing, Enron in electricity trading.

The stock market meltdown of 2001 and 2002 and the demise of many of the brightest stars of the TMT (technology, media, and telecommunications) sector – including giants such as Enron and WorldCom – marked the end of "irrational exuberance" and deflated optimism over the power of strategic innovation to create new markets and new sources of competitive advantage. Nevertheless, digital technologies have continued to be major drivers of change and sources of new threats and opportunities – the networked economy, battles over rival technical standards (e.g. HD-DVD vs. BluRay),[17] and the rise of "winner-take-all markets" (e.g. eBay in internet auctions).[18] The turbulence and unpredictability caused by technology, competition and geopolitical forces has meant that strategy has become as much about managing uncertainty as a quest for profit. One outcome has been increased interest in the application of real option thinking to the management of flexibility.[19]

In terms of new developments, the reaction against excesses of greed and unbridled shareholder value maximization has taken the form of renewed interest in business ethics and corporate social responsibility (CSR).[20] These trends have been reinforced by greater awareness of the fragility of Earth's ecosystem, stimulated by accelerating global warming. As optimism over the capacity of the "new economy" to generate new business opportunities waned, companies looked elsewhere for new business opportunities. Increasingly, Western companies looked to emerging countries – India and China in particular – as sources of future growth.[21]

Figure 1.3 summarizes the main developments in strategic management over the past 60 years.

Strategic Management Today

What Is Strategy?

In its broadest sense, strategy is the means by which individuals or organizations achieve their objectives. By "means" I am referring not to detailed actions but the plans, policies, and principles that guide and unify a number of specific actions. Table 1.1 presents a number of definitions of the term strategy. Common to definitions of business strategy is the notion that strategy is focused on achieving certain *goals*; that the critical actions that make up a strategy involve *allocation of resources*; and that strategy implies some *consistency*, *integration*, or *cohesiveness*.

TABLE 1.1 Some definitions of strategy

- Strategy: a plan, method, or series of actions designed to achieve a specific goal or effect.
  —*Wordsmyth Dictionary*

- Lost Boy: "Injuns! Let's go get 'em!"
  John Darling: "Hold on a minute. First we must have a strategy."
  Lost Boy: "Uhh? What's a *strategy*?"
  John Darling: "It's, er . . . it's a plan of attack."
  —Walt Disney's *Peter Pan*

- The determination of the long-run goals and objectives of an enterprise, and the adoption of courses of action and the allocation of resources necessary for carrying out these goals.
  —Alfred Chandler, *Strategy and Structure* (Cambridge, MA: MIT Press, 1962)

- A strategy is the pattern or plan that integrates an organization's major goals, policies and action sequences into a cohesive whole. A well-formulated strategy helps marshal and allocate an organization's resources into a unique and viable posture based upon its relative internal competencies and shortcomings, anticipated changes in the environment, and contingent moves by intelligent opponents.
  —James Brian Quinn, *Strategies for Change: Logical Incrementalism* (Homewood, IL: Irwin, 1980)

- Strategy is the pattern of objectives, purposes, or goals and the major policies and plans for achieving these goals, stated in such a way as to define what business the company is in or is to be in and the kind of company it is or is to be.
  —Kenneth Andrews, *The Concept of Corporate Strategy* (Homewood, IL: Irwin, 1971)

FIGURE 1.3 Evolution of strategic management: dominant themes

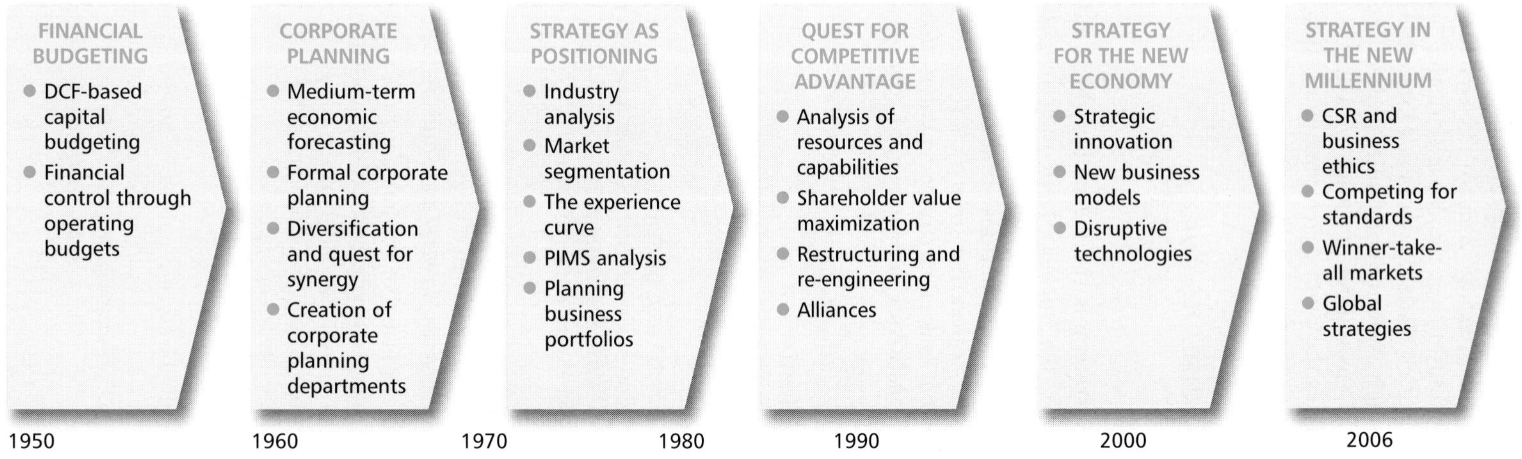

FINANCIAL BUDGETING	CORPORATE PLANNING	STRATEGY AS POSITIONING	QUEST FOR COMPETITIVE ADVANTAGE	STRATEGY FOR THE NEW ECONOMY	STRATEGY IN THE NEW MILLENNIUM
• DCF-based capital budgeting • Financial control through operating budgets	• Medium-term economic forecasting • Formal corporate planning • Diversification and quest for synergy • Creation of corporate planning departments	• Industry analysis • Market segmentation • The experience curve • PIMS analysis • Planning business portfolios	• Analysis of resources and capabilities • Shareholder value maximization • Restructuring and re-engineering • Alliances	• Strategic innovation • New business models • Disruptive technologies	• CSR and business ethics • Competing for standards • Winner-take-all markets • Global strategies
1950	1960	1970 1980	1990	2000	2006

Yet, as we have seen in our historical review, the conception of firm strategy has changed greatly over the past half century. As the business environment has become more unstable and unpredictable, so strategy has become less concerned with detailed plans, and more about mission, vision, principles, guidelines, and targets. This is consistent with our starting point to the chapter. If we think back to our three introductory examples – Madonna, General Giap, and Lance Armstrong – none wrote detailed strategic plans, but all possessed clear ideas of what they wanted to achieve and how they would achieve it. This shift in emphasis from strategy as plan to strategy as direction does not imply any downgrading of the role of strategy. Certainly, in a turbulent environment, strategy must embrace flexibility and responsiveness. But it is precisely in these conditions that strategy becomes more rather than less important. When the firm is buffeted by unforeseen threats and where new opportunities are constantly appearing, then strategy becomes a vital tool to navigate the firm through stormy seas.

In an environment of uncertainty and change, a clear sense of direction is essential to the pursuit of objectives. As Michael Porter has emphasized, strategy is not about doing things better – this is the concern of operational effectiveness – strategy is about doing things *differently*; hence, the essence of strategy is *making choices*.[22]

Strategic choices can be distilled to two basic questions:

- *Where* to compete?
- *How* to compete?

The answers to these questions also define the major areas of a firm's strategy: *corporate strategy* and *business strategy*.

Corporate and Business Strategy

If we start from basics, the purpose of strategy is to achieve certain goals. For the firm, the basic goal is to survive and prosper. Survival, over the long term, requires that the firm earns a rate of return on its capital that exceeds its cost of capital. There are two possible ways of achieving this. First, the firm may locate within an industry where overall rates of return are attractive. Second, the firm may attain a position of advantage vis-à-vis its competitors within an industry, allowing it to earn a return in excess of the industry average (see Figure 1.4).

These two sources of superior performance define the two basic levels of strategy within an enterprise:

- *Corporate strategy* defines the scope of the firm in terms of the industries and markets in which it competes. Corporate strategy decisions include investment in diversification, vertical integration, acquisitions, and new ventures; the allocation of resources between the different businesses of the firm; and divestments.
- *Business strategy* is concerned with how the firm competes within a particular industry or market. If the firm is to prosper within an industry, it must establish a competitive advantage over its rivals. Hence, this area of strategy is also referred to as *competitive strategy*.

Using different terminology, Jay Bourgeois has referred to corporate strategy as the task of *domain selection* and business strategy as the task of *domain navigation*.[23]

FIGURE 1.4 The sources of superior profitability

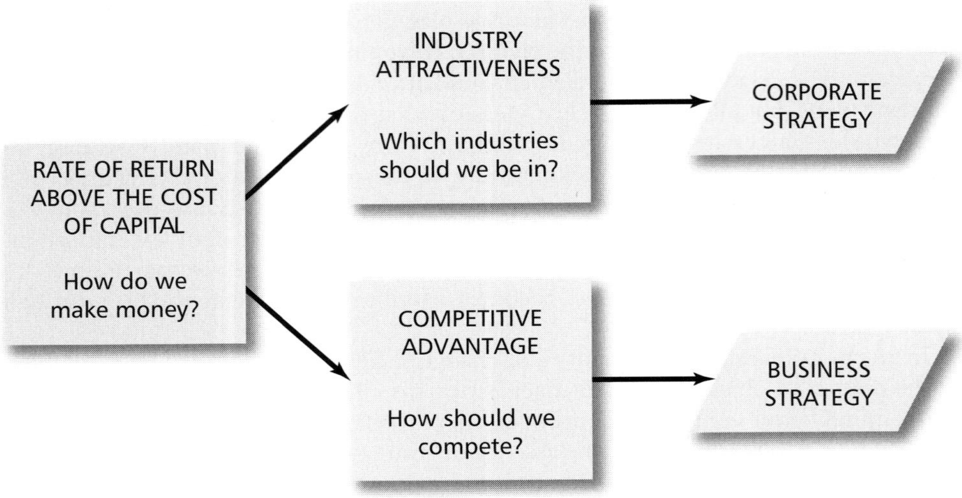

This distinction may be expressed in even simpler terms. The basic question facing the firm is: "How do we make money?" The answer to this question corresponds to the two basic strategic choices we identified above: "Where to compete" (i.e. "In which industries and markets should we be?") and "How should we compete?"

The distinction between corporate strategy and business strategy corresponds to the organization structure of most large companies. Corporate strategy is the responsibility of the top management team and the corporate strategy staff. Business strategy is primarily the responsibility of divisional management.

As an integrated approach to firm strategy, this book deals with both business and corporate strategy. However, my primary emphasis will be business strategy. This is because the critical requirement for a company's success is its ability to establish competitive advantage. Hence, issues of business strategy precede those of corporate strategy. At the same time, these two dimensions of strategy are closely linked: the scope of a firm's business has implications for the sources of competitive advantage, and the nature of a firm's competitive advantage determines the range of businesses it can be successful in.

Describing a Firm's Strategy

Where do we go looking for a firm's strategy? Strategy resides primarily within the minds of top managers. In the case of an entrepreneurial startup, strategy will exist primarily within the mind of the founder. However, to learn about firm strategies we do not need to be mind readers – most companies find it helpful to articulate their strategies in one form or another. In the case of the startup enterprise, strategy is usually written down in the business plan that was prepared to raise finance. In the case of established companies, strategy is communicated in a number of ways:

- *Vision* is an aspirational view of what the organization will be like in the future. Charlotte Villiers defines vision as: "an ideal picture of what the company could be if it fulfilled all of its potential and all the human potential of its staff." However, the vision statements found on most companies' websites tend to be too idealized to offer clear guidance to their strategies.

- *Mission* is a statement of purpose: what the organization seeks to achieve over the long term. Like vision, mission does not provide a distinct statement of strategy but offers a pointer to the overall direction in which strategy will take the organization.

- *Business models.* As noted earlier, business models came into vogue during the e-commerce boom of the late 1990s when firms were devising innovative ways for harvesting profit from internet-based businesses. A business model is a statement of the basis on which a business will generate revenue and profit. Most firms operate with a very simple business model: supply a product that meets a consumer need and sell it at a price that exceeds the cost of production. Other companies have more complex business models. Broadcasters supply radio and TV programming free to consumers, but charge for advertising (hence the threat to this business model posed by TiVo and other technologies that allow consumers to eliminate advertising from their viewing and listening). A business model is a preliminary to a strategy: it is only concerned with the viability of the basic business concept; even if the business model is sound, the firm still needs a strategy that will allow it to survive against competitors that are using the same business model.[24]

- *Strategic plans.* A firm's strategic plan documents its strategy in terms of performance goals, approaches to achieving those goals, and planned resource commitments over a specific time period (typically three to five years). For large, multibusiness companies, strategic plans comprise business plans for individual businesses and divisions and the overall corporate plan. Companies may formulate regional, country, and functional plans as well. Most large companies create their strategic plans through a regular, sequential process – the strategic planning cycle. In most large companies there is an annual cycle.

Strategy Capsules 1.5 and 1.6 give examples of how two companies have articulated their strategies.

Suppose that a firm is not explicit about its strategy, how do we go about describing a firm's strategy? A useful starting point is the two basic questions we identified as defining a firm's basic strategic position: *where is the firm competing? how is it competing?* Strategy Capsule 1.7 uses basic information about the Coca-Cola Company to describe its strategy.

How Is Strategy Made? Design vs. Emergence

So far, the picture I have painted has involved strategies being created deliberately by top management utilizing the tools and techniques of strategic analysis. But is this how strategies are really made? When we examined Madonna's career, we discerned a consistency and pattern to her career decisions that we described as a strategy, yet there is no evidence that she engaged in any systematic strategic planning or articulated her strategy. Similarly with many successful companies, Wal-Mart's incredibly successful strategy based on large store formats, hub-and-spoke distribution system,

STRATEGY CAPSULE 1.5

Nokia's Strategy

OUR VISION: Life goes Mobile!

Ten years ago, we had a vision that seemed revolutionary for the times: Voice Goes Mobile! As history shows, this vision became reality in an incredibly short amount of time. With more than 1.6 billion mobile phone subscriptions globally – and more mobile phones than fixed-line phones in use – we see that mobility has transformed the way people live their lives.

Today, Nokia sees mobility expanding into new areas such as imaging, games, entertainment, media, and enterprises. There are new mobile services already taking our industry forward and creating new opportunities. At the same time, major opportunities still exist in bringing mobile voice to completely new users.

If it can go mobile – it will!

MISSION: Connecting People

By connecting people, we help fulfill a fundamental human need for social connections and contact. Nokia builds bridges between people – both when they are far apart and face-to-face – and also bridges the gap between people and the information they need.

STRATEGY

The Nokia Strategy continues to focus on three activities to expand mobile communications in terms of volume and value:

- **Expand mobile voice**: We can further develop the mobile voice market – both in markets where mobile telephony is just taking off as well as in more mature markets. Nokia estimates the number of mobile subscriptions to surpass three billion in 2008. Nokia's position in mobile voice is strong thanks to our key assets and excellent logistics capabilities.

- **Drive consumer multimedia**: Nokia is playing a key role in shaping this emerging complex market by focusing on the fastest growth areas: imaging, music, and games, to name a few.

- **Bring extended mobility to enterprises**: Nokia will provide a range of competitive, specifically targeted handsets, platforms, and connectivity solutions so enterprises can boost productivity through the power of mobility.

Source: www.nokia.com/P11879 accessed March 22, 2006.

small-town locations, and unique approach to employee motivation was not the result of grand design – it was the result of Sam Walton's hunches and intuition plus a series of historical accidents.

How organizations make strategy has emerged as an area of intense debate within the strategy field. Henry Mintzberg distinguishes *intended*, *realized*, and *emergent* strategies. *Intended strategy* is strategy as conceived of by the top management team. Even here, rationality is limited and the intended strategy is the result of a process of negotiation, bargaining, and compromise, involving many individuals and groups within the organization. However, *realized strategy* – the actual strategy that is implemented – is only partly related to that which was intended (Mintzberg suggests

STRATEGY CAPSULE 1.6

Apple Computer, Inc.: Business Strategy

The Company is committed to bringing the best personal computing and music experience to students, educators, creative professionals, businesses, government agencies, and consumers through its innovative hardware, software, peripherals, services, and internet offerings. The Company's business strategy leverages its unique ability, through the design and development of its own operating system, hardware, and many software applications and technologies, to bring to its customers new products and solutions with superior ease-of-use, seamless integration, and innovative industrial design. The Company believes continual investment in research and development is critical to facilitate innovation of new and improved products and technologies. Besides updates to its existing line of personal computers and related software, services, peripherals, and networking solutions, the Company continues to capitalize on the convergence of digital consumer electronics and the computer by creating innovations like the iPod and iTunes Music Store. The Company's strategy also includes expanding its distribution network to effectively reach more of its targeted customers and provide them a high-quality sales and after-sales support experience.

Source: Apple Computer, Inc., 10-K Report, 2005.

only 10–30 percent of intended strategy is realized). The primary determinant of realized strategy is what Mintzberg terms *emergent strategy* – the decisions that emerge from the complex processes in which individual managers interpret the intended strategy and adapt to changing external circumstances.[25]

Analysis of Honda's successful entry into the US motorcycle market has provided a battleground for the debate between those who view strategy making as primarily a rational, analytical process of deliberate planning (the *design school*) and those that envisage strategy as emerging from a complex process of organizational decision making (the *emergence* or *learning school* of strategy).[26] Boston Consulting Group identified Honda as pursuing a global strategy based on exploiting economies of scale and volume to establish unassailable cost leadership.[27] However, subsequent interviews with the Honda managers in charge of US market entry revealed a different story: a haphazard approach to entry, with little analysis and no clear plan.[28] As Mintzberg observes: "Brilliant as its strategy may have looked after the fact, Honda's managers made almost every conceivable mistake until the market finally hit them over the head with the right formula."[29]

Henry Mintzberg's critique over analytical approaches to strategy design goes further. Not only is rational design an inaccurate account of how strategies are actually formulated, it is a poor way of making strategy. "The notion that strategy is something that should happen way up there, far removed from the details of running an organization on a daily basis, is one of the great fallacies of conventional strategic management."[30] At the basis of this fallacy is that it fails to allow for learning though a continuous interaction between strategy formulation and strategy implementation in which strategy is constantly being adjusted and revised in light of experience.

STRATEGY CAPSULE 1.7
Describing the Strategy of the Coca-Cola Company

Coca-Cola's mission statement – "To refresh the world . . . To inspire moments of optimism . . . To create value in everything we do . . ." – is ethereal, but doesn't say much about how these lofty goals are translated into strategy. However, on the basis of some fundamental facts about the company's operation and intentions, we can provide a more explicit statement of its strategy. Our starting point is to answer the two basic questions of *where* and *how* it competes.

The *where* question can be answered as follows:

- Coca-Cola competes in the soft drinks industry where it supplies concentrate for its branded carbonated drinks (e.g. Coca-Cola, Sprite, Fanta, Tab, and Fresca) and supplies other drinks (e.g. Minute Maid, Hi-C, and Fiver Alive fruit juices and Dasani bottled water).

- Geographically, Coca-Cola competes in 200 countries, with 27% of sales in the US and a further 27% in its next four biggest markets (Mexico, Brazil, Japan, and China).

- In terms of vertical scope, Coca-Cola is primarily engaged in product development, brand management, and the manufacture of concentrate. It relies on franchised local bottlers for bottling and distribution. Coca-Cola holds equity interest in over half of its larger bottlers.

With regard to *how*: Coca-Cola pursues a differentiation strategy in which it relies on brand image developed through heavy advertising and promotion. It seeks market share leadership through its mass marketing and through close relationships with the leading bottlers in every country where it does business.

These facts outline Coca-Cola's strategy only in the *static* sense of describing its current competitive stance. Strategy is also *dynamic* – it's about the direction in which a company is developing. Coca-Cola's company reports tell us a good deal about what the company is currently doing to change its competitive position. In particular, it is committed to continuous growth of both volume and earnings, and to the reinforcement of its world leadership. Its major growth opportunities will be in fast-growing countries outside the US, such as China, Russia, and Turkey. (During 2001–5, the international portion of its capital expenditure budget increased from 56% to 71%.) Coca-Cola also sought to capitalize on increasing demand for low carbohydrate and natural ingredient drinks. However, its primary emphasis will be on marketing its core brands – particularly targeting younger consumers through linking Coca-Cola products with sport and music. Acquisition will play an important role in building and reinforcing Coca-Cola's international market position.

Source: www2.coca-cola.com/investors/index.html

While the debate between these schools rumbles on,[31] it is apparent that the central issue is not "who is right?" but "how can the two views complement one another to give us a richer understanding of how strategy is made?" In most organizations, strategy is made through a combination of design and emergence. At the formal, deliberate level, strategy is made in board meetings, meetings of the top management team, and within the strategic planning process. At the same time, strategy is being continually enacted through decisions that are made by every member of the organization – by middle management especially. The decentralized, bottom–up process of strategy emergence may lead formal, top–down strategy formulation. Intel's historic decision to abandon memory chips and concentrate on microprocessors was initiated through a host of decentralized decisions taken by divisional and plant managers that were subsequently acknowledged by top management and promulgated into strategy.[32] Maximizing responsiveness and adaptability requires that strategic management processes combine design and emergence. Thus, the strategic planning process typically combines both top–down and bottom–up strategy making. Corporate headquarters sets guidelines in the form of mission statements, business principles, and performance targets while the individual business units take the lead in formulating strategic plans. Within the strategic plans that are decided, divisional and business unit managers have considerable freedom to adjust, adapt, and experiment. This predominant pattern of strategic planning may be described as one of "planned emergence."[33]

This idea of strategy providing overall direction for an emergent, adaptive, responsive process of strategic decision making is central to Bain & Company's advocacy of *strategic principles* to guide the organization. A strategic principle is a "pithy, memorable distillation of strategy that guides employees as it empowers them." Thus, America's most successful airline, Southwest, encapsulates its strategy in a simple statement: "Meet customers' short-haul travel needs at fares competitive with the cost of automobile travel." This principle provides a clear strategy focus of the company while allowing employees to enact the strategy in adaptive, innovative ways.[34]

The notion of fostering strategic adaptation through establishing a few broad principles and directives to guide decentralized decision making is consistent with the tenets of complexity theory. Jack Welch's management of General Electric combined simple directives ("Be number 1 or number 2 in your sector," "Simplicity . . . Self-confidence," "Achieve six-sigma quality"), strong performance incentives, and considerable autonomy for divisional managers. The result was that one of the world's biggest and most complex companies achieved outstanding financial performance, rapid response to change, and a high level of internal cohesiveness.[35] We shall explore the implications of complexity theory more fully in Chapter 17.

The optimal balance between design and emergence depends on the stability of the external environment. The Roman Catholic church and the US Postal Service inhabit relatively stable environments. They can use top–down, formalized approaches to planning strategy. Organizations whose environments are fast changing and unpredictable – Google Inc. or the Baghdad Home Security Services Ltd – must limit their strategic planning to a few principles and guidelines; the rest must emerge as circumstances unfold.

Multiple Roles of Strategy

What emerges from this discussion is that strategy making is not some abstract analysis for devising the optimal strategy for the firm. Strategy making is part of an ongoing management process. The reason that *strategic management* has displaced the terms *long-range planning* and *corporate planning* is partly to disassociate strategy from planning, but also to emphasize that strategy making is a central component of what managers do. Viewing strategy making as a part of the management process helps us to see that strategy plays multiple roles within organizations.

Strategy as Decision Support I have described strategy as a pattern or theme that gives coherence to the decisions of an individual or organization. But why can't individuals or organizations make optimal decisions in the absence of such a unifying theme? Consider the 1997 "man-versus-computer" chess epic in which Garry Kasparov was defeated by IBM's "Deep Blue." Deep Blue did not need strategy. Its phenomenal memory and computing power allowed it to identify its optimal moves based on a huge decision tree.[36] Kasparov – although the world's greatest chess player – was subject to *bounded rationality*: his decision analysis was subject to the cognitive limitations that constrain all human beings.[37] For chess players, a strategy offers guidelines and decision criteria that assist positioning and help create opportunities.

Strategy improves decision making in several ways. First, strategy simplifies decision making by *constraining* the range of decision alternatives considered and by acting as a *heuristic* – a rule of thumb that reduces the search required to find an acceptable solution to a decision problem. Second, a strategy-making process permits the knowledge of different individuals to be pooled and integrated. Third, a strategy-making process facilitates the use of analytic tools – the frameworks and techniques that we will encounter in the ensuing chapters of this book.

Strategy as a Coordinating Device The greatest challenge of managing an organization is coordinating the actions of different organizational members. Strategy can promote coordination in several ways. First, it is a communication device. Statements of strategy are a powerful means through which the CEO can communicate the identity, goals, and competitive stance of the company to all organizational members. However, communication alone is not enough. For coordination to be effective, buy-in is essential from the different groups and functions that make up the organization. The strategic planning process can provide a forum in which views are exchanged and consensus developed. Once formulated, the implementation of strategy through goals, commitments, and performance targets that are monitored over the strategic planning period also provides a mechanism to ensure that the organization moves forward in a consistent direction.

Strategy as Target Strategy is forward looking. It is concerned not only with how the firm will compete now, but also with what the firm will become in the future. A key purpose of a forward-looking strategy is not only to establish a direction of the firm's development, but also to set aspirations that can motivate and inspire the members of the organization. Gary Hamel and C. K. Prahalad use the term "strategic intent" to describe the articulation of a desired leadership position. They argue that: ". . . strategic intent creates an extreme misfit between resources and ambitions. Top management then challenges the organization to close the gap by building new competitive advantages."[38] The implication they draw is that strategy should be less about fit and resource allocation, and more about *stretch* and *resource leverage*.[39] The evidence from Toyota, Virgin, and Southwest Airlines is that resource scarcity may engender ambition, innovation, and a "success-against-the-odds" culture. Jim Collins and Jerry Porras make a similar point: US companies that have been sector leaders for 50 years or more – Merck, Walt Disney, 3M, IBM, and Ford – have all generated commitment and drive through setting "Big, Hairy, Ambitious Goals."[40] Striving, inspirational goals are typical of most organizations' statements of vision and mission. One of the best known is the goal set by President Kennedy for NASA's space program: ". . . before this decade is out, of landing a man on the moon and returning him safely to Earth." British Airways aspires to be "The World's Favorite Airline," while Coca-Cola's drive for growth is driven by the quest to "have a Coca-Cola within arm's reach of everyone in the world."

The Role of Analysis in Strategy Formulation

Despite the criticism of rational, analytical approaches to strategy formulation by Henry Mintzberg and others, the approach of this book is to emphasize analytic approaches to strategy formulation. This is not because I wish to downplay the role of intuition, creativity and spontaneity – these qualities are essential ingredients of successful strategies. Nevertheless, whether strategy formulation is formal or informal, whether strategies are deliberate or emergent, systematic analysis is a vital input into the strategy process. Without analysis, strategic decisions are susceptible to power battles, individual whims, fads, and wishful thinking. Concepts, theories, and analytic tools are complements not substitutes for experience, commitment, and creativity. Their role is to provide frameworks for organizing discussion, processing information and opinions, and assisting communication and consensus.

This is not to endorse current approaches to strategy analysis. The weakness of our existing toolbox of strategy concepts and techniques is that they have failed to take adequate account of expertise and experiential knowledge, of creativity, and of the merits of decentralized, emergent processes of strategy making. My purpose is not to defend conventional approaches to business strategy analysis, but to do better. The challenge is to extend our analytic tools to take account of the role of values and goals, the drivers of innovation, the value of flexibility and adaptability, and the conditions conducive to the rapid evolution of complex adaptive systems. In the course of the book you will encounter concepts such as real options, tacit knowledge, hypercompetition, and complexity science that can help us extend our tools of strategy analysis to remedy many of the inadequacies addressed by Mintzberg and others.

We must also recognize the nature of strategy analysis. Unlike many of the analytical techniques in accounting, finance, market research, or production management, strategy analysis does not generate solutions to problems. It does not yield rules, algorithms, or formulae that tell us the optimal strategy to adopt. The strategic questions that companies face (like those that we face in our own careers and lives) are simply too complex to be programmed.

The purpose of strategy analysis is not to provide answers but to help us understand the issues. Most of the analytic techniques introduced in this book are frameworks that allow us to identify, classify, and understand the principal factors relevant to strategic decisions. Such frameworks are invaluable in allowing us to come to terms with the complexities of strategy decisions. In some instances, the most useful contribution may be in assisting us to make a start on the problem. By guiding us to the questions we need to answer, and by providing a framework for organizing the information gathered, we are in a superior position to a manager who relies exclusively on experience and intuition. Finally, analytic frameworks and techniques can improve our flexibility as managers. The analysis in this book is general in its applicability; it is not specific to particular industries, companies, or situations. Hence, it can help increase our confidence and effectiveness in understanding and responding to new situations and new circumstances. By encouraging depth of understanding in fundamental issues concerning competitive advantage, customer needs, organizational capabilities, and the basis of competition, the concepts, frameworks, and techniques in this book will encourage rather than constrain innovation, flexibility, and opportunism.

Summary

This chapter has covered a great deal of ground – I hope that you are not suffering from indigestion. If you are feeling a little overwhelmed, not to worry: we shall be returning to most of the themes and issues raised in this chapter in the subsequent chapters of the book.

The next stage is to delve further into the basic strategy framework shown in Figure 1.2. Each element of this framework – goals and values, the industry environment, resources and capabilities,

and structure and systems – comprises the basic components of strategy analysis. Part II of the book will devote a separate chapter to each. (In the case of industry analysis – two chapters.) We then deploy these tools in the analysis of competitive advantage (Part III), in the formulation and implementation of business strategies in different industry contexts (Part IV), and then in the development of corporate strategy (Part V). Figure 1.5 shows the framework for the book.

FIGURE 1.5 The structure of the book

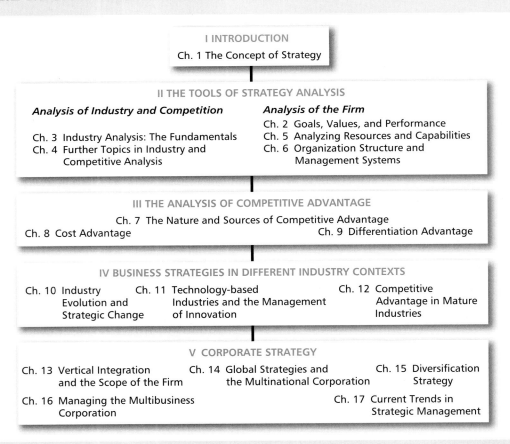

I INTRODUCTION
Ch. 1 The Concept of Strategy

II THE TOOLS OF STRATEGY ANALYSIS

Analysis of Industry and Competition

Ch. 3 Industry Analysis: The Fundamentals
Ch. 4 Further Topics in Industry and
        Competitive Analysis

Analysis of the Firm

Ch. 2 Goals, Values, and Performance
Ch. 5 Analyzing Resources and Capabilities
Ch. 6 Organization Structure and
        Management Systems

III THE ANALYSIS OF COMPETITIVE ADVANTAGE
Ch. 7 The Nature and Sources of Competitive Advantage
Ch. 8 Cost Advantage   Ch. 9 Differentiation Advantage

IV BUSINESS STRATEGIES IN DIFFERENT INDUSTRY CONTEXTS
Ch. 10 Industry   Ch. 11 Technology-based   Ch. 12 Competitive
        Evolution and   Industries and the Management   Advantage in Mature
        Strategic Change   of Innovation   Industries

V CORPORATE STRATEGY
Ch. 13 Vertical Integration   Ch. 14 Global Strategies and   Ch. 15 Diversification
        and the Scope of the Firm   the Multinational Corporation   Strategy
Ch. 16 Managing the Multibusiness   Ch. 17 Current Trends in
        Corporation   Strategic Management

Self-Study Questions

1   In relation to the four characteristics of successful strategies (clear, consistent, long-term objectives; profound understanding of the environment; objective appraisal of resources; and effective implementation), assess the US strategy towards Iraq during 2003–7.

2   To what extent does McDonald's Corporation achieve a close *strategic fit* between its strategy, the characteristics of its external environment, and its internal resources and capabilities? Are changes occurring in its external environment weakening this strategic fit? If so, how should McDonald's adjust its strategy?

3   My discussion of the evolution of business strategy ("From Corporate Planning to Strategic Management") established that the characteristics of a firm's strategic plans and its strategic planning process are strongly influenced by the volatility and unpredictability of its external environment. On this basis, what differences would you expect in the strategic plans and strategic planning processes of Coca-Cola Company and Google Inc.?

4   I have noted that a firm's strategy can be described in terms of the answers to two questions: where are we competing? and how are we competing? ("Describing a Firm's Strategy"). Applying these two questions, provide a concise description of Madonna's career strategy (see Strategy Capsule 1.1).

5   What is your career strategy for the next five years? To what extent does your strategy fit with your long-term goals, the characteristics of the external environment, and your own strengths and weaknesses?

Notes

1 P. F. Drucker, "Managing Oneself," *Harvard Business Review* (March–April 1999): 65–74.

2 Stephen Covey (*The Seven Habits of Highly Effective People*, Simon & Schuster, 1989) advises us to start at the end – to visualize our own funerals and imagine what we would like the funeral speakers to say about us and our lives. On this basis, he recommends that we develop lifetime mission statements based on the multiple roles that we occupy in life.

3 On SWOT analysis see entries in Wikipedia (http://en.wikipedia.org/wiki/SWOT) or Mindtools (www.mindtools.com/pages/articles/newTMC_05.htm).

4 Sun Tzu, *The Art of Strategy: A New Translation of Sun Tzu's Classic "The Art of War,"* trans. R. L. Wing (New York: Doubleday, 1988).

5 On the links between military and business strategy, see R. Evered, "So What Is Strategy?" *Long Range Planning* 16, no. 3 (June 1983): 57–72; E. Clemons and J. Santamaria, "Maneuver Warfare," *Harvard Business Review* (April 2002): 46–53.

6 On the contribution of game theory to business strategy analysis, see F. M. Fisher, "Games Economists Play: A Non-cooperative View," *RAND Journal of Economics* 20 (Spring 1989): 113–24; and C. F. Camerer, "Does Strategy Research Need Game Theory?" *Strategic Management Journal* 12, Special Issue (Winter 1991): 137–52.

7 For practical and accessible introductions to the application of game theory, see T. C. Schelling, *The Strategy of Conflict*, 2nd edn (Cambridge, MA: Harvard University Press, 1980); A. K. Dixit and B. J. Nalebuff, *Thinking Strategically* (New York: W. W. Norton, 1991); and A. Brandenburger and B. J. Nalebuff, *Co-opetition* (New York: Doubleday, 1996).

8 During the late 1950s, *Harvard Business Review* featured a number of articles on corporate planning, e.g. D. W. Ewing, "Looking Around: Long-range Business Planning," *Harvard Business Review* (July–August 1956): 135–46; B. Payne, "Steps in Long-range Planning," *Harvard Business Review* (March–April 1957): 95–101.

9   I. Ansoff, *Corporate Strategy* (London: Penguin, 1985): 18.

10 M. E. Porter, *Competitive Strategy* (New York: Free Press, 1980).

11 Boston Consulting Group, *Perspectives on Experience* (Boston: Boston Consulting Group, 1978).

12 R. D. Buzzell and B. T. Gale, *The PIMS Principles* (New York: Free Press, 1987).

13 R. M. Grant, "The Resource-based Theory of Competitive Advantage: Implications for Strategy Formulation," *California Management Review* 33 (Spring 1991): 114–35; D. J. Collis and C. Montgomery, "Competing on Resources: Strategy in the 1990s," *Harvard Business Review* (July–August 1995): 119–28.

14 M. E. Porter, "What is Strategy?" *Harvard Business Review* (November–December 1996): 64.

15 C. Christensen, *The Innovator's Dilemma* (Boston: Harvard Business School Press, 1997).

16 T. Peters, *The Pursuit of Wow* (New York: Vintage Books, 1994); G. Hamel, *Leading the Revolution* (Boston: Harvard Business School Press, 2000).

17 C. Shapiro and H. R. Varian, *Information Rules* (Boston: Harvard Business School Press, 1998).

18 R. H. Frank and P. J. Cook, *The Winner-Take-All Society* (New York: Penguin, 1997).

19 On option theory and strategy see: T. Copeland and V. Antikarov, *Real Options: A Practitioner's Guide* (Texere, 2001); A. van Putten and I. C. Macmillan, "Making Real Options Really Work," *Harvard Business Review* (December 2004): 134–41.

20 C. Smith, "Corporate Social Responsibility: Whether or How?" *California Management Review* 45, no. 4 (Summer 2003): 52–76.

21 "Survey: India and China," *Economist* (March 3, 2005).

22 M. E. Porter, "What is Strategy?" op. cit.

23 L. J. Bourgeois, "Strategy and the Environment: A Conceptual Integration," *Academy of Management Review* 5 (1980): 25–39.

24 J. Magretta, "Why Business Models Matter," *Harvard Business Review* (May 2002): 86–92; George Yip, "Using Strategy to Change Your Business Model," *Business Strategy Review* 15, issue 2 (Summer 2004): 17–24.

25 See H. Mintzberg, "Patterns of Strategy Formulation," *Management Science* 24 (1978): 934–48; "Of Strategies: Deliberate and Emergent," *Strategic Management Journal* 6 (1985): 257–72; and *Mintzberg on Management: Inside Our Strange World of Organizations* (New York: Free Press, 1988).

26 The two views of Honda are captured in two Harvard cases: *Honda [A]* (Boston: Harvard Business School, Case No. 384049, 1989) and *Honda [B]* (Boston: Harvard Business School, Case No. 384050, 1989).

27 Boston Consulting Group, *Strategy Alternatives for the British Motorcycle Industry* (London: Her Majesty's Stationery Office, 1975).

28 R. T. Pascale, "Perspective on Strategy: The Real Story Behind Honda's Success," *California Management Review* 26, no. 3 (Spring 1984): 47–72.

29 H. Mintzberg, "Crafting Strategy," *Harvard Business Review* 65 (July–August 1987): 70.

30 H. Mintzberg, "The Fall and Rise of Strategic Planning," *Harvard Business Review* (January–February 1994): 107–14.

31 H. Mintzberg, R. T. Pascale, M. Goold, and R. P. Rumelt, "The Honda Effect Revisited," *California Management Review* 38 (Summer 1996): 78–117.

32 R. A. Burgelman and A. Grove, "Strategic Dissonance," *California Management Review* 38 (Winter 1996): 8–28.

33 R. M. Grant, "Strategic Planning in a Turbulent Environment: Evidence from the Oil and Gas Majors," *Strategic Management Journal* 14 (June 2003): 491–517.

34 O. Gadiesh and J. Gilbert, "Transforming Corner-office Strategy into Frontline Action," *Harvard Business Review* (May 2001): 73–80.

35 W. McKelvey, "Energising Order-Creating Networks of Distributed Intelligence: Improving the Corporate Brain," *International Journal of Innovation Management* 5(2) (June 2001): 181–212.

36 "Strategic Intensity: A Conversation with Garry Kasparov," *Harvard Business Review* (April 2005): 105–13.

37 The concept of bounded rationality was developed by Herbert Simon ("A Behavioral Model of Rational Choice," *Quarterly Journal of Economics* 69 (1955): 99–118).

38 G. Hamel and C. K. Prahalad, "Strategic Intent," *Harvard Business Review* (May–June 1989): 63–77.

39 G. Hamel and C. K. Prahalad, "Strategy as Stretch and Leverage," *Harvard Business Review* (March–April 1993): 75–84.

40 J. C. Collins and J. I. Porras, *Built to Last: Successful Habits of Visionary Companies* (New York: HarperCollins, 1995).

II

THE TOOLS OF STRATEGY ANALYSIS

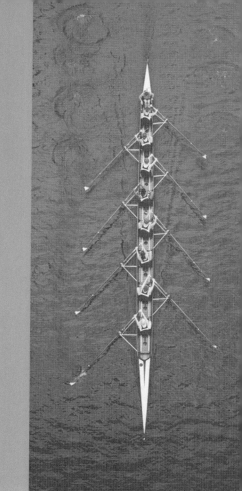

2

Goals, Values, and Performance

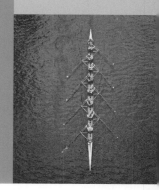

The strategic aim of a business is to earn a return on capital, and if in any particular case the return in the long run is not satisfactory, then the deficiency should be corrected or the activity abandoned for a more favorable one.

—ALFRED P. SLOAN JR., MY YEARS WITH GENERAL MOTORS

OUTLINE

Introduction and Objectives

Our framework for strategy analysis (Figure 1.2) comprises four components: the firm's goals and values, its resources and capabilities, its structure and management systems, and its industry environment. The five chapters that form Part II of the book outline these four components of strategy analysis (I devote two chapters to the industry environment). We begin with goals and values, and, by extension, we consider the performance of the firm in attaining its goals.

Firms possess multiple goals. A firm's choice of goals is influenced by its values. However, in this book we make a bold and simple assumption – that the primary goal of the firm is to maximize profit over the long term. Business strategy then becomes a quest for profit. Hence, most of the frameworks and techniques of strategy analysis we will cover are concerned with identifying and exploiting the sources of profitability open to the firm.

Yet, here we face a fundamental dilemma: businesses that have been most successful in generating profits have typically been those driven by ambitions other than profit. Profit is the life-blood of the organization, but it is not a goal that inspires organizational members to outstanding achievement. Linking a sense of mission to the pursuit of profit represents one of the greatest challenges of strategic management.

By the time you have completed this chapter you will be able to:

- Appreciate the main arguments in the debate over shareholder versus stakeholder goals for the firm.

- Recognize how profit maximization relates to shareholder value maximization.

- Diagnose a company's performance problems systematically and strategically.

- Translate the overall goals of long-term profit maximization into meaningful performance targets that can be measured and monitored.

- Understand the linkages between financial analysis and strategic analysis, and how they can be used to complement one another.

- Comprehend the role of values, mission, and vision in formulating and implementing strategy.

Strategy as a Quest for Value

Business is about creating value. Value, in its broadest sense, refers to the amount of money customers are willing to pay for a good or service. The challenge for business strategy is, first, to create value for customers and, second, to extract some of that value in the form of profit for the firm.

Value can be created in two ways: by production and by commerce. Production creates value by physically transforming products that are less valued by consumers into products that are more valued by consumers – turning clay into coffee mugs, for example. Commerce creates value not by physically transforming products, but by repositioning them in space and time. Trade involves transferring products from individuals and places where they are less valued to individuals and locations where they are more valued. Similarly, speculation involves transferring products from a point in time where the product is valued less to a point in time where it is valued more. Thus, the essence of commerce is creating value through arbitrage across time and space.[1]

The difference between the value of a firm's output and the cost of its material inputs is its *value added*. Value added is equal to the sum of all the income paid to the suppliers of factors of production. Thus:

Value Added = Sales revenue from output *less* Cost of material inputs
= Wages/Salaries + Interest + Rent + Royalties/License fees
+ Taxes + Dividends + Retained profit

In Whose Interest? Shareholders vs. Stakeholders

The value added created by firms is distributed among different parties: employees (wages and salaries), lenders (interest), landlords (rent), government (taxes), and owners (profit). In addition, firms also create value for their customers to the extent that the satisfaction customers gain exceeds the price they pay (i.e., they derive *consumer surplus*). It is tempting, therefore, to think of the firm as operating for the benefit of multiple constituencies. This view of the business enterprise as a coalition of interest groups where top management's role to balance these different – often conflicting – interests is referred to as the *stakeholder* approach to the firm.[2]

The notion of the corporation balancing the interests of multiple stakeholders has a long tradition, especially in Asia and continental Europe. By contrast, most English-speaking countries have endorsed *shareholder capitalism*, where companies' overriding duty is to produce profits for owners. These differences are reflected in international differences in companies' legal obligations. In the US, Canada, the UK, and Australia, company boards are required to act in the interests of shareholders. By contrast, French boards are required to pursue the national interest, Dutch boards are required to ensure the continuity of the enterprise, and German supervisory boards are constituted to include representatives of both shareholders and employees.

Whether companies should operate exclusively in the interests of their owners or should also pursue the goals of other stakeholders is an ongoing debate. During the late 1990s, "Anglo-Saxon" shareholder capitalism was in the ascendant – many continental European and Japanese companies changed their strategies and corporate governance to increase their responsiveness to shareholder interests. However, the catastrophic failure of some of the most prominent advocates of shareholder value creation – Enron and WorldCom in particular – and widespread distaste over the excessive top management remuneration resulting from efforts to align managers' interests with those of shareholders has greatly undermined the case for shareholder capitalism.

The responsibilities of business to employees, customers, society, and the natural environment remain central ethical and social issues. Nevertheless, in order to make progress in developing analytical tools for designing successful strategies, I shall avoid these issues by adopting the simplifying assumption that companies operate in the interests of their owners by seeking to maximize profits over the long term. Why do I make this assumption and how do I justify it? Let me point to four key considerations:

1 *Competition*. Competition erodes profitability. As competition increases, the interests of different stakeholders converge around the goal of survival. Survival requires that, over the long term, the firm earns a rate of profit that covers its cost of capital: otherwise it will not be able to replace its assets. Among 2,717 companies included in the Russell 3000 index, Stern Stewart calculated that well over half were earning negative economic profit, i.e. they were not covering their cost of capital.[3] Across many sectors of industry, the heat of international competition is such that few companies have the luxury of pursuing goals that diverge substantially from profit maximization.

2 *The market for corporate control*. Management teams that fail to maximize the profits of their companies will be replaced by teams that do. The past 20 years have seen a more active "market for corporate control" in which acquisition provides a mechanism for management change. Underperforming companies may be acquired by other public companies – in 2005 a languishing Sears Roebuck was acquired by a newly revitalized Kmart. Increasingly, private equity groups are the main threat to underperforming public companies. In addition, activist investors, both individuals (Carl Icahn at Time Warner and Kirk Kerkorian at General Motors) and institutions (such as California Public Employees' Retirement System), put pressure on boards of directors to improve shareholder returns. One result has been increased turnover of chief executives.[4]

3 *Convergence of stakeholder interests*. Even beyond a common interest in the survival of the firm, there is likely to be more community of interests than conflict of interests among different stakeholders. Long-term profitability is likely to require that a company gains loyalty from its employees, builds trusting relationships with suppliers and customers, and gains support from governments and communities. The evidence from research is that companies that adhere to strong ethical principles, that support sustainable development, and engage in corporate philanthropy are also those that are the most capable in building capabilities, adapting to new external circumstances, and – ultimately – delivering the strongest financial performance.[5]

4 *Simplicity*. In terms of analysis, the key problem of a stakeholder approach is the need to consider multiple goals and specify tradeoffs between goals. The result is vastly increased complexity.[6] Virtually all the major tools of business decision making, from pricing rules to discounted cash flow analysis, are rooted in the assumption of profit maximization.

Assuming that firm strategy is directed primarily toward making profit doesn't mean that we have to accept that profit is the sole motivation driving business enterprises.

As we noted in the last chapter when discussing strategic intent, the forces driving the architects of some of the world's greatest enterprises – Henry Ford at Ford Motor Company, Bill Gates at Microsoft, and Akio Morita at Sony – are seldom financial. The dominant drivers tend to be the fulfillment of a vision and the desire to make a difference in the world. Nevertheless, even when enterprises and their leaders have motives that transcend mere money making, achieving these goals requires enterprises that are commercially successful – this requires the adoption of profit-oriented strategies. Steve Jobs and Steve Wozniak founded Apple Computer with the goal of changing the world through taking computers to the people. Despite pioneering personal computing, Apple lost out to IBM and Microsoft during the 1980s and 1990s not because of a faulty vision, but of a faulty strategy. Apple's strategy did not take sufficient account of technological changes and shifting customer requirements in the personal computer industry.

What Is Profit?

Thus far, we have referred to firms' quest for profit in loose terms. It is time to look more carefully at what we mean by profit and how it relates to shareholder value.

Profit is the surplus of revenues over costs available for distribution to the owners of the firm. But, if profit maximization is to be a realistic goal, the firm must know what profit is and how to measure it. Otherwise, instructing managers to maximize profit offers little guidance. What is the firm to maximize: total profit or rate of profit? Over what time period? With what kind of adjustment for risk? And what is profit anyway – accounting profit, cash flow, or economic profit? The ambiguity is apparent once we consider the profit performance of companies. Table 2.1 shows that any ranking of companies by performance depends critically on how profitability is measured. There are several uncertainties that need to be resolved:

- Does profit maximization mean maximizing total profit or rate of profit? If the latter, are we concerned with profit as a percentage of sales (return on sales), total assets (return on assets), or shareholders' equity (return on equity)?

- Over what time period is profitability being maximized? The specification of time period is critical. If management becomes committed to maximizing quarterly earnings, there is a danger that long-term profitability may be undermined through cutting investment in fixed assets and R&D.

- How is profit to be measured? Accounting profit is defined by the accounting principles under which a company's financial statements are drawn up. Not only does a company's profit vary by country, but a company has considerable discretion as to how it applies accounting principles. Accounting scandals at Enron, Ahold, and other companies, and earnings restatements at many blue-chip companies have undermined the credibility of accounting profit as a meaningful performance indicator.

From Accounting Profit to Economic Profit

A major problem of accounting profit is that it combines two types of returns: the *normal return to capital* that rewards investors for the use of their capital; and *economic profit*, which is the pure surplus available after all inputs (including capital)

TABLE 2.1 Performance of the world's biggest companies using different profitability measures (2006 data)

FT global 500 rank[1]	Company	Market capitalization ($BN)	Net income ($BN)[2]	Return on sales (%)[3]	Return on equity (%)[4]	Return on assets (%)[5]	Return to shareholders (%)[6]
1	Exxon Mobil	372	36.1	19.9	34.9	17.8	11.7
2	General Electric	363	16.4	10.7	22.2	14.7	(1.5)
3	Microsoft	281	12.3	40.3	30.0	18.8	(0.9)
4	Citigroup	239	24.6	22.0	21.9	1.5	4.6
5	BP	233	22.3	9.9	27.9	10.7	10.2
6	Bank of America	212	16.5	27.0	14.1	1.2	2.4
7	Royal Dutch Shell	211	25.3	14.7	26.7	11.6	11.8
8	Wal-Mart	197	11.2	5.5	21.4	8.1	(10.3)
9	Toyota Motor	197	12.1	10.7	13.0	4.8	(22.1)
10	Gazprom	196	7.3	28.1	9.8	7.1	n.a.
11	HSBC	190	15.9	23.0	16.3	1.0	(11.8)
12	Procter & Gamble	190	8.7	17.3	13.7	6.4	7.2

Notes:

1 Ranked by market capitalization. Source: *Financial Times*.

2 Source: *Fortune*.

3 Pre-tax profit as a percentage of sales revenues. Source: Hoovers.

4 Net income as a percentage of (year end) shareholders' equity. Source: Hoovers.

5 Net income as a percentage of (year end) total assets. Source: Hoovers.

6 Dividend + Share price appreciation. Source: *Fortune*.

have been paid for. Economic profit represents a purer and more reliable measure of profit that is a better measure of performance. To distinguish economic profit from accounting profit, economic profit is often referred to as *rent* or *economic rent*.

A widely used measure of economic profit is economic value added (EVA), devised and popularized by the New York consulting firm Stern Stewart & Company.[7] EVA is measured as net operating profit after tax (NOPAT) less cost of capital, where cost of capital is calculated as: capital employed *multiplied by* the weighted average cost of capital (WACC).[8]

Economic profit has two main advantages over accounting profit as a performance measure. First, it sets a more demanding performance discipline for managers. As Stern Stewart's calculations show, many major corporations' apparent profitability disappears once cost of capital is taken into account. James Meenan, chief financial officer of AT&T, reported:

> The effect of adopting EVA on AT&T's businesses is staggering. "Good" is no longer a positive operating earnings. It's only when you beat the cost of capital.[9]

Second, using economic profit improves the allocation of capital between the different businesses of the firm by taking account of the real costs of more capital-intensive businesses (see Strategy Capsule 2.1).

STRATEGY CAPSULE 2.1

Economic Value Added at Diageo plc.

At Guinness-to-Johnny-Walker drinks giant Diageo, EVA provided the basis for a complete management system that transformed the way in which Diageo measured its performance, allocated its capital and advertising expenditures, and evaluated its managers.

For example, taking account of the costs of the capital tied up in slow-maturing, vintage drinks such as Talisker and Lagavulin malt whisky, Hennessey cognac, and Dom Perignon champagne showed that these high-margin drinks were often not as profitable as the company had believed. The result was that Diageo's advertising expenditures were reallocated towards Smirnoff vodka, Gordon's gin, Bailey's, and other drinks that could be sold within weeks of distillation.

More generally, once managers had to report profits after deduction of the cost of the capital tied up in their businesses, they took measures to reduce their capital bases and make their assets work harder. At Diageo's Pillsbury food business, the economic profit of every product and every major customer was scrutinized. The result was the elimination of many products and renewed efforts to expand sales to unprofitable customers. Ultimately, EVA analysis resulted in Diageo selling Pillsbury to General Foods. This was followed by the sale of Diageo's Burger King chain to Texas Pacific, a private equity group.

Value-based management was extended throughout the organization through making EVA the primary determinant of the incentive pay earned by 1,400 Diageo managers.

Sources: John McGrath, "Tracking Down Value," *Financial Times Mastering Management Review*, December 1998; www.diageo.com

Linking Profit to Enterprise Value

There is also the problem of time. Once we consider multiple periods of time, then profit maximization means maximizing the net present value of profits over the lifetime of the firm.

Thus, profit maximization translates into maximizing the value of the firm. This means that the value of the firm is calculated in the same way as for any other asset: it is the net present value (NPV) of the returns to that asset. The relevant returns are the cash flows to the firm. Hence, firms are valued using the same discounted cash flow (DCF) methodology that we apply to the valuation of investment projects. Thus, the value of an enterprise (V) is the sum of its free cash flows (C) in each year t, discounted at the enterprise's cost of capital (r).[10] The relevant cost of capital is the weighted average cost of capital (r_{e+d}) that averages the cost of equity (r_e) and the cost of debt (r_d):

$$V = \sum_t \frac{C_t}{(1 + r_{e+d})^t}$$

where *free cash flow* (C) is measured as:

Net Operating Profit *plus* Depreciation *less* Taxes *less* Investment
in Fixed and Working Capital.

To maximize its value, a firm must maximize its future net cash flows (its *free cash flow*) while also managing its finances to minimize its cost of capital.

This value-maximizing approach implies that *cash flow* rather than *accounting profit* is the relevant performance measure. In practice, valuing companies by discounting economic profit gives the same result as by discounting net cash flows. The difference is in the treatment of the capital consumed by the business. The cash flow approach deducts capital at the time when the capital expenditure is made; the EVA approach follows the accounting convention of charging capital as it is consumed (through charging depreciation). In principle, a full DCF approach is the most satisfactory approach to valuing companies. In practice, however, for DCF analysis to be meaningful requires forecasting cash flows several years ahead, since cash flow for a single year is a poor indicator of underlying profitability. Thus, profitable companies are likely to have negative cash flows for the whole of their growth phase. The preference of many financial analysts for cash-based accounting is also based on the fact that cash flows are less easily manipulated by company managers for cosmetic purposes than are accounting profits. For the same reason, operating earnings, EBIT (earnings before interest and tax) and EBITDA (earnings before interest, tax, depreciation, and amortization) are often preferred to net income as an indicator of profit.

For assessing firm performance in a single year or over a finite number of years, economic profit is usually preferable to free cash flow. Economic profit shows the surplus being generated by the firm in each year, whereas free cash flow depends on management choices over the level of capital expenditure. Thus, a firm can easily boost its free cash flow by slashing its capex budget.

Enterprise Value and Shareholder Value How does maximizing enterprise value relate to the much-lauded goal of *maximizing shareholder value*? In the 1950s, Modigliani and Miller laid the foundations of modern financial theory by showing that the value of a company's assets must equal the value of the claims against those assets.[11] Hence, for public companies, the DCF value of the firm is equal to the market value of the firm's securities (plus any other financial claims such as debt and pension fund deficits). Thus, shareholder value is calculated by subtracting the debt (and other non-equity financial claims) from the DCF value of the firm.

Does enterprise value less debt really equal the stock market value of a firm's equity? So long as full information about a firm's prospects reaches the stock market and this information is efficiently reflected in stock prices – yes. But isn't the stock market subject to bubbles, fads, and crashes? Yes – but we need to remember that no one knows what a firm's cash flows over its lifetime are likely to be. In the case of the technology internet bubble of the late 1990s, stock prices of technology, media, and telecommunications companies were inflated by over-optimistic expectations of their future earnings.

Our emphasis in this book will be on maximization of enterprise value rather than maximization of shareholder value. This is principally for convenience: distinguishing debt from equity is not always straightforward due to the presence of preference stock and convertible debt, while junk bonds share the characteristics of both equity and debt. Also, focusing on the value of the enterprise as a whole assists us in identifying the fundamental drivers of firm value. In practice, however, maximization of enterprise value and maximization of shareholder value mean much the same in terms of our strategy analysis.

Applying DCF Analysis to Valuing Companies, Businesses, and Strategies

Applying DCF to Uncertain Future Cash Flows The biggest difficulty in using DCF analysis to value companies and business units is forecasting cash flows sufficiently far into the future. Given the level of uncertainty affecting most businesses, even one-year forecasts of profits and cash flows may be difficult. To estimate future cash flows we may need to make assumptions. For example in a stable, growth business (the sole dairy in an expanding village) it may be reasonable to assume that the current year's cash flow (C_0) will grow at a constant rate (g) to infinity. In this case, the above equation becomes:

$$V = \frac{C_0}{(r_{e+d} - g)^t}$$

A slightly more sophisticated approach is to forecast free cash flow over the medium term – say five years – then to calculate a horizon value (H) based either on the book value of the firm at that time or on some more arbitrary forecast of cash flows beyond the medium term:

$$V = C_0 + \frac{C_1}{(1 + r)^1} + \frac{C_2}{(1 + r)^2} + \frac{C_3}{(1 + r)^3} + \frac{C_4}{(1 + r)^4} + \frac{H_4}{(1 + r)^4}$$

Valuing Strategies The same approach used to value companies and business units can be applied to evaluating alternative strategies. Thus, different strategy options can be appraised by forecasting the cash flows under each strategy and then selecting the strategy that produces the highest NPV.[12] Since the early 1990s, companies have increasingly integrated value analysis into their strategic planning processes. At PepsiCo, for example, value maximization provides the basis on which strategic plans are formulated, divisional and business unit targets are set, and performance is monitored. A key merit of value maximization is its consistency. The same DCF methodology is used to value individual projects, individual business units, alternative business strategies, and the company as a whole.

Applying enterprise value analysis to appraising business strategies involves several steps:

- Identify strategy alternatives (the simplest approach is to compare the current strategy with the preferred alternative strategy).
- Estimate the cash flows associated with each strategy.
- Estimate the implications of each strategy for the cost of capital – according to the risk characteristics of different strategies and their financing implications, different strategies will be associated with a different cost of capital.
- Select the strategy that generates the highest NPV.

Though in principle simple, applying DCF analysis to strategy selection runs into major practical difficulties. The central problem is forecasting cash flows. A strategy that is implemented today is likely to influence a company's cash flows over its entire life. Given the volatility and unpredictability of the business conditions facing most companies, making any reasonable forecast of the costs and revenues resulting from a particular strategy is exceedingly difficult. But even if we ignore the problems associated with forecasting an uncertain future, the feasibility of linking a strategy with specific cash flow outcomes is doubtful. As we discussed in the first chapter, a strategy is not a detailed plan, it is a direction and a set of guidelines. As such, a strategy will be consistent with a range of specific outcomes in terms of product introductions, output levels, prices, and investments in new plant. Once we recognize that strategy is about reconciling flexibility with direction in an uncertain environment, there are two key implications as far as strategy analysis is concerned: first, it may be better to view strategy as a portfolio of options rather than a portfolio of investment projects; second, qualitative approaches to strategy analysis may be more useful than quantitative ones. We take up each of these themes in the next two sub-sections.

Strategy and Real Options

The simple idea that there is value to having the option to do something has important implications for how we value firms. In recent years, the principles of option pricing have been extended from financial securities to investment projects and business enterprises. The resulting field of *real option analysis* has emerged as one of the most important developments in financial theory over the past decade, with far-reaching implications for strategy analysis. The technical details of valuing real options are complex. However, the underlying principles are intuitive. Let me outline the basic ideas of real options theory and what they mean for strategy analysis.

In November 2005, BP announced the doubling of capital expenditure at its newly formed BP Alternative Energy division. Yet returns to this investment could not conceivably match those of BP's oil and gas businesses. How could investing in renewable energy – wind and solar power – be consistent with shareholder interests?

The answer lies in the *option value* of alternative energy investments. BP's $600 million in alternative energy represented only 0.4% of overall 2006 capital expenditure. By developing a leading position in solar, wind, and hydrogen energy technologies, BP was buying the option to become a leading player in these energy sources should hydrocarbon use be restricted by Middle East conflict, reserve exhaustion, or environmental concerns.

In a world of uncertainty, where investments, once made, are irreversible, flexibility is valuable. Instead of committing to an entire project, there is virtue in breaking the project into a number of phases, where the decision of whether and how to embark on the next phase can be made in the light of prevailing circumstances and the learning gained from the previous stage of the project. Most large companies have a *phases and gates* approach to product development in which the development process is split into distinct phases, at the end of which the project is reassessed before being allowed through the "gate." Such a phased approach creates option values. Option value arises from the potential to amend the project during the development process or even abandon it. One of the key buzz-words of the e-commerce boom of 1998–2000 was "scalability" – the potential to scale up or replicate a project or business model should the initial version be successful. In evaluating new business proposals, venture capitalists look for "scalability" – the potential to scale up or replicate the business if it proves successful. Scalability is a source of option value. Strategy Capsule 2.2 addresses the calculation of real option values.

Calculating Real Option Value[1]

The adoption of real option valuation to value investment projects and strategies has been limited by the complexity of the techniques: modeling uncertainty and taking account of multiple sources of flexibility soon immerses the analyst in complex mathematics.

However, the basic process is logical and straightforward. McKinsey & Company outline a four-stage process for valuing flexibility in a project (the same analysis can be used in valuing a strategy for the business):

1 Apply a standard DCF analysis to the project without taking account of any flexibility options.

2 Model uncertainty in the project using event trees. This requires identifying the key uncertainties facing the project at each point of time and identifying the cash flows associated with different outcomes.

3 Model flexibility using a decision tree. Identify the key managerial decisions with regard to flexibility at each stage of the development of the project in order to convert the event tree into a decision tree. Flexibility may relate to abandonment, deferring investment, or changing the scale of the project.

4 Estimate the value of flexibility. For this, the following two approaches can be used.

Real Option Valuation applies the principles of financial option valuation developed by Fischer Black, Myron Scholes,[2] and Robert Merton[3] to real options. The *Black–Scholes option-pricing formula* comprises six variables, each of which has analogies in the valuation of real options (see the figure below).[4] The key

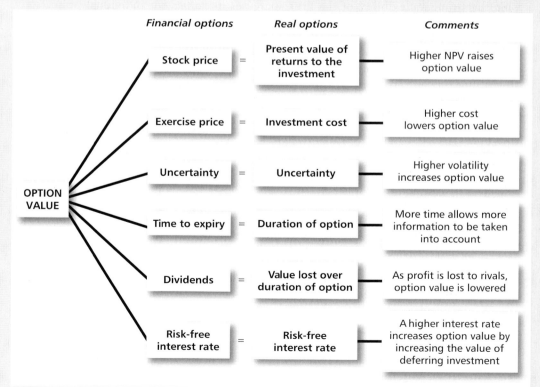

Financial options		Real options	Comments
Stock price	=	Present value of returns to the investment	Higher NPV raises option value
Exercise price	=	Investment cost	Higher cost lowers option value
Uncertainty	=	Uncertainty	Higher volatility increases option value
Time to expiry	=	Duration of option	More time allows more information to be taken into account
Dividends	=	Value lost over duration of option	As profit is lost to rivals, option value is lowered
Risk-free interest rate	=	Risk-free interest rate	A higher interest rate increases option value by increasing the value of deferring investment

OPTION VALUE

challenge in using this method is in creating a portfolio of securities that replicates the returns of the project.

Decision Tree Analysis values a project through aggregating and discounting all the possible returns to the project at the cost of capital of the project. The key challenge of this approach is in calculating the appropriate cost of capital to the project.

Notes:

1 For more on this topic see T. Koller, M. Goedhart, and D. Wessels, *Valuation: Measuring and Managing the Value of Companies*, 4th edn (Hoboken, NJ: Wiley, 2005), Chapter 20.

2 F. Black and M. Scholes, "The Pricing of Options and Corporate Liabilities," *Journal of Political Economy* 81 (1993): 637–54.

3 R. C. Merton, "The Theory of Rational Option Pricing," *Bell Journal of Economics and Management Science* 4 (1973): 141–83.

4 K. J. Leslie and M. P. Michaels, "The Real Power of Real Options," *McKinsey Quarterly Anthology: On Strategy* (McKinsey & Company, 2000). Also: A. Dixit and R. Pindyck, "The Options Approach to Capital Investment," *Harvard Business Review* (May–June 1995): 105–15.

Strategy as Options Management

From the viewpoint of strategy formulation, our primary interest is not the technicalities of options valuation, but how we can use the principles of option valuation to create shareholder value. The key observation is that creating options, by increasing the strategic flexibility of the firm, increases its value. For individual projects, this means avoiding commitment to the complete project and introducing decision points at multiple stages, where the main options are to delay, modify, scale up, or abandon the project. Merck, an early adopter of option pricing, noted, "When you make an initial investment in a research project, you are paying an entry fee for a right, but you are not obligated to continue that research at a later stage."[13] In designing projects, options thinking implies comparing the costs of flexibility with the options value that such flexibility creates. New plants that allow different products to be manufactured, permit easy capacity expansion, and can be operated with different types of raw material are more valuable than specialized plants.

For complete strategies, as opposed to individual projects, creating option value means positioning the firm such that a wide array of opportunities become available. Such strategies might include:

- "Platform investments," which are investments that create a stream of additional options.[14] 3M's investment in nanotechnology offers the opportunity to create new products across a wide range of its businesses, from dental restoratives and drug-delivery systems to adhesives and protective coatings. Google's creation of its Google China (www.google.cn) website and censored Chinese search engine offers the opportunity for Google to become a major player in offering a wide range of internet-based services in China.

- Strategic alliances and joint ventures, which are limited investments that offer options for the creation of whole new strategies.[15] Virgin Group has used joint ventures as the basis for creating a number of new businesses: with Stagecoach to create Virgin Rail, with AMP to create Virgin Money (financial services), with Deutsche Telecom to form Virgin Mobile. Joint-venture investments can act as both a call and a put option: in some cases Virgin has bought out its JV partner; in other cases it has sold out to its JV partner. General Motors' network of alliances with other car producers (including Suzuki, Daewoo, and Fiat) has similarly created a range of options for internationalization and new products.

- Organizational capabilities, which can also be viewed as options offering the potential to create competitive advantage across multiple products and businesses.[16] Sharp's miniaturization capability has provided a gateway to success in calculators, CD screens, solar cells, and PDAs.

Putting Performance Analysis Into Practice

Our discussion so far has established the following:

- For the purposes of strategy formulation, profit maximization is a convenient and reasonable assumption. Once we look beyond a single period, maximizing profit translates into maximizing enterprise value.
- Profit can be measured in many different ways. In principle, free cash flow is the appropriate measure of profit for calculating the net present value of the firm. In practice, economic profit may be a better indicator of profit performance.
- Discounted cash flow (DCF) valuation of enterprises, projects, and strategies underestimates their value where significant option values are present.
- Using value maximization as a basis for selecting optimal strategy is difficult. DCF approaches to valuing strategy encounter difficulties of estimating cash flows far into the future. Real option approaches to valuing strategy are problematic because of the complexity and information requirements of real option valuation.

Given these challenges, what practical guidance can I offer about using financial analysis to appraise and choose business strategies? Let me deal with four questions. First, how can we best appraise overall firm (or business unit) performance? Second, how can we diagnose the sources of poor performance? Third, how can we select strategies on the basis of their profit prospects? Lastly, how do we set performance targets?

Appraising Current and Past Performance

The first task of any strategy formulation exercise is to assess the current situation. This requires that we identify the current strategy of the firm and assess how well that strategy is doing in terms of the financial performance of the firm. The next stage is diagnosis – identifying the sources of unsatisfactory performance. Thus, good strategic practice emulates good medical practice: the first task is to determine the state of health of the patient, and then to determine the reasons for any sickness.

Forward-Looking Performance Measures: Stock Market Value If our goal is maximizing profit over the lifetime of the firm, then to evaluate the performance of a firm we need to look at its stream of profit (or cash flows) over the rest of its life.

The problem, of course, is that we don't know what these will be. However, for public companies we do have a good indicator: stock market valuation, which represents the best available estimate of expected cash flows into the future. Thus, to evaluate the effectiveness of the firm's top management team or of the strategies they have implemented, growth in the market value of the firm over the relevant time period is a good indicator. However, there are two main problems of using stock market valuation as a performance indicator. First, the information upon which the stock market values companies is imperfect. Second, expectations about a firm's future earnings tend to be volatile and strongly influenced by expectations about the economy in general and individual sectors.

Backward-Looking Performance Measures: Accounting Ratios Given the volatility and imperfections of stock market values, evaluation of firm performance for the purposes of assessing the current strategy or evaluating management effectiveness tends to concentrate on current indicators of financial performance. All of these are inevitably historical – financial reports appear, at minimum, three weeks after the quarter to which they relate.

In the light of our discussion over accounting profit vs. economic profit vs. cash flow, which are the best indicators to use? McKinsey & Company argue that, for practical purposes, the DCF value of the firm may be viewed as a function of three variables: the return on the firm's invested capital (ROIC), its weighted average cost of capital, and the rate at which it grows its operating profit.[17] Hence, return on invested capital, or its close relatives return on capital employed (ROCE), return on assets (ROA), and return on equity (ROE), are useful indicators of the effectiveness of the firm in generating profits from its assets. However, evaluating this return requires that it is compared with cost of capital, and also takes account of growth – one easy means of boosting a firm's return on capital is by reducing its capital base through disposing of less profitable businesses.

While the debate over different profitability measures emphasizes the advantages of some measures over others, in practice they are all related. Moreover, the longer the time period under consideration, the greater their convergence.[18] Over shorter periods, the key issues are, first, to be aware of the limitations and biases inherent in any particular profitability measure and, second, to utilize multiple measures of profitability so that their consistency can be judged. Table 2.2 outlines some commonly used performance indicators.

Interpreting probability ratios requires benchmarks. Longitudinal comparisons examine whether a profitability ratio is improving or deteriorating. Interfirm comparisons tell us how a firm is performing relative to a competitor, relative to its industry average, or relative to firms in general (e.g. the average for the Fortune 500 or FT 500). Another key benchmark is cost of capital. To determine whether a firm is earning economic profit, ROIC and ROCE should be compared with WACC, and ROE compared with the cost of equity capital.

Performance Diagnosis

If profit performance is unsatisfactory, we need to identify the sources of poor performance so that management can take corrective action. Diagnosis primarily involves disaggregation of return on capital in order to identify the fundamental "value drivers." A useful approach is to use the *Du Pont Formula* to disaggregate return on

TABLE 2.2 Profitability ratios

Ratio	Formula	Comments
Return on Invested Capital (ROIC)	$$\frac{\text{Operating profit before interest after tax}}{\text{Fixed assets} + \text{Net current assets}}$$	ROIC measures the return on the capital invested in the business. ROIC is also referred to as return on capital employed (ROCE). ROCE is sometimes calculated pre-tax and sometimes post-tax.
Return on Equity (ROE)	$$\frac{\text{Net income}}{\text{Shareholders' equity}}$$	ROE measures the success of the company in using shareholders' capital to generate profits that are available for remunerating investors. Net income should ideally be measured net of dividends on preferred stock. Net income is often measured net of income from discontinued operations and before any special items.
Return on Assets (ROA)	$$\frac{\text{Operating profit}}{\text{Total assets}}$$	Different measures of the numerator are common. Ideally the numerator should be a broad-based measure of profit: operating profit, EBITDA (earnings before interest, tax, depreciation, and amortization), or EBIT (earnings before interest and tax).
Gross margin	$$\frac{\text{Sales} - \text{Cost of bought-in goods and services}}{\text{Sales}}$$	Gross margin measures the extent to which a firm adds value to the goods and services it buys in.
Operating margin	$$\frac{\text{Operating profit}}{\text{Sales}}$$	Operating margin and net margin measure a firm's ability to extract profit from its sales, but for comparing firm's performance, these ratios reveal little because margins vary so much between different sectors (see Table 2.1).
Net margin	$$\frac{\text{Net income}}{\text{Sales}}$$	

Notes:

1 Few accounting ratios have agreed definitions. Hence, it is always advisable to be explicit about how you have calculated the ratio you are using.

2 A general guideline for rate of return ratios is that the numerator should be the profits that are available to remunerate the owners of the assets in the denominator.

3 Profits are measured over a period of time (typically over a year). Assets are valued at a point of time. Hence, in rate of return calculations, assets and capital employed need to be averaged between the end of the period and the end of the previous period.

invested capital into sales margin and capital turnover. But we can go further: as Figure 2.1 shows, sales margin and capital productivity can be further disaggregated into their constituent items. This analysis allows us to identify the sources of poor performance in terms of specific activities.

Strategy Capsule 2.3 investigates the performance of Ford's automotive operations compared with those of the industry's top performer, Toyota. By disaggregating

FIGURE 2.1 Disaggregating return on capital employed

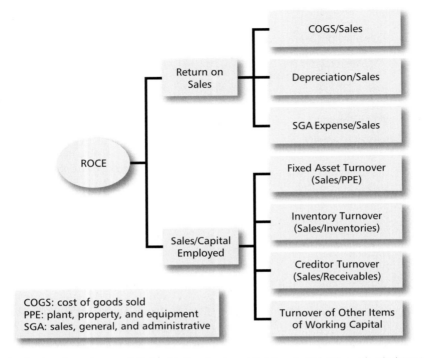

Note: For further discussion, see T. Koller, M. Goedhart, and D. Wessels, *Valuation*, 4th edn (New York: Wiley, 2005): Chapter 7.

STRATEGY CAPSULE 2.3
Diagnosing Performance: What Ails Ford?

During the early years of the twenty-first century, Ford Motor Company continued the declining trend that had begun during the 1980s. During the five-year period 2001–5, return on equity averaged a negative 0.9% while operating losses in its automotive business totaled over $14 billion. Ford's share of the US car and truck market declined from 22.8% to 18.2%. The ousting of CEO Jacques Nasser by Bill Ford (great-grandson of founder Henry Ford) had brought about a change of strategy and significant cost cutting, but no major upturn in profitability.

To understand the sources of Ford's poor financial performance, it is useful to compare Ford's automotive operations with those of the company that had displaced it as the world's second largest auto manufacturer (by volume) – Toyota. We can disaggregate Ford and Toyota's return on capital employed into sales margin and capital turnover, then disaggregate further into individual cost and asset productivity ratios:

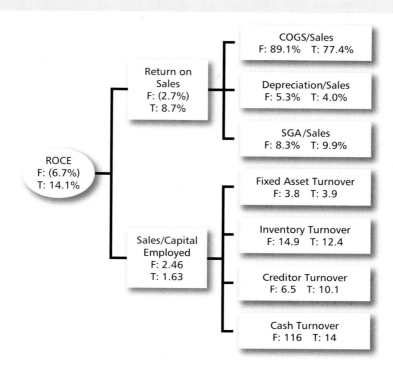

Note: These ratios relate to the automotive businesses only; financial services are excluded.

The analysis reveals the following:

- Ford's lower ROCE is wholly the result of a lower margin on sales than Toyota. This lower margin results from a substantially higher ratio of cost of goods sold to sales. This could be the result of higher costs (e.g. of labor and parts), or lower unit prices, or both. Additional analysis suggests that Ford's higher COGS/sales ratio is the result of lower productivity of labor – Ford produced 23.8 vehicles per employee compared with 31.9 for Toyota. Also, Toyota with just 17 manufacturing plants worldwide is likely to exploit scale economies more effectively than Ford with its 113 plants. Although Ford received more revenue per vehicle than Toyota ($22,514 vs. $20,642), the difference seems to be accounted for by Toyota's greater emphasis on small cars. For comparable models, it appears that Toyota's prices are higher than Ford's – possibly the result of higher quality and better features.

- Ford's capital productivity is higher than Toyota's. Yet, when we review the disaggregated asset productivity ratios, it is difficult to find the source of this higher capital turnover. Certainly Ford is leaner in terms of cash and inventory, but not in turning over plant and equipment and creditors. The real explanation for Ford's apparent efficiency in capital utilization derives from its higher current liabilities – especially short-term debt – which reduce its capital employed.

overall return on assets we can begin to pinpoint the sources of Ford's dismal profitability. We can also disaggregate performance by business and geographical segments. If we then combine the financial data with qualitative data on Ford's business strategy, its operations, its product strategy, the organizational issues it has faced, and the conditions in the world market for motor vehicles, we can begin to formulate hypotheses as to why Ford has performed so poorly. This can then provide the basis for identifying corrective measures.

Evaluating Alternative Strategies

A probing diagnosis of a firm's current performance – as outlined above – provides a useful starting point for strategy formulation. If a firm is making losses or is performing worse than its major competitors, then the main priority for strategy is to address sources of deficient performance. If current performance is so bad that the survival of the enterprise is in question, then strategy must adopt a short-term orientation and focus, at least initially, on staunching cash flow drain.

Even if a firm is performing well, it is not enough to conclude that the present strategy is working well and should therefore be continued. The world of business is one of constant change, and the role of strategy is to assist the firm to adapt to changing market and competitive conditions. The sustained, outstanding success of companies such as Wal-Mart, Dell, Nokia, Canon, HSBC, and Toyota has been achieved by their continual strategic adaptation rather than sticking with previous winning formulae. But, as we have already noted, we cannot simply test out alternative strategies by calculating which one will yield the greatest net present value of the firm. The problems of estimating future cash flows are simply too daunting. In practice, therefore, strategy formulation requires more qualitative tools of strategic analysis. We may not be able to forecast the profits that might result from Ford consolidating its plants, shifting production to lower cost countries, or introducing more fuel-efficient cars, but we can analyze the industry trends, product market conditions, and sources of competitive advantage that are likely to determine Ford's future profit streams and then make soundly based judgments about which strategy offers the best prospects.

Setting Performance Targets

As discussed in Chapter 1, an important role for strategic planning systems is to drive corporate performance through setting performance aspirations then monitoring and assessing results against targets. To be effective, performance management needs to be consistent with long-term goals, closely linked to strategy, and address individuals throughout the organization. While the overall corporate performance goal is to increase long-run profits with a view to maximizing the value of the firm, such a goal is meaningless outside the top echelon of management. Corporate targets need to be translated into more specific goals that are meaningful for managers further down the organization. The key is to match performance targets to the variables over which different managers exert some control. Thus, for the CEO, it may make sense to set the overall goal of maximizing enterprise value. For the chief operating officer and divisional heads, it makes more sense to set more specific financial goals (such as maximizing ROCE on existing assets and investing in projects whose rate of return

FIGURE 2.2 Linking value drivers to performance

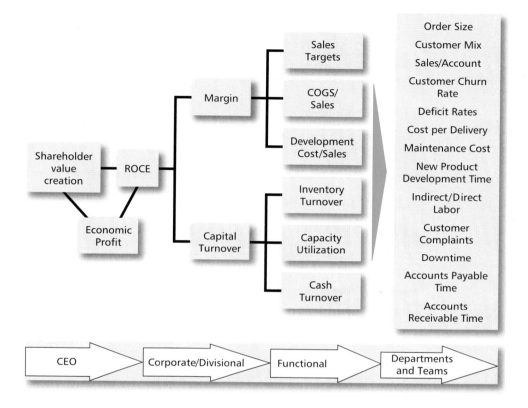

exceeds the cost of capital). For functional, departmental, and unit managers, more specific operating targets are preferable. Thus, in a retailing company, store managers might be given targets with regard to sales per square foot and gross margins. Warehouse managers might be required to achieve target levels of inventory turns. Purchasing managers might be required to reduce the cost of goods purchased as a percentage of sales revenue. The chief financial officer might be required to minimize average cost of capital and reduce cash balances.

The same procedure that we used to disaggregate return on capital for appraising past performance can be used to set performance targets appropriate to different levels and functions within the organization. Figure 2.2 uses the same breakout of the drivers of return on capital as Figure 2.1. The difference is that Figure 2.2 provides a basis for identifying the financial and operating ratios appropriate to managers at the different levels and in the different functions of the company.

Balanced Scorecards   The problem with any system of performance management is that the performance goals are long term (e.g. maximizing profits over the lifetime of the company) but to act as an effective control system, performance targets need to be monitored over the short term. The problem with the above financially based

FIGURE 2.3 Balanced scorecard for Mobil North American Marketing and Refining

		Strategic Objectives	Strategic Measures
Financially Strong	Financial	F1 Return on Capital Employed F2 Cash Flow F3 Profitability F4 Lowest Cost F5 Profitable Growth F6 Manage Risk	● ROCE ● Cash Flow ● Net Margin ● Full cost per gallon delivered to customer ● Volume growth rate vs. industry ● Risk index
Delight the Consumer **Win–Win Relationship**	Customer	C1 Continually delight the targeted consumer C2 Improve dealer/distributor profitability	● Share of segment in key markets ● Mystery shopper rating ● Dealer/distributor margin on gasoline ● Dealer/distributor survey

Safe and Reliable
 	
Competitive Supplier
 	
Good Neighbor
On Spec
On time
	Internal	I1 Marketing
		  1. Innovative products and services
		  2. Dealer/distributor quality
		
		I2 Manufacturing
		  1. Lower manufacturing costs
		  2. Improve hardware and performance
		I3 Supply, Trading, Logistics
		  1. Reducing delivered cost
		  2. Trading organization
		  3. Inventory management
		
		I4 Improve health, safety, and environmental performance
		I5 Quality
			● Non-gasoline revenue and margin per square foot
			● Dealer/distributor acceptance rate of new programs
			● Dealer/distributor quality ratings
			● ROCE on refinery
			● Total expenses (per gallon) vs. competition
			● Profitability index
			● Yield index
			Delivered cost per gallon vs. competitors
			● Trading margin
			● Inventory level compared to plan and to output rate
			● Number of incidents
			● Days away from work
			● Quality index

Motivated and Prepared	Learning and growth	L1 Organization involvement L2 Core competencies and skills L3 Access to strategic information	● Employee survey ● Strategic competitive availability ● Strategic information availability

approach of disaggregating profitability into its constituent ratios is that the short-term pursuit of financial targets is unlikely to result in long-term profit maximization. One solution to this dilemma is to link the overall corporate goal of value maximization to strategic and operational targets to ensure that the pursuit of financial goals is not at the expense of the longer term strategic position of the company. The most widely used method for doing this is the *balanced scorecard* developed by Robert Kaplan and David Norton.[19] The balanced scorecard methodology provides an integrated framework for balancing financial and strategic goals, and extending these balanced performance measures down the organization to individual business units and departments. The performance measures combine the answers to four questions:

1 *How do we look to shareholders?* The financial perspective is composed of measures such as cash flow, sales and income growth, and return on equity.

2 *How do customers see us?* The customer perspective comprises measures such as goals for new products, on-time delivery, and defect and failure levels.

3 *What must we excel at?* The internal business perspective relates to internal business processes such as productivity, employee skills, cycle time, yield rates, and quality and cost measures.

4 *Can we continue to improve and create value?* The innovation and learning perspective includes measures related to new product development cycle times, technological leadership, and rates of improvement.

By balancing a set of strategic and financial goals, the scorecard methodology allows the strategy of the business to be linked with the creation of shareholder value while providing a set of measurable targets to guide this process. Thus, at machinery and chemicals conglomerate FMC, Kaplan and Norton report:

> *Strategists came up with five- and ten-year plans, controllers with one-year budgets and near-term forecasts. Little interplay occurred between the two groups. But the scorecard now bridges the two. The financial perspective builds on the traditional function performed by controllers. The other three perspectives make the division's long-term strategic objectives measurable.*[20]

Mobil Corporation's North American Marketing and Refining business (NAM&R) was a pioneer of the balanced scorecard during the 1990s. Faced with pressures of unsatisfactory profit performance, the business adopted the scorecard methodology as a means of linking strategy with financial performance goals and translating these into operating objectives tailored to the specific performance requirements of individual business units and functional departments. The scorecard provided a mechanism for "cascading down" divisional strategy into specific operating goals. The result was an integrated system where scorecards provided the measurements by which the performance of each unit and department was appraised and against which performance-related pay bonuses were determined.[21] Figure 2.3 shows NAM&R's scorecard.

Beyond Profit: Values and Social Responsibility

It is time to look more deeply and more realistically at the goals of the firm. In Chapter 1 we introduced the simplifying assumption that the primary goal of the firm is long-run profitability. In this chapter we have developed techniques of performance appraisal and analysis based on this assumption. Yet, lurking in the shadows is the recognition that, in reality, firms are motivated by goals other than maximizing profit. Even more worrying, such alternative goals may be better, both for society and maybe even for the firm itself. Let us address these issues directly.

The Paradox of Profit

There is more to business than making money. Profit maximization (enterprise value maximization, to be more precise) provides a convenient foundation for building our tools of strategy analysis, yet it is not the goal that inspired Henry Ford to build a business that precipitated a social revolution. Ford Motor Company was the outcome of Henry's mission and vision:

> I will build a motor car for the great multitude . . . It will be so low in price that no man making good wages will be unable to own one and to enjoy with his family the blessing of hours of pleasure in God's great open spaces . . . When I'm through, everyone will be able to afford one, and everyone will have one.[22]

Similar remarks can be made about most of the great entrepreneurs that have shaped the world of business. It seems unlikely that it is the quest to make more money that causes the world's richest person, Bill Gates, to show up for work most days at Microsoft.

As we recognized in Chapter 1 (see Strategy as Target), the world's most consistently successful companies in terms of profits and shareholder value tend to be those that are motivated by factors other than profit. A succession of studies have pointed to the role of strategic intent, vision, and "big, hairy, ambitious goals" in driving sustained corporate success.[23] Indeed, the converse may also be true – the companies that are most focused on profitability and the creation of shareholder value are often remarkably unsuccessful at achieving those goals. The case of Boeing during the 1990s is instructive (see Strategy Capsule 2.4).

Why is it that the pursuit of profit so often fails to generate adequate returns? First, profit will only be an effective guide to management action if managers know what determines profit. Obsession with profitability can blinker managers' perception of the real drivers of superior performance. Conversely, a strategic goal "to build a motor car for the great multitude that everyone will be able to afford" (Ford), or to "build great planes" (Boeing), or to "become the company most known for changing the worldwide poor quality image associated with Japanese products" (Sony, 1950s) may lead a company to direct its efforts towards the sources of competitive advantage within its industry – ultimately leading to superior long-term profitability.

The second factor concerns motivation. Success is the result of coordinated effort. The goal of maximizing the return to stockholders is unlikely to inspire employees and other company stakeholders and it's unlikely to be especially effective in inducing cooperation and unity between them. Dennis Bakke, founder of the international power company AES, offers the following analogy:

> Profits are to business as breathing is to life. Breathing is essential to life, but is not the purpose for living. Similarly, profits are essential for the existence of the corporation, but they are not the reason for its existence.

To consider these issues more specifically, let us look more generally at values, ideals and principles.

STRATEGY CAPSULE 2.4

The Pitfalls of Pursuing Shareholder Value: Boeing

Boeing was one of the most financially successful members of the Dow Jones Industrial Index between 1960 and 1990. Yet, financial goals or financial controls had little role in Boeing's management over this period. CEO Bill Allen was interested in building great planes and leading the world market with them: "Boeing is always reaching out for tomorrow. This can only be accomplished by people who live, breathe, eat and sleep what they are doing." Allen bet the company on the 747, yet when asked by non-executive director Crawford Greenwalt for financial projections on the project, Allen was utterly vague. "My God," muttered Greenwalt, "these guys don't even know what the return on investment will be on this thing."

The change came in the mid-1990s when Boeing acquired McDonnell Douglas and a new management team of Harry Stonecipher and Phil Condit took over. Mr. Condit proudly talked of taking the company into "a value-based environment where unit cost, return on investment, shareholder return are the measures by which you'll be judged."

The result was lack of investment in major new civil aviation projects and diversification into defense and satellites. Under Condit, Boeing relinquished market leadership in passenger aircraft to Airbus, while faltering as a defense contractor due partly to ethical lapses by key executives. When Condit resigned on December 1, 2003, Boeing's stock price was 20 percent lower than when he was appointed.

Source: Adapted from John Kay, "Forget how the Crow Flies," *Financial Times Magazine* (January 17, 2004): 17–27.

Values and Principles

Even when a company recognizes profit or the creation of shareholder value as its primary goal, its pursuit of that goal is likely to be constrained by values, ideals, and principles to which the members of the company subscribe. It has become popular for public companies – and some private companies too – to be explicit about the values and principles that guide their business conduct. This may even be formulated into specific rules or a code of conduct. Strategy Capsule 2.5 summarizes Shell's values and business principles.

At one level, statements of values and principles may be regarded as instruments of companies' external image management. Yet, to the extent that companies are consistent and sincere in their commitments, values and principles can be integral to an organization's sense of what it is, what it represents, what it wants to achieve, and how it intends to achieve it. Values and principles not only condition, constrain, and even transcend the pursuit of profit, they influence employees' motivation, propensity to collaborate, and their own sense of identity. To the extent that values are shared among organizational members, they form a central component of organizational culture.

STRATEGY CAPSULE 2.5

Shell's Values and Principles

Our Values

Shell employees share a set of core values – honesty, integrity, and respect for people. We also firmly believe in the fundamental importance of trust, openness, teamwork and professionalism, and pride in what we do.

Principles

1 *Economic*. Long-term profitability is essential to achieving our business goals and to our continued growth. It is a measure both of efficiency and of the value that customers place on Shell products and services.

2 *Competition*. Shell companies support free enterprise. We seek to compete fairly and ethically and within the framework of applicable competition laws; we will not prevent others from competing freely with us.

3 *Business Integrity*. Shell companies insist on honesty, integrity, and fairness in all aspects of our business and expect the same in our relationships with all those with whom we do business. The direct or indirect offer, payment, soliciting or acceptance of bribes in any form is unacceptable.

4 *Political Activities*. Shell companies act in a socially responsible manner within the laws of the countries in which we operate in pursuit of our legitimate commercial objectives. Shell companies do not make payments to political parties, organizations or their representatives.

5 *Health, Safety, Security, and the Environment*. Shell companies have a systematic approach to health, safety, security, and environmental management in order to achieve continuous performance improvement.

6 *Local Communities*. Shell companies aim to be good neighbors by continuously improving the ways in which we contribute directly or indirectly to the general wellbeing of the communities within which we work.

7 *Communication and Engagement*. Shell companies recognize that regular dialog and engagement with our stakeholders is essential. We are committed to reporting of our performance by providing full relevant information to legitimately interested parties, subject to any overriding considerations of business confidentiality.

8 *Compliance*. We comply with all applicable laws and regulations of the countries in which we operate.

Source: Extracted from Royal Dutch Shell plc, *General Business Principles*, 2005 (www.shell.com/static/royal-en/downloads/sgbp/sgbp_300805.pdf).

In terms of providing the basis for firm strategy, a company's values complement its vision. Thus, Jim Collins and Jerry Porras argue that "core values" and "core purpose" – the organization's most fundamental reason for being – unite to form an organization's "core ideology" which "defines an organization's timeless character" and is "the glue that holds the organization together."[24] When core ideology is put together with an "envisioned future" for the enterprise, the result is a powerful sense of strategic direction.

The Debate Over Corporate Social Responsibility

Values and principles can enhance a sense of identity and self-worth, but what values and principles should companies adopt? The risk is that, rather than focus and enhance a firm's sense of identity and purpose, commitment to values may conflict with the commercial interests of the company. At cosmetics and toiletries retailer Body Shop, faltering performance during the 1990s could be traced to the excessive commitment of top management to environmental and social activism. Founder and CEO Anita Roddick became increasingly involved in campaigns against globalization and threats to biodiversity and the rights of indigenous peoples. The head of finance was detailed to help set up windmills in Wales to ecologically balance the electricity used by the corporate head office.[25] The danger is that a company's purpose becomes manipulated to serve the values and beliefs of a powerful leader. Silvio Berlusconi is the most recent in a long line of media barons who have used their companies as vehicles for their political aspirations. The history of Hughes Aircraft under the leadership of aviator and playboy Howard Hughes is an even more salutary example of the risks of business strategy becoming dominated by the personal interests of the CEO.

The debate over corporate social responsibility provides a particularly interesting arena for the discussion of goals, values, and principles. Like many free-market economists, Milton Friedman was suspicious of any influences that cause a firm to deviate from profit maximization:

> There is one and only one social responsibility of business – to use its resources and engage in activities designed to increase its profits so long as it stays within the rules of the game, which is to say, engages in open and free competition without deception or fraud.[26]

Socially responsible acts by a CEO – whether it is improving the natural environment, hiring disadvantaged individuals rather than better qualified workers, or holding down prices in the interest of supporting inflation goals – involve management spending owners' money for a general social interest. According to Friedman, this is an unjustified abuse of executive power.

Conflicting views of the responsibilities of the firm reflect different concepts of the nature and role of the public corporation. William Allen identifies two different concepts of the public corporation: "the property conception," which views the firm as a collection of assets owned by the stockholders, and the "social entity conception," which views the firm as the community of individuals that is sustained and supported by its relationships with its social, political, economic, and natural environment.[27] While the "firm as property" view implies a narrow focus by management on maximizing shareholder value, the "firm as social entity" implies the fundamental requirements for the survival and prosperity of the firm are the maintenance of the firm's social relationships, which, in turn, requires coexistence with the external environment. Thus, Charles Handy argues that the property view is a legal hangover from the nineteenth century, when shareholders really did own and run their companies. In the twenty-first century, shareholders invest in companies; they are not "owners" in any meaningful sense. Certainly it is important to reward shareholders, but to regard profit as the purpose for which companies exist is a tragic confusion, argues Handy – companies exist to do something that is better or different than anyone else.[28]

While Charles Handy, Sumantra Ghoshal, and other critics of shareholder value maximization view seek to emphasize the conflicts between shareholder interests and the interests of other stakeholders, in practice it would appear that their interests converge, especially over the longer term. If a firm is to maximize profitability over its lifetime, it is helpful if it lives a long time. Former Shell strategist, Arie De Geus, argues that long-living companies are ones that build strong communities, have a strong sense of identity, commit to learning, and are sensitive to the world around them. In short, the company is a living organization whose lifespan depends on recognizing its organic nature and ensuring its effective adaptation to its changing environment.[29] Adaptation to a changing environment is enhanced by close interactions and supportive relations between the firm and customers, employees, governments, local communities, and the natural environment. Beyond these broad generalizations that social responsibility is typically compatible with business survival and prosperity, Strategy Capsule 2.6 examines BP's approach to social and environmental responsibilities, while Strategy Capsule 2.7 summarizes the views of leading strategy gurus on the convergence of profitability and corporate social responsibility.

STRATEGY CAPSULE 2.6
Social and Environmental Responsibility at BP

In a 1997 speech at Stanford University, John Browne, BP's CEO, committed the company to an active role in the quest for solutions to the problem of global warming. Since then, sustainability has become a central theme of BP's corporate strategy. Given BP's position as one of the world's leading extractors of fossil fuels, this has inevitably meant a focus on the natural environment – climate change in particular. In response, BP has pursued aggressive targets for emissions reduction, pioneered R&D into environmentally friendly technologies (including reformulated fuels), and invested in alternative energy (notably solar). However, BP's sustainability initiatives also extend to other aspects of human development – in the countries where it does business, BP supports education,

poverty relief, and the "development of human talent."

At the same time, in a 2006 bulletin to shareholders, "Maintaining our Strategy, Maximizing our Returns," Lord Browne emphasized that: "Our core objective is to grow sustainable free cash flow and to distribute it so as to grow shareholder returns." With a 28% return on equity in 2005 and a five-year growth in earnings per share of 26%, BP has done well for its shareholders. Future returns look even better: at its 2006 AGM, Lord Browne outlined the potential for BP to return $65 billion to shareholders during 2006–8.

So, how does BP reconcile its quest for social and environmental responsibility with its focus on shareholder returns? Some cynics claim that

BP's program of sustainable development is simply a front to deflect criticism from governments and environmental and antiglobalization activists, to sustain the feel-good factor among corporate executives while allowing BP to continue feeding the flow of greenhouse gases and earning outrageous profits. Certainly BP puts its eco-friendly image at the forefront of its external communications. It spent $7 million to develop its new "sunburst" corporate logo and over $100 million annually integrating the new logo into its marketing efforts. Associating BP with "Beyond Petroleum" rather than British Petroleum was another major marketing initiative.

Lord Browne is resolute in his argument that the theme of sustainability applies equally to the planet, human society, and to BP's own profit stream. In his 2000 BBC Reith Lecture, Browne outlined his concept of "enlightened self interest":

> The simple fact is that business needs sustainable societies in order to protect its own sustainability . . . And I say this because very few businesses are short-term activities. Most want to do business again and again over many decades. And this is especially true of the businesses which are most often criticized – those, like mine, which are in the business of extracting and developing the world's natural resources. We are by definition – whether we like it or not – long-term players. We have to live with the consequences of what we do for decades. We can't pack up and go home when the going gets tough. But in order to sustain what we value, we have to be prepared to change. And the sort of change which business promotes is the application of technical advances to meet human needs.

By pioneering the quest for eco-friendly technologies and ambitious environmental targets, BP has discovered a number of commercial benefits – many of them unexpected. Its aggressive program of reducing emissions from its refineries resulted in wider improvements in refinery processes that generated cost savings that exceeded the investment costs of the refinery upgrades. In pioneering reformulated fuels, BP has gained early-mover advantages over competitors. In gaining access to exploration licenses and joint ventures with national oil companies, BP has established itself as a preferred partner of producer countries.

By mid-2006, BP's reputation as the petroleum sector's pioneer of social responsibility was tarnished by its inability to match its actions to its words. In 2005, an explosion at its Texas refinery killed 15 employees and during summer 2006, BP was rocked by an oil spill in Alaska and allegations of price fixing in its natural gas liquids business.

Sources: www.bp.com; Craig Smith, "BP's failure of execution, not strategy," *Financial Times* (August 9, 2006): 11.

STRATEGY CAPSULE 2.7

Strategic Philanthropy and Serving the Bottom of the Pyramid

In contrast to Milton Friedman's denunciation of corporate social responsibility, strategy gurus Michael Porter and C. K. Prahalad point to the strategic use of social responsibility as a means of furthering the long-term profit goals of the firm.

Strategic Philanthropy

Michael Porter and Mark Fuller argue that: "There is no inherent contradiction between improving competitive context and making a sincere commitment to bettering society." Yet, all too often corporate philanthropy fails to look beyond public relations and employee morale. Charity and social responsibility efforts need to align with the firm's strategy to improve its competitive environment or enhance competitive advantage. Companies often make available both finance and employees' time to support collaborative initiatives with local schools. Improvements in the education and training of the local labor force are clearly in companies' own interests. Aardman Productions, creators of animated films such as the *Wallace and Gromit* series, collaborated with the University of the West of England to establish the Bristol School of Animation – a rich source of future employees. Apple's computers-for-schools program helped build it a strong position in the educational sector during the 1980s. To be effective, many of these initiatives must be collaborative. Multinational companies throughout the world are major sources of funding for Transparency International.

Serving the World's Poor

C. K. Prahalad and Allen Hammond argue that multinational companies tend to overlook the world's poor. This is shortsighted on two counts. First, although poor, the lowest economic tier of world society – "the bottom of the pyramid" – can offer attractive market opportunities. The shanty towns of Rio de Janeiro, Johannesburg, and Mumbai house millions of people, vibrant economies, and substantial collective purchasing power. On a smaller scale, Grameen Telecom's payphones sited in Bangladeshi villages generate strong profit margins. Second, looking long term, it is through engaging with the world's poor that they will grow their way out of poverty and be the growth markets of the future. The challenges of serving the "bottom of the pyramid" market can stimulate innovations with more general applicability. The wind-up, batteryless radio was developed by British inventor Trevor Bayliss to give poor, Third-World communities access to radio broadcasts. Wind-up radios have been one of the most successful audio products of the past decade.

Sources: M. E. Porter and M. Fuller, "The Competitive Advantage of Corporate Philanthropy," *Harvard Business Review* (September 2002): 57–68. C. K. Prahalad and A. Hammond, "Serving the World's Poor, Profitably," *Harvard Business Review* (September 2002).

Summary

Chapter 1 established that strategy is about success and provided a framework for viewing strategy as a link between the firm and its industry environment. This chapter has explored the first component of that framework – the goals, values, and performance of the firm. The key assumption in this chapter is that the firm operates in the interests of its owners through maximizing their returns (profits), which implies maximizing the net present value of the firm. At the same time, we must recognize that profit, while essential, is not the *raison d'être* for most business enterprises. Strategy is also about creating purpose and unifying the energy and creativity of organizational members in pursuing that purpose.

While every business venture has a unique purpose and vision, common to all is the need to generate profit for that vision to be realized. Hence, the challenge we address in this book is to develop strategies that can help the firm generate profit over the long term.

Financial analysis can help us understand how return on capital, cost of capital, growth, and option values determine the value of the firm. But, ultimately, creating value depends on identifying and exploiting the fundamental drivers of firm value. That is the challenge we address in the next three chapters of the book. We begin with the industry environment of the firm.

Self-Study Questions

1 Table 2.1 compares companies according to different profitability measures:

   a) Which two of the six performance measures do you think are the most useful indicators of how well a company is being managed?
   b) Is return on sales or return on equity a better basis on which to compare the performance of the companies listed?
   c) Several companies are highly profitable, yet have delivered negative returns to their shareholders. How is this possible?

2 Nike, supplier of sports footwear and apparel, is interested in actions it might take to increase its option value. What advice would you give to its top management?

3 Some of the most prominent adopters of EVA (and other measures of economic profit) for the purposes of setting targets, monitoring performance, and allocating capital expenditure have been in capital-intensive industries (automobiles, energy, engineering, hotels). Why might companies in capital-intensive industries find EVA a more useful tool than companies in sectors with low capital intensity?

4 With regard to Strategy Capsule 2.3, what additional data would you seek and additional cost and productivity ratios would you calculate to shed further light on the reasons for Ford's inferior ROCE relative to Toyota?

5   A listed public company is considering developing a program of corporate social responsibility (CSR). One group of board directors believes that the company should embrace CSR as part of a "stakeholder" orientation in which the company explicitly pursues the interests of investors, customers, employees, and the community. Another group believes that the company should develop a program of CSR initiatives as a means by which the company pursues investor interests through the long-term maximization of profitability. Which group would you support and why?

Notes

1   In this chapter, I use the term "value" in two distinct senses. Here I am referring to *economic value*, which is worth as measured in monetary units. We shall also be discussing *values* as moral principles or standards of behavior.

2   T. Donaldson and L. E. Preston, "The stakeholder theory of the corporation," *Academy of Management Review* 20 (1995): 65–91.

3   Stern Stewart & Co. Russell 3000 Annual Ranking Data, 2003.

4   M. Wiersema, "Holes at the Top: Why CEO Firings Backfire," *Harvard Business Review* (December 2002): 66–78.

5   S. L. Hart and M. B. Milstein, "Global Sustainability and the Creative Destruction of Industries," *Sloan Management Review* 41 (Fall 1999): 23–33. M. Orlitzky, F. L. Schmidt, and S. L. Rynes, "Corporate Social and Financial Performance: A Meta-Analysis," *Organization Studies* 24 (Summer 2003): 403–41.

6   See K. R. MacCrimmon, "An Overview of Multiple Objective Decision Making," in J. L. Cochrane and M. Zeleny (eds), *Multiple Criteria Decision Making* (Columbia, SC: University of South Carolina Press, 1973).

7   Go to www.sternstewart.com. See also: G. Bennett Stewart III and A. Ehrbar, *EVA: The Real Key to Creating Wealth* (New York: Wiley, 1999).

8   EVA is one of several measures of economic profit. A similar measure is *value added*, proposed by J. Kay in *Foundations of Corporate Success: How Corporate Strategies Add Value* (Oxford: Oxford University Press, 1993).

9   S. Tully, "EVA: The Real Key to Creating Wealth," *Fortune* (September 20, 1993): 42.

10   The cost of equity capital is calculated using the capital asset pricing model: Firm X's cost of equity = the risk-free rate of interest + a risk premium. The risk premium is the excess of the stock market rate of return over the risk-free rate multiplied by Firm X's beta coefficient (its measure of *systematic risk*). See T. Koller, M. Goedhart, and D. Wessels, *Valuation: Measuring and Managing the Value of Companies*, 4th edn (New York: Wiley, 2005): Chapter 10.

11   F. Modigliani and M. H. Miller, "The Cost of Capital, Corporation Finance, and the Theory of Investments," *American Economic Review* 48 (1958): 261–97.

12   This "shareholder value" approach to strategy appraisal is outlined by A. Rappaport in *Creating Shareholder Value: The New Standard for Business Performance* (New York: Free Press, 1986); and "CFOs and Strategists: Forging a Common Framework," *Harvard Business Review* (May–June 1992): 84–91.

13   N. Nichols, "Scientific Management at Merck: An Interview with CFO Judy Lewent," *Harvard Business Review* (January–February 1994): 89–105.

14   B. Kogut and N. Kulatilaka, "Options Thinking and Platform Investments: Investing in Opportunity," *California Management Review* (Winter 1994): 52–69.

15   T. Chi, "Option to Acquire or Divest a Joint Venture," *Strategic Management Journal* 21 (2000): 665–87.

16   B. Kogut and N. Kulatilaka, "Capabilities as Real Options," *Organization Science* 12 (2001): 744–58; R. G. McGrath, W. Furrier, and A. Mendel, "Real Options as Engines of Choice and Heterogeneity," *Academy of Management Review* 29, no. 1 (2004).

17   Koller, Goedhart, and Wessels, *Valuation* op. cit.: Chapter 13.

18   J. A. Kay and C. Meyer, "On the Application of Accounting Rates of Return," *Economic Journal* 96 (1986): 199–207; J. A. Kay, *Foundations of Corporate Success: How Business Strategies Create Value* (Oxford: Oxford University Press, 1993): 207.

19   The approach is in a stream of publications by R. S. Kaplan and D. P. Norton. See "The Balanced Scorecard: Measures That Drive Performance," *Harvard Business Review* (January–February 1992); *Balanced Scorecard: Translating Strategy into Action* (Boston: Harvard Business School Press, 1996); "Using the Balanced Scorecard as a Strategic Management System," *Harvard Business Review* (January–February 1996).

20   R. S. Kaplan and D. P. Norton, "Putting the Balanced Scorecard to Work," *Harvard Business Review* (September–October 1993): 147.

21   R. S. Kaplan and D. P. Norton, *The Strategy-focused Organization* (Boston: Harvard Business School Press,

2001): Chapter 2, "How Mobil Became a Strategy-focused Organization."

22 www.abelard.org/ford

23 T. Peters and R. Waterman identified "shared values" as a key ingredient in corporate excellence (*In Search of Excellence*, HarperCollins, 1982); G. Hamel and C. K. Prahalad introduced "Strategic Intent" (*Harvard Business Review*, May–June 1989: 63–76); J. Collins and J. Porras, "Building Your Company's Vision," *Harvard Business Review* (September–October 1996): 65–77.

24 Collins and Porras, "Building Your Company's Vision," op. cit.

25 "Can the Body Shop Shape Up?" *Fortune* (April 15, 1996).

26 M. Friedman, *Capitalism and Freedom* (University of Chicago Press, Chicago, 1963). See also: M. Friedman, "The Social Responsibility of Business is to Increase its Profits," *New York Times Magazine* (September 13, 1970).

27 W. T. Allen, "Our Schizophrenic Conception of the Business Corporation," *Cardozo Law Review* 14 (1992): 261–81.

28 C. Handy, "What's a Business For?" *Harvard Business Review* (December 2002): 133–43.

29 A. De Geus, "The Living Company," *Harvard Business Review* (March–April 1997): 51–9.

Industry Analysis: The Fundamentals

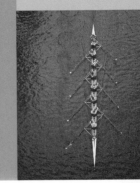

3

When a management with a reputation for brilliance tackles a business with a reputation for poor fundamental economics, it is the reputation of the business that remains intact.

—WARREN BUFFETT, CHAIRMAN, BERKSHIRE HATHAWAY

The reinsurance business has the defect of being too attractive-looking to new entrants for its own good and will therefore always tend to be the opposite of, say, the old business of gathering and rendering dead horses that always tended to contain few and prosperous participants.

—CHARLES T. MUNGER, CHAIRMAN, WESCO FINANCIAL CORP.

OUTLINE

Introduction and Objectives

In this chapter and the next we explore the external environment of the firm. In Chapter 1 we observed that profound understanding of the competitive environment is a critical ingredient of a successful strategy. We further noted that business strategy is essentially a quest for profit. The primary task for this chapter is to identify the sources of profit in the external environment. The firm's proximate environment is its industry environment; hence the focus of our environmental analysis will be industry analysis.

Industry analysis is relevant both to corporate-level and business-level strategy.

- Corporate strategy is concerned with deciding which industries the firm should be engaged in and how it should allocate its resources among them. Such decisions require assessment of the attractiveness of different industries in terms of their profit potential. The main objective of this chapter is to understand how the competitive structure of an industry determines its profitability.

- Business strategy is concerned with establishing competitive advantage. By analyzing customer needs and preferences and the ways in which firms compete to serve customers, we identify the general sources of competitive advantage in an industry – what we call *key success factors*.

By the time you have completed this chapter you will be able to:

- Identify the main structural features of an industry that influence competition and profitability.

- Use industry analysis to explain why in some industries competition is more intense and profitability lower than in other industries.

- Use evidence on structural trends within industries to forecast changes in competition and profitability in the future.

- Develop strategies to influence industry structure in order to improve industry profitability.

- Analyze competition and customer requirements in order to identify opportunities for competitive advantage within an industry (*key success factors*).

From Environmental Analysis to Industry Analysis

The business environment of the firm consists of all the external influences that affect its decisions and performance. Given the vast number and range of external influences, how can managers hope to monitor, let alone analyze, environmental conditions? The starting point is some kind of system or framework for organizing information. For example, environmental influences can be classified by *source* – e.g. into political, economic, social, and technological factors ("PEST analysis") – or by *proximity* – the "micro-environment" or "task environment" can be distinguished from the wider influences that form the "macro-environment".[1] Though systematic, continuous scanning of the whole range of external influences might seem desirable, such extensive environmental analysis is unlikely to be cost effective and creates information overload.

The prerequisite for effective environmental analysis is to distinguish the vital from the merely important. To do this, let's return to first principles. For the firm to make profit it must create value for customers. Hence, it must understand its customers. Second, in creating value, the firm acquires goods and services from suppliers. Hence, it must understand its suppliers and manage relationships with them. Third, the ability to generate profitability depends on the intensity of competition among firms that vie for the same value-creating opportunities. Hence, the firm must understand competition. Thus, the core of the firm's business environment is formed by its relationships with three sets of players: customers, suppliers, and competitors. This is its industry environment.

This is not to say that macro-level factors such as general economic trends, changes in demographic structure, or social and political trends are unimportant to strategy analysis. These factors may be critical determinants of the threats and opportunities a company will face in the future. The key issue is how these more general environmental factors affect the firm's industry environment (Figure 3.1). Consider the threat of global warming. For most companies this is not an important strategic issue (at least, not for the next hundred years). However, for the producers of automobiles, global warming is a vital issue. But, to analyze the strategic implications of global warming, the automobile manufacturers need to trace its implications for their industry environment. For example, what will be the impact on demand – will consumers switch to more fuel-efficient cars? Will they abandon their cars in favor of public

FIGURE 3.1 From environmental analysis to industry analysis

transportation? With regard to competition, will there be new entry by manufacturers of electric vehicles into the car industry? Will increased R&D costs cause the industry to consolidate?

The Determinants of Industry Profit: Demand and Competition

If the purpose of strategy is to help a company to survive and make money, the starting point for industry analysis is a simple question: what determines the level of profit in an industry?

As already noted, business is about the creation of value for the customer, either by production (transforming inputs into outputs) or commerce (arbitrage). Value is created when the price the customer is willing to pay for a product exceeds the costs incurred by the firm. But value creation does not translate directly into profit. The surplus of value over cost is distributed between customers and producers by the forces of competition. The stronger is competition among producers, the more of the surplus is received by customers in *consumer surplus* (the difference between the price they actually pay and the maximum price they would have been willing to pay) and the less is the surplus received by producers (as *producer surplus* or *economic rent*). A single supplier of bottled water at an all-night rave can charge a price that fully exploits the dancers' thirst. If there are many suppliers of bottled water, then, in the absence of collusion, competition causes the price of bottled water to fall toward the cost of supplying it.

The surplus earned by producers over and above the minimum costs of production is not entirely captured in profits. Where an industry has powerful suppliers – monopolistic suppliers of components or employees united by a strong labor union – a substantial part of the surplus may be appropriated by these suppliers (the profits of suppliers or premium wages of union members).

The profits earned by the firms in an industry are thus determined by three factors:

- The value of the product to customers.
- The intensity of competition.
- The bargaining power of the producers relative to their suppliers.

Industry analysis brings all three factors into a single analytic framework.

Analyzing Industry Attractiveness

Table 3.1 shows the profitability of different US industries. Some industries (such as tobacco and pharmaceuticals) consistently earn high rates of profit; others (airlines, paper, and food production) fail to cover their cost of capital. The basic premise that underlies industry analysis is that the level of industry profitability is neither random nor the result of entirely industry-specific influences – it is determined by the systematic influences of the industry's structure. The US pharmaceutical industry and the US food production industry not only supply very different products, they also have very different structures, which make one highly profitable and the other a nightmare of price competition and weak margins. The pharmaceutical industry produces highly

TABLE 3.1 The profitability of US industries, 1999–2005

Industry	Median ROE 1999–2005 (%)	Leading companies
Household and Personal Products	22.7	Procter & Gamble, Kimberley-Clark, Colgate-Palmolive
Pharmaceuticals	22.3	Pfizer, Johnson & Johnson, Merck
Tobacco	21.6	Altria, Reynolds American, Universal
Food Consumer Products	19.6	PepsiCo, Sara Lee, Conagra
Securities	18.9	Morgan Stanley, Merrill Lynch, Goldman Sachs
Diversified Financials	18.3	General Electric, American Express
Beverages	17.5	Coca-Cola, Anheuser-Busch
Mining, Crude Oil Production	17.8	Occidental Petroleum, Devon Energy
Petroleum Refining	17.3	ExxonMobil, Chevron, ConocoPhillips
Medical Products and Equipment	17.2	Medtronic, Baxter International
Commercial Banks	15.5	Citigroup, Bank of America
Food Services	15.3	McDonald's, Yum Brands
Scientific, Photographic, and Control Equipment	15.0	Eastman Kodak, Danaher, Aligent
Apparel	14.4	Nike, VF, Jones Apparel
Computer Software	13.9	Microsoft, Oracle, CA
Publishing, Printing	13.5	R. R. Donnelley & Sons, Gannett
IT Services	13.5	EDS, Computer Sciences, Science Applications Intl.
Healthcare	13.1	United Health Group, Wellpoint, HCA, Medco
Electronics, Electrical Equipment	13.0	Emerson Electric, Whirlpool
Specialty Retailers	13.0	Home Depot, Costco, Lowe's
Chemicals	12.9	Dow Chemical, Du Pont
Engineering, Construction	12.0	Flour, Jacobs Engineering
Trucking, Truck Leasing	11.8	YRC Worldwide, Ryder System
Aerospace and Defense	11.7	Boeing, United Technologies, Lockheed Martin
Computers, Office Equipment	11.7	IBM, Hewlett-Packard, Dell Computer
Furniture	11.6	Leggett & Platt, Steelcase
Automotive Retailing and Services	11.3	AutoNation, United Auto Group
Wholesalers: Food and Grocery	11.3	Sysco, Supervalu, CHS
General Merchandisers	11.0	Wal-Mart, Target, Sears Holdings
Pipelines	11.0	Plains All-American Pipeline, Enterprise Products
Industrial and Farm Equipment	10.8	Caterpillar, Deere, Illinois Tool Works
Oil and Gas Equipment and Services	10.7	Halliburton, Baker Hughes
Utilities: Gas and Electric	10.4	Duke Energy, Dominion Resources
Energy Production	10.6	Constellation Energy, ONEOK
Food and Drug Stores	10.0	Kroger, Walgreen, Albertson's
Motor Vehicles and Parts	9.8	GM, Ford, Johnson Controls
Hotels, Casinos, Resorts	9.7	Marriott International, Harrah's Entertainment
Insurance: Life and Health	8.6	MetLife, New York Life
Packaging and Containers	8.6	Smurfit-Stone Container, Owens-Illinois
Real Estate	8.5	Cendant, Host Marriott, Simon Property Group
Insurance: Property and Casualty	8.3	American Intl. Group, Berkshire Hathaway

TABLE 3.1 (*cont'd*)

Industry	Median ROE 1999–2005 (%)	Leading companies
Building Materials, Glass	8.3	Owens Corning, USG, Armstrong Holdings
Metals	8.0	Alcoa, US Steel, Nucor
Food Production	7.2	Archer Daniels Midland, Tyson Foods
Forest and Paper Products	6.6	International Paper, Weyerhaeuser
Semiconductors and Electronic Components	5.9	Intel, Texas Instruments, Sanmina-SCI
Telecommunications	4.6	Verizon, AT&T, Sprint-Nextel
Network and Communications Equipment	1.2	Motorola, Cisco Systems, Lucent
Entertainment	0.4	Time Warner, Walt Disney, News Corp.
Airlines	(22.0)	AMR, UAL, Delta Airlines

Notes:

1   Median ROE for each industry averaged across the 7 years 1999–2005.

2   Industries with five or fewer firms were excluded. Also omitted were industries that were substantially redefined during 1999–2005.

SOURCE: DATA FROM FORTUNE 1000 BY INDUSTRY

differentiated products with price-insensitive consumers and each new product receives monopoly privileges in the form of 17-year patents. The food industry produces commodity products with slow-growing demand and overcapacity, and is squeezed by powerful retail customers.

These industry patterns tend to be fairly consistent across countries. Figure 3.2 shows return on capital for a number of global industries.

Particularly high rates of profit often result from industry segments dominated by a single firm. These niche markets provide attractive havens from the rigors of fierce competition. Strategy Capsule 3.1 offers some examples.

The underlying theory of how industry structure drives competitive behavior and determines industry profitability is provided by industrial organization (IO) economics. The two reference points are the *theory of monopoly* and the *theory of perfect competition* which form end points of the spectrum of industry structures. *Monopoly* exists where an industry comprises a single firm protected by high barriers to entry. The monopolist can appropriate in profit the full amount of the value it creates. At the other extreme, *perfect competition* exists where there are many firms supplying an identical product with no restrictions on entry or exit. Here, the rate of profit falls to a level that just covers firms' cost of capital. In the real world, industries fall between these two extremes. The US market for chewing tobacco is close to being a monopoly; the Chicago grain markets are close to being perfectly competitive. Most manufacturing industries and many service industries tend to be *oligopolies*: they are dominated by a small number of major companies. Table 3.2 identifies some key points on the spectrum. By examining the principal structural features and their interactions for any particular industry, it is possible to predict the type of competitive behavior likely to emerge and the resulting level of profitability.

FIGURE 3.2 Profitability of global industries

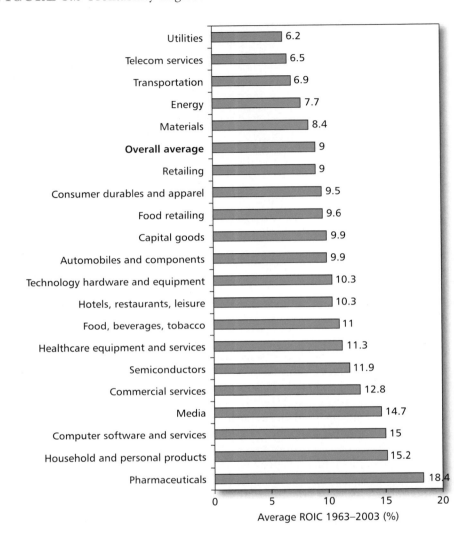

SOURCE: T. KOLLER, M. GOEDHART, AND D. WESSELS, VALUATION: MEASURING AND MANAGING THE VALUE OF COMPANIES, 4TH EDN. (WILEY, HOBOKEN NJ, 2005). REPRINTED BY PERMISSION OF JOHN WILEY & SONS, INC. © 2005.

STRATEGY CAPSULE 3.1

Chewing Tobacco, Sausage Skins, and Slot Machines: The Joys of Niche Markets

UST Inc. (formerly US Tobacco) has been the most profitable company in the S&P500 over the past 10 years. During 2003–5 UST earned an ROIC (operating profit as percentage of total assets less current liabilities) of 68%. What's the secret of UST's success? It controls 78% of the US market for "smokeless tobacco" (chewing tobacco and snuff), with brands such as Skoal, Copenhagen, Long Cut, and Red Seal. Despite its association with a bygone era of cowboys and farm workers, chewing tobacco has been a growth market over the past two decades with a surprisingly large number of young consumers. UST's long-established brands, its distribution through tens of thousands of small retail outlets, and the unwillingness of major tobacco companies to enter this market (due to the poor image and social unacceptability of the product) have made UST's market position unassailable. Restrictions on advertising of smokeless tobacco products have further buttressed UST's market dominance by making it more difficult for would-be entrants to establish their brands.

Devro plc, based in the Scottish village of Moodiesburn, is the world's leading supplier of collagen sausage skins ("casings"). "From the British 'Banger' to the Chinese Lap Cheong, from the French Merguez to the South American Chourizo, Devro has a casing to suit all product types." Its overall world market share is around 60%, rising to 94% in the UK market and 83% in Australia. In recent years its ROIC has averaged 18% and its return on equity 30%.

International Game Technology (IGT) based in Reno, Nevada, is the world's dominant manufacturer of slot machines for casinos and other establishments that allow gambling machines. With a continuous flow of new gaming machines – 2005 saw 172 new products launched, including Megabucks, Persian Princess, and Lucky Larry's Lobstermania – IGT has over 70% of the US market share and market leadership in several European countries, including the UK. With heavy investment in R&D, new product saturation, tight control over distribution and servicing, and a policy of leasing rather than selling machines, IGT's market leadership appears well-entrenched. During 2004–6, IGT earned an average ROE of 25%.

Sources: www.ustinc.com, www.devro.com, www.igt.com

Porter's Five Forces of Competition Framework

Table 3.2 identifies four structural variables influencing competition and profitability. In practice, there are many features of an industry that determine the intensity of competition and the level of profitability. A helpful, widely used framework for classifying and analyzing these factors was developed by Michael Porter of Harvard Business School.[2] Porter's five forces of competition framework views the profitability of an industry (as indicated by its rate of return on capital relative to its cost of capital) as determined by five sources of competitive pressure. These five forces of competition include three sources of "horizontal" competition: competition from substitutes, competition from entrants, and competition from established rivals; and

TABLE 3.2 The spectrum of industry structures

	Perfect Competition	Oligopoly	Duopoly	Monopoly
Concentration	Many firms	A few firms	Two firms	One firm
Entry and Exit Barriers	No barriers	Significant barriers		High barriers
Product Differentiation	Homogeneous product (Commodity)	Potential for product differentiation		
Information Availability	No impediments to information flow	Imperfect availability of information		

two sources of "vertical" competition: the power of suppliers and power of buyers (see Figure 3.3).

The strength of each of these competitive forces is determined by a number of key structural variables, as shown in Figure 3.4.

Competition from Substitutes

The price customers are willing to pay for a product depends, in part, on the availability of substitute products. The absence of close substitutes for a product, as in the case of gasoline or cigarettes, means that consumers are comparatively insensitive to

FIGURE 3.3 Porter's five forces of competition framework

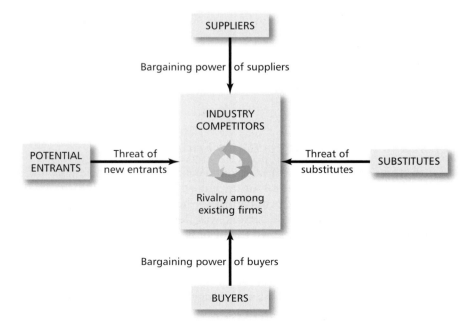

FIGURE 3.4 The structural determinants of the five forces of competition

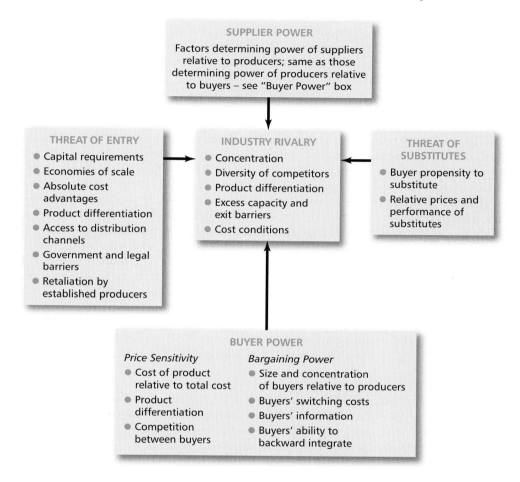

price (i.e., demand is inelastic with respect to price). The existence of close substitutes means that customers will switch to substitutes in response to price increases for the product (i.e., demand is elastic with respect to price). The internet has provided a new source of substitute competition that has proved devastating for a number of established industries. Travel agencies, newspapers, and telecommunication providers have all suffered devastating competition from internet-based substitutes.

The extent to which substitutes depress prices and profits depends on the propensity of buyers to substitute between alternatives. This, in turn, is dependent on their price–performance characteristics. If city-center to city-center travel between Washington and New York is 50 minutes quicker by air than by train and the average traveler values time at $30 an hour, the implication is that the train will be competitive at fares of $25 below those charged by the airlines. The more complex the product and the more difficult it is to discern performance differences, the lower the extent of substitution by customers on the basis of price differences. The failure of low-priced imitations of leading perfumes to establish significant market share reflects consumers' difficulty in recognizing the performance characteristics of different fragrances.

Threat of Entry

If an industry earns a return on capital in excess of its cost of capital, it will act as a magnet to firms outside the industry. If the entry of new firms is unrestricted, the rate of profit will fall toward its competitive level. The US bagel industry faced a flood of new entrants in the late 1990s that caused a sharp decline in profitability.[3] Why is it that my wife, a psychotherapist, earns much less than our niece, a recently qualified medical doctor? Barriers to entry are one factor. In psychotherapy there are multiple accrediting bodies and limited state licensing, hence the entry barriers to psychotherapy are much lower than in medicine.

Threat of entry rather than actual entry may be sufficient to ensure that established firms constrain their prices to the competitive level. Only American Airlines offers a direct service between Dallas-Fort Worth and Santa Barbara, California, for example. Yet, American may be unwilling to exploit its monopoly power to the full if Southwest or another airline can easily extend its routes to cover the same two cities. An industry where no barriers to entry or exit exist is *contestable*: prices and profits tend towards the competitive level, regardless of the number of firms within the industry.[4] Contestability depends on the absence of sunk costs – investments whose value cannot be recovered on exit. An absence of sunk costs makes an industry vulnerable to "hit-and-run" entry whenever established firms raise their prices above the competitive level.

In most industries, however, new entrants cannot enter on equal terms with those of established firms. A barrier to entry is any advantage that established firms have over entrants. The height of a barrier to entry is usually measured as the unit cost disadvantage faced by would-be entrants. The principal sources of barriers to entry are discussed below.

Capital Requirements The capital costs of getting established in an industry can be so large as to discourage all but the largest companies. The duopoly of Boeing and Airbus in large passenger jets is protected by the huge capital costs of establishing R&D, production, and service facilities for supplying these planes. Similarly with the business of launching commercial satellites: the costs of developing rockets and launch facilities make new entry highly unlikely. In other industries, entry costs can be modest. One reason why the e-commerce boom of the late 1990s ended in financial disaster for most participants is that the initial setup costs of new internet-based ventures were typically very low. Across the service sector more generally, startup costs tend to be low. For example, startup costs for a franchised pizza outlet begin at $141,000 for a Domino's, $250,000 for a Papa John's, and $1.1 million for a Pizza Hut.[5]

Economies of Scale In industries that are capital or research or advertising intensive, efficiency requires large-scale operation. The problem for new entrants is that they are faced with the choice of either entering on a small scale and accepting high unit costs, or entering on a large scale and bearing the costs of underutilized capacity. In automobiles, cost efficiency means producing at least three million vehicles a year. As a result, the only recent entrants into volume car production have been state-supported companies (e.g., Proton of Malaysia and Maruti of India). The main source of scale economies is new product development costs. Thus, developing and launching a new model of car typically costs over $1.5 billion. Airbus's A380 superjumbo cost about $15 billion to develop and must sell over 300 planes to break even. Once

Airbus had committed to the project, then Boeing was effectively excluded from the superjumbo segment of the market.

Absolute Cost Advantages Established firms may have a unit cost advantage over entrants irrespective of scale. Absolute cost advantages often result from the acquisition of low-cost sources of raw materials. Saudi Aramco's access to the world's biggest and most accessible oil reserves give it an unassailable cost advantage over Shell, Exxon Mobil, and BP, whose costs per barrel are at least three times those of Saudi Aramco. Absolute cost advantages may also result from economies of learning. Sharp's cost advantage in LCD flat screen TVs results from its early entry into LCDs and its speed in moving down the learning curve.

Product Differentiation In an industry where products are differentiated, established firms possess the advantages of brand recognition and customer loyalty. The percentage of US consumers loyal to a single brand varies from under 30% in batteries, canned vegetables, and garbage bags, up to 61% in toothpaste, 65% in mayonnaise, and 71% in cigarettes.[6] New entrants to such markets must spend disproportionately heavily on advertising and promotion to gain levels of brand awareness and brand goodwill similar to that of established companies. One study found that, compared to early entrants, late entrants into consumer goods markets incurred additional advertising and promotional costs amounting to 2.12% of sales revenue.[7]

Access to Channels of Distribution For many new suppliers of consumer goods, the principal barrier to entry is likely to be gaining distribution. Limited capacity within distribution channels (e.g., shelf space), risk aversion by retailers, and the fixed costs associated with carrying an additional product result in retailers being reluctant to carry a new manufacturer's product. The battle for supermarket shelf space between the major food processors (typically involving "slotting fees" to reserve shelf space) further disadvantages new entrants. One of the most important economic impacts of the internet has been allowing new businesses to circumvent barriers to distribution.

Governmental and Legal Barriers Economists from the Chicago School claim that the only effective barriers to entry are those created by government. In taxicabs, banking, telecommunications, and broadcasting, entry usually requires the granting of a license by a public authority. From medieval times to the present day, companies and favored individuals have benefitted from governments granting them an exclusive right to ply a particular trade or offer a particular service. In knowledge-intensive industries, patents, copyrights, and other legally protected forms of intellectual property are major barriers to entry. Xerox Corporation's monopolization of the plain-paper copier industry until the late 1970s was protected by a wall of over 2,000 patents relating to its xerography process. Regulatory requirements and environmental and safety standards often put new entrants at a disadvantage to established firms because compliance costs tend to weigh more heavily on newcomers.

Retaliation Barriers to entry also depend on the entrants' expectations as to possible retaliation by established firms. Retaliation against a new entrant may take the form of aggressive price-cutting, increased advertising, sales promotion, or litigation. The major airlines have a long history of retaliation against low-cost entrants.

Southwest and other budget airlines have alleged that selective price cuts by American and other major airlines amounted to predatory pricing designed to prevent its entry into new routes.[8] To avoid retaliation by incumbents, new entrants may seek initial small-scale entry into less visible market segments. When Toyota, Nissan, and Honda first entered the US auto market, they targeted the small car segments, partly because this was a segment that had been written off by the Detroit Big Three as inherently unprofitable.[9]

The Effectiveness of Barriers to Entry   Empirical research shows industries protected by high entry barriers tend to earn above average rates of profit.[10] Capital requirements and advertising appear to be particularly effective impediments to entry.[11]

The effectiveness of barriers to entry depends on the resources and capabilities that potential entrants possess. Barriers that are effective against new companies may be ineffective against established firms that are diversifying from other industries. George Yip found no evidence that entry barriers deterred new entry.[12] Some entrants possessed resources that allowed them to surmount barriers and compete against incumbent firms using similar strategies. Thus, Mars used its strong position in confectionery to enter the ice cream market, while Virgin has used its brand name to enter a wide range of industries from airlines to telecommunications.

Rivalry Between Established Competitors

For most industries, the major determinant of the overall state of competition and the general level of profitability is competition among the firms within the industry. In some industries, firms compete aggressively – sometimes to the extent that prices are pushed below the level of costs and industry-wide losses are incurred. In other industries, price competition is muted and rivalry focuses on advertising, innovation, and other nonprice dimensions. The intensity of competition between established firms is the result of interactions between six factors. Let us look at each of them.

Concentration   Seller concentration refers to the number and size distribution of firms competing within a market. It is most commonly measured by the *concentration ratio*: the combined market share of the leading producers. For example, the four-firm concentration ratio (*CR4*) is the market share of the four largest producers. In markets dominated by a single firm (e.g., Microsoft in PC operating systems, or UST in the US smokeless tobacco market), the dominant firm can exercise considerable discretion over the prices it charges. Where a market is dominated by a small group of leading companies (an oligopoly), price competition may also be restrained, either by outright collusion, or more commonly through "parallelism" of pricing decisions.[13] Thus, in markets dominated by two companies, such as alkaline batteries (Duracell and Energizer), color film (Kodak and Fuji), and soft drinks (Coke and Pepsi), prices tend to be similar and competition focuses on advertising, promotion, and product development. As the number of firms supplying a market increases, coordination of prices becomes more difficult, and the likelihood that one firm will initiate price-cutting increases. However, despite the common observation that the elimination of a competitor reduces price competition, while the entry of a new competitor stimulates it, systematic evidence of the impact of seller concentration on profitability is surprisingly weak. Richard Schmalensee concluded that: "The relation, if any, between seller concentration and profitability is weak statistically and the estimated effect is usually small."[14]

Diversity of Competitors The extent to which a group of firms can avoid price competition in favor of collusive pricing practices depends on how similar they are in their origins, objectives, costs, and strategies. The cozy atmosphere of the US auto industry prior to the advent of import competition was greatly assisted by the similarities of the companies in terms of cost structures, strategies, and top management mindsets. The intense competition that affects the car markets of Europe and North America today is partly due to the different national origins, costs, strategies, and management styles of the competing firms. Similarly, the key challenge faced by OPEC is agreeing and enforcing output quotas among member countries that are sharply different in terms of objectives, production costs, politics, and religion.

Product Differentiation The more similar the offerings among rival firms, the more willing customers are to substitute and the greater the incentive for firms to cut prices to increase sales. Where the products of rival firms are virtually indistinguishable, the product is a commodity and price is the sole basis for competition. Commodity industries such as agriculture, mining, and petrochemicals tend to be plagued by price wars and low profits. By contrast, in industries where products are highly differentiated (perfumes, pharmaceuticals, restaurants, management consulting services), price competition tends to be weak, even though there may be many firms competing.

Excess Capacity and Exit Barriers Why does industry profitability tend to fall so drastically during periods of recession? The key is the balance between demand and capacity. Unused capacity encourages firms to offer price cuts to attract new business in order to spread fixed costs over a greater sales volume. Excess capacity may be cyclical (e.g. the boom–bust cycle in the semiconductor industry); it may also be part of a structural problem resulting from overinvestment and declining demand. In these latter situations, the key issue is whether excess capacity will leave the industry. *Barriers to exit* are costs associated with capacity leaving an industry. Where resources are durable and specialized, and where employees are entitled to job protection, barriers to exit may be substantial.[15] In the European and North American auto industry excess capacity together with high exit barriers have devastated industry profitability. Conversely, rapid demand growth creates capacity shortages that boost margins. Between 2001 and 2005, bulk cargo shipping rates increased sevenfold as a result of increased world demand for commodities.[16] On average, companies in growing industries earn higher profits than companies in slow growing or declining industries (see Figure 3.5).

Cost Conditions: Scale Economies and the Ratio of Fixed to Variable Costs When excess capacity causes price competition, how low will prices go? The key factor is cost structure. Where fixed costs are high relative to variable costs, firms will take on marginal business at any price that covers variable costs. The consequences for profitability can be disastrous. Between 2001 and 2003, the total losses of the US airline industry exceeded the cumulative profits earned during the entire previous history of the industry. The willingness of airlines to offer heavily discounted tickets on flights with low bookings reflects the very low variable costs of filling empty seats. Similarly, the devastating impact of excess capacity on profitability in tires, hotels, and semiconductors is a result of high fixed costs in these businesses and the willingness of firms to accept additional business at any price that covers variable costs.

Scale economies may also encourage companies to compete aggressively on price in order to gain the cost benefits of greater volume. If scale efficiency in the auto

FIGURE 3.5 The impact of growth on profitability

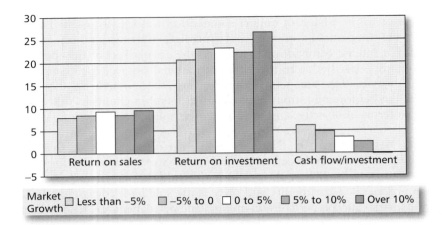

SOURCE: R. D. BUZZELL AND B. T. GALE, *THE PIMS PRINCIPLES* (NEW YORK: FREE PRESS, 1987): 56–7. © 1987 BY THE FREE PRESS. ALL RIGHTS RESERVED. REPRINTED BY PERMISSION OF THE FREE PRESS, A DIVISION OF SIMON & SCHUSTER, INC.

industry means producing four million cars a year, a level that is achieved by only six of the nineteen international auto companies, the outcome is a battle for market share as each firm tries to achieve critical mass.

Bargaining Power of Buyers

The firms in an industry operate in two types of markets: in the markets for inputs and the markets for outputs. In input markets firms purchase raw materials, components, and financial and labor services. In the markets for outputs firms sell their goods and services to customers (who may be distributors, consumers, or other manufacturers). In both markets the transactions create value for both buyers and sellers. How this value is shared between them in terms of profitability depends on their relative economic power. Let us deal first with output markets. The strength of buying power that firms face from their customers depends on two sets of factors: buyers' price sensitivity and relative bargaining power.

Buyers' Price Sensitivity   The extent to which buyers are sensitive to the prices charged by the firms in an industry depends on four main factors:

- The greater the importance of an item as a proportion of total cost, the more sensitive buyers will be about the price they pay. Beverage manufacturers are highly sensitive to the costs of aluminum cans because this is one of their largest single cost items. Conversely, most companies are not sensitive to the fees charged by their auditors, since auditing costs are such a small proportion of overall company expenses.

- The less differentiated the products of the supplying industry, the more willing the buyer is to switch suppliers on the basis of price. The manufacturers of T-shirts and light bulbs have much more to fear from Wal-Mart's buying power than have the suppliers of perfumes.

- The more intense the competition among buyers, the greater their eagerness for price reductions from their sellers. As competition in the world automobile industry has intensified, so component suppliers face greater pressures for lower prices.

- The more critical an industry's product to the quality of the buyer's product or service, the less sensitive are buyers to the prices they are charged. The buying power of personal computer manufacturers relative to the manufacturers of microprocessors (Intel and AMD) is limited by the vital importance of these components to the functionality of PCs.

Relative Bargaining Power Bargaining power rests, ultimately, on refusal to deal with the other party. The balance of power between the two parties to a transaction depends on the credibility and effectiveness with which each makes this threat. The key issue is the relative cost that each party sustains as a result of the transaction not being consummated. A second issue is each party's expertise in managing its position. Several factors influence the bargaining power of buyers relative to that of sellers:

- *Size and concentration of buyers relative to suppliers.* The smaller the number of buyers and the bigger their purchases, the greater the cost of losing one. Because of their size, health maintenance organizations (HMOs) can purchase healthcare from hospitals and doctors at much lower cost than can individual patients. Several empirical studies show that buyer concentration lowers prices and profits in the supplying industry.[17]
- *Buyers' information.* The better informed buyers are about suppliers and their prices and costs, the better they are able to bargain. Doctors and lawyers do not normally display the prices they charge, nor do traders in the bazaars of Tangier and Istanbul. Keeping customers ignorant of relative prices is an effective constraint on their buying power. But knowing prices is of little value if the quality of the product is unknown. In the markets for haircuts, interior design, and management consulting, the ability of buyers to bargain over price is limited by uncertainty over the precise attributes of the product they are buying.
- *Ability to integrate vertically.* In refusing to deal with the other party, the alternative to finding another supplier or buyer is to do it yourself. Large food-processing companies such as Heinz and Campbell Soup have reduced their dependence on the manufacturers of metal cans by manufacturing their own. The leading retail chains have increasingly displaced their suppliers' brands with their own-brand products. Backward integration need not necessarily occur – a credible threat may suffice.

Bargaining Power of Suppliers

Analysis of the determinants of relative power between the producers in an industry and their suppliers is precisely analogous to analysis of the relationship between producers and their buyers. The only difference is that it is now the firms in the industry that are the buyers and the producers of inputs that are the suppliers. The key issues are the ease with which the firms in the industry can switch between different input suppliers and the relative bargaining power of each party.

Because raw materials, semi-finished products, and components are often commodities supplied by small companies to large manufacturing companies, their suppliers usually lack bargaining power. Hence, commodity suppliers often seek to boost their bargaining power through cartelization (e.g., OPEC, the International Coffee Organization, and farmers' marketing cooperatives). A similar logic explains labor unions. Conversely, the suppliers of complex, technically sophisticated components may be able to exert considerable bargaining power. The dismal profitability of the

FIGURE 3.6 The impact of unionization on profitability

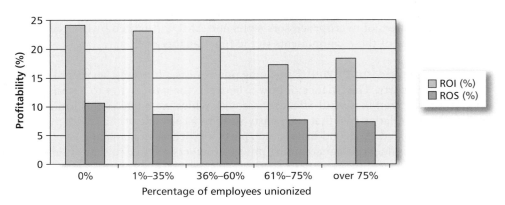

SOURCE: R. D. BUZZELL AND B. T. GALE, *THE PIMS PRINCIPLES: LINKING STRATEGY TO PERFORMANCE* (NEW YORK: FREE PRESS, 1987): 67 © 1987 BY THE FREE PRESS, ALL RIGHTS RESERVED. REPRINTED BY PERMISSION OF THE FREE PRESS, A DIVISION OF SIMON & SCHUSTER, INC.

personal computer industry may be attributed to the power exercised by the suppliers of key components (processors, disk drives, LCD screens) and the dominant supplier of operating systems (Microsoft).

Labor unions are important sources of supplier power. Where an industry has a high percentage of its employees unionized – as in steel, airlines, and automobiles – profitability is reduced (see Figure 3.6).

Applying Industry Analysis

Once we understand how industry structure drives competition, which, in turn, determines industry profitability, we can apply this analysis, first to forecasting industry profitability in the future, and second to devising strategies for changing industry structure.

Describing Industry Structure

The first stage of industry analysis is to identify the key elements of the industry's structure. In principle, this is a simple task. It requires identifying who are the main players – the producers, the customers, the suppliers, and the producers of substitute goods – then examining some of the key structural characteristics of each of these groups that will determine competition and bargaining power.

In most manufacturing industries the identity of the different groups of players is usually straightforward, in other industries – particularly in service industries – building a picture of the industry may be more difficult. Consider the supply of television programming. There are a number of different types of player and establishing which are buyers, which are sellers, and where the industry boundaries lie is not simple. In terms of industry definition, do we consider all forms of TV distribution or identify separate industries for broadcast TV, cable TV, and satellite TV? In terms of identifying buyers and sellers, we see that there the industry has quite a complex value chain with the producers of the individual shows, networks that put together program schedules, and local broadcasting and cable companies that undertake final distribution. For the distribution companies there are two buyers – viewers and advertisers. Some companies are vertically integrated across several stages of the value chain – thus, networks such as Fox and NBC not only create and distribute program schedules, they are also backward integrated into producing some TV shows and they are forward integrated into local distribution through ownership of local TV stations.

Sorting out the different players and their relationships therefore involves some critical issues of industry definition. Which activities within the value chain do we include in the industry? What are the horizontal boundaries of the industry in terms of both products and geographical scope? We shall return to some of these issues of industry definition in a subsequent section.

Forecasting Industry Profitability

We can use industry analysis to understand why profitability has been low in some industries and high in others but, ultimately, our interest in industry analysis is not to explain the past, but to *predict the future*. Investment decisions made today will commit resources to an industry for a decade or more – hence, it is critical that we are able to predict what industry profitability is likely to be in the future. Current profitability tends to be a poor indicator of future profitability. However, if an industry's profitability is determined by the structure of that industry, then we can use observations of the structural trends in an industry to forecast the likely changes in competition and profitability. Given that changes in industry structure tend to be long term and are the result of fundamental shifts in customer buying behavior, technology, and firm strategies, we can use our current observations to identify emerging structural trends.

To predict the future profitability of an industry, our analysis proceeds in three stages:

1 Examine how the industry's current and recent levels of competition and profitability are a consequence of the industry's present structure.

2 Identify the trends that are changing the industry's structure. Is the industry consolidating? Are new players seeking to enter? Are the industry's products becoming more differentiated or more commoditized? Does it look as though additions to industry capacity will outstrip the industry's growth of demand?

3 Identify how these structural changes will affect the five forces of competition and resulting profitability of the industry. Compared with the present, does it seem as though the changes in industry structure will cause competition to intensify or to weaken? Rarely do all the structural changes move competition in a consistent direction – typically, some factors will cause competition to increase; others will cause competition to moderate. Hence, determining the overall impact on profitability is likely to be a matter of judgment.

Strategy Capsule 3.2 discusses the future profitability of the US casino industry. During the past 20 years industry profitability has been undermined by two major forces: increasing international competition and accelerating technological change. Despite widespread optimism that the "TMT" (technology, media, and telecommunication) boom of the late 1990s would usher in a new era of profitability, the reality was very different. Digital technologies and the internet both increased competitive pressures through lowering entry barriers and causing industries to converge. (See Strategy Capsule 3.3.)

STRATEGY CAPSULE 3.2
Prospects for the US Casino Industry

The early years of the 21st century saw a continuation of the US casino boom that had begun during the mid-1990s. Between 1991 and 2005, the installed base of gaming machines increased from 184,000 to 829,000 machines, while US expenditure on gambling revenues rose from $304 billion to $850 billion over the same period. Despite the costs of expansion, the two industry leaders continued to earn good profits. Harrah's Entertainment (Grand Casino, Caesar's, Bally's, Paris) earned an average ROE of 14.8% during 2003–5, while MGM Mirage (Bellagio, New York New York, Luxor, Excalibur, MGM Grand) earned an average ROE of 12.6%. However, the bankruptcy of Trump Hotels and Casinos at the end of 2004 had raised a question mark over the industry. Was Trump's entry into Chapter 11 an isolated case of bad management, or did it point to an industry future of intensifying competition and declining margins?

The most visible sign of expansion was the race to build the "biggest and best" hotel-casino complexes in Las Vegas. Between 1996 and 2000, the number of hotel rooms in Las Vegas casinos more than doubled. New "mega-casinos" in Vegas included the MGM Grand, the Bellagio, New York New York, and the Venetian. Competition between the casinos involved ever more ambitious differentiation in terms of spectacle, entertainment, theming, and sheer scale. Price competition was also evident in terms of subsidized travel packages, free rooms, and other perks for "high rollers."

However, by far the greater part of industry expansion was outside the traditional centers in Las Vegas and Atlantic City, NJ. The municipalities and state governments saw gambling as a new source of tax revenue and a stimulus to economic development. The result was the introduction of riverboat casinos and the licensing of casinos in Mississippi and seven other states. Most important was the opening of new casinos on Indian reservations. By 2006 there were some 120 casinos on Indian reservations across 17 states. One of the biggest was Foxwood's, owned by the Mashantucket Pequot tribe in Ledyard, CT. At the end of 2005, there were 287,000 gaming machines in casinos located on tribal lands compared with 459,000 in "traditional" casinos (including riverboats and cruise ships).

During 2006–7, geographical expansion of gambling seemed set to continue with several new casinos in Indian reservations in California and more permissive approaches to gambling in California, Washington State, Florida, and Oklahoma.

A further source of new competition was the internet. Although illegal in the US, internet gambling (especially poker) through non-US internet gambling companies grew massively during 2000–5.

With the growth of casino capacity and new gambling opportunities far outstripping growth in demand, what would the implications be for competition and profitability? Much would depend on how the leading casino companies responded to the deteriorating competitive situation. During 2005, the industry had experienced another merger wave. Former industry leader Park Place was acquired by Harrah's, while MGM Mirage acquired the number 4 in the industry, Mandalay Resorts. As a result, two companies, Harrah's and MGM Mirage, dominated the industry with the reconstituted Trump Entertainment Resorts a distant third.

The Internet: Value Creator or Value Destroyer?

The diffusion of the internet during the late 1990s and the creation of a host of businesses that sought to exploit its economic potential resulted in one of the most spectacular stock market booms in history. Pets.com, Webvan.com, Kozmo.com, and Boo.com all burned through hundreds of millions of dollars of venture capital and, in several cases, achieved stock market values over $1 billion before descending into bankruptcy.

So what are the true industrial economics of e-business? What can Porter's five forces analysis tell us about the likely profit potential of new internet-based businesses?

The first thing to note is that most new electronic businesses were not fundamentally new businesses. For the most part they used a new distribution channel for existing goods and services: books (Amazon), airline tickets (Expedia), groceries (Peapod), and securities (E-Trade). As such, the main features of these markets are: strong substitute competition from traditional retail distribution, low entry barriers (setting up a website costs little), and weak product differentiation. The principal structural features of these "e-tailing" businesses are shown below:

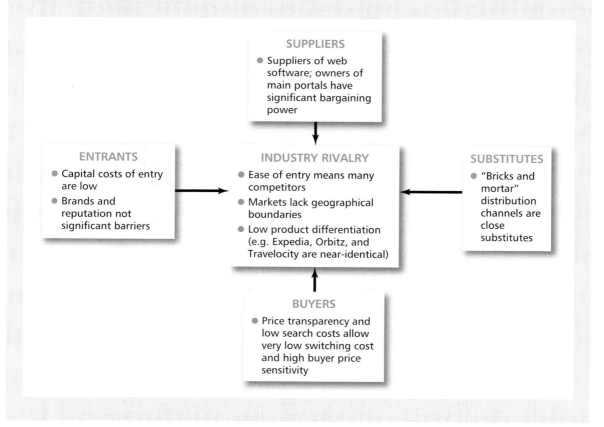

SUPPLIERS
- Suppliers of web software; owners of main portals have significant bargaining power

ENTRANTS
- Capital costs of entry are low
- Brands and reputation not significant barriers

INDUSTRY RIVALRY
- Ease of entry means many competitors
- Markets lack geographical boundaries
- Low product differentiation (e.g. Expedia, Orbitz, and Travelocity are near-identical)

SUBSTITUTES
- "Bricks and mortar" distribution channels are close substitutes

BUYERS
- Price transparency and low search costs allow very low switching cost and high buyer price sensitivity

The implication is that most "e-tailing" markets – whether for books, securities, household goods, or hotel accommodation – will tend to be highly competitive and, on average, will generate low margins and low rates of return on capital. Will any e-businesses offer high profitability? The key is the potential to reduce rivalry and raise barriers to entry through strategies that exploit network effects, economies of scale, or product differentiation. For example, eBay exploits network effects to dominate the person-to-person auction business; in books, Amazon relies on scale economies and product differentiation through its range of customer services; Google exploits scale economies and differentiation based on rapid innovation to dominate web search.

Sources: M. E. Porter, "Strategy and the Internet," *Harvard Business Review* (March 2001): 63–77; "The E-Commerce Winners," *Business Week* (August 3, 2001).

Strategies to Alter Industry Structure

Understanding how the structural characteristics of an industry determine the intensity of competition and the level of profitability provides a basis for identifying opportunities for changing industry structure to alleviate competitive pressures. The first issue is to identify the key structural features of an industry that are responsible for depressing profitability. The second is to consider which of these structural features are amenable to change through appropriate strategic initiatives. For example:

- The remarkable profit revival in the world steel industry since 2002 owes much to the rapid consolidation of the industry, led by Mittal Steel.[18]
- Excess capacity was a major problem in the European petrochemicals industry. Through a series of bilateral plant exchanges, each company built a leading position within a particular product area.[19]
- In the US airline industry, the major airlines have struggled to change an unfavorable industry structure. In the absence of significant product differentiation, the airlines have used frequent-flier schemes to build customer loyalty. Through hub-and-spoke route systems, the companies have achieved dominance of particular airports: American at Dallas-Fort Worth, US Airways at Charlotte NC, and Northwest at Detroit and Memphis. Mergers and alliances have reduced the numbers of competitors on many routes.[20]
- Building entry barriers is a vital strategy for preserving high profitability in the long run. A primary goal of the American Medical Association has been to maintain the incomes of its members by controlling the numbers of doctors trained in the United States and imposing barriers to the entry of doctors from overseas.

Defining Industries: Where to Draw the Boundaries

In our earlier discussion of the structure of the television broadcasting industry, I noted that a key challenge in industry analysis is defining the relevant industry. The Standard Industrial Classification (SIC) offers an official guide, but this provides limited practical assistance. Suppose Jaguar, a subsidiary of Ford Motor Company, is assessing its future prospects. In forecasting the profitability of its industry, should Jaguar consider itself part of the "motor vehicles and equipment" industry (SIC 371), the automobile industry (SIC 3712), or the luxury car industry? Should it view its industry as national (UK), regional (Europe), or global?

Industries and Markets

The first issue is clarifying what we mean by the term "industry." Economists define an industry as a group of firms that supplies a market. Hence, a close correspondence exists between markets and industries. So, what's the difference between analyzing industry structure and analyzing market structure? The principal difference is that industry analysis – notably five forces analysis – looks at industry profitability being determined by competition in two markets: product markets and input markets.

Everyday usage makes a bigger distinction between industries and markets. Typically, industry is identified with relatively broad sectors, while markets refer to specific products. Thus, the firms within the packaging industry compete in many distinct product markets – glass containers, steel cans, aluminum cans, paper cartons, plastic containers, and so on.

Similar issues arise in relation to geographical boundaries. From an economist's viewpoint, the US automobile industry would denote all companies supplying the US auto market – irrespective of their location. In everyday usage, the term "US auto industry" typically refers to auto manufacturers located within the US, and is often restricted to US-owned automakers (which now includes primarily Ford and General Motors).

For the purposes of industry analysis, we need to adopt the economist's approach to identifying and defining industries. Thus, our starting point is the market – which are the groups of firms that compete to supply a particular service? The result may be that, for the purposes of industry analysis, we may wish to disregard conventional concepts of industry. For example, if we are examining competition within the banking industry, it is likely that we would want to regard banking as comprising a number of industries – banks supply a number of distinct services and competition in each product market comprises different sets of firms. Most basic is the distinction between retail banking and investment banking. Even within retail banking we can distinguish different product groups. For example, credit cards and consumer lending are closely related products, but they involve distinct product offerings and different groups of competing firms.

Given the conventional view of industries as broad economic sectors, it can be revealing to focus on competition using a micro-level approach that begins with customers choosing between rival offerings (see Strategy Capsule 3.4).

Defining Markets: Substitution in Demand and Supply

I have argued that the key to defining industry boundaries is identifying the relevant market. By focusing on the relevant market, we do not lose sight of the critical relationship among firms within an industry: competition. But how do we define markets?

A market's boundaries are defined by *substitutability*. There are two dimensions to this – substitutability on the demand side and the supply side. Let us consider once more the market within which Jaguar competes. Starting with the demand side, if customers are unwilling to substitute trucks for cars on the basis of price differences,

STRATEGY CAPSULE 3.4
Analyzing Competition in Markets for Offerings

Mathur and Kenyon argue that our conventional concept of industry is fundamentally flawed. In order to analyze competition, we must begin with customer choice. Customers do not choose a product or a company, their unit of choice is the single *offering*. Competitive strategy is the "positioning of a single offering vis-à-vis a unique set of potential customers and competitors." To analyze competition, it makes no sense to talk about the "watch market" or the "watch industry" – the Patek Philippe Sky Moon Tourbillon that sells at about half a million dollars does not compete with the $35 Timex Sport Watch. Similarly, a $1,400 Swatch Lustrous Bliss Sapphire Watch is not a close competitor to Swatch's $39.95 Pampas Rider. Each model by each watch maker is a separate offering and each offering forms a distinct market where competitors can be ranked according to how closely they compete with the focal offering. Thus, if we consider the Seiko Men's Steel Watch ($81), we can view the Citizen Men's Steel Watch ($78) and Timex T29771 ($60) as close competitors; the Bulova Infinity ($150) and Swatch Once Again ($45) are more distant competitors.

This micro approach to analyzing competition focuses on customer choices and contrasts sharply with Porter's industry analysis that examines competition at a much higer level of aggregation.

Should we abandon our more aggregated industry analysis in favor of the meticulously micro analysis advocated by Mathur and Kenyon? The critical consideration is the type of question that we want our competitive analysis to answer. For decisions relating to marketing strategy – including product design, pricing, advertising, distribution, and entry into specific market segments – analysis of competition between narrowly defined offerings in relation to specific customers and customer groups is likely to be particularly revealing.

For understanding and predicting medium-term profit trends, the conventional five forces analysis of fairly broadly defined industries has two virtues. First, it allows us to consider competition in two markets simultaneously – the market for outputs and markets for inputs. Second, it takes account of supply-side substitution. Thus, different Swatch models are produced at the same plants using many of the same components. Indeed, the parent company – Swatch Group – owns 16 brands, including Swatch, Omega, Longines, and Tissot. Even between brands there is scope for reallocating resources. Hence, for analyzing broad questions of profitability and competitive advantage, it is useful to consider the global watch industry – though probably excluding the luxury watch segment, which in terms of demand conditions and production is closer to the jewelry industry than to the watch industry.

Based on: Shiv Mathur and Alfred Kenyon, *Winning Business Strategies* (Oxford: Butterworth-Heinemann, 2007).

Jaguar's market should be viewed as automobiles rather than all motor vehicles. Again, if customers are only willing to substitute between Jaguars and other makes of luxury cars, then Jaguar's relevant market is luxury cars rather than the automobile market as a whole.

But this fails to take account of substitutability on the supply side. If manufacturers find it easy to switch their production from luxury cars to family sedans to sports cars and the like, such supply-side substitutability would suggest that Jaguar is competing within the broader automobile market. The ability of Toyota, Nissan, and Honda to penetrate the luxury car market suggests that supply-side substitutability between mass-market autos and specialty autos is moderately high. Similarly, the automobile industry is frequently defined to include vans and light trucks, since these can be manufactured at the same plants as automobiles (often using the same platforms and engines). So too with "major appliance" manufacturers. They tend to be classified as a single industry, not because consumers are willing to substitute between refrigerators and dishwashers, but because the manufacturers can use the same manufacturing plants and distribution channels for different appliances.

The same considerations apply to the geographical boundaries of markets. Should Jaguar view itself as competing in a single global market or in a series of separate national or regional markets? The criterion here again is substitutability. If customers are willing and able to substitute cars available on different national markets, or if manufacturers are willing and able to divert their output among different countries to take account of differences in margins, then a market is global. The key test of the geographical boundaries of a market is price: if price differences for the same product between different locations tend to be eroded by demand-side and supply-side substitution, then these locations lie within a single market.

In practice, drawing the boundaries of markets and industries is a matter of judgment that depends on the purposes and context of the analysis. If Ford is considering the pricing and market positioning of its Jaguar cars, it must take a micro-level approach that defines markets around each model, in each country, and in relation to different categories of customer (e.g., distinguishing between sales to car rental companies and sales to individual consumers). In considering decisions over investments in fuel cell technology, the location of engine plants, and which new products to develop over the next five years, Ford will view Jaguar as one part of its auto and light truck business and will define its market as global and extending across its full range of models. The longer term the decisions are that it is considering, the more broadly it will wish to consider its markets, since substitutability is higher in the long run than in the short term.

Second, the precise delineation of the boundaries of a market or industry is seldom critical to the outcome of our analysis so long as we remain wary of external influences. The market in which an offering competes is a continuum rather than a bounded space. Thus, we may view the competitive market of Disneyland, Anaheim as a set of concentric circles. Closest is Universal Studios Tour. Slightly more distant competitors are Sea World and Six Flags. Further still might be a trip to Las Vegas, or a skiing weekend. Beyond these would be the broader entertainment market that might include cinemas, the beach, or playing video games.

For the purposes of applying the five forces framework, industry definition is not critical. We define an industry "box" within which industry rivals compete, but because we include competitive forces outside the industry box – notably entrants and substitutes – the precise boundaries of the industry box are not greatly important. Whether we view Harley-Davidson as competing in the "retro" segment of the heavyweight motorcycle industry, in the heavyweight motorcycle industry, or in the motorcycle industry as a whole is not critical to the outcome of our analysis. Even if we define Harley's market narrowly, we can still take into account competition from

Triumph and Ducati as substitute competition. Indeed, we might want to consider competition from more distant substitutes – sports cars, motorized water craft, and participation in "extreme sports."[21]

From Industry Attractiveness to Competitive Advantage: Identifying Key Success Factors

The five forces framework allows us to determine an industry's potential for profit. But how is industry profit shared between the different firms competing in that industry? As we have noted in our discussion of industry dynamics, competition between industry participants is ultimately a battle for competitive advantage in which firms rival one another to attract customers and maneuver for positional advantage. Let us look explicitly at the sources of competitive advantage within an industry. In subsequent chapters we develop a more comprehensive analysis of competitive advantage. Our goal here is to identify those factors within the firm's market environment that determine the firm's ability to survive and prosper – its *key success factors*.[22] In Strategy Capsule 3.5, Kenichi Ohmae of McKinsey's Tokyo office discusses key success factors in forestry and their link with strategy.

Like Ohmae, our approach to identifying key success factors is straightforward and commonsense. To survive and prosper in an industry, a firm must meet two criteria: first, it must supply what customers want to buy; second, it must survive competition. Hence, we may start by asking two questions:

- What do our customers want?
- What does the firm need to do to survive competition?

To answer the first question we need to look more closely at customers of the industry and to view them not so much as a source of bargaining power, and hence as a threat to profitability, but more as the basic rationale for the existence of the industry and as the underlying source of profit. This implies that the firm must identify who its customers are, what are their needs, and how they choose between competing offerings. Once we have identified the basis of customers' preference, this is merely the starting point for a chain of analysis. For example, if consumers' choice of supermarkets is based primarily on which charges the lowest prices and if the ability to charge low prices depends on low costs, the key issues concern the determinants of costs among supermarkets.

The second question requires that the firm examines the basis of competition in the industry. How intense is competition and what are its key dimensions? Thus, in the luxury car market, consumers select primarily on the basis of prestige, design, quality, and exclusiveness. However, these qualities are an insufficient basis for success. In this intensely competitive market, survival requires a strong financial position (to finance new product development) and costs that are sufficiently low to allow a company to cover its cost of capital.

A basic framework for identifying key success factors is presented in Figure 3.7. Application of the framework to identify key success factors in three industries is outlined in Table 3.3.

Key success factors can also be identified through the direct modeling of profitability. In the same way that the five forces analysis models the determinants of industry-level profitability, we can also attempt to model firm-level profitability in terms of

Probing for Key Success Factors

As a consultant faced with an unfamiliar business or industry, I make a point of first asking the specialists in the business, "What is the secret of success in this industry?" Needless to say, I seldom get an immediate answer, and so I pursue the inquiry by asking other questions from a variety of angles in order to establish as quickly as possible some reasonable hypotheses as to key factors for success. In the course of these interviews it usually becomes quite obvious what analyses will be required in order to prove or disprove these hypotheses. By first identifying the probable key factors for success and then screening them by proof or disproof, it is often possible for the strategist to penetrate very quickly to the core of a problem.

Traveling in the United States last year, I found myself on one occasion sitting in a plane next to a director of one of the biggest lumber companies in the country. Thinking I might learn something useful in the course of the five-hour flight, I asked him, "What are the key factors for success in the lumber industry?" To my surprise, his reply was immediate: "Owning large forests and maximizing the yield from them." The first of these key factors is a relatively simple matter: purchase of forest land. But his second point required further explanation. Accordingly, my next question was: "What variable or variables do you control in order to maximize the yield from a given tract?"

He replied: "The rate of tree growth is the key variable. As a rule, two factors promote growth: the amount of sunshine and the amount of water. Our company doesn't have many forests with enough of both. In Arizona and Utah, for example, we get more than enough sunshine but too little water, and so tree growth is very low. Now, if we could give the trees in those states enough water, they'd be ready in less than fifteen years instead of the thirty it takes now. The most important project we have in hand at the moment is aimed at finding out how to do this."

Impressed that this director knew how to work out a key factor strategy for his business, I offered my own contribution: "Then under the opposite conditions, where there is plenty of water but too little sunshine – for example, around the lower reaches of the Columbia River – the key factors should be fertilizers to speed up the growth and the choice of tree varieties that don't need so much sunshine."

Having established in a few minutes the general framework of what we were going to talk about, I spent the rest of the long flight very profitably hearing from him in detail how each of these factors was being applied.

Source: Kenichi Ohmae, *The Mind of the Strategist* (Harmondsworth: Penguin, 1982): 85. © 1982. Reprinted by permission of McGraw-Hill Companies.

FIGURE 3.7 Identifying key success factors

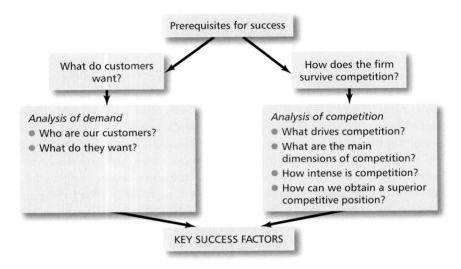

identifying the key factors that drive a firm's relative profitability within an industry. In Chapter 2, we made some progress on this front. By disaggregating a firm's return on capital employed into individual operating factors and ratios, we can pinpoint the most important determinants of firm success (see Figure 2.1). In many industries, these primary drivers of firm-level profitability are well known and widely used as performance targets. Strategy Capsule 3.6 begins with a well-known profitability formula used in the airline industry, then identifies the factors that drive this ratio. More generally, the approach introduced in Chapter 2 to disaggregate return on capital into its component ratios can be extended to identify the specific operational and strategic drivers of superior profitability. Figure 3.8 applies this analysis to identifying success factors in retailing.

The value of success factors in formulating strategy has been scorned by some strategy scholars. Pankaj Ghemawat observes that the "whole idea of identifying a success factor and then chasing it seems to have something in common with the ill-considered medieval hunt for the philosopher's stone, a substance that would transmute everything it touched into gold."[23] Our objective in identifying key success factors is less ambitious. There is no universal blueprint for a successful strategy and, even in individual industries, there is no "generic strategy" that can guarantee success. However, each market is different in terms of what motivates customers and how competition works. Understanding these aspects of the industry environment is a prerequisite for an effective business strategy. Nevertheless, this does not imply that firms within an industry adopt common strategies. Since every firm comprises a unique set of resources and capabilities, even when an industry is subject to common success factors (e.g. low costs), firms will select unique strategies to link their resources and capabilities to industry success factors.

TABLE 3.3 Identifying key success factors: steel, fashion clothing, and supermarkets

	WHAT DO CUSTOMERS WANT? (Analysis of demand)	HOW DO FIRMS SURVIVE COMPETITION? (Analysis of competition)	KEY SUCCESS FACTORS
Steel	● Low price ● Product consistency ● Reliability of supply ● Specific technical specifications for special steels	● Commodity products, excess capacity, high fixed costs, excess capacity, exit barriers, and substitute competition mean intense price competition and cyclical profitability ● Cost efficiency and financial strength essential	● Cost efficiency requires: large-scale plants, low-cost location, rapid capacity adjustment ● Alternatively, high technology, small-scale plants can achieve low costs through flexibility and high productivity ● Differentiation through technical specifications and service quality
Fashion clothing	● Diversity of customer preferences in terms of garment type, style, quality, color ● Customers willing to pay premium for brand, style, exclusivity, and quality ● Mass market highly price sensitive	● Low barriers to entry and exit, low seller concentration, and buying power of retail chains imply intense competition ● Differentiation can yield substantial price premium, but imitation is rapid	● Combining differentiation with low costs ● Differentiation requires speed of response to changing fashions, style, reputation, and quality ● Cost efficiency requires manufacture in low wage countries
Supermarkets	● Low prices ● Convenient location ● Wide range of products adapted to local preferences ● Fresh/quality produce; good service; ease of parking; pleasant ambience	● Intensity of price competition depends on number and proximity of competitors ● Bargaining power a critical determinant of cost of bought-in goods	● Low costs require operational efficiency, scale-efficient stores, large aggregate purchases, low wage costs ● Differentiation requires large stores (to allow wide product range), convenient location, familiarity with local customer preferences

STRATEGY CAPSULE 3.6

Identifying Key Success Factors by Modeling Profitability: Airlines

Profitability, as measured by operating income per available seat-mile (ASM), is determined by three factors: yield, which is total operating revenues divided by the number of revenue passenger miles (RPMs); load factor, which is the ratio between RPMs and ASMs; and unit cost, which is total operating expenses divided by ASMs. Thus:

$$\frac{\text{Income}}{\text{ASMs}} = \frac{\text{Revenue}}{\text{RPMs}} \times \frac{\text{RPMs}}{\text{ASMs}} \: less \: \frac{\text{Expenses}}{\text{ASMs}}$$

Some of the primary determinants of each of these measures are the following:

- Revenue/RPMs
  - Intensity of competition on routes flown.
  - Effective yield management to permit quick price adjustment to changing market conditions.
  - Ability to attract business customers.
  - Superior customer service.
- Load factors
  - Competitiveness of prices.
  - Efficiency of route planning (e.g., through hub-and-spoke systems).
  - Building customer loyalty through quality of service, frequent-flier programs.

- Matching airplane size to demand for individual flights.
- Expenses/ASMs
  - Wage rates and benefit levels.
  - Fuel efficiency of aircraft.
  - Productivity of employees (determined partly by their job flexibility).
  - Load factors.
  - Level of administrative cost.

In their battle for survival, the airlines have sought to optimize as many of these factors as possible in order to improve their profitability. To enhance revenue, several airlines have withdrawn from their most intensely competitive routes; others have sought to achieve a fare premium over the cut-price airlines through superior punctuality, convenience, comfort, and services. To improve load factors, companies have become more flexible in their pricing and in allocating different planes to different routes. Most notably, companies have sought to cut costs by increasing employee productivity, reducing overhead, sharing services with other airlines, and reducing salaries and benefits.

FIGURE 3.8 Identifying key success factors through analyzing profit drivers: the case of retailing

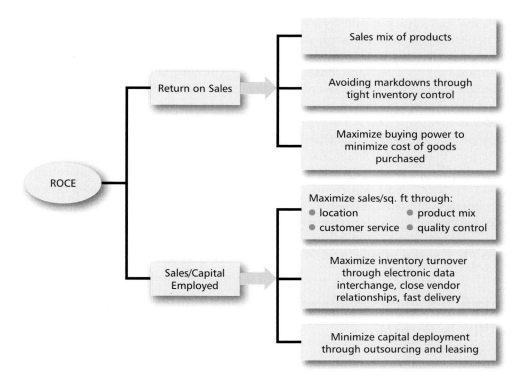

Summary

In Chapter 1, we established that profound understanding of the competitive environment is a critical ingredient of a successful strategy. In this chapter, we have developed a systematic approach to analyzing a firm's industry environment in order to evaluate that industry's profit potential and to identify the sources of competitive advantage. The centerpiece of our approach is Porter's *five forces of competition* framework, which links the structure of an industry to the competitive intensity within it and to the profitability that it realizes. Although every industry is unique, competition and profitability are the result of the systematic influences of the structure of that industry. The Porter framework provides a simple, yet powerful organizing framework for classifying the relevant features of an industry's structure and predicting their implications for competitive behavior. The framework is particularly useful for predicting industry profitability and for identifying how the firm can influence industry structure in order to improve industry profitability.

As with most of the tools for strategy analysis that we shall consider in this book, the Porter five forces framework is easy to comprehend. While its basis is a substantial body of microeconomic theory, the relationships it posits are straightforward and consistent with commonsense. However, the real learning about industry analysis, and about the Porter framework in particular, derives from its *application*. It is only when we apply the Porter framework to analyzing competition and diagnosing the causes of high or low profitability in an industry that we are forced to confront the complexities and subtleties of the model. What industry (or industries) does a company compete in? Where do the industry's boundaries lie? How wide a range of substitutes do we consider? How do excess capacity, cost structures, and exit barriers interact with one another?

I urge you to put the tools of industry analysis to work – not just in your strategic management coursework, but also in your interpretation of everyday business events. What will be the impact of Linux, Apache, and other open-source software on Microsoft's hugely profitable sales of operating systems and server software? What are the prospects for the fixed-line telecom providers currently battered by wireless and internet telephony? Is your cousin's plan to leave her law firm to take up the position of legal counsel with a major airline a good idea given the different competitive circumstances of the two industries?

Through practical applications of the Porter framework, we shall also become aware of its limitations. In the next chapter we shall consider some of these limitations and look to ways in which we can extend and augment our analysis with additional concepts, tools, and frameworks.

Self-Study Questions

1   The major forces shaping the business environment of the fixed-line telecom industry are technology and government policy. The industry has been influenced by fiber-optics (greatly increasing transmission capacity), new modes of telecommunication (wireless and internet telephony), deregulation, and privatization. Using the five forces of competition framework, show how each of these developments has influenced competition in the fixed-line telecom industry.

2   From Table 3.1, select a high-profit industry and a low-profit industry. From what you know of the structure of your selected industry, use the five forces framework to explain why profitability has been either high or low.

3   With reference to Strategy Capsule 3.1, use the five forces framework to explain why the US smokeless tobacco industry is so profitable (as indicated by the profitability of its dominant firm).

4   Despite high fuel costs, profitability in the world airline industry increased substantially during 2005 and 2006 – even while fuel costs were rising sharply. Why?

5   Wal-Mart (like Carrefour, Ahold, and Metro) competes in several countries of the world, yet most shoppers choose between retailers within a radius of a few miles. For the purposes of analyzing profitability and competitive strategy, should Wal-Mart consider the discount retailing industry to be global, national, or local?

6   What do you think are key success factors in:

a)   The delivered pizza industry?
b)   The investment banking industry?

Notes

1   B. Eilert, "Ignite your Strategic Planning Process with a PEST Analysis," *Strategy Knowledge* (http://strategyknowhow.bnet.com/PEST_analysis_primer.html), September 2004.

2   M. E. Porter, *Competitive Strategy: Techniques for Analyzing Industries and Competitors* (New York: Free Press, 1980): Chapter 1. For a summary, see his article, "How Competitive Forces Shape Strategy," *Harvard Business Review* 57 (March–April 1979): 86–93.

3   "For Bagel Chains, Investment May Be Money in the Hole," *Wall Street Journal* (December 30, 1997): B8.

4   W. J. Baumol, J. C. Panzar, and R. D. Willig, *Contestable Markets and the Theory of Industry Structure* (New York: Harcourt Brace Jovanovich, 1982). See also Michael Spence, "Contestable Markets and the Theory of Industry Structure: A Review Article," *Journal of Economic Literature* 21 (September 1983): 981–90.

5   "Annual Franchise 500," *Entrepreneur* (January 2006).

6   "Brand Loyalty Is Rarely Blind Loyalty," *Wall Street Journal* (October 19, 1989): B1.

7   R. D. Buzzell and P. W. Farris, "Marketing Costs in Consumer Goods Industries," in H. Thorelli (ed.), *Strategy + Structure = Performance* (Bloomington, IN: Indiana University Press, 1977): 128–9.

8   In October 1999, the Dept. of Justice alleged that American Airlines was using unfair means in attempting to monopolize air traffic out of Dallas-Fort Worth (http://www.aeroworldnet.com/1tw05179.htm).

9   M. Lieberman ("Excess Capacity as a Barrier to Entry," *Journal of Industrial Economics* 35, June 1987: 607–27) argues that, to be credible, the threat of retaliation needs to be supported by incumbents holding excess capacity giving them the potential to flood the market.

10 See for example: J. S. Bain, *Barriers to New Competition* (Cambridge, MA: Harvard University Press, 1956) and H. M. Mann, "Seller Concentration, Entry Barriers, and Rates of Return in Thirty Industries," *Review of Economics and Statistics* 48 (1966): 296–307.

11 W. S. Comanor and T. A. Wilson, *Advertising and Market Power* (Cambridge: Harvard University Press, 1974); J. L. Siegfried and L. B. Evans, "Empirical Studies of Entry and Exit: A Survey of the Evidence," *Review of Industrial Organization* 9 (1994): 121–55.

12 G. S. Yip, "Gateways to Entry," *Harvard Business Review* 60 (September–October 1982): 85–93.

13 F. M. Scherer and D. R. Ross, *Industrial Market Structure and Economic Performance*, 3rd edn (Boston:

Houghton Mifflin, 1990); R. M. Grant, "Pricing Behavior in the UK Wholesale Market for Petrol. A 'Structure-Conduct Analysis'," *Journal of Industrial Economics* 30 (March 1982).

14 R. Schmalensee, "Inter-Industry Studies of Structure and Performance," in R. Schmalensee and R. D. Willig, *Handbook of Industrial Organization*, 2nd edn (Amsterdam: North Holland, 1988): 976; M. A. Salinger, "The Concentration–Margins Relationship Reconsidered," *Brookings Papers: Microeconomics* (1990): 287–335.

15 The problems caused by excess capacity and exit barriers are discussed in C. Baden-Fuller (ed.), *Strategic Management of Excess Capacity* (Oxford: Basil Blackwell, 1990).

16 "Boom and Bust at Sea," *Economist* (August 18, 2005).

17 S. H. Lustgarten, "The Impact of Buyer Concentration in Manufacturing Industries," *Review of Economics and Statistics* 57 (1975): 125–32; T. Kelly and M. L. Gosman, "Increased Buyer Concentration and its Effects on Profitability in the Manufacturing Sector," *Review of Industrial Organization* 17 (2000): 41–59.

18 "Globalization or Concentration?" *Business Week* (November 8, 2004): 54; "Mittal: Blood, Steel and Empire Building," *Business Week* (February 13, 2006).

19 J. Bower, *When Markets Quake* (Boston: Harvard Business School Press, 1986).

20 M. Carnall, S. Berry, and P. Spiller, "Airline Hubbing, Costs and Demand," in D. Lee (ed.), *Advances in Airline Economics* vol. 1 (Elsevier, 2006).

21 For a concise discussion of market definition see Office of Fair Trading, Market Definition (London: December 2004), especially pp. 7–17.

22 The term was coined by Chuck Hofer and Dan Schendel – *Strategy Formulation: Analytical Concepts* (St. Paul: West Publishing, 1977): 77 – who defined key success factors as "those variables that management can influence through its decisions and that can affect significantly the overall competitive positions of the firms in an industry . . . Within any particular industry they are derived from the interaction of two sets of variables, namely, the economic and technological characteristics of the industry . . . and the competitive weapons on which the various firms in the industry have built their strategies."

23 P. Ghemawat, *Commitment: The Dynamic of Strategy* (New York: Free Press, 1991): 11.

4

Further Topics in Industry and Competitive Analysis

Introduction and Objectives

The Porter five forces model offers a systematic approach to analyzing competition. At the same time, it offers a highly simplified view of industry and competition. Consider the following:

- The only relationships between products that we have considered are substitute relations. Many products – both goods and services – have *complementary* relationships with one another. What do complements imply for competition and the potential for profit?

- In many sectors, industry structure may be much less stable than envisaged by the Porter model. Rather than structure determining competition in some predictable way, competition – particularly technological competition – may reshape industry structure very rapidly. How do we analyze industries where structure is continually being recreated by technology and firms' strategies?

- We have not explored the dynamic rivalry that characterizes business competition in the real world. Pepsi-Cola's competitive environment is determined more by the strategy and marketing tactics of Coca-Cola than by the structure of the world soft drinks industry. Similarly, Reuter's competitive environment is dominated by the competitive strategy of Bloomberg, as is Boeing's by Airbus Industrie. To understand competition as a dynamic, personalized process we shall draw upon the tools of game theory and competitor analysis.

- In our discussion of the problems of drawing industry boundaries, we noted the advantages of analyzing competition at different levels. American Airlines competes in the world airline industry. However, each route comprises a different market with a different set of competitors. To take account of the internal heterogeneity of industries, we shall disaggregate industries into segments and analyze each segment as a separate market.

This chapter will extend the analysis of industry and competition to address the above topics. In doing so, you will acquire the following capabilities:

- To analyze the impact of goods and services that are *complements* to those supplied by a firm, and to identify the potential for the firm to make profit through managing relationships with the suppliers of complements.

- To recognize the implications of *game theory* for competitive analysis, in particular, the potential gains to cooperative strategies and the use of threats, commitments, signaling, deterrence, and preemption to gain and sustain competitive advantage.

- To use *competitor analysis* to predict the competitive moves rivals are likely to initiate and likely responses by rivals to our own competitive initiatives.

- To *segment* an industry into its constituent markets, to appraise the relative attractiveness of different segments, and identify differences in key success factors among them.

- To classify the firms within an industry into *strategic groups* based on similarities in their strategies.

Extending the Five Forces Framework

Does Industry Matter?

Porter's five forces of competition framework has been the subject of constant criticism. Some have attacked its theoretical foundations, arguing that the structure–conduct–performance approach to industrial organization that underlies it lacks rigor (especially when compared with the logical robustness of game theory). The main defense of industry analysis is that it is useful in allowing us to understand competition and to predict changes in profitability on the basis of changes in industry structure.

A more serious attack is that, irrespective of its theoretical rigor, in reality a firm's industry environment is a relatively minor determinant of that firm's profitability. A series of studies measuring the proportion of interfirm differences in profitability attributable to industry factors has produced very different results (see Table 4.1). Despite major differences in the findings of different studies, a common conclusion emerges very clearly: industry factors account for a minority of interfirm differences in profitability (less than 20% in all the studies).

These sobering findings have several implications. First, they point to the need to understand more deeply the determinants of competitive behavior between companies and how competition influences industry-level profitability. We need to reconsider the relationship between industry structure and competition and explore more rigorous and sophisticated approaches to analyzing competition – game theory in particular. Second, we need to disaggregate broad industry groupings and examine competition at the level of particular segments and strategic groupings of firms. Let us begin by considering the possibilities of extending the Porter framework.

Complements: A Missing Force in the Porter Model?

The Porter framework identifies the suppliers of substitute goods and services as one of the forces of competition that reduces the profit available to the firms within an industry. However, economic theory identifies two types of relationship between different products: substitutes and complements. While the presence of substitutes reduces the value of a product, complements increase value. The availability of ink cartridges for my printer transforms its value to me.

TABLE 4.1 What determines interfirm differences in profitability? The role of industry

	Percentage of variance in firms' return on assets explained by:		
	Industry effects	Firm effects	Unexplained variance
Schmalensee (1985)	19.6%	0.6%	79.9%
Rumelt (1991)	4.0%	44.2%	44.8%
McGahan & Porter (1997)	18.7%	31.7%	48.4%
Hawawini et al. (2003)	8.1%	35.8%	52.0%
Roquebert et al. (1996)	10.2%	55.0%	32.0%
Misangyi et al. (2006)	7.6%	43.8%	n.a.

Notes:

1   "Firm effects" combine business unit and corporate effects.
2   The rows do not sum to 100% because other sources of variance are not reported.

SOURCES: R. SCHMALENSEE, "DO MARKETS DIFFER MUCH?" AMERICAN ECONOMIC REVIEW, 75 (1985): 341–51; R. P. RUMELT, "DOES INDUSTRY MATTER MUCH?" STRATEGIC MANAGEMENT JOURNAL 12 (1991): 167–85; A. M. MCGAHAN AND M. E. PORTER, "HOW MUCH DOES INDUSTRY MATTER, REALLY?" STRATEGIC MANAGEMENT JOURNAL 18 (1997): 15–30; G. HAWAWINI, V. SUBRAMANIAN, AND P. VERDIN, "IS FIRMS' PROFITABILITY DRIVEN BY INDUSTRY OR FIRM-SPECIFIC FACTORS? A NEW LOOK AT THE EVIDENCE," STRATEGIC MANAGEMENT JOURNAL 24 (2003): 1–16; J. A. ROQUEBERT, R. L. PHILLIPS, AND P. A. WESTFALL, "MARKETS VS. MANAGEMENT: WHAT DRIVES PROFITABILITY?" STRATEGIC MANAGEMENT JOURNAL 17 (1996): 633–64; V. F. MISANGYI, H. ELMS, T. GRECKHAMER, AND J. A. LEPINE," A NEW PERSPECTIVE ON A FUNDAMENTAL DEBATE: A MULTILEVEL APPROACH TO INDUSTRY, CORPORATE AND BUSINESS UNIT EFFECTS," STRATEGIC MANAGEMENT JOURNAL 27 (2006): 571–90.

Given the importance of complements to most products – the value of my car depends on the availability of gasoline, insurance, and repair services – our analysis of the competitive environment needs to take them into account. The simplest way is to add a sixth force to Porter's framework (see Figure 4.1).[1]

Having introduced complements into our competitive analysis, the key issue is analyzing their impact. Where products are close complements, they have little value to customers individually – customers value the whole system. But how is the value shared between the producers of the different complementary products? Bargaining power and its deployment are the key. During the early 1990s, Nintendo video game consoles earned it huge profits. Although most of the revenue and consumer value was in the software – mostly supplied by independent developers – Nintendo was able to appropriate most of the profit potential of the entire system. Nintendo's strategic genius was in the management of its relationships with games developers. Nintendo established a dominant relationship with games developers by controlling its operating system, by issuing developer licenses to many producers of games software, and by maintaining tight control over the manufacture and distribution of games cartridges (from which Nintendo earned a hefty royalty).[2]

In PCs, by contrast, power has been on the side of the software suppliers – Microsoft in particular. IBM's adoption of open architecture meant that Microsoft Windows became a proprietary standard, while PCs were gradually reduced to commodity status. This is a very different situation from video games, where hardware suppliers keep proprietary control over their operating systems.

Where two products are complements to one another, profit will accrue to the supplier that builds the stronger market position and reduces the value contributed by the other. How is this done? The key is to achieve monopolization, differentiation, and shortage of supply in one's own product, while encouraging competition, commoditization, and excess capacity in the production of the complementary product. IBM is

FIGURE 4.1 Five forces, or six?

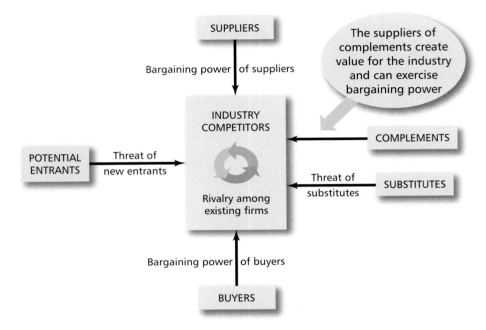

attempting to shift the balance of power between hardware and software producers through its promotion of Linux and other open-source software programs. By pressing to differentiate its hardware products while commoditizing software, it can reduce the power of Microsoft and garner a bigger share of the profit returns from systems of hardware and software.[3]

Dynamic Competition: Creative Destruction and Hypercompetition

The notion that industry structure is relatively stable and determines competitive behavior in a predictable way ignores the dynamic forces of innovation and entrepreneurship. Joseph Schumpeter viewed competition as a "perennial gale of creative destruction" through which favorable industry structures – monopoly in particular – contain the seeds of their own destruction by attracting incursions from new and established firms deploying innovatory strategies and innovatory products to unseat incumbents.[4]

This view of Schumpeter (and the "Austrian school" of economics) that competition is a dynamic process of rivalry that constantly reformulates industry structure suggests that it may be more appropriate to view structure as the outcome of competitive behavior rather than vice versa.[5] The key consideration is the speed of structural change in the industry – if structural transformation is rapid, the five forces model is of limited use in predicting competition and profitability.

In practice, Schumpeter's process of "creative destruction" tends to be more of a breeze than a gale. In established industries, entry occurs so slowly that profits are undermined only gradually,[6] while changes in industrial concentration tend to be slow.[7] One survey observed: "the picture of the competitive process . . . is, to say the least, sluggish in the extreme."[8] Another study found a "lack of widespread evidence . . . that markets are more unstable now than in the recent past."[9] As a result, both at the firm and the industry level, profits tend to be highly persistent in the long run.[10]

However, some industries show clear evidence of "creative destruction." Jeffrey Williams defines "Schumpeterian industries" as those subject to rapid product innovation with relatively steep experience curves – they include semiconductors, consumer electronics, and computers.[11] In other industries, deregulation has been an important source of instability.[12] Rich D'Aveni uses the term *hypercompetition* to describe industry environments characterized by intense and rapid competitive moves, where competitors must move quickly to build advantages and erode the advantages of their rivals.[13] Hypercompetitive behavior involves continuously generating new competitive advantages and destroying, obsoleting, or neutralizing the opponent's competitive advantage, thereby disrupting the status quo of the marketplace by creating disequilibrium. If competitive advantage is transitory, the only route to sustained superior performance is through continually recreating and renewing competitive advantage. We shall return to this issue in Chapter 7 when we consider competitive advantage in greater depth.

The Contribution of Game Theory

Central to the criticisms of Porter's five forces as a static framework is its failure to take full account of competitive interactions among firms. In Chapter 1, we noted that the essence of strategic competition is the interaction among players, such that the decisions made by any one player are dependent on the actual and anticipated decisions of the other players. By relegating competition to a mediating variable that links industry structure with profitability, the five forces analysis offers little insight into competition as a process of interactive decision making by rival firms. Game theory allows us to model competitive interaction. In particular, it offers two especially valuable contributions to strategic management:

1 *It permits the framing of strategic decisions.* Apart from any theoretical value of the theory of games, game theory provides a structure, a set of concepts, and a terminology that allows us to describe a competitive situation in terms of:
   - identity of the players;
   - specification of each player's options;
   - specification of the payoffs from every combination of options;
   - the sequencing of decisions using game trees.

   This permits us to understand the structure of the competitive situation and facilitates a systematic, rational approach to decision making.

2 *It can predict the outcome of competitive situations and identify optimal strategic choices.* Through the insight it offers into situations of competition and bargaining, game theory can predict the equilibrium outcomes of competitive situations and the consequences of strategic moves by any one player. Game theory provides penetrating insights into central issues of strategy that go well beyond pure intuition. Simple game models (e.g.

"prisoners' dilemma") predict cooperative versus competitive outcomes, whereas more complex games permit analysis of the effects of reputation,[14] deterrence,[15] information,[16] and commitment[17] – especially within the context of multiperiod games. Particularly important for practicing managers, game theory can indicate strategies for improving the structure and outcome of the game through manipulating the payoffs to the different players.

Despite exploding interest and rapid development of game theory during the 1980s, its influence on strategic management practice remained limited until the 1990s. Since then, practical applications of game theory have grown as a result of a number of practical guides to the application of game theory's tools and insights.[18] Game theory has provided illuminating insights into a wide variety of situations, including the Cuban missile crisis of 1962,[19] rivalry between Boeing and Airbus Industrie,[20] NASCAR race tactics,[21] auctions of airwave spectrum,[22] and the reasons why evolution has conferred such magnificent tails upon male peacocks.[23]

Cooperation

One of the key merits of game theory is its ability to encompass both competition and cooperation. A key deficiency of the five forces framework is in viewing interfirm relations as exclusively competitive in nature. The central message of Adam Brandenburger and Barry Nalebuff's book *Co-opetition* is recognizing the competitive/cooperative duality of business relationships.[24] Whereas Coca-Cola's relationship with Pepsi-Cola is essentially competitive, that between Intel and Microsoft is primarily cooperative.

However, there is no simple dichotomy between competition and cooperation: all business relationships combine elements of both. For all their intense rivalry, Coca-Cola and PepsiCo cooperate on multiple fronts, including common policies on sales of soda drinks with schools, environmental issues, and health concerns. There is also some evidence of coordination in both pricing and product introductions.[25] Exxon and Shell have battled for over a century for leadership of the world petroleum industry. At the same time, Exxon and Shell cooperate in a number of joint ventures, including NAM, one of Europe's biggest natural gas producers. The desire of competitors to cluster together – antique dealers in London's Bermondsey Market and movie studios in Hollywood – points to the complementary relations among competitors in growing the size of their market and developing its infrastructure. Similarly, with customers and suppliers, they are partners in creating value, but also rivals in sharing that value.

In many business relationships, competition results in an inferior outcome for the players compared with cooperation. The prisoners' dilemma game analyzes this predicament (see Strategy Capsule 4.1).

Deterrence

One way of changing a game's equilibrium through adjusting its payoffs is through *deterrence*. The principle behind deterrence is to impose costs on the other players for actions that we deem to be undesirable. By establishing the certainty that deserters would be shot, the British army provided a strong incentive to its troops to participate in advances on heavily fortified German trenches during World War I.

STRATEGY CAPSULE 4.1

The Prisoners' Dilemma

The classic prisoners' dilemma game involves a pair of crime suspects who are arrested and interrogated separately. The dilemma is that each will "rat" on the other with the result that both end up in jail despite the fact that, if both had remained silent, both would have been released for lack of evidence.

The dilemma arises in almost all competitive situations – everyone could be better off with collusion. Consider competition between Coca-Cola and Pepsi-Cola in Ukraine where each has the choice of spending big or small on advertising. The matrix below shows the payoffs to each firm.

Clearly, the best solution for both firms is for them to each restrain their advertising expenditure (the upper left cell). However, in the absence of cooperation, the outcome for both firms is to adopt big budgets (the lower right cell) – the reason being that each will fear that any restraint will be countered by the rival seeking advantage by shifting to a big advertising budget. The resulting *maxi-min* choice of strategies (each company chooses the strategy that maximizes the minimum payoff) is a *Nash equilibrium*: no player can increase his/her payoff by a unilateral change in strategy. Even if collusion can be achieved, it will be unstable because of the incentives for cheating – a constant for problem for OPEC, where the member countries agree quotas, but then cheat on them.

COKE (Payoffs in $ millions)

		Small Advertising Budget	Big Advertising Budget
PEPSI	Small Advertising Budget	10 10	15 −2
	Big Advertising Budget	−2 15	4 4

How can a firm escape from such prisoners' dilemmas? One answer is to change a one-period game (single transaction) into a repeated game. In the case of the supplier–buyer relationship, moving from a spot transaction to a long-term vendor relationship gives the supplier the incentive to offer a better-quality product and the buyer to offer a price that offers the seller a satisfactory return. In the case of price competition, markets dominated by two or three suppliers tend to converge toward patterns of price leadership where price competition is avoided.

A second solution is to change the payoffs in the game. In the classic prisoners' dilemma, the Mafia shifts the equilibrium from the suspects implicating one another to the suspects not talking by enforcing its "code of silence" through draconian reprisals. Similarly, if both Coke and Pepsi were to threaten one another with an aggressive price war should the other seek advantage through a big advertising budget, this could shift the equilibrium to the top left cell.

Sources: A. Dixit and B. Nalebuff, "Prisoners' Dilemma," *The Concise Encyclopedia of Economics* (www.econlib.org/library/Enc/PrisonersDilemma.html); "Prisoners' Dilemma," *Stanford Encyclopedia of Philosophy* (http://plato.stanford.edu/entries/prisoner-dilemma/).

The key to the effectiveness of any deterrent is that it must be credible. The problem here is that if administering the deterrent is costly or unpleasant for the threatening party, the deterrent is not credible. Incumbents in a market may threaten a would-be entrant with aggressive price cuts. However, the entrant may rationalize that, once it has entered the market, it is no longer in the incumbent firm's best interest to engage in a costly price war. The key is that threats will only deter if they are credible. Investing in excess capacity is an effective means of discouraging entry. Prior to the expiration of its Nutrasweet patents, Monsanto invested heavily in unneeded plant capacity to deter manufacturers of generic aspartame.[26] Conversely, in compact disks, the reluctance of the dominant firm (Philips) to invest heavily in new capacity to meet growing demand allowed the entry of a wave of newcomers.[27] However, Marvin Lieberman has cast doubt on the effectiveness of excess capacity in deterring new entry.[28]

Deterrence has provided a central theme in military strategy. The nuclear arms race between the US and the then Soviet Union was based on the logic of "mutual assured destruction." However, the ability for deterrence to produce a stable, peaceful equilibrium depends on the willingness of the adversaries to be deterred. The central weakness of George W. Bush's "war on terror" was that ideologically motivated terrorists are not susceptible to deterrence.[29]

Commitment

For deterrence to be effective it must be credible, which means being backed by commitment. Commitment involves the elimination of strategic options – hence it means accepting increased risk. When Hernan Cortes destroyed his ships on arrival in Mexico in 1519, he achieved, first, motivation for his men to conquer the Aztec empire, and second, a signal to Montezuma that any Aztec aggression could not lead to Spanish withdrawal. Airbus's investments in advertising, research, and supply contracts during 2000–2 for its A380 superjumbo was to signal its commitment both to airlines and to Boeing, so that the airlines would be encouraged to place orders, and Boeing would be discouraged from developing a rival plane. Don Sull argues that commitments are the essence of strategic decision making since they "bind an organization to a future course of action."[30]

These commitments to aggressive competition have been described as "hard commitments." A company may also make commitments that moderate competition; these are called "soft commitments."[31] The airlines' frequent-flier programs commit the airlines to redeem miles flown with free tickets. They also signal to other airlines a willingness to avoid price competition and indicate less vulnerability to a rival's price cuts. How these different types of commitment affect the profitability of the firm making the commitment depends on the type of game being played. Where companies compete on price, game theory shows that they tend to match one another's price changes.[32] Hence, under price adjustments, hard commitments (e.g., a commitment to cut price) tend to have a negative profit impact and soft commitments (e.g., a commitment to raise prices) have a positive impact. Conversely, where companies compete on output, game theory shows that increases in output by one firm results in output reductions by the other.[33] Hence, under quantity adjustments, a hard commitment (e.g., a commitment to build new plants) will tend to have a positive effect on the committing firm's profitability, since it will tend to be met by other firms reducing their output.[34]

Changing the Structure of the Game

Creative strategies can change the structure of the competitive game. A company may seek to change the structure of the industry within which it is competing in order to increase the profit potential of the industry or to appropriate a greater share of the profit available. Thus, establishing alliances and agreements with competitors can increase the value of the game by increasing the size of the market and building joint strength against possible entrants. There may be many opportunities for converting win–lose (or even lose–lose) games into win–win games. A cooperative solution was found to Norfolk Southern's competition with CSX for control of Conrail, for example. The 1997 bidding war was terminated when CSX and Norfolk Southern agreed to cooperate in acquiring and dismembering Conrail.

In some cases, it may be advantageous for a firm to create competition for itself. By offering second-sourcing licenses to AMD, Intel gave up its potential monopoly over its x86 microprocessors. Although Intel was creating competition for itself, it was also encouraging the adoption of the x86 chip by computer manufacturers (including IBM) who were concerned about overdependence on Intel. As we shall see in Chapter 11, standards battles typically involve the deliberate creation of competition by the main contestants.

Signaling

How a competitor will react to a company's strategic initiative depends on how the competitor perceives the initiative. The term *signaling* is used to describe the selective communication of information to competitors (or customers) designed to influence their perception and hence to provoke or avoid certain types of reaction.[35] The use of diversionary attacks and misinformation is well developed in military warfare. In 1944, Allied deception was so good that even during the D-Day landings in Normandy, the Germans believed that the main invasion would occur near Calais. The principal role of signaling is to deter and mislead competitors. But, as noted in discussing deterrence, information on its own is not enough: signals need to be credible. Thus, Allied misinformation concerning the invasion of Europe included the marshaling of a phantom army designed to convince the German high command that the Normandy invasion was merely a diversionary mission.

The credibility of threats is critically dependent on the company's reputation.[36] Even though carrying out threats against rivals is costly and depresses short-term profitability, exercising such threats can build a reputation for aggressiveness that deters competitors in the future. The benefits of building a reputation for aggressiveness may be particularly great for diversified companies where reputation can be transferred from one market to another.[37] Hence, Procter & Gamble's protracted market share wars in disposable diapers and household detergents have established a reputation for toughness that protects it from competitive attacks in other markets. Other companies whose aggressive quest for market share has gained them reputations as "killer competitors" include Coca-Cola in soft drinks, Anheuser-Busch in beer, and Emerson Electric in sink disposal units. Faced with such formidable and unrelenting rivals, smaller competitors have typically retreated to niches or given up the fight altogether.

Signaling through price announcement may also be a means to facilitate collaborative pricing among firms.[38]

Is Game Theory Useful?

The value of game theory to strategic management has generated lively debate. For economists this seems paradoxical, since to them game theory *is* the theory of strategy. The great virtue of game theory is its rigor. In microeconomics, the game theory revolution of the past quarter-century has established the analysis of markets and firm behavior on a much more secure theoretical foundation.

However, the price of mathematical rigor has been limited applicability to real world situations. Game theory provides clear prediction in highly stylized situations involving few external variables and highly restrictive assumptions. The result is a mathematically sophisticated body of theory that suffers from unrealistic assumptions, lack of generality, and an analysis of dynamic situations through a sequence of static equilibriums.[39] When applied to more complex (and more realistic) situations, game theory frequently results in either no equilibrium or multiple equilibriums, and outcomes that are highly sensitive to small changes in the assumptions. In general, game theory has not developed to the point where it permits us to model real business situations in a level of detail that can generate precise predictions.

In terms of empirical application, game theory has done a much better job of explaining the past than of predicting the future. In diagnosing Nintendo's domination of the video games industry in the 1980s, Monsanto's efforts to prolong Nutrasweet's market leadership beyond the expiration of its patents, or Airbus's wresting of market leadership from Boeing, game theory provides penetrating insight into the competitive situation and deep understanding of the rationale behind the strategies deployed. However, in predicting outcomes and designing strategies, game theory has been much less impressive – the use of game theory by US and European governments to auction wireless spectrum has produced mixed results.[40]

So, where can game theory assist us in designing successful strategies? As with all our theories and frameworks, game theory is useful not because it gives us answers, but because it can help us understand business situations. Game theory provides a set of tools that allows us to structure our view of competitive interaction. If we identify the players in a game, identify the decision choices available to each player, specify the performance implications of each combination of decisions, and predict how each player is likely to react to the decision choices of the other, then we have made huge progress in understanding the dynamics of competition. Most importantly, by describing the structure of the game we are playing, we have a basis for suggesting ways of changing the game and thinking through the likely outcomes of such changes.

Although game theory continues its rapid development, it is still a long way from providing the central theoretical foundation for strategic management. Though we draw on game theory in several places in this book (particularly in exploring competitive dynamics in highly concentrated markets), our emphasis in strategy formulation will be less on achieving advantage through influencing the behavior of competitors and much more on transforming competitive games through building positions of unilateral competitive advantage. The competitive market situations with which we shall be dealing will, for the most part, be different from those considered by game theory. Game theory typically deals with competitive situations with closely matched players where each has a similar range of strategic options (typically relating to price changes, advertising budgets, capacity decisions, and new product introductions). The outcome of these games is highly dependent on order of moves, signals, bluffs, and threats. Our emphasis will be less on managing competitive interactions and more on establishing competitive advantage through exploiting uniqueness.

Competitor Analysis

We have argued that in highly concentrated industries, the key characteristics of a company's external environment are determined by the behavior of a few rivals – possibly a single firm. In household detergents, Unilever's industry environment is dominated by the strategy of Procter & Gamble. The same is true in soft drinks (Coke and Pepsi), jet engines (GE, United Technologies, and Rolls-Royce), and business news periodicals (*Business Week*, *Fortune*, and *Forbes*). Similar circumstances exist in more local markets. The competitive environment of my local Costa Coffee house is dominated by the presence of Starbucks across the road. Game theory provides a theoretical apparatus for analyzing competitive interaction between small numbers of rivals but, for everyday business situations, a more empirically based approach to predicting competitor behavior may be more useful. Let us examine how information about competitors can help us to predict their behavior.

Competitive Intelligence

Competitive intelligence involves the systematic collection and analysis of public information about rivals for informing decision making. It has three main purposes:

- To forecast competitors' future strategies and decisions.
- To predict competitors' likely reactions to a firm's strategic initiatives.
- To determine how competitors' behavior can be influenced to make it more favorable.

For all three purposes, the key requirement is to understand competitors in order to predict their responses to environmental changes and our own competitive moves. To understand competitors, it is important to be informed about them. Competitive intelligence is a growth field, with a flood of recent books,[41] a dedicated journal,[42] specialist consulting firms, and professional associations.[43] About one-quarter of large US corporations have set up competitive intelligence units.

The distinction between legitimate competitive intelligence and illegal industrial espionage is blurred. The boundaries between public and private information are not always clear. The scope of trade secrets law is murky. Several well publicized cases of information theft have underlined the dangers. In 2001, Procter & Gamble acknowledged that its efforts to acquire information on Unilever's hair care business had transgressed the limits of propriety and legality in trespassing on Unilever's property and taking documents from Unilever dumpsters.[44]

A Framework for Predicting Competitor Behavior

Competitive intelligence is not simply about collecting information. The problem is likely to be too much rather than too little information. The key is a systematic approach that makes clear what information is required and for what purposes it will be used. The objective is to *understand* one's rival. A characteristic of great generals from Hannibal to Patton has been their ability to go beyond military intelligence and

FIGURE 4.2 A framework for competitor analysis

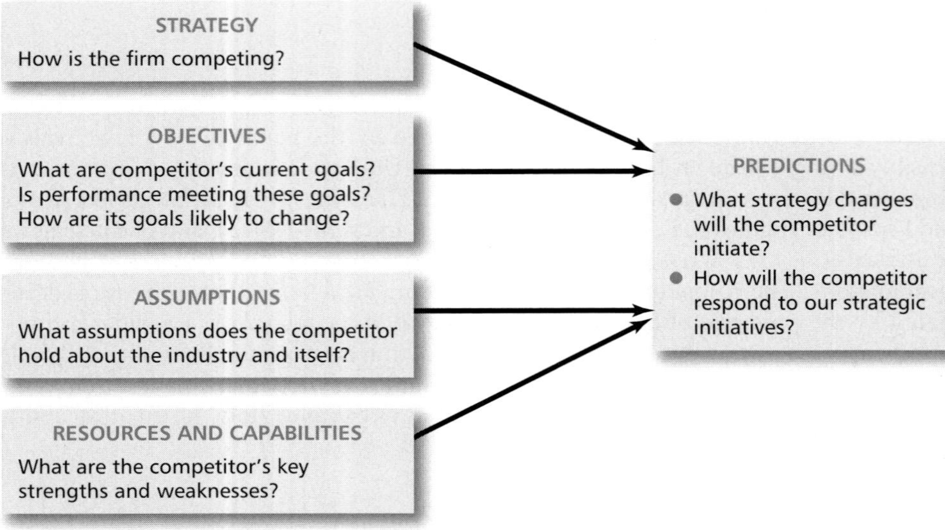

to "get inside the heads" of their opposing commanders. Michael Porter proposes a four-part framework for predicting competitor behavior (see Figure 4.2).

1. Competitor's Current Strategy To predict how a rival will behave in the future, we must understand how that rival is competing at present. A company's strategy may be identified on the basis of what it says and what it does. These two are not necessarily the same. As we noted in Chapter 1, a company's statements of strategy intentions (e.g., in its annual reports – especially the chairman's letter to shareholders – and in presentations to financial analysts) may deviate from its realized strategy as indicated by its capital expenditures, its new product launches, its R&D initiatives, and its HR decisions. Thus, in building a picture of a company's strategy, the key is to link the content of top management communication (with investors, the media, and financial analysts) with the evidence of strategic actions – particularly those that involve commitment of resources. For both sources of information, company websites are invaluable.

2. Competitor's Objectives To forecast how a competitor might change its strategy, we must identify its goals. A key issue is whether a company is driven by financial goals or market goals. A company whose primary goal is attaining market share is likely to be much more aggressive a competitor than one that is mainly interested in profitability. The willingness of the US automobile and consumer electronics producers to cede market share to Japanese competitors was partly a result of their preoccupation with short-term profitability. By comparison, companies like Procter & Gamble and Coca-Cola are obsessed with market share and tend to react aggressively when rivals step on their turf. The most difficult competitors are likely to be those that are not subject to profit disciplines at all – state-owned enterprises in particular.

The level of current performance in relation to the competitor's objectives is important in determining the likelihood of strategy change. The more a company is satisfied with present performance, the more likely it is to continue with its present strategy. But if performance is falling well short of target, radical strategic change, possibly accompanied by a change in top management, is likely.

3. Competitor's Assumptions about the Industry   A competitor's strategic decisions are conditioned by its perceptions of itself and the outside world. The perceptions are guided by its assumptions concerning the industry and business in general. Both are likely to reflect the beliefs that senior managers hold about their industry and the success factors within it. Evidence suggests that not only do these systems of belief tend to be stable over time, they also tend to converge among the firms within an industry. J.-C. Spender has described them as "industry recipes."[45]

Industry recipes may engender "blindspots" that limit the capacity of a firm – even an entire industry – to respond to an external threat. During the 1960s, the Big Three US automobile manufacturers firmly believed that small cars were unprofitable. This belief was partly a product of their own overhead allocation procedures. The result was a willingness to yield the fastest-growing segment of the US automobile market to imports. The complacency of British and US motorcycle manufacturers in the face of Japanese competition reflects similar beliefs (see Strategy Capsule 4.2).

STRATEGY CAPSULE 4.2
Motorcycle Myopia

During the 1960s, BSA was the leading motorcycle manufacturer in Britain, while Harley-Davidson was the leader in the US. During the 1960s, both markets experienced increased import penetration from Japan, but given the emphasis by Honda, Suzuki, and Yamaha on smaller motorcycles, the Japanese challenge was largely discounted.

Eric Turner, chairman of BSA Ltd. (manufacturer of Triumph and BSA motorcycles), commented in 1965:

> The success of Honda, Suzuki, and Yamaha has been jolly good for us. People start out by buying one of the low-priced Japanese jobs. They get to enjoy the fun and exhilaration of the open road and they frequently end up buying one of our more powerful and expensive machines.

Similar complacency was expressed by William Davidson, president of Harley-Davidson:

> Basically, we do not believe in the lightweight market. We believe that motorcycles are sports vehicles, not transportation vehicles. Even if a man says he bought a motorcycle for transportation, it's generally for leisure time use. The lightweight motorcycle is only supplemental. Back around World War I, a number of companies came out with lightweight bikes. We came out with one ourselves. We came out with another in 1947 and it just didn't go anywhere. We have seen what happens to these small sizes.

By the end of the 1970s, BSA and Triumph had ceased production and Harley-Davidson was barely surviving. The world motorcycle industry, including the large bike segments, was dominated by the Japanese.

Sources: *Advertising Age* (December 27, 1965); *Forbes* (September 15, 1966); Richard T. Pascale, *Honda A* (Harvard Business School Case No. 9-384-049, 1983).

4. Competitor's Resources and Capabilities Evaluating the likelihood and seriousness of a competitor's potential challenge requires assessing the strength of that competitor's resources and capabilities. If our rival has a massive cash pile, it would be unwise for our company to unleash a price war by initiating price cuts. Conversely, if we direct our competitive initiative towards our rivals' weaknesses, it may be difficult for them to respond. Richard Branson's Virgin Group has launched a host of entrepreneurial new ventures, typically in markets dominated by a powerful incumbent – British Airways in airlines, EMI in music, Vodafone in wireless telecommunications. Branson's strategy has been to adopt innovative forms of differentiation that are difficult for established incumbents to respond to.

Segmentation Analysis[46]

The Uses of Segmentation

In Chapter 3 we noted the difficulty of drawing industry boundaries and the need to define industries both broadly and narrowly according to the types of question we are seeking to answer. Initially it may be convenient to define industries broadly, but for a more detailed analysis of competition we need to focus on markets that are drawn more narrowly in terms of both products and geography. This process of disaggregating industries into specific markets we call *segmentation*.

Segmentation is particularly important if competition varies across the different submarkets within an industry such that some are more attractive than others. A company can avoid some of the problems of an unattractive industry by judicious segment selection. Consider Dell Computer in the intensely competitive personal computer industry. One of the ways in which Dell has maintained its margins is by continuously shifting towards higher margin products, customer groups, and geographical areas. During 2000–6, Dell shifted resources from desktop PCs to servers, storage systems, laptops, conumables (e.g. ink cartridges), and consumer electronic products (e.g. TVs); and from the more mature markets of North America and Europe to the growth markets of the Asia-Pacific region. Its direct distribution model allows highly detailed segmentation – to the point of analyzing probability at the level of the individual customer. "We cut the market and then cut it again, looking for the most profitable customers to serve," says CEO Kevin Rollins.[47]

Key success factors also differ by segment. In the restaurant industry, the requirements for success are almost totally different between the fast-food segment and luxury restaurants. The result is that within a single industry, very different companies with very different strategies coexist.

Stages in Segmentation Analysis

The purpose of segmentation analysis is to identify attractive segments, to select strategies for different segments, and to determine how many segments to serve. The analysis proceeds in five stages (see Strategy Capsule 4.3 for a summary and application).

1. Identify Key Segmentation Variables The first stage of segmentation analysis is to determine the basis of segmentation. Segmentation decisions essentially are choices about which customers to serve and what to offer them: hence segmentation variables relate to the characteristics of customers and the product (see Figure 4.3). The most appropriate segmentation variables are those that partition the market most distinctly in terms of limited substitutability among both customers (demand-side substitutability) and producers (supply-side substitutability). Distinct market segments tend to be recognizable from price differentials. Thus, in the auto industry, color is

STRATEGY CAPSULE 4.3

Segmenting the European Metal Can Industry

1. Identify Key Segmentation Variables and Categories

- Identify possible segmentation variables

  Raw material, can design, can size, customer size, customer's industry, location

- Reduce the number of segmentation variables: Which are most significant? Which are closely correlated and can be combined?

  Type of can, customer industry, customer location

- Identify discrete categories for each segmentation variable.

  Type of can: steel 3-piece, steel 2-piece, aluminum 2-piece, general cans, composite cans, aerosols. Type of customer: food processing, fruit juice, pet food, soft drink, toiletries, beer, oil. Location: France, Germany, Spain/Portugal, Italy, UK, Benelux.

2. Construct a Segmentation Matrix

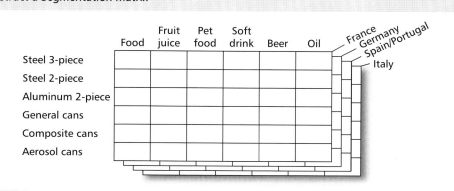

3. Analyze Segment Attractiveness

Apply five forces analysis to individual segments. For example, the market for aluminum 2-piece cans to soft drink canners in Italy may be analyzed as follows:

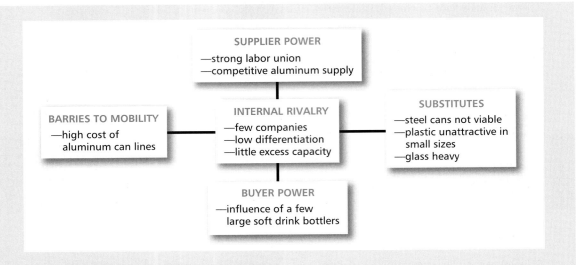

4. Identify Key Success Factors in Each Segment

Within each segment, how do customers choose, and what is needed to survive competition?

5. Analyze Attractions of Broad versus Narrow Segment Scope

● What is the potential to share costs and transfer skills across segments?

● How similar are key success factors between segments?

● Are there benefits of segment specialization?

probably not a good segmentation variable (white and red Honda Civics sell at much the same price); size is a better segmentation variable (full-size cars sell at a price premium over sub-compact cars).

Typically, segmentation analysis generates far too many segmentation variables. For our analysis to be manageable, we need to reduce these to two or three. To do this we need to:

● Identify the most *strategically significant* segmentation variables. Which variables are most important in creating meaningful divisions in a market?

● Combine segmentation variables that are closely correlated. Thus, in the restaurant industry, price level, service level (waiter service/self-service), cuisine (fast-food/full meals), and alcohol license (wine served/soft drinks only) are likely to be closely related. We could use a single variable, restaurant type, with three categories – full-service restaurants, cafés, and fast-food outlets – as a proxy for all of these variables.

2. Construct a Segmentation Matrix Once the segmentation variables have been selected and discrete categories determined for each, the individual segments may be identified using a two- or three-dimensional matrix. Thus, the European metal container industry might be analyzed in a three-dimensional segmentation matrix (see

FIGURE 4.3 The basis for segmentation: the characteristics of buyers and products

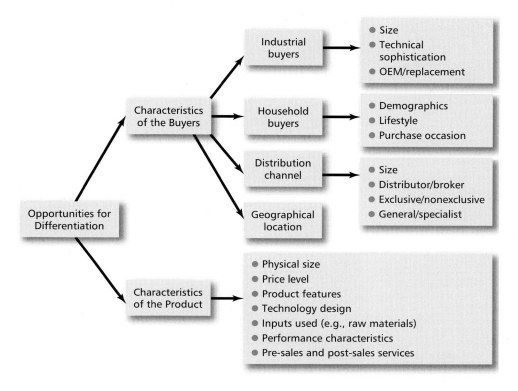

Strategy Capsule 4.3), whereas the world automobile industry might be segmented simply by vehicle type and geographical region (see Strategy Capsule 4.4).

3. Analyze Segment Attractiveness Profitability within an industry segment is determined by the same structural forces that determine profitability within an industry as a whole. As a result, Porter's five forces of competition framework is equally effective in relation to a segment as to an entire industry. Strategy Capsule 4.4 points to some implications of a five forces analysis for certain segments of the world automobile industry.

There are, however, a few differences. First, when analyzing the pressure of competition from substitute products, we are concerned not only with substitutes from other industries, but, more importantly, substitutes from other segments within the same industry. Second, when considering entry into the segment, the main source of entrants is likely to be producers established in other segments within the same industry. The barriers that protect a segment from firms located in other segments are called *barriers to mobility* to distinguish them from the *barriers to entry* that protect the industry as a whole.[48] When barriers to mobility are low, then the superior returns of high-profit segments tend to be quickly eroded. Thus, the high margins earned on sport utility vehicles during the mid-1990s were competed away once most of the world's main auto producers had entered the segment.

STRATEGY CAPSULE 4.4
Segmenting the World Automobile Market

A global automobile producer such as Ford or Toyota might segment the world auto market by product type and geography. A first-cut segmentation might be along the following lines:

REGIONS

PRODUCTS	North America	Western Europe	Eastern Europe	Asia	Latin America	Australia & NZ	Africa
Luxury cars							
Full-size cars							
Mid-size cars							
Small cars							
Station wagons							
Minivans							
Sports cars							
Sport utility							
Pickup trucks							
Hybrids							

To identify segments with the best profit prospects for the future, we need to understand why, in the past, some segments have been more profitable than others. For example, during the 1990s:

● The North American market for small cars was unprofitable due to many competitors (all the world's major auto producers were represented), lack of clear product differentiation, and customers' price sensitivity.

● Sport utility vehicles and passenger minivans were highly profitable segments due to strong demand relative to capacity, and comparatively few participants. However, the influx of companies into these segments has eroded margins.

● The luxury car segment is traditionally a high-margin segment due to few players, high product differentiation, and price insensitivity of buyers. However, new entry and excess capacity has increased competition.

● Hybrids have earned big margins due to few players and shortage of capacity relative to demand.

Once we understand the factors that determined segment profitability in the past, we can predict segment profitability in the future.

Segmentation analysis can also be useful in identifying unexploited opportunities in an industry. For example, a segmentation matrix of the restaurant industry in a town or locality might reveal a number of empty segments. Companies that have built successful strategies by concentrating on unoccupied segments include Wal-Mart (discount stores in small towns), Enterprise Rent-A-Car (suburban locations), and Edward Jones (full-service brokerage for small investors in smaller cities). This can be an intermediate step in the quest for "blue oceans" – new markets untainted by competition.[49]

4. Identify the Segment's Key Success Factors Differences in competitive structure and in customer preferences between segments result in different key success factors. By analyzing buyers' purchase criteria and the basis of competition within individual segments, we can identify key success factors for individual segments. For example, the US bicycle market can be segmented on the basis of the age group of the customer (infants, children, youths, adults), price, branding, and distribution channel. Combining and categorizing these segmentation variables results in four major segments, each with different key success factors (see Figure 4.4).

FIGURE 4.4 Segmentation and key success factors: the US bicycle market

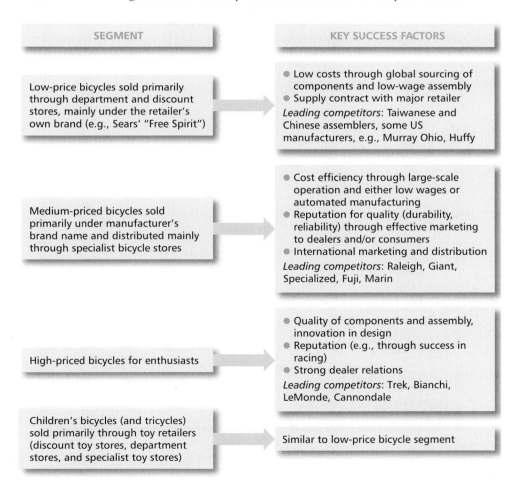

5. Select Segment Scope Finally, a firm needs to decide whether it wishes to be a segment specialist, or compete across multiple segments. The advantages of a broad over a narrow segment focus depend on two main factors: similarity of key success factors and the presence of shared costs. If key success factors are different across segments, a firm will need to deploy distinct strategies and may have difficulties in drawing upon the same capabilities. Harley-Davidson's attempt to compete in sports motorcycles through its Buell brand has met limited success.

The ability to share costs across different segments has been a major factor in automobiles where very few specialist manufacturers survive and most of the world's main automakers offer a full range of vehicles allowing them to share costs through common platforms and components. The analysis of a company's optimal segment range is similar to the analysis of diversification versus specialization. We shall return to this issue in Chapter 15.

Vertical Segmentation: Profit Pools

Segmentation is usually horizontal – markets are disaggregated according to products, geography, and customer groups. An industry can also be segmented vertically by identifying different value chain activities. Bain & Company show that profitability varies greatly between different vertical activities and proposes *profit pool mapping* as a technique for analyzing the vertical structure of profitability.[50] For example, in the US automobile industry, downstream activities such as finance, leasing, insurance, and service and repair are much more profitable than manufacturing (see Figure 4.5). During 2003–6, all of Ford and GM's profits were derived from the financial services they offered to dealers and car buyers.

FIGURE 4.5 The US auto industry profit pool

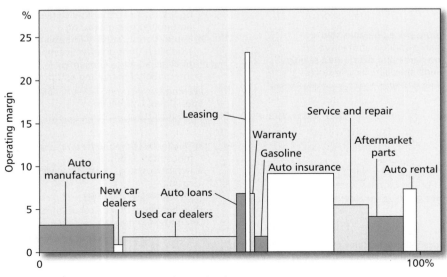

SOURCE: O. GADIESH AND J. L. GILBERT, "PROFIT POOLS: A FRESH LOOK AT STRATEGY," *HARVARD BUSINESS REVIEW* (MAY-JUNE 1998): 142. © 1998 BY THE HARVARD BUSINESS SCHOOL PUBLISHING CORPORATION, ALL RIGHTS RESERVED. REPRINTED BY PERMISSION OF HARVARD BUSINESS SCHOOL PUBLISHING.

To map an industry's profit pool, Bain & Company identifies four steps:

1 *Define the pool's boundaries.* What is the range of value-adding activities that your business sector encompasses? It may be useful to look upstream and downstream beyond conventional industry boundaries.

2 *Estimate the pool's overall size.* Total industry profit may be estimated by applying the average margin earned by a sample of companies to an estimate of industry total revenues.

3 *Estimate profit for each value chain activity in the pool.* Here is the key challenge. It requires gathering data from companies that are "pure players" – specialized in the single value chain activity – and disaggregating data for "mixed players" – those performing multiple activities.

4 *Check and reconcile the calculations.* Compare the aggregation of profits in each activity (stage 3) with the total for the industry (stage 2).

Strategic Groups

Whereas segmentation analysis concentrates on the characteristics of markets as the basis for disaggregating industries, strategic group analysis segments an industry on the basis of the strategies of the member firms. A strategic group is "the group of firms in an industry following the same or a similar strategy along the strategic dimensions."[51] These strategic dimensions might include product range, geographical breadth, choice of distribution channels, level of product quality, degree of vertical integration, choice of technology, and so on. By selecting the most important strategic dimensions and locating each firm in the industry along them, it is possible to identify groups of companies that have adopted more or less similar approaches to competing within the industry. Figure 4.6 identifies strategic groups within the world automobile industry; Figure 4.7 shows strategic groups within the oil industry.[52]

Strategic group analysis developed out of initial work on the domestic appliance[53] and brewing industries.[54] Most of the empirical research into strategic groups has been concerned with analyzing differences in profitability among firms.[55] The basic argument is that mobility barriers between strategic groups permit some groups of firms to be persistently more profitable than other groups. In general, the proposition that profitability differences *within* strategic groups are less than differences *between* strategic groups has not received robust empirical support.[56] The inconsistency of empirical findings may reflect the fact that the members of a strategic group, though pursuing similar strategies, are not necessarily in competition with one another. For example, within the European airline industry, budget airlines such as EasyJet, BalticAir, SkyEurope, Volare, and Ryanair pursue similar strategies, but do not, for the most part, compete on the same routes. Strategic group analysis is very useful in identifying strategic niches within an industry and the strategic positioning of different firms; it is less useful as a tool for analyzing interfirm profitability differences.[57]

FIGURE 4.6 Strategic groups within the world automobile industry

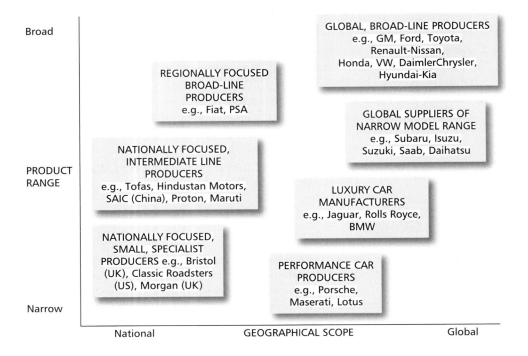

FIGURE 4.7 Strategic groups within the world petroleum industry

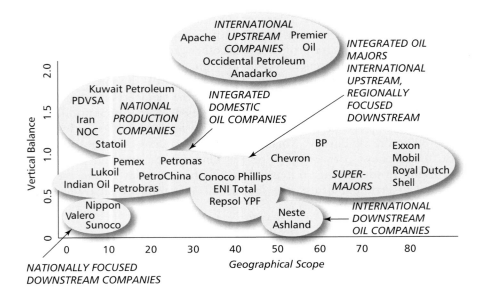

Summary

The purpose of this chapter has been to go beyond the basic analysis of industry structure, competition and profitability presented in Chapter 3, and consider the interactive nature of competition and the complexities of industries and markets.

In terms of our capabilities in analyzing industry and competition, we have extended our strategy tool kit in a number of directions:

● We have recognized the potential for complementary products to add value and noted the importance of developing strategies that can exploit this source of value.

● We have noted the importance of competitive interactions between close rivals and learned a structured approach to analyzing competitors and predicting their behavior. At a more sophisticated theoretical level, we have recognized some of the findings of game theory that we can use to understand competition and develop winning strategies.

● We examined the microstructure of industries and markets and the value of segmentation analysis, profit pool analysis, and strategic group analysis in understanding industries at a more detailed level and in selecting an advantageous strategic position within an industry.

Self-Study Questions

1   HP, Canon, Lexmark, and other manufacturers of inkjet printers make most of their profits on the sales of ink cartridges. Why are cartridges more profitable than printers? If cartridges were manufactured by different firms from those which make printers, would the situation be different?

2   In November 2005, six of Paris's most luxurious hotels – including George V, Le Bristol, the Ritz, and Hotel de Crillon – were fined for colluding on room rates. Several regular guests were unsurprised and noted that at these hotels it was always possible to negotiate substantial discounts for the listed rates. How do you think that the hotels involved were able to overcome the "prisoners' dilemma" problem of colluding over rates and how does the "prisoners' dilemma" model explain the eagerness of the hotels to offer individually negotiated discounts?

3   In August 2006, Rupert Murdoch's News International announced its intention of launching a free evening newspaper, *TheLondonPaper*, to challenge Associated Newspapers' London *Evening Standard* (daily sales 390,000). Given that the *Evening Standard* was already believed to be loss making, the new competition could be fatal for the paper. What steps might Associated Newspapers take to deter News International from launching its new paper, and if it goes ahead with the launch, what would Associated Newspapers' best response be?

4   During 2006–7, Sony was locked in a ferocious war with Microsoft for leadership in the market for video game consoles. Because of its early lead, Microsoft's XBox had a substantial lead in installed base, but Sony's PS3 had superior specifications. Sony is anxious to predict how aggressive Microsoft is likely to be in this market. Using the competitor analysis framework in Figure 4.2 and what you know about Microsoft, what predictions can you make about Microsoft's likely competitive strategy in the game console market?

5   How would you segment the restaurant market in your home town? Which segments do you consider to be the most attractive in terms of profit potential?

Notes

1   Adam Brandenburger and Barry Nalebuff (*Co-opetition*, New York: Doubleday, 1996) propose an alternative framework, the *value net*, for analyzing the impact of complements.

2   See A. Brandenburger and B. Nalebuff, "The Right Game: Use Game Theory to Shape Strategy," *Harvard Business Review* (July–August 1995): 63–4; and A. Brandenburger, J. Kou, and M. Burnett, *Power Play (A): Nintendo in 8-bit Video Games* (Harvard Business School Case No. 9-795-103, 1995).

3   C. Baldwin, S. O'Mahony, and J. Quinn, *IBM and Linux (A)* (Harvard Business School Case No. 903-083, 2003).

4   J. A. Schumpeter, *The Theory of Economic Development* (Cambridge, MA: Harvard University Press, 1934).

5   See R. Jacobson, "The Austrian School of Strategy," *Academy of Management Review* 17 (1992): 782–807; and Greg Young, Ken Smith, and Curtis Grimm, "Austrian and Industrial Organization Perspectives on Firm-Level Competitive Activity and Performance," *Organization Science* 7 (May–June 1996): 243–54.

6   R. T. Masson and J. Shaanan, "Stochastic Dynamic Limit Pricing: An Empirical Test," *Review of Economics and Statistics* 64 (1982): 413–22; R. T. Masson and J. Shaanan, "Optimal Pricing and Threat of Entry: Canadian Evidence," *International Journal of Industrial Organization* 5 (1987).

7   R. Caves and M. E. Porter, "The Dynamics of Changing Seller Concentration," *Journal of Industrial Economics* 19 (1980): 1–15; P. Hart and R. Clarke, *Concentration in British Industry* (Cambridge: Cambridge University Press, 1980).

8   P. A. Geroski and R. T. Masson, "Dynamic Market Models in Industrial Organization," *International Journal of Industrial Organization* 5 (1987): 1–13.

9   G. McNamara, P. M. Vaaler, and C. Devers, "Same as it Ever Was: The Search for Evidence of Increasing Hypercompetition," *Strategic Management Journal* 24 (2003): 261–78.

10   D. C. Mueller, *Profits in the Long Run* (Cambridge: Cambridge University Press, 1986).

11   J. R. Williams, "The Productivity Base of Industries," working paper (Carnegie-Mellon Graduate School of Industrial Administration, 1994) and *Renewable Advantage: Crafting Strategy through Economic Time* (New York: Free Press, 1999).

12   R. R. Wiggins and T. W. Ruefli, "Sustained Competitive Advantage," *Organizational Science* 13 (2002): 81–105.

13   R. D'Aveni, *Hypercompetition: Managing the Dynamics of Strategic Maneuvering* (New York: Free Press, 1994): 217–18.

14   K. Weigelt and C. F. Camerer, "Reputation and Corporate Strategy: A Review of Recent Theory and Applications," *Strategic Management Journal* 9 (1988): 137–42.

15   A. K. Dixit, "The Role of Investment in Entry Deterrence," *Economic Journal* 90 (1980): 95–106.

16   P. Milgrom and J. Roberts, "Informational Asymmetries, Strategic Behavior and Industrial Organization," *American Economic Review* 77, no. 2 (May 1987): 184–9; J. Tirole, *The Theory of Industrial Organization* (Cambridge, MA: MIT Press, 1988).

17   P. Ghemawat, *Commitment: The Dynamic of Strategy* (New York: Free Press, 1991).

18   There are several outstanding introductions to the principles and applications of game theory: T. C. Schelling, *The Strategy of Conflict*, 2nd edn (Cambridge: Harvard University Press, 1980); A. K. Dixit and B. J. Nalebuff, *Thinking Strategically: The Competitive Edge in Business, Politics, and Everyday Life* (New York: W. W. Norton, 1991); J. McMillan, *Games, Strategies, and Managers* (New York: Oxford University Press, 1992).

19   G. T. Allison and P. Zelikow, *Essence of Decision: Explaining the Cuban Missile Crisis*, 2nd edn (Boston: Little Brown, 1999).

20 B. C. Esty and P. Ghemawat, "Airbus vs. Boeing in Superjumbos: A Case of Failed Preemption," *Harvard Business School Working Paper* No. 02-061 (2002).

21 D. Ronfelt, "Social Science at 190 mph on NASCAR's Biggest Superspeedways," *First Monday* 5 (February 7, 2000).

22 "Game Theory in Action: Designing the US Airwaves Auction," *Financial Times* Mastering Strategy Supplement (October 11, 1999): 4.

23 J. Maynard Smith, "Sexual Selection and the Handicap Principle," *Journal of Theoretical Biology* 57 (1976): 239–42.

24 Adam Brandenburger and Barry Nalebuff (1996), op. cit.

25 T. Dhar, J.-P. Chatas, R. W. Collerill, and B. W. Gould, Strategic Pricing Between Coca-Cola Company and PepsiCo, *Journal of Economics and Management Strategy* 14 (2005): 905–31.

26 *Bitter Competition: Holland Sweetener vs. Nutrasweet (A)* (Harvard Business School Case No. 9-794-079, 1994).

27 A. M. McGahan, "The Incentive not to Invest: Capacity Commitments in the Compact Disk Introduction," in R. A. Burgelman and R. S. Rosenbloom (eds), *Research on Technological Innovation Management and Policy*, vol. 5 (Greenwich, CT: JAI Press, 1994).

28 M. B. Lieberman, "Excess Capacity as a Barrier to Entry: An Empirical Appraisal," *Journal of Industrial Economics* 35 (1987): 607–27.

29 D. K. Levine and R. A. Levine, "Deterrence in the Cold War and the War on Terror," UCLA Dept. of Economics (2006).

30 D. N. Sull, "Managing by Commitments," *Harvard Business Review* (June 2003).

31 J. Chevalier, "When It Can Be Good to Burn Your Boats," *Financial Times* Mastering Strategy Supplement (October 25, 1999): 2–3.

32 Games where price is the primary decision variable are called Bertrand models after the 19th-century French economist Joseph Bertrand.

33 Games where quantity is the primary decision variable are called Cournot models after the 19th-century French economist Augustin Cournot.

34 F. Scott Morton, "Strategic Complements and Substitutes," *Financial Times* Mastering Strategy Supplement (November 8, 1999): 10–13.

35 For a review of research on competitive signaling, see O. Heil and T. S. Robertson, "Toward a Theory of Competitive Market Signaling: A Research Agenda," *Strategic Management Journal* 12 (1991): 403–18.

36 For a survey of the strategic role of reputation, see K. Weigelt and C. Camerer, "Reputation and Corporate Strategy: A Review of Recent Theory and Applications," *Strategic Management Journal* 9 (1988): 443–54.

37 P. Milgrom and J. Roberts, "Predation, Reputation, and Entry Deterrence," *Journal of Economic Theory* 27 (1982): 280–312.

38 R. M. Grant, "Pricing Behavior in the UK Wholesale Market for Petrol," *Journal of Industrial Economics* 30 (1982): 271–92; L. Miller, "The Provocative Practice of Price Signaling: Collusion versus Cooperation," *Business Horizons* (July–August 1993).

39 There are numerous critiques of the usefulness of game theory. F. M. Fisher, "The Games Economists Play: A Noncooperative View," *Rand Journal of Economics* 20 (Spring 1989): 113–24, points to the ability of game theory to predict almost any equilibrium solution. Colin Camerer describes this as the "Pandora's Box Problem." See C. F. Camerer, "Does Strategy Research Need Game Theory?" *Strategic Management Journal*, special issue, 12 (Winter 1991): 137–52. Steve Postrel illustrates this problem by developing a game theory model to explain the rationality of bank presidents setting fire to their trousers. See S. Postrel, "Burning Your Britches Behind You: Can Policy Scholars Bank on Game Theory?" *Strategic Management Journal*, special issue, 12 (Winter 1991): 153–5. Michael E. Porter ("Toward a Dynamic Theory of Strategy," *Strategic Management Journal*, special issue, 12 (Winter 1991): 95–117) notes that game theory "stops short of a dynamic theory of strategy . . . these models explore the dynamics of a largely static world."

40 P. Milgrom, *Putting Auction Theory to Work* (Cambridge: Cambridge University Press, 2004); J. McMillan, *Reinventing the Bazaar* (New York: Norton, 2002).

41 L. Field, *The Secret Language of Competitive Intelligence* (New York: Random House, 2006); J. E. Prescott and S. H. Miller, *Proven Strategies in Competitive Intelligence: Lessons from the Trenches* (Wiley: New York, 2001).

42 *Competitive Intelligence Review* (New York: John Wiley).

43 The Society of Competitive Intelligence Professionals (www.scip.org).

44 "P&G's Covert Operation," *Fortune* (September 17, 2001).

45 J.-C. Spender, *Industry Recipes: The Nature and Sources of Managerial Judgement* (Oxford: Basil Blackwell, 1989). How social interaction promotes convergence of perceptions and beliefs is discussed by Anne Huff in "Industry Influences on Strategy Reformulation," *Strategic Management Journal* 3 (1982): 119–31.

46 This section draws heavily on M. E. Porter, *Competitive Advantage* (New York: Free Press, 1985): Chapter 7.

47 O. Gadiesh and J. L. Gilbert, "Profit Pools: A Fresh Look at Strategy," *Harvard Business Review* (May–June 1998): 146.

48 R. E. Caves and M. E. Porter, "From Entry Barriers to Mobility Barriers: Conjectural Decisions and Contrived Deterrence to New Competition," *Quarterly Journal of Economics* 91 (1977): 241–62.

49 W. C. Kim and R. Mauborgne, "Blue Ocean Strategy: From Theory to Practice," *California Management Review* 47 (Spring 2005): 105–21.

50 O. Gadiesh and J. L. Gilbert, "How to Map Your Industry's Profit Pools," *Harvard Business Review* (May–June 1998): 149–62.

51 M. E. Porter, *Competitive Strategy* (New York: Free Press, 1980): 129.

52 For more on strategic groups, see John McGee and Howard Thomas's "Strategic Groups: Theory, Research, and Taxonomy," *Strategic Management Journal* 7 (1986): 141–60.

53 M. Hunt, "Competition in the Major Home Appliance Industry," doctoral dissertation (Harvard University, 1973).

54 K. Hatten, D. Schendel, and A. Cooper, "A Strategic Model of the US Brewing Industry," *Academy of Management Journal* 21 (1978): 592–610.

55 K. Cool and D. Schendel, "Strategic Group Formation and Performance: The Case of the US Pharmaceutical Industry," *Management Science* 33 (1987): 1102–24; A. Feigenbaum and H. Thomas, "Strategic Groups and Performance: The US Insurance Industry," *Strategic Management Journal* 11 (1990): 197–215.

56 K. Cool and I. Dierickx, "Rivalry, Strategic Groups, and Firm Profitability," *Strategic Management Journal* 14 (1993): 47–59.

57 K. Smith, C. Grimm, and S. Wally, "Strategic Groups and Rivalrous Firm Behavior: Toward a Reconciliation," *Strategic Management Journal* 18 (1997): 149–57.

5

Analyzing Resources and Capabilities

Analysts have tended to define assets too narrowly, identifying only those that can be measured, such as plant and equipment. Yet the intangible assets, such as a particular technology, accumulated consumer information, brand name, reputation, and corporate culture, are invaluable to the firm's competitive power. In fact, these invisible assets are often the only real source of competitive edge that can be sustained over time.

—HIROYUKI ITAMI, MOBILIZING INVISIBLE ASSETS

You've gotta do what you do well.

—LUCINO NOTO, FORMER VICE CHAIRMAN, EXXON MOBIL

OUTLINE

- Introduction and Objectives

- The Role of Resources and Capabilities in Strategy Formulation

  Basing Strategy on Resources and Capabilities

  Resources and Capabilities as Sources of Profit

- The Resources of the Firm

  Tangible Resources
  Intangible Resources
  Human Resources

- Organizational Capabilities

  Classifying Capabilities
  The Architecture of Capability

- Appraising Resources and Capabilities

  Establishing Competitive Advantage
  Sustaining Competitive Advantage
  Appropriating the Returns to Competitive Advantage

- Putting Resource and Capability Analysis to Work: A Practical Guide

  Step 1 Identify the Key Resources and Capabilities

Introduction and Objectives

In Chapter 1, I noted that the focus of strategy thinking has been shifted from the external environment towards its internal environment. In this chapter, we will make the same transition. In looking within the firm, we will concentrate our attention on the resources and capabilities that firms possess. In doing so, we shall build the foundations for our analysis of competitive advantage (which began in Chapter 3 with the discussion of key success factors).

By the time you have completed this chapter you will be able to:

● Appreciate the role of a firm's resources and capabilities as a basis for formulating strategy.

● Identify and appraise the resources and capabilities of a firm.

● Evaluate the potential for a firm's resources and capabilities to confer sustainable competitive advantage.

● Use the results of resource and capability analysis to formulate strategies that exploit internal strengths while defending against internal weaknesses.

● Identify the means through which a firm can develop its resources and capabilities.

We begin by explaining why a company's resources and capabilities are so important to its strategy.

The Role of Resources and Capabilities in Strategy Formulation

Strategy is concerned with matching a firm's resources and capabilities to the opportunities that arise in the external environment. So far, the emphasis of the book has been the identification of profit opportunities in the external environment of the firm. With this chapter, our emphasis shifts from the interface between strategy and the external environment towards the interface between strategy and the internal environment of the firm – more specifically, with the resources and capabilities of the firm (see Figure 5.1).

Increasing emphasis on the role of resources and capabilities as the basis for strategy is the result of two factors. First, as firms' industry environments have become more unstable, so internal resources and capabilities rather than external market focus has been viewed as a securer base for formulating strategy. Second, it has become increasingly apparent that competitive advantage rather than industry attractiveness is the primary source of superior profitability. Let us consider each of these factors.

Basing Strategy on Resources and Capabilities

During the 1990s, ideas concerning the role of resources and capabilities as the principal basis for firm strategy and the primary source of profitability coalesced into what has become known as the *resource-based view of the firm*.[1]

To understand why the resource-based view has had a major impact on strategy thinking, let us go back to the starting point for strategy formulation: typically some statement of the firm's identity and purpose (often expressed in a mission statement). Conventionally, firms have answered the question "what is our business?" in terms of the market they serve: "who are our customers?" and "which of their needs are we seeking to serve?" However, in a world where customer preferences are volatile and the identity of customers and the technologies for serving them are changing, a market-focused strategy may not provide the stability and constancy of direction needed to guide strategy over the long term.[2] When the external environment is in a

FIGURE 5.1 Analyzing resources and capabilities: the interface between strategy and the firm

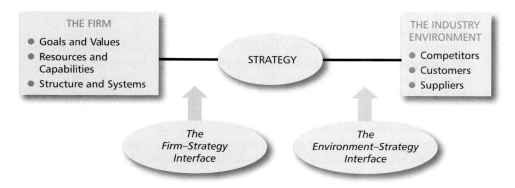

FIGURE 5.2 Honda Motor Company: product development milestones

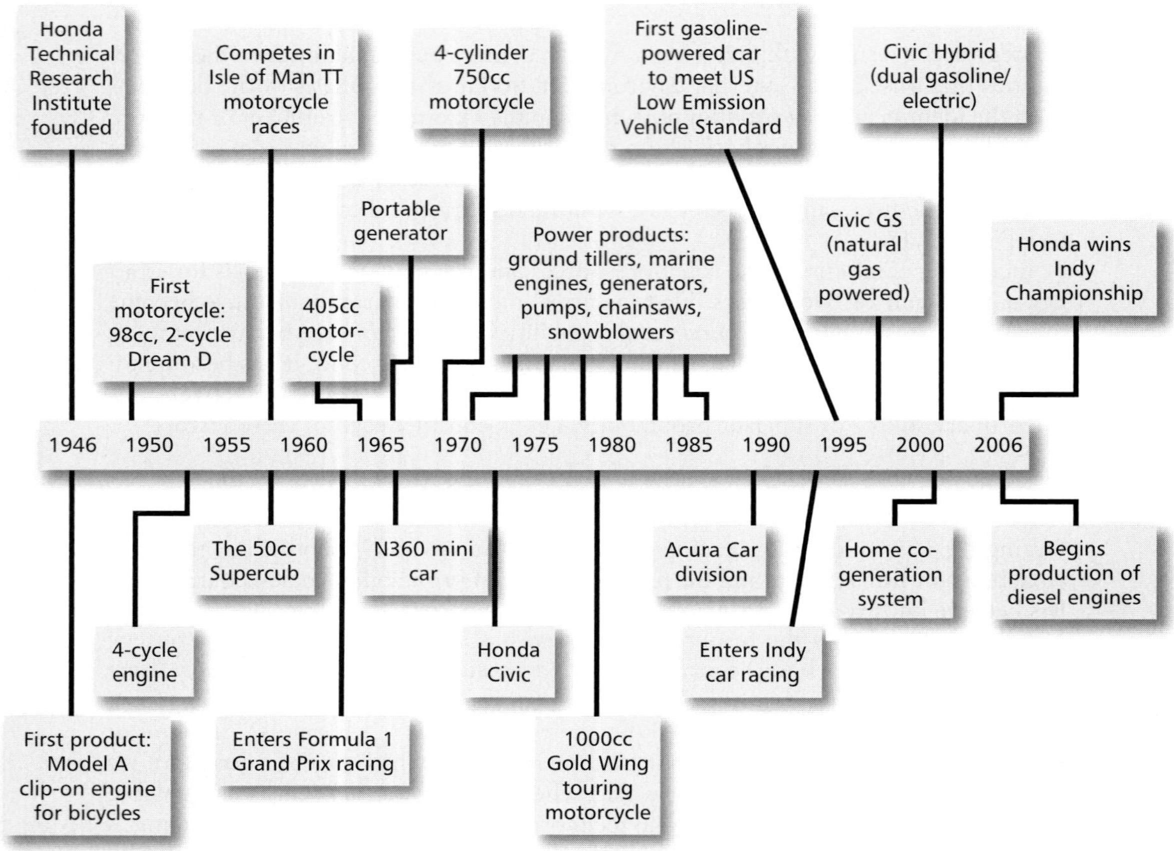

state of flux, the firm itself, in terms of its bundle of resources and capabilities, may be a much more stable basis on which to define its identity.[3]

In their 1990 landmark paper, "The Core Competence of the Corporation," C. K. Prahalad and Gary Hamel pointed to the potential for capabilities to be the "roots of competitiveness," source of new products, and foundation for strategy.[4] For example:

● Honda Motor Company is the world's biggest motorcycle producer and a lead supplier of automobiles. But it has never defined itself either as a motorcycle company or a motor vehicle company. Since its founding in 1948, its strategy has been built around its expertise in the development and manufacture of engines; this capability has successfully carried it from motorcycles to a wide range of gasoline-engined products (see Figure 5.2).

● Canon Inc. had its first success producing 35 mm cameras. Since then it has gone on to develop fax machines, calculators, copy machines, printers, video cameras, camcorders, semiconductor manufacturing equipment, and many other products. Almost all Canon's products involve the application of three areas of technological capability: precision mechanics, microelectronics, and fine optics.

FIGURE 5.3 The evolution of capabilities and products: 3M

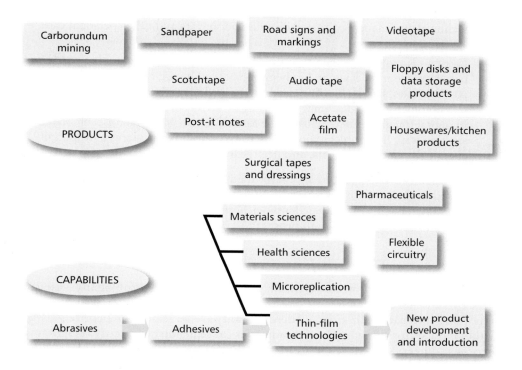

- 3M Corporation has expanded from sandpaper, into adhesive tapes, audiotapes and videotapes, road signs, medical products, and floppy disks. Its product list comprises over 30,000 separate products. Is it a conglomerate? Certainly not, claims 3M. Its vast product range rests on a foundation of key technologies relating to adhesives and thin-film coatings, and its remarkable ability to manage the development and marketing of new products (see Figure 5.3).

In general, the greater the rate of change in a firm's external environment, the more likely it is that internal resources and capabilities will provide a secure foundation for long-term strategy. In fast-moving, technology-based industries, new companies are built around specific technological capabilities. The markets where these capabilities are applied are a secondary consideration. Motorola, the Texas-based supplier of wireless telecommunications equipment, semiconductors, and direct satellite communications, has undergone many transformations, from being a leading provider of TVs and car radios to its current focus on telecom equipment. Yet, underlying these transformations has been a consistent focus on wireless electronics.

When a company faces the imminent obsolescence of its core product, should its strategy focus on continuing to serve fundamental customer needs or on deploying its resources and capabilities in other markets?

- When Olivetti, the Italian typewriter manufacturer, faced the displacement of typewriters by microcomputers during the 1980s, it sought to maintain its focus on serving the word processing needs of businesses by expanding into PCs. The venture was a costly failure.[5] By contrast, Remington, another leading typewriter manufacturer, moved into products that required similar technical and manufacturing skills: electric shavers and other personal care appliances.[6]

● Eastman Kodak's dominance of the world market for photographic products based on chemical imaging has been threatened by digital imaging. Over the past 25 years, Kodak has invested billions of dollars developing digital technologies and digital imaging products. Yet profits and market leadership in digital imaging remain elusive for Kodak. Might Kodak have been better off sticking with its chemical know-how and developing its interests in specialty chemicals, pharmaceuticals, and healthcare?[7]

The difficulties experienced by established firms in adjusting to technological change within their own markets are well documented – in typesetting and in disk-drive manufacturing, successive technological waves have caused market leaders to falter and allowed new entrants to prosper.[8]

Resources and Capabilities as Sources of Profit

In Chapter 1, we identified two major sources of superior profitability: industry attractiveness and competitive advantage. Of these, competitive advantage is the more important. Internationalization and deregulation have increased competitive pressure within most sectors; as a result, few industries (or segments) offer cozy refuges from vigorous competition. As we observed in the previous chapter (see Table 4.1), industry factors account for only a small proportion of interfirm profit differentials. Hence, establishing competitive advantage through the development and deployment of resources and capabilities, rather than seeking shelter from the storm of competition, has become the primary goal for strategy.

The distinction between industry attractiveness and competitive advantage (based on superior resources) as sources of a firm's profitability corresponds to economists' distinction between different types of profit (or *rent*). The profits arising from market power are referred to as *monopoly rents*; those arising from superior resources are *Ricardian rents*, after the 19th-century British economist David Ricardo. Ricardo showed that, even when the market for wheat was competitive, fertile land would yield high returns. Ricardian rent is the return earned by a scare resource over and above the cost of bringing it into production.[9]

In practice, distinguishing between profit arising from market power and profit arising from resource superiority is less clear in practice than in principle. A closer look at Porter's five forces framework suggests that industry attractiveness derives ultimately from the ownership of resources. Barriers to entry, for example, are the result of patents, brands, distribution channels, learning, or some other resource possessed by incumbent firms. Similarly, the lack of rivalry resulting from the dominance of a single firm (monopoly) or a few firms (oligopoly) is usually based on the concentrated ownership of key resources such as technology, manufacturing facilities, or distribution facilities.

The resource-based approach has profound implications for companies' strategy formulation. When the primary concern of strategy was industry selection and positioning, companies tended to adopt similar strategies. The resource-based view, by contrast, emphasizes the uniqueness of each company and suggests that the key to profitability is not through doing the *same* as other firms, but rather through exploiting *differences*. Establishing competitive advantage involves formulating and implementing a strategy that exploits the uniqueness of a firm's portfolio of resources and capabilities.

The remainder of this chapter outlines a resource-based approach to strategy formulation. Fundamental to this approach is recognizing that a firm must seek a thorough and profound understanding of its resources and capabilities. Such understanding provides a basis for:

1 Selecting a strategy that exploits an organization's key strengths. Mariah Carey's disastrous 2001–2 was the result of her straying from her core competences (see Strategy Capsule 5.1). Walt Disney's turnaround under Michael Eisner's leadership was the result of exploiting its underlying resources more effectively (see Strategy Capsule 5.2).

2 Developing the firm's resources and capabilities. Resource analysis is not just about deploying existing resources, it is also concerned with filling resource gaps and building capability for the future. Toyota, Microsoft, Johnson & Johnson, and British Petroleum are all companies whose long-term success

STRATEGY CAPSULE 5.1

Focusing Strategy around Core Capabilities: Lyor Cohen on Mariah Carey

2001 was a disastrous year for Mariah Carey. Her first movie, *Glitter*, was a flop, the soundtrack was Carey's most poorly received album in a decade, her $80 million recording contract was dropped by EMI, and she suffered a nervous breakdown.

Lyor Cohen, the aggressive, workaholic chief executive of Island Def Jam records was quick to spot an opportunity:

> "I cold-called her on the day of her release from EMI and I said, I think you are an unbelievable artist and you should hold your head up high," says Cohen. "What I said stuck on her and she ended up signing with us."

His strategic analysis of Carey's situation was concise:

> "I said to her, what's your competitive advantage? A great voice, of course. And what else? You write every one of your songs – you're a great writer. So why did you stray from your competitive advantage? If you have this magnificent voice and you write such compelling songs, why are you dressing like that, why are you using all these collaborations [with other artists and other songwriters]? Why? It's like driving a Ferrari in first – you won't see what that Ferrari will do until you get into sixth gear."

Cohen signed Carey in May 2002. Under Universal Music's Island Def Jam Records, Carey returned to her core strengths: her versatile voice, song-writing talents, and ballad style. Her new album, *The Emancipation of Mimi*, was the biggest-selling album of 2005, and in 2006 she won a Grammy award.

STRATEGY CAPSULE 5.2
Resource Utilization: Revival at Walt Disney

In 1984, Michael Eisner became CEO of the Walt Disney Company. Between 1984 and 1988, Disney's sales revenue increased from $1.66 billion to $3.75 billion, net income from $98 million to $570 million, and the stock market's valuation of the company from $1.8 billion to $10.3 billion.

The key to the Disney turnaround was the mobilization of Disney's considerable resource base. Prominent among Disney's underutilized resources were 28,000 acres of land in Florida. With the help of the Arvida Corporation, a land development company acquired in 1984, Disney began hotel, resort, and residential development of these landholdings. New attractions were added to the Epcot Center, and a new theme park, the Disney-MGM Studio Tour, was built. Disney World expanded beyond theme parks into resort vacations, the convention business, and residential housing.

To exploit its huge film library, Disney introduced videocassette sales of Disney movies and licensed packages of movies to TV networks. The huge investments in the Disney theme parks were more effectively exploited through heavier marketing effort and increased admission charges. Encouraged by the success of Tokyo Disneyland, Disney embarked on further international duplication of its US theme parks with Euro Disneyland just outside Paris, France. A chain of Disney Stores was established to push sales of Disney merchandise.

The most ambitious feature of the turnaround was Disney's regeneration as a movie studio. Eisner began a massive expansion of its Touchstone label, which had been established in 1983 with the objectives of putting Disney's film studios to fuller use and establishing the company in the teenage and adult markets. Disney Studios doubled the number of movies in production. In 1988, it became America's leading studio in terms of box office receipts. Studio production was further boosted by Disney's increasing TV presence, both through the Disney Channel and programs for network TV.

Above all, the new management team was exploiting Disney's most powerful and enduring asset: the affection of millions of people of different nations and different generations for the Disney name and the Disney characters.

owes much to their commitment to nurturing talent, developing technologies, and building capabilities that allow adaptability to their changing business environments.

Our starting point is to identify and assess the resources and capabilities available to the firm.

The Resources of the Firm

It is important to distinguish between the resources and the capabilities of the firm: resources are the productive assets owned by the firm; capabilities are what the firm

FIGURE 5.4 The links among resources, capabilities, and competitive advantage

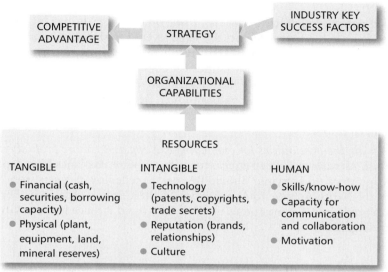

can do. Individual resources do not confer competitive advantage, they must work together to create *organizational capability*. It is capability that is the essence of superior performance. Figure 5.4 shows the relationship among resources, capabilities, and competitive advantage.

Drawing up an inventory of a firm's resources can be surprisingly difficult. No such document exists within the accounting or management information systems of most corporations. The corporate balance sheet provides a limited view of a firm's resources – it comprises mainly financial and physical resources. To take a wider view of a firm's resources it is helpful to identify three principal types of resource: tangible, intangible, and human resources.

Tangible Resources

Tangible resources are the easiest to identify and evaluate: financial resources and physical assets are identified and valued in the firm's financial statements. Yet, balance sheets are renowned for their propensity to obscure strategically relevant information, and to under- or overvalue assets. Historic cost valuation can provide little indication of an asset's market value. Disney's movie library had a balance sheet value of $4.6 billion in 2005, based on production cost less amortization. Its land assets (including its 28,000 acres in Florida) were valued at a paltry $1.1 billion.

However, the primary goal of resource analysis is not to value a company's assets, but to understand their potential for creating competitive advantage. Information that British Airways possesses tangible fixed assets with a book value of £8.2 billion is of little use in assessing their strategic value. To assess British Airways' ability to compete effectively in the world airline industry we need to know about the composition of these assets, the location of land and buildings, the types of plane and their age, and so on.

Once we have fuller information on a company's tangible resources we explore how we can create additional value from them. This requires that we address two key questions:

1   *What opportunities exist for economizing on their use?* It may be possible to use fewer resources to support the same level of business, or to use the existing resources to support a larger volume of business. In the case of British Airways, there may be opportunities for consolidating administrative offices and engineering and service facilities. Improved inventory control may allow economies in inventories of parts and fuel. Better control of cash and receivables permits a business to operate with lower levels of cash and liquid financial resources.

2   *What are the possibilities for employing existing assets more profitably?* Could British Airways generate better returns on some of its planes by redeploying them into cargo carrying? Should BA seek to redeploy its assets from Europe and the North Atlantic to Asia-Pacific? Might it reduce costs in its European network by reassigning routes to small franchised airlines (such as GB Airways and Loganair)?

Intangible Resources

For most companies, intangible resources are more valuable than tangible resources. Yet, in company financial statements, intangible resources remain largely invisible – particularly in the US where R&D is expensed. The exclusion or undervaluation of intangible resources is a major reason for the large and growing divergence between companies' balance sheet valuations ("book values") and their stock market valuations (see Table 5.1). Among the most important of these undervalued or unvalued intangible resources are brand names. Table 5.2 shows companies owning brands valued at $15 billion or more.

Brand names and other trademarks are a form of *reputational asset*: their value is in the confidence they instill in customers. This value is reflected in the price premium that customers are willing to pay for the branded product over that for an unbranded or unknown brand. Brand value (or "brand equity") can be estimated by taking the price premium attributable to a brand, multiplying it by the brand's annual sales volume, then calculating the present value of this revenue stream. The brand valuations in Table 5.2 involve estimating the operating profits for each brand (after taxation and a capital charge), estimating the proportion of net operating income attributable to the brand, then capitalizing these returns. The value of a company's brands can be increased by extending the product/market scope over which the company markets those brands. Philip Morris is an expert at internationalizing its brand franchises. Harley-Davidson's brand strength has not only permitted the company to obtain a price premium of about 40% above that of comparable motorcycles, but also to license its name to the manufacturers of clothing, coffee mugs, cigarettes, and restaurants.

Reputation may be attached to a company as well as to its brands. Companies depend on support from employees, customers, investors, and governments.[10] Harris Interactive shows Johnson & Johnson followed by Coca-Cola, Google, UPS, and 3M to have the highest "reputation quotients."[11]

Like reputation, technology is an intangible asset whose value is not evident from most companies' balance sheets. Intellectual property – patents, copyrights, trade

TABLE 5.1 Major companies with the highest market-to-book ratios, December 2005

Company	Valuation ratio	Country	Company	Valuation ratio	Country
Yahoo! Japan	72.0	Japan	Coca-Cola	7.8	US
Colgate-Palmolive	20.8	US	Diageo	7.4	UK
GlaxoSmithKline	13.4	UK	3M	7.3	US
Anheuser-Busch	12.6	US	Nokia	6.7	Finland
eBay	11.2	US	Sanofi-Aventis	6.3	France
SAP	10.8	Germany	AstraZeneca	5.9	UK
Yahoo!	10.7	US	Johnson & Johnson	5.7	US
Dell Computer	10.0	US	Boeing	5.7	US
Sumitomo Mitsui Financial	8.8	Japan	Eli Lily	5.6	US
Procter & Gamble	8.4	US	Cisco Systems	5.5	US
Qualcomm	8.3	US	Roche Holding	5.5	Switz.
Schlumberger	8.2	US	L'Oreal	5.3	France
Unilever	8.1	Neth./UK	Altria	5.2	US
PepsiCo	8.0	US	Novartis	5.1	Switz.

Note: The table includes companies with the highest market capitalization as a proportion of balance sheet net asset value among the top 200 companies of the world with the largest market capitalization at the end of 2005.

secrets, and trademarks – comprise technological and artistic resources where ownership is defined in law. Over the past 20 years, companies have become more attentive to the value of their intellectual property. Texas Instruments was one of the first companies to begin managing its patent portfolio in order to maximize its licensing revenues. For some companies, their ownership of intellectual property is a key source of their market value. For example, Qualcomm's patents relating to CDMA digital wireless telephony make it one of the most valuable companies in the telecom sector, while IBM's position as the world's biggest patent holder results in a royalty stream of over $1.2 billion a year.

Human Resources

The human resources of the firm are the expertise and effort offered by its employees. Human resources do not appear on corporate balance sheets for the simple reason that people are not owned: they offer their services under employment contracts. Identifying and appraising the stock of human resources within a firm is complex and difficult. Human resources are appraised at the time of recruitment and throughout the period of employment, e.g. through annual performance reviews.

Companies are continually seeking more effective methods to assess the performance and potential of their employees. Over the past decade, human resource appraisal has become far more systematic and sophisticated. Organizations are relying less on formal qualifications and years of experience and more on attitude, motivation, learning capacity, and potential for collaboration. *Competency modeling*

TABLE 5.2 The world's most valuable brands, 2006

Rank	Brand	Brand value in 2006, $ billion	Change from 2004	Country of origin
1	Coca-Cola	67.5	0%	USA
2	Microsoft	59.9	−2%	USA
3	IBM	53.4	−1%	USA
4	GE	47.0	+7%	USA
5	Intel	35.6	+6%	USA
6	Nokia	26.5	+10%	Finland
7	Disney	26.4	−2%	USA
8	McDonald's	26.0	+4%	USA
9	Toyota	24.8	+10%	Japan
10	Marlboro	21.2	−4%	USA
11	Mercedes Benz	20.0	−6%	Germany
12	Citi	20.0	0%	USA
13	Hewlett-Packard	18.9	−10%	USA
14	American Express	18.6	+5%	USA
15	Gillette	17.5	+5%	USA
16	BMW	17.1	+8%	Germany
17	Cisco	16.6	+4%	USA
18	Louis Vuitton	16.1	n.a.	France
19	Honda	15.8	+6%	Japan
20	Samsung	15.0	19%	S. Korea

Note: Brand values are calculated as the net present value of future earnings generated by the brand.

SOURCE: INTERBRAND.

involves identifying the set of skills, content knowledge, attitudes, and values associated with superior performers within a particular job category, then assessing each employee against that profile.[12] The results of such competency assessments can then be used to identify training needs, make selections for hiring or promotion, and determine compensation. A key outcome of systematic assessment has been recognition of the importance of psychological and social aptitudes in linking technical and professional abilities to overall job performance. Recent interest in *emotional intelligence* reflects growing recognition of the importance of social and emotional skills and values.[13]

The ability of employees to harmonize their efforts and integrate their separate skills depends not only on their interpersonal skills but also the organizational context. This organizational context as it affects internal collaboration is determined by a key intangible resource: the *culture* of the organization. The term *organizational culture* is notoriously ill defined. It relates to an organization's values, traditions, and social norms. Building on the observations of Peters and Waterman that "firms with sustained superior financial performance typically are characterized by a strong set of core managerial values that define the ways they conduct business," Jay Barney identifies organizational culture as a firm resource of great strategic importance that is potentially very valuable.[14]

Organizational Capabilities

Resources are not productive on their own. A brain surgeon is close to useless without a radiologist, anesthetist, nurses, surgical instruments, imaging equipment, and a host of other resources. To perform a task, a team of resources must work together. An *organizational capability* is a "firm's capacity to deploy resources for a desired end result."[15] Just as an individual may be capable of playing the violin, ice skating, and speaking Mandarin, so an organization may possess the capabilities needed to manufacture widgets, distribute them throughout Latin America, and hedge the resulting foreign exchange exposure. We use the terms *capability* and *competence* interchangeably.[16]

Our primary interest is in those capabilities that can provide a basis for competitive advantage. Selznick used *distinctive competence* to describe those things that an organization does particularly well relative to its competitors.[17] Prahalad and Hamel coined the term *core competences* to distinguish those capabilities fundamental to a firm's strategy and performance.[18] Core competences, according to Hamel and Prahalad, are those that:

- Make a disproportionate contribution to ultimate customer value, or to the efficiency with which that value is delivered, and
- Provide a basis for entering new markets.[19]

Prahalad and Hamel criticize US companies for emphasizing product management over competence management. They compare the strategic development of Sony and RCA in consumer electronics. Both companies were failures in the home video market. RCA introduced its videodisk system, Sony its Betamax videotape system. For RCA, the failure of its first product marked the end of its venture into home video systems and heralded a progressive retreat from the consumer electronics industry. RCA was acquired by GE, which then sold off the combined consumer electronics division to Thomson of France. Sony, on the other hand, acknowledged the failure of Betamax, but continued to develop its capabilities in video technology. This continuous development and upgrading of its video capabilities resulted in a string of successful video products from camcorders and digital cameras to the PlayStation game console.

Classifying Capabilities

To identify a firm's capabilities, we need to have some basis for classifying and dis-aggregating its activities. Two approaches are commonly used:

1. A *functional analysis* identifies organizational capabilities in relation to each of the principal functional areas of the firm. Table 5.3 classifies the principal functions of the firm and identifies organizational capabilities pertaining to each function.

2. A *value chain analysis* separates the activities of the firm into a sequential chain. Michael Porter's representation of the value chain distinguishes between *primary activities* (those involved with the transformation of inputs and interface with the customer) and *support activities* (see Figure 5.5). Porter's generic value chain identifies a few broadly defined activities that can be disaggregated to provide a more detailed identification of the firm's

TABLE 5.3 A functional classification of organizational capabilities

Functional area	Capability	Exemplars
CORPORATE FUNCTIONS	● Financial control	Exxon Mobil, PepsiCo
	● Strategic management of multiple businesses	General Electric, Procter & Gamble
	● Strategic innovation	BP, Google
	● Multidivisional coordination	Unilever, Shell
	● Acquisition management	Cisco, Bank of America
	● International management	Shell, Citigroup
MANAGEMENT INFORMATION	● Comprehensive, integrated MIS network linked to managerial decision making	Wal-Mart, Capital One, Dell Computer
RESEARCH & DEVELOPMENT	● Research	IBM, Merck
	● Innovative new product development	3M, Apple
	● Fast-cycle new product development	Canon, Inditex (Zara)
OPERATIONS	● Efficiency in volume manufacturing	Briggs & Stratton, YKK
	● Continuous improvements in operations	Toyota, Harley-Davidson
	● Flexibility and speed of response	Four Seasons Hotels
PRODUCT DESIGN	● Design capability	Nokia, Apple Computer
MARKETING	● Brand management	P&G, Altria
	● Promoting reputation for quality	Johnson & Johnson
	● Responsiveness to market trends	MTV, L'Oreal
SALES AND DISTRIBUTION	● Effective sales promotion and execution	PepsiCo, Pfizer
	● Efficiency and speed of order processing	L. L. Bean, Dell Computer
	● Speed of distribution	Amazon.com
	● Quality and effectiveness of customer service	Singapore Airlines, Caterpillar

FIGURE 5.5 Porter's value chain

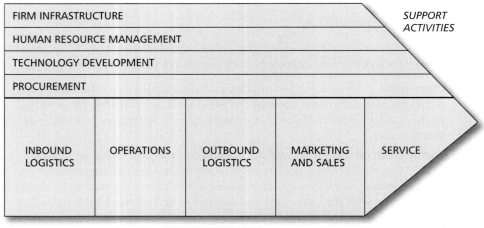

activities (and the capabilities that correspond to each activity). Thus, marketing might include market research, test marketing, advertising, promotion, pricing, and dealer relations.[20]

The Architecture of Capability

Why is 3M so good at developing new products for a variety of home, office, and medical needs? How is Wal-Mart able to combine relentless cost focus and high levels of flexibility and adaptability? Why is Toyota so superior to either Ford or GM in developing new models of car and launching them globally? We can guess, but the fact remains: we don't really know how organizational capabilities are created or why one company performs a capability more effectively than another. To begin to understand organizational capabilities, let us look at their structure.

Capability as Routine Organizational capability requires the expertise of various individuals to be integrated with capital equipment, technology, and other resources. But how does this integration occur? Virtually all productive activities involve teams of people undertaking closely coordinated actions – typically without detailed direction. Richard Nelson and Sidney Winter have used the term *organizational routines* to refer to these regular and predictable patterns of activity made up of a sequence of coordinated actions by individuals.[21] Such routines form the basis of most organizational capabilities. At the manufacturing level, a series of routines governs the passage of raw materials and components through the production process to the factory gate. Sales, ordering, distribution, and customer service activities are similarly organized through a number of standardized, complementary routines. Even top management functions comprise routines for monitoring business unit performance, capital budgeting, and strategic planning.

Like individual skills, organizational routines develop through learning-by-doing. Just as individual skills become rusty when not exercised, so it is difficult for organizations to retain coordinated responses to contingencies that arise only rarely. Hence, there may be a tradeoff between efficiency and flexibility. A limited repertoire of routines can be performed highly efficiently with near-perfect coordination. The same organization may find it extremely difficult to respond to novel situations.[22]

Routinization is an essential step in translating directions and operating practices into capabilities. In every McDonald's hamburger restaurant, operating manuals provide precise directions for the conduct of every activity undertaken, from the placing of the pickle on the burger to the maintenance of the milk-shake machine. In practice, the operating manuals are seldom referred to in the course of day-to-day operations – through continuous repetition, tasks become routinized.

The Hierarchy of Capabilities Whether we examine capabilities from a functional or value chain approach, it is evident that broad functions or value chain activities can be disaggregated into more specialist capabilities performed by smaller teams of resources. What we observe is a hierarchy of capabilities where more general, broadly defined capabilities are formed from the integration of more specialized capabilities. For example:

- A hospital's capability in treating heart disease depends on its integration of capabilities pertaining to a patient's diagnosis, physical medicine, cardiovascular surgery, pre- and post-operative care, as well as capabilities relating to various administrative and support functions.

● Toyota's manufacturing capability – its system of "lean production" – integrates capabilities relating to the manufacture of components and subassemblies, supply-chain management, production scheduling, assembly, quality control procedures, systems for managing innovation and continuous improvement, and inventory control.

Figure 5.6 offers a partial view of the hierarchy of capabilities of a telecom equipment maker. At the highest level of integration are those capabilities which integrate across multiple functions. New product development draws upon a broad range of functional capabilities – which is why it is so difficult to manage. One solution to the problems of integrating functional know-how into new product development is the creation of cross-functional product development teams. The use of such product development teams (led by a "heavyweight" team leader) by Toyota, Nissan, and

FIGURE 5.6 The hierarchical nature of capabilities: a manufacturer of PBXs

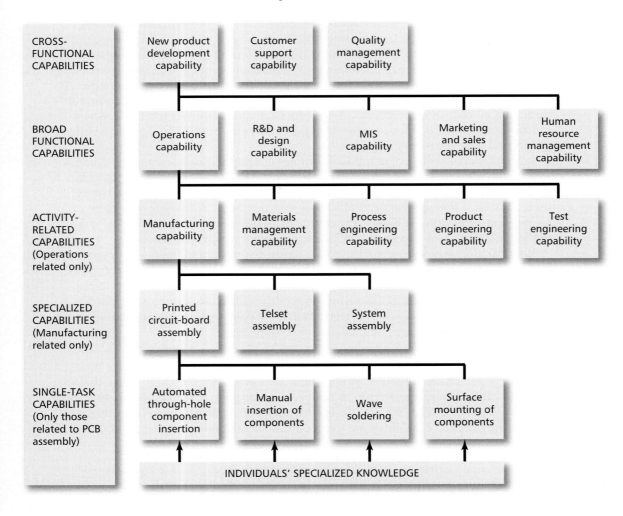

Honda has been a key reason for these firms' fast-cycle new product development compared with US and European car companies.[23]

Appraising Resources and Capabilities

So far, we have established what resources and capabilities are, how they can provide a long-term focus for a company's strategy, and how we can go about identifying them. However, if the focus of this book is the pursuit of profit, we also need to appraise the potential for resources and capabilities to earn profits for the company.

The profits that a firm obtains from its resources and capabilities depend on three factors: their abilities to *establish* a competitive advantage, to *sustain* that competitive advantage, and to *appropriate* the returns to that competitive advantage. Each of these depends on a number of resource characteristics. Figure 5.7 shows the key relationships.

Establishing Competitive Advantage

For a resource or capability to establish a competitive advantage, two conditions must be present:

1 *Scarcity*. If a resource or capability is widely available within the industry, then it may be essential to compete, but it will not be a sufficient basis for competitive advantage. In oil and gas exploration, new technologies such as directional drilling and 3-D seismic analysis are critical to reducing the costs

FIGURE 5.7 Appraising the strategic importance of resources and capabilities

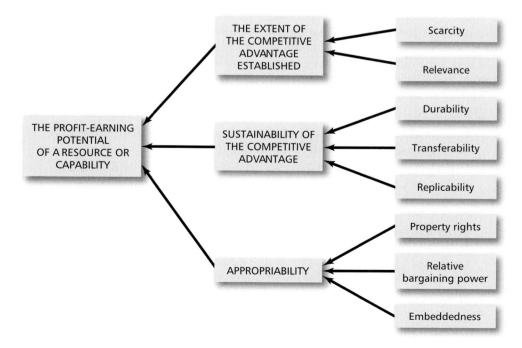

of finding new reserves. However, these technologies are widely available from oilfield service and IT companies. As a result, such technologies are "needed to play," but they are not sufficient to win.

2 *Relevance*. A resource or capability must be relevant to the key success factors in the market. British coal mines produced some wonderful brass bands. Unfortunately, musical capabilities did little to assist the mines in meeting competition from cheap imported coal and North Sea gas. As retail banking shifts toward automated teller machines and online transactions, so the retail branch networks of the banks have become less relevant for customer service.

Sustaining Competitive Advantage

The profits earned from resources and capabilities depend not just on their ability to *establish* competitive advantage, but also on how long that advantage can be *sustained*. This depends on whether resources and capabilities are *durable* and whether rivals can *imitate* the competitive advantage they offer. Resources and capabilities are imitable if they are *transferable* or *replicable*.

Durability Some resources are more durable than others and, hence, are a more secure basis for competitive advantage. The increasing pace of technological change is shortening the useful life span of most resources including capital equipment and proprietary technologies. Brands, on the other hand, can show remarkable resilience to time. Heinz sauces, Kellogg's' cereals, Campbell's soup, Hoover vacuum cleaners, and Coca-Cola have been market leaders for over a century.

Transferability The simplest means of acquiring the resources and capabilities necessary for imitating another firm's strategy is to buy them. The ability to buy a resource or capability depends on its *transferability* – the extent to which it is mobile between companies. Some resources, such as finance, raw materials, components, machines produced by equipment suppliers, and employees with standardized skills (such as short-order cooks and auditors), are transferable and can be bought and sold with little difficulty. Some resources are not easily transferred – either they are entirely firm specific, or their value depreciates on transfer.[24]

Sources of immobility include:

- Geographical immobility of natural resources, large items of capital equipment, and some types of employees may make it difficult for firms to acquire these resources without relocating themselves.

- Imperfect information regarding the quality and productivity of resources creates risks for buyers. Such imperfections are especially important in relation to human resources – hiring decisions are typically based on very little knowledge of how the new employee will perform. Sellers of resources have better information about the characteristics of the resources on offer than potential buyers – this creates a "lemons problem" for firms seeking to acquire resources.[25] Jay Barney has shown that different valuations of resources by firms can result in their being either underpriced or overpriced, giving rise to differences in profitability between firms.[26]

- Complementarity between resources means that the detachment of a resource from its "home team" causes it to lose productivity and value. Thus, if brand reputation is associated with the company that created it, a change in ownership of the brand erodes its value. The transfer of the *Thinkpad* brand of notebook computers from IBM to Lenovo almost certainly eroded its value.[27]

● Organizational capabilities, because they are based on teams of resources, are less mobile than individual resources. Even if the whole team can be transferred (in investment banking it has been commonplace for whole teams of analysts or M&A specialists to defect from one bank to another), the dependence of the team on a wider network of relationships and corporate culture may pose difficulties for recreating the capability in the new company.

Replicability If a firm cannot buy a resource or capability, it must build it. In financial services, most innovations in new derivative products can be imitated easily by competitors. In retailing too, competitive advantages that derive from store layout, point-of-sale technology, charge cards, and extended opening hours can also be copied easily by competitors.

Less easily replicable are capabilities based on complex organizational routines. Federal Express's national, next-day delivery service and Nucor's system for steel manufacturing that combines efficiency with flexibility are complex capabilities based on unique corporate cultures. Some capabilities appear simple but prove difficult to replicate. Just-in-time scheduling and quality circles are relatively simple techniques used effectively by Japanese companies. Although neither require advanced manufacturing technologies or sophisticated information systems, their dependence on high levels of collaboration through communication and trust meant that many American and European firms had difficulty implementing them.

Even where replication is possible, incumbent firms may benefit from the fact that resources and capabilities that have been accumulated over a long period can only be replicated at disproportionate cost by would-be imitators. Dierickx and Cool identify two major sources of incumbency advantage:

● *Asset mass efficiencies* occur where a strong initial position in technology, distribution channels, or reputation facilitates the subsequent accumulation of these resources.

● *Time compression diseconomies* are the additional costs incurred by imitators when attempting to accumulate rapidly a resource or capability. Thus, "crash programs" of R&D and "blitz" advertising campaigns tend to be less productive than similar expenditures made over a longer period.[28]

Appropriating the Returns to Competitive Advantage

Who gains the returns generated by superior capabilities? We should normally expect that such returns accrue to the owner of that capability. However, ownership is not always clear-cut: capabilities depend heavily on the skills and efforts of employees – who are not owned by the firm. For companies dependent on human ingenuity and know-how, the mobility of key employees represents a constant threat to their competitive advantage (see Strategy Capsule 5.3). In investment banks and other human capital-intensive firms, the struggle between employees and shareholders to appropriate rents is reminiscent of the war for surplus value between labor and capital that

STRATEGY CAPSULE 5.3

When Your Competitive Advantage Walks Out the Door: Gucci

On September 10, 2001, French retailer Pinault Printemps Redoute (PPR) agreed to acquire Gucci Group – the Italian-based fashion house and luxury goods maker. On November 4, 2003 the managers and shareholders of the two companies were stunned to learn that Chairman Domenico De Sole and Vice Chairman Tom Ford would be leaving Gucci in April 2004.

The duo had masterminded Gucci's transformation from a chaotic, near-bankrupt family firm with an over-licensed brand into a close rival to LVMH – the luxury goods powerhouse. As creative director, Tom Ford had established Gucci as the hottest label around, through fashion shows that were practically rock shows, associations with famous faces, and hiring young designers such as Stella McCartney and Alexander McQueen. De Sole's astute leadership had instituted careful planning and financial discipline, and built Gucci's global presence (especially in Asia).

How great a blow was De Sole and Ford's departure to the parent PPR? In principle, a new CEO and new head of design could be hired. In practice, talent of the ilk of De Sole and Ford was a rare commodity. Especially rare was the combination of a designer and a CEO who could work together with the harmony and shared vision of De Sole and Ford.

The stock market's reaction was ominous. On November 3, 2003 Gucci's share price was $86.10; on November 6 it had fallen to $84.60, however, in the absence of PPR's guarantee to acquire their shares at $85.52, analysts estimated that Gucci would be trading at around $74. The implication is that Gucci was worth $1.2 billion less without De Sole and Ford than with them.

Source: Adapted from articles in the *Financial Times* during November 5–8, 2003.

Marx analyzed. It is notable that in 2005, average employee pay among Goldman Sachs' 24,000 staff (including secretaries and janitors) was $520,000.[29] The prevalence of partnerships (rather than joint-stock companies) in professional service industries (lawyers, accountants, and management consultants) reflects the desire to avoid conflict between owners and its human resources.

The less clearly defined are property rights in resources and capabilities, the greater the importance of relative bargaining power in determining the division of returns between the firm and its individual members. In the case of team-based organizational capabilities, this balance of power between the firm and an individual employee depends crucially on the relationship between individuals' skills and organizational routines. The more deeply embedded are individual skills and knowledge within organizational routines, and the more they depend on corporate systems and reputation, the weaker the employee is relative to the firm.

Conversely, the closer an organizational capability is identified with the expertise of individual employees, and the more effective those employees are at deploying their bargaining power, the better able employees are to appropriate rents. If the individual employee's contribution to productivity is clearly identifiable, if the employee is mobile, and if the employee's skills offer similar productivity to other firms, the employee is in a strong position to appropriate most of his or her contribution to the firm's value added. Does the $27.7 million paid to Shaquille O'Neal fully exploit his value to the Miami Heat? In most professional sports, it appears that strategies based exclusively on signing superstar players result in the players appropriating most of the rents, with little surplus available for the clubs – this was certainly the fate of Real Madrid during 2002–6.[30] In recent years investment banks and consulting companies have emphasized the team-based nature of their capabilities. In downplaying the role of individual expertise, they can improve their firm's potential for appropriating the returns to their capabilities.

Putting Resource and Capability Analysis to Work: A Practical Guide

We have covered the principal concepts and frameworks for analyzing resources and capabilities. How do we put this analysis into practice? Let me offer a simple, step-by-step approach to how a company can appraise its resources and capabilities and then use the appraisal to guide strategy formulation.

Step 1 Identify the Key Resources and Capabilities

To draw up a list of the firm's resources and capabilities, we can begin from outside or inside the firm. From an external focus, we begin with key success factors (see Chapter 3). What factors determine why some firms in an industry are more successful than others and on what resources and capabilities are these success factors based? Suppose we are evaluating the resources and capabilities of Volkswagen AG, the German-based automobile manufacturer. We can start with key success factors in the world automobile industry: low-cost production, attractively designed new models embodying the latest technologies, and the financial strength to weather the cyclicality and heavy investment requirements of the industry. What capabilities and resources do these key success factors imply? They would include manufacturing capabilities, new product development capability, effective supply chain management, global distribution, brand strength, scale-efficient plants with up-to-date capital equipment, a strong balance sheet, and so on. To organize and categorize these various resources and capabilities, it is helpful to switch to the inside of VW and look at the company's value chain, identifying the sequence of activities from new product development to purchasing, to supply chain management, to component manufacture, assembly, and right the way through to dealership support and after-sales service. We can then look at the resources that underpin the capabilities at each stage of the value chain. Table 5.4 lists VW's principal resources and capabilities.

Step 2 Appraising Resources and Capabilities

Resources and capabilities need to be appraised against two key criteria. First is their *importance*: which resources and capabilities are most important in conferring sustainable competitive advantage? Second, where are our strengths and weaknesses as compared with competitors?

Assessing Importance The temptation in assessing which resources and capabilities are most important is to concentrate on customer choice criteria. What we must bear in mind, however, is that our ultimate objective is not to attract customers, but to make superior profit through establishing a sustainable competitive advantage. For this purpose we need to look beyond customer choice to the underlying strategic characteristics of resources and capabilities. To do this we need to look at the set of appraisal criteria outlined in the previous section on "Appraising Resources and Capabilities." In the case of VW, many resources and capabilities are essential to compete in the business, but several of them are not scarce (for example, total quality management capability and technologically advanced assembly plants have become widely diffused within the industry), while others (such as IT capability and design capability) are outsourced to external providers – either way, they are "needed to play" but not "needed to win." On the other hand, resources such as brand strength and a global distribution network, and capabilities such as fast-cycle new product development and global logistics capability, cannot be easily acquired or internally developed – they are critical to establishing and sustaining advantage.

Assessing Relative Strengths Objectively appraising the comparative strengths and weaknesses of a company's resources and capabilities relative to competitors is difficult. In assessing their own competencies, organizations frequently fall victim to past glories, hopes for the future, and their own wishful thinking. The tendency toward hubris among companies – and their senior managers – means that business success often sows the seeds of its own destruction.[31] Among the failed industrial companies in America and Europe are many whose former success blinded them to their stagnating capabilities and declining competitiveness: examples include the cutlery producers of Sheffield, England and the integrated steel giants of the United States.

To identify and appraise a company's capabilities, managers must look both inside and outside. Internal discussion can be valuable in sharing insights and evidence and building consensus regarding the organization's resource and capability profile. The evidence of history can be particularly revealing in reviewing instances where the company has performed well and those where it has performed poorly: do any patterns appear?

Finally, to move the analysis from the subjective to the objective level, *benchmarking* is a powerful tool for quantitative assessment of performance relative to that of competitors. Benchmarking is "the process of identifying, understanding, and adapting outstanding practices from organizations anywhere in the world to help your organization improve its performance."[32] Benchmarking offers a systematic framework and methodology for identifying particular functions and processes and then for comparing their performance with other companies. Strategy Capsule 5.4 offers some examples. As McKinsey & Co. has shown, performance difference between top-performing and average-performing companies in most activities tends to be wide.[33]

Ultimately, appraising resources and capabilities is not about data, it's about insight and understanding. Every organization has some activity where it excels or has the potential to excel. For Federal Express, it is a system that guarantees next-day delivery anywhere within the United States. For BMW it is the ability to integrate world-class engineering with design excellence and highly effective marketing. For McDonald's, it is the ability to supply millions of hamburgers from thousands of outlets throughout the world, with remarkable uniformity of quality, customer service, and hygiene. For General Electric, it is a system of corporate management that

STRATEGY CAPSULE 5.4
Using Benchmarking to Assess Capabilities

Benchmarking allows companies, first, to make objective assessments of their capabilities relative to competitors and, second, to put into place programs to imitate other companies' superior capabilities. For example:

- Xerox Corporation is the pioneer of benchmarking. Losing market share during the 1980s, logistics engineer Robert Camp performed detailed comparisons that showed the massive superiority of Japanese competitors in cost efficiency, quality, and new product development over American companies. Looking beyond direct competitors, every department was encouraged to look globally to identify best-in-class companies against which to benchmark. For inventory control and customer responsiveness, Xerox benchmarked L. L. Bean, the direct-mail clothing company.

- During the early 1980s, a benchmarking study by General Motors discovered that Toyota could make a changeover from one model to another on an automobile assembly line in eight minutes. The comparable time at GM plants was eight hours. The result was profound inquiry within GM as to the appropriateness of its manufacturing strategy and the state of its operational capabilities.

- At Bank of America, Vice Chairman, Martin Sheen, commented, "We have worked a lot with the Royal Bank of Canada on benchmarking because our sizes and philosophies are comparable and we're not direct competitors. We have had some particularly good exchanges with them on processes. We can also benchmark through the Research Board against an array of competitors reported in a disguised fashion. What these do is to highlight anomalies. You can't get down to a unit cost or systems task level. But if a comparable company has 22 people and we have 60, we can sit down and try to figure out what's going on."

The key stages in the benchmarking process are: first, deciding what to benchmark; second, identifying partners; third, establishing benchmarking metrics; fourth, gathering data; and fifth, analysis.

Sources: Robert C. Camp, *Benchmarking: The Search for Industry Best Practices that Lead to Superior Performance* (Milwaukee: Quality Press, 1989); American Productivity & Quality Center, *The Benchmarking Management Guide* (Cambridge, MA: Productivity Press, 1993); R. S. Kaplan, "Limits to Benchmarking," *Balanced Scorecard Report*, November–December, 2005.

reconciles coordination, innovation, flexibility, and financial discipline in one of the world's largest and most diversified corporations. All these companies are examples of highly successful enterprises. One reason why they are successful is that they have recognized what they can do well and have based their strategies on their strengths. For poor-performing companies, the problem is not necessarily an absence of distinctive capabilities, but a failure to recognize what they are and to deploy them effectively.

TABLE 5.4 Appraising VW's resources and capabilities

	Importance[1]	VW's relative strength[2]	Comments
RESOURCES			
R1. Finance	6	6	A– credit rating is above average for the industry, but free cash flow remains negative
R2. Technology	7	5	Despite technical strengths, VW is not a leader in automotive technology
R3. Plant and equipment	8	8	Has invested heavily in upgrading plants
R4. Location	4	4	Plants in key low-cost, growth markets (China, Mexico, Brazil), but German manufacturing base is very high cost
R5. Distribution (dealership network)	8	5	Geographically extensive distribution with special strength in emerging markets. Historically weak position within the US
R6. Brands	6	5	VW, Audi, Bentley, and Bugatti are strong brands, but together with Skoda and Seat, VW's brand portfolio lacks coherence and clear market positioning
CAPABILITIES			
C1. Product development	9	4	Traditionally weak at VW, with few big hits: Beetle (introduced 1938), Golf (1974), Passat (1974), Vanagon (1979). Despite major upgrading, product development still weak compared to industry leaders
C2. Purchasing	7	5	Traditionally weak – strengthened by senior hires from Opel and elsewhere
C3. Engineering	7	9	The core technical strength of VW
C4. Manufacturing	8	4	VW is a high-cost producer with below average quality
C5. Financial management	6	4	Has traditionally lacked a strong financial orientation
C6. R&D	5	4	Despite several technical strengths, VW is not a leader in automotive innovation
C7. Marketing and sales	9	4	Despite traditional weakness in recognizing and meeting customer needs in different national markets, VW has increased its sensitivity to the market, improved brand management, and managed its advertising and promotion with increasing dexterity
C8. Government relations	4	8	Important in emerging markets
C9. Strategic management	7	4	Effective restructuring and cost cutting, but lack of consistency and consensus at top management level

1   Both scales range from 1 to 10 (1 = very low, 10 = very high).
2   VW's resources and capabilities are compared against those of GM, Ford, Toyota, DaimlerChrysler, Nissan, Honda, Fiat, and PSA, where 5 represents parity. The ratings are based on the author's subjective judgment.

FIGURE 5.8 Appraising VW's resources and capabilities (hypothetical)

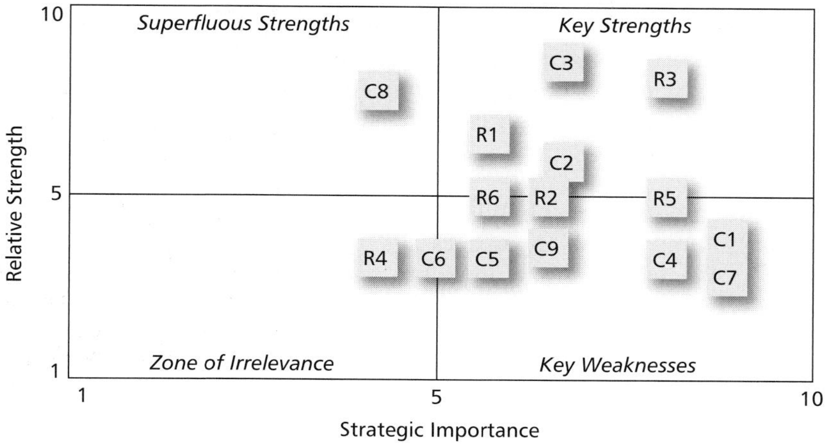

Note: The table is based on the ratings of resources and capabilities in Table 5.4.

Bringing Together Importance and Relative Strength Putting together the two criteria – importance and relative strength – allows us to highlight a company's key strengths and key weaknesses. Consider, for example, Volkswagen AG. Table 5.4 provides a partial (and hypothetical) identification and appraisal of VW's resources and capabilities during the late 1990s in relation to the two criteria of importance and relative strength outlined above. Figure 5.8 then brings the two criteria together into a single display. Dividing this display into four quadrants allows us to identify those resources and capabilities that we may regard as key strengths and those that we may identify as key weaknesses. For example, our assessment suggests that plant and equipment, engineering capability, and supply chain management are key strengths of VW, while distribution (a relatively weak presence in the US and Japan), new product development (no consistent record of fast-cycle development of market-winning new models), and financial management are key weaknesses.

Step 3 Developing Strategy Implications

Our key focus is on the two right-hand quadrants of Figure 5.8. How do we exploit our key strengths most effectively? What do we do about our key weaknesses in terms of both upgrading them and reducing our vulnerability to them? Finally, what about our "inconsequential" strengths? Are these really superfluous, or are there ways in which we can deploy them to greater effect?

Exploiting Key Strengths Having identified resources and capabilities that are important and where our company is strong relative to competitors, the key task is to formulate our strategy to ensure that these resources are deployed to the greatest effect. If engineering is a key strength of VW, then it may wish to seek differentiation advantage through technical sophistication and safety features. If VW is effective in managing government relations and is well positioned in the potential growth markets of China, Eastern Europe, and Latin America, exploiting this strength may require developing models that will appeal to these markets.

To the extent that different companies within an industry have different capability profiles, this implies differentiation of strategies within the industry. Thus, Toyota's outstanding manufacturing capabilities and fast-cycle new product development, Hyundai's low-cost manufacturing capability that derives from its South Korean location, and Peugeot's design flair suggest that each company should be pursuing a distinctively different strategy.

Managing Key Weaknesses What does a company do about its key weaknesses? It is tempting to think of how companies can upgrade existing resources and capabilities to correct such weaknesses. However, converting weakness into strength is likely to be a long-term task for most companies. In the short to medium term, a company is likely to be stuck with the resources and capabilities that it inherits from the previous period.

The most decisive – and often most successful – solution to weaknesses in key functions is to outsource. Thus, in the automobile industry, companies have become increasingly selective in the activities they perform internally. During the 1930s, Ford was almost completely vertically integrated. At its massive River Rouge plant, coal and iron ore entered at one end, completed cars exited at the other. By 2003, Ford had outsourced most component manufacture, much of its design work was being undertaken by independent design studios, and services ranging from IT to security were being provided by third parties. In athletic shoes and clothing, Nike undertakes product design, marketing, and overall "systems integration," but manufacturing, logistics, and many other functions are contracted out. We shall consider the vertical scope of the firm at greater depth in Chapter 13.

Through clever strategy formulation a firm may be able to negate the impact of its key weaknesses. Consider Harley-Davidson: in competition with Honda, Yamaha, and BMW, and with sales of 300,000 bikes a year (compared with 10 million at Honda), Harley is unable to compete on technology. How has it dealt with this problem? It has made a virtue out of its outmoded technology and traditional designs. Harley-Davidson's obsolete push-rod engines and recycled designs have become central to the retro-look appeal of the "hog."

What about Superfluous Strengths? What about those resources and capabilities where a company has particular strengths, but these don't appear to be important sources of sustainable competitive advantage? One response may be to lower the level of investment from these resources and capabilities. If a retail bank has a strong, but increasingly underutilized, branch network, this may be an opportunity to prune its real estate assets and invest in IT approaches to customer services.

However, in the same way that companies can turn apparent weaknesses into competitive strengths, so it is possible to develop innovative strategies that turn apparently inconsequential strengths into valuable resources and capabilities. Edward Jones' network of brokerage offices and 8,000-strong sales force looked increasingly irrelevant in an era when brokerage transactions were increasingly going on-line. However, by emphasizing personal service, the trustworthiness of its brokers, and its traditional, conservative investment virtues, Edward Jones has continued to build market share.[34]

Consider too my own institution, Georgetown University's McDonough School of Business. A distinctive characteristic of the school is its Jesuit heritage, at first glance an unlikely source of competitive advantage in the fiercely competitive MBA market. Yet, to the extent that a fundamental principle of Jesuit education is developing the whole person and that success as a manager is not just about what you know but also about who you are, Georgetown's Jesuit tradition can provide a key differentiating factor through the MBA program's emphasis on developing the values, integrity, and emotional intelligence necessary to be a successful business leader.

Developing Resources and Capabilities

Conventional approaches to developing resources and capabilities have emphasized *gap analysis* – identifying discrepancies between the current position and the desired future position, then adopting policies to fill those gaps. Such approaches are of limited value. In the case of resources, investing in areas of weakness – whether it is proprietary technology or manufacturing facilities – can be very expensive and, because of the complex complementarities between different resources, such investments may deliver limited returns. In the case of capabilities, because we know little about their structure or operation, developing them is a hazardous endeavor.

The Relationship between Resources and Capabilities

Possibly the most difficult problem in developing capabilities is that we know little about the linkage between resources and capabilities. In most sports, the relationship between the skills of the individual players and team performance is weak. In European football (soccer), teams built with modest expenditures (Bayern Munich, PSV Eindhoven, and Valencia) have often outplayed star-studded, big-budget teams (Real Madrid, Chelsea, and Inter Milan). In international competitions, small, resource-poor countries often humiliate the preeminent national teams. Despite dominating the ranks of the world's best basketball players, the US has won the World Basketball Championship just once since 1990.

Similarly in business, the firms that demonstrate the most outstanding capabilities are not necessarily those with the greatest resource endowments:

- In automobiles, GM has four times the output of Honda and four times the R&D expenditure, yet it is Honda, not GM, that is world leader in power train technology.
- In animated movies, the most successful productions in recent years were by newcomers Pixar (*Toy Story, The Incredibles*) and Aardman Animations (*Wallace and Gromit*) rather than by industry giant, Walt Disney.
- In telecom equipment it was the upstart Cisco rather than industry leaders Lucent, Nortel Networks, and Alcatel that established leadership in the new world of package switching.

According to Hamel and Prahalad, it is not the size of a firm's resource base that is the primary determinant of capability, but the firm's ability to *leverage* its resources. Resources can be leveraged in the following ways:

- *Concentrating resources* through the processes of *converging* resources on a few clearly defined and consistent goals; *focusing* the efforts of each group, department, and business unit on individual priorities in a sequential fashion; and *targeting* those activities that have the biggest impact on customers' perceived value.

- *Accumulating resources* through *mining experience* in order to achieve faster learning, and *borrowing* from other firms – accessing their resources and capabilities through alliances, outsourcing arrangements, and the like.

- *Complementing resources* involves increasing their effectiveness through linking them with complementary resources and capabilities. This may involve *blending* product design capabilities with the marketing capabilities needed to communicate these to the market, and *balancing* to ensure that limited resources and capabilities in one area do not hold back the effectiveness of resources and capabilities in another.

- *Conserving resources* involves utilizing resources and capabilities to the fullest by *recycling* them through different products, markets, and product generations; and *co-opting* resources through collaborative arrangements with other companies.[35]

Replicating Capabilities

Growing capabilities requires that the firm replicates them internally.[36] Some of the world's most successful corporations are those that have been able to replicate their capabilities in different product and geographical markets. Ray Kroc's genius was to take the original McDonald's formula and replicate it thousands of times over in building a global chain of hamburger restaurants. Other leading service companies – Starbucks, Mandarin Oriental Hotels, IKEA, eBay – have built global presence on the principle that once a capability has been developed, its replication in another location can be achieved at a low cost.

If routines develop learning-by-doing, and the knowledge that underpins them is tacit, replication is far from easy. Replication requires *systematization* of the knowledge that underlies the capability – typically through the formulation of standard operating procedures. Thus, McDonald's has distilled its business system into operating procedures and training manuals that govern the operation and maintenance of every aspect of its restaurants. This systematization presumes that the firm can more fully articulate the processes that underlie its capabilities. In the case of semiconductor fabrication, these processes are so complex and the know-how involved so deeply embedded that the only way that Intel can replicate its production capabilities is by replicating its lead plant in every detail – a process called "Copy Exactly."[37]

Developing New Capabilities

Creating certain resources – a brand or an overseas distribution network – may be difficult, costly, and time consuming, but at least the challenge can be comprehended and planned. Creating organizational capability poses a much higher level of difficulty. If capabilities are based on routines that develop through practice and learning, what can the firm do to establish such routines within a limited time period? We know that capabilities involve teams of resources working together, but, even with the tools of business process mapping, we typically have sketchy understanding of how people, machines, technology, and organizational culture fit together to achieve a particular level of performance. In the same way that we can only speculate about what makes Tiger Woods the greatest golfer of our time, we are unable fully to diagnose how Dell achieves its brilliance at logistics management or how Electronic Arts has been able to develop video games that continue to set new standards in complexity, sophistication, and player involvement.

Capability as a Result of Early Experiences   Organizational capability is *path dependent* – a company's capabilities today are the result of its history. More importantly, this history will constrain what capabilities the company can perform in the future. To understand the origin of a company's capabilities, a useful starting point is to study the circumstances that existed and events that occurred at the time of the company's founding and early development. How did Wal-Mart develop its super-efficient system of warehousing and distribution? This system was not the result of careful planning and design, but of initial conditions: because of its rural locations, the company was unable to get reliable distribution from its suppliers, and so it established its own distribution system. How does one explain Wal-Mart's amazing commitment to cost efficiency? Its management systems are undoubtedly important, but ultimately it is Wal-Mart's origins in small-town Arkansas and the values and personality of its founder, Sam Walton, that sustains its obsession with efficiency and cost cutting.

Consider too the world's largest oil and gas majors (see Table 5.5). Despite long histories of competing together in the same markets, with near-identical products, and

TABLE 5.5 Distinctive capabilities as a consequence of childhood experiences: the oil majors

Company	Distinctive capability	Early history
Exxon	Financial management	Exxon's predecessor, Standard Oil (NJ), was the holding company for Rockefeller's Standard Oil Trust
Royal Dutch Shell	Coordinating a decentralized global network of 200+ operating companies	Shell Transport & Trading headquartered in London and founded to sell Russian oil in China and the Far East Royal Dutch Petroleum headquartered in The Hague; founded to exploit Indonesian reserves
BP	"Elephant hunting"	Discovered huge Persian reserves, went on to find Forties field (North Sea) and Prudhoe Bay (Alaska)
ENI	Deal making in politicized environments	The Enrico Mattei legacy; the challenge of managing government relations in post-war Italy
Mobil	Lubricants	Vacuum Oil Co. founded in 1866 to supply patented petroleum lubricants

similar strategies, the majors display very different capability profiles. Exxon and the Royal Dutch Shell Group have shared parallel development for over a century yet have very different capability profiles. Exxon is known for its financial management capabilities exercised through rigorous investment controls and emphasis on cost efficiency. Shell is known for its decentralized, international management capabilities, in particular its adaptability to a wide variety of national environments. These differences can be traced back to the companies' 19th-century origins. Exxon (then Standard Oil New Jersey) was part of Rockefeller's Standard Oil Trust, where it played a key holding company role with responsibilities for the financial management of other parts of the Standard Oil empire. Shell was established to sell Russian oil in China and the Far East, while Royal Dutch was established to exploit Indonesian oil reserves. With head offices thousands of miles away in Europe, it was imperative that the group developed a decentralized, adaptable management style.

Organizational Capability: Rigid or Dynamic? These long periods over which capabilities develop have important implications for firms' capacity for change. The more highly developed a firm's organizational capabilities are, the narrower its repertoire and the more difficult it is for the firm to adapt them to new circumstances. Dorothy Leonard argues that core capabilities are simultaneously *core rigidities* – they inhibit firms' ability to access and develop new capabilities.[38] Nevertheless, some companies appear to have the capacity to continually upgrade, extend, and reconfigure their organizational capabilities. David Teece and his colleagues have referred to *dynamic capabilities* as the "firm's ability to integrate, build, and reconfigure internal and external competences to address rapidly changing environments."[39] There is little consensus in the literature as to what dynamic capabilities are. Eisenhardt and Martin identify dynamic capabilities as routines that enable a firm to reconfigure its resources – these include R&D, new product development and acquisition capabilities. Zollo and Winter define dynamic capabilities as higher level processes through which the firm modifies its operating routines.[40]

What is agreed is that dynamic capabilities are far from common. For most companies highly developed capabilities in existing products and technologies create barriers to developing capabilities in new products and new technologies. When adapting to radical change within an industry, or in exploiting entirely new business opportunities, are new firms at an advantage or disadvantage to established firms? It depends on whether the change or the innovation is competence enhancing or competence destroying. In TV manufacturing, the most successful new entrants were existing producers of radios – the new technology was compatible with their capabilities. However, in most new industries, the most successful firms tend to be startups rather than established firms. In personal computers, it was newcomers such as Dell, Acer, Compaq, and Gateway that emerged as most successful during the 1990s. Among established firms, relatively few (IBM, Hewlett-Packard, and Toshiba) went on to significant success. Many others (e.g., Xerox, GE, Texas Instruments, AT&T, and Olivetti) exited. In wireless telephony, too, it was startups – Vodafone, McCaw Cellular, Orange – that were more successful than established telephone companies.[41]

Approaches to Capability Development

So, how do companies go about developing new capabilities? Let us review three approaches commonly utilized.

Acquiring Capabilities: Mergers and Acquisitions If new capabilities can only be developed over long periods, then acquiring a company that has already developed the desired capability can short-circuit the tortuous process of capability development. In technologically fast-moving environments, established firms typically use acquisitions as a means of acquiring specific technical capabilities – Cisco Systems and Microsoft have each benefitted substantially from such acquisitions. Microsoft's adaptation to the internet and its entry into video games was achieved through multiple acquisitions. Each year, Microsoft hosts its VC Summit, where venture capitalists from all over the world are invited to market their companies.

However, using acquisitions as a means of extending a company's capability base involves major risks. On its own, acquisition does not achieve the intended goal. Once the acquisition has been made, the acquiring company must find a way to integrate the acquiree's capabilities with its own. All too often, culture clashes, personality clashes between senior managers, or incompatibility of management systems can result in the degradation or destruction of the very capabilities that the acquiring company was seeking.

Accessing Capabilities: Strategic Alliances Given the high cost of acquiring companies, alliances offer a more targeted and cost effective means to access another company's capabilities. A *strategic alliance* is a cooperative relationship between firms involving the sharing of resources in pursuit of common goals. Long-running technical collaboration between HP and Canon has allowed both firms to enhance their printer technology. Prior to acquisition in 2005, Pixar's alliance with Disney allowed it to access Disney's marketing and distribution capabilities. Strategic alliances comprise a wide variety of collaborative relationships, which include joint research, technology-sharing arrangements, shared manufacturing, joint marketing and/or distribution arrangements, and vertical partnerships, to mention but a few. Alliances may involve formal agreements or they may be entirely informal; they may or may not involve ownership links. Alliances may also be for the purpose of *acquiring* the partner's capabilities through organizational learning.[42] When General Motors formed its NUMMI joint venture with Toyota, its motive was to learn Toyota's "lean" approach to manufacturing.[43] Where both alliance partners are trying to acquire one another's capabilities, the result may well be a "competition for competence" that ultimately destabilizes the relationship.[44]

Creating Capabilities Creating organizational capability requires, first, acquiring the necessary resources and, second, integrating these resources. With regard to resource acquisition, particular attention must be given to *organizational culture* – values and behavioral norms are critically important influences on motivation and collaboration. In general, however, it is *integration* that presents the greatest challenge. We know that capabilities are based on routines – coordinated patterns of activity – but we know little about how routines are established. The assumption has been that they "emerge" as a result of learning-by-doing. Recent research, however, has emphasized the role of management in developing organizational capability through motivation and deliberate learning.[45] Organizational structure and management systems are of particular importance:

● Capabilities need to be housed within dedicated organizational units if organizational members are to achieve high levels of coordination. Thus, product development is facilitated when undertaken within product development units rather than through a sequence of "over-the-wall" transfers from one functional department to another. Similarly, capabilities in quality management, change management, corporate social responsibility, and customer service are all best developed when organizational units are dedicated to such activities. Inevitably, aligning organizational structure with the multiple capabilities creates organizational complexity. However, as we shall see in the next chapter, many capabilities are suited to informal structural arrangements.

● Organizations need to take systematic approaches to capability development – the need to create, develop, and maintain organizational capabilities must be built into the design of management systems. The literature emphasizes the roles of search, experimentation, and problem solving in capability development.[46] Systematic approaches to capability development – including the creation of organizational routines for defensive and offensive maneuvers – are central to the management and coaching of sports teams, but in most business organizations the heavy emphasis on maintaining current operations means that limited attention is devoted to explicit capability development. The management of motivation and incentives is one area that is relatively well developed. The literature places heavy emphasis on the role of strategic intent and performance aspirations in driving capability development. This has implications for both leadership and the design of incentives.

Organizations often discover that the organizational structure, management systems, and culture that support existing capabilities may be unsuitable for new capabilities. To resolve this problem, companies may find it easier to develop new capabilities in new organizational units that are geographically separated from the main company – Strategy Capsule 5.5 offers examples.

Given the complexity and uncertainty of programs to develop new organizational capabilities, an indirect approach may be preferable. If we cannot design new capabilities from scratch, but if we know what types of capabilities are required for different products, then by *pushing* the development of particular products we can *pull* the development of the capabilities that those products require. For such an approach to be successful it must be systematic and incremental. Developing complex capabilities over a significant period of time requires a sequencing of products, where each stage of the sequence has specific capability development goals.[47] Strategy Capsule 5.6 provides an example. This parallel development of a firm's product portfolio and its base of resources and capabilities is referred to by Hiroyuki Itami as *dynamic resource fit*.[48] Matsushita utilized this in its international expansion strategy, moving from simple to more complex products:

> *In every country batteries are a necessity, so they sell well. As long as we bring a few advanced automated pieces of equipment for the processes vital to final product quality, even unskilled labor can produce good products. As they work on this rather simple product, the workers get trained, and this increased skill level then permits us to gradually expand production to items with increasingly higher technology levels, first radios, then televisions.*[49]

Ultimately, developing organizational capabilities is about building the know-how of the company, which requires integrating the knowledge of multiple organizational members. One of the most powerful tools for managing such a process is *knowledge management*. We shall consider the role and potential of knowledge management in the appendix to this chapter.

STRATEGY CAPSULE 5.5

Incubating Capabilities in Separate Organizational Units

The model for organizationally separate development units was Lockheed's "skunk works" – a product development team established in Burbank, California during WWII to develop innovative new military aircraft. Since then, a number of companies have used satellite units to develop new organizational capabilities:

● IBM developed its PC at a new unit led by veteran executive Bill Lowe and located in Florida – a thousand miles from IBM's corporate headquarters in New York. Lowe claimed that isolation from IBM's main organization was critical to the team's creation of a product design and business system that were radically different from those of IBM's mainframe business.[1]

● The pioneering online financial services company Egg was established by its London-based parent, Prudential Insurance, in the Midlands towns of Dudley and Derby – well away from the London headquarters.

These separate incubator units combine the flexibility and autonomy of a startup, while drawing on the resources and capabilities of the parent. However, the critical challenge is in reintegrating the new capabilities back into the parent company. Xerox's Palo Alto Research Center (PARC) pioneered many of the technologies that formed the basis of the microcomputer revolution of the 1980s. However, it was much easier for these technologies to flow to nearby competitors – Hewlett-Packard, Apple, Microsoft, and Sun Microsystems – than it was for them to be absorbed by Xerox's east coast establishment.[2] GM's Saturn has had a similar experience. The Tennessee-based subsidiary achieved its objective of developing new manufacturing and marketing capabilities, but, as yet, these seem to have had little impact on the parent organization.[3]

Notes:

1 T. Elder, "Lessons from Xerox and IBM," *Harvard Business Review* (July–August 1989): 66–71.
2 *Xerox PARC: Innovation without Profit?* ICMR Case Study, 2004.
3 J. O'Toole, *Forming the Future: Lessons from the Saturn Corporation* (New York: Harper, 1996).

STRATEGY CAPSULE 5.6

Hyundai Motor: Developing Capabilities through Product Sequencing

Hyundai's emergence as a world class automobile producer is a remarkable example of capability development over a sequence of compressed phases. Each phase of the development process was characterized by a clear objective in terms of product outcome, a tight time deadline, responsibility allocated to a development team, a clear recognition of the capabilities that

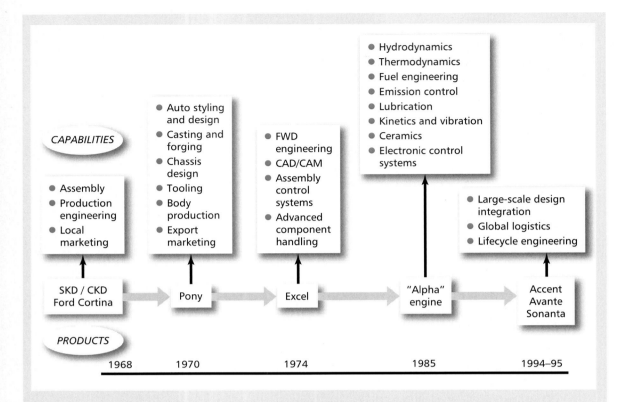

CAPABILITIES

- Assembly
- Production engineering
- Local marketing

- Auto styling and design
- Casting and forging
- Chassis design
- Tooling
- Body production
- Export marketing

- FWD engineering
- CAD/CAM
- Assembly control systems
- Advanced component handling

- Hydrodynamics
- Thermodynamics
- Fuel engineering
- Emission control
- Lubrication
- Kinetics and vibration
- Ceramics
- Electronic control systems

- Large-scale design integration
- Global logistics
- Lifecycle engineering

PRODUCTS

| SKD / CKD Ford Cortina | Pony | Excel | "Alpha" engine | Accent Avante Sonanta |

| 1968 | 1970 | 1974 | 1985 | 1994–95 |

needed to be developed in each phase, and an atmosphere of impending crisis should the project not succeed. The first phase was the construction of an assembly plant in the unprecedented time of 18 months in order to build Hyundai's first car – a Ford Cortina imported in parts. The figure shows the principal phases of Hyundai Motor's development.

Source: L. Kim, "Crisis construction and organizational learning: Capability building and catching up at Hyundai Motor," *Organizational Science* 9 (1998): 506–21.

Summary

We have shifted the focus of our attention from the external to the internal environment of the firm. This internal environment comprises many features of the firm, but for the purposes of strategy analysis, the key issue is what the firm *can do*. This means looking at the resources of the firm and the way resources combine to create organizational capabilities. Our interest is the potential for resources and capabilities to establish sustainable competitive advantage. Systematic appraisal of a company's resources and capabilities provides the basis for formulating (or reformulating) strategy. How can the firm deploy its strengths to maximum advantage? How can it

FIGURE 5.9 Summary: a framework for analyzing resources and capabilities

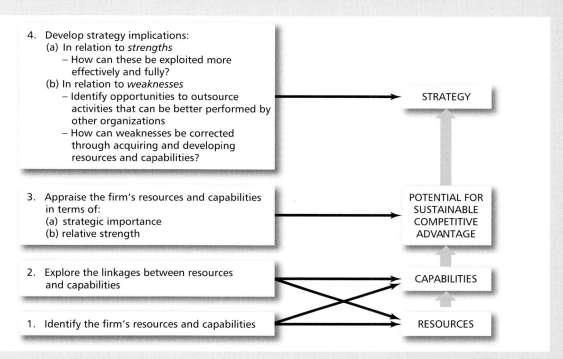

minimize its vulnerability to its weaknesses? How can it develop and extend its capabilities to meet the challenges of the future? Figure 5.9 provides a simplified view of the approach to resource analysis developed in this chapter.

Despite the progress that has been made in the last ten years in our understanding of resources and capabilities, there is much that remains unresolved. We know little about the microstructures of organizational capabilities and how they are established and develop. Can firms develop entirely new capabilities, or must top management accept that distinctive capabilities are the result of experience-based learning over long periods of time through processes that are poorly understood? If that is the case, strategy must be concerned with exploiting, preserving, and developing the firm's existing pool of resources and capabilities, rather than trying to change them. We have much to learn in this area.

Although much of the discussion has been heavy on concepts and theory, the issues are practical. The management systems of most firms devote meticulous attention to the physical and financial assets that are valued on their balance sheets; much less attention has been paid to the critical intangible and human resources of the firm, and even less to the identification and appraisal of organizational capability. Most senior managers are now aware of the importance of their resources and capabilities, but the techniques of identifying, assessing, and developing them are woefully underdeveloped.

Because the resources and capabilities of the firm form the foundation for building competitive advantage, we shall return again and again to the concepts of this chapter. Our next port of call is the structures and systems through which the firm deploys its resources, builds and exercises its capabilities, and implements its strategy.

Self-Study Questions

1 In recent years Google has expanded from internet search across a broad range of internet services, including email, photo management, satellite maps, digital book libraries, blogger services, and telephony. To what extent has Google's strategy focused on its resources and capabilities rather than specific customer needs? What are Google's principal resources and capabilities?

2 Microsoft's main capabilities relate to the development and marketing of complex computer software and its greatest resource is its huge installed base of its Windows operating system. Does Microsoft's entry into video game consoles indicate that its strategy is becoming divorced from its principal resources and capabilities?

3 During 1984–8, Michael Eisner, the newly installed CEO of Walt Disney Company, successfully exploited Disney's existing resources to boost profitability (see Strategy Capsule 5.2). During the last eight years of Eisner's tenure (1998–2005), however, profitability stagnated and share price declined. To what extent did Eisner focus too much on exploiting existing resources and not enough on developing Disney's capabilities to meet the entertainment needs of a changing world?

4 Many companies announce in their corporate communications: "Our people are our most important resource." In terms of the criteria listed in Figure 5.7, can employees be considered to be of the utmost strategic importance?

5 Given the profile of VW's resources and capabilities outlined in Table 5.4 and Figure 5.8, what strategy recommendations would you offer VW?

6 Apply the approach outlined in the section "Putting Resource and Capability Analysis to Work" to your own business school. Begin by identifying the resources and capabilities relevant to success in the market for business education, appraise the resources and capabilities of your school, then make strategy recommendations regarding such matters as the programs to be offered and the overall positioning and differentiation of the school and its offerings.

7 Identify two sports teams: one that is rich in resources (e.g. talented players) but whose capabilities (as indicated by performance) have been poor; one that is resource-poor but has displayed strong team capabilities. What clues can you offer as to the determinants of capabilities among sports teams?

8 In 2006, Disney completed its acquisition of the film animation company Pixar for $7.4 billion. The high purchase price reflected Disney's eagerness to gain Pixar's animation capabilities, its talent (animators, technologists, and storytellers), and its culture of creativity. What risks does Disney face in achieving the goals of this acquisition?

Appendix: Knowledge Management and the Knowledge-based View of the Firm

During the past ten years our thinking about resources and capabilities and their management has been extended and reshaped by a surge of interest in knowledge management. Knowledge management refers to processes and practices through which organizations generate value from knowledge. Initially, knowledge management was primarily concerned with information technology – especially the use of intranets, groupware, and databases for storing, analyzing, and disseminating information. Subsequent developments in knowledge management have been concerned less with data and more with organizational learning – especially the transfer of best practices – and the management of intellectual property. The level of interest in knowledge management is indicated by the number of large corporations that have created the position of chief knowledge officer, the spawning of knowledge management practices by consulting firms, and a flood of books on the subject.

Academic interest in the role of knowledge within organizations represents the confluence of several research streams including resource-based theory, the economics of information, epistemology, evolutionary economics, and the management of technology. The outcome has been a *knowledge-based view of the firm* that considers the firm as a set of knowledge assets with the purpose of deploying these assets to create value.[50]

Is knowledge management a major breakthrough in management practice or mere fad? A growing body of evidence points to the ability of knowledge management to generate substantial gains in performance. At the same time many of its manifestations are highly dubious. *The Wall Street Journal* reports that Saatchi & Saatchi's director of knowledge management is "absorbing everything under the sun," including the implications of breakthrough products such as Japanese pantyhose "embedded with millions of microcapsules of vitamin C and seaweed extract that burst when worn to provide extra nourishment for the limbs."[51] Lucy Kellaway of the *Financial Times* observes that "The subject [of knowledge management] has attracted more needless obfuscation and wooly thinking by academics and consultants than any other."[52]

My approach is to regard knowledge management and the knowledge-based view of the firm as important extensions of our analysis of resources and capabilities. In terms of resources, knowledge is acknowledged to be the overwhelmingly important productive resource; indeed, the value of people and machines lies primarily in the fact that they embody knowledge. From the strategic viewpoint, knowledge is a particularly interesting resource: many types of knowledge are scarce, much of it is difficult to transfer, and complex forms of knowledge may be very difficult to replicate. Capabilities may be viewed as the manifestation of the knowledge of the organization. Knowledge management offers valuable tools for creating, developing, maintaining, and replicating organizational capabilities.

Types of Knowledge

The single most useful contribution of knowledge management is the recognition that different types of knowledge have very different characteristics. A key distinction is between *knowing how* and *knowing about*. *Know-how* is primarily *tacit* in nature – it involves skills that are expressed through their performance (riding a bicycle, playing the piano). *Knowing about* is primarily *explicit* – it comprises facts, theories, and sets of instructions. The primary difference between tacit and explicit knowledge lies in their transferability. Explicit knowledge is revealed by its communication: it can be transferred across individuals, across space, and across time. This ease of communication means that explicit knowledge – information especially – has the characteristics of a *public good*: once created, it can be replicated among innumerable users at very low marginal cost (IT has driven these costs to near zero for most types of information). Tacit knowledge, on the other hand, cannot be codified; it can only be observed through its application and acquired through practice, hence its transfer between people is slow, costly, and uncertain.

This distinction has major implications for strategy. If explicit knowledge can be transferred so easily, it is seldom the foundation of sustainable competitive advantage. Because explicit knowledge leaks so quickly to competitors, it is only secure when it is protected, either by intellectual property rights (patents, copyrights, trade secrets) or by secrecy ("The formula for Coca-Cola will be kept in a safe in the vault of our Atlanta headquarters guarded by armed Coca-Cola executives"). The challenge of tacit knowledge is the opposite: if Ms. Jenkins is an incredibly successful salesperson, how can the skills embedded in her brain be transferred to the rest of the salesforce of Acme Delights? For consulting companies, the distinction between tacit ("personalized") and explicit ("systematized") knowledge defines their business model and is a central determinant of their strategy.[53]

The tacit/explicit distinction has important implications for the distribution of decision-making authority within the company. If the knowledge relevant to decisions is explicit, it can be easily transferred and assembled in one place, hence permitting centralized decision making (treasury activities within companies are typically centralized). If knowledge is primarily tacit, it cannot be transferred and decision making needs to be located among the people where the knowledge lies. If each salesperson's knowledge of how to make sales is based on their intuition and their understanding of their customers' idiosyncrasies, such knowledge cannot be easily transferred to their sales managers. It follows that decisions about their working hours and selling tactics should be made by them, not by the sales manager.

Types of Knowledge Process

A second component of knowledge management is understanding the processes through which knowledge is developed and applied. Two categories of knowledge processes can be identified: those that are concerned with increasing the stock of knowledge available to the organization, and those that are concerned with the application of the organization's knowledge. J.-C. Spender refers to the former as *knowledge generation* and the latter as *knowledge application*. James March's distinction between *exploration* and *exploitation* recognizes a similar dichotomy.[54] Within these two broad areas we can identify a number of different knowledge processes, each of which has been associated with particular techniques and approaches to knowledge management (see Figure 5.10).

The best-developed and most widely applied techniques of knowledge management have focused on some of the most basic aspects of knowledge application and exploitation. For example:

FIGURE 5.10 Knowledge processes within the organization

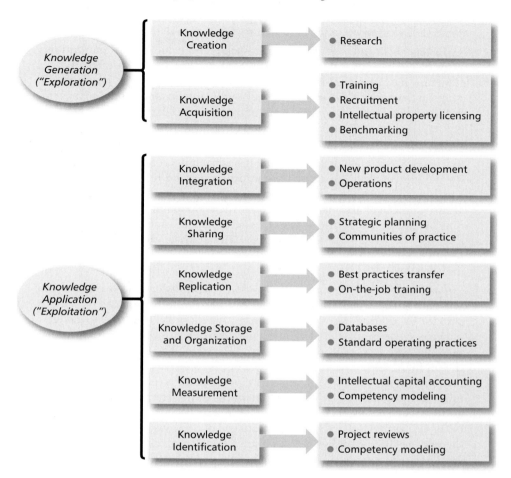

In the area of *knowledge identification*, companies are increasingly assembling and systematizing information on their knowledge assets. These include assessments and reviews of patent portfolios and providing personnel data that allows each employee to identify the skills and experience of other employees in the organization. A key aspect of such knowledge identification is the recognition of knowledge that is being generated within the organization so that it can subsequently be stored for future use. Such knowledge identification is especially important in project-based organizations to ensure that knowledge developed in one project is not lost to the organization. Systematic post-project reviews are a central theme in the US Army's "lessons learned" procedure, which distils the results of practice maneuvers and simulated battles into tactical guidelines and recommended procedures. A process is applied to learning from actual operations. During the military intervention in Bosnia in 1995, the results of every operation were forwarded to the Center for Lessons Learned to be collected and codified. Resulting lessons learned were distributed to active units every 72 hours.[55] By the late 1990s, every major management consulting firm had introduced a system whereby learning from each consulting project was identified, written up, and submitted to a common database.

● *Knowledge measurement* involves measuring and valuing the organization's stock of knowledge and its utilization. Skandia, the Swedish insurance company, has pioneered knowledge metrics with its system of intellectual capital accounting.[56] Dow Chemical also uses intellectual capital management to link its intellectual property portfolio to shareholder value.

● For knowledge to be efficiently utilized within the organization, *knowledge storage and organization* are critical. The key contribution of information technology to knowledge management has been in creating databases for storing information, for organizing information, and for accessing and communicating information, to facilitate the transfer of and access to knowledge. The backbone of the Booz-Allen & Hamilton's "Knowledge-On-Line" system,[57] Accenture's "Knowledge Xchange," and AMS's "Knowledge Express"[58] is an IT system that comprises a database, groupware, dedicated search engine, and an intranet that permits employees to input and access information.

● *Knowledge sharing and replication* involves the transfer of knowledge from one part of the organization (or from one person) to be replicated in another part (or by another individual). A central function of IT-based knowledge management systems is to facilitate such transfer. However, tacit knowledge is not amenable to codification within an IT system. The traditional answer to the problem of replicating tacit knowledge is to use apprenticeships and other forms of on-the-job training. Recently, organizations have discovered the important role played by informal networks in transferring experiential knowledge. These self-organizing *communities of practice* are increasingly being deliberately established and managed as a means of facilitating knowledge sharing and group learning.[59] Replicating capabilities poses an even greater challenge. Transferring best practices within companies is not simply about creating appropriate incentives; complexity and credibility of the knowledge involved are key impediments.[60]

● *Knowledge integration* represents one of the greatest challenges to any company. Producing most goods and services requires bringing together the knowledge of multiple individuals. The essential task of almost all organizational processes is integrating individual knowledge in an effective and efficient manner. For example, a strategic planning system may be seen as a vehicle for integrating the different knowledge bases of managers at different levels of the organization and from different functions in order to create the best strategy for the company. Similarly with new product development: the key is to integrate the knowledge of many technical experts and across a range of functions. A wide body of evidence points to the effectiveness of project teams in integrating knowledge.[61]

Within knowledge generation, it is possible to distinguish between the internal creation of knowledge (*knowledge creation*) and the search to identify and absorb existing knowledge from outside the organization (*knowledge acquisition*). The mechanisms through which knowledge is acquired from outside the organization are typically well known: hiring skilled employees, acquiring companies or their knowledge resources, benchmarking companies that are recognized as "best-in-class" for certain practices, and learning through alliances and joint ventures. Creativity remains a key challenge for most companies. While most studies of creativity emphasize the role of the individual and the types of environment conducive to individual creativity, Dorothy Leonard has explored the role of groups and group processes in stimulating innovation.[62] We shall return to creativity and innovation in Chapter 11.

Knowledge Conversion

In practice, knowledge generation and application are not distinct. For example, the application of existing knowledge creates opportunities for learning that increase the stock of knowledge.[63] Nonaka's theory of knowledge creation identifies the processes of *knowledge conversion* – between tacit and explicit and between individual and organizational knowledge – as central to the organization's building of its knowledge base.[64] The conversion of knowledge between the different knowledge types (the "epistemological dimension") and knowledge levels (the "ontological dimension") forms a knowledge spiral in which the stock of knowledge broadens and deepens (see Figure 5.11). Thus, explicit knowledge is *internalized* into tacit knowledge in the form of intuition, know-how, and routines, while tacit knowledge is *externalized* into explicit knowledge through articulation and codification.

Converting tacit into explicit knowledge is critical to companies that wish to replicate their capabilities:

● Henry Ford's Model T was initially produced on a small scale by skilled metal workers one car at a time. Ford's assembly-line mass-production technology systematized that tacit knowledge, built it into machines and a business process, and replicated it in Ford plants throughout the world. With the

FIGURE 5.11 Nonaka's spiral of knowledge creation

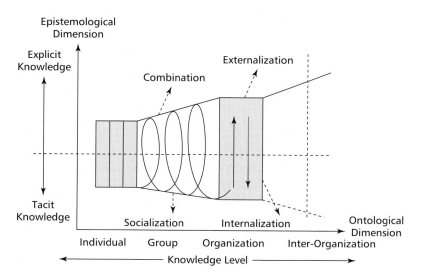

SOURCE: I. NONAKA, "ON A KNOWLEDGE CREATING ORGANIZATION," PAPER PRESENTED AT AIF NATIONAL CONGRESS (POSMA, OCTOBER 1993).

FIGURE 5.12 Knowledge types and the transformation from craft to industrial enterprises

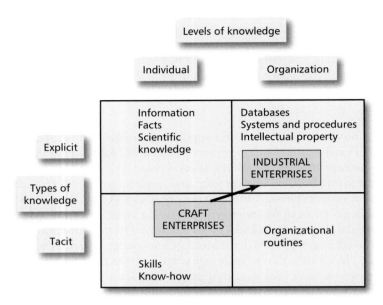

SOURCE: I. NONAKA, "ON KNOWLEDGE CREATING ORGANIZATION," PAPER PRESENTED AT AIR NATIONAL CONGRESS (POSMA, OCTOBER 1993). © 1993 BY I. NONAKA. REPRINTED BY PERMISSION OF THE AUTHOR.

knowledge built into the system, car workers no longer needed to be skilled craftsmen.

● When Ray Kroc discovered the McDonald brothers' hamburger stand in Riversdale, California, he quickly recognized the potential for systematizing and replicating their process through operating manuals, videos, and training programs. It allows thousands of McDonald's outlets worldwide to produce fast food to exacting standards by a labor force that, for the most part, possesses few culinary skills.

This shift in the knowledge base of the firm, from tacit knowledge located in individuals to explicit knowledge held by the organization, is fundamental to the transformation of craft enterprises into industrial enterprises. In addition to Ford and McDonald's, Marriott in hotels, Andersen Consulting (now Accenture) in IT consulting, and Starbucks in coffee shops have pioneered transformation through systematization (see Figure 5.12).

Conclusion

Analysis of the characteristics of knowledge and the processes through which it is created and deployed offers striking insights into the principles and practices of management – including the development of organizational capability.

Given the scope of knowledge management and the vast range of tools, techniques, and frameworks that have been developed, where does a company begin to incorporate knowledge management within its management systems? A useful starting point is to identify the linkage between knowledge and the basis on which the firm creates value. This can then highlight the key processes through which knowledge is generated and applied. Consider the following examples:

- For Dow Chemical, the core of its value creation is generating intellectual property in new chemical products and processes, and exploiting them through worldwide manufacturing, marketing, and sales. Dow's "Intellectual Capital Management" places its central emphasis on the company's patent portfolio and links its intellectual property to a broad range of intellectual capital variables and processes and ultimately to the company's total value.[65]

- For McKinsey & Co., creating value for clients requires continually building on the knowledge it generates from client assignments, and conceptualizing and sharing that knowledge base. This is achieved through a system that ensures the knowledge generated from each project is captured and made available for subsequent client projects; a matrix structure of industry and functional practices that permits specialized knowledge to be created and stored; and an R&D function in the form of the McKinsey Global Institute.[66]

- For McDonald's Corporation, knowledge management is primarily concerned with implementing the McDonald's system. This is a detailed set of operating practices that extend from the company's values down to the placing of a pickle on the bun of a Big Mac and the procedure for servicing a McDonald's milkshake machine. The essence of the McDonald's system is the systematization of knowledge into a detailed set of rules that are followed in every McDonald's outlet. These explicit operating practices are internalized within employees' cognition and behavior through rigorous attention to training, both in formal training programs at Hamburger University, and in training at individual restaurants.[67]

The design of every knowledge process must take account of the characteristics of the knowledge being deployed. The fundamental distinction here is between explicit and tacit knowledge. Take a simple example of the transfer of best practice between the different fabrication plants of a multinational semiconductor plant. If the knowledge is explicit, then such knowledge can be disseminated in the form of reports, or directives requiring every plant to adopt a new standard operating procedure. If the knowledge is tacit – it is the result of the experience or intuition of a single plant manager – the task is more difficult. Transferring the best practice is likely to require either visits by other plant managers to the innovating plant, or for the innovating plant manager to adopt a consulting role and visit other plants in the group for the purpose of teaching employees there.

It is in the area of managing tacit knowledge (which includes, typically, the major part of the knowledge relevant to organizational capability) where the major challenges and opportunities in knowledge management lie. Information technology has made huge strides in the storage, analysis, and systematization of explicit knowledge. However, the greater part of organizational learning is experience based and intuitive. Identifying this knowledge, and transferring it to other parts of the organization in order to utilize it more effectively, remains a fundamental management challenge.

Notes

1 The "resource-based view" is described in J. B. Barney, "Firm Resources and Sustained Competitive Advantage," *Journal of Management* 17 (1991): 99–120; J. Mahoney and J. R. Pandian, "The Resource-Based View within the Conversation of Strategic Management," *Strategic Management Journal* 13 (1992): 363–80; M. A. Peterlaf, "The Cornerstones of Competitive Advantage: A Resource-Based View," *Strategic Management Journal* 14 (1993): 179–92; D. Collis and C. Montgomery, "Competing on Resources: Strategy in the 1990s," *Harvard Business Review* (July–August 1995): 119–28.

2 Ted Levitt ("Marketing Myopia," *Harvard Business Review*, July–August 1960: 24–47) proposed that the answer to such volatility was for firms to define their markets broadly rather than narrowly. Railroad companies should view themselves as in the transportation business; oil companies should think of themselves as energy companies. The fact is that railroad companies that entered airlines and road transportation generally performed poorly, as did the oil companies that went into coal, nuclear energy, and solar power.

3 J. Kay, "Resource Based Strategy," *Financial Times* (September 27, 1999).

4 C. K. Prahalad and G. Hamel, "The Core Competence of the Corporation," *Harvard Business Review* (May–June 1990): 79–91.

5 "Olivetti: On the Ropes," *Economist* (May 20, 1995): 60–1; "Olivetti Reinvents Itself Once More," *Wall Street Journal* (February 22, 1999): A.1.

6 www.remington-products.com

7 "Eastman Kodak: Meeting the Digital Challenge," in R. M. Grant, *Cases to Accompany* Contemporary Strategy Analysis 6th edn (Oxford, Blackwell, 2008).

8 M. Tripsas, "Unraveling the Process of Creative Destruction: Complementary Assets and Incumbent Survival in the Typesetter Industry," *Strategic Management Journal* 18, Summer Special Issue (1997): 119–42; J. Bower and C. M. Christensen, "Disruptive Technologies: Catching the Wave," *Harvard Business Review* (January–February 1995): 43–53.

9 J. W. Trailer, "On the Theory of Rent and the Mechanics of Profitability," CSU Chico, 2002 (www.csuchico.edu/~jtrailer/Trailer.doc).

10 C. Fombrun, "The Value to be Found in Corporate Reputation," *Financial Times* Mastering Management Series (December 4, 2000): 8–10.

11 www.harrisinteractive.com

12 E. Lawler, "From Job-Based to Competency-Based Organizations," *Journal of Organizational Behavior* 15 (1994): 3–15; L. Spencer, D. McClelland, and S. Spencer, *Competency Assessment Methods: History and State of the Art* (Hay/McBer Research Group, 1994); L. Spencer and S. Spencer, *Competence At Work: Models for Superior Performance* (New York, Wiley: 1993).

13 D. Goleman, *Emotional Intelligence* (New York: Bantam, 1995).

14 J. Barney, "Organizational Culture: Can It Be a Source of Sustained Competitive Advantage?" *Academy of Management Review* 11 (1986): 656–65.

15 C. E. Helfat and M. Lieberman, "The Birth of Capabilities: Market Entry and the Importance of Prehistory," *Industrial and Corporate Change* 12 (2002): 725–60.

16 G. Hamel and C. K. Prahalad argue (*Harvard Business Review*, May–June 1992: 164–5) that "the distinction between competencies and capabilities is purely semantic."

17 P. Selznick, *Leadership in Administration: A Sociological Interpretation* (New York: Harper & Row, 1957).

18 C. K. Prahalad and G. Hamel, "The Core Competence of the Corporation," op. cit.

19 G. Hamel and C. K. Prahalad, letter, *Harvard Business Review* (May–June 1992): 164–5.

20 Porter's value chain is the main framework of his *Competitive Advantage* (New York: Free Press, 1984). McKinsey & Company refers to the firm's value chain as its "business system." See: C. F. Bates, P. Chatterjee, F. W. Gluck, D. Gogel, and A. Puri, "The Business System: A New Tool for Strategy Formulation and Cost Analysis," in *McKinsey on Strategy* (Boston: McKinsey & Company, 2000).

21 R. R. Nelson and S. G. Winter, *An Evolutionary Theory of Economic Change* (Cambridge, MA: Belknap, 1982).

22 As a result, specialists perform well in stable environments while generalists do well in variable conditions. (J. Freeman and M. Hannan, "Niche Width and the Dynamics of Organizational Populations," *American Journal of Sociology* 88, 1984: 1116–45).

23 K. B. Clark and T. Fujimoto, *Product Development Performance* (New York: Free Press, 1991).

24 See Richard Caves' discussion of "specific assets" in "International Corporations: The Industrial Economics of Foreign Investment," *Economica* 38 (1971): 1–27.

25 G. Akerlof, "The Market for Lemons: Qualitative Uncertainty and the Market Mechanism," *Quarterly Journal of Economics* 84 (1970): 488–500.

26 J. B. Barney, "Strategic Factor Markets: Expectations, Luck and Business Strategy," *Management Science* 32 (October 1986): 1231–41.

27 "Lenovo Makes Break With IBM Brand," *New York Times* (April 11, 2006).

28 I. Dierickx and K. Cool, "Asset Stock Accumulation and Sustainability of Competitive Advantage," *Management Science* 35 (1989): 1504–13.

29 "Goldman Sachs," *Economist* (April 29, 2006): 77–80.

30 "Real Madrid: A Contingency Theory Explanation of How to Fail," www.davidbruceallen.com/strategyoped

31 D. Miller, *The Icarus Paradox: How Exceptional Companies Bring About Their Own Downfall* (New York: Harper-Business, 1990).

32   Benchnet: The Benchmarking Exchange
     (www.benchnet.com).

33   S. Walleck, D. O'Halloran, and C. Leader,
     "Benchmarking World-Class Performance," *McKinsey
     Quarterly* 1 (1991); "The Link Between Management
     and Productivity," *McKinsey Quarterly* (February 2006).

34   C. Markides, *All the Right Moves* (Boston: Harvard
     Business School Press, 1999).

35   G. Hamel and C. K. Prahalad, *Competing for the Future*
     (Boston: Harvard Business School Press, 1994).

36   S. Winter, "The Four Rs of Profitability: Rents,
     Resources, Routines, and Replication," in C.
     Montgomery (ed.), *Resource-Based and Evolutionary
     Theories of the Firm* (Boston: Kluwer, 1995): 147–78.

37   "Copy Exactly Factory Strategy"
     (www.intel.com/pressroom/kits/manufacturing/
     copy_exactly.htm). See also: G. Szulanski and S. Winter,
     "Getting it Right the Second Time," *Harvard Business
     Review* (January 2002): 62–9; and C. Baden-Fuller and
     S. G. Winter, "Replicating Organizational Knowledge:
     Principles or Templates?" Papers on Economics and
     Evolution, Max Planck Institute, 2005.

38   D. Leonard-Barton, "Core Capabilities and Core
     Rigidities," *Strategic Management Journal*, Summer
     Special Issue (1992): 111–26.

39   D. J. Teece, G. Pisano, and A. Shuen, "Dynamic
     Capabilities and Strategic Management," *Strategic
     Management Journal* 18 (1997): 509–33. The nature of
     dynamic capability is further explored in K. M.
     Eisenhardt and J. A. Martin, "Dynamic Capabilities:
     What Are They?" *Strategic Management Journal* 21
     (2000): 1105–21 and H. Volberda, *Building the Flexible
     Firm* (Oxford: Oxford University Press, 1998).

40   M. Zollo and S. G. Winter, "Deliberate Learning and the
     Evolution of Dynamic Capabilities," *Organization
     Science* 13 (2002): 339–51. See also: M. Feldman and
     B. Pentland, "Reconceptualizing Organizational
     Routines as a Source of Flexibility and Change,"
     Administrative Science Quarterly 48 (March 2003).

41   Established firms typically fail to survive radical
     innovation. See, for example, R. M. Henderson and
     K. B. Clark, "Architectural Innovation: The
     Reconfiguration of Existing Product Technologies and
     Failure of Established Firms," *Administrative Science
     Quarterly* 35 (1990): 9–30; C. Christensen, "The Rigid
     Disk Drive Industry: A History of Commercial and
     Technological Turbulence," *Business History Review* 67
     (1993): 531–88; M. Tripsas, "Unravelling the Process of
     Creative Destruction: Complementary Assets and
     Incumbent Survival in the Typesetter Industry," *Strategic
     Management Journal* 18 (Summer Special Issue, 1997):
     119–42; A. Henderson, "Firm Strategy and Age
     Dependence: A Contingent View of the Liabilities of
     Newness, Adolescence and Obsolescence,"
     Administrative Science Quarterly 44 (1999): 281–314;
     S. Karim and W. Mitchell, "Path-Dependent and Path-
     Breaking Change: Reconfiguring Business Resources
     Following Acquisitions in the US Medical Sector,

     1978–1995," *Strategic Management Journal* 21 (2000):
     1016–81.

42   See, for example, M. Lyles, "Learning Among Joint-
     venture Sophisticated Firms," *Management International
     Review* 28, Special Issue (1988): 85–98; A. Mody,
     "Learning Through Alliances," *Journal of Economic
     Behavior and Organization* 20 (1993): 151–70; D. C.
     Mowery, J. E. Oxley, and B. S. Silverman, "Strategic
     Alliances and Interfirm Knowledge Transfer," *Strategic
     Management Journal* 17, Winter Special Issue (1996):
     77–93; A. C. Inkpen and M. M. Crossan, "Believing Is
     Seeing: Joint Ventures and Organizational Learning,"
     Journal of Management Studies 32 (1995): 595–618.

43   J. A. Badaracco, *The Knowledge Link: How Firms
     Compete Through Strategic Alliances* (Boston: Harvard
     Business School Press, 1991).

44   G. Hamel, "Competition for Competence and Inter-
     partner Learning within International Strategic
     Alliances," *Strategic Management Journal* 12, Summer
     Special Issue (1991): 83–103.

45   S. G. Winter, "The Satisficing Principle in Capability
     Learning," *Strategic Management Journal* 21 (2000):
     981–96; G. Gavetti and D. Levinthal, "Looking Forward
     and Looking Backward: Cognitive and Experiential
     Search," *Administrative Science Quarterly* 45 (2000):
     113–37.

46   G. Dosi, R. R. Nelson, and S. G. Winter (eds), *The
     Nature and Dynamics of Organizational Capabilities*
     (Oxford: Oxford University Press, 2001).

47   C. E. Helfat and Ruth S. Raubitschek, "Product
     Sequencing: Co-evolution of Knowledge, Capabilities
     and Products," *Strategic Management Journal* 21 (2000):
     961–79.

48   H. Itami, *Mobilizing Invisible Assets* (Boston: Harvard
     University Press, 1987): 125.

49   A. Takahashi, *What I Learned from Konosuke Matsushita*
     (Tokyo: Jitsugyo no Nihonsha, 1980); in Japanese,
     quoted by Itami, op. cit.: 25.

50   "The knowledge-based view" offers a rationale for the
     firm that is based on its effectiveness as an institution for
     creating, assembling, and transforming knowledge into
     goods and services. See: B. Kogut and U. Zander,
     "Knowledge of the Firm, Combinative Capabilities and
     the Replication of Technology, *Organization Science*
     3 (1992): 387–99; R. M. Grant, "Toward a Knowledge-
     based Theory of the Firm," *Strategic Management
     Journal* 17, Winter Special Issue (1996): 109–22.

51   "Saatchi's 'Manager of Knowledge' Keeps Track of
     What's Trendy," *Wall Street Journal* (February 28, 1997):
     B.16.

52   Lucy Kellaway column, *Financial Times* (June 23,
     1999): 13.

53   M. Hansen, N. Nohria, and T. Tierney, "What's Your
     Strategy for Managing Knowledge?" *Harvard Business
     Review* (March 1999): 106–16.

54   J.-C. Spender, "Limits to Learning from the West," *The
     International Executive* 34 (September/October 1992):
     389–410; J. G. March, "Exploration and Exploitation in

Organizational Learning," *Organization Science* 2 (1991): 71–87.

55 "Lessons Learned: Army Devises System to Decide What Does and What Does Not Work," *Wall Street Journal* (May 23, 1997): A1 and A10.

56 L. Edvinsson and S. Malone, *Intellectual Capital: Realizing Your Company's True Value by Finding its Hidden Brainpower* (New York: Harper Business, 1997); D. Marchand and J. Roos, *Skandia AFS: Measuring and Visualizing Intellectual Capital*, Case No. GM 624 (Lausanne: IMD, 1996).

57 *Cultivating Capabilities to Innovate: Booz-Allen & Hamilton*, Case No. 9-698-027 (Boston: Harvard Business School, 1997).

58 *American Management Systems: The Knowledge Centers*, Case No. 9-697-068 (Boston: Harvard Business School, 1997).

59 E. C. Wenger and W. M. Snyder, "Communities of Practice: The Organizational Frontier," *Harvard Business Review* (January–February 2000).

60 G. Szulanski, "Exploring Internal Stickiness: Impediments to the Transfer of Best Practices within the Firm," *Strategic Management Journal* 17, Winter Special Issue (1996): 27–44.

61 See, for example, K. B. Clark and T. Fujimoto, *Product Development Performance* (New York: Free Press, 1991); and K. Imai, I. Nonaka, and H. Takeuchi, "Managing the New Product Development Process: How Japanese Companies Learn and Unlearn," in K. Clark, R. Hayes, and C. Lorenz (eds), *The Uneasy Alliance* (Boston: Harvard Business School Press, 1985).

62 D. Leonard and S. Sensiper, "The Role of Tacit Knowledge in Group Innovation," *California Management Review* 40 (Spring 1998): 112–32; D. Leonard, *The Wellsprings of Knowledge* (Boston: Harvard Business School Press, 1996).

63 P. McNamara, "Managing the Tension Between Knowledge Exploration and Exploitation: The Case of UK Biotechnology," Ph.D. thesis (City University Business School, London, 2000).

64 I. Nonaka and H. Takeuchi, *The Knowledge-Creating Company* (Oxford: Oxford University Press, 1995).

65 G. Petrash, "Dow's Journey to a Knowledge Value Management Culture," *European Management Journal* 14 (August 1996): 365–73.

66 *McKinsey & Company: Managing Knowledge and Learning*, Case No. 9-396-357 (Boston: Harvard Business School, 1996).

67 As McDonald's has faced new challenges – internationalization and trends towards healthier eating – it has changed its systems for managing knowledge, emphasizing decentralized product development and internal knowledge sharing through Food Improvement Teams and corporate blogs.

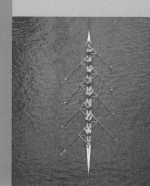

Organization Structure and Management Systems

6

Ultimately, there may be no long-term sustainable advantage other than the
ability to organize and manage.

—JAY GALBRAITH AND ED LAWLER

I'd rather have first-rate execution and second-rate strategy anytime than
brilliant ideas and mediocre management.

—JAMIE DIMON, CEO, JP MORGAN CHASE & CO.

OUTLINE

Introduction and Objectives

"Great strategy; lousy implementation," is an epithet applied to organizational failures from Philip II of Spain's disastrous attack on England with the Spanish Armada[1] to the unraveling of the "merger made in heaven" between carmakers Daimler-Benz and Chrysler.[2] The idea that the formulation of strategy can be separated from its implementation has become institutionalized by the numerous strategic management texts that devote separate sections to strategy formulation and strategy implementation.

This supposed division between formulation and implementation is fiction. At the most obvious level, formulating a strategy without taking into account the conditions under which it will be implemented will result in a poorly designed strategy. A fundamental flaw in the corporate planning systems of 25 years ago was separating strategy formulation – the task of corporate executives and strategic planners – from its implementation by divisional heads and middle managers.

The design of organization structure and management form key components of strategy implementation. Hence, the view of strategy formulation and strategy implementation as a sequential process is summed up in the adage "structure follows strategy." Yet, management guru Tom Peters argues the reverse: if capabilities are the primary basis of strategy, and if capabilities are a product of organizational structure, then *strategy follows structure*.[3] The key point, however, is not whether strategy or structure takes precedence, but the recognition that the two are closely interdependent.[4] For companies, such as Benetton, with its closely coordinated network of local suppliers and worldwide network of franchised retailers, or Amway, with its pyramid of commission-based, independent distributors, strategy is defined by these firms' organizational structures.

Having established that how companies organize themselves is fundamental to their strategy and their performance, the goal of this chapter is to introduce the key concepts and ideas necessary to understand and design companies' structures and systems. The approach is concise and selective. I do not intend to offer a potted overview of organizational theory. My aim is to introduce some basic principles of organizational design and to apply these to key aspects of firm structure. The principles outlined here will be further developed in later chapters when we consider strategies within particular business contexts. For example, Chapter 11 considers the organizational conditions conducive to innovation; Chapter 12 considers organization and organizational change within mature industries; Chapter 13 discusses vertical structures and outsourcing; Chapter 14 examines the structure and systems of the multinational corporation; and Chapter 16 deals with organizing the multibusiness company.

By the time you have completed this chapter you will be able to:

- Recognize the key organizational innovations that have shaped the evolution of the modern corporation.

- Understand the basic principles that determine the structural characteristics of complex human organizations.

- Apply the principles of organizational design to recommend the types of organizational structure suited to particular tasks and particular business environments.

- Understand the role of information systems, strategic planning, financial control, and human resource management in the coordination and control of corporations.

- Appreciate the forces that are causing companies to seek new organizational structures and management systems.

The Evolution of the Corporation

Firms and Markets

Most of the world's production of goods and services is undertaken by corporations – enterprises with a legal identity that is distinct from the individuals that own the enterprise. The main exceptions include agriculture and crafts in the developing world, where family-based production predominates, and services such as defense, policing, and education that are usually provided by government organizations.

This has not always been so. Until the late 19th century, the world's only large-scale organizations were the Roman Catholic church and national armies (see Strategy Capsule 6.1). The only large firms were colonial trading companies such as the Dutch East India Company, Hudson's Bay Company, and the United Africa Company. As late as the 1850s, the largest enterprises in the US in terms of numbers of workers were agricultural plantations.[5] Most manufacturing was organized through networks of self-employed, home-based workers. The English woolen industry once consisted of home-based spinners who purchased raw wool (on credit) from a merchant to whom

STRATEGY CAPSULE 6.1

Reorganizing the Prussian Army, 1857–1870

In 1857, Helmuth von Moltke was the appointed commander-in-chief of the Prussian army. During the next 12 years he completely reorganized it. His new structure was based on *divisions* that were controlled and coordinated by a *general staff*. Each division was a standardized unit with the same composition of infantry, cavalry, and artillery and the same size, structure, equipment, and training methods. The general staff comprised headquarters generals and specialist units: engineering, intelligence, training, and supply.

A key role of the general staff was officer training. Each year 120 young officers were selected from the whole officer corps for intensive training at a war academy that placed a strong emphasis on strategic and tactical planning. Each year, the top 12 graduates of the war academy were selected for several years' further training and development with Moltke at the general staff before being assigned to one of the divisions. The idea was that, through common training, each officer would react with similar responses to new situations,

even without direct instruction from the general staff. Moreover, individual officers were interchangeable.

The test of the new organization came with the Franco-Prussian War of 1870. The French army was one of the biggest and most experienced in Europe, yet within weeks it was routed. The French were defeated not by superior numbers, armaments, or valor, but by a superior organizational system.

Like the Prussian army, the French army had decentralized by creating formations that included units of infantry, cavalry, and artillery. Yet no standardization had been achieved. The units had different sizes, structures, and methods. Most serious were the deficiencies of the French general staff, which comprised the commander-in-chief supported by messengers and clerks, but with no effective means of co-ordinating the different army units.

Sources: M. Howard, *The Franco-Prussian War: The German Invasion of France, 1870–1871* (London: Routledge, 1991); R. Stark, *Sociology*, 10th edn (Wadsworth Publishing, 2006).

they sold the yarn; the merchant resold the yarn to home-based weavers from whom he purchased cloth. This "putting-out" system survived until the introduction of powered looms, when weavers relocated to factories and eventually became employees rather than independent contractors.

The business corporation is one of the greatest innovations of modern civilization. The rise of the corporation as the predominant institution for organizing production is one of the central features of modern economic development. This rise reflects the efficiency and effectiveness of corporations – relative to other institutions – in organizing economic activity. In the capitalist economy, production is organized in two ways: in *markets* – by the price mechanism – and in *firms* – by managerial direction. The relative roles of firms and markets are determined by efficiency: if the *administrative costs* of firms are less than the *transaction costs* of markets (as occurred in the English textile industry after the introduction of the factory system), transactions will tend to be organized within firms rather than across markets. We shall revisit the *transaction cost theory* when we consider vertical integration in Chapter 13.

Emergence of the Modern Corporation

According to business historian Alfred Chandler, the modern corporation emerged as a result of two "critical transformations."[6]

Line-and-Staff Structure Initially, most companies were small and operated from a single plant or office. Lack of transportation limited each firm's market to its immediate vicinity, while lack of communication prevented firms from operating in multiple locations. The railroad and the telegraph changed all that – but to operate over a wider geographical area, firms needed new organizational structures and management techniques. In the US, the railroad companies were the first to create geographically separate operating units managed by an administrative headquarters. This organizational form was termed a *line-and-staff* structure. Employees are either *line*, allocated to operational tasks within the operating units, or *staff*, administrators and functional specialists located at head office.

By the end of the late 19th century, simple line-and-staff structures had developed into more complex *functional structures* – companies such as DuPont, Sears Roebuck and Company, and Shell Transport and Trading managed a number of separate operating units with large functional departments that conducted sales, finance, R&D, legal affairs, and other specialist activities. Other large business enterprises were organized as *holding companies* – Standard Oil (of the US), Mitsui (of Japan), and the British South Africa Company were created by a series of acquisitions in which the parent company bought controlling equity stakes in a number of other companies.

The Multidivisional Corporation The second critical transformation was the emergence during the 1920s of the divisionalized corporation, which, over time, replaced both the centralized, functional structures that characterized most industrial corporations and the loose-knit holding companies created in the merger wave of the early 20th century. The pioneers were DuPont and General Motors.

- At DuPont, increasing size and a widening product range strained the functional structure and overloaded top management:

    . . . the operations of the enterprise became too complex and the problems of coordination, appraisal and policy formulation too intricate for a small number of top officers to handle both long-run, entrepreneurial and short-run, operational administrative activities.[7]

    The solution devised by Pierre Du Pont was to decentralize: ten product divisions were created, each with their own sales, R&D, and support activities. The corporate head office headed by an Executive Committee took responsibility for coordination, strategy, and resource allocation.[8]

- General Motors, which had grown by acquisition into a loose holding company, adopted a similar structure as a solution to the problems of weak financial control and a confused product line. The new structure (shown in Figure 6.1) was based on two principles: the chief executive of each division was fully responsible for the operation and performance of that division,

FIGURE 6.1 General Motors Corporation: organizational structure, 1921

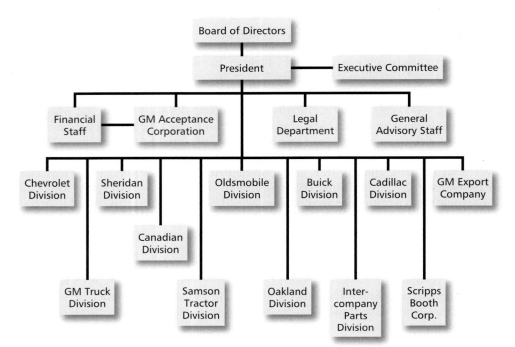

SOURCE: A. P. SLOAN, MY YEARS WITH GENERAL MOTORS (ORBIT PUBLISHING, 1972): 57. © 1963 BY ALFRED P. SLOAN. © RENEWED 1991, ALFRED P. SLOAN FOUNDATION. REPRINTED BY PERMISSION OF HAROLD MATSON CO., INC.

while the general office, headed by the president, was responsible for the development and control of the corporation as a whole, including:

- monitoring return on invested capital within the divisions;
- coordinating the divisions (including establishing terms for interdivisional transactions);
- establishing a product policy.[9]

The primary feature of the divisionalized corporation was the separation of operating responsibilities, which were vested in general managers at the divisional level, from strategic responsibilities, which were located at the head office. The divisionalized corporation reconciled central coordination with the efficiencies and responsiveness of operational decentralization.

Organizational Change Since the Mid-Twentieth Century

Since the end of the Second World War, business enterprises have continued to evolve their structures and systems at a rapid rate. Increased scope and complexity has resulted in the multidivisional form developing into the *matrix organization* – where separate hierarchies coordinate around products, functions, and geographical areas.

The quest for flexibility and responsiveness has resulted in the *delayering* of hierarchies, the shift from functionally organized headquarters staff to *shared services organizations*, and the creation of flexibility and responsiveness through alliances, networks, and outsourcing partnerships.

Most striking has been the rapid evolution of management systems – operational and capital expenditure budgeting, corporate planning, and management-by-objectives – during the 1950s and 1960s, through to knowledge management and corporate social responsibility during recent years.

However, our purpose is not to review history nor to identify best practice. Our challenge is to appreciate the basic principles of organizational design so that we can design organizations that are appropriate to specific purposes and circumstances and recognize the fit between strategy, structure, and the business environment.

The Organizational Problem: Reconciling Specialization With Coordination and Cooperation

According to Henry Mintzberg:

Every organized human activity – from making pots to placing a man on the moon – gives rise to two fundamental and opposing requirements: the division of labor into various tasks, and the coordination of these tasks to accomplish the activity. The structure of the organization can be defined simply as the ways in which labor is divided into distinct tasks and coordination is achieved among these tasks.[10]

We begin with these two fundamental organizational requirements: *specialization* and *coordination*.

Specialization and Division of Labor

Firms exist because they are efficient institutions for the organization of economic activities, particularly the production of goods and services. The fundamental source of efficiency in production is *specialization*, especially the *division of labor* into separate tasks. The classic statement on the gains due to specialization is Adam Smith's description of pin manufacture:

One man draws out the wire, another straightens it, a third cuts it, a fourth points it, a fifth grinds it at the top for receiving the head; to make the head requires two or three distinct operations; to put it on is a peculiar business, to whiten the pins is another; it is even a trade by itself to put them into the papers.[11]

Smith's pin makers produced about 4,800 pins per person each day. "But if they had all wrought separately and independently, and without any of them having been educated to this peculiar business, they certainly could not each have made 20, perhaps not one pin, in a day." Similarly, Henry Ford experienced huge productivity gains by installing moving assembly lines and assigning individuals to highly specific production tasks. Between the end of 1912 and early 1914, the time taken to assemble a Model T fell from 106 hours to just over six hours. More generally, the difference in human productivity between modern industrial society and primitive subsistence society is the result of the efficiency gains from individuals specializing.

But specialization comes at a cost. The more a production process is divided between different specialists, the greater are the costs of coordination. The more volatile and unstable the external environment, the greater the number of decisions that need to be made and the higher are these coordination costs. Hence, the more stable is the environment, the greater is the optimal division of labor. This is true both for firms and for entire societies. Civilizations are built on increased division of labor, which is only possible through stability. As Somalia, Afghanistan, and the Congo have demonstrated so tragically, once chaos reigns, societies regress toward subsistence mode where each family unit must be self-sufficient.

The Coordination Problem

No matter how great the specialist skills possessed by individuals, unless these individuals can coordinate their efforts, production doesn't happen. The current challenge for every coach of a national soccer team is how to coordinate the efforts of a group of talented individuals within a limited time before the 2010 World Cup finals. Conversely, the exceptional performance of organizations such as Wal-Mart, the Cirque du Soleil, and the Berlin Philharmonic Orchestra are primarily the result of superb coordination between organizational members. How do individuals within organizations coordinate their efforts? Let us look at the operation of four different coordination mechanisms:

- *Price*. In the market, coordination is achieved through the *price mechanism*. Price mechanisms also exist within firms. Different departments and divisions may trade on an arm's-length basis, where internal prices (*transfer prices*) are either negotiated or set by corporate headquarters.

- *Rules and directives*. A key feature of firms is the existence of employment contracts. Unlike self-employed workers, who negotiate market contracts for individual tasks, employees enter general employment contracts where they agree to perform a range of duties as required by their employer. Authority is exercised by means of general rules ("Employees will report for work not later than 8.30 a.m.") and specific directives ("Miss Moneypenny, show Mr. Bond his new cigarette case with 3G communication and a concealed death ray").

- *Mutual adjustment*. The simplest form of coordination involves the mutual adjustment of individuals engaged in related tasks. In soccer or doubles tennis, each player coordinates with fellow team members without any authority relationship among them. Such mutual adjustment occurs in all teams and work groups where there is no formal leader.

- *Routines*. Where activities are performed recurrently, coordination based on mutual adjustment and rules becomes institutionalized within organizational routines. As we noted in the previous chapter, these "regular and predictable sequences of coordinated actions by individuals" are the foundation of organizational capability. If organizations are to perform complex activities at extreme levels of efficiency and reliability, coordination by rules, directives, or mutual adjustment is not enough – coordination must become embedded in routines.

The relative roles of these different coordination devices depend on the types of activity being performed and the intensity of collaboration required. Price mechanisms work well in situations of "arm's-length" coordination. For example, in coordinating production and sales, it may be sufficient to offer sales personnel simple price incentives such as higher commission rates on those products where inventories are high. Rules tend to work well for activities where standardized outcomes are required and the decision-making abilities of the operatives involved may be limited – most quality control procedures involve the application of simple rules. Routines form the basis for coordination in most activities where close interdependence exists between individuals, whether a basic production task (supplying customers at Starbucks) or a more complex activity (performing a heart by-pass operation or implementing a systems integration project for a multinational corporation).

The Cooperation Problem: Incentives and Control

The discussion of coordination has dealt only with the technical problem of integrating the actions of different individuals. However, coordination problems are not entirely solved by implementing coordination mechanisms, there is also the problem of different organizational members having conflicting goals. This is referred to as the *cooperation problem*. Overcoming goal conflict requires creating incentives and controls.

The economics literature analyzes goal misalignment in terms of *agency problems*.[12] An *agency relationship* exists when one party (the principal) contracts with another party (the agent) to act on behalf of the principal. The problem is ensuring that the agent acts in the principal's interest. Within the firm, the major agency problem is between owners (shareholders) and managers. The problem of ensuring that managers operate companies to maximize shareholder wealth is at the center of the corporate governance debate. During the 1990s, changes in top management remuneration – in particular the increasing emphasis given to stock options – were intended to align the interests of managers with those of shareholders.[13] However, at Enron, WorldCom, and other companies, these incentives encouraged managers to manipulate reported earnings rather than to work for long-term profitability.

Agency problems exist throughout the hierarchy. For individual employees, systems of incentives, monitoring, and appraisal are designed to encourage pursuit of organizational objectives and overcome employees' tendency to do their own thing or simply shirk. The organization structure may create its own problems. Organizational departments create their own subgoals that do not align with one another. The classic conflicts are between different functions: sales wishes to please customers, production wishes to maximize output, R&D wants to introduce mind-blowing new products, while finance worries about profit and loss.

Several mechanisms are available to management for achieving goal alignment within organizations:

- *Control mechanisms* typically operate on the basis of managers supervising groups of subordinates. Managerial supervision involves monitoring behavior and performance, while subordinates are obliged to seek approval for actions that lie outside their area of authority. Such hierarchical supervision and control rests on both positive and negative incentives. Positive incentives are typically the reward of promotion up the hierarchy in return for compliance; negative incentives are dismissal and demotion for failing to acquiesce to rules and directives.

- *Financial incentives* are designed to reward performance. Such incentives extend from piece-rates for production workers to stock options and profit bonuses for executives. Such performance-related incentives have two main benefits: first, they are *high powered* – they relate rewards directly to output – and second, they economize on the need for costly monitoring and supervision of employees. The problems of pay-for-performance arise where employees work in teams or on activities where output is difficult to measure. Linking pay to individual performance may discourage collaboration; linking it to group performance may encourage free riding.

- *Shared values*. Some organizations are able to achieve high levels of cooperation and low levels of goal conflict without extensive control mechanisms or performance-related incentives. Churches, charities, clubs, and most voluntary organizations fall into this category. The reason is the commonality of goals between organizational members. Since Peters and Waterman's *In Search of Excellence*, the role of shared core values in sustained organizational success is well documented.[14] The role of culture as a control mechanism that is an alternative to bureaucratic control or the price mechanism is central to Bill Ouchi's concept of *clan control*.[15] The role of corporate culture in encouraging conformity to organizational goals has long been recognized among Japanese corporations. However, in western companies too – in Wal-Mart, Four Seasons Hotels, Amway, and the Shell Group – the presence of shared values and principles encourages the alignment of individual and corporate goals without necessarily undermining the individuality of organizational members. Such control saves on monitoring costs: self-control and informal monitoring by co-workers substitute for managerial supervision and financial incentives. Similar observations can be made about companies driven by a common technological vision. At Apple Computer in the 1980s, the belief that Apple was leading a computer revolution that would transform and democratize society permitted intense cooperation with very little formal control. As one cynic noted: "What's the difference between Apple and the Boy Scouts? In the Boy Scouts, the kids have adult supervision!"

We shall return to these issues of incentives and control when we consider the management systems of companies.

Hierarchy in Organizational Design

How have companies addressed these basic needs for specialization, coordination, and cooperation? The traditional approach to large-scale organization has been to create *hierarchy*. Despite the negative associations that currently attach to hierarchy, I shall argue that hierarchical structures are essential for creating efficient and flexible coordination in complex organizations. The critical issue is not whether or not to organize by hierarchy – there is little alternative – but how the hierarchy should be structured and how the different parts of it should relate to one another. Hierarchies come in many forms. Traditionally, hierarchy is associated with bureaucratic approaches to management control. However, hierarchical structures may also be organized along *organic* lines. The past decade has seen important changes in how companies structure and manage hierarchical structures.

Hierarchy as Coordination: Modularity

Hierarchy is fundamental to the structure of all organizations; indeed, according to Herbert Simon, hierarchy is present in virtually all complex systems.[16] If a hierarchy is defined as a system composed of interrelated subsystems, examples of hierarchy include:

- The human body, which is composed of a hierarchy of cells, organs, and subsystems such as the respiratory system, nervous system, digestive system, and so on.
- Physical systems are composed at the macro level of planets, stars, and galaxies, and at the micro level of subatomic particles, atoms, and molecules.
- Social systems consist of individuals, families, communities, tribes or socio-economic groups, and nations.
- A book consists of letters, words, sentences, paragraphs, and chapters.

Note that this is a broader concept of hierarchy than that encountered in most discussions of organization design, where hierarchy is identified with *administrative hierarchy*, in which organizational members are arranged in superior–subordinate relationships and authority flows downward from the top.

Viewed in this broad context of subsystems and component units, there are two key advantages to hierarchical structures:

1   *Economizing on coordination.* As we have noted, the gains from specialization come at the cost of coordination. Suppose there are five programmers designing a piece of customized computer software. If they are structured as a "self-organized team," where coordination is by mutual adjustment (see Figure 6.2a), ten bilateral interactions must be managed. Alternatively, suppose the programmer with the biggest feet is selected to be supervisor. In this simple hierarchy (Figure 6.2b), there are only four relationships to be managed. Of course, this says nothing about the quality of the coordination: if the programmers' work is highly interdependent, hierarchical relationships may not allow for the richness of communication and collaboration that a team structure would permit. As an organization increases in size and complexity, so the communication-economizing benefits of hierarchically arranged modules increase:

    > By breaking up a complex system into discrete pieces – which can then communicate with one another through standard interfaces within a standardized architecture – one can eliminate what would otherwise be an unmanageable spaghetti tangle of interconnections.[17]

FIGURE 6.2 How hierarchy economizes on coordination

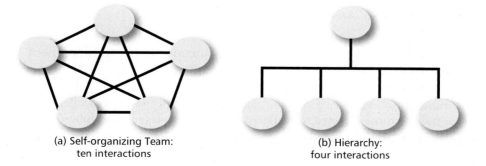

(a) Self-organizing Team:
ten interactions

(b) Hierarchy:
four interactions

2 *Adaptability*. Hierarchical, modular systems are able to evolve more rapidly than unitary systems that are not organized into subsystems. Such adaptability requires some degree of *decomposability*: the ability of each component subsystem to operate with some measure of independence from the other subsystems. Modular systems that allow significant independence for each module are referred to as *loosely coupled*.[18] In developing a new model of automobile, a modular structure permits different subassemblies (engine, brakes, steering, electricals, etc.) to be developed by separate teams that do not need constant communication and coordination with the designers of every other unit.[19] Once developed, defects can be corrected by replacing a single subunit – the engine, the gearbox, or the exhaust system – without having to scrap the entire car. Similar advantages exist for modular organizations. In a divisionalized firm, such as GE, decisions can be made in GE's jet engines business that do not require coordination with GE's other business areas. Similarly, GE can acquire a new business or dispose of an existing subsidiary without having to redesign the entire company.[20]

The efficiency and flexibility advantages of modularity and hierarchical communication are evident in Nelson Mandela's restructuring of the ANC (see Strategy Capsule 6.2). Let's look more closely at administrative hierarchies associated with *bureaucratic* or *mechanistic* organizational forms.

Hierarchy as a Control: Bureaucracy

I have shown that hierarchy is an efficient solution to the problem of *coordination* in organizing complex tasks. To the extent that hierarchy is also a device for exercising control, it is also one solution to the problem of *cooperation* in organizations. The *administrative hierarchy*, in which power is located at the apex of the hierarchy and delegated downward, has been the basic design for large organizations since the Ch'in dynasty of China in 220 BC. Administrative hierarchies operate as *bureaucracies*. According to Max Weber, writing at the end of the 19th century, bureaucracy is based on the following principles:

1 *Specialization* through a "systematic division of labor" with clear job definitions and individual authority limited to the sphere of work responsibilities.

2 *Hierarchical structure* with "each lower office under the control and supervision of a higher one."

3 *Coordination* and *control* through rules and standard operating procedures.

4 *Standardized employment rules and norms.*

5 *Separation of management and ownership.*

6 *Separation of jobs and people*, where the organization is defined by positions and their associated responsibilities and authority, not by individuals; there is no ownership of the position by the individual.

7 *Rational-legal authority* based on "belief in the legality of enacted rules and the right of those elevated to authority under such rules to issue commands."

8 *Formalization* in writing of "administrative acts, decisions, and rules."[21]

STRATEGY CAPSULE 6.2

Hierarchical Structures: The 1952 Mandela Plan for the ANC

Along with many others, I had become convinced that the government intended to declare the ANC (African National Congress) and the SAIC (South African Indian Congress) illegal organizations, just as it had done with the Communist Party. It seemed inevitable that the state would attempt to put us out of business as a legal organization. With this in mind, I approached the National Executive with the idea that we must come up with a contingency plan . . . They instructed me to draw up a plan that would enable the organization to operate from underground. This strategy came to be known as the Mandela-Plan, or simply, M-Plan.

The idea was to set up organizational machinery that would allow the ANC to take decisions at the highest level, which could then be swiftly transmitted to the organization as a whole without calling a meeting. In other words, it would allow the organization to continue to function and enable leaders who were banned to continue to lead. The M-Plan was designed to allow the organization to recruit new members, respond to local and national problems and maintain regular contact between the membership and the underground leadership.

I worked on it for a number of months and came up with a system that was broad enough to adapt itself to local conditions and not fetter individual initiative, but detailed enough to facilitate order. The smallest unit was the cell, which in urban townships consisted of roughly ten houses on a street. A cell steward would be in charge of each of these units. If a street had more than ten houses, a street steward would take charge and the cell stewards would report to him. A group of streets formed a zone directed by a chief steward, who was in turn responsible to the secretariat of the local branch of the ANC. The secretariat was a subcommittee of the branch executive, which reported to the provincial secretary. My notion was that every cell and street steward would know every person and family in his area, so that he would be trusted by his people and know whom to trust. The cell steward arranged meetings, organized political classes, and collected dues. He was the linchpin of the plan.

The plan was accepted and was implemented immediately. Word went out to the branches to begin to prepare for this covert restructuring . . . As part of the M-Plan, the ANC introduced an elementary course of political lectures for its members throughout the country. These lectures were meant not only to educate but to hold the organization together. They were given in secret by branch leaders. Those members in attendance would in turn give the same lectures to others in their homes and communities.

Source: Nelson Mandela, *Long Walk to Freedom* (London: Little, Brown, 1994): 134–5. © 1994, 1995 by Nelson Rolihlahla Mandela. Reprinted by permission of Little, Brown and Co.

Bureaucracies attempt to minimize most of the traits that characterize human beings and their interaction: creativity, personality, variation, and emotion. For this reason, Burns and Stalker describe bureaucratic organizations as *mechanistic*,[22] while Mintzberg calls them *machine bureaucracies*.[23]

Mechanistic and Organic Forms

During the first half of the 20th century, the bureaucratic model dominated thinking about organizational structure. This reflected Weber's clear articulation of the principles of bureaucracy and the fact that most large-scale organizations – the military and civil service in particular – embodied these principles. However, as management theory developed, interest grew in alternatives to bureaucracy.

During the 1950s and 1960s, the *human relations school* recognized that cooperation and coordination within organizations was about social relationships as well as bureaucratic principles. A study of Scottish engineering companies by Burns and Stalker identified two organizational forms: *mechanistic* forms, characterized by bureaucracy, and *organic* forms that were less formal, where coordination relied on mutual adjustment and interaction was more flexible. The mechanistic form was found mainly in stable markets; the organic form predominated in unstable markets with rapid technological change.

Table 6.1 contrasts key characteristics of the two forms.

The relative merits of the two organizational forms depend on the activities undertaken and the surrounding environment. Where an organization is supplying standardized goods or services (beverage cans, blood tests, or haircuts for army inductees) using well-understood processes in an environment where change is slow and predictable, the bureaucratic model with its standard operating procedures and high levels of specialization offers efficiency advantages. The problems occur when the bureaucratic model has to produce heterogeneous outputs from heterogeneous inputs, using poorly understood technologies, in an environment where change requires constant adjustment. Here, the bureaucracy fails because greater organizational flexibility is required.

But even when faced with variability in the outside environment, firms may attempt to retain the advantages of bureaucracy by trying to control variation. McDonald's business system is highly mechanistic, relying heavily upon standardized, formalized working practices that are carefully documented in the company's operating procedures. Making this system work requires that McDonald's carefully controls its inputs to reduce variation: potatoes are carefully selected for size and

TABLE 6.1 Mechanistic vs. organic organizational forms

Feature	Mechanistic	Organic
Task definition	Rigid and highly specialized	Flexible and less narrowly defined
Coordination and control	Rules and directives vertically imposed	Mutual adjustment, common culture
Communication	Vertical	Vertical and horizontal
Knowledge	Centralized	Dispersed
Commitment and loyalty	To immediate superior	To the organization and its goals
Environmental context	Stable with low technological uncertainty	Unstable with significant technological uncertainty and ambiguity

SOURCE: ADAPTED FROM RICHARD BUTLER, *DESIGNING ORGANIZATIONS: A DECISION-MAKING PERSPECTIVE* (LONDON: ROUTLEDGE, 1991): 76.

shape, managers are carefully selected and trained, consumer tastes and expectations are carefully managed through advertising and promotion.

Within companies, the organization of different functions and departments depends on these same variables. Stable, standardized activities such as payroll, treasury, taxation, customer support, and purchasing activities tend to operate well when organized along bureaucratic principles; research, new product development, marketing, and strategic planning require more organic modes of organization.

Rethinking Hierarchy

Hierarchical organizations add layers as they get bigger. Thus, with a fixed span of control of three, a firm with four employees (including the CEO) is organized into two layers, five to 13 employees requires three layers, from 14 to 41 employees requires four layers, and 42 to 122 employees requires five layers. (Sketch this for yourself.) If the hierarchy is run as a bureaucracy with centralized power, growth implies an increasing ratio of managers to operatives, slower decision making, and increased loss of control.[24]

In a stable environment with limited decision-making pressure on top management, such ponderousness is of little consequence. However, in a fast-paced business environment, the slow movement of information up the hierarchy and decisions down the hierarchy can be fatal. As the business environment has become increasingly turbulent, so administrative hierarchy organized along bureaucratic principles has become increasingly unpopular.

At the same time, efforts to reform and restructure corporate hierarchies do not amount to a rejection of hierarchy as an organizing principle. So long as there are benefits from the division of labor, hierarchy is inevitable.[25] The critical issue is to reorganize hierarchies in order to increase responsiveness to external change. The organizational changes that have occurred in giant corporations such as BP and General Electric have retained the basic multidivisional structures of the companies, but reduced the number of hierarchical layers, decentralized decision making, shrunk headquarters staffs, emphasized horizontal rather than vertical communication, and shifted the emphasis of control from *supervision* to *accountability*.[26]

The trend towards decentralization has not been one way. Some companies engage in decentralization followed by a phase of centralization. Thus, BP pursued radical decentralization during 1994–8, but by 2000–4 was re-centralizing decision making and control. Nickerson and Zenger argue that this type of "structural modulation" in a company's formal structure is effective in achieving an optimal balance between centralization and decentralization.[27]

Applying the Principles of Organizational Design

We have established that the fundamental problem of organization is reconciling specialization with coordination and cooperation. The basic design for complex organizations – whether they are business enterprises, religious orders, political associations, or criminal organizations – is hierarchy. The essence of hierarchy is creating specialized units coordinated and controlled by a superior unit. But this does not take us very far. On what basis should specialized units be defined? How should decision-making authority be allocated? And what kind of relationships should there be between different organizational units?

In this section, we will tackle the first two of these questions: the basis of grouping and the allocation of decision-making power. In the next section, we identify some typical organizational structures found in business enterprises. Then, in the following section we shall look at structuring relations between units – the operation and design of management systems.

Defining Organizational Units

In creating a hierarchical structure, on what basis are individuals assigned to organizational units within the firm? This issue is fundamental and complex. Multinational, multiproduct companies are continually grappling with the issue of whether they should be structured around product divisions, country subsidiaries, or functional departments, and periodically they undergo the disruption of changing from one to another. Some of the principal bases for grouping employees are common tasks, products, geography, and process:

- *Tasks*. Organizational units can be created around common tasks. This usually means grouping together employees who do the same job – thus, a firm might create a machine shop, a maintenance department, a secretarial pool, and a sales office.
- *Products*. Where a company offers multiple products, these can provide a basis for structure. In a department store, departments are defined by products: kitchen goods, bedding, lingerie, and so on. PepsiCo comprises three main product groups: PepsiCo Beverages, Frito-Lay (snack foods), and Quaker Foods (cereals and processed foods).
- *Geography*. Where a company serves multiple local markets, organizational units can be defined around these localities. Wal-Mart is organized by individual stores, groups of stores within an area, and groups of areas within a region. The Roman Catholic church is organized into parishes, dioceses, and archdioceses.
- *Process*. A process is a sequence of interlinked activities. An organization may be viewed as a set of processes: the product development process, the manufacturing process, the sales and distribution process, and so on. A process may correspond closely with an individual product, or a process may be dominated by a single task. Functional organizations tend to combine task-based and process-based grouping.

Organizing on the Basis of Coordination Intensity

How do we decide whether to use task, product, geography, or process to define organizational units? The fundamental issue is achieving the coordination necessary to integrate the efforts of different individuals. This implies grouping individuals according to the intensity of their coordination needs. Those individuals whose tasks require the most intensive coordination should work within the same organizational unit.

- In a geographically dispersed organization where communication across distance is difficult, the organization must be built on local units. The ANC is an example (see Strategy Capsule 6.2).

● Where an organization is not particularly diversified in relation to products and does not need to be differentiated by location, but possesses strong functional specializations, then a grouping around functional tasks is appropriate. For example, British Airways is organized primarily around functions: flight operations, engineering, marketing, sales, customer service, human resources, information, and finance.

● Where a company is diversified over many products and these products are substantially different in terms of technology and markets, it is vital that individuals who work on the same product should interact closely – a product-based organization is the appropriate structure. Virtually all diversified companies – General Electric, 3M, Sony, Siemens, and Unilever – are organized by product divisions.

Having created organizational units that bring together individuals whose coordination needs are most intense, the next challenge is to create hierarchical control that permits effective coordination while giving as much operational autonomy as possible to the subordinate units. Oliver Williamson refers to this as the *principle of hierarchical decomposition*. At the operating level (where decision making is high frequency), organization units are created where the interactions are strong. At the strategic level (where decision making is low frequency), a separate organization unit is created to exercise coordination and direction. Hence:

> The hierarchical decomposition principle can be stated as follows: Internal organization should be designated in such a way as to effect quasi-independence between the parts, the high frequency dynamics (operating activities) and low frequency dynamics (strategic planning) should be clearly distinguished, and incentives should be aligned within and between components so as to promote both local and global effectiveness.[28]

To organize according to coordination needs requires understanding the nature of interdependence within an organization. James Thompson distinguished three levels of interdependence: *pooled interdependence* (the loosest), where individuals operate independently but depend on one another's performance; *sequential interdependence*, where the output of one individual is the input of the other; and *reciprocal interdependence* (the most intense), where individuals are mutually dependent. Thompson argued that organizational design needed to begin with creating organizational units where interdependence was the most intense.[29]

Over time, the relative importance of these different dependencies change. Hence, companies need to change the basis on which they define their structure. For example, as trade and communication between countries has become easier and consumer preferences between countries have become more homogeneous, multinational corporations have shifted from geographically based structures to worldwide product divisions.

Other Factors Influencing the Definition of Organizational Units

Coordination requirements are not the only consideration in deciding how to group together employees and activities within the firm. Additional factors that influence the efficiency of different organizational arrangements include:

● *Economies of scale*. There may be advantages in grouping together activities where scale economies are present. Thus, it may be desirable to group together research activities even if there is little coordination among different research projects, simply to exploit scale economies in specialized facilities and technical personnel.

● *Economies of utilization*. It may also be possible to exploit efficiencies from grouping together similar activities that result from fuller utilization of employees. Even though there may be little need for individual maintenance engineers to coordinate with one another, establishing a single maintenance department permits maintenance personnel to be utilized more fully than assigning a maintenance engineer to each manufacturing cell.

● *Learning*. If establishing competitive advantage requires building distinctive capabilities, firms must be structured to maximize learning. Typically, it was assumed that learning was best achieved by grouping together individuals doing similar jobs – creating a manufacturing engineering department, a quality control department, and a finance function. More recently, it has been observed that the specialized functional and discipline-based knowledge may be less important than *architectural knowledge* – knowing how to link together specialized knowledge from different fields. This implies the creation of multifunctional work groups comprising experts from different knowledge bases.

● *Standardization of control systems*. Tasks may be grouped together to achieve economies in standardized control mechanisms. An advantage of the typing pool and the sales department was that employees doing near-identical jobs could be subject to the same system of monitoring, performance measurement, training, and behavioral norms. Creative activities such as research and new product development need to be managed in a different way from routine activities such as manufacturing and accounting – hence they should be located in different organizational units.[30]

Alternative Structural Forms

On the basis of these alternative approaches to grouping tasks and activities, we can identify three basic organizational forms: the functional structure, the multidivisional structure, and the matrix structure.

The Functional Structure

Single-business firms tend to be organized along functional lines. Grouping together functionally similar tasks is conducive to exploiting scale economies, promoting learning and capability building, and deploying standardized control systems. Since cross-functional integration occurs at the top of the organization, functional structures are conducive to a high degree of centralized control by the CEO and top management team.

However, even for single-product firms, functional structures are subject to the problems of cooperation and coordination. Different functional departments develop their own goals, values, vocabularies, and behavioral norms which make cross-functional integration difficult. As the size of the firm increases, the pressure on top management to achieve effective integration increases. Because the different functions of the firm tend to be *tightly coupled* rather than *loosely coupled*, there is limited scope for decentralization. In particular, it is very difficult to operate individual functions as semi-autonomous profit centers.

The real problems arise when the firm grows its range of products and businesses. As we noted with DuPont during the early 20th century, once a functionally organized company expands its product range, coordination within each product area becomes difficult.

Although the long-term trend among very large companies has been for product-based, divisionalized companies to replace functionally organized companies, the trend is not entirely one way. As companies mature, the need for strong centralized control and well-developed functional capabilities has caused some companies to revert to functional structures. For example:

- When John Scully became CEO of Apple in 1984, the company was organized by product: Apple II, Apple III, Lisa, and Macintosh. Despite strong cross-functional coordination within each product group, there was little integration across products. Each product was completely incompatible with the others, and the structure failed to exploit scale economies within functions. Scully's response was to reorganize Apple along functional lines to gain control, reduce costs, and achieve a more coherent product strategy.
- General Motors, pioneer of the multidivisional structure, has adopted a more functional structure. As its strategic priorities have shifted from differentiation and segmentation toward cost efficiency, it has maintained its brand names (Cadillac, Oldsmobile, Chevrolet, Buick), but merged the separate divisions into a more functionally based structure to exploit scale economies and faster technical transfer (see Figure 6.3 and compare it with Figure 6.1).

The Multidivisional Structure

We have seen how the product-based, multidivisional structure emerged during the 20th century in response to the coordination problems caused by diversification. The key advantage of divisionalized structures (whether product based or geographically based) is the potential for decentralized decision making. The multidivisional structure is the classic example of a loose-coupled, modular organization where business-level strategies and operating decisions can be made at the divisional level, while the corporate headquarters concentrates on corporate planning, budgeting, and providing common services.

Central to the efficiency advantages of the multidivisional corporation is the ability to apply a common set of corporate management tools to a range of different businesses. At ITT, Harold Geneen's system of "managing by the numbers" allowed him to cope with over 50 divisional heads reporting directly to him. At British Petroleum, John Browne's system of "performance contracts" allows direct reporting by over 20 "strategic performance units." Divisional autonomy also fosters the development of top management leadership capability among divisional heads – an important factor in CEO succession.

The large, divisionalized corporation is typically organized into three levels: the corporate center, the divisions, and individual business units, each representing a

FIGURE 6.3 General Motors Corporation: organizational structure, 1997

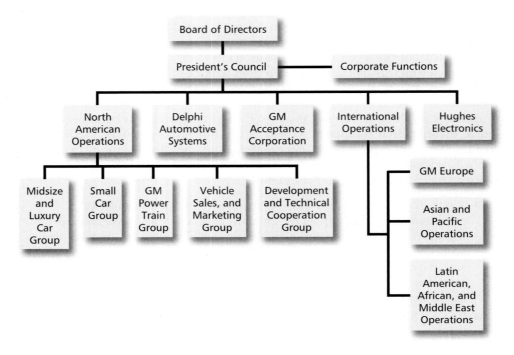

FIGURE 6.4 General Electric: organizational structure, 2002

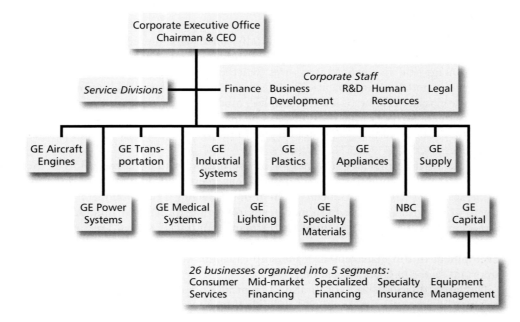

SOURCE: BASED ON INFORMATION IN GENERAL ELECTRIC ANNUAL REPORT, 2001.

distinct business for which financial accounts can be drawn up and strategies formulated. Figure 6.4 shows General Electric's organizational structure at the corporate and divisional levels.

In Chapter 16, we shall look in greater detail at the organization of the multi-business corporation.

Matrix Structures

Whatever the primary basis for grouping, all companies that embrace multiple products, multiple functions, and multiple locations must coordinate across all three dimensions. Organizational structures that formalize coordination and control across multiple dimensions are called *matrix structures*.

Figure 6.5 shows the Shell management matrix (prior to reorganization in 1996). Within this structure, the general manager of Shell's Berre refinery in France reported to his country manager, the managing director of Shell France, but also to his business

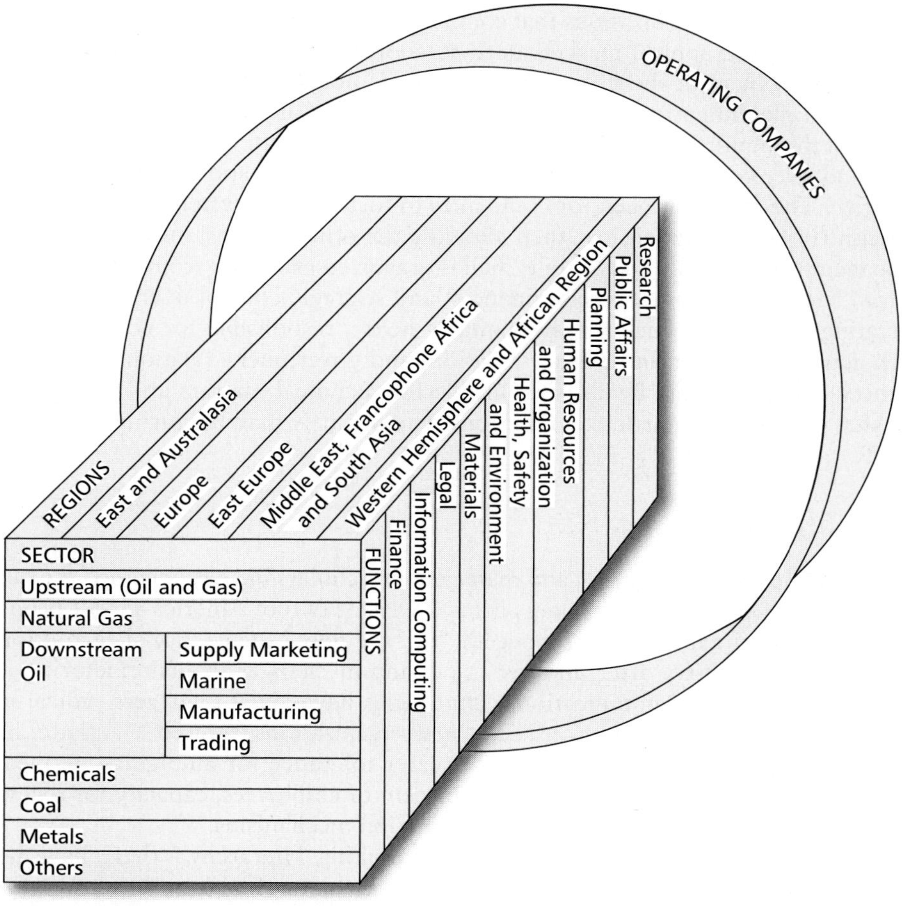

FIGURE 6.5 Royal Dutch Shell Group: pre-1996 matrix structure

sector head, the coordinator of Shell's refining sector, as well as having a functional relationship with Shell's head of manufacturing.

Many diversified, multinational companies, including Philips, Nestlé, and Unilever, adopted matrix structures during the 1960s and 1970s, although in all cases one dimension of the matrix tended to be dominant in terms of authority. Thus, in the old Shell matrix the geographical dimension, as represented by country heads and regional coordinators, had primary responsibility for budgetary control, personnel appraisal, and strategy formulation.

During the past two decades, most large corporations have dismantled or reorganized their matrix structures. Shell abandoned its matrix during 1995–6 in favor of a structure based on four business sectors: upstream, downstream, chemicals, and gas and power. During 2001–2, the Swiss–Swedish engineering giant ABB abandoned its much-lauded matrix structure in the face of plunging profitability and mounting debt. In fast-moving business environments companies have found that the benefits from formally coordinating across multiple dimensions have been outweighed by excessive complexity, larger head office staffs, slower decision making, and diffused authority. Bartlett and Ghoshal observed that matrix structures "led to conflict and confusion; the proliferation of channels created informational logjams as a proliferation of committees and reports bogged down the organization; and overlapping responsibilities produced turf battles and a loss of accountability."[31]

Yet, all complex organizations that comprise multiple products, multiple functions, and multiple geographical markets need to coordinate within each of these dimensions. The problem of the matrix organization is not that it attempts to coordinate across multiple dimensions – in complex organizations such coordination is essential – but that this multiple coordination is over-formalized, resulting in excessive corporate staffs and over-complex systems that slow decision making and dull entrepreneurial initiative. The trend has been for companies to focus formal systems of coordination and control on one dimension, then allowing the other dimensions of coordination to be mainly informal.[32] Thus, while Shell is organized primarily around four business sectors and these sectors exercise financial and strategic control over the individual operating companies, Shell still has country heads, responsible for coordinating all Shell activities in relation to legal, taxation, and government relations within each country, and functional heads, responsible for technical matters and best-practice transfer within their particular function, whether it is manufacturing, marketing, or HR.

Beyond Hierarchy?

For several decades consultants and management scholars have proclaimed the death of hierarchical structures in business firms. In 1993, two of America's most prominent scholars of organization announced: ". . . the new organizational revolution is sweeping one industry after another . . . quantum changes in manufacturing and computer-mediated communication technologies have given managers radical new options for designing organizations." The new organizations featured ". . . flatter hierarchies, decentralized decision making, greater tolerance for ambiguity, permeable internal and external boundaries, empowerment of employees, capacity for renewal, self-organizing units, self-integrating coordination mechanisms."[33]

As I noted in the earlier section on "Rethinking Hierarchy," there have been substantial changes in the way in which corporate hierarchies have been organized.

Layers have been removed; mechanistic formality has been replaced by organic informality. Yet, hierarchy remains as the basic structural form of almost all companies. Are there alternative modes of organization?

Several organizational forms have been identified which, although they comprise some hierarchical elements, are sufficiently distinctive to be regarded as alternative organizational forms:

- *Adhocracies*. In some organizations, the presence of shared values, motivation and willingness to participate, mutual respect, and communication effectiveness may allow a high level of coordination with little need for hierarchy, authority, or tools of control. These organizations, which Henry Mintzberg calls *adhocracies*,[34] feature flexible, spontaneous coordination and collaboration around problem solving and other nonroutine activities. Adhocracies tend to exist among organizations where expertise is prized. In research organizations, new product development groups, jazz bands, and consulting firms, each specialist is valued for his or her expertise and there is little exercise of authority.

- *Team-based and project-based organizations*. Adhocracies are one example of an organizational form based on informal structure with flexible patterns of coordination. Flexibility and adaptability can also be achieved in project-based organizations – common in sectors such as construction, consulting, oil exploration, and engineering services – where business takes the form of projects of limited duration. Because every project is different, and every project goes through a changing sequence of activities, each project needs to be undertaken by a closely interacting team that relies on problem solving and mutual adjustment as well as rules and routines. Increasingly, companies are introducing elements of team- and project-based organizations into their conventional divisional and functional structures. For example, in most divisionalized corporations, new product development, change management, knowledge management, and research is organized in projects and undertaken by teams.

- *Networks*. Localized networks of small, closely interdependent firms have been a feature of manufacturing for many hundreds of years. In Italy such networks are prominent in the clothing industry of Prato, near Florence, and in packaging equipment.[35] Hollywood movie making[36] and microelectronics in Silicon Valley have similar structures – highly specialized firms that coordinate to design and produce complex products. Often these networks feature a central firm that acts as a "systems integrator,"[37] as in the case of Benetton and Toyota.[38] In fast-moving industries, the ability of highly specialized, know-how intensive firms to reconfigure their relationships can be conducive to innovation, product differentiation, and rapid new product development. In the developing world, such networks can be a viable alternative to industrial development where large enterprises are lacking.[39]

These different organizational forms share several common characteristics:

1 *A focus on coordination rather than control*. In contrast to the "command-and-control" hierarchy, these structures focus almost wholly upon achieving coordination. Financial incentives, culture, and social controls take the place of hierarchical control.

2   *Reliance on coordination by mutual adjustment.* Central to all nonhierarchical structures is their dependence on voluntaristic coordination through bilateral and multilateral adjustment. The capacity for coordination through mutual adjustment has been greatly enhanced by information technology.

3   *Individuals in multiple organizational roles.* Reconciling complex patterns of coordination with high levels of flexibility and responsiveness is difficult if job designs and organizational structures are rigidly defined. Adhocracies and team-based organizations feature individuals switching their organizational roles and occupying multiple roles simultaneously. For example, for most of the 1990s, AES had no finance function, no HR function, no safety or environmental affairs functions, and no public relations department. These functions were performed by teams of operatives and line managers.

Management Systems for Coordination and Control

The relationship between management systems and organizational structure is similar to that between the skeleton and bodily systems in the human body. The skeleton provides the framework; the respiratory system, digestive system, and nervous system are the means by which the body operates. Computer networks offer another analogy: the hardware provides the structure and the software provides the systems that make the network operational.

Management systems provide the mechanisms of communication, decision making, and control that allow companies to solve the problems of achieving both coordination and cooperation. Four management systems are of primary importance: the information systems, the strategic planning systems, the financial systems, and the human resource management systems.

Information Systems

Information is fundamental to the operation of all management systems. Communication technology – the telephone and telegraphy – were essential for the emergence of the modern corporation. The computer has had an equally dramatic impact during the past half century. Accounting systems are key components of firms' information systems. They collect, organize, and communicate financial information to top management and other parts of the organization.

Administrative hierarchies are founded on vertical information flows: the upward flow of information to the manager and the downward flow of instructions. The trend towards decentralization and informality in organizations rests on two key aspects of increased information availability: *information feedback* to the individual on job performance, which has made self-monitoring possible, and *information networking*, which has allowed individuals to coordinate their activities voluntarily without hierarchical supervision. For example, a central element of total quality management has been recognition that regular, real-time, performance feedback to employees permits them to take responsibility for quality control, reducing or eliminating the need for supervisors and quality controllers. During the past decade, corporate intranets, web-based information systems, and groupware have transformed organizations' capacity for decentralized coordination.

Strategic Planning Systems

Small enterprises can operate successfully without an explicit strategy. The firm's strategy may exist only in the head of the founder and, unless the founder needs to write a business plan in order to attract outside financing, the strategy may never be articulated. Most large companies have a regular (normally annual) strategic planning process. For a multibusiness company, the strategic planning process creates business plans for the individual divisions that are then integrated into a corporate plan.

Whether formal or informal, systematic or ad hoc, documented or not, the strategy formulation process is an important vehicle for achieving coordination within a company. As discussed in Chapter 1, the strategy process brings together knowledge from different parts of the company, ensures consistency between the decisions being made at different levels and in different parts of the company, and commits managers to ambitious performance targets.

The system through which strategy is formulated varies considerably from company to company. Even after the entrepreneurial startup has grown into a large company, strategy making may remain the preserve of the chief executive. Functional managers may provide key inputs such as financial projections and market analysis, but the key elements of strategy – goals, new business developments, capital investment, and key competitive initiatives – are often decided by the chief executive.[40] At MCI Communications former CEO Orville Wright observed: "We do it strictly top–down at MCI."[41] The first director of strategic planning was warned: "If you ever write a strategic plan, you will be fired!"

As companies mature, their strategic planning processes become more systematized and typically follow an annual cycle. Strategic plans tend to be for three to five years and combine top–down initiatives (indications of performance expectations and identification of key strategic initiatives) and bottom–up business plans (proposed strategies and financial forecasts for individual divisions and business units). After discussion between the corporate level and the individual businesses, the business plans are amended and agreed and integrated into an overall corporate plan that is presented to and agreed by the board of directors. Figure 6.6 shows a typical strategic planning cycle.

The resulting strategic plan typically comprises the following elements:

- *A statement of the goals* the company seeks to achieve over the planning period with regard to both financial targets (e.g., targets for revenue growth, cost reduction, operating profit, return on capital employed, return to shareholders) and strategic goals (e.g., market share, new products, overseas market penetration, and new business development). For example, in BP's February 2006 strategy statement, the company established its "primary objective is to deliver sustainable growth in free cash flow," which it would achieve through "growing production by about 4% a year to 2010" and "delivering further improvements in return on average capital employed relative to our peer group."[42]

- *A set of assumptions or forecasts* about key developments in the external environment to which the company must respond. For example, BP's 2006–10 strategic plan assumed an oil price of $40 a barrel.

FIGURE 6.6 The generic strategic planning cycle

- *A qualitative statement* of how the shape of the business will be changing in relation to geographical and segment emphasis, and the basis on which the company will be establishing and extending its competitive advantage. For example, BP's 2006–10 strategy emphasized capital discipline (capex to increase by $0.5 billion per year) and upgrading BP's asset portfolio by selective divestments of about $3 billion per year.
- *Specific action steps* with regard to decisions and projects, supported by a set of mileposts stating what is to be achieved by specific dates. For example, BP's strategic commitments included 24 start-ups of upstream projects during 2006–8, $6 billion capital expenditure on its Russian joint venture, and growth in wind power to 450 MW.
- *A set of financial projections*, including a capital expenditure budget and outline operating budgets. For example, BP's 2006 strategy statement set a capital expenditure budget of $15–16 billion per year, shareholder distribution of $50 billion during 2006–8, and operating costs to increase at less than the rate of inflation.

Although strategic planning tends to emphasize the specific commitments and decisions that are documented in written strategic plans, the most important aspect of strategic planning is the *strategy process*: the dialog through which knowledge is shared and ideas communicated, the consensus that is established, and the commitment to action and results that is built.

Increasing turbulence in the business environment has caused strategic planning processes to become less formalized and more flexible. For example, among the world's largest petroleum majors, the key changes have been as follows:

- Strategic plans have become less concerned with specific actions and became more heavily focused on performance targets, especially on financial goals such as profitability and shareholder return. Planning horizons have also shortened (two to five years is the typical planning period).

- Companies recognized the impossibility of forecasting the future and based their strategies less on medium- and long-term economic and market forecasts of the future and more on more general issues of strategic direction (in the form of vision, mission, and strategic intent) and alternative views of the future (e.g., using scenario analysis).

- Strategic planning shifted from a *control perspective*, in which senior management used the strategic planning mechanisms as a means of controlling decisions and resource deployments by divisions and business units and departments, toward more of a *coordination perspective*, in which the strategy process emphasized dialog involving knowledge sharing and consensus building. As a result, the process became increasingly informal and put less emphasis on written documents.

- A diminishing role for strategic planning staff as responsibility for strategic decisions and the strategy-making process become located among senior managers.[43]

Financial Planning and Control Systems

Financial flows form the life blood of the enterprise. Revenues from customers provide the funds to pay suppliers and employees and any surplus remunerates owners. If inflows are insufficient to cover outflows, the firm becomes insolvent. Hence, financial systems are inevitably the primary mechanism through which top management seeks to control the enterprise. At the center of financial planning is the *budgetary process*. This involves setting and monitoring financial estimates with regard to income and expenditure over a specified time period, both for the firm as a whole and for divisions and departments. Budgets are in part an estimate of incomes and expenditures for the future, in part a target of required financial performance in terms of revenues and profits, and in part a set of authorizations for expenditure up to specified budgetary limits. Two types of budget are set: the capital expenditure budget and the operating budget.

The Capital Expenditure Budget *Capital expenditure budgets* are established through both top–down and bottom–up processes. From the top down, strategic plans establish annual capital expenditure budgets for the planning period both for the company as a whole and for individual divisions. From the bottom up, capital expenditures are determined by the approval of individual capital expenditure projects. Companies have standardized processes for evaluating and approving projects. Requests for funding are prepared according to a standardized methodology, typically based on a forecast of cash flows discounted at the relevant cost of capital (adjusted for project risk). The extent to which the project's returns are sensitive to key environmental uncertainties is also estimated. Capital expenditure approvals take place at different levels of a company according to their size. Projects up to $5 million might be approved by a business unit head, projects up to $25 million might be approved by divisional top management, larger projects might need to be approved by the top management committee, while the biggest projects require approval by the board of directors.

The Operating Budget The *operating budget* is a pro forma profit and loss statement for the company as a whole and for individual divisions and business units for the upcoming year. It is usually divided into quarters and months to permit continual monitoring and the early identification of variances. The operating budget is part forecast and part target. It is set within the context of the performance targets established by the strategic plan. Each business typically prepares an operating budget for the following year that is then discussed with the top management committee and, if acceptable, approved. At the end of the financial year, business-level divisional managers are called upon to account for the performance over the past year.

Human Resource Management Systems

Strategies may arise from principles, formulae, or divine inspiration, but their implementation depends on people. Ultimately, strategic and financial plans come to nothing unless they influence the ways in which people within the organization behave. To support strategic and financial plans, companies need systems for setting goals, creating incentives and monitoring performance at the level of the individual employee. Human resource management has the task of establishing an incentive system that supports the implementation of strategic plans and performance targets through aligning employee and company goals, and ensuring that each employee has the skills necessary to perform his or her job. The general problem, we have noted, is one of agency: how can a company induce employees to do what it wants?

The problem is exacerbated by the imprecision of employment contracts. Unlike most contracts, employment contracts are vague about employee performance expectations. The employer has the right to assign the employee to a particular category of tasks for a certain number of hours per week, but the amount of work to be performed and the quality of that work are unspecified. Employment contracts give the right to the employer to terminate the contract for unsatisfactory performance by the employee, but the threat of termination is an inadequate incentive: it imposes costs on the employer and only requires the employee to perform better than a new hire would. Moreover, the employer has imperfect information as to employees' work performance – in team production, individual output is not separately observable.[44]

The firm can ensure the employee's compliance with organizational goals using direct supervision of the type that administrative hierarchies are designed to do. The weaknesses of such administrative supervision are, first, there is little incentive for performance in excess of minimum requirements, second, supervision imposes costs, and third, the system presupposes that the supervisor has the knowledge required to direct the employee effectively.

The key to promoting more effective cooperation is for more sophisticated incentives than the threat of dismissal. The principal incentives available to the firm for promoting cooperation are compensation and promotion. The key to designing compensation systems is to link pay either to the inputs required for effective job performance (hours of work, punctuality, effort, numbers of customers visited) or to outputs. The simplest form of output-linked pay is piecework (paying for each unit of output produced) or commission (paying a percentage of the revenue generated).

Relating pay to individual performance is suitable for tasks performed individually. However, firms exist primarily to permit complex coordination among individuals; encouraging such collaboration requires linking pay to team or departmental performance. Where broad-based, enterprise-wide collaboration is required, there may be little alternative to linking pay to company performance through some form of profit sharing.

Corporate Culture as a Control Mechanism

We have already noted how shared values can align the goals of different stakeholders within the organization. More generally, we can view the culture of the organization as a mechanism for achieving coordination and control. *Corporate culture* comprises the beliefs, values, and behavioral norms of the company, which influence how employees think and behave.[45] It is manifest in symbols, ceremonies, social practices, rites, vocabulary, and dress. It is embedded within national cultures, and incorporates elements of social and professional cultures. As a result, a corporate culture may be far from homogeneous: very different cultures may be evident in the research lab, on the factory floor, and within the accounting department. To this extent, culture is not necessarily an integrating device – it can contribute to divisiveness.

Culture can play an important role in facilitating both cooperation and coordination. In companies such as Starbucks, Shell, Nintendo, and Google, strong corporate cultures create a sense of identity among employees that facilitates communication and the building of organizational routines, even across national boundaries. The unifying influence of corporate culture is likely to be especially helpful in assisting coordination through mutual adjustment in large cross-functional teams of the type required for new product development. One of the advantages of culture as a co-ordinating device is that it permits substantial flexibility in the types of interactions it can support.

The extent to which corporate culture assists coordination depends on the characteristics of the culture. Salomon Brothers (now part of Citigroup) was renowned for its individualistic, internally competitive culture; this was effective in motivating drive and individual effort, but did little to facilitate cooperation. The British Broadcasting Corporation has a strong culture that reflects internal politicization, professional values, internal suspicion, and a dedication to the public good, but without a strong sense of customer focus.[46] The culture of a leading British bank was described as one of complaint, negativity, and pessimism.[47] However, culture is far from being a flexible management tool. Cultures take a long time to develop and cannot easily be changed. As the external environment changes, a highly effective culture may become dysfunctional. The Los Angeles Police Department's culture of professionalism and militarism, which made it one of the most admired and effective police forces in America, later contributed to problems of isolation and unresponsiveness to community needs.[48]

Integrating Different Control Mechanisms

The past ten years have seen substantial progress in integrating different control systems. As strategy has become more and more focused on creating shareholder value, so financial planning has become more closely integrated with strategic planning. Performance management systems have also done much to link strategic and financial planning with human resource management – especially in terms of goal setting and performance appraisal. The central aspect of the "metrics" movement within management is the ability not just to establish quantitative goals for individual employees and groups, but to create mechanisms for measuring and reporting the attainment of these targets. The balanced scorecard system outlined in Chapter 2 is but one approach to this linking of employee goals to company-wide goals.

Summary

The internal structure and systems of the firm are not simply a matter of "strategy implementation," which can be separated from the hard analytics of strategy formulation. Not only is strategy implementation inseparable from strategy formulation, but issues of structure and systems are central to the fundamental issues of competitive advantage and strategy choice – the existence of organizational capability in particular.

Despite the importance of these issues, this chapter provides only a brief introduction to some of the key issues in organization design. Subsequent chapters develop many of the themes more fully in relation to particular areas of strategy and particular business contexts. Nevertheless, our progress is limited by the weakness of theory in

this area. Organization theory is an exceptionally rich field that still lacks adequate integration of its component disciplines: sociology, psychology, organizational economics, systems theory, population ecology, and organizational evolution. While business enterprises continue to experiment with new organizational forms, we business school academics are still struggling to articulate general principles of organizational design.

The chapters that follow will have more to say on the organizational structures and management systems appropriate to different strategies and different business contexts. In the final chapter (Chapter 17) we shall explore some of the new trends and new ideas that are reshaping our thinking about organizational design.

Self-Study Questions

1   As DuPont expanded its product range (from explosives into paints, dyes, plastics, and synthetic fibers) why do you think that the functional structure (organized around manufacturing plants and other functions such as sales, finance, and R&D) became unwieldy? Why did the multidivisional structure based on product groups facilitate administration?

2   Explain (with reference to a diversified, divisionalized company such as General Electric) the extent to which the multidivisional company may be regarded as a modular organization. To what degree is each division an independent entity? What are the "standardized interfaces" that allow the divisions to fit together into a coherent whole?

3   Within your own organization (whether a university, company, or not-for-profit organization), which departments or activities are organized mechanistically and which organically? To what extent does the mode of organization fit the different environmental contexts and technologies of the different departments or activities?

4   The examples of Apple Computer and General Motors (see section on "Functional Structure") point to a more general feature of organizational structure over the product life cycle. During the growth phase many companies adopt multidivisional structures, during maturity and decline many companies revert to functional structures. Why might this be?

(*Note*: you may wish to refer to Chapter 10, which outlines the main features of the life cycle model.)

5   Draw an organizational chart for a business school that you are familiar with. Does the school operate with a matrix structure (e.g. are there functional/discipline-based departments together with units managing individual programs)? Which dimension of the matrix is more powerful, and how effectively do the two dimensions coordinate? How would you reorganize the structure to make the school more efficient and effective?

Notes

1   G. Parker, *The Grand Strategy of Philip II* (New Haven: Yale University Press, 1998).

2   "Daimler Open the Door to Disposal of Chrysler," *Financial Times*, February 15, 2007: 1; S. Finkelstein, *The Daimler Chrysler Merger*, Tuck School of Business, Dartmouth College, 2002.

3   T. Peters, "Strategy Follows Structure," *California Management Review*, 26 (Spring 1984): 114–28.

4   R. Whittington, A. Pettigrew, S. Peck, E. Fenton, and M. Conyon, "Change and Complementarities in the New Competitive Landscape," *Organization Science* 10 (1999): 583–96.

5   A. D. Chandler, *The Visible Hand: The Managerial Revolution in American Business* (Cambridge, MA: MIT Press, 1977): Chapter 2.

6   A. D. Chandler, *Strategy and Structure* (Cambridge: MIT Press, 1962); Chandler, *The Visible Hand*, op. cit.

7   Chandler, *Strategy and Structure*, op. cit.: 382–3.

8   http://heritage.dupont.com/floater/fl_management/floater.shtml

9   A. P. Sloan, *My Years at General Motors* (London: Sidgwick & Jackson, 1963): 42–56.

10   H. Mintzberg, *Structure in Fives: Designing Effective Organizations* (Englewood Cliffs: Prentice Hall, 1993): 2.

11   A. Smith, *The Wealth of Nations* (London: Dent, 1910): 5.

12   S. Ross, "The Economic Theory of Agency," *American Economic Review*, 63 (1973): 134–9; K. Eisenhardt, "Agency Theory: An Assessment and Reviews," *Academy of Management Review*, 14 (1989): 57–74.

13   M. Conyon, S. Peck, G. Sadler, and L. Read, "The Structure of Executive Compensation Contracts: UK Evidence," *Long Range Planning* 33 (2000): 478–503.

14   T. Peters and R. Waterman, *In Search of Excellence* (New York: Harper & Row, 1982).

15   W. G. Ouchi, *Theory Z* (Reading, MA: Addison-Wesley, 1981).

16   H. A. Simon, "The Architecture of Complexity," *Proceedings of the American Philosophical Society* 106 (1962): 467–82.

17   R. N. Langlois, "Modularity in Technology and Organization," *Journal of Economic Behavior and Organization* 49 (September 2002): 19–37.

18   J. D. Orton and K. E. Weick, "Loosely Coupled Systems: A Reconceptualization," *Academy of Management Review* 15 (1990): 203–23.

19   M. Sako and F. Murray, "Modular Strategies in Car and Computers," *Financial Times*, Mastering Strategy Part 11 (December 6, 1999): 4–7.

20   Modularity in organizations is explored in a number of articles. See R. Sanchez and J. T. Mahoney, "Modularity, Flexibility, and Knowledge Management in Product and Organizational Design," *Strategic Management Journal* 17, Winter Special Issue (1996): 63–76; M. A. Schilling, "Toward a General Modular Systems Theory and its Application to Interfirm Product Modularity," *Academy of Management Review* 25 (2000): 312–34; C. Baldwin and K. Clark, "Managing in an Age of Modularity," *Harvard Business Review* (September–October 1997): 84–93.

21   The quotes in this section are from Max Weber's *Economy and Society: An Outline of Interpretive Sociology* (Berkeley: University of California Press, 1968).

22   T. Burns and G. M. Stalker, *The Management of Innovation* (London: Tavistock Institute, 1961).

23   H. Mintzberg, op. cit.: Chapter 9.

24   The control loss phenomenon in hierarchies is analyzed in O. E. Williamson, "Hierarchical Control and Optimal Firm Size," *Journal of Political Economy* 75 (1967): 123–38.

25   H. J. Leavitt, "Why Hierarchies Thrive," *Harvard Business Review* (March 2003): 97–102.

26   R. Whittington and A. Pettigrew, "New Notions of Organizational Fit," *Financial Times*, Mastering Strategy Part 10 (November 29, 1999): 8–10.

27   J. Nickerson and T. Zenger, "Being Efficiently Fickle: A Dynamic Theory of Organizational Choice," *Organization Science* 13 (September–October 2002): 547–67.

28 O. E. Williamson, "The Modern Corporation: Origins, Evolution, Attributes," *Journal of Economic Literature* 19 (1981): 1537–68.

29 J. D. Thompson, *Organizations in Action* (New York: McGraw-Hill, 1967). The nature of interdependence in organizational processes is revisited in T. W. Malone, K. Crowston, J. Lee, and B. Pentland, "Tools for Inventing Organizations: Toward a Handbook of Organizational Processes," *Management Science* 45 (March 1999): 489–504.

30 The need for organizations to differentiate management and organization between different functional departments and product units is discussed in P. R. Lawrence and J. W. Lorsch, *Organization and Environment* (Boston: Harvard Business School Press, 1986).

31 C. A. Bartlett and S. Ghoshal, "Matrix Management: Not a Structure, a Frame of Mind," *Harvard Business Review* (July–August 1990): 138–45.

32 "A Survey of the Company: The New Organization," *Economist* (January 21, 2006).

33 R. Daft and A. Lewin, "Where are the theories for the new organizational forms?" *Organization Science* 3 (1993): 1–6.

34 H. Mintzberg, op. cit.: Chapter 12.

35 M. H. Lazerson and G. Lorenzoni, "The Firms that Feed Industrial Districts: A Return to the Italian Source," *Industrial and Corporate Change* 8 (1999): 235–66; G. Lorenzoni and A. Lipparini, "The leveraging of interfirm relationships as a distinctive organizational capability: a longitudinal study," *Strategic Management Journal* 20 (1999): 317–38; A. Grandori, *Interfirm Networks* (London: Routledge, 1999).

36 R. J. DeFilippi and M. B. Arthur, "Paradox in Project-based Enterprise: The Case of Film Making," *California Management Review* 42 (1998): 186–91.

37 G. Lorenzoni and C. Baden-Fuller, "Creating a Strategic Center to Manage a Web of Partners,"

38 J. H. Dyer and K. Nobeoka, "Creating and managing a high-performance knowledge-sharing network: the Toyota case," *Strategic Management Journal* 21 (2000): 345–67; A. Camuffo, P. Romano, and A. Vinelli, "Back to the Future: Benetton Transforms Its Global Network," *Sloan Management Review* 43 (Fall 2001): 46–52.

39 D. Wheeler, K. McKague, J. Thomson, R. Davies, J. Medalye, and M. Prada, "Sustainable Local Enterprise Networks," *Sloan Management Review* (Fall 2005): 33–40.

40 W. C. Finnie, *Hands-On Strategy: The Guide to Crafting Your Company's Strategy* (New York: John Wiley, 1994).

41 *MCI Communications: Planning for the 1990s*, Case No. 9-190-136 (Boston: Harvard Business School, 1990): 1.

42 BP Strategy and Fourth Quarter 2005 Results Presentation, February 7, 2006 (www.bp.com).

43 R. M. Grant, "Strategic Planning in a Turbulent Environment: Evidence from the Oil Majors," *Strategic Management Journal* 24 (2003): 491–518. Similar findings have been reported by the American Productivity and Quality Center among "best practice companies" (*Strategic Planning: Final Report*, Houston: APQC, 1996).

44 A. Alchian and H. Demsetz, "Production, Information Costs, and Economic Organization," *American Economic Review* 62 (1972): 777–97.

45 E. H. Schein, "Organizational Culture," *American Psychologist* 45 (1990): 109–19.

46 Tom Burns, *The BBC: Public Institution and Private World* (London: Macmillan, 1977).

47 J. Weeks, *Unpopular Culture: The Ritual of Complaint in a British Bank* (Chicago: University of Chicago Press, 2004).

48 "LAPD: Storming the Rampart," *Economist* (December 2, 2000): 72.

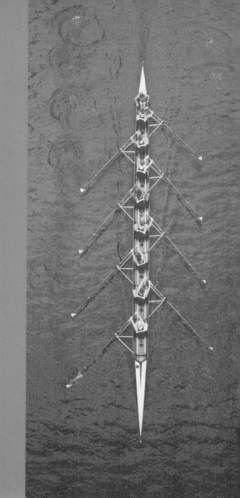

III

THE ANALYSIS OF COMPETITIVE ADVANTAGE

7

The Nature and Sources of Competitive Advantage

One Saturday afternoon in downtown Chicago, Milton Friedman, the famous free-market economist, was shopping with his wife.

"Look, Milton!" exclaimed Mrs. Friedman. "There's a $20 bill on the sidewalk!"

"Don't be foolish, my dear," replied the Nobel laureate. "If that was a $20 bill, someone would have picked it up by now."

—ECONOMIST'S ANECDOTE OF DOUBTFUL AUTHENTICITY

OUTLINE

Introduction and Objectives

In this chapter, we integrate and develop the elements of competitive advantage that we have analyzed in prior chapters. Chapter 1 noted that a firm can earn superior profitability either by locating in an attractive industry or by establishing a competitive advantage over its rivals. Of these two, competitive advantage is the more important. As competition has intensified across almost all industries, very few industry environments can guarantee secure returns; hence, the primary goal of a strategy is to establish a position of competitive advantage for the firm.

Chapters 3 and 5 provided the two primary components of our analysis of competitive advantage. The last part of Chapter 3 analyzed the external sources of competitive advantage: customer requirements and the nature of competition determine the *key success factors* within a market. Chapter 5 analyzed the internal sources of competitive advantage: the potential for the firm's resources and capabilities to establish and sustain competitive advantage.

This chapter looks more deeply at competitive advantage. We focus on the relationship between competitive advantage and the competitive process. Competition provides the incentive for establishing advantage and is the means by which advantage is eroded. Only by understanding the characteristics of competition in a market can we identify the opportunities for competitive advantage.

By the time you have completed this chapter you will be able to:

● Identify the circumstances in which a firm can create a competitive advantage over a rival.

● Understand how responsiveness and innovation can create competitive advantage.

● Predict the potential for competition to erode competitive advantage through imitation.

● Recognize the role of resource conditions in creating imperfections in the competitive process and, therefore, opportunities for competitive advantage.

● Distinguish the two primary types of competitive advantage: cost advantage and differentiation advantage.

● Apply this analysis to assess the potential for a business strategy to establish and sustain competitive advantage given the characteristics of the industry setting.

The Emergence of Competitive Advantage

To understand how competitive advantage emerges, we must first understand what competitive advantage is. Most of us can recognize competitive advantage when we see it: Dell Computer has a competitive advantage in the supply of personal computers, Wal-Mart has a competitive advantage in discount retailing, Toyota has a competitive advantage in making cars. Defining competitive advantage is troublesome. At a basic level we can define it as follows:

> When two or more firms compete within the same market, one firm possesses a competitive advantage over its rivals when it earns (or has the potential to earn) a persistently higher rate of profit.

The problem here is that, if we identify competitive advantage with superior profitability, why do we need the concept of competitive advantage at all? The key difference is that competitive advantage may not be revealed in higher profitability – a firm may forgo current profit in favor of investment in market share, technology, customer loyalty, or executive perks.[1]

External Sources of Change

Differences in profitability between competing firms are a disequilibrium phenomenon[2] – hence, competitive advantage emerges when change occurs. The source of the change may be external or internal to the industry: Figure 7.1 illustrates several sources. For an external change to create competitive advantage, the change must have differential effects on companies because of their different resources and capabilities or strategic positioning. For example, during 2000–3, General Motors' return on equity was 14.4%; Toyota's was 8.8%. During 2004–5, General Motors' ROE was −14.4%; Toyota's was 13.5%. Over the period oil prices had tripled and demand had shifted, increasing to the transitional economies. Toyota, with its fuel-efficient product range and superior distribution in Asia and Eastern Europe, was the advantaged competitor.

FIGURE 7.1 The emergence of competitive advantage

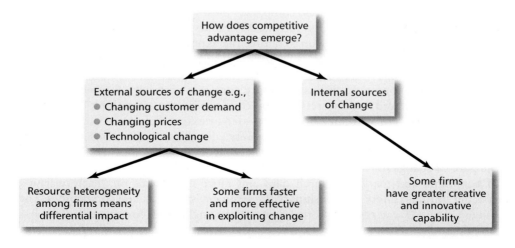

The extent to which external change creates competitive advantage and disadvantage depends on the magnitude of the change and the extent of firms' strategic differences. The more turbulent an industry's environment, the greater the number of sources of change, and the greater the differences in firms' resources and capabilities, the greater the dispersion of profitability within the industry. In the world tobacco industry, the external environment is comparatively stable and the leading firms pursue similar strategies with similar resources and capabilities. The result is that competitive advantages, as reflected in interfirm profit differentials, tend to be small. The toy industry, on the other hand, experiences rapid and unpredictable changes in demand, technology, and fashion. The leading companies pursue different strategies and have different resources and capabilities. As a result, profitability differences are wide and variable over time.

Competitive Advantage from Responsiveness to Change

The impact of external change on competitive advantage also depends on firms' ability to respond to change. Any external change creates opportunities for profit. The ability to identify and respond to opportunity lies in the core management capability that we call *entrepreneurship*.[3] To the extent that external opportunities are fleeting or subject to first-mover advantage, speed of response is critical to exploiting business opportunity. An unexpected rain shower creates an upsurge in the demand for umbrellas. Those street vendors who are quickest to position themselves outside a busy railroad station will benefit most.

As markets become increasingly turbulent, so responsiveness to external change has become increasingly important as a source of competitive advantage.

- Wal-Mart's ability consistently to outperform Kmart and other discount retailers is based on a business system that responds quickly and effectively to changes in demand. Wal-Mart's distribution and purchasing are driven by point-of-sale data, resulting in low inventories, few stockouts, and few forced markdowns. However, at the heart of Wal-Mart's fast-response capability is the encouragement and rewarding of initiative at all levels of the company.

- Nokia's continued market and profit leadership in mobile phones owes much to its rapid response to changes in technology and customer preferences.

Responsiveness also involves anticipating changes in the basis of competitive advantage. As an industry evolves, companies must adjust their strategies and their capabilities to shifting key success factors. Monsanto showed considerable foresight in building its competitive position to outlive the expiration in 1992 of its patents on its artificial sweetener Nutrasweet. In addition to heavy promotion of the Nutrasweet brand name and its "swirl" logo, Monsanto invested in scale-efficient production facilities, signed long-term exclusive supply contracts with key customers (such as Coca-Cola), and used trade secrets to protect its production know-how.[4]

Responsiveness to the opportunities provided by external change requires one key resource – information – and one key capability – flexibility. Information is necessary to identify and anticipate external changes. This requires environmental scanning. As the pace of change has accelerated, firms are less dependent on conventional analysis of economic and market research data and more dependent on "early warning systems" through direct relationships with customers, suppliers, and competitors. The faster a company can respond in real time to changing market circumstances, the less

TABLE 7.1 New product development performance by Japanese, US, and European auto producers

	Japanese volume producer	US volume producer	European volume producer	European high-end specialist
Average lead time (months)	42.6	61.9	57.6	71.5
Engineering hours (in millions)	1.2	3.5	3.4	3.4
Total product quality index	58	41	41	84

it needs to forecast the future. Short cycle times are a key requirement for fast response capability:

- Dell Computer is a master of speed and agility. A custom order placed at 9 a.m. on Monday can be on a delivery truck by 9 p.m. Tuesday. This permits Dell to customize each computer to the customer's specifications and to operate with under 10 days' inventory, which not only cuts costs but permits Dell to adjust rapidly to changes in market demand and technology.[5]
- The Zara chain of retail clothing stores owned by the Spanish company Inditex has a tightly integrated vertical structure that cuts the time between a garment's design and retail delivery to under three weeks – the industry norm is six to nine months. This allows Zara to identify emerging fashion trends and launch new styles on the market far quicker than its mass-market competitors.[6]

Emphasis on speed as a source of competitive advantage is central to the Boston Consulting Group's concept of *time-based competition.*[7] The premise that speed is the only real source of advantage in today's economy was the primary rationale behind the founding of *Fast Company* magazine in 1995. In automobiles, speed of new product development has been a major advantage of Japanese companies (see Table 7.1). However, only with the advent of the internet, real-time electronic data exchange, and business process reengineering have companies been able to reduce cycle times drastically through radical changes in operations, strategy, and organization.

Competitive Advantage from Innovation: "New Game" Strategies

The changes that create competitive advantage may be internal as well as external. Internal change is generated by innovation. Innovation not only creates competitive advantage, it provides a basis for overturning the competitive advantage of other firms. Schumpeter's view of the competitive process as "a gale of creative destruction" viewed market leadership as being destroyed by innovation rather than eroded by imitation. Innovation is typically thought of in its technical sense: the new products or processes that embody new ideas and new knowledge. In a business, however, innovation includes new approaches to doing business – *strategic innovation* – including new business models (see Strategy Capsule 7.1).

STRATEGY CAPSULE 7.1

Gary Hamel on the Quest for New Business Models

In *Leading the Revolution*, Gary Hamel, chairman of the consulting firm Strategos and visiting professor at London Business School, argues that the age of continuity is over and we have now entered the age of revolution where the value of incumbency is being eroded and those companies that embrace discontinuous change will be the winners. The revolutionaries will win through innovatory business concepts embodied in new business models:

In the new economy, the unit of analysis for innovation is not a product or a technology – it's a business concept. The building blocks of a business concept and a business model are the same – a business

model is simply a business concept that has been put into practice. Business concept innovation is the capacity to imagine dramatically different business concepts or dramatically new ways of differentiating existing business concepts. Business concept innovation is thus the key to creating new wealth. Competition within a broad domain – be it financial services, communications, entertainment, publishing, education, energy, or any other field – takes place not between products or companies, but between business models.

Source: G. Hamel, *Leading the Revolution* (Boston: Harvard Business School Press, 2000).

What does "strategic innovation" involve? Most commonly it involves creating value for customers from novel experiences, products, or product delivery or bundling. The competition in the retail sector is driven by a constant quest for new retail concepts and formats. This may take the form of: bigger stores with greater variety (Toys-R-Us, Home Depot); augmented customer service (Nordstrom); novel approaches to display and store layout (Sephora in cosmetics).

Strategic innovation may also be based on redesigned processes and novel organizational designs:

- In the US steel industry, Nucor achieved unrivaled productivity and flexibility by combining new process technologies, flat and flexible organizational structures, and innovative management systems. Since 1997, it has been the biggest steel producer in the US.

- Southwest Airlines' point-to-point, no-frills airline service using a single type of plane and flexible, nonunion employees has made it the only consistently profitable airline in North America and the model for budget airlines throughout the world.

- Nike built its large and successful businesses on a business system that totally reconfigured the traditional shoe-manufacturing value chain. To begin with, Nike does not manufacture shoes – indeed, it manufactures little of anything. It designs, markets, and distributes shoes, but its primary activity is the coordination of a vast and complex global network involving design and market research (primarily in the US), the production (under contract) of components

(primarily in Korea and Taiwan), and the contract assembly of shoes (in China, the Philippines, India, Thailand, and other low-wage countries).
- Apple Computer's resurgence during 2003–6 is the result of its reinvention of the recorded music business by combining an iconic MP3 player with its iTunes music download service.

How do we go about formulating innovative strategies? Are new approaches to competing and delivering superior value the result of pure creativity, or are there analyses and ways of thinking that can lead us in the right direction? The management literature suggests several approaches:

- McKinsey & Company's concept of *new game strategy* involves reconfiguring the industry value chain in order to change the "rules of the game." Strategy Capsule 7.2 outlines a successful new game strategy.
- Charles Baden-Fuller and John Stopford argue that strategic innovation often involves delivering unprecedented customer satisfaction through combining performance dimensions that were previously viewed as conflicting. For example, Toyota's "lean production system" combines low cost, high quality, and innovative product differentiation. Richardson, a Sheffield-based cutlery manufacturer, uses process technology, innovatory design, and an entrepreneurial culture to supply kitchen knives that combine low price, sharpness, durability, and attractive designs.[8]
- Kim and Mauborgne's *blue ocean strategy* emphasizes the attractions of creating new markets. Blue oceans may comprise entirely new industries (Apple's pioneering of the personal computer industry), or recreating existing industries (Cirque du Soleil in the circus business).[9]
- Gary Hamel argues that strategic innovation extends beyond new products, new markets and new technologies. Innovations in management – Procter & Gamble's invention of brand management, General Electric's unique approach to management development, Toyota's lean production system – are the strongest foundation for competitive advantage.[10]

Sustaining Competitive Advantage

Once established, competitive advantage is subject to erosion by competition. The speed with which competitive advantage is undermined depends on the ability of competitors to challenge either by imitation or innovation. Imitation is the most direct form of competition; thus, for competitive advantage to be sustained over time, barriers to imitation must exist. Rumelt uses the term *isolating mechanisms* to describe "barriers that limit the *ex post* equilibration of rents among individual firms."[11] The more effective these isolating mechanisms are, the longer competitive advantage can be sustained against the onslaught of rivals. In most industries the erosion of the competitive advantage of industry leaders is a slow process. Even over periods of a decade and more, interfirm profit differentials tend to persist, with little change in the identities of the leaders and the laggards.[12]

To identify the sources of isolating mechanisms, we need to examine the process of competitive imitation. For one firm successfully to imitate the strategy of another, it must meet four conditions:

STRATEGY CAPSULE 7.2

Reconfiguring the Value Chain for New Game Strategies: Savin and Xerox

For most of the 1970s, Xerox possessed a near monopoly position in the North American market for plain-paper copiers. Xerox's dominance rested, first, upon the wall of patents that the company had built over several decades and, second, on the scale economies and reputation that its market dominance conferred. The first company to compete effectively with Xerox during the late 1970s was Savin. The basis of Savin's challenge was an approach that sought not to imitate Xerox's success but to compete in an entirely different manner.

Savin developed and patented a new low-cost technology. Its product design permitted the use of standardized parts that could be sourced in volume from Japan. Assembly was also undertaken in Japan. The result was a product whose cost was about half that of Xerox's. To avoid the costs of leasing and the need for a costly direct sales force, Savin distributed through existing office equipment dealers.

The principal differences between the approach of Savin and that of Xerox can be seen by comparing the main activities of the companies:

Value chain activity	Xerox	Savin
Technology and design	Dry xerography High copy speed Many features	Liquid toner Low copy speed Few features and options
Manufacture	Most manufacturing (including components) in house	Machines sourced from Ricoh in Japan
Product range	Wide range of machines	Narrow range of machines for different volumes and uses
Marketing	Machines leased to customers	Machines sold to customers
Distribution	Direct sales force	Distribution through dealers
Service	Directly operated service organization	Service by dealers and independent service engineers

Source: Roberto Buaron, "New-Game Strategies," *McKinsey Staff Paper* (March 1980); reprinted in *On Strategy* (McKinsey Quarterly Anthologies, 2000): 34–6.

● *Identification.* The firm must be able to identify that a rival possesses a competitive advantage.

● *Incentive.* Having identified that a rival possesses a competitive advantage (as shown by above-average profitability), the firm must believe that by investing in imitation, it too can earn superior returns.

● *Diagnosis.* The firm must be able to diagnose the features of its rival's strategy that give rise to the competitive advantage.

FIGURE 7.2 Sustaining competitive advantage: types of isolating mechanism

REQUIREMENT FOR IMITATION	ISOLATING MECHANISM
Identification	—*Obscure* superior performance
Incentives for imitation	—*Deterrence*: signal aggressive intentions to imitators —*Preemption*: exploit all available investment opportunities
Diagnosis	—Rely on multiple sources of competitive advantage to create "*causal ambiguity*"
Resource acquisition	—Base competitive advantage on resources and capabilities that are *immobile* and *difficult to replicate*

- *Resource acquisition.* The firm must be able to acquire through transfer or replication the resources and capabilities necessary for imitating the strategy of the advantaged firm.

Figure 7.2 illustrates these stages and the types of isolating mechanism that exist at each stage.

Identification: Obscuring Superior Performance

A simple barrier to imitation is to obscure the firm's superior profitability. In the 1948 movie classic *The Treasure of the Sierra Madre*, Humphrey Bogart and his partners went to great lengths to obscure their find from other gold prospectors.[13] The Mongolian Gold Rush of 2002–3 also featured secretive behavior as companies with good initial test results sought to acquire exploration rights on nearby properties.[14]

Avoiding competition through avoiding disclosure of a firm's profits is much easier for a private than a public company. For Mars Ltd., the nondisclosure of financial results may help the firm in protecting its highly profitable pet food and confectionery businesses.

The desire to avoid competition may be so strong as to cause companies to forgo short-run profits. The *theory of limit pricing*, in its simplest form, postulates that a firm in a strong market position sets prices at a level that just fails to attract entrants.[15]

Deterrence and Preemption

A firm may avoid competition by undermining the incentives for imitation. If a firm can persuade rivals that imitation will be unprofitable, it may be able to avoid competitive challenges. In Chapter 4 we discussed strategies of deterrence and the role of signaling and commitment in supporting them.[16]

As we have seen, reputation is critically important in making threats credible. Brandenburger and Nalebuff argue that in the aspartame market, Nutrasweet's aggressive price war against the Holland Sweetener Company deterred other would-be entrants.[17]

A firm can also deter imitation by preemption – occupying existing and potential strategic niches to reduce the range of investment opportunities open to the challenger. Preemption can take many forms:

- Proliferation of product varieties by a market leader can leave new entrants and smaller rivals with few opportunities for establishing a market niche. Between 1950 and 1972, for example, the six leading suppliers of breakfast cereals introduced 80 new brands into the US market.[18]

- Large investments in production capacity ahead of the growth of market demand also preempt market opportunities for rivals. Monsanto's heavy investment in plants for producing Nutrasweet ahead of its patent expiration was a clear threat to would-be producers of generic aspartame.

- Patent proliferation can protect technology-based advantage by limiting competitors' technical opportunities. In 1974, Xerox's dominant market position was protected by a wall of over 2,000 patents, most of which were not used. When IBM introduced its first copier in 1970, Xerox sued it for infringing 22 of these patents.[19]

The ability to sustain competitive advantage through preemption depends on the presence of two imperfections of the competitive process. First, the market must be small relative to the minimum efficient scale of production, such that only a very small number of competitors is viable. Second, there must be first-mover advantage that gives an incumbent preferential access to information and other resources, putting rivals at a disadvantage.

Diagnosing Competitive Advantage: "Causal Ambiguity" and "Uncertain Imitability"

If a firm is to imitate the competitive advantage of another, it must understand the basis of its rival's success. In most industries, there is a serious identification problem in linking superior performance to the resources and capabilities that generate that performance. Consider the remarkable success of Wal-Mart in discount retailing. It is easy for Kmart to point to the differences between Wal-Mart and itself. As one Wal-Mart executive commented: "Retailing is an open book. There are no secrets. Our competitors can walk into our stores and see what we sell, how we sell it, and for how much." The difficult task is to identify which differences are the critical determinants of superior profitability. Is it Wal-Mart's store locations (typically in small towns with little direct competition)? Its tightly integrated supply chain? Its unique management system? The information system that supports Wal-Mart's logistics and decision-making practices? Or is it the culture that combines rural American values of thrift, simplicity, and hard work with company traditions of family-like unity, customer attentiveness, and entrepreneurial drive?

The problem for Kmart and other wannabe Wal-Marts is what Lippman and Rumelt refer to as *causal ambiguity*.[20] The more multidimensional a firm's competitive advantage and the more each dimension of competitive advantage is based on complex bundles of organizational capabilities rather than individual resources, the more difficult it is for a competitor to diagnose the determinants of success. The outcome of causal ambiguity is *uncertain imitability*: where there is ambiguity associated with the causes of a competitor's success, any attempt to imitate that strategy is subject to uncertain success.

Acquiring Resources and Capabilities

Having diagnosed the sources of an incumbent's competitive advantage, the imitator can mount a competitive challenge only by assembling the resources and capabilities necessary for imitation. As we saw in Chapter 5, a firm can acquire resources and capabilities in two ways: it can buy them or it can build them. The period over which a competitive advantage can be sustained depends critically on the time it takes to acquire and mobilize the resources and capabilities needed to mount a competitive challenge.

There is little to add here to the discussion of transferability and replicability in Chapter 5. The ability to buy resources and capabilities from outside factor markets depends on their transferability between firms. Even if resources are mobile, the market for a resource may be subject to transaction costs – costs of buying and selling arising from search costs, negotiation costs, contract enforcement costs, and transportation costs. Transaction costs are greater for highly differentiated (or "idiosyncratic") resources.[21]

The alternative to buying a resource or capability is to create it through internal investment. As we noted in Chapter 5, where capabilities are based on organizational routines, accumulating the coordination and learning required for their efficient operation can take considerable time.

Businesses that require the integration of a number of complex, team-based routines may take years to reach the standards set by industry leaders. GM's attempt to transfer Toyota-style, team-based production from its NUMMI joint venture at Fremont, California, to the GM Van Nuys plant 400 miles to the south involved complex problems of learning and adjustment that remained unsolved two years after the program had begun.[22]

Conversely, where a competitive advantage does not require the application of complex, firm-specific resources, imitation is likely to be easy and fast. In financial services, many new products such as money market checking accounts, exchange traded funds, zero coupon bonds, interest rate swaps, and other derivatives require resources and capabilities that are widely distributed among banks. Hence, imitation of financial innovations is swift. Despite the boom in the demand for personal organizers in the 1990s, the originator, Filofax, faced many imitators. In 2001, Filofax was sold for a mere £17 million.

First-mover Advantage

A firm's ability to challenge an incumbent depends on the extent and the sources of first-mover advantage in the market. The idea of first-mover advantage is that the initial occupant of a strategic position or niche gains access to resources and capabilities that a follower cannot match. The simplest form of first-mover advantage is a patent or copyright. First movers can also gain preferential access to scarce resources. For example, Starbucks has taken prime locations in shopping malls and airports for its coffee shops. First movers may also be able to use the profit streams from their early entry to build resources and capabilities more rapidly than latecomers.[23]

We shall return to the issue of first-mover versus follower advantages when we consider competitive advantage in emerging and technology-based industries (Chapter 11).

Competitive Advantage in Different Market Settings

Profiting from competitive advantage requires that the firm first establishes a competitive advantage, and then sustains its advantage for long enough to reap the rewards. To identify opportunities for establishing and sustaining competitive advantage requires that we understand the competitive process in the specific market. For competitive advantage to exist, there must be some imperfection of competition. To understand these imperfections in the competitive process, we need to identify the types of resources and capabilities necessary to compete and the circumstances of their availability.

Our initial discussion of the nature of business in Chapter 1 identified two types of value-creating activity: trading and production. Trading involves arbitrage across space (trade) and time (speculation). Production involves the physical transformation of inputs into outputs. These different types of business activity correspond to different market types: trading markets and production markets (see Figure 7.3). We begin with a discussion of a special type of trading market: an efficient market.

FIGURE 7.3 Competitive advantage in different industry settings: trading and production

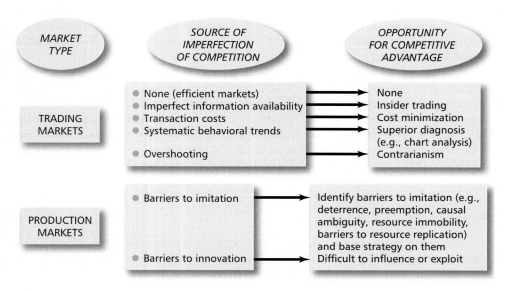

Efficient Markets: The Absence of Competitive Advantage

In Chapter 3, we introduced the concept of perfect competition. Perfect competition exists where there are many buyers and sellers, no product differentiation, no barriers to entry or exit, and free flow of information. In equilibrium, all firms earn the competitive rate of profit, which equals the cost of capital. The closest real-world examples of perfect competition are financial and commodity markets (for example, the markets for securities, foreign exchange, and grain futures). These markets are sometimes described as *efficient*. An *efficient market* is one in which prices reflect all available information. Because prices adjust instantaneously to newly available information, no market trader can expect to earn more than any other. Any differences in *ex post* returns reflect either different levels of risk selected by different traders or purely random factors (luck). Because all available information is reflected in current prices, no trading rules based on historical price data or any other available information can offer excess returns: it is not possible to "beat the market" on any consistent basis. In other words, competitive advantage is absent.

The absence of competitive advantage in efficient markets can be linked to resource availability. If financial markets are efficient, it is because only two types of resource are required to participate – finance and information. If both are equally available to all traders, there is no basis for one to gain competitive advantage over another.

Competitive Advantage in Trading Markets

For competitive advantage to exist, imperfections (or "inefficiencies") must be introduced into the competitive process. Focusing on the relatively simple case of trading markets, let us introduce different sources of imperfection to the competitive process, showing how these imperfections create opportunities for competitive advantage, and how the imperfections relate to the conditions of resource availability.

Imperfect Availability of Information Financial markets (and most other trading markets) depart from the conditions for efficiency because of imperfect availability of information. Competitive advantage, therefore, depends on superior access to information. The most likely source of superior information is privileged access to private information. Trading on the basis of such information normally falls within the restrictions on "insider trading." Though insider information creates advantage, such competitive advantage tends to be of short duration. Once a market participant begins acting on the basis of insider information, other operators are alerted to the existence of the information. Even though they may not know its content, they are able to imitate the behavior of the market leader. A commonly followed strategy in stock markets is to detect and follow insider transactions by senior company executives.

Transaction Costs If markets are efficient except for the presence of transaction costs, then competitive advantage accrues to the traders with the lowest transaction costs. In stock markets, low transaction costs are attained by traders who economize on research and market analysis and achieve efficient portfolio diversification. Studies of mutual fund performance show that, on average, managed funds underperform index funds and the amount of that underperformance is roughly equal to the additional expenses incurred by the managed funds.[24]

Systematic Behavioral Trends If the current prices in a market fully reflect all available information, then price movements are caused by the arrival of new information and follow a random walk.[25] If, however, other factors influence price movements, there is scope for a strategy that uses an understanding of how prices really do move. Some stock market anomalies are well documented, notably the "small firm effect," the "January effect," and "weekend effects."[26] More generally, there is evidence that prices in financial markets follow systematic patterns that are the result of "market psychology," the trends and turning points of which can be established from past data. Chart analysis uses hypotheses concerning the relationship between past and future price movements for forecasting. Standard chartist tools include Elliott wave theory, Gann theories, momentum indicators, and patterns such as "support and resistance levels," "head and shoulders," "double tops," "flags," and "candlesticks." Despite mixed evidence on the success of chart analysis in financial markets,[27] systematic behavioral trends do occur in most markets, which implies that competitive advantage is gained by traders with superior skill in diagnosing such behavior.

Overshooting One well-documented behavioral aberration is the propensity of market participants to overreact to new information, with the result that prices overshoot.[28] Such overreaction is typically the result of imitative behavior resulting in the creation of bandwagon effects. On the assumption that overshooting is temporary and is eventually offset by an opposite movement back to equilibrium, then advantage can be gained through a contrarian strategy: doing the opposite of the mass-market participants. Two of the world's richest men, Warren Buffett (number 2) and Prince Alwaleed bin Talal Alsaud (number 8), are prominent contrarians. Both have made their fortunes by opposing market forces and acquiring large stakes in temporarily depressed companies.

Competitive Advantage in Production Markets

The transitory nature of competitive advantage in trading markets is a result of the characteristics of the resources required to compete: finance and information. Finance is a relatively homogeneous resource that is widely available. Information, although highly differentiated, is transferable easily and at very low cost; hence, the competitive advantage it offers tends to be fleeting.

Production markets are quite different. Production activities require complex combinations of resources and capabilities, and these resources and capabilities are highly differentiated. The result, as we have noted, is that each producer possesses a unique combination of resources and capabilities. The greater the heterogeneity of firms' endowments of resources and capabilities, the greater the potential for competitive advantage. In the European airline industry, the growing diversity of companies – state-owned airlines (e.g. Alitalia), privately owned international airlines (British Airways), budget airlines (Ryanair), regional carriers (Skyways), and charter airlines (Monarch) – has expanded opportunities for competitive advantage and widened the profit differentials between them.

Differences in resource endowments among firms also have an important impact on the process by which competitive advantage is eroded. Where firms possess very similar bundles of resources and capabilities, imitation of the competitive advantage of the incumbent firm is most likely. Where resource bundles are highly differentiated, competition is likely to be less direct. Using different resources and capability, a firm may substitute a rival's competitive advantage.[29] For example:

- Canon substituted for Xerox's technical service capability in copiers by developing high-reliability copiers that needed little service.
- Online discount brokers have used the internet to substitute for networks of retail offices of established brokerage companies, such as Merrill Lynch and Charles Schwab, and online research to substitute for the established brokers' research departments.

Since substitute competition can come from many directions – alternative resources, technological innovations, new business models – it is difficult to counter. The key is to persuade potential competitors that substitution is unlikely to be profitable. This can be achieved through committing the firm to continuous improvement, locking in customers and suppliers, and market deterrence.[30]

Industry Conditions Conducive to Emergence and Sustaining of Competitive Advantage In analyzing the potential for creating and sustaining advantage in production markets, I have focused on the role of interfirm differences in resources. However, the characteristics of the industry also play a role in determining the means by which competitive advantage emerges and is eroded.

Thus, the opportunities for establishing competitive advantage in production markets depend on the number and diversity of the sources of change in the business environment. Industries subject to a wide range of unpredictable external changes offer a multiplicity of opportunities for competitive advantage. Consider the wireless telecommunication services. The industry is subject to a vast array of dynamic forces – regulatory change, technological change, changing customer preferences, to mention but a few. All of these forces offer opportunities for competitive advantage. The complexity of the industry also determines the variety of opportunities for competitive advantage: complex products such as IT consulting offer greater scope than cement.

The extent to which competitive advantage is eroded through imitation will also depend on the characteristics of the industry. For example:

- *Information complexity*. The more difficult it is to diagnose the basis of the success of advantaged firms, the more difficult it is to imitate their success. Industries where competitive advantage is based on complex, multilayered capabilities tend to have more sustainable competitive advantages. In movie production, the long-established leadership of studios such as Paramount, Columbia (Sony), Universal, Fox, and Disney reflects the difficult-to-diagnose secrets of producing "blockbuster" movies, even though the individual resources (scripts, actors, technicians, and directors) can be hired from the market.
- *Opportunities for deterrence and preemption*. Industries where the market is small (relative to the minimum efficient scale of production), essential resources are scarce or tightly held, or economies of learning are important, allow first movers to establish and sustain competitive advantage by preemption and deterrence.
- *Difficulties of resource acquisition*. Industries differ according to the availability of strategically important resources. In the bicycle messenger business in London or New York, competitive advantage is easily eroded because the key resources (cyclists, wireless communication, and marketing) are easily acquired. The securities underwriting business (whether for IPOs or corporate bond issues) offers more sustainable advantages because the key resources and capabilities (market expertise, reputation, relationships, retail distribution links, and massive financial reserves) are difficult to assemble.

Types of Competitive Advantage: Cost and Differentiation

A firm can achieve a higher rate of profit (or potential profit) over a rival in one of two ways: either it can supply an identical product or service at a lower cost, or it can supply a product or service that is differentiated in such a way that the customer is willing to pay a price premium that exceeds the additional cost of the differentiation. In the former case, the firm possesses a cost advantage; in the latter, a differentiation advantage. In pursuing cost advantage, the goal of the firm is to become the cost leader in its industry or industry segment. Cost leadership requires that the firm "must find and exploit all sources of cost advantage . . . [and] . . . sell a standard, no-frills product."[31] Differentiation by a firm from its competitors is achieved "when it provides something unique that is valuable to buyers beyond simply offering a low price."[32] Figure 7.4 illustrates these two types of advantage.

The two sources of competitive advantage define two fundamentally different approaches to business strategy. A firm that is competing on low cost is distinguishable from a firm that competes through differentiation in terms of market positioning, resources and capabilities, and organizational characteristics. Table 7.2 outlines some of the principal features of cost and differentiation strategies.

By combining the two types of competitive advantage with the firm's choice of scope – broad market versus narrow segment – Michael Porter has defined three generic strategies: cost leadership, differentiation, and focus (see Figure 7.5). Porter views cost leadership and differentiation as mutually exclusive strategies. A firm that attempts to pursue both is "stuck in the middle":

> The firm stuck in the middle is almost guaranteed low profitability. It either loses the high-volume customers who demand low prices or must bid away its profits to get this business from the low-cost firms. Yet it also loses high-margin business – the cream – to the firms who are focused on high-margin targets or have achieved differentiation overall. The firm that is stuck in the middle also probably suffers from a blurred corporate culture and a conflicting set of organizational arrangements and motivation system.[33]

In practice, few firms are faced with such stark alternatives. Differentiation is not simply an issue of "to differentiate or not to differentiate." All firms must make

FIGURE 7.4 Sources of competitive advantage

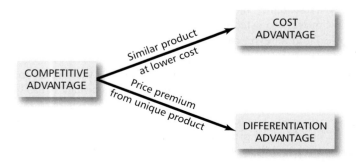

TABLE 7.2 Features of cost leadership and differentiation strategies

Generic strategy	Key strategy elements	Resource and organizational requirements
Cost leadership	Scale-efficient plants Design for manufacture Control of overheads and R&D Process innovation Outsourcing (especially overseas) Avoidance of marginal customer accounts	Access to capital Process engineering skills Frequent reports Tight cost control Specialization of jobs and functions Incentives linked to quantitative targets
Differentiation	Emphasis on branding advertising, design, service, quality, and new product development	Marketing abilities Product engineering skills Cross-functional coordination Creativity Research capability Incentives linked to qualitative performance targets

FIGURE 7.5 Porter's generic strategies

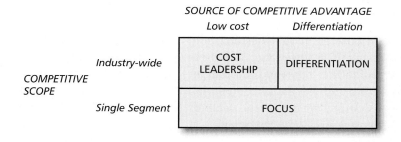

decisions as to which customer requirements to focus on, and where to position their product or service in the market. A cost leadership strategy typically implies a narrow-line, limited-feature, standardized offering. However, such a positioning does not necessarily imply that the product or service is an undifferentiated commodity. In the case of IKEA furniture and Southwest Airlines, a low-price, no-frills offering is also associated with clear market positioning and a unique brand image. The VW Beetle shows that a low-cost, utilitarian, mass-market product can achieve cult status. At the same time, firms that pursue differentiation strategies cannot be oblivious to cost.

In most industries, market leadership is held by a firm that maximizes customer appeal by reconciling effective differentiation with low cost – Toyota, Dell, and Canon are classic examples. In many industries, the cost leader is not the market leader but is a smaller competitor with minimal overheads, nonunion labor, and cheaply acquired assets. In oil refining, the cost leaders tend to be independent refining companies rather than integrated giants such as Exxon Mobil or Shell. In car rental, the cost leader is more likely to be Rent-A-Wreck (a division of Bundy American Corporation) rather than Hertz or Avis.

Kim and Mauborgne view the simultaneous pursuit of differentiation and low cost as a key element in the creation of "blue ocean" opportunities. Common to the success of Japanese companies in consumer goods industries such as cars, motorcycles, consumer electronics, and musical instruments has been the ability to reconcile low costs with high quality and technological progressiveness. New management techniques have helped. Total quality management has exploded the myth that there is a tradeoff between high quality and low cost. Innovations in manufacturing technology and manufacturing management have produced simultaneous increases in productivity and quality.[34] Tom Peters observes an interesting asymmetry:

> Cost reduction campaigns do not often lead to improved quality; and, except for those that involve large reductions in personnel, they don't usually result in long-term lower costs either. On the other hand, effective quality programs yield not only improved quality but lasting cost reductions as well.[35]

Having conquered the cost/quality tradeoff, companies such as Honda, Toyota, Sony, and Canon have gone on to reconcile world-beating manufacturing efficiency and outstanding quality with flexibility, fast-paced innovation, and effective marketing.

Summary

Making money in business requires establishing and sustaining competitive advantage. Both these conditions for profitability demand profound insight into the nature and process of competition within a market. Competitive advantage depends critically on the presence of some imperfection in the competitive process – under perfect competition, profits are transitory. Our analysis of the imperfections of the competitive process has drawn us back to the resources and capabilities that are required to compete in different markets and to pursue different strategies. Sustaining competitive advantage depends on the existence of isolating mechanisms: barriers to rivals' imitation of successful strategies. The greater the difficulty that rivals face in accessing the resources and capabilities needed to imitate or substitute the competitive advantage of the incumbent firm, the greater the sustainability of that firm's competitive advantage. Hence, one outcome of our analysis is to reinforce the argument made in Chapter 5: the characteristics of a firm's resources and capability are fundamental to its strategy and its performance in decision making and long-term success.

In the next two chapters, we analyze the two primary dimensions of competitive advantage: cost advantage and differentiation advantage. In both of these areas we emphasize the importance of a deep understanding of both the firm and its industry environment. To this end, it is useful to disaggregate the firm into a series of separate but interlinked activities. A useful and versatile framework for this purpose is the value chain, which is an insightful tool for understanding the sources of competitive advantage in an industry, for assessing the competitive position of a particular firm, and for suggesting opportunities to enhance a firm's competitiveness.

Self-Study Questions

1   Figure 7.1 implies that stable industries where firms have similar resources and capabilities offer less opportunity for competitive advantage than industries where change is rapid and firms are heterogeneous. Select examples of these two types of industry, and look for any evidence that interfirm profit differences are wider in dynamic, heterogeneous industries than in stable, homogeneous industries.

2   Apple has been successful in dominating the market for both MP3 players with its iPod, and for music downloads with its iTunes service. How can Apple best sustain its leadership in these markets?

3   Illy, the Italian-based supplier of quality coffee and coffee-making equipment, is launching an international chain of gourmet coffee shops. What advice would you offer Illy for how it can best build competitive advantage in the face of Starbucks' dominance of this market?

4   Do you believe that some mutual funds ("unit trusts" in British parlance) can deliver consistently superior returns (once adjusted for risk)? If so, what is the basis for such superior performance and what can fund managers do to achieve superior performance?

5   Target (the US discount retailer), H&M (the Swedish fashion clothing chain), and Primark (the UK discount clothing chain) have pioneered "cheap chic" – combining discount store prices with fashion appeal. What are the principal challenges of designing and implementing a "cheap chic" strategy? Design a "cheap chic" strategy for a company entering another market, e.g. restaurants, sports shoes, cosmetics, or office furniture.

Notes

1   Richard Rumelt argues that competitive advantage lacks a clear and consistent definition ("What in the World is Competitive Advantage," Policy Working Paper 2003-105, Anderson School, UCLA, August 2003).

2   In long-run industry equilibrium, firms with competitive disadvantage are eliminated.

3   According to Edith Penrose (*Theory of the Growth of the Firm*, Oxford: Blackwell, 1959): "Entrepreneurial activity involves identifying opportunities within the economic system."

4   *Bitter Competition: The Holland Sweetener Co. vs. Nutrasweet* (A), Case No. 9-794-079 (Boston: Harvard Business School: 1998). See also D. J. Teece, "Profiting from Technological Innovation: Implications for Integration, Collaboration, Licensing, and Public Policy," in David J. Teece (ed.), *The Competitive Challenge: Strategies for Industrial Innovation and Renewal* (Cambridge, MA: Ballinger, 1987).

5   J. Magretta, "The Power of Virtual Integration: An Interview with Dell Computer's Michael Dell," *Harvard Business Review* (March–April 1998): 73–84.

6   K. Ferdows, M. A. Lewis, and J. Machuca, "Rapid-Fire Fulfillment," *Harvard Business Review* (November 2004): 104–10.

7   G. Stalk Jr., "Time – The Next Source of Competitive Advantage," *Harvard Business Review* (July–August 1988): 41–51.

8   C. Baden-Fuller and J. M. Stopford, *Rejuvenating the Mature Business* (London and New York: Routledge, 1992).

9   C. Kim and R. Mauborgne, "Blue Ocean Strategy," *Harvard Business Review* (October 2004).

10 G. Hamel, "The Why, What, and How of Management Innovation," *Harvard Business Review* (February 2006).

11 R. P. Rumelt, "Toward a Strategic Theory of the Firm," in R. Lamb (ed.), *Competitive Strategic Management* (Englewood Cliffs, NJ: Prentice Hall, 1984): 556–70.

12 See J. Cubbin and P. Geroski, "The Convergence of Profits in the Long Run: Interfirm and Interindustry Comparisons," *Journal of Industrial Economics* 35 (1987): 427–42; R. Jacobsen, "The Persistence of Abnormal Returns," *Strategic Management Journal* 9

(1988): 415–30; and D. C. Mueller, "Persistent Profits among Large Corporations," in L. G. Thomas (ed.), *The Economics of Strategic Planning* (Lexington, MA: Lexington Books, 1986): 31–61.

13 The film was based on the book, by B. Traven, *The Treasure of the Sierra Madre* (New York: Knopf, 1947).

14 "The Great Mongolian Gold Rush," *Fortune Investors Guide 2004* (December 2003).

15 S. Martin, *Advanced Industrial Economics*, 2nd edn (Oxford: Blackwell Publishers, 2001): Chapter 8.

16 T. C. Schelling, *The Strategy of Conflict*, 2nd edn (Cambridge: Harvard University Press, 1980): 35–41.

17 A. Brandenburger and B. Nalebuff, *Co-opetition* (New York: Doubleday, 1996): 72–80.

18 R. Schmalensee, "Entry Deterrence in the Ready-to-Eat Breakfast Cereal Industry," *Bell Journal of Economics* 9 (1978): 305–27.

19 Monopolies and Mergers Commission, *Indirect Electrostatic Reprographic Equipment* (London: Her Majesty's Stationery Office, 1976): 37, 56.

20 S. A. Lippman and R. P. Rumelt, "Uncertain Imitability: An Analysis of Interfirm Differences in Efficiency under Competition," *Bell Journal of Economics* 13 (1982): 418–38. The analysis of causal ambiguity has been further developed by R. Reed and R. DeFillippi, "Causal Ambiguity, Barriers to Imitation, and Sustainable Competitive Advantage," *Academy of Management Review* 15 (1990): 88–102.

21 See O. E. Williamson, "Transaction Cost Economics: The Governance of Contractual Relations," *Journal of Law and Economics* 19 (1979): 153–6.

22 C. Brown and M. Reich, "When Does Union–Management Cooperation Work? A Look at NUMMI and GM-Van Nuys," *California Management Review* 31 (Summer 1989): 26–44.

23 For an analysis of first-mover advantage, see M. Lieberman and D. Montgomery, "First-Mover Advantages," *Strategic Management Journal* 9 (1988): 41–58; and M. Lieberman and D. Montgomery, "First-Mover (Dis)Advantages: Retrospective and Link with the Resource-based View," *Strategic Management Journal* 19 (1998): 1111–25.

24 www.travismorien.com/indexactive.htm

25 E. F. Fama, "Efficient Capital Markets: A Review of Theory and Empirical Work," *Journal of Business* 35 (1970): 383–417.

26 S. Keane, "The Efficient Market Hypothesis on Trial," *Financial Analysts Journal* (March–April 1986): 58–63.

27 S. N. Neftci, "Naive Trading Rules in Financial Markets and Wilner-Kolmogorov Prediction Theory: A Study of Technical Analysis," *Journal of Business* 64 (1991): 549–71.

28 W. De Bondt and R. Thaler, "Does the Stock Market Overreact?" *Journal of Finance* 42 (1985): 793–805.

29 J. B. Barney, "Firm Resources and Sustained Competitive Advantage," *Journal of Management* 17 (1991): 99–120.

30 S. K. McEvily, S. Das, and K. McCabe, "Avoiding Competence Substitution Through Knowledge Sharing," *Academy of Management Review* 25 (2000): 294–311.

31 M. E. Porter, *Competitive Advantage* (New York: Free Press, 1985): 13.

32 Ibid.: 120.

33 M. E. Porter, *Competitive Strategy* (New York: Free Press, 1980): 42.

34 See, for example, J. R. Meredith, "Strategic Advantages of the Factory of the Future," *California Management Review* (Winter 1989): 129–45.

35 T. Peters, *Thriving on Chaos* (New York: Knopf, 1987): 80.

Cost Advantage

8

SEARS MOTOR BUGGY: $395
For car complete with rubber tires, Timken roller bearing axles, top, storm front, three oil-burning lamps, horn, and one gallon of lubricating oil. Nothing to buy but gasoline.

. . . We found there was a maker of automobile frames that was making 75 percent of all the frames used in automobile construction in the United States. We found on account of the volume of business that this concern could make frames cheaper for automobile manufacturers than the manufacturers could make them themselves. We went to this frame maker and asked him to make frames for the Sears Motor Buggy and then to name us prices for those frames in large quantities. And so on throughout the whole construction of the Sears Motor Buggy. You will find every piece and every part has been given the most careful study; you will find that the Sears Motor Buggy is made of the best possible material; it is constructed to take the place of the top buggy; it is built in our own factory, under the direct supervision of our own expert, a man who has had fifteen years of automobile experience, a man who has for the past three years worked with us to develop exactly the right car for the people at a price within the reach of all.

—EXTRACT FROM AN ADVERTISEMENT IN THE SEARS ROEBUCK & CO.
CATALOG, 1909: 1150

Introduction and Objectives

For some industries, cost advantage is the predominant basis for competitive advantage: in commodities there is limited opportunity for competing on anything else. But even where competition focuses on product differentiation, intensifying competition has resulted in cost efficiency becoming a prerequisite for profitability. Some of the most dramatic examples of companies and industries being transformed through the pursuit of cost efficiency are in sectors where competition has increased sharply due to deregulation, such as airlines, telecommunications, banking, and electrical power generation.

By the time you have completed this chapter, you will be able to:

- Identify the determinants of relative cost within the industry or activity ("cost drivers").

- Assess a firm's cost position relative to its competitors and identify the factors responsible for cost differentials.

- Recommend cost-reduction measures.

The analysis in this chapter is oriented around these objectives. In pursuing these objectives, we shall examine techniques for:

- Identifying the basic sources of cost advantage in an industry.

- Appraising the cost position of a firm within its industry by disaggregating the firm into its separate activities.

- Using the analysis of costs and relative cost position as a basis for recommending strategies for enhancing cost competitiveness.

Strategy and Cost Advantage

Historically, strategic management has emphasized cost advantage as the primary basis for competitive advantage in an industry. This focus on cost reflected the traditional emphasis by economists on price as the principal medium of competition – competing on price depends on cost efficiency. It also reflected the strategy preoccupations of large industrial corporations. For much of the 20th century, the development of large corporations was dominated by the quest for economies of scale and scope through investments in mass production and mass distribution. During the 1960s, the quest for scale efficiency provided the driving force for mergers in automobiles, steel, textiles, shipbuilding, and other manufacturing industries.

In 1968 the Boston Consulting Group (BCG) published *Perspectives in Experience*, which documented the relationship between cost and accumulated experience. The result was a profound shift in thinking about cost analysis and the emergence of the *experience curve* as one of the best-known and most influential concepts in the history of strategic management (see Strategy Capsule 8.1).

STRATEGY CAPSULE 8.1
BCG and the Experience Curve

The experience curve has its basis in the systematic reduction in the time taken to build airplanes and Liberty ships during World War II.[1] The relationship was generalized by BCG to encompass not just economies in direct labor, but in all costs (excluding materials). In a series of studies, ranging from bottle caps and refrigerators to long-distance calls and insurance policies, BCG observed a remarkable regularity in the reductions in unit costs with increased cumulative output. BCG summarized its observations in its "Law of Experience":

> The unit cost of value added to a standard product declines by a constant percentage (typically between 20 and 30%) each time cumulative output doubles.

("Unit cost of value added" is total cost per unit of production less the cost per unit of production of bought-in components and materials.) The figure below shows examples of experience curves.

The relationship between unit cost and production volume may be expressed as follows:

$$C_n = C_1 \cdot n^{-a}$$

where C_1 is the cost of the first unit of production
C_n is the cost of the nth unit of production
n is the cumulative volume of production
a is the elasticity of cost with regard to output.

The experience curve has important implications for business strategy. If a firm can expand its output faster than its competitors, it can move down the experience curve more rapidly and open up a widening cost differential. The inference drawn by BCG was that a firm's primary strategic goal should be maximizing market share.[2]

To achieve this, firms should price not on the basis of current costs, but on the basis of anticipated costs – *penetration pricing* rather than *full-cost pricing*. In the British motorcycle industry, BCG observed that British motorcycle

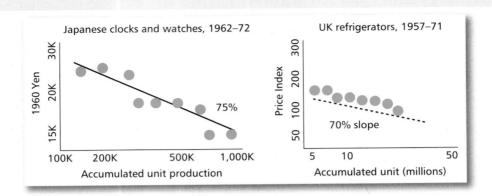

SOURCE: BOSTON CONSULTING GROUP

manufacturers adopted cost-plus pricing, whereas Honda priced to meet market share objectives.[3] The quest for experience-based economies also points to the advantages of increasing volume by broadening product range and expanding internationally.[4]

Empirical studies confirm a positive relationship between profitability and market share.[5] However, this does not mean that pursuing market share necessarily leads to higher profits. It could be that causation runs the other way (profitable companies use their profits to build market share) or that both profitability and market share are the joint outcome of some underlying factor – innovation or cheaper labor.[6] Even if market share does lead to higher profitability, it could be that the costs of increasing market share outweigh the profitability advantages achieved.[7] This is especially likely if a number of companies are competing to grow their market shares.

Notes:

1 Louis E. Yelle, "The Learning Curve: Historical Review and Comprehensive Survey," *Decision Sciences* 10 (1979): 302–28.

2 For an analysis of the effect of market share on profit under differently sloped experience curves, see David Ross, "Learning to Dominate," *Journal of Industrial Economics* 34 (1986): 337–53.

3 Boston Consulting Group, *Strategy Alternatives for the British Motorcycle Industry* (London: Her Majesty's Stationery Office, 1975).

4 Charles Baden-Fuller, "The Implications of the Learning Curve for Firm Strategy and Public Policy," *Applied Economics* 15 (1983): 541–51.

5 Robert D. Buzzell, Bradley T. Gale, and Ralph Sultan, "Market Share – A Key to Profitability," *Harvard Business Review* (January–February 1975); Robert Jacobsen and David Aaker, "Is Market Share All That It's Cracked up to Be?" *Journal of Marketing* 49 (Fall 1985): 11–22.

6 Richard Rumelt and Robin Wensley, using PIMS data, found the relationship between market share and profitability to be the result of both being joint outcomes of a risky competitive process. "In Search of the Market Share Effect," Paper MGL-63 (Graduate School of Management, UCLA, 1981).

7 Robin Wensley, "PIMS and BCG: New Horizons or False Dawn?" *Strategic Management Journal* 3 (1982): 147–58.

In recent decades, companies have been forced to think more broadly and radically about cost efficiency. Cost advantage has shifted to companies benefitting from low labor costs (e.g. Chinese companies) and those taking advantage of new technologies (Skype and Vonage in telephony). The result has been more dramatic and innovative approaches to cost reduction involving outsourcing, process reengineering, and organizational delayering.

Cost analysis has also adjusted to a more explicit recognition that cost advantage is the result of multiple factors, the balance of which varies greatly from industry to industry. In the clothing industry, wage rates are the critical factor; in petrochemicals, it is feedstock costs; while in semiconductors, it is yield rates. In some industries there may be alternative routes to low cost – in the steel industry, Severstal of Russia with its low input costs and Nucor of the US with its advanced technologies and high productivity are both low-cost producers. The key to analyzing cost advantage is to identify the key cost drivers within a particular industry.

The Sources of Cost Advantage

The key to cost analysis is to go beyond mechanistic approaches such as the experience curve and probe the factors that determine a firm's cost position. There are seven principal determinants of a firm's unit costs (cost per unit of output) relative to its competitors; we refer to these as *cost drivers* (see Figure 8.1).

FIGURE 8.1 The drivers of cost advantage

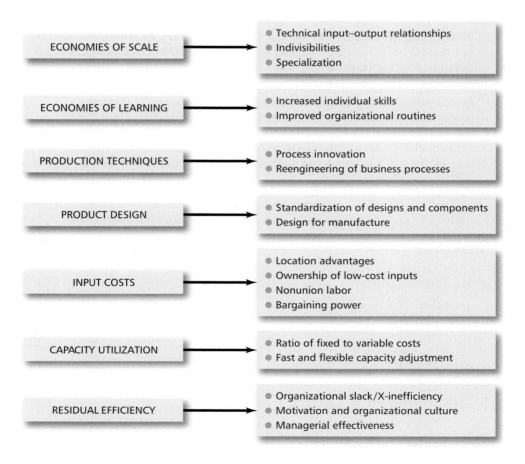

The relative importance of these different cost drivers varies across industries, across firms within an industry, and across the different activities within a firm. By examining each of these different cost drivers, in relation to a particular firm we can do the following:

- Analyze a firm's cost position relative to its competitors and diagnose the sources of inefficiency.
- Make recommendations as to how a firm can improve its cost efficiency.

Let's examine the nature and the role of each of these cost drivers.

Economies of Scale

The predominance of large corporations in most manufacturing and service industries is a consequence of economies of scale. Economies of scale exist wherever proportionate increases in the amounts of inputs employed in a production process result in lower unit costs. Economies of scale have been conventionally associated with manufacturing. Figure 8.2 shows a typical relationship between unit cost and plant capacity. The point at which most scale economies are exploited is the Minimum Efficient Plant Size (MEPS). Scale economies are also important in nonmanufacturing operations such as purchasing, R&D, distribution, and advertising.

Scale economies arise from three principal sources:

1 *Technical input–output relationships*. In many activities, increases in output do not require proportionate increases in input. A 10,000-barrel oil storage tank does not cost five times as much as a 2,000-barrel tank. Similar volume-related economies exist in ships, trucks, and steel and petrochemical plants.

2 *Indivisibilities*. Many resources and activities are "lumpy" – they are unavailable in small sizes. Hence, they offer economies of scale, as firms are able to spread the costs of these items over larger volumes of output. A national TV advertising campaign or a research program into fuel cell technology will cost much the same whether it is being undertaken by Toyota

FIGURE 8.2 The long-run average cost curve for a plant

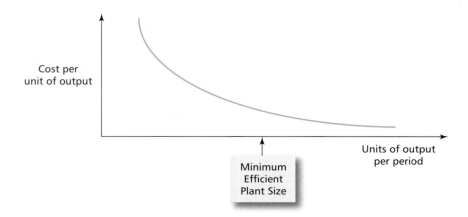

or Daihatsu. However, the costs as a percentage of sales will be much lower for Toyota because it has almost 20 times the sales of Daihatsu.

3   *Specialization.* Increased scale permits greater task specialization that is manifest in greater *division of labor.* Mass production – whether in Adam Smith's pin factory or Henry Ford's auto plants (see Chapter 6) – involves breaking down the production process into separate tasks performed by specialized workers using specialized equipment. Specialization promotes learning, avoids time loss from switching activities, and assists in mechanization and automation. Similar economies are important in knowledge-intensive industries such as investment banking, management consulting, and design engineering, where large firms are able to offer specialized expertise across a broad range of know-how.

Scale Economies and Industry Concentration   Scale economies are a key determinant of an industry's level of concentration (the proportion of industry output accounted for by the largest firms). However, the critical scale advantages of large companies are seldom in production. In packaged consumer goods – cigarettes, household detergents, beer, and soft drinks – economies of scale in marketing are the key factor causing world markets to be dominated by a few giant companies. Advertising is a key indivisibility: a 60-second TV commercial can cost over $5 million to produce, but the real cost is in showing it – Sony's launch of its PlayStation 3 will incur advertising costs of about half a billion dollars. Figure 8.3 shows the relationship between sales volume and average advertising costs for different brands of soft drinks.

Consolidation in the world car industry has been driven by the huge costs associated with new model development (see Table 8.1). Small and medium-sized auto companies have been acquired by larger rivals simply because they lacked the necessary volume over which to amortize the costs of developing new models. Thus, VW acquired Skoda, Seat, and Rolls-Royce, while Ford acquired Jaguar, Mazda, Land Rover, and Volvo. To survive, smaller auto producers must license technology and designs from their bigger competitors.[1]

FIGURE 8.3   Economies of scale in advertising: US soft drinks

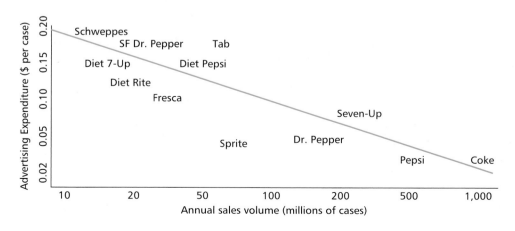

TABLE 8.1 The development cost (including plant and tooling) of new automobile models

Model	Estimated development cost
Ford Mondeo/Contour	$6 billion
GM Saturn	$5 billion
Ford Taurus (1996 model)	$2.8 billion
Ford Escort (new model, 1996)	$2 billion
Renault Clio (1999 model)	$1.3 billion
Chrysler Neon	$1.3 billion
Honda Accord (1997 model)	$0.6 billion
BMW Mini	$0.5 billion
Rolls Royce Phantom (2003 model)	$0.3 billion

SOURCE: R. M. GRANT, "DAIMLERCHRYSLER AND THE WORLD AUTOMOBILE INDUSTRY," IN GRANT AND NEUPERT (EDS), CASES IN CONTEMPORARY STRATEGY ANALYSIS, 3RD EDN (OXFORD: BLACKWELL PUBLISHING, 2003).

Similar scale economies exist in passenger aircraft production. The $18 billion development cost of the Airbus A380 Superjumbo will require sales of 400 planes to reach break-even.

Limits to Scale Economies Despite the prevalence of scale economies, small and medium-sized companies continue to survive and prosper in competition with much bigger rivals. In the automobile industry, the most profitable companies in recent years have been medium-sized producers such as Peugeot, Renault, and BMW. In US and European banking, smaller banks have consistently been more profitable on average than the big boys. The efficiency advantages of scale are offset by three factors: first, the ability of smaller companies to differentiate their offerings more effectively; second, the greater flexibility of smaller companies; third, the greater difficulty of achieving motivation and coordination in large units.[2]

Economies of Learning

The experience curve is based primarily on learning-by-doing on the part of individuals and organizations. Repetition develops both individual skills and organizational routines. In 1943 it took 40,000 labor-hours to build a Convair B-24 bomber. By 1945 it took only 8,000 hours.[3] The more complex a process or product, the greater the potential for learning. Learning curves are exceptionally steep in semiconductor fabrication. When IBM introduced 0.18 micron, copper-interconnector chips, yields increased from zero to over 50% within the first two months. LCD flat screens are notoriously difficult to manufacture – a single defective chip may render an entire screen useless. The dominant position of Sharp and Samsung in flat screens is primarily a result of volume-based learning resulting in exceptionally high yields.[4] Learning occurs both at the individual level through improvements in dexterity and problem solving, and at the group level through the development and refinement of organizational routines.[5]

Process Technology and Process Design

For most goods and services, alternative process technologies exist. A process is technically superior to another when, for each unit of output, it uses less of one input without using more of any other input. Where a production method uses more of some inputs but less of others, then cost efficiency depends on the relative prices of the inputs. Hence, in the assembly of desktop PCs, Dell's Palmer North 2 plant in Austin, Texas is highly automated, while its two plants in Xiamen, China (where wages are about 90% lower) are much more labor intensive.

New process technology may radically reduce costs. Pilkington's float glass process gave it (and its licensees) an unassailable cost advantage in glass production. Ford's moving assembly line reduced the time taken to assemble a Model T from 106 hours to six hours between 1912 and 1913.

When process innovation is embodied in new capital equipment, diffusion is likely to be rapid. However, the full benefits of new processes typically require system-wide changes in job design, employee incentives, product design, organizational structure, and management controls.[6] Between 1979 and 1986, General Motors spent $40 billion on new process technology with the goal of becoming the world's most efficient manufacturer of automobiles. Yet, in the absence of fundamental changes in organization and management, the productivity gains were meager. After a tour of Cadillac's state-of-the-art Hamtramck plant in Detroit, Toyota chairman Eiji Toyoda told a colleague, "It would have been embarrassing to comment on it."[7] By contrast, Toyota, Nucor, Dell Computer, McDonald's, and Wal-Mart have established cost leadership through adapting their organizations and human resource management to the requirements of their new process technologies.

Indeed, the greatest productivity gains from process innovation typically are the result of organizational improvements rather than technological innovation and new hardware. The central components of Toyota's system of lean production are just-in-time scheduling, total quality management, continuous improvement (*kaisan*), team-working, job flexibility, and supplier partnerships rather than robotics or IT.[8] Harley-Davidson's gains in productivity during the late 1980s and early 1990s resulted from reorganizing its production processes, human resource management, and control systems, but with limited investment in automation and new manufacturing hardware.[9]

Business Process Reengineering During the 1990s, recognition that the redesign of operational processes could achieve substantial efficiency gains stimulated a surge of interest in a new management tool called *business process reengineering* (BPR). "Reengineering gurus" Michael Hammer and James Champy defined BPR as:

> *the fundamental rethinking and radical redesign of business processes to achieve dramatic improvements in critical contemporary measures of performance, such as cost, quality, service, and speed.*[10]

BPR recognizes that production and commercial processes involve complex interactions among many individuals and evolve over time with little conscious or consistent direction. With information technology, the temptation is to automate existing processes – "paving over cowpaths," as Michael Hammer calls it.[11] The key is to detach from the way in which a process is currently organized and to begin with the question: "If we were starting afresh, how would we design this process?" Hammer and Champy point to the existence of a set of "commonalities, recurring themes, or characteristics" that can guide BPR. These include:

- Combining several jobs into one.
- Allowing workers to make decisions.

- Performing the steps of a process in a natural order.
- Recognizing that processes have multiple versions and designing processes to take account of different situations.
- Performing processes where it makes the most sense, e.g., if the accounting department needs pencils, it is probably cheaper for such a small order to be purchased directly from the office equipment store along the block than to be ordered via the firm's purchasing department.
- Reducing checks and controls to the point where they make economic sense.
- Minimizing reconciliation.
- Appointing a case manager to provide a single point of contact at the interface between processes.
- Reconciling centralization with decentralization in process design – e.g., via a shared database, decentralized decisions can be made while permitting overall coordination simply through information sharing.

BPR has resulted in major gains in efficiency, quality, and speed (see Strategy Capsule 8.2), but in many instances has produced disappointing results. One of the major realizations to emerge from BPR is that most business processes are complex. To redesign a process one must first understand it. Process mapping exercises reveal that even seemingly simple business processes, such as the procurement of office supplies, involve complex and sophisticated systems of interactions among a number of organizational members. As we noted in Chapter 5, many organizational routines operate without any single person fully understanding the mechanism. Hammer and Champy's recommendation to "obliterate" existing processes and start with a "clean sheet of paper" runs the risk of destroying organizational capabilities that have been nurtured over a long period of time.

Product Design

Design-for-manufacture – designing products for ease of production rather than simply for functionality and esthetics – can offer substantial cost savings, especially when linked to the introduction of new process technology.

- Volkswagen cut product development and component costs by redesigning its 30+ different models around just four separate platforms. The VW Beetle, Audi TT, Golf, and Audi A3, together with several Seat and Skoda models, all share a single platform.
- The IBM "Proprinter," one of the most successful computer printers of the 1980s, owed its low costs (and reliability) to an innovative design that:
  – reduced the number of parts from 150, found in the typical PC printer, to 60;
  – designed the printer in layers so that robots could build it from the bottom up;
  – eliminated all screws, springs, and other fasteners that required human insertion and adjustment and replaced them with molded plastic components that clipped together.[12]

STRATEGY CAPSULE 8.2

Process Reengineering at IBM Credit

IBM Credit provides credit to customers of IBM for the purchase of IBM hardware and software. Under the old system, five stages were involved:

1 The IBM salesperson telephoned a request for financing. The request was logged on a piece of paper.

2 The request was sent to the Credit Department where it was logged onto a computer and the customer's creditworthiness was checked. The results of the credit check were written on a form and passed to the Business Practices Department.

3 There the standard loan covenant would be modified to meet the terms of customer loan.

4 The request was passed to the pricer who determined the appropriate interest rate.

5 The clerical group took all the information and prepared a quote letter, which was sent to the salesperson.

Because the process took an average of six days, it resulted in a number of lost sales and delayed the sales staff in finalizing deals.

After many efforts to improve the process, two managers undertook an experiment. They took a financing request and walked it around through all five steps. The process took 90 minutes!

On this basis, a fundamental redesign of the credit approval process was achieved. The change was replacing the specialists (credit checkers, pricers, and so on) with generalists who undertook all five processes. Only where the request was nonstandard or unusually complex were specialists called in. The basic problem was that the system had been designed for the most complex credit requests that IBM received, whereas in the vast majority of cases no specialist judgment was called for – simply clerical work involving looking up credit ratings, plugging numbers into standard formulae, etc.

The result was that credit requests are processed in four hours compared to six days, total employees were reduced slightly, while the total number of deals increased one hundred times.

Source: Adapted from M. Hammer and J. Champy, *Reengineering the Corporation: A Manifesto for Business Revolution* (New York: HarperBusiness, 1993): 36–9.

● Service offerings too can be designed for ease and efficiency of production. Motel 6, cost leader in US budget motels, carefully designs its product to keep operating costs low. Its motels occupy low-cost, out-of-town locations, it uses standard motel designs, it avoids facilities such as pools and restaurants, and it designs rooms to facilitate easy cleaning and low maintenance.

Capacity Utilization

Over the short and medium term, plant capacity is more or less fixed, and variations in output cause capacity utilization to rise or fall. Underutilization raises unit costs because fixed costs must be spread over fewer units of production. In businesses where virtually all costs are fixed (e.g., airlines, theme parks), profitability is highly sensitive to shortfalls in demand. During periods of peak demand, output may be pushed beyond the normal full-capacity operation. As Boeing discovered in 1997 and then in 2006, pushing output beyond capacity operation increases unit costs due to overtime pay, premiums for night and weekend shifts, increased defects, and higher maintenance costs.

In cyclical industries, the ability to speedily adjust capacity to downturns in demand can be a major source of cost advantage. During the 2001–2 stock market slump, the online brokerage companies that remained profitable were those that adjusted their operations to reduced transactions. Critical to effective adjustment is the ability to distinguish *cyclical* overcapacity – common to all cyclical industries, from semiconductors and construction to hotels and railroads – from the *structural* overcapacity that affects automobiles, gasoline retailing, and the US hospital industry.[13]

Input Costs

The firms in an industry do not necessarily pay the same price for identical inputs. There are several sources of lower input costs:

- *Locational differences in input prices.* The prices of inputs may vary between locations, the most important being differences in wage rates from one country to another. In the US, software engineers earned an average of $82,000 in 2005. In India the average was $24,000. In less-skilled occupations, differentials are much wider: in Suzhou, China, workers assembling iPods and laptop computers for Asustek earned $54 a month in 2006.[14]

- *Ownership of low-cost sources of supply.* In raw material-intensive industries, ownership or access to low-cost sources can offer crucial cost advantage. In oil and gas, finding and development costs for the three "supermajors" (Exxon Mobil, Royal Dutch Shell, and BP) were over $9 per barrel in 2005; for Saudi Aramco they were under $2.

- *Nonunion labor.* Where employment costs account for a major part of total costs, cost leaders are often the firms that have avoided unionization. In the US airline industry, nonunion Jet Blue had average salary and benefit cost per employee of $50,700 in 2005 compared with $70,200 for United (80% unionized).

- *Bargaining power.* Where bought-in products are a major cost item, differences in buying power among the firms in an industry can be an important source of cost advantage.[15] Wal-Mart's UK entry (with its acquisition of Asda) was greeted with dismay by British retailers – they recognized that Wal-Mart would be able to use its massive bargaining power to extract additional discounts from Asda's suppliers, which it could use to fuel aggressive price competition.

Residual Efficiency

In many industries, the basic cost drivers – scale, technology, product and process design, input costs, and capacity utilization – fail to provide a complete explanation for why one firm in an industry has lower unit costs than a competitor. Even after taking all these cost drivers into account, unit cost differences between firms remain. These residual efficiencies relate to the extent to which the firm approaches its efficiency frontier of optimal operation. Residual efficiency depends on the firm's ability to eliminate "organizational slack"[16] or "X-inefficiency"[17] – surplus costs that keep the firm from maximum-efficiency operation. These costs are often referred to as "organizational fat" and build up unconsciously as a result of employees – both in management and on the shop floor – maintaining some margin of slack in preference to the rigors of operating at maximum efficiency.

Eliminating excess costs is difficult. It may take a shock to a company's very survival to provide the impetus for rooting out institutionalized inefficiencies. When faced with bankruptcy or a precipitous fall in profitability, companies can demonstrate a remarkable capacity for paring costs. For example, as part of the rescue of Nissan Motor by Renault, the ensuing cost cutting implemented by turnaround CEO Carlos Ghosn cut Nissan's operating costs by 20% during his first year.[18]

In the absence of a threat to survival, high levels of residual efficiency are typically the result of an organizational culture and management style that are intolerant toward all manifestations of unnecessary costs. At Wal-Mart, for example, parsimony and frugality are virtues that take on a near-religious significance.

Using the Value Chain to Analyze Costs

To analyze costs and make recommendations for building cost advantage, the company or even the business unit is too big a level for us to work at. As we saw in Chapter 5, every business may be viewed as a chain of activities. In most value chains each activity has a distinct cost structure determined by different cost drivers. Analyzing costs requires disaggregating the firm's value chain to identify:

- The relative importance of each activity with respect to total cost.
- The cost drivers for each activity and the comparative efficiency with which the firm performs each activity.
- How costs in one activity influence costs in another.
- Which activities should be undertaken within the firm and which activities should be outsourced.

The Principal Stages of Value Chain Analysis

A value chain analysis of a firm's cost position comprises the following stages:

1 *Disaggregate the firm into separate activities.* Determining the appropriate value chain activities is a matter of judgment. It requires understanding the chain of processes involved in the transformation of inputs into output and its delivery to the customer. Very often, the firm's own divisional and departmental structure is a useful guide. Key considerations are:
   - the separateness of one activity from another;
   - the importance of an activity;
   - the dissimilarity of activities in terms of cost drivers;

- the extent to which there are differences in the way competitors perform the particular activity.

2 *Establish the relative importance of different activities in the total cost of the product.* Our analysis needs to focus on the activities that are the major sources of cost. In disaggregating costs, Michael Porter suggests the detailed assignment of operating costs and assets to each value activity. Though the adoption of activity-based costing has made such cost data more available, detailed cost allocation can be a major exercise.[19] Even without such detailed cost data, it is usually possible to identify the critical activities, establish which activities are performed relatively efficiently or inefficiently, identify cost drivers, and offer recommendations.

3 *Compare costs by activity.* To establish which activities the firm performs relatively efficiently and which it does not, benchmark unit costs for each activity against those of competitors.

4 *Identify cost drivers.* For each activity, what factors determine the level of cost relative to other firms? For some activities, cost drivers are evident simply from the nature of the activity and the composition of costs. For capital-intensive activities such as the operation of a body press in an auto plant, the principal factors are likely to be capital equipment costs, weekly production volume, and downtime between changes of dies. For labor-intensive assembly activities, critical issues are wage rates, speed of work, and defect rates.

5 *Identify linkages.* The costs of one activity may be determined, in part, by the way in which other activities are performed. Xerox discovered that its high service costs relative to competitors reflected the complexity of design of its copiers, which required 30 different interrelated adjustments.

6 *Identify opportunities for reducing costs.* By identifying areas of comparative inefficiency and the cost drivers for each, opportunities for cost reduction become evident. For example:

- If scale economies are a key cost driver, can volume be increased? One feature of Caterpillar's cost-reduction strategy was to broaden its model range and begin selling diesel engines to other vehicle manufacturers in order to expand its sales base.
- Where wage costs are the issue, can wages be reduced either directly or by relocating production?
- If a certain activity cannot be performed efficiently within the firm, can it be outsourced?

Figure 8.4 shows how the application of the value chain to automobile manufacture can yield suggestions for possible cost reductions.

FIGURE 8.4 Using the value chain in cost analysis: an automobile manufacturer

SEQUENCE OF ANALYSIS	VALUE CHAIN	COST DRIVERS

SEQUENCE OF ANALYSIS

1. IDENTIFY ACTIVITIES
Establish the basic framework of the value chain by identifying the principal activities of the firm.

2. ALLOCATE TOTAL COSTS
For a first-stage analysis, a rough estimate of the breakdown of total cost by activity is sufficient to indicate which activities offer the greatest scope for cost reductions.

3. IDENTIFY COST DRIVERS
(See diagram)

4. IDENTIFY LINKAGES
Examples include:
1. Consolidating purchase orders to increase discounts increases inventories.
2. High-quality parts and materials reduce costs of defects at later stages.
3. Reducing manufacturing defects cuts warranty costs.
4. Designing different models around common components and platforms reduces manufacturing costs.

5. MAKE RECOMMENDATIONS FOR COST REDUCTION
For example:
Purchasing: Concentrate purchases on fewer suppliers to maximize purchasing economies. Institute just-in-time component supply to reduce inventories.

R&D/Design/Engineering: Reduce frequency of model changes. Reduce number of different models (e.g., single range of global models). Design for commonality of components and platforms.

Component manufacture: Exploit economies of scale through concentrating production of each component on fewer plants. Outsource wherever scale of production or run lengths are suboptimal or where outside suppliers have technology advantages. For labor-intensive components (e.g., seats, dashboards, trim), relocate production in low-wage countries. Improve capacity utilization through plant rationalization or supplying components to other manufacturers.

VALUE CHAIN

SUPPLIES OF COMPONENTS AND MATERIALS

PURCHASING

INVENTORY HOLDING

R&D/DESIGN/ENGINEERING

COMPONENT MANUFACTURE

ASSEMBLY

TESTING/QUALITY CONTROL

INVENTORIES OF FINAL GOODS

SALES AND MARKETING

DISTRIBUTION

DEALER AND CUSTOMER SUPPORT

COST DRIVERS

Prices of brought-in components depend upon:
Order sizes
Total value of purchases over time per supplier
Location of suppliers
Relative bargaining power
Extent of cooperation

Size of R&D commitment
Productivity of R&D/design
Number and frequency of new models
Sales per model

Scale of plant for each type of component
Vintage of the process technology used
Location of plants
Run length per component
Level of capacity utilization

Scale of plants
Number of models per plant
Degree of automation
Level of wages
Employee commitment and flexibility
Level of capacity utilization

Level of quality targets
Frequency of defects

Cyclicality and unpredictability of sales
Flexibility and responsiveness of production
Customers' willingness to wait

Number of dealers
Sales per dealer
Desired level of dealer support
Frequency and seriousness of defects requiring warranty repairs or recalls

Summary

Cost efficiency may no longer be a guarantee of profitability in today's hypercompetitive markets, but in almost all industries it is a prerequisite for success. In industries where competition has always been primarily price based – steel, textiles, and mortgage loans – increased intensity of competition requires relentless cost-reduction efforts. In industries where price competition was once muted – airlines, banking, and electrical power – firms have been forced to reconcile the pursuit of innovation, differentiation, and service quality with vigorous cost reduction.

The foundation for a cost-reduction strategy must be an understanding of the determinants of a company's costs. The principal message of this chapter is the need to look behind cost accounting data and beyond simplistic approaches to the determinants of cost efficiency, and to analyze the factors that drive relative unit costs in each of the firm's activities in a systematic and comprehensive manner.

Increasingly, approaches to cost efficiency are less about incremental efficiencies, and more about fundamentally rethinking the activities undertaken by the firm and the ways in which it organizes them. By focusing on those activities in which the firm possesses a cost advantage and outsourcing others, and by extensively reengineering manufacturing and administrative processes, firms have succeeded in achieving dramatic reductions in operating costs.

Given multiple drivers of relative cost, cost management implies multiple initiatives at different organizational levels. Careful analysis of existing activities relative to competitors can pinpoint cost-reduction opportunities by lowering input costs, accessing scale economies, and better utilizing capacity. At the same time, the firm must seek opportunities for innovation and process redesign to exploit new sources of dynamic efficiency.

Self-Study Questions

1   A number of industries have experienced rapidly increasing global concentration in recent years: commercial aircraft (led by Boeing and Airbus), steel (led by Mittal Steel), beer (led by SAB-Miller, Anheuser-Busch, and Heineken), investment banking (led by Citigroup, Goldman Sachs, UBS, and Morgan Stanley), defense equipment (led by Lockheed Martin and Northrop Grumman), and delivery services (led by UPS, Federal Express, and Deutsche Post/DHL). For each industry, are economies of scale the major rationale for increasing concentration? If so, identify the sources of economies of scale. If not, how can increasing global concentration be explained?

2   In Strategy Capsule 2.3 (Chapter 2), we observed that Ford's profitability was low primarily because its costs were high. Using the value chain shown in Figure 8.4 and what you know about Ford (including the information in Strategy Capsule 2.3), what suggestions would you offer as to how Ford might lower its costs of producing cars?

3   To what extent are the seven cost drivers shown in Figure 8.1 relevant in analyzing the costs per student at your business school? What recommendations would you make to your dean for improving the cost efficiency of the school?

Notes

1 To be more precise, the economies of amortizing product development costs are *economies of volume* rather than *economies of scale*. The product development cost per unit depends on the total volume of production over the life of the model.

2 D. Schwartzman, "Uncertainty and the Size of the Firm," *Economica* (August 1963).

3 L. Rapping, "Learning and World War II Production Functions," *Review of Economics and Statistics* (February 1965): 81–6. See also K. B. Clark and R. H. Hayes, "Recapturing America's Manufacturing Heritage," *California Management Review* (Summer 1988): 25.

4 "Exploiting the Flat Screen Frenzy," Forbes.com (December 12, 2003, http://www.forbes.com/business/manufacturing/2003/12/12/cz_bf_1211tv.html); "Japan Watches Display Market Go Flat," RedHerring.com (January 10, 2001).

5 L. Argote, S. L. Beckman, and D. Epple, "The Persistence and Transfer of Learning in Industrial Settings," *Management Science* 36 (1990): 140–54; M. Zollo and S. G. Winter, "Deliberate Learning and the Evolution of Dynamic Capabilities," *Organization Science* 13 (2002): 339–51.

6 R. H. Hayes and R. Jaikumar, "Manufacturing's Crisis: New Technologies, Obsolete Organizations," *Harvard Business Review* (September–October 1988): 85; and R. M. Grant, A. B. Shani, R. Krishnan, and R. Baer, "Appropriate Manufacturing Technology: A Strategic Approach," *Sloan Management Review* 33, no. 1 (Fall 1991): 43–54.

7 M. Keller, *Collision* (New York: Doubleday, 1993): 169–71.

8 J. Womack and D. T. Jones, "From Lean Production to Lean Enterprise," *Harvard Business Review* (March–April 1994); J. Womack and D. T. Jones, "Beyond Toyota: How to Root Out Waste and Pursue Perfection," *Harvard Business Review* (September–October 1996).

9 R. M. Grant, "Harley-Davidson Inc.," in R. M. Grant (ed.), *Cases to Accompany* Contemporary Strategy Analysis, 6th edn (Oxford: Blackwell, 2008).

10 M. Hammer and J. Champy, *Reengineering the Corporation: A Manifesto for Business Revolution* (New York: HarperBusiness, 1993): 32. See also M. Hammer, *Beyond Reengineering: How the Processed Centered Organization Is Changing our Work and our Lives* (New York: HarperBusiness, 1996).

11 M. Hammer, "Reengineering Work: Don't Automate, Obliterate," *Harvard Business Review* (July–August 1990).

12 R. E. Gomory, "From the Ladder of Science to the Product Development Cycle," *Harvard Business Review* (November–December 1989): 103.

13 J. Billington, "Listening to Overcapacity – Lessons from the Auto and Health Care Industries," *Harvard Management Update* (Boston: Harvard Business School, 1998, Reprint # U98068).

14 C. Joseph, "I-Pod City," *Mail on Sunday* (London: June 11, 2006): 56–7.

15 See R. M. Grant, "Manufacturer–Retailer Relations: The Shifting Balance of Power," in G. Johnson (ed.), *Retailing and Business Strategy* (New York: John Wiley, 1987).

16 R. Cyert and J. March, *A Behavioral Theory of the Firm* (Englewood Cliffs, NJ: Prentice Hall, 1963).

17 H. Leibenstein, "Allocative Efficiency Versus X-Efficiency," *American Economic Review* 54 (June 1966).

18 K. Kase, F. J. Saez, and H. Riquelme, *The New Samurais of Japanese Industry* (Edward Elgar, 2006).

19 On activity-based costing, see R. S. Kaplan and S. R. Anderson, "Time-Driven Activity-based Costing," *Harvard Business Review* (November 2004): 131–8; J. Billington, "The ABCs of ABC: Activity-based Costing and Management," *Harvard Management Update* (Boston: Harvard Business School Publishing, May 1999).

9

Differentiation Advantage

If the three keys to selling real estate are location, location, location, then the three keys of selling consumer products are differentiation, differentiation, differentiation.

—ROBERT GOIZUETA, FORMER CHAIRMAN, COCA-COLA COMPANY

If you gave me $100 billion and said, "Take away the soft drink leadership of Coca-Cola in the world," I'd give it back to you and say, "It can't be done."

—WARREN BUFFETT, CHAIRMAN, BERKSHIRE HATHAWAY,
AND COCA-COLA'S BIGGEST SHAREHOLDER

OUTLINE

Introduction and Objectives

A firm differentiates itself from its competitors "when it provides something unique that is valuable to buyers beyond simply offering a low price."[1] Differentiation advantage occurs when a firm is able to obtain from its differentiation a price premium in the market that exceeds the cost of providing the differentiation.

Every firm has opportunities for differentiating its offering to customers, although the range of differentiation opportunities depends on the characteristics of the product. An automobile or a restaurant offers greater potential for differentiation than cement, wheat, or memory chips. These latter products are called "commodities" precisely because they lack physical differentiation. Yet, even commodity products can be differentiated in ways that create customer value: "Anything can be turned into a value-added product or service for a well-defined or newly created market," claims Tom Peters.[2]

During the 1990s, desktop PCs became commodity items identified by their technical specifications more than by their brand names. Yet, Dell Computer's direct sales model allowed it to differentiate its PCs by permitting customers to design their own computer system and offering complementary services such as online customer support, three-year on-site warranty, web hosting, installation and configuration of customers' hardware and software. Gasoline and diesel fuel are also commodities, yet Shell has established retail market leadership both through introducing premium fuels (V-Power) and upgrading facilities and service at its filling stations.[3] The lesson is this: differentiation is not simply about offering different product features, it is about identifying and understanding every possible interaction between the firm and its customers, and asking how these interactions can be enhanced or changed in order to deliver additional value to the customer.

Analyzing differentiation requires looking at both the firm (the supply side) and its customers (the demand side). While supply-side analysis identifies the firm's potential to create uniqueness, the critical issue is whether such differentiation creates value for customers, and whether the value created exceeds the cost of the differentiation. Hence, in this chapter we shall be concerned especially with the demand side of the market. By understanding what customers want, how they choose, and what motivates them, we can identify opportunities for profitable differentiation.

Differentiation strategies are not about pursuing uniqueness for the sake of being different. Differentiation is about understanding customers and how our product can meet their needs. To this extent, the quest for differentiation advantage takes us to the heart of business strategy. The fundamental issues of differentiation are also the fundamental issues of business strategy: Who are our customers? How do we create value for them? And how do we do it more effectively and efficiently than anyone else?

Because differentiation is about uniqueness, establishing differentiation advantage requires creativity – it cannot be achieved simply through applying standardized frameworks and techniques. This is not to say that differentiation advantage is not amenable to systematic analysis. As we have observed, there are two requirements for creating profitable differentiation. On the supply side, the firm must be aware of the resources and capabilities through which it can create uniqueness (and do it better than competitors). On the demand side, the key is insight into customers and their needs and preferences. These two sides form the major components of our analysis of differentiation.

By the time you have completed this chapter you will be able to:

● Understand what differentiation is, recognize its different forms, and appreciate its potential for creating competitive advantage.

● Analyze the sources of differentiation in terms of customers' preferences and characteristics, and of the firm's capacity for supplying differentiation.

● Formulate strategies that create differentiation advantage by linking the firm's differentiation capability to customers' demand for differentiation.

The Nature of Differentiation and Differentiation Advantage

Let us begin by exploring what differentiation is and why it is such an important basis for competitive advantage.

Differentiation Variables

The potential for differentiating a product or service is partly determined by its physical characteristics. For products that are technically simple (a pair of socks, a brick), that satisfy uncomplicated needs (a corkscrew, a nail), or must meet rigorous technical standards (a spark plug, a thermometer), differentiation opportunities are constrained by technical and market factors. Products that are technically complex (an airplane), that satisfy complex needs (an automobile, a vacation), or that do not need to conform to particular technical standards (wine, toys) offer much greater scope for differentiation.

Beyond these constraints, the potential in any product or service for differentiation is limited only by the boundaries of the human imagination. For seemingly simple products such as shampoo, toilet paper, and bottled water, the proliferation of brands on any supermarket's shelves is testimony both to the ingenuity of firms and the complexity of customer preferences. Differentiation extends beyond the physical characteristics of the product or service to encompass everything about the product or service that influences the value customers derive from it. This means that differentiation includes every aspect of the way in which a company relates to its customers. Starbucks' ability to charge up to $4 for a cup of coffee rests not just on the characteristics of the coffee but also on the overall "Starbucks' Experience," which encompasses the retail environment, the values the company projects, and a sense of community that customers feel a part of. Differentiation is not an activity specific to particular functions such as design and marketing; it infuses all activities within the organization and is built into the identity and culture of a company.

In analyzing differentiation opportunities, we can distinguish *tangible* and *intangible* dimensions of differentiation. Tangible differentiation is concerned with the observable characteristics of a product or service that are relevant to customers' preferences and choice processes. These include size, shape, color, weight, design, material, and technology. Tangible differentiation also includes the performance of the product or service in terms of reliability, consistency, taste, speed, durability, and safety.

Tangible differentiation extends to products and services that complement the product in question. There is little that is distinctive about Dell's computers. The differentiation lies in the speed with which they are delivered, the flexibility with which customers can configure their own systems, and after-sales services including technical support, online training courses, repair service, upgrading service, and customer discussion forum – to mention but a few.

Opportunities for intangible differentiation arise because the value that customers perceive in a product or service does not depend exclusively on the tangible aspects of the offering. There are few products where customer choice is determined solely by observable product features or objective performance criteria. Social, emotional, psychological, and esthetic considerations are present in choices over all products and services. The desires for status, exclusivity, individuality, and security are powerful motivational forces in choices relating to most consumer goods. Where a product or service is meeting complex customer needs, differentiation choices involve the overall image of the firm's offering. Image differentiation is especially important for those products and services whose qualities and performance are difficult to ascertain at the time of purchase ("experience goods"). These include cosmetics, medical services, and education.

Differentiation and Segmentation

Differentiation is different from segmentation. Differentiation is concerned with *how* a firm competes – the ways in which it can offer uniqueness to customers. Such uniqueness might relate to consistency (McDonald's), reliability (Federal Express), status (American Express), quality (BMW), and innovation (Sony). Segmentation is concerned with *where* a firm competes in terms of customer groups, localities, and product types.

Whereas segmentation is a feature of market structure, differentiation is a strategic choice by a firm. A segmented market is one that can be partitioned according to the characteristics of customers and their demand. Differentiation is concerned with a firm's positioning within a market (or market segment) in relation to the product, service, and image characteristics that influence customer choice.[4] By locating within a segment, a firm does not necessarily differentiate itself from its competitors within the same segment. Ameritrade, E-Trade, and T. D. Waterhouse are all located within the online segment of the brokerage industry, yet are not significantly differentiated from one another. Conversely, Toyota, McDonald's, Amazon, and Starbucks pursue differentiation, but position themselves within the mass market and span multiple segments.

Nevertheless, differentiation decisions tend to be closely linked to choices over the segments in which a firm competes. By offering uniqueness in its offerings, a firm may inevitably target certain market niches. By selecting performance, engineering, and style as the basis on which BMW competes in the automobile industry, it inevitably appeals to different market segments than does VW. To the extent that differentiation is imitated by other companies, the result can be the creation of new market segments. In the beer industry innovative differentiation to offer light beer, high-alcohol beer, microbrews, and brewpubs has resulted in the emergence of new market segments.[5]

The Sustainability of Differentiation Advantage

Although strategy analysis has traditionally emphasized cost advantage as the primary basis for competitive advantage, low cost offers a less secure basis for competitive advantage than does differentiation. The growth of international competition has revealed the fragility of seemingly well-established positions of domestic cost leadership. The cost advantages of Ford in autos, Honda in motorcycles, Indesit in domestic appliances, and Matsushita in consumer electronics have all been overturned by the emergence of new competitors from countries with low labor costs.

In addition, cost advantage is highly vulnerable to unpredictable external forces. The rise of the euro against the US dollar during 2002 to 2006 has seriously affected the cost competitiveness of most European companies.

Cost advantage is also vulnerable to new technology and strategic innovation. US integrated iron and steel producers lost ground to the minimill producers – Nucor, Chaparral Steel, and Steel Dynamics. Discount brokers such as Quick and Reilly, Brown & Company, Olde, and Seibert were undercut by online brokers such as Ameritrade and E-Trade. Internet telephony (VoIP) offered by Skype, Vonage, and other upstarts has potentially devastating implications for the fixed-line businesses of established providers such as Verizon, AT&T, and British Telecom.

Hence, sustained high profitability is associated more with differentiation than cost leadership. Large companies that consistently earn a high return on equity – such as Colgate-Palmolive, Microsoft, Anheuser-Busch, Yum Brands, Kellogg's, Procter & Gamble, 3M, and Wyeth – tend to be those that have pursued differentiation through quality, branding, and innovation.

Analyzing Differentiation: The Demand Side

Successful differentiation involves matching customers' demand for differentiation with the firm's capacity to supply differentiation. Let's begin with the demand side. Analyzing customer demand enables us to determine which product characteristics have the potential to create value for customers, customers' willingness to pay for differentiation, and a company's optimal competitive positioning in terms of differentiation variables.

Analyzing demand begins with understanding why customers buy a product or service. What are the needs and requirements of a person who is purchasing a personal computer? What is motivating a company when it hires management consultants? Market research systematically explores customer preferences and customer perceptions of existing products. However, the key to successful differentiation is to understand customers. In gaining insight into customer requirements and preferences, simple, direct questions about the purpose of a product and its performance attributes can often be far more illuminating than objective market research data obtained from

STRATEGY CAPSULE 9.1
Understanding What a Product Is About

Getting back to strategy means getting back to a deep understanding of what a product is about. Some time back, for example, a Japanese home appliance company was trying to develop a coffee percolator. Should it be a General Electric-type percolator, executives wondered? Should it be the same drip-type that Philips makes? Larger? Smaller? I urged them to ask a different kind of question: Why do people drink coffee? What are they looking for when they do? If your objective is to serve the customer better, then shouldn't you understand why that customer drinks coffee in the first place? Then you would know what kind of percolator to make.

The answer came back: good taste. Then I asked the company's engineers what they were doing to help the consumer enjoy good taste in a cup of coffee. They said they were trying to design a good percolator. I asked them what influences the taste in a cup of coffee. No one knew. That became the next question we had to answer. It turns out that lots of things can affect taste – the beans, the temperature, the water. We did our homework and discovered all the things that affect taste . . .

Of all the factors, water quality, we learned, made the greatest difference. The percolator in design at the time, however, didn't take water quality into account at all . . . We discovered next the grain distribution and the time between grinding the beans and pouring in the water were crucial. As a result we began to think about the product and its necessary features in a new way. It had to have a built-in dechlorinating function. It had to have a built-in grinder. All the customer should have to do is pour in water and beans . . .

To start you have to ask the right questions and set the right kinds of strategic goals. If your only concern is that General Electric has just brought out a percolator that brews coffee in ten minutes, you will get your engineers to design one that brews it in seven minutes. And if you stick to that logic, market research will tell you that instant coffee is the way to go . . . Conventional marketing approaches won't solve the problem. If you ask people whether they want their coffee in ten minutes or seven, they will say seven, of course. But it's still the wrong question. And you end up back where you started, trying to beat the competition at its own game. If your primary focus is on the competition, you will never step back and ask what the customers' inherent needs are, and what the product really is about.

large samples of actual and potential customers. Strategy Capsule 9.1 offers a striking example of the value of simplicity and directness in probing customer requirements.

Product Attributes and Positioning

Virtually all products and services serve multiple customer needs. As a result, understanding customer needs requires the analysis of multiple attributes. Market research

FIGURE 9.1 Consumer perceptions of competing pain relievers: a multidimensional scaling mapping

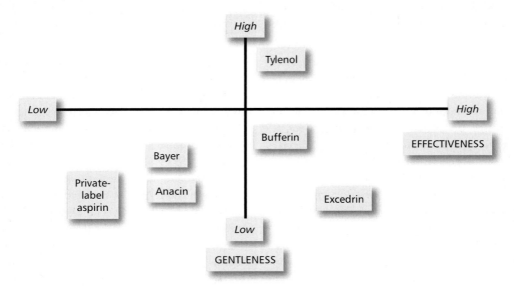

has developed numerous techniques for analyzing customer preferences in relation to different product attributes. These techniques – including multidimensional scaling, conjoint analysis, and hedonic price analysis – can guide the positioning of new products, repositioning of existing products, and setting product prices.

Multidimensional Scaling Multidimensional scaling (MDS) permits customers' perceptions of competing products' similarities and dissimilarities to be represented graphically and for the dimensions to be interpreted in terms of key product attributes.[6] For example, a survey of consumer ratings of competing pain relievers resulted in the mapping shown in Figure 9.1. MDS has also been used to classify 109 single-malt Scotch whiskies according to the characteristics of their color, nose, palate, body, and finish.[7]

Conjoint Analysis Conjoint analysis is a powerful means of analyzing the strength of customer preferences for different product attributes. The technique requires, first, an identification of the underlying attributes of a product and, second, market research to rank hypothetical products that contain alternative bundles of attributes. The results can then be used to estimate the proportion of customers who would prefer a hypothetical new product to competing products already available in the market.[8] Conjoint analysis has been used to predict market shares of forthcoming new models of personal computer, to analyze windsurfer preferences, and to design new products, including Marriott's Courtyard hotel chain and nature tourism in the Amazon basin.

Hedonic Price Analysis The demand for a product may be viewed as the demand for the underlying attributes that the product provides.[9] The price at which a product can sell in the market is the aggregate of the values derived from each of these individual attributes. Hedonic price analysis observes price differences for competing products, relates these differences to the different combinations of attributes offered by each product, and calculates the implicit market price for each attribute. For example:

- For European automatic washing machines, price differences were related to differences in capacity, spin speed, energy consumption, number of programs, and reliability. For example, a machine that spins at 1000 rpm sold at about a $200 price premium to one that spins at 800 rpm.[10]

- In the case of personal computers, hedonic price analysis showed that price differences between models reflected differences in processor speed, memory, and hard drive capacity.[11]

Value Curve Analysis Selecting the optimal combination of attributes depends not only on which attributes are valued by customers, but also on where competitors' offerings are positioned in relation to different attributes. Chan Kim and Renee Mauborgne argue that to position products or to create a whole new market space it is useful to position competitive offerings according to a set of basic performance characteristics that deliver value to customers. Presented graphically, they call such a mapping a *value curve*. Thus, in book retailing key value metrics include price, knowledge levels of staff, selection of books, store ambiance, store hours, and facilities such as cafés and reading areas. By viewing the positioning of independent book stores and chain bookstores along these dimensions we can identify the opportunity for a new combination of attributes – such as those offered by Borders and Barnes and Noble.[12] The key to deploying the value curve in order to create differentiation advantage, they argue, is to look beyond the conventionally defined boundaries of competition and consider competitive offerings from different industries, strategic groups, and buyer segments.

The Role of Social and Psychological Factors

The problem with analyzing product differentiation in terms of measurable performance attributes is that it does not delve very far into customers' underlying motivations. Very few goods or services are acquired to satisfy basic needs for survival: most buying reflects social goals and values in terms of the desire to find community with others, to establish one's own identity, and to make sense of what is happening in the world. Psychologist Abraham Maslow proposed a hierarchy of human needs. Once basic needs for survival are established, there is a progression from security needs, to belonging needs, to esteem needs, to self-actualization needs.[13] Most suppliers of branded goods recognize that their brand equities have much more to do with status and conformity than to survival or security. The disastrous introduction of "New Coke" in 1985 was the result of Coca-Cola giving precedence to tangible differentiation (taste preferences) over intangible differentiation (authenticity).[14] Harley-Davidson harbors no such illusions: it recognizes quite clearly that it is in the business of selling lifestyle, not transportation.

If the key customer needs that a product satisfies are self-identity and social affiliation, the implications for differentiation are far reaching. In particular, to understand customer demand and identify profitable differentiation opportunities requires

FIGURE 9.2 Identifying differentiation potential: the demand side

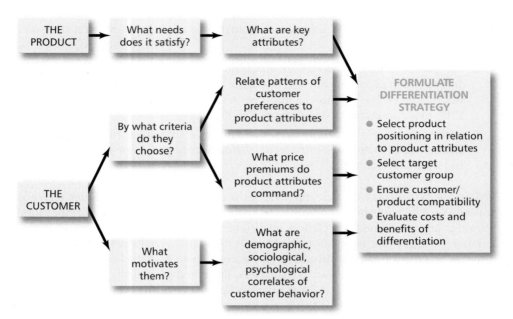

that we analyze the product and its characteristics, but also customers, their lifestyles and aspirations, and the relationship of the product to these lifestyles and aspirations. Market research that looks behind the product and explores the demographic (age, sex, race, location), socioeconomic (income, education), and psychographic (lifestyle, personality type) characteristics of potential customers may be of some value. However, effective differentiation is likely to depend on an understanding of what customers want and how they behave rather than the results of statistical market research. While the phenomenon is complex, the answer, according to Tom Peters, is simple: business people need to "get out from behind their desks to where the customers are . . . [and] construct settings so as to maximize 'naive' listening."[15]

In practice, understanding customer needs and preferences is likely to require more than listening. Typically, consumers cannot clearly articulate the motives that drive them and the emotions that different products trigger. Companies must observe their customers to understand their lives and their use of the product. The implication is that, for companies to understand their customers, they need to become involved with them. Going beyond functionality to explore the emotional and esthetic aspects of consumers' relationships with products is central to Japanese companies' approaches to marketing.[16]

Figure 9.2 summarizes the key points of this discussion by posing some basic questions that explore the potential for demand-side differentiation.

Analyzing Differentiation: The Supply Side

Demand analysis identifies customers' demands for differentiation and their willingness to pay for it, but creating differentiation advantage also depends on a firm's ability to offer differentiation. To identify the firm's potential to supply differentiation, we need to examine the activities the firm performs and the resources it has access to.

The Drivers of Uniqueness

Differentiation is concerned with the provision of uniqueness. A firm's opportunities for creating uniqueness in its offerings to customers are not located within a particular function or activity, but can arise in virtually everything that it does. Michael Porter identifies a number of drivers of uniqueness that are decision variables for the firm:

- Product features and product performance.
- Complementary services (e.g., credit, delivery, repair).
- Intensity of marketing activities (e.g., rate of advertising spending).
- Technology embodied in design and manufacture.
- The quality of purchased inputs.
- Procedures influencing the conduct of each of the activities (e.g., rigor of quality control, service procedures, frequency of sales visits to a customer).
- The skill and experience of employees.
- Location (e.g., with retail stores).
- The degree of vertical integration (which influences a firm's ability to control inputs and intermediate processes).[17]

Most offerings do not involve a single product or a single service, but are a combination of products and services. In analyzing the potential for differentiation, we can distinguish between differentiation of the product ("hardware") and ancillary services ("software"). On this basis, four transaction categories can be identified (see Figure 9.3).[18]

As markets mature, so systems comprising both hardware and software tend to "unbundle." Products become commoditized while complementary services become provided by specialized suppliers. However, as customer preferences become increasingly sophisticated and companies seek new opportunities for differentiation advantage, so hardware and software is repackaged into new systems. Service stations once offered a comprehensive array of services to motorists – gasoline, oil changes, car repair, tires, car washing, and so on. As more and more of these services have become commodities provided by specialist suppliers, so the oil companies have

FIGURE 9.3 Differentiation of merchandise (hardware) and support (software)

		SUPPORT (SOFTWARE) Differentiated	SUPPORT (SOFTWARE) Undifferentiated
MERCHANDISE (HARDWARE)	Differentiated	SYSTEM	PRODUCT
	Undifferentiated	SERVICE	COMMODITY

SOURCE: SHIV MATHUR AND ALFRED KENYON, *CREATING VALUE* (OXFORD: BUTTERWORTH-HEINEMANN, 1997). © 1997 REPRINTED BY PERMISSION OF ELSEVIER.

sought differentiation through creating new bundles of retail services at their service stations.

A critical issue is whether such bundling really creates customer value. Thus, the offer of "one-stop shopping" by financial service companies through diversifying across personal banking, brokerage services, fund management, and insurance has had limited appeal to customers. The advent of internet-based electronic commerce has greatly reduced customers' transaction costs, allowing them to assemble their own bundles of goods and services at low cost. The declining fortunes of European tour operators that organize vacations comprising flights, hotel bookings, car hire, insurance, and other services is the result of the increasing consumer preference to use on-line information and reservations systems to create their own customized vacations.[19] The result, according to McKinsey consultants Hagel and Singer, is not just unbundling of products, but the unbundling of the corporation itself.[20]

Product Integrity

All companies face a range of differentiation opportunities. The primary issue is likely to be determining which forms of differentiation may be most successful in distinguishing the firm in the market and which are most valued by customers. However, such choices cannot be made on a piecemeal basis. Establishing a coherent and effective differentiation position requires that the firm assemble a complementary package of differentiation measures. If Beck's beer wishes to differentiate itself on the basis of the quality of its ingredients, then it must adopt production methods that are consistent with quality ingredients, and packaging, advertising, and distribution appropriate to a quality, premium-priced product.

Product integrity refers to the consistency of a firm's differentiation; it is the extent to which a product achieves:

> *total balance of numerous product characteristics, including basic functions, esthetics, semantics, reliability, and economy . . . Product integrity has both internal and external dimensions. Internal integrity refers to consistency between the function and structure of the product – e.g., the parts fit well, components match and work well together, layout achieves maximum space efficiency. External integrity is a measure of how well a product's function, structure, and semantics fit the customer's objectives, values, production system, lifestyle, use pattern, and self-identity.*[21]

In their study of product development in the auto industry, Clark and Fujimoto argue that simultaneously achieving internal and external integrity is the most complex organizational challenge facing automakers, since it requires linking close cross-functional collaboration with intimate customer contact. The organizational changes among US and European automakers, including the growing role of product managers, have attempted to imitate the success of Toyota and Honda in achieving internal–external integration.[22]

Combining internal and external product integrity is especially important to those supplying "lifestyle" products whose differentiation is based on customers' social and psychological needs. Here, the credibility of the image depends critically on the consistency of the image presented. A critical factor in such differentiation is the ability of employees and customers to identify with one another. Thus:

● Harley-Davidson's ability to develop its image of ruggedness, independence, and individuality is supported by a top management team that dons biking leathers and rides its "hogs" to owners' group rallies, and a management system that empowers shop-floor workers and fosters quality, initiative, and responsibility.

● MTV's capacity to stay at the leading edge of popular culture and embody "coolness" for new generations of young people owes much to its internal culture and human resource management, which rely heavily on the ideas and enthusiasm of its youngest employees.[23]

Maintaining integrity of differentiation is ultimately dependent on a company's ability to live the values embodied in the images with which its products are associated (see Strategy Capsule 9.2).

STRATEGY CAPSULE 9.2

Body Shop: The Role of Values in Differentiation

Anita Roddick opened her first Body Shop in Brighton, England in 1976. With the rapid expansion that followed its IPO in 1985, Body Shop became the world's leading "alternative" cosmetics and toiletries brand.

Two key strategic lessons can be drawn from Body Shop's success. First, a contrarian strategy can be highly effective in creating a new market space. Roddick contradicted most of the industry's long-established, most deeply held conventions. Rather than peddle the allure of beauty, youth, and sexual attractiveness, Body Shop rejects this "magic" – "My products can only cleanse, moisten, and protect," says Roddick. She is equally scornful of the business practices that characterize the industry. In selecting franchisees, Body Shop typically rejects those with prior business experience in favor of those with energy, enthusiasm, and commitment to Body Shop ideals.

Second, for all its apparent naivety and opposition to typical business methods, Body Shop demonstrates a comprehensive and sophisticated approach to differentiation.

Roddick created a clear, distinctive identity and personality for Body Shop and its brand, reinforced and projected through its products, packaging, promoting, retail environment, and business system. For example, the products contain only natural ingredients; the packaging emphasizes simplicity and economy; the retail stores are open, unostentatious, and designed to encourage customers to interact with the products and sales personnel; the business system emphasizes commitment, open communication, loyalty, and individual accountability. Guiding all these aspects of differentiation are the Body Shop's principles and values relating to environmental and social responsibility. The result is that Body Shop is not just a supplier of skin creams and shampoo; it is engaged in creating identity with its customers through commitment to naturalness, honesty, global environmental responsibility, economic support for indigenous people through fair trade, and a rejection of business methods that involve exploiting the natural environment and the economically weak.

Differentiation that embodies ennobling principles and values can be very powerful. But it also creates vulnerability. During the past 10 years, Body Shop has faced many allegations concerning lapses in its ethical standards including departures from "all natural" ingredients, the use of animal-tested ingredients, unfair treatment of franchisees and employees, and lack of commitment to its community support and fair trade initiatives. However, the biggest threat to Body Shop's continued success was its acquisition by L'Oreal – one of the world's biggest and most successful personal care giants – in 2006.

While many of Body Shop's most loyal customers regarded the acquisition as a sellout by Roddick to the enemy, Ms. Roddick was adamant that Body Shop's values would not just be protected, but that the merger offered Body Shop the opportunity to influence the way that L'Oreal did business. To help safeguard Body Shop's values and brand integrity, L'Oreal committed to operating Body Shop as an independent entity within the group and to appoint Ms. Roddick as adviser to L'Oreal's chairman on fair trade policies. Others were skeptical fearing that attacks on Body Shop by consumer activist groups – including Nature-watch's boycott of Body Shop and *Ethical Consumer* magazine's cutting Body Shop's ethical rating from 11 out of 20 to 2.5 – would weaken the brand, undermine morale, and lead to the disintegration of Body Shop's unique corporate culture.

Source: *Body Shop International*, Case No. 9-392-032 (Boston: Harvard Business School, 1992); "Body Shop: Shrewd Sale or Sell-out?" *Financial Times* (March 18, 2006).

Signaling and Reputation

Differentiation is only effective if it is communicated to customers. But information about the qualities and characteristics of products is not always readily available to potential customers. The economics literature distinguishes between *search goods*, whose qualities and characteristics can be ascertained by inspection, and *experience goods*, whose qualities and characteristics are only recognized after consumption. This latter class of goods includes medical services, baldness treatments, frozen TV dinners, and wine. Even after purchase, performance attributes may be slow in revealing themselves – it took me almost ten years to reach the conclusion that my dentist was incompetent and my financial adviser was a charlatan.

In the terminology of game theory (see Chapter 4), the market for experience goods corresponds to a classic "prisoners' dilemma." A firm can offer a high-quality or a low-quality product. The customer can pay either a high or a low price. If quality cannot be detected, then equilibrium is established, with the customer offering a low price and the supplier offering a low-quality product, even though both would be better off with a high-quality product sold at a high price (see Figure 9.4).

The resolution of this dilemma is for producers to find some credible means of signaling quality to the customer. The most effective signals are those that change the payoffs in the prisoners' dilemma. Thus, an extended warranty is effective because providing such a warranty would be more expensive for a low-quality than a high-quality producer. Brand names, warranties, expensive packaging, money-back guarantees, sponsorship of sports and cultural events, and a carefully designed retail environment in which the product is sold are all signals of quality. Their effectiveness

FIGURE 9.4 The problem of quality in experience goods: a "prisoners' dilemma"

		Producer's strategies	
		High quality	Low quality
Consumer's strategies	High price	7 7	10 −5
	Low price	−5 10	3 3

Note: In each cell, the lower-left number is the payoff to the consumer and the upper-right number the payoff to the producer.

stems from the fact that they represent significant investments by the manufacturer that will be devalued if the product proves unsatisfactory to customers.

The need for signaling variables to complement performance variables in differentiation depends on the ease with which performance can be assessed by the potential buyer. The more difficult it is to ascertain performance prior to purchase, the more important signaling is.

- A perfume can be sampled prior to purchase and its fragrance assessed, but its ability to augment the identity of the wearer and attract attention remains uncertain. Hence, the key role of branding, packaging, advertising, and lavish promotional events in establishing an identity for the perfume in terms of the implied personality, lifestyle, and aspirations of the user.
- In financial services, the customer cannot easily assess the honesty, financial security, or competence of a broker, fund manager, or insurance company. Hence, financial service companies emphasize symbols of security and stability: imposing head offices, conservative office decor, smartly dressed employees, and trademarks such as Prudential's rock and Travelers' red umbrella.

Strategies for reputation building have been subjected to extensive theoretical analysis.[24] Some of the propositions that arise from this research include the following:

- Quality signaling is primarily important for products whose quality can only be ascertained after purchase ("experience goods").
- Expenditure on advertising is an effective means of signaling superior quality, since suppliers of low-quality products will not expect repeat buying and hence it is not profitable for them to spend money on advertising.
- A combination of premium pricing and advertising is likely to be superior in signaling quality than either price or advertising alone.
- The higher the sunk costs required for entry into a market and the greater the total investment of the firm, the greater the incentives for the firm not to cheat customers through providing low quality at high prices.

Brands

Brand names and the advertising that supports them are especially important as signals of quality and consistency – because a brand is a valuable asset, it acts as a disincentive to provide poor quality. For many consumer goods (and some producer goods) companies, their brand is their most important asset.

Brands fulfill multiple roles. Most importantly, a brand provides a guarantee by the producer to the consumer of the quality of the product. It does so in several ways. At its most basic, a brand identifies the producer of a product. This ensures that the producer is legally and morally accountable for the products supplied to market. Further, the brand represents an investment that provides an incentive to maintain quality and customer satisfaction. Hence, the brand represents a guarantee to the customer that reduces uncertainty and search costs. The more difficult it is to discern quality on inspection, and the greater the cost to the customer of purchasing a defective product, the greater the value of a brand. Thus, a well-known brand name is likely to be more important to us when we purchase mountaineering equipment than when we buy a pair of socks.

The traditional role of the brand as a guarantor of reliability is particularly significant in e-commerce. Internet transactions are characterized by the anonymity of buyers and sellers and lack of government regulation. As a result, well-established players in e-commerce – Amazon, Microsoft, eBay, and Yahoo! – can use their brand to reduce consumers' perceived risk.

By contrast, the value conferred by leading consumer brands such as Coca-Cola, Harley-Davidson, Mercedes-Benz, Gucci, Virgin, and American Express is less a guarantee of reliability and more an embodiment of identity and lifestyle. For these brands, advertising and promotion have long been the primary means of influencing and reinforcing customer perceptions. Increasingly, consumer goods companies are seeking new approaches to brand development that focus less on product characteristics and more on "brand experience," "tribal identity," "shared values," and "emotional dialogue."

The Costs of Differentiation

Differentiation adds cost. The direct costs of differentiation include higher quality inputs, better-trained employees, higher advertising, and better after-sales service. The indirect costs of differentiation arise through the interaction of differentiation variables with cost variables. If differentiation narrows a firm's segment scope, it also limits the potential for exploiting scale economies. If differentiation requires continual product redesign, it hampers the exploitation of learning economies.

One means of reconciling differentiation with cost efficiency is to postpone differentiation to later stages of the firm's value chain. Economies of scale and the cost advantages of standardization are frequently greatest in the manufacturing of basic components. Modular design with common components permits scale economies while maintaining considerable product variety. All the major automakers have reduced the number of platforms and engine types and increased the commonality of components across their model ranges, while offering customers a greater variety of colors, trim, and accessory options.

New manufacturing technology and the internet have redefined traditional trade-offs between efficiency and variety. Flexible manufacturing systems and just-in-time scheduling have increased the versatility of many plants, made model changeovers less costly, and made the goal of an "economic order quantity of one" increasingly realistic. More and more automobile, motorcycle, and domestic appliance plants are producing multiple models on a single assembly line.[25] Internet communication allows consumers to design their own products and quickly communicate their requirements to manufacturers. Pioneers of mass-customization include Capital One, which offers a unique package of credit facilities and interest rate charges to its credit card customers,[26] and Adidas, whose *mi adidas* program offers individually customized sports shoes through foot scanners installed in its retail stores.[27]

Bringing It All Together: The Value Chain in Differentiation Analysis

There is little point in identifying the product attributes that customers value most if the firm is incapable of supplying those attributes. Similarly, there is little purpose in identifying a firm's ability to supply certain elements of uniqueness if these are not valued by customers. The key to successful differentiation is matching the firm's capacity for creating differentiation to the attributes that customers value most. For this purpose, the value chain provides a particularly useful framework. Let's begin with the case of a producer good, i.e., one that is supplied by one firm to another.

Value Chain Analysis of Producer Goods

Using the value chain to identify opportunities for differentiation advantage involves four principal stages:

1 *Construct a value chain for the firm and the customer.* It may be useful to consider not just the immediate customer, but also firms further downstream in the value chain. If the firm supplies different types of customers – for example, a steel company may supply steel strip to automobile manufacturers and white goods producers – draw separate value chains for each of the main categories of customer.

2 *Identify the drivers of uniqueness in each activity.* Assess the firm's potential for differentiating its product by examining each activity in the firm's value chain and identifying the variables and actions through which the firm can achieve uniqueness in relation to competitors' offerings. Figure 9.5 identifies sources of differentiation within Porter's generic value chain.

3 *Select the most promising differentiation variables for the firm.* Among the numerous drivers of uniqueness that we can identify within the firm, which one should be selected as the primary basis for the firm's differentiation strategy? On the supply side, there are three important considerations.

● First, we must establish where the firm has greater potential for differentiating from, or can differentiate at lower cost than, rivals. This requires some analysis of the firm's internal strengths in terms of resources and capabilities.

FIGURE 9.5 Using the value chain to identify differentiation potential on the supply side

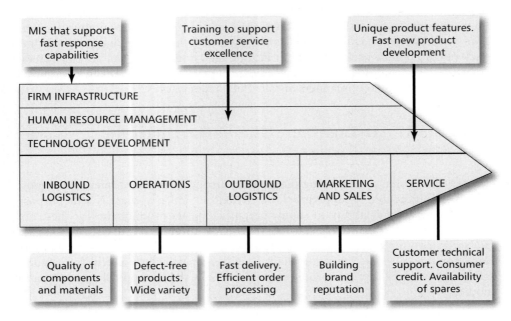

- Second, to identify the most promising aspects of differentiation, we also need to identify linkages among activities, since some differentiation variables may involve interaction among several activities. Thus, product reliability is likely to be the outcome of several linked activities: monitoring purchases of inputs from suppliers, the skill and motivation of production workers, and quality control and product testing.
- Third, the ease with which different types of uniqueness can be sustained must be considered. The more differentiation is based on resources specific to the firm or skills that involve the complex coordination of a large number of individuals, the more difficult it will be for a competitor to imitate the particular source of differentiation. Thus, offering business-class passengers wider seats and more legroom is an easily imitated source of differentiation. Achieving high levels of punctuality represents a more sustainable source of differentiation.

4 *Locate linkages between the value chain of the firm and that of the buyer.* The objective of differentiation is to yield a price premium for the firm. This requires that the firm's differentiation creates value for the customer. Creating value for customers requires either that the firm lowers customers' costs, or that customers' own product differentiation is facilitated. Thus, by reorganizing its product distribution around quick response technologies, Procter & Gamble has radically reduced distribution time and increased delivery reliability. This permits retailers to reduce costs of inventory while

simultaneously increasing their reliability to shoppers through lowering the risk of stockouts. To identify the means by which a firm can create value for its customers it must locate the linkages between differentiation of its own activities and cost reduction and differentiation within the customer's activities. Analysis of these linkages can also evaluate the potential profitability of differentiation. The value differentiation created for the customer represents the maximum price premium the customer will pay. If the provision of just-in-time delivery by a component supplier costs an additional $1,000 a month but saves an automobile company $6,000 a month in reduced inventory, warehousing, and handling costs, then it should be possible for the component manufacturer to obtain a price premium that easily exceeds the costs of the differentiation.

Strategy Capsule 9.3 demonstrates the use of value chain analysis in identifying differentiation opportunities available to a manufacturer of metal containers.

STRATEGY CAPSULE 9.3
Analyzing Differentiation Opportunities for a Manufacturer of Metal Containers

The metal container industry is a highly competitive, low-growth, low-profit industry. Cans lack much potential for differentiation and buyers (especially beverage and food canning companies) are very powerful. Clearly, cost efficiency is essential, but are there also opportunities for differentiation advantage? A value chain analysis can help a metal can manufacturer identify profitable opportunities for differentiation.

STAGE 1. Construct a value chain for firm and customers. The principal activities of the can manufacturer and its customers are shown in the diagram below.

STAGE 2. Identify the drivers of uniqueness. For each of the canmaking activities it is possible to suggest several possible differentiation variables. Examples are shown on the diagram.

STAGE 3. Select key variables. To select the most promising differentiation

variables, the company's internal strengths must be considered. If the firm has strong technical capabilities, then it might design and manufacture products to meet difficult technical and design specifications, and provide sophisticated technical services to customers. If its logistics capabilities are strong it might offer fast and reliable delivery, possibly extended to electronic data interchange with customers.

STAGE 4. Identify linkages. To determine differentiation likely to create value for the customer, identify linkages between the canmaker's potential for differentiation and the potential for reducing cost or enhancing differentiation within the customer's value chain. The diagram identifies five such linkages:

Identifying differentiation opportunities through linking the value chains of the firm and its customers: can manufacture

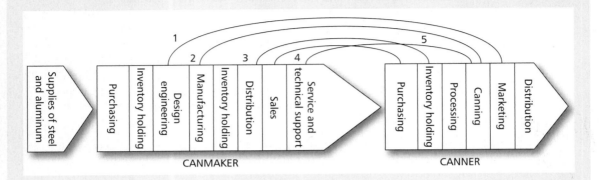

1. Distinctive can designs support canners' own marketing activities.
2. High manufacturing tolerances minimize breakdowns on customers' canning lines.
3. Frequent, punctual deliveries enable canners to minimize inventories.
4. Efficient order processing system reduces canners' ordering costs.
5. Speedy, competent technical support increases capacity utilization of canning lines.

Value Chain Analysis of Consumer Goods

Value chain analysis of differentiation opportunities can also be applied to consumer goods. Few consumer goods are consumed directly; in most cases consumers are involved in a chain of activities involving the acquisition and purchase of the product. Hence, even when the customer is a consumer, it is still feasible to draw a value chain showing the activities that the consumer engages in when purchasing and consuming a product.

In the case of consumer durables, customers are involved in a long chain of activities from search, purchase, financing, acquiring accessories, operation, service and repair, and eventual disposal. Complex consumer value chains offer many potential linkages with the manufacturer's value chain, with considerable opportunity for innovative differentiation. Japanese producers of automobiles, consumer electronics, and domestic appliances have a long tradition of observing their customers' behavior in selecting and utilizing products, then using the information of customer usage and selection processes in planning product design and marketing. Harley-Davidson has been particularly effective at achieving differentiation advantage through careful examination of the activities that customers undertake in selecting, purchasing, using, and maintaining their motorcycles. Harley creates value for its customers through providing test ride facilities at its dealerships, financing, driving instruction, insurance, service and repair facilities, owners' club activities, and various sponsored events for Harley riders. Even nondurables involve the consumer in a chain of activities. Consider a frozen TV dinner: it must be purchased, taken home, removed from the package, heated, and served before it is consumed. After eating, the consumer must clean any used dishes, cutlery, or other utensils. A value chain analysis by a frozen foods producer would identify ways in which the product could be formulated, packaged, and distributed to assist the consumer in performing this chain of activities.

Summary

The attraction of differentiation over low cost as a basis for competitive advantage is its potential for sustainability. It is less vulnerable to being overturned by changes in the external environment, and it is more difficult to replicate.

The potential for differentiation in any business is vast. It may involve physical differentiation of the product, it may be through complementary services, it may be intangible. Differentiation extends beyond technology, design, and marketing to include all aspects of a firm's interactions with its customers.

The essence of differentiation advantage is to increase the perceived value of the offering to the customer either more effectively or at lower cost than do competitors. This requires that the firm match the requirements and preferences of customers with its own capacity for creating uniqueness.

The value chain provides a useful framework for analyzing differentiation advantage. By analyzing how value is created for customers and by systematically appraising the scope of each of the firm's activities for achieving differentiation, the value chain permits matching demand-side and supply-side sources of differentiation.

Successful differentiation requires a combination of astute analysis and creative imagination. The two are not antithetical. A systematic framework for the analysis of differentiation can act as a stimulus to creative ideas.

Self-Study Questions

1   What examples of differentiated consumer products and service offerings can you think of that are differentiated but also succeed in attracting customers across multiple market segments? What advice would you offer companies that are attempting to differentiate their consumer offerings while maintaining a broad market appeal?

2   During 2004–7, Sony struggled to challenge the Apple iPod's dominance of the market for portable MP3 music players. Using the framework outlined in Figure 9.2, suggest opportunities for how Apple might differentiate its MP3 Walkman to increase its customer appeal.

3   What advice would you offer L'Oreal for how it should maintain (or possibly adjust) Body Shop's differentiation and overall competitive positioning (see Strategy Capsule 9.2)?

4   During 2006, Dell Computer faced shrinking margins and a declining share price as the computer market became increasingly commoditized and price competitive. Use the value chain framework outlined in Strategy Capsule 9.3 to identify potential linkages between Dell's value chain and that of the customer in order to spot new differentiation opportunities for Dell.

Notes

1   M. E. Porter, *Competitive Advantage* (New York: Free Press, 1985): 120.

2   T. Peters, *Thriving on Chaos* (New York: Knopf, 1987): 56.

3   P. Barwise and S. Meehan, "Making Differentiation Make a Difference," *Strategy and Business* (September 30, 2004).

4   These distinctions are developed in more detail by P. R. Dickson and J. L. Ginter, "Market Segmentation, Product Differentiation and Marketing Strategy," *Journal of Marketing* 51 (April 1987): 1–10.

5   G. R. Carroll and A. Swaminathan, "Why the Microbrewery Movement?" *American Journal of Sociology* 106 (2000): 715–62.

6   See S. Schiffman, M. Reynolds, and F. Young, *Introduction to Multidimensional Scaling: Theory, Methods, and Applications* (Cambridge, MA: Academic Press, 1981).

7   F.-J. Lapointe and P. Legendre, "A Classification of Pure Malt Scotch Whiskies," *Applied Statistics* 43 (1994): 237–57. On principles of MDS, see I. Borg and P. Groenen, *Modern Multidimensional Scaling: Theory and Application* (Springer Verlag, 1997).

8   See P. Cattin and D. R. Wittink, "Commercial Use of Conjoint Analysis: A Survey," *Journal of Marketing* (Summer 1982): 44–53.

9   K. Lancaster, *Consumer Demand: A New Approach* (New York: Columbia University Press, 1971).

10 P. Nicolaides and C. Baden-Fuller, "Price Discrimination and Product Differentiation in the European Domestic Appliance Market," discussion paper (London: Center for Business Strategy, London Business School, 1987).

11 A. Pates, "A Reconsideration of Hedonic Price Indexes With an Application to PCs," *American Economic Review* 93 (2003): 1578–96.

12 C. Kim and R. Mauborgne, "Creating New Market Space," *Harvard Business Review* (January–February 1999): 83–93.

13 A. Maslow, "A Theory of Human Motivation," *Psychological Review* 50 (1943): 370–96.

14 M. Bastedo and A. Davis, "God, What a Blunder: The New Coke Story," December 17, 1993 (http://members.lycos.co.uk/thomassheils/newcoke.htm).

15 T. Peters, op. cit.: 149.

16 J. K. Johansson and I. Nonaka, *Relentless: The Japanese Way of Marketing* (New York: HarperBusiness, 1996).

17 M. E. Porter, op. cit.: 124–5.

18 S. Mathur, "Competitive Industrial Marketing Strategies," *Long Range Planning* 17, no. 4 (1984): 102–9.

19 "Turbulent times for air charters," *Financial Times* (October 21, 2003): 21.

20 J. Hagel and M. Singer, "Unbundling the Corporation," *McKinsey Quarterly* no. 3 (2000).

21 K. Clark and T. Fujimoto, *Product Development Performance* (Boston: Harvard Business School Press, 1991): 29–30.

22 Ibid.: 247–85; K. B. Clark and T. Fujimoto, "The Power of Product Integrity," *Harvard Business Review* (November–December, 1990): 107–18.

23 J. Seabrook, "Rocking in Shangri-La," *The New Yorker* (October 10, 1994): 64–78.

24 For a survey, see K. Weigelt and C. Camerer, "Reputation and Corporate Strategy: A Review of Recent Theory and Applications," *Strategic Management Journal* 9 (1988): 443–54.

25 R. J. Schonberger, *World Class Manufacturing Casebook: Implementing JIT and TQC* (New York: Free Press, 1987): 120–3; J. Pine, B. Victor, A. Boynton, "Making Mass-customization Work," *Harvard Business Review* (September–October 1993): 108–16.

26 *Capital One Financial Corporation*, Harvard Business School Case No. 7–900–124 (2000).

27 R. Seifert, *The* mi adidas *Mass Customization Initiative*, IMD Case 159 (2002).

IV

BUSINESS STRATEGIES IN DIFFERENT INDUSTRY CONTEXTS

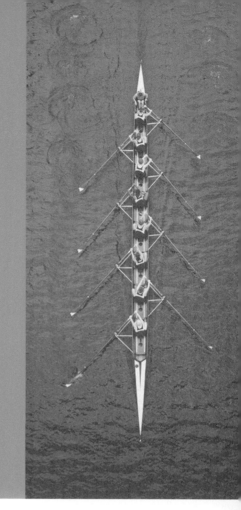

10

Industry Evolution and Strategic Change

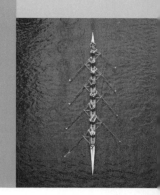

No company ever stops changing ... Each new generation must meet changes – in the automotive market, in the general administration of the enterprise, and in the involvement of the corporation in a changing world. The work of creating goes on.

—ALFRED P. SLOAN JR., PRESIDENT OF GENERAL MOTORS 1923–37, CHAIRMAN 1937–56

OUTLINE

Introduction and Objectives

Everything is in a state of constant change – the business environment especially. The greatest challenge of management is to ensure that adaptation of the enterprise matches the changes occurring within the business environment.

Change in the industry environment is driven by the forces of technology, consumer preferences, economic growth, and a host of other influences. In some cases these forces for change may combine to create massive, unpredictable changes. For example, in telecommunications new digital and wireless technologies combined with regulatory changes have resulted in the telecom industry of 2007 being almost unrecognizable from that which existed 20 years previously. In other industries – food processing, aircraft production, and funeral services – change is more gradual and more predictable. Change is the result both of external forces and the competitive strategies of the firms within the industry. As we have seen, competition is a dynamic process in which firms vie for competitive advantage, only to see it eroded through imitation and innovation by rivals. The outcome of this process is an industry environment that is continually being reshaped by the forces of competition.

The purpose of this chapter is to help us to understand, predict, and manage change. To do this we shall explore the forces that drive change and look for patterns of change that can help us to predict how industries are likely to evolve over time. While recognizing that every industry follows a unique development path, we shall examine the extent to which there are commonalities to the life cycles of industry evolution that are the result of common driving forces. Understanding these patterns can help us to identify and exploit emerging opportunities for competitive advantage.

However, understanding and predicting changes in the industry environment is only one aspect of the management challenge. By far the greater challenge is ensuring the adaptation of the firm to these changes. Change is disruptive, costly, and uncomfortable for individuals and for organizations the forces of inertia are even stronger. As a result, the life cycles of firms tend to be much shorter than the life cycles of industries. This implies that changes at the industry level tend to occur through the death of existing firms and birth of new firms rather than through continuous adaptation by a constant population of firms.

Our starting point is the *industry life cycle*. We shall consider the extent to which industries follow a common development pattern, examine the changes in industry structure over the cycle, and explore the implications for business strategy. We will then study the challenges of managing organizational change, including threats posed by technological change. While our main emphasis will be on the problems of adaptation to changing external circumstances, we shall also investigate the potential for firms to become agents of change – using strategy as a means of transforming their business environments.

By the time you have completed this chapter, you will be able to:

● Recognize the different stages of industry development and understand the factors that drive the process of industry evolution.

● Identify the key success factors associated with industries at different stages of their development.

● Identify the strategies, organizational structures, and management systems appropriate to different stages of industry development.

● Use scenarios to explore industry futures.

● Appreciate the challenges of managing organizational change and be familiar with alternative approaches to strategic change.

The Industry Life Cycle

One of the best-known and most enduring marketing concepts is the *product life cycle*.[1] Products are born, their sales grow, they reach maturity, they go into decline, and they ultimately die. If products have life cycles, so too do the industries that produce them. The *industry life cycle* is the supply-side equivalent of the product life cycle. To the extent that an industry produces a range and sequence of products, the industry life cycle is likely to be of longer duration than that of a single product. Sony's PS3 video game console has a probable life cycle of six or seven years; the life cycle of the electronic games industry extends back to the release of the Atari 2600 in 1977.

The life cycle comprises four phases: *introduction* (or *emergence*), *growth*, *maturity*, and *decline* (see Figure 10.1). Before we examine the features of each of these

FIGURE 10.1 The industry life cycle

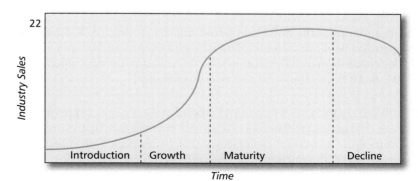

stages, let us examine the forces that are driving industry evolution. Two factors are fundamental: demand growth and the production and diffusion of knowledge.

Demand Growth

The life cycle and the stages within it are defined primarily by changes in an industry's growth rate over time. The characteristic profile is an S-shaped growth curve.

- In the *introduction stage*, sales are small and the rate of market penetration is low because the industry's products are little known and customers are few. The novelty of the technology, small scale of production, and lack of experience means high costs and low quality. Customers for new products tend to be affluent, innovation-oriented, and risk-tolerant.
- The *growth stage* is characterized by accelerating market penetration as product technology becomes more standardized and prices fall. Ownership spreads from higher income customers to the mass market.
- Increasing market saturation causes the onset of the *maturity stage* and slowing growth as new demand gives way to replacement demand. Once saturation is reached, demand is wholly for replacement, either direct replacement (customers replacing old products with new products) or indirect replacement (new customers replacing old customers).
- Finally, as the industry becomes challenged by new industries that produce technologically superior substitute products, the industry enters its *decline stage*.

Creation and Diffusion of Knowledge

The second driving force of the industry life cycle is knowledge. New knowledge in the form of product innovation is responsible for an industry's birth, and the dual processes of knowledge creation and knowledge diffusion exert a major influence on industry evolution.

In the introduction stage, product technology advances rapidly. There is no dominant product technology, and rival technologies compete for attention. Competition is primarily between alternative technologies and design configurations:

- The first 30 years of steam ships featured competition between paddles and propellers, wooden hulls and iron hulls, and, eventually, between coal and oil.
- The beginnings of the home computer industry during 1978–82 saw competition between different data storage systems (audio tapes vs. floppy disks), visual displays (TV receivers vs. dedicated monitors), operating systems (CPM vs. DOS vs. Apple II), and microprocessors.

Dominant Designs and Technical Standards   The outcome of competition between rival designs and technologies is usually convergence by the industry around a *dominant design* – a product architecture that defines the look, functionality, and production method for the product and becomes accepted by the industry as a whole. Dominant designs have included the following:

- The IBM PC launched in 1981 established the basic design parameters of the personal computer as well as the key technical standard that was eventually to dominate the industry (the so-called "Wintel" standard).

- Leica's Ur-Leica 35mm camera developed by Oskar Barnack and launched in Germany in 1924 established what would become the dominant design for cameras, though it was not until Canon began mass-producing cameras based on the Leica design that the 35mm camera came to dominate still photography.[2]

- When Ray Kroc opened his first McDonald's hamburger restaurant in Illinois in 1955, he established what would soon become a dominant design for the fast-food restaurant industry: a limited menu, no waiter service, eat-in and take-out options, roadside locations for motorized customers, and a franchise system of ownership and control.

A dominant design may or may not embody a technical standard. IBM's PC established the MS-DOS operating system and Intel x86 series of microprocessor as technical standards for personal computing. Conversely, the Boeing 707 was a dominant design for large passenger jets, but did not set industry standards in aerospace technology that would dominate subsequent generations of airplanes. Technical standards emerge where there are *network effects* – the need for users to connect in some way with one another. Network effects cause each customer to choose the same technology as everyone else to avoid being stranded. Unlike a proprietary technical standard, which is typically embodied in patents or copyrights, a firm that sets a dominant design does not normally own intellectual property in that design. Hence, except for some early-mover advantage, there is not necessarily any profit advantage from setting a dominant design.

Dominant designs are present in business models as well as products. In many new markets, competition is between rival *business models*. In home grocery delivery, dot.com startups such as Webvan and Peapod soon succumbed to competition from "bricks 'n' clicks" retailers such as Albertson's and Giant. In the retailing of air travel, conventional travel agents such as American Express compete with the airlines' direct sales and online travel agents such as Expedia and Travelocity.

From Product to Process Innovation The emergence of a dominant design marks a critical juncture in an industry's evolution. Once the industry coalesces around a leading technology and design, there's a shift from radical to incremental product innovation. This transition may be necessary to inaugurate the industry's growth phase: greater standardization reduces risks to customers and encourages firms to invest in manufacturing. The shift in emphasis from design to manufacture typically involves increased attention to process innovation as firms seek to reduce costs and increase product reliability through large-scale production methods (see Figure 10.2). The combination of process improvements, design modifications, and scale economies results in falling costs and greater availability that drives rapidly increasing market penetration. Strategy Capsule 10.1 uses the history of the automobile industry to illustrate these patterns of development.

Knowledge diffusion is also important on the customer side. Over the course of the life cycle, customers become increasingly informed. As they become more knowledgeable about the performance attributes of rival manufacturers' products, so they are better able to judge value for money and become more price sensitive.

FIGURE 10.2 Product and process innovation over time

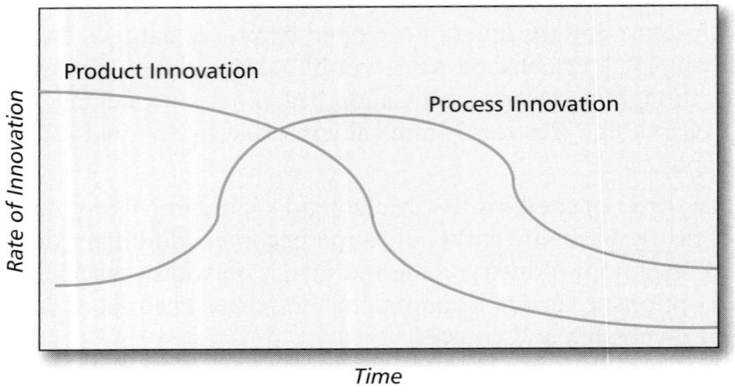

STRATEGY CAPSULE 10.1
Evolution of the Automobile Industry

The period 1890–1912 was one of rapid product innovation in the auto industry. After 1886, when Karl Benz received a patent on his three-wheel motor carriage, a flurry of technical advances occurred in Germany, France, the US, and Britain. Developments included:

- The first four-cylinder four-stroke engine (by Karl Benz in 1890).
- The honeycomb radiator (by Daimler in 1890).
- The speedometer (by Oldsmobile in 1901).
- Automatic transmission (by Packard in 1904).
- Electric headlamps (by General Motors in 1908).
- The all-steel body (adopted by General Motors in 1912).

Ford's Model T, introduced in 1908, with its front-mounted, water-cooled engine and transmission with a gearbox, wet clutch, and rear-wheel drive, acted as a dominant design for the industry. During the remainder of the 20th century, automotive technology and design converged. A key indicator of this was the gradual elimination of alternative technologies and designs. Volkswagen's Beetle was the last mass-produced car with a rear-mounted, air-cooled engine. Citroën abandoned its distinctive suspension and braking systems. Four-stroke engines with four or six inline cylinders became dominant. Distinctive national differences eroded as American cars became smaller and Japanese and Italian cars became bigger. The fall of the Iron Curtain extinguished the last outposts of nonconformity: by the mid-1990s, East German two-stroke Wartburgs and Trabants were collectors' items.

As product innovation slowed, so process innovation took off. In October 1913, Ford opened its Highland Park Assembly Plant, with its revolutionary production methods based on interchangeable parts and a moving assembly line. In the space of one year, chassis assembly time was cut from 12 hours and 8 minutes to

1 hour and 33 minutes. The price of the Model T fell from $628 in 1908 to $260 in 1924. Between 1908 and 1927 over 15 million Model Ts had been produced.

The second revolutionary process innovation in automobile manufacturing was Toyota's system of "lean production," involving a tightly integrated "pull" system of production embodying just-in-time scheduling, team-based produc-

tion, flexible manufacturing, and total quality management. During the 1970s and 1980s, lean production diffused throughout the world vehicle industry in the same way that Ford's mass-production system had transformed the industry half a century before.

Sources: www.daimlerchrysler.com; www.ford.com

How General Is the Life Cycle Pattern?

To what extent do industries conform to this life cycle pattern? To begin with, the duration of the life cycle varies greatly from industry to industry:

- The introduction phase of the US railroad industry extended from the building of the first railroad, the Baltimore and Ohio in 1827, to the growth phase of the 1870s. By the late 1950s, the industry was entering its decline phase.
- The introduction stage of the US automobile industry lasted about 25 years, from the 1890s until growth took off in 1913–15. Maturity, in terms of slackening growth, set in during the mid-1950s.
- In personal computers, the introduction phase lasted only about four years before growth took off in 1978. Between 1978 and 1983 a flood of new and established firms entered the industry. Toward the end of 1984, the first signs of maturity appeared: growth stalled, excess capacity emerged, and the industry began to consolidate around a few companies; however, it remained strong until the end of the 1990s.
- Digital audio players (MP3 players) were first introduced by Seehan Information Systems and Diamond Multimedia during 1997–8. With the launch of Apple's iPod in 2001 the industry entered its growth phase. By 2007, the industry appeared to be entering its mature phase.

The tendency over time has been for life cycles to become compressed. This is evident for all consumer electronic products, communication products, and also pharmaceuticals. In e-commerce, life cycles have become even more compressed. Businesses such as online gambling, business-to-business online auctions, and online travel services have gone from initial introduction to apparent maturity within a few years. Such time compression has required a radical rethink of strategies and management processes – "competing on internet time" is how Michael Cusumano and David Yoffie refer to the challenge.[3]

Patterns of evolution also differ. Industries supplying basic necessities such as residential construction, food processing, and clothing may never enter a decline phase because obsolescence is unlikely for such needs. Some industries may experience a rejuvenation of their life cycle. In the 1960s, the world motorcycle industry, in decline

FIGURE 10.3 Innovation and renewal in the industry life cycle: retailing

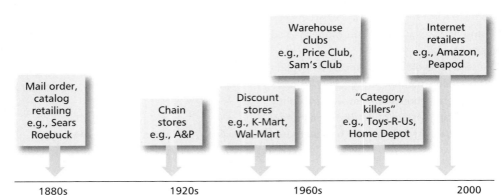

in the US and Europe, re-entered its growth phase as Japanese manufacturers pioneered the recreational use of motorcycles. The market for TV receivers has experienced multiple revivals: color TVs, computer monitors, flat-screen TVs, and, most recently, HDTVs. Similar waves of innovation have revitalized retailing (see Figure 10.3). These rejuvenations of the product life cycle are not natural phenomena – they are typically the result of companies resisting the forces of maturity through breakthrough product innovations or developing new markets.

An industry is likely to be at different stages of its life cycle in different countries. Although the US auto market is in the early stages of its decline phase, markets in China, India, and Russia are in their growth phases. Multinational companies can exploit such differences: developing new products and introducing them into the advanced industrial countries, then shifting attention to other growth markets once maturity sets in.

Structure, Competition, and Success Factors over the Life Cycle

Changes in demand growth and technology over the cycle have implications for industry structure, competition, and the sources of competitive advantage (key success factors). Table 10.1 summarizes the principal features of each stage of the industry life cycle.

Product Differentiation

Emerging industries are characterized by a wide variety of product types that reflect the diversity of technologies and designs – and the lack of consensus over customer requirements. Standardization during growth and maturity phases increases product uniformity, with the result that a product may evolve toward commodity status unless producers are effective in developing new dimensions for differentiation, such as marketing variables, ancillary services (e.g., credit facilities, after-sales service),

TABLE 10.1 The evolution of industry structure and competition over the life cycle

	Introduction	Growth	Maturity	Decline
Demand	Limited to early adopters: high-income, avant-garde.	Rapidly increasing market penetration.	Mass market, replacement/repeat buying. Customers knowledgeable and price sensitive.	Obsolescence.
Technology	Competing technologies. Rapid product innovation.	Standardization around dominant technology. Rapid process innovation.	Well-diffused technical know-how: quest for technological improvements.	Little product or process innovation.
Products	Poor quality. Wide variety of features and technologies. Frequent design changes.	Design and quality improve. Emergence of dominant design.	Trend to commoditization. Attempts to differentiate by branding, quality, bundling.	Commodities the norm: differentiation difficult and unprofitable.
Manufacturing and distribution	Short production runs. High-skilled labor content. Specialized distribution channels.	Capacity shortages Mass production. Competition for distribution.	Emergence of overcapacity. Deskilling of production. Long production runs. Distributors carry fewer lines.	Chronic overcapacity. Re-emergence of specialty channels.
Trade	Producers and consumers in advanced countries.	Exports from advanced countries to rest of world.	Production shifts to newly industrializing then developing countries.	Exports from countries with lowest labor costs.
Competition	Few companies.	Entry, mergers, and exits.	Shakeout. Price competition increases.	Price wars, exits.
Key success factors	Product innovation. Establishing credible image of firm and product.	Design for manufacture. Access to distribution. Brand building. Fast product development. Process innovation.	Cost efficiency through capital intensity, scale efficiency, and low input costs.	Low overheads. Buyer selection. Signaling commitment. Rationalizing capacity.

and product options.[4] A feature of the markets for personal computers, credit cards, securities broking, and internet access is their increasing commodity status in which buyers select primarily on price.

Organizational Demographics and Industry Structure

Industry evolution is associated with high rates of entry and exit and considerable changes in firm population. The field of *organizational ecology*, founded by Michael Hannan, John Freeman, and Glen Carroll, has examined the evolution of industries as a Darwinian process in which the size and composition of the population of firms in an industry are determined by the process through which firms are founded and the process of selection through which they compete for survival.[5] Some of the main findings of the organizational ecologists in relation to industry evolution are:

- The number of firms in an industry increases rapidly during the early stages of an industry's life. Initially an industry may be pioneered by a few firms. However, as these firms gain legitimacy, failure rates decline and the rate of new-firm foundings increases. New entrants have very different origins. Some are startup companies ("*de novo*" entrants); others are established firms diversifying from related industries ("*de alio*" entrants). The US automobile industry featured several hundred producers in the early years of the 20th century,[6] while in TV receivers there were 92 companies in 1951.[7]

- With the onset of maturity, the number of firms begins to fall. Very often, industries go through one or more "shakeout" phases during which the rate of firm failure increases sharply. After this point, rates of entry and exit decline and the survival rate for incumbents increases substantially.[8] The shakeout phase of intensive acquisition, merger, and exit occurs, on average, 29 years into the life cycle and results in the number of producers being halved.[9] In the US tire industry, the number of players increased during the first 25 years, before waves of consolidation, typically triggered by technological and strategic changes within the industry.[10]

- As industries become increasingly concentrated and the leading firms focus on the mass market, so a new phase of entry may take place as new firms take advantage of opportunities in peripheral regions of the market. An example of this "resource partitioning" is the US brewing industry: as the mass market became dominated by a handful of national brewers, so opportunities arose for new types of brewing companies – microbreweries and brew pubs – to establish themselves in specialist niches.[11]

However, different industries follow very different evolutionary paths. While in most industries, maturity is associated with increasing concentration, in industries where scale economies are unimportant and entry barriers are low, maturity and commoditization may cause concentration to decline (as in credit cards, television broadcasting, and frozen foods). Some industries, especially where the first-mover achieves substantial patent protection, may start out as near-monopolies, then become increasingly competitive. Plain-paper copiers were initially monopolized by Xerox Corporation and it was not until the early 1980s that the industry was transformed by a wave of new entry. Seemingly stable mature industries can be transformed within a few years by a wave of mergers. The world petroleum industry consolidated considerably during 1998–2001, as did the world steel industry during 2001–6.

Location and International Trade

The industry life cycle involves the international migration of production.[12] The life cycle theory of trade and direct investment is based on two assumptions. First, that demand for new products emerges first in the advanced industrialized countries of North America, western Europe, and Japan and then diffuses internationally. Second, that with maturity, products require fewer inputs of technology and sophisticated skills. The result is the following development pattern:

1 New industries begin in high-income countries (United States, Japan, and western Europe) because of the presence of a market and the availability of technical and scientific resources.

2 As demand grows in other countries, they are serviced initially by exports.

3 Continued growth of overseas markets and reduced need for inputs of technology and sophisticated labor skills make production attractive in newly industrialized countries. The advanced industrialized countries begin to import.

4 With maturity, commoditization, and de-skilling of production processes, production shifts to developing countries where labor costs are lowest.

For example, consumer electronics were initially dominated by the United States and Germany. During the early 1960s, production shifted towards Japan. The 1980s saw the rise of Korea, Hong Kong, and Taiwan as leading exporters. By the mid-1990s, assembly had moved to lower-wage countries such as China, the Philippines, Thailand, Mexico, and Brazil. We return to these issues of national-level competitiveness in Chapter 14.

The Nature and Intensity of Competition

Competition changes in two ways over the course of the industry life cycle. First, there is a shift from nonprice to price competition. Second, the intensity of competition grows, causing margins to narrow. During the introduction stage, competitors battle for technological leadership and competition focuses on technology and design. Gross margins can be high, but heavy investments in innovation and market development tend to depress return on capital. The growth phase is more conducive to profitability as market demand outstrips industry capacity – especially if incumbents are protected by barriers to entry. With the onset of maturity, increased product standardization and excess capacity stimulates price competition. How intense this is depends a great deal on the capacity/demand balance and the extent of international competition. In food retailing, airlines, motor vehicles, metals, and insurance, maturity was associated with strong price competition and slender profitability. In household detergents, breakfast cereals, cosmetics, and investment banking, high levels of seller concentration and successful maintenance of product differentiation resulted in positive economic profits. The decline phase is almost always associated with strong price competition (often degenerating into destructive price wars) and dismal profit performance.

Key Success Factors and Industry Evolution

These changes in structure, demand, and technology over the industry life cycle have important implications for the primary sources of competitive advantage at each stage of industry evolution:

● During the introductory stage, product innovation is the basis for initial entry and for subsequent success. Soon, however, knowledge alone is not enough. As the industry begins its evolution and technological competition intensifies, other requirements for success emerge. In moving from the first generation of products to subsequent generations, investment requirements tend to grow, and financial resources become increasingly important. Capabilities in product development soon need to be matched by capabilities in manufacturing, marketing, and distribution. Hence, in an emerging industry, firms need to support their innovation with a broad array of vertically integrated capabilities.

● Once the growth stage is reached, the key challenge is scaling up. As the market expands, the firm needs to adapt its product design and its manufacturing capability to large-scale production. As Figure 10.4 shows, investment in R&D, plant and equipment, and sales tends to be high during the growth phase. To utilize increased manufacturing capability, access to distribution becomes critical. At the same time, the tensions that organizational growth impose create the need for internal administrative and strategic skills. We consider these issues in Chapter 11.

FIGURE 10.4 Differences in strategy and performance between businesses at different stages of the industry life cycle

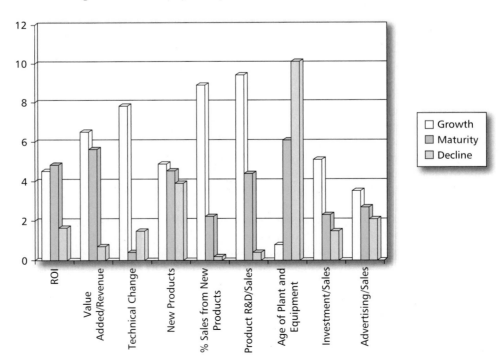

SOURCE: C. ANDERSON AND C. ZEITHAML, "STAGE OF THE PRODUCT LIFE CYCLE, BUSINESS STRATEGY AND BUSINESS PERFORMANCE," ACADEMY OF MANAGEMENT JOURNAL 27 (1984): 5–24.

Note: The figure shows standardized means for each variable for businesses at each stage of the life cycle.

- With the maturity stage, competitive advantage is increasingly a quest for cost efficiency – particularly in those mature industries that tend toward commoditization. Cost efficiency through scale economies, low wages, and low overheads become the key success factors. Figure 10.4 shows that R&D, capital investment, and marketing are lower in maturity than during the growth phase.

- The transformation to the decline phase raises the potential for destructive price competition. While cost advantage is essential, it is also important to maintain a stable industry environment. Hence, company strategies focus on encouraging the orderly exit of industry capacity and building a strong position in relation to residual market demand. We consider the strategic issues presented by mature and declining industries more fully in Chapter 12.

Organizational Adaptation and Change

In Chapter 1, I emphasized the importance of *fit*. For companies to be successful, their strategies and organizational structures need to be aligned with their industry environments. This concept of fit has its origin in *contingency* approaches to organization theory.[13] Industry evolution poses a huge challenge to managers: strategy and structure must adapt to keep pace with the rate of change in the external environment. The faster the pace of industry evolution, the more daunting is the challenge of organizational change.

Evolutionary Theory and Organizational Change

Theories of organizational evolution draw heavily upon biological theories of evolution. Organizations – like biological organisms – adapt to external change through *variation*, *selection*, and *retention*. The critical issue that divides organizational theorists is the level at which these evolutionary processes occur:

- *Organizational ecologists* emphasize evolution at the industry level. Individual organizations are subject to *inertia* – the resistance to change that accompanies the processes of institutionalization.[14] Hence, evolutionary processes work at the level of the industry. The competitive process is a *selection mechanism*, in which organizations whose characteristics match the requirements of their environment survive, and organizations whose characteristics do not are eliminated through acquisition or liquidation. The implication is that industry evolution involves a changing population of companies. As we shall see, a number of empirical studies support this contention that industry evolution is achieved more by the changes in the composition of firms than by adaptation by companies in response to external change.[15]

- *Evolutionary theorists* (such as Nelson and Winter) view evolution as occurring within individual organizations where the process of variation, selection, and retention takes place at the level of the *organizational routine*.[16] As we discussed in Chapter 5, these patterns of coordinated activity are the basis for organizational capability. While evolutionary theorists view firms as adapting to external change through the search for new routines, replication of successful routines, and abandonment of unsuccessful routines, such adaptation is neither fast nor costless. The search for new routines is triggered by declining performance; when companies are performing well there is little impetus for change.

The Sources of Organizational Inertia

Common to all the different analyses of organizational change is the recognition that for organizations – as for individuals – change is difficult and painful. Indeed, it is more difficult for organizations than for individuals because change upsets patterns of social interaction and requires coordinated action among multiple individuals. Different theories emphasize different barriers to change:

- *Organizational capabilities and routines.* Evolutionary economists emphasize the fact that capabilities are based on organizational routines – patterns of interaction among organizational members that develop through continual repetition. The more highly developed are an organization's routines, the more difficult it is to develop new routines. Hence, organizations get caught in *competency traps*[17] where "core capabilities become core rigidities."[18]

- *Social and political structures.* Organizations develop social patterns of interaction that make organizational change stressful and disruptive.[19] Similarly, organizations create stable systems of political power. To the extent that change disrupts social patterns and threatens the power of those in positions of authority, organizations tend to resist change.

- *Conformity.* Institutional sociologists emphasize the propensity of firms to imitate one another to gain legitimacy.[20] The process of *institutional isomorphism* locks organizations into common structures and strategies that make it difficult for them to adapt to change. External pressures for conformity arise from governments, investment analysts, banks, and other sources of resources and legitimacy, but also through voluntary imitation – risk aversion encourages companies to adopt similar strategies and structures to their peers.[21]

- *Complementarities between strategy, structure, and systems.* Both organizational economists[22] and sociotechnical systems scholars[23] emphasize the importance of *fit* between an organization's strategy, structure, management systems, culture, employee skills – indeed, all the characteristics of an organization. Organizations establish complex, idiosyncratic combinations of multiple characteristics during their early phases of development in order to match the conditions of their business environment. However, once established, this complex configuration becomes a barrier to change because of the need to change all the elements of the organization. The implication is that organizations tend to evolve through a process of *punctuated equilibrium* involving long periods of stability during which the widening misalignment between the organization and its environment ultimately forces radical and comprehensive change on the company.[24]

- *Limited search and blinkered perceptions.* Organizations' capacity for large-scale change is also limited by their propensity to limit search to areas close to their existing activities and operations. According to the Carnegie School of organizational theory, most organizations are limited to incremental changes because of *bounded rationality* (limited information processing capacity constrains human beings in their search activities), *satisficing* (the quest for satisfactory rather than optimal performance), and the preference for *exploitation* of existing knowledge over *exploration* for new opportunities.[25]

Empirical Evidence on Organizational Adaptation

The ability of some companies to adapt is indicated by the fact that many have been leaders in their industries for a century or more – Siemens has been a leading player in communications equipment since the founding of Telegraphen-Bau-Anstalt von Siemens & Halske in 1847, Exxon (now Exxon Mobil) and Royal Dutch Shell have dominated the petroleum industry for the whole of the 20th century, General Motors has been the world's biggest automobile maker since the mid-1920s. Yet these companies are exceptions. Among the companies forming the original Dow Jones Industrial Average in 1896, only General Electric remains in the index today. Of the world's 12 biggest companies in 1912, just three were in the top 12 in 2006 (see Table 10.2).

The ability of a firm to adapt to external change depends on the nature of that change. Evolutionary change over the typical industry life cycle is less threatening than radical technological change. Let us review evidence on adaptation to both types of change.

Adapting to changes over the life cycle   Even though the industry life cycle involves changes that are largely predictable, the different stages of the life cycle require different capabilities that established forms may struggle to develop. Markides and Geroski show that steps through the different stages of an industry's development are usually undertaken by different companies – the "innovators" that pioneer the creation of a new industry are typically different companies from the "consolidators" that develop it:

TABLE 10.2   World's biggest companies in terms of market capitalization, 1912 and 2006

1912	$ bn	2006	$ bn
US Steel	0.74	Exxon Mobil	372
Exxon	0.39	General Electric	363
J&P Coates	0.29	Microsoft	281
Pullman	0.20	Citigroup	239
Royal Dutch Shell	0.19	BP	233
Anaconda	0.18	Bank of America	212
General Electric	0.17	Royal Dutch Shell	211
Singer	0.17	Wal-Mart Stores	197
American Brands	0.17	Toyota Motor	197
Navistar	0.16	Gazprom	196
BAT	0.16	HSBC	190
De Beers	0.16	Procter & Gamble	190

SOURCES: FINANCIAL TIMES, ECONOMIST.

The fact that the firms that create new product and service markets are rarely the ones that scale them into mass markets has serious implications for the modern corporation. Our research points to a simple reason for this phenomenon: the skills, mind-sets, and competences needed for discovery and invention are not only different from those needed for commercialization; they conflict with the needed characteristics. This means that the firms good at invention are unlikely to be good at commercialization and vice versa.[26]

In personal computers the pioneers were Apple, Commodore, and Xerox; 25 years later, the leaders were Dell, Lenova, Acer, and Hewlett-Packard. In US wireless telephony the pioneer was McCaw Communications; the current market leaders are Cingular and Verizon.

Adapting to technological change   The ability of firms to adapt to technological change depends to a great extent on the implications of the new technology. Some new technologies may enhance a company's existing capabilities, others may be "competence destroying."[27] This depends, in part, on whether the technology's impact is at the "component" or the "architectural" level – i.e. whether it involves a single process or product feature or whether it necessitates a new configuration of the product.[28] In many sectors of e-commerce – online grocery purchases and online banking – the internet involved innovation at the component level (it provided a new channel of distribution for existing products). Hence, existing supermarket chains and established retail banks with their "clicks and bricks" business models have dominated online groceries and online financial services.

Where more radical technological change involves architectural innovation then established firms have difficulty adapting and new startups tend to be more successful. But even here, ownership of key resources (e.g. brands, customer relationships, and distribution systems) can support established firms while they overcome the disruptive effects of radical technological change. Since the late 19th century, the typesetter industry has undergone three waves of wrenching technological change. Yet, although new entrants had advantages in technology and new product development, incumbent firms' customer relationships, sales and service networks, and font libraries allowed many to survive and prosper.[29]

Elsewhere, technological changes – even the apparently modest technological changes associated with new product generations – can give newcomers the ability to unseat established market leaders. In disk drives, Clayton Christensen found that with every new product generation – from 14″ to 8″ to 5.25″ to 3.5″ drives – the established companies were on average two years behind newcomers in launching new products.[30] The barriers to change were twofold: first, at the time of their introduction, new technologies are initially inferior to existing technologies; second, established companies listen to their customers, most of whom don't want the new technology – typically, it is fringe customers that are lead adopters of new technologies. The result is that new technologies tend to be disruptive to established firms even when they do not embody architectural innovations. The critical feature of these *disruptive technologies*, according to Christensen, is that they offer a very different package of attributes from the existing technology. For example:

● Sony's early transistor radios sacrificed sound fidelity but offered portability through small size and light weight.

- Nucor pioneered minimill technology, which initially was lower quality and higher cost than integrated steel production but offered flexible, small-scale production close to customers.
- In telecommunications equipment, it was newcomers Cisco Systems and Juniper Networks, rather than established leaders such as Lucent Technologies and Alcatel, that were most successful in exploiting the packet switching technologies associated with the internet.[31]

What about technological changes that create new industries? Again, we see the same phenomenon: new startup companies (*de novo* entrants) competing with established companies that have diversified from other sectors (*de alio* entrants). The issues are the same as within an industry undergoing change: are the flexibility advantages of new startups more important than the more substantial resources and capabilities of established firms? The evidence suggests that, where the resources and capabilities of one industry are closely related to those required in a new industry, then diversifying entrants from that established industry will tend to be at an advantage over new startups. Thus:

- In the US automobile industry, former bicycle, carriage, and engine manufacturers tended to be the best performers.[32]
- The US television manufacturing industry was dominated by former producers of radios.[33]

However, often some of the best performing firms in a new industry are spinoffs from existing companies within that industry – i.e. new ventures established by former employees of existing companies. This was evident in the US auto industry,[34] the Akron tire industry,[35] and the Silicon Valley semiconductor industry – where most of the leading players, including Intel, trace their origins to Shockley Semiconductor Laboratories, the initial producer of integrated circuits.[36]

Managing Organizational Change

Given the many barriers to organizational change, how can companies adapt to changes in their environment? The fundamental requirement is that managers recognize the sources of inertia – existing routines and capabilities, power structures, and entrenched perceptions regarding the nature of the business. Once the rigidities of the status quo are acknowledged, then we can embark on the challenge of initiating and guiding strategic change.

Dual Strategies and Separate Organizational Units Given the rigidities of prevailing strategies and structures, it may be easier to effect change by creating new organizational units rather than trying to change the existing organization. Thus, faced with the challenge of disruptive technologies, Christensen and Overdorf suggest that established companies develop products and businesses that embody the new technologies in organizationally separate units.[37]

Costas Markides argues that the critical issue is not so much the allocation of new strategic initiatives to separate organizational units, but the firm's capacity to simultaneously pursue multiple strategies. Despite several well-publicized failures of dual strategies – notably the budget airlines initiated by British Airways, Continental, and United – he finds that a surprisingly large number of companies have successfully pursued dual business models. Success had little to do with whether the new strategy was organizationally separated; the key was the ability of the new business model to access and deploy the company's existing resources and capabilities.[38]

To some extent all companies need to pursue dual strategies to the extent that they must maximize current performance by deploying existing resources and capabilities most effectively while at the same time developing the business to meet the challenges of competing in the business environment of the future. According to Derek Abell, pursuing such dual strategies requires dual planning systems: short-term planning that focuses on strategic fit and performance over a one- or two-year period, and longer term planning to develop vision, reshape the corporate portfolio, redefine and reposition individual businesses, develop new capabilities, and redesign organizational structures over periods of five years or more.[39] In companies, strategic management is biased towards the exploitation of current resources and capabilities and insufficient management time is devoted towards the exploration of new opportunities and new capabilities for the future.

Bottom–up Processes of Decentralized Organizational Change

In Chapter 6, we noted that the appeal of modular, loosely coupled organizational structures was the potential for decentralized adaptation that avoided disrupting the whole organization. Yet, typically, simply decentralizing decision making is not enough to speed the processes of organizational adaptation. The strategy literature points to the need for top management to manage the conditions that foster and extend the processes of change. For example:

- If search for new strategies and new opportunities is limited by satisficing behavior, then top management needs to stimulate performance by raising performance expectations – establishing "stretch targets" for example.

- Corporate top management can challenge divisional and business unit managers to seek new opportunities by issuing specific company-wide initiatives. General Electric's former CEO, Jack Welch, would periodically issue such challenges: "Be number 1 or number 2 in your industry," "six-sigma quality," "destroy-your-business.com."

- Andy Grove of Intel has pointed to the necessity for top management to be alert to the emergence of "strategic dissonance" created by divergent strategic directions within the company. Such dissonance is likely to signal a "strategic inflection point" – a fundamental change in industry dynamics – at which point the company must be willing to make a radical strategic shift. For Intel, such an inflection point occurred when it recognized that its future lay in microprocessors rather than its initial business of DRAM chips.[40]

- By periodically changing organizational structure, a company can stimulate decentralized search and local initiatives while encouraging more effective exploitation of the outcomes of such search.[41] A typical pattern is to oscillate from periods of decentralization to periods of centralization.[42]

Imposing Top–down Organizational Change

If organizational change occurs periodically through a punctuated equilibrium process, the implication is that these instances of concentrated organizational change must be orchestrated from the top. Most large companies exhibit periodic restructuring involving simultaneous changes in strategy, structure, management systems, and top management personnel. Such restructuring typically follows declining performance. For example, the oil and gas majors all experienced far-reaching restructuring during 1986–92 following depressed profitability that accompanied the oil price decline of 1986.[43] The challenge for top management is to undertake large-scale change before the company is pressured by declining performance. This may require that the CEO manufactures a perception of impending crisis within the company.

Using Scenarios to Prepare for the Future A company's ability to adapt to changes in its environment depends on its capacity to anticipate such changes. Yet predicting the future is hazardous, if not impossible. "Only a fool would make predictions – especially about the future," remarked movie mogul Samuel Goldwyn. But the inability to predict does not mean that it is not useful to think about what might happen in the future. *Scenario analysis* is a systematic way of thinking about how the future might unfold that builds on what we know about current trends and signals. Scenario analysis is not a forecasting technique, but a process for thinking and communicating about the future.

Herman Kahn, who pioneered their use first at the Rand Corporation and subsequently at the Hudson Institute, defined scenarios as "hypothetical sequences of events constructed for the purpose of focusing attention on causal process and decision points."[44] The multiple scenario approach constructs several distinct, internally consistent views of how the future may look five to 25 years ahead (shorter in the case of fast-moving sectors). Its key value is in combining the interrelated impacts of a wide range of economic, technological, demographic, and political factors into a few distinct alternative stories of how the future might unfold. Scenario analysis can be either qualitative or quantitative, or involve some combination of the two. Quantitative scenario analysis models events and runs simulations to identify likely outcomes. Qualitative scenarios typically take the form of narratives and can be particularly useful in engaging the insight and imagination of decision makers.

For the purposes of strategy making, scenario analysis is used to explore likely paths of industry evolution, to examine developments in particular country markets, to think about the impact of new technologies, and to analyze prospects for specific investment projects. Applied to industry evolution, scenarios can clarify and develop alternative views of how changing customer requirements, emerging technologies, government policies, and competitor strategies might have an impact on industry structure, and what the implications for competition and competitive advantage might be.

However, as with most strategy techniques, the value of scenario analysis is not in the results, but in the process. Scenario analysis is a powerful tool for bringing together different ideas and insights, for surfacing deeply held beliefs and assumptions, for identifying possible threats and opportunities, for generating and evaluating alternative strategies, for generating more flexible thinking by managers, and for building consensus. Evaluating the likely performance of different strategies under different scenarios can help identify which strategies are most robust and can assist in contingency planning by forcing managers to address "what if?" questions. Strategy Capsule 10.2 outlines the use of scenarios at Shell.

Shaping the Future

A succession of management gurus from Tom Peters to Gary Hamel have argued that the key to organizational change is not to adapt to external change but to create the

STRATEGY CAPSULE 10.2
Multiple Scenario Development at Shell

Royal Dutch Shell has pioneered the use of scenarios as a basis for long-term strategic planning in an industry where the life of investment projects (up to 50 years) far exceeds the time horizon for forecasting (two or three years). In 1967, a "Year 2000" study was inaugurated and scenario development soon became fundamental to Shell's planning process. Mike Pocock, Shell's former chairman, observed: "We believe in basing planning not on single forecasts, but on deep thought that identifies a coherent pattern of economic, political, and social development."

Shell views its scenarios as critical to its transition from planning toward strategic management, in which the role of the planning function is not so much to produce a plan, but to manage a process, the outcome of which is improved decision making by managers. This involves continually challenging current thinking within the group, encouraging a wider look at external influences on the business, promoting learning, and forging coordination among Shell's 200-odd subsidiaries.

Shell's global scenarios are prepared about every four years by a team comprising corporate planning staff, executives, and outside experts. Economic, political, technological, and demographic trends are analyzed 20 years into the future. Shell's 2005–25 scenarios were based on three sets of forces – market incentives, community, and coercion and regulation; and three objectives – efficiency, social cohesion, and security. Their interactions produced three scenarios each embodying different social, political, and economic conditions:

- *Low Trust Globalization*. A legalistic world where emphasis is on security and efficiency at the expense of social cohesion.
- *Open Doors*. A pragmatic world emphasizing social cohesion and efficiency with the market providing built-in solutions to crises of security and trust.
- *Flags*. A dogmatic world where community and security values are emphasized at the expense of efficiency.

Once approved by top management, the scenarios are disseminated by reports, presentations, and workshops, where they form the basis for long-term strategy discussion by business sectors and operating companies.

Shell is adamant that its scenarios are not forecasts. They represent carefully thought-out stories of how the various forces shaping the global energy environment of the future might play out. Their value is in stimulating the social and cognitive processes through which managers think about the future. CEO Van Der Veer commented: ". . . the imperative is to use this tool to gain deeper in sights into our global business environment and to achieve the cultural change that is at the heart of our group strategy . . . I know that they broaden one's mindset and stimulate discussions."

Sources: Pierre Wack, "Scenarios: Uncharted Waters Ahead," *Harvard Business Review* (September–October 1985): 72 and "Scenarios: Shooting the Rapids," *Harvard Business Review* (November–December 1985): 139; Arie De Geus, "Planning as Learning," *Harvard Business Review* (March–April 1988): 70–4; Paul Schoemacher, "Multiple Scenario Development: Its Conceptual and Behavioral Foundation," *Strategic Management Journal* 14 (1993): 193–214; *Shell Global Scenarios to 2025* (Shell International, 2005).

FIGURE 10.5 Shaking the foundations

ADAPTED FROM: GARY HAMEL, *LEADING THE REVOLUTION* (BOSTON: HARVARD BUSINESS SCHOOL PRESS, 2000): 280–1.

OLD BRICK	NEW BRICK
Top management is responsible for setting strategy	Everyone is responsible for setting strategy
Getting better, getting faster is the way to win	Rule-busting innovation is the way to win
IT creates competitive advantage	Unconventional business concepts create competitive advantage
Being revolutionary is high risk	More of the same is high risk
We can merge our way to competitiveness	There's no correlation between size and competitiveness
Innovation equals new products and new technology	Innovation equals entirely new business concepts
Strategy is the easy part; implementation the hard part	Strategy is the easy part only if you're content to be an imitator
Change starts at the top	Change starts with activists
Our real problem is execution	Our real problem is incrementalism
Big companies can't innovate	Big companies can become gray-haired revolutionaries

future. Companies that adapt to change are doomed to playing catch-up; competitive advantages accrue to those companies that act as leaders and initiate change. Hamel and Prahalad's "new strategy paradigm" emphasizes the role of strategy as a systematic and concerted approach to redefining both the company and its industry environment in the future.[45]

According to Gary Hamel, in an age of revolution, "the company that is evolving slowly is already on its way to extinction."[46] The only option is to give up incremental improvement and adapt to a nonlinear world – revolution must be met by revolution. Achieving internal revolution requires changing the psychological and sociological norms of an organization that restrict innovation (see Figure 10.5).

Hamel's challenge for managers to cast off their bureaucratic chains and become revolutionaries is invigorating and inspiring. But is revolution among established companies either feasible or desirable? Some established companies have achieved radical change:

- Nokia underwent a metamorphosis from a manufacturer of paper and rubber goods into the world's leading supplier of mobile phones.
- BP transformed itself from a bureaucratic state-owned oil company to one of the most flexible and innovative of the supermajors.
- Microsoft has successfully ridden a series of disruptive changes in the world's computer industry, including the transition to object-oriented computing and the networking revolution of the late 1990s, and is currently positioning itself for the conversion of computing, telecommunications, and home entertainment.

However, for most established companies, efforts at radical change have resulted in disaster:

- Enron's transformation from a utility and pipeline company to a trader and market-maker in energy futures and derivatives ended in disaster in 2001.
- Vivendi's multimedia empire built on the base of French water and waste utility fell apart in 2002.
- GEC's reincarnation as Marconi, a telecom equipment supplier, was swiftly followed by bankruptcy in 2002.
- ICI, the former British chemical giant, has yet to recover from its attempt to reinvent itself as a specialty chemical company.
- Skandia's quest to become one of the world's most innovative insurance companies ended in top management scandal and the sale of most of the company's businesses outside of Sweden.

The perils of radical strategic change are not difficult to understand. We have noted that competitive advantage depends on the deployment of superior organizational capabilities and these capabilities develop slowly. Strategic changes that take a company beyond its competence domain involve massive risks.

Summary

Strategy is about establishing an identity and a direction for the development of a business into the future. How can we formulate a strategy for the future if the future is unknown and difficult to predict?

In this chapter we have learned that some regularities are evident in the evolutionary paths that industries follow. The life cycle model is a useful approach to exploring the impact of temporal processes of market saturation and technology development and dissemination and their impact on industry structure and the basis of competitive advantage. Classifying industries according to their stage of development can in itself be an insightful exercise:

- It acts as a shortcut in strategy analysis. Categorizing an industry according to its stage of development can alert us to the type of competition likely to emerge and the kinds of strategy likely to be effective.

- Classifying an industry encourages comparison with other industries. By highlighting similarities and differences with other industries, such comparisons can help us gain a deeper understanding of the strategic characteristics of an industry.

- It directs attention to the forces of change and direction of industry evolution, thereby helping us to anticipate and manage change.

Even if we can identify certain regularities in the pattern of industry evolution, adapting to change presents a huge challenge to companies. Organizational theories that emphasize inertia and conformity among organizations suggest that industry adjustment may occur more through the birth of new firms and death of old ones, rather than through adaptation by established firms. This analysis is supported by empirical evidence that points to the limited success of established firms in dealing with industry evolution and disruptive technologies.

While various management consultants and commentators advocate radical and continuous change among established companies, there is little evidence that most companies have the capacity to manage such change. Certain tools and techniques – scenario analysis, in particular – may help managers understand and cope with change in the external environment; nevertheless, the fundamental truth is that, so long as developing new capabilities is slow and risky, a firm's capacity to successfully undergo radical change is inherently uncertain.

In the next two chapters, we discuss strategy formulation and strategy implementation in industries at different stages of their development: emerging industries, those characterized by technology-based competition, and mature industries.

Self-Study Questions

1 Consider the changes that have occurred in a comparatively new industry (e.g. wireless communications, video game consoles, medical diagnostic imaging, PDAs, online auctions, bottled water, courier delivery services). To what extent has the evolution of the industry followed the pattern predicted by the industry life cycle model? At what stage of development is the industry today? How is the industry likely to evolve in the future?

2 Select a product that has become a *dominant design* for its industry (e.g. the IBM PC in personal computers, the Boeing 707 in passenger jets, McDonald's in fast food, Harvard in MBA education, Southwest in budget airlines). What forces caused one firm's product architecture to become dominant? Why did other firms imitate this dominant design? To what extent has the dominant design evolved or been displaced?

3 The "resource partitioning" model argues that as industries become dominated by a few major companies whose strategies and products converge, so opportunities open for new entrants to build specialist niches. Identify an opportunity for establishing a specialist new business in an industry dominated by mass market giants.

4 Consider an industry facing fundamental technology change (e.g. fixed-point telecommunications and internet protocols, the recorded music industry and digitalization, computer software and open-source, newspapers and the internet, automobiles and alternative fuels). Develop two alternative scenarios for the future evolution of your chosen industry. In relation to one leading player in the industry, identify the problems posed by the new technology and develop a strategy for how the company might adapt to and exploit the changes you envisage.

Notes

1   For early work on the product life cycle, see
    E. M. Rogers, *The Diffusion of Innovations* (New York:
    Free Press, 1962); T. Levitt, "Exploit the Product Life
    Cycle," *Harvard Business Review* (November–December
    1965): 81–94; G. Day, "The Product Life Cycle:
    Analysis and Applications," *Journal of Marketing* 45
    (Autumn 1981): 60–7.

2   Thanks to Bob Edwards for information on the
    development of camera design.

3   M. A. Cusumano and D. B. Yoffie, *Competing on
    Internet Time: Lessons From Netscape and Its Battle
    with Microsoft* (New York: Free Press, 1998).

4   In Shiv Mathur and Alfred Kenyon's "transaction cycle,"
    differentiation re-emerges as products and service are
    bundled into new systems. See "Competitive System
    Dynamics," in *Creating Wealth: Shaping Tomorrow's
    Business* (Oxford: Butterworth-Heinemann, 1997):
    Chapter 9.

5   G. Carroll and M. Hannan, *The Demography of
    Corporations and Industries* (Princeton: Princeton
    University Press, 2000). For a survey see: J. Baum,
    "Organizational Ecology," in S. R. Clegg, C. Hardy, and
    W. R. Nord, *Handbook of Organizational Studies*
    (Thousand Oaks: Sage, 1996); D. Barron, "Evolutionary
    Theory," in D. O. Faulkner and A. Campbell (eds),
    The Oxford Handbook of Strategy (Oxford: Oxford
    University Press, 2003) vol. 1: 74–97.

6   G. R. Carroll, L. S. Bigelow, M.-D. Seidel, and B. Tsai,
    "The Fates of *de novo* and *de alio* Producers in the
    American Automobile Industry, 1885–1981," *Strategic
    Management Journal* 17, Summer Special Issue (1996):
    117–37.

7   S. Klepper and K. L. Simons, "Dominance by Birthright:
    Entry of Prior Radio Producers and Competitive
    Ramifications in the US Television Receiver Industry,"
    Strategic Management Journal 17 (2000): 997–1016.

8   High rates of entry and exit may continue well into
    maturity. In US manufacturing industries in any given
    year, it was found that 39 percent of larger companies
    were not industry participants five years earlier and 40
    percent would not be participants five years later. See
    T. Dunne, M. J. Roberts, and L. Samuelson, "Patterns
    of Firm Entry and Exit in US Manufacturing Industries,"
    Rand Journal of Economics 19 (1988): 495–515.

9   S. Klepper and E. Grady, "The Evolution of New
    Industries and the Determinants of Industry Structure,"
    Rand Journal of Economics (1990): 27–44.

10 S. Klepper and K. Simons, "The Making of an
    Oligopoly: Firm Survival and Technological Change in
    the Evolution of the US Tire Industry," *Journal of
    Political Economy* 108 (2000).

11 G. Carroll and A. Swaminathan, "Why the
    Microbrewery Movement? Organizational Dynamics of
    Resource Partitioning in the American Brewing
    Industry," *American Journal of Sociology* 106 (2000):
    715–62.

12 R. Vernon, "International Investment and International
    Trade in the Product Cycle," *Quarterly Journal of
    Economics* 80 (1966): 190–207.

13 Contingency theory has its origins in P. R. Lawrence
    and J. W. Lorsch's book *Organization and Environment*
    (Boston: Harvard Business School, 1967). See also
    A. Ginsberg and N. Venkatraman, "Contingency
    Perspectives of Organizational Strategy," *Academy of
    Management Review* 10 (1985): 421–34.

14 P. J. DiMaggio and W. W. Powell, "The Iron Cage
    Revisited: Institutional Isomorphism and Collective
    Rationality," in W. W. Powell and P. J. DiMaggio, *The
    New Institutionalism and Organizational Analysis*
    (Chicago: University of Chicago Press, 1991): 63–82.

15 For an introduction to organizational ecology, see:
    M. T. Hannan and G. R. Carroll, "An introduction to
    organizational ecology," in *Organizations in Industry*
    (Oxford: Oxford University Press, 1995): 17–31.

16 For a survey of evolutionary approaches, see
    R. R. Nelson, "Recent Evolutionary Theorizing About
    Economic Change," *Journal of Economic Literature* 33
    (March 1995): 48–90.

17 J. G. March, "Exploration and Exploitation in
    Organizational Learning," *Organizational Science* 2
    (1991): 71–87.

18 D. Leonard-Barton, "Core Capabilities and Core
    Rigidities: A Paradox in Managing New Product
    Development," *Strategic Management Journal*, Summer
    Special Issue (1992): 111–25.

19 M. T. Hannan, L. Polos, and G. R. Carroll, "Structural
    Inertia and Organizational Change Revisited III: The
    Evolution of Organizational Inertia," Stanford GSB
    Research Paper 1734 (April 2002).

20 P. J. DiMaggio and W. Powell, "'The Iron Cage
    Revisited': Institutional Isomorphism and Collective
    Rationality in Organizational Fields," *American
    Sociological Review* 48 (1983): 147–60.

21 J.-C. Spender, *Industry Recipes* (Oxford: Blackwell,
    1989).

22 P. R. Milgrom and J. Roberts, "Complementarities and
    Fit: Strategy, Structure, and Organizational Change in
    Manufacturing," *Journal of Accounting and Economics*
    19 (1995): 179–208; M. E. Porter and N. Siggelkow,
    "Contextual Interactions within Activity Systems and
    Sustainable Competitive Advantage," Working Paper,
    Harvard Business School, Boston, 2002.

23 A. B. Shani and J. A. Sena, "Information Technology
    and the Integration of Change: A Sociotechnical Systems
    Approach," *Journal of Applied Behavioral Science* 30
    (1994): 247–70; E. Trist, "The Sociotechnical
    Perspective." In Van de Ven and Joyce (eds), *Perspectives
    on Organization Design and Behavior* (New York: Wiley,
    1984).

24 M. L. Tushman and E. Romanelli, "Organizational
    Evolution: A Metamorphosis Model of Convergence
    and Reorientation," in L. L. Cummins and B. M. Staw

(eds), *Research in Organizational Behavior* 7 (1985): 171–26; E. Romanelli and M. L. Tushman, "Organizational Transformation as Punctuated Equilibrium: An Empirical Test," *Academy of Management Journal* 37 (1994): 1141–66.

25 J. G. March and H. A. Simon, *Organizations* (New York: Wiley, 1958); J. G. March, "Exploration and Exploitation in Organizational Learning," *Organization Science* 2 (1991): 71–87.

26 C. Markides and P. Geroski, "Colonizers and Consolidators: The Two Cultures of Corporate Strategy," *Strategy & Business* 32 (Fall 2003).

27 M. L. Tushman and P. Anderson, "Technological Discontinuities and Organizational Environments," *Administrative Science Quarterly* 31 (1986): 439–65.

28 R. M. Henderson and K. B. Clark, "Architectural Innovation: The Reconfiguration of Existing Systems and the Failure of Established Firms," *Administrative Science Quarterly* (1990): 9–30.

29 M. Tripsas, "Unravelling the Process of Creative Destruction: Complementary Assets and Incumbent Survival in the Typesetter Industry," *Strategic Management Journal* 18, Summer Special Issue (July 1997): 119–42.

30 C. M. Christensen and J. L. Bower, "Customer Power, Strategic Investment, and the Failure of Leading Firms," *Strategic Management Journal* 17 (March 1996): 197–218.

31 J. Bower and C. M. Christensen, "Disruptive Technologies: Catching the Wave," *Harvard Business Review* (January–February 1995): 43–53.

32 S. Klepper, "The Capabilities of New Firms and the Evolution of the US Automobile Industry," *Industrial and Corporate Change* 11 (2002): 645–66.

33 S. Klepper and K. L. Simons, "Dominance by Birthright: Entry of Prior Radio Producers and Competitive Ramifications in the U.S. Television Receiver Industry," *Strategic Management Journal* 21 (2000): 997–1016.

34 Klepper 2002, op. cit.

35 G. Buenstorf and S. Klepper, "Heritage and Agglomeration: The Akron Tire Cluster Revisited," Department of Social and Decision Sciences Working Paper, Carnegie Mellon University, March 2005.

36 D. A. Kaplan, *The Silicon Boys and Their Valley of Dreams* (New York: Morrow, 1999).

37 C. M. Christensen and M. Overdorf, "Meeting the Challenge of Disruptive Change," *Harvard Business Review* (March–April 2000): 66–76.

38 C. Markides and C. D. Charitou, "Competing with Dual Strategies," *Academy of Management Executive* 18 (2004): 22–36.

39 D. F. Abell, *Managing with Dual Strategies* (New York: Free Press, 1993).

40 A. Grove, *Only the Paranoid Survive* (New York: Doubleday, 1996).

41 N. Siggelkow and D. A. Levinthal, "Escaping Real (Non-benign) Competency Traps: Linking the Dynamics of Organizational Structure to the Dynamics of Search," *Strategic Organization* 3 (2005): 85–115.

42 J. Nickerson and T. Zenger, "Being Efficiently Fickle: A Dynamic Theory of Organizational Choice," *Organization Science* 13 (September–October 2002): 547–67.

43 R. Cibin and R. M. Grant, "Restructuring among the World's Leading Oil Companies," *British Journal of Management* 7 (1996): 283–308.

44 H. Kahn, *The Next 200 Years: A Scenario for America and the World* (New York: William Morrow, 1976). For a guide to the use of scenarios in strategy making, see K. van der Heijden, *Scenarios: The Art of Strategic Conversation* (Chichester: Wiley, 2005).

45 G. Hamel and C. K. Prahalad, *Competing for the Future* (Boston: Harvard Business School Press, 1995).

46 G. Hamel, *Leading the Revolution* (Boston: Harvard Business School Press, 2000): 5.

Technology-based Industries and the Management of Innovation

11

Whereas a calculator on the ENIAC is equipped with 18,000 vacuum tubes and weighs 30 tons, computers in the future may have only 1,000 vacuum tubes and perhaps weigh only 1.5 tons.

—POPULAR MECHANICS, *MARCH 1949*

I can think of no conceivable reason why an individual should wish to have a computer in his own home.

—KENNETH OLSEN, CHAIRMAN, DIGITAL EQUIPMENT CORPORATION, 1977

OUTLINE

Introduction and Objectives

Industries where competition centers on innovation and the application of technology provide some of the most fascinating and complex competitive environments in which to apply the concepts of strategy analysis. Consider the upheaval that wireless communication and internet protocols have caused in the telecom sector:

- In 1996, the world's three most valuable telecom companies were AT&T, Nippon Telephone and Telegraph (NTT), and British Telecom (BT). By the end of 2006, the top three (in terms of market value) were China Mobile, Vodafone, and AT&T – although the new AT&T was a renamed SBC Communication, not the direct descendant of the old AT&T.

- A similar upheaval occurred on the manufacturing side of the telecom industry. In 1996, the world's leading producers of telecom equipment were AT&T, Alcatel, NEC, Siemens, and GTE. By the end of 2006, three companies – Cisco Systems, Nokia, and Qualcomm – accounted for two-thirds of the stock market value of the world's top 10 telecom equipment producers.

- During 2006–7, the fixed-line telecom business was being rocked by new waves of competition from cable operators and internet telecom providers.

There are few industries that have seen as much technological upheaval as has the telecom industry over the past ten years. At the same time, technological change has been a feature of almost every sector of the economy, not least because of the pervasive influence of microelectronics, digitization, new materials, and new communication modes. In this chapter, we concentrate on the strategic management of innovation and technological change. Our focus is on technology-intensive industries, which include both emerging industries (those in the introductory and growth phases of their life cycle) and established industries (such as pharmaceuticals, chemicals, telecommunications, and electronics) where technology continues to be the major driver of competition. The issues we examine, however, are also relevant to a much broader range of industries. Although industries such as food processing, fashion goods, domestic appliances, and financial services are not technology based to the same extent as consumer electronics or pharmaceuticals, innovation and the application of new technologies are important sources of competitive advantage.

In the last chapter, we saw how innovation is responsible for the creation of new industries, how innovation changes over the course of the industry life cycle, and the implications of this industry structure and competitive advantage. In this chapter we shall be looking at innovation and technology as weapons of competitive strategy. Our focus is the firm: how does the firm use technology and innovation to establish competitive advantage, to survive the brutal competition that characterizes so many technology-based industries and, ultimately, to earn superior profits over the long term?

By the time you have completed this chapter, you will be able to:

● Analyze how technology affects industry structure and competition.

● Identify the factors that determine the returns to innovation, and evaluate the potential for an innovation to establish competitive advantage.

● Formulate strategies for exploiting innovation and managing technology, focusing in particular on:

   – the relative advantages of being a leader or a follower in innovation;

   – identifying and evaluating strategic options for exploiting innovation;

   – how to win standards battles;

   – how to manage risk.

● Design the organizational conditions needed to implement such strategies successfully.

This chapter is organized as follows. First, we examine the links between technology and competition in technology-intensive industries. Second, we explore the potential for innovation to establish sustainable competitive advantage. Third, we deal with key issues in designing technology strategies, including timing (to lead or to follow), alternative strategies for exploiting an innovation, setting industry standards, and managing risk. Finally, we examine the organizational conditions for the successful implementation of technology-based strategies.

Competitive Advantage in Technology-intensive Industries

Our focus is innovation. Innovation is responsible for industries coming into being, and innovation – if successful – creates competitive advantage. Let us begin by exploring the linkage between innovation and profitability.

The Innovation Process

Invention is the creation of new products and processes through the development of new knowledge or from new combinations of existing knowledge. Most inventions are the result of novel applications of existing knowledge. Samuel Morse's telegraph, patented in 1840, was based on several decades of research into electromagnetism from Ben Franklin to Orsted, Ampere, and Sturgion. The compact disc embodies knowledge about lasers developed several decades previously.

Innovation is the initial commercialization of invention by producing and marketing a new good or service or by using a new method of production. Once introduced, innovation diffuses: on the demand side, through customers purchasing the good or service; on the supply side, through imitation by competitors. An innovation may be the result of a single invention (most product innovations in chemicals and pharmaceuticals involve discoveries of new chemical compounds) or it may combine many inventions. The first automobile, introduced by Benz in 1885, embodied a multitude of inventions, from the wheel, invented some 5,000 years previously, to the internal combustion engine, invented nine years earlier. Not all invention progresses into innovation: among the patent portfolios of most technology-intensive firms are numerous inventions that have yet to find a viable commercial application. Many innovations may involve little or no new technology: the personal computer brought together existing components and technologies, but no fundamental scientific breakthroughs; most new types of packaging – including the vast array of anti-tamper packages – involve clever design but little in the way of new technology. Most business method patents are process innovations with little technological content.

Figure 11.1 shows the pattern of development from knowledge creation to invention and innovation. Historically, the lags between knowledge creation and innovation have been long:

- Chester F. Carlson invented xerography in 1938 by combining established knowledge about electrostatics and printing. The first patents were awarded in 1940. Xerox purchased the patent rights and launched its first office copier in 1958. By 1974, the first competitive machines were introduced by IBM, Kodak, Ricoh, and Canon.
- The jet engine, employing Newtonian principles of forces, was patented by Frank Whittle in 1930. The first commercial jet airliner, the Comet, flew in 1957. Two years later, the Boeing 707 was introduced.

Recently, the innovation cycle has speeded up:

- The mathematics of *fuzzy logic* were developed by Lofti Zadeh at Berkeley during the 1960s. By the early 1980s, Dr. Takeshi Yamakawa of the Kyushu

FIGURE 11.1 The development of technology: from knowledge creation to diffusion

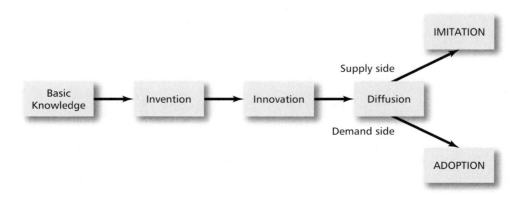

Institute of Technology had registered patents for integrated circuits embodying fuzzy logic, and in 1987 a series of fuzzy logic controllers for industrial machines was launched by Omron of Kyoto. By 1991, the world market for fuzzy logic controllers was estimated at $2 billion.[1]

● MP3, the audio file compression software, was developed at the Fraunhofer Institute in Germany in 1987; by the mid-1990s, the swapping of MP3 music files had taken off in US college campuses and in 1998 the first MP3 player, Diamond Multimedia's *Rio*, was launched.

The Profitability of Innovation

"If a man . . . make a better mousetrap than his neighbor, though he build his house in the woods, the world will make a beaten path to his door," claimed Emerson. Yet, the inventors of new mousetraps, and other gadgets too, are more likely to be found at the bankruptcy courts than in the millionaires' playgrounds of the Caribbean. Certainly, innovation is no guarantor of fame and fortune, either for individuals or for companies. The empirical evidence on technological intensity, innovation, and profitability confirms this mixed picture. Across companies, R&D intensity and frequency of new product introductions tend to be negatively associated with profitability.[2]

The profitability of an innovation to the innovator depends on the value created by the innovation and the share of that value that the innovator is able to appropriate. The value created by an innovation is distributed among a number of different parties (see Figure 11.2). In the case of the personal computer, the innovators – MITS, Tandy, Apple, and Xerox – earned modest profits from their innovation. The imitators – IBM, Dell, Compaq, Acer, Toshiba and a host of other followers into the PC industry earned rather more in total profits. Nevertheless, their returns were overshadowed by the huge profits earned by the suppliers to the industry: Intel in microprocessors, Seagate Technology and Quantum Corp. in disk drives, Sharp in flat-panel displays, and Microsoft in operating systems. However, because of strong competition in the industry, the greatest part of the value created by the personal computer was

FIGURE 11.2 Appropriation of value: who gets the benefits from innovation?

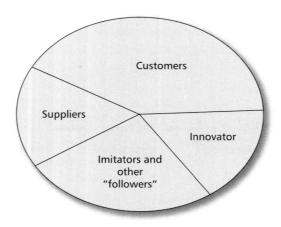

appropriated by customers, who typically paid prices for their PCs that were far below the value that they derived.[3]

The term *regime of appropriability* is used to describe the conditions that influence the distribution of returns to innovation. In a strong regime of appropriability, the innovator is able to capture a substantial share of the value created: Nutrasweet artificial sweetener (developed by Searle, subsequently acquired by Monsanto), Pfizer's Viagra, and Pilkington's float glass process generated huge profits for their owners. In a weak regime of appropriability, other parties derive most of the value. In internet telephony (VoIP), ownership of technologies is diffused and standards are public, with the result that no players are likely to earn massive profits. Four factors are critical in determining the extent to which innovators are able to appropriate the value of their innovation: property rights, the tacitness and complexity of the technology, lead-time, and complementary resources.

Property Rights in Innovation Appropriating the returns to innovation depends, to a great extent, on the ability to establish property rights in the innovation. It was the desire to protect the returns to inventors that prompted the English Parliament to pass the 1623 Statute of Monopolies, which established the basis of patent law. Since then, the law has been extended to several areas of *intellectual property*, including:

- *Patents* – exclusive rights to a new and useful product, process, substance, or design. Obtaining a patent requires that the invention is novel, useful, and not excessively obvious. Patent law varies from country to country. In the United States, a patent is valid for 17 years (14 for a design).
- *Copyrights* – exclusive production, publication, or sales rights to the creators of artistic, literary, dramatic, or musical works. Examples include articles, books, drawings, maps, photographs, and musical compositions.
- *Trademarks* – words, symbols, or other marks used to distinguish the goods or services supplied by a firm. In the US and UK, they are registered with the Patent Office. Trademarks provide the basis for brand identification.
- *Trade secrets* – offer a modest degree of legal protection for recipes, formulae, industrial processes, customer lists, and other knowledge acquired in the course of business.

The effectiveness of these legal instruments of protection depends on the type of innovation being protected. For some new chemical products and basic mechanical inventions, patents can provide effective protection. For products that involve new configurations of existing components or new manufacturing processes, patents may be less effective due to opportunities to innovate around the patent. Patents granted on dubious grounds may later be revoked or challenged in the courts. The US courts and Patent Office have continually broadened the scope of the patent laws. In 1980 patent law was extended to new plants created by biotechnology, in 1981 to software, and in 1998 to business methods. Thus, Netflix has a patent covering the method by which customers choose titles and the process by which Netflix distributes movies, while Amazon holds a patent on its "one-click-to-buy" internet purchasing.[4] While patents and copyright establish property rights, their disadvantage (from the inventor's viewpoint) is that they make information public. Hence, companies may prefer secrecy to patenting as a means of protecting innovations.

Whatever the imperfections of patents and copyrights, companies have become increasingly attentive to the economic value of their intellectual property and, in the process, more careful about protecting and exploiting these knowledge assets. During the 1950s and 1960s, the leading companies in electronics research – RCA, IBM, and AT&T – pursued liberal patent licensing policies, almost to the point of giving away access to their technologies.

When Texas Instruments began exploiting its patent portfolio as a revenue source during the 1980s, the technology sector as a whole woke up to the value of its knowledge assets. During the 1990s, TI's royalty income exceeded its operating income from other sources. An average of 180,000 patents were granted by the US Patent Office in each year between 2000 and 2006 – well over double the annual rate during the 1980s.

Tacitness and Complexity of the Technology   In the absence of effective legal protection through patents and copyrights, the extent to which an innovation can be imitated by a competitor depends on the ease with which the technology can be comprehended and communicated. Two characteristics are especially important. The first is the extent to which the technical knowledge is tacit or codifiable. *Codifiable knowledge*, by definition, is that which can be written down. Hence, if it is not effectively protected by patents or copyright, diffusion is likely to be rapid and the competitive advantage not sustainable. Financial innovations such as mortgage-backed securities, zero-interest bonds, and new types of index options embody readily codifiable knowledge that can be copied very quickly. Similarly, Coca-Cola's recipe is codifiable and, in the absence of trade secret protection, is easily copied. Intel's designs for advanced microprocessors are codified and copyable; however, the processes for manufacturing these integrated circuits are based on deeply tacit knowledge. Sharp was able to sustain its leadership in flat screen manufacture primarily because of the experiential knowledge required to make these difficult products.

The second characteristic is *complexity*. Most new toys, from the hula-hoop of 1958 to Powerizer jumping shoes, and every new fashion, from the Mary Quant miniskirt of 1962 to Alexander McQueen's frilly dresses of 2007, involve simple, easy-to-copy ideas. Airbus's A380 and Intel's Xeon microprocessor represent entirely different challenges for the would-be imitator.

Lead-Time   Tacitness and complexity do not provide lasting barriers to imitation, but they do offer the innovator *time*. Innovation creates a *temporary* competitive advantage that offers a window of opportunity for the innovator to build on the initial advantage.

The innovator's *lead-time* is the time it will take followers to catch up. The challenge for the innovator is to use initial lead-time advantages to build the capabilities and market position to entrench industry leadership. Microsoft, Intel, and Cisco Systems were brilliant at exploiting lead-time to build advantages in efficient manufacture, quality, and market presence. By contrast, a number of innovative British companies have squandered their initial lead-time advantage: DeHavilland with the Comet (the world's first jet airliner), EMI with its CT scanner, Clive Sinclair and the home computer, all failed to capitalize on their lead-time with large-scale investments in production, marketing, and continued product development.

A key advantage of lead-time is the ability to move down the learning curve ahead of followers. In new generations of microprocessors, Intel has traditionally been first

FIGURE 11.3 Complementary resources

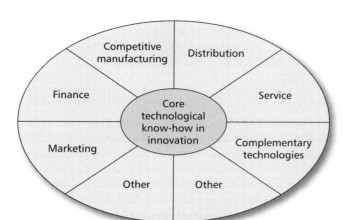

to market, allowing it to move quickly down its experience curve, cut prices, and so pressure the profit margins of AMD. The ability to turn lead-time into cost advantage is thus a key aspect of the innovator's advantage.[5]

Complementary Resources[6] Innovation brings new products and processes to market. This requires more than invention, it requires the diverse resources and capabilities needed to finance, produce, and market the innovation. These are referred to as *complementary resources* (see Figure 11.3). Chester Carlson invented xerography, but was unable for many years to bring his product to market because he lacked the complementary resources needed to develop, manufacture, market, distribute, and service his invention. Conversely, Searle (and its later parent, Monsanto) was able to provide almost all the development, manufacturing, marketing, and distribution resources needed to exploit its Nutrasweet innovation. As a result, Carlson was able to appropriate only a tiny part of the value created by his invention of the plain-paper Xerox copier, while Searle/Monsanto was successful in appropriating a major part of the value created by its new artificial sweetener.

When an innovation and the complementary resources that support it are supplied by different firms, the division of value between them depends on their relative power. A key determinant of this is whether the complementary resources are *specialized* or *unspecialized*. Fuel cells may eventually displace internal combustion engines in many of the world's automobiles. However, the problem for the developers of fuel cells is that their success depends on automobile manufacturers making specialized investments in designing a whole new range of cars, oil companies providing specialized refueling facilities, and service and repair firms investing in training and new equipment. For fuel cells to be widely adopted will require that the benefits of the innovation are shared widely with the different providers of these complementary resources. Where complementary resources are generic, the innovator is in a much stronger position to capture value. Because Adobe Systems' Acrobat Portable Document Format (pdf) works with files created in almost any software application, Adobe is well positioned to capture most of the value created by its innovatory software product. However, one advantage of co-specialized complementary resources is that they raise barriers to imitation. Consider the threat that Linux presents to Microsoft Window's dominance of PC operating systems. Because Intel has adapted its microprocessors to the needs of Windows and most applications software is written to run on Windows, the challenge for the Linux community is not just to develop a workable operating system, but also to encourage the development of applications software and hardware that are compatible with the Linux operating system.

Which Mechanisms are Effective at Protecting Innovation?

How effective are these different mechanisms in protecting innovations? The evidence in Table 11.1 shows that, despite considerable variation across industries, patent protection is of limited effectiveness as compared with lead-time, secrecy, and complementary manufacturing and sales/service resources. Indeed, since the late 1980s, the effectiveness of patents appeared to have declined despite the strengthening of patent law. Although patents are effective in increasing the lead-time before competitors are able to bring imitative products to market, the lead-time gains tend to be small. The great majority of patented products and processes are duplicated within three years.[7]

Given the limited effectiveness of patents, why do firms continue to engage in patenting? As shown in Table 11.2, although protection from imitation is the principal motive, several others are also very important. In particular, much patenting activity appears to be strategic – it is directed towards blocking the innovation efforts of other companies and establishing property rights in technologies that can then be used in bargaining with other companies for access to their proprietary technologies. In semiconductors and electronics, cross-licensing arrangements – where one company gives access to its patents across a field of technology in exchange for access

TABLE 11.1 The effectiveness of mechanisms for protecting innovation: percentage of innovations for which different mechanisms were considered effective

	Product innovations					Process innovations				
	Secrecy (%)	Patents (%)	Lead-time (%)	Sales/service (%)	Manufacturing (%)	Secrecy (%)	Patents (%)	Lead-time (%)	Sales/service[1] (%)	Manufacturing[1] (%)
Food	59	18	53	40	51	56	16	42	30	47
Chemicals	53	37	49	45	41	54	20	27	28	42
Drugs	54	50	50	33	49	68	36	36	25	44
Computers	44	41	61	35	42	43	30	40	24	36
Electronic components	34	21	46	50	51	47	15	43	42	56
Telecom equipment	47	26	66	42	41	35	15	43	34	41
Medical equipment	51	55	58	52	49	49	34	45	32	50
All industries	51	35	53	43	46	51	23	38	31	43

1   Shows the percentage of companies that reported that complementary capabilities in sales and service, and in manufacturing, were effective in protecting their innovations.

SOURCE: W. M. COHEN, R. R. NELSON, AND J. P. WALSH, "PROTECTING THEIR INTELLECTUAL ASSETS: APPROPRIABILITY CONDITIONS AND WHY US MANUFACTURING FIRMS PATENT (OR NOT)," NBER WORKING PAPER NO. W7552 (FEBRUARY 2000). © 2000. REPRINTED BY PERMISSION OF THE AUTHORS.

SOURCE: W. M. COHEN, R. R. NELSON, AND J. P. WALSH, "PROTECTING THEIR INTELLECTUAL ASSETS: APPROPRIABILITY CONDITIONS AND WHY US MANUFACTURING FIRMS PATENT (OR NOT)," NBER WORKING PAPER NO. W7552 (FEBRUARY 2000).

TABLE 11.2 Why do companies patent? (Responses by 674 US manufacturers)

	Product Innovations (%)	Process Innovations (%)
To prevent copying	95	77
For licensing revenue	28	23
To prevent law suits	59	47
To block others	82	64
For use in negotiations	47	43
To enhance reputation	48	34
To measure performance	6	5

to another company's patents – are critical in permitting "freedom to design": the ability to design products that draw on technologies owned by different companies.[8]

Strategies to Exploit Innovation: How and When to Enter

Having established some of the key factors that determine the returns to innovation, let us consider some of the main questions concerning the formulation of strategies to manage technology and exploit innovation.

Alternative Strategies to Exploit Innovation

How should a firm maximize the returns to its innovation? A number of alternative strategies are available. Figure 11.4 orders them according to the size of the commitment of resources and capabilities that each requires. Thus, licensing requires little involvement by the innovator in subsequent commercialization; hence a limited investment. Internal commercialization – possibly through creating a new enterprise or business unit – involves a much greater investment of resources and capabilities. In between, there are various opportunities for collaboration with other companies. Joint ventures and strategic alliances typically involve substantial resource sharing between companies. On a more limited scale, specific activities may be outsourced to other companies.

The choice of strategy mode depends on two main sets of factors: the characteristics of the innovation, and the resources and capabilities of the firm.

Characteristics of the Innovation The extent to which a firm can establish clear property rights in an innovation critically determines the choice of strategy options. Licensing is only viable where ownership in an innovation is clearly defined by patent or copyrights. Thus, in pharmaceuticals, licensing is widespread because patents are clear and defensible. Many biotech companies engage only in R&D and license their drug discoveries to large pharmaceutical companies that possess the necessary complementary resources. Royalties from licensing its sound-reduction technologies accounted for 76% of Dolby Laboratories' 2006 revenues. Conversely, Steve Jobs and Steve Wozniak, developers of the Apple I and Apple II computers, had little

FIGURE 11.4 Alternative strategies for exploiting innovation

	Licensing	Outsourcing certain functions	Strategic alliance	Joint venture	Internal commercialization
Risk and return	Little investment risk but returns also limited. Risk that the licensee either lacks motivation or steals the innovation	Limits capital investment, but may create dependence on suppliers/partners	Benefits of flexibility. Risks of informal structure	Shares investment and risk. Risk of partner disagreement and culture clash	Biggest investment requirement and corresponding risks. Benefits of control
Resource requirements	Few	Permits external resources and capabilities to be accessed	Permits pooling of the resources and capabilities of more than one firm		Substantial requirements in terms of finance, production capability, marketing capability, distribution, etc.
Examples	Ericsson with its Bluetooth wireless technology; Dolby Labs with its sound reduction technology; Qualcomm and CDMA	Microsoft's XBox was largely designed by other companies and Flextronics does the manufacturing	Ballard's strategic alliance with DaimlerChrysler to develop fuel cells	Psion created Symbian as a joint venture with Ericsson, Nokia, and Motorola to develop the Symbian mobile phone operating system	Larry Page and Sergey Brin established Google Inc. to develop and market their internet search technology

option other than to go into business themselves – the absence of proprietary technology ruled out licensing as an option.

The advantages of licensing are, first, that it relieves the company of the need to develop the full range of complementary resources and capabilities needed for commercialization, and second, that it can allow the innovation to be commercialized quickly. If the lead-time offered by the innovation is short, multiple licensing can allow for a fast global rollout. The problem, however, is that the success of the innovation in the market is totally dependent on the commitment and effectiveness of the licensees. Strategy Capsule 11.1 outlines two examples of companies that met difficulties in licensing their inventions.

STRATEGY CAPSULE 11.1

To License or Commercialize Internally? Dyson Vacuum Cleaners and Benecol Margarine

The Dyson Vacuum Cleaner

In 1981, British inventor James Dyson patented his "dual cyclone" bagless vacuum cleaner. For four years, Dyson tried unsuccessfully to interest US and European appliance manufacturers in his prototype before finally licensing to a Japanese appliance maker where it was successfully launched as the "G-Force." Meanwhile, in the US, Amway, with whom Dyson had negotiated over a license, introduced its own bagless vacuum cleaner – the "Amagram." In 1990, after incurring $4 million in legal costs, Dyson won his case against Amway for patent infringement. In Europe, Dyson decided to go it alone. Using his licensing royalties from Japan, Dyson opened a plant in Wiltshire, England in June 1993. Within two years, Dyson had established UK market leadership. By 1999, Dyson was back in court claiming that Hoover with its "Vortex" vacuum cleaner had infringed his patents. Dyson won his case forcing Hoover to withdraw its offending product. In 2002, Dyson entered the US market. By the beginning of 2005, Dyson had gained market share leadership – mainly at the expense of Hoover which was now incurring substantial losses for its owner, Maytag.

Raisio and Benecol

At the end of 1995, Raisio, a 57-year-old grain milling and vegetable oils company based in Finland, launched "Benecol" – a patented, cholesterol-reducing margarine that contained plant stanol. The phenomenal success of Benecol encouraged Raisio to sell international licensing rights to Johnson & Johnson. In 1999, Benecol was launched in the US and Europe after several years of delay caused by regulatory hurdles in the US and J&J's indecision as to whether to launch Benecol as a food, a food supplement, or a pharmaceutical. In the meantime, Raisio's lead-time had been lost. Unilever launched its own cholesterol reducing margarine ("Take Control" in the US; "Flora ProActif" in Europe) at about the same time as Benecol and quickly established a strong market share lead.

Sources: James Dyson, *Against the Odds*, 2nd edn (Texere, 2003); "Dyson's Magic Carpet Ride," *Business Week* (April 1, 2005); "Raisio and the Benecol Launch," in R. M. Grant, *Cases to Accompany* Contemporary Strategy Analysis, 6th edn (Blackwell, 2008).

Resources and Capabilities of the Firm As Figure 11.4 shows, the different strategic options require very different resources and capabilities. Business startups and other small firms possess few of the complementary resources and capabilities needed to commercialize their innovations. Inevitably they will be attracted to licensing or to accessing the resources of larger firms through outsourcing, alliances, or joint ventures. Yet, for all their advantages in commercializing innovation, evidence suggests that most invention is the result of individual creativity – often by mavericks and eccentrics who do not fit easily into large corporations. Most of the major innovations of the 20th century, were contributed by individual inventors – frequently working in their garage or garden shed.[9] Among 27 key inventions of the post-WWII period, only seven emerged from the R&D departments of established corporations.[10] Hence, in many sectors it seems that different stages of the innovation process are best conducted by different types of firm. In biotechnology and electronics, a two-stage model for innovation is common: the technology is developed initially by a small, technology-intensive startup, which then licenses to, or is acquired by, a larger concern.

Conversely, large, established corporations, which can draw on their wealth of resources and capabilities, are better placed for internal commercialization. Companies such as Sony, GE, Siemens, Hitachi, and IBM have traditionally developed innovations internally – yet, as technologies evolve, converge, and splinter, even these companies have increasingly resorted to joint ventures, strategic alliances, and outsourcing arrangements in order to access technical capabilities outside their corporate boundaries.

In the video games software industry, an industry structure has emerged that allows different types of firm to specialize in different stages of the innovation process according to their different resources and capabilities. Large video games publishers such as Electronic Arts and Sega undertake marketing, financing, and distribution. Video game software is produced by game developers – often quite small firms.

Timing Innovation: To Lead or to Follow?

To gain competitive advantage in emerging and technologically intensive industries, is it best to be a leader or a follower in innovation? As Table 11.3 shows, the evidence is mixed: in some products the leader has been the first to grab the prize, in others the leader has succumbed to the risks and costs of pioneering. Optimal timing of entry into an emerging industry and the introduction of new technology are complex issues. The extent of first-mover advantages (or disadvantages) associated with pioneering depends on the following factors:

1 *The extent to which innovation can be protected by property rights or lead-time advantages.* If an innovation is appropriable through a patent, copyright, or lead-time advantage, there is advantage in being an early mover. This is especially the case where patent protection is important, as in pharmaceuticals. Here, competition can take the form of a patent race.

2 *The importance of complementary resources.* The more important are complementary resources in exploiting an innovation, the greater the costs and risks of pioneering. Several firms – from Clive Sinclair with a battery-driven car to General Motors with a fuel-cell car – have already failed in their attempts to develop and market an electric automobile. The problem for the

TABLE 11.3 Leaders, followers, and success in emerging industries

Product	Innovator	Follower	The winner
Helicopter	Sikorsky	Augusta Westland	Leader
Jet airliner	De Havilland (Comet)	Boeing (707)	Follower
Float glass	Pilkington	Corning	Leader
X-ray scanner	EMI	General Electric	Follower
Office PC	Xerox	IBM	Follower
VCRs	Ampex/Sony	Matsushita	Follower
Instant camera	Polaroid	Kodak	Leader
Pocket calculator	Bowmar	Texas Instruments	Follower
Microwave oven	Raytheon	Samsung	Follower
Fiber-optic cable	Corning	Many companies	Leader
Video games player	Atari	Nintendo/Sony	Followers
Disposable diaper	Procter & Gamble	Kimberley-Clark	Leader
Ink jet printer	IBM and Siemens	Hewlett Packard	Follower
Web browser	Netscape	Microsoft	Follower
MP3 music players	Diamond Multimedia	Apple (iPod)	Follower
Operating systems for mobile phones	Symbian	Microsoft	Leader
Flash memory	Toshiba	Samsung, Intel	Followers

SOURCE: BASED IN PART ON DAVID TEECE, THE COMPETITIVE CHALLENGE: STRATEGIES FOR INDUSTRIAL INNOVATION AND RENEWAL (CAMBRIDGE: BALLINGER, 1987): 186–8.

pioneer is that the development costs are huge because of the need to orchestrate multiple technologies and establish facilities for service and recharging. Followers are also favored by the fact that, as an industry develops, specialist firms emerge as suppliers of complementary resources. Thus, in pioneering the development of the British frozen foods industry, Unilever's Bird's Eye subsidiary had to set up an entire chain of cold stores and frozen distribution facilities. Later entrants were able to rely on the services of public cold stores and refrigerated trucking companies.

3 *The potential to establish a standard.* As we shall see later in this chapter, some markets converge toward a technical standard. The greater the importance of technical standards, the greater the advantages of being an early mover in order to influence those standards and gain the market momentum needed to establish leadership. Once a standard has been set, displacing it becomes exceptionally difficult. IBM had little success with its PS2 operating system against the entrenched position of Microsoft Windows. However, there is also a risk of entering too early, before the direction of technological development is clear.

Optimal timing depends also on the resources and capabilities that the individual firm has at its disposal. Different companies have different *strategic windows* – periods in time when their resources and capabilities are aligned with the opportunities available in the market. A small, technology-based firm may have no choice but to pioneer the introduction of an innovation. Given its lack of complementary resources, its only chance of building sustainable competitive advantage is to grab first-mover advantage and use this to develop the necessary complementary resources before more power-ful rivals appear. For the large, established firm with financial resources and strong production, marketing, and distribution capabilities, the strategic window is likely to be both longer and later. The risks of pioneering are greater for an established firm with a reputation and brands to protect, while to exploit its complementary resources effectively typically requires a more developed market. Consider the following examples:

- In personal computers, Apple was a pioneer, IBM a follower. The timing of entry was probably optimal for each. Apple's resources were its imagination and its technology. Its strategic window occurred at the very beginning of the industry when these strengths could make the biggest impact. IBM had enormous strengths in manufacturing, distribution, and reputation. It could use these resources to establish competitive advantage even without a clear technological advantage. What was important for IBM was to delay its entry to the point when market and technological risks had been reduced and the industry had reached a stage of development where strengths in large-scale manufacturing, marketing, and distribution could be brought to bear.

- In the browser war between Netscape and Microsoft, Microsoft had the luxury of being able to follow the pioneer, Netscape. Microsoft's huge product development, marketing, and distribution capabilities, and – most important – its vast installed base of the Windows operating system allowed it to overhaul Netscape's initial lead.

- Although General Electric entered the market for CT scanners some four years after EMI, GE was able to overtake EMI within a few years because of its ability to apply vast technological, manufacturing, sales, and customer service capabilities within the field of medical electronics.

To exploit strategic windows effectively, Don Sull argues that companies need to engage in a process of *active waiting*:

During periods of active waiting, leaders must probe the future and remain alert to anomalies that signal potential threats or opportunities; exercise the restraint to preserve their war chests; and maintain the discipline to keep the troops battle ready. When a golden opportunity or sudden-death threat emerges, they must have the courage to declare the main effort and concentrate resources to seize the moment.[11]

Managing Risks

Emerging industries are risky. There are two main sources of uncertainty:

- *Technological uncertainty* arises from the unpredictability of technological evolution and the complex dynamics through which technical standards and dominant designs are selected. Hindsight is always 20/20, but ex ante it is difficult to predict how technologies and the industries that deploy them will evolve.

- *Market uncertainty* relates to the size and growth rates of the markets for new products. When Xerox introduced its first plain-paper copier in 1959, Apple its first personal computer in 1977, or Sony its Walkman in 1979, none had any idea of the size of the potential market. Forecasting demand for new products is hazardous since all forecasting is based on some form of extrapolation or modeling based on past data. One approach is to use analogies.[12] Another is to draw on the combined insight and experience of experts through the *Delphi technique*.[13]

If reliable forecasting is impossible, the keys to managing risk are alertness and responsiveness to emerging trends together with limiting vulnerability to mistakes through avoiding large-scale commitments. Useful strategies for limiting risk include:

- *Cooperating with lead users*. During the early phases of industry development, careful monitoring of and response to market trends and customer requirements is essential to avoid major errors in technology and design. Von Hippel argues that lead users provide a source of leading market indicators, they can assist in developing new products and processes, and offer an early cash flow to fund development expenditures.[14] In computer software, "beta versions" are released to computer enthusiasts for testing; in footwear, Nike test markets new product ideas with inner-city gangs; in communications and aerospace, government defense contracts play a crucial role in developing new technologies.[15]

- *Limiting risk exposure*. The high level of risk in emerging industries requires that firms adopt financial practices that minimize their exposure to adversity. Uncertainties over development costs and the timing and amount of future cash flows require a strong balance sheet with limited debt financing. Restricting risk exposure also requires economizing on capital expenditure commitments and other sources of fixed cost. Smaller players in high-tech, high-risk industries from biotechnology to computer games typically concentrate on research and development and rely on larger companies for manufacture, marketing and distribution. Even large companies are resorting increasingly to strategic alliances and joint ventures in developing major new initiatives.

- *Flexibility*. The high level of uncertainty in emerging industries makes flexibility critical to long-term survival and success. Because technological and market changes are difficult to forecast, it is essential that top management closely monitors the environment and responds quickly to market signals. For Sichiro Honda, the founder of Honda Motor Company, a key aspect of flexibility was learning from failure: "Many people dream of success. To me success can only be achieved through repeated failure and introspection. In fact, success represents the 1% of your work that only comes from the 99% that is called failure."[16] Flexibility also means keeping options open and delaying commitment to a specific technology until its potential becomes clear. Microsoft is well known for its strategy of investing in alternative technologies (see Strategy Capsule 11.2).

Competing for Standards

In the previous chapter, I noted that the establishment of standards is a key event in industry evolution. The emergence of the digital, networked economy has made

Keeping Your Options Open: Microsoft in Operating Systems

In 1988, as I wandered about the floor of Comdex, the computer industry's vast annual trade show, I could feel the anxiety among the participants. Since the birth of the IBM PC, six years earlier, Microsoft's Disk Operating System (DOS) had been the de facto standard for PCs. But DOS was now starting to age. Everyone wanted to know what would replace it.

Apple Computer, at the peak of its powers, had one of the largest booths showcasing the brilliantly graphical Macintosh operating system . . . Two different alliances of major companies, including AT&T, HP, and Sun Microsystems, offered graphical versions of Unix . . . And IBM was touting its new OS/2.

Amid the uncertainty, there was something very curious about the Microsoft booth . . . [which] resembled a Middle Eastern bazaar. In one corner, the company was previewing the second version of its highly criticized Windows system . . . In another, Microsoft touted its latest release of DOS. Elsewhere it was displaying OS/2, which it had developed with IBM. In addition, Microsoft was demonstrating new releases of Word and Excel that ran on Apple's Mac. Finally, in a distant corner, Microsoft displayed SCO Unix . . .

"What am I supposed to make of this?" grumbled a corporate buyer standing next to me. Columnists wrote that Microsoft was adrift, that its chairman and chief operating officer, Bill Gates, had no strategy.

Although the outcome of this story is now well known, to anyone standing on the Comdex floor in 1988 it wasn't obvious which operating system would win. In the face of this uncertainty, Microsoft followed the only robust strategy: betting on every horse.

Source: E. D. Beinhocker, "Robust Adaptive Strategies," *Sloan Management Review* (Spring 1999): 95–106. © 1999 by Massachusetts Institute of Technology. All rights reserved. Distributed by Tribune Media Services.

standards increasingly important and companies that own and influence industry standards are capable of earning returns that are unmatched by any other type of competitive advantage. The shareholder value generated by Microsoft and Intel from the "Wintel" PC standard, by Qualcomm from its CDMA digital wireless communications technology, and Cisco from its leadership role in setting internet protocol standards are examples of this potential. Table 11.4 lists several companies whose success is closely associated with their control of standards within a particular product category.

Types of Standard

A standard is a format, an interface, or a system that allows interoperability. It is adherence to standards that allow us to browse millions of different web pages, that ensure the light bulbs made by any manufacturer will fit any manufacturer's lamps, and that keep the traffic moving in Los Angeles (most of the time). Standards can be *public* or *private*.

TABLE 11.4 Examples of companies that own de facto industry standards

Company	Product category	Standard
Microsoft	PC operating systems	Windows
Intel	PC microprocessors	x86 series
Matsushita	Videocassette recorders	VHS system
Sony/Philips	Compact disks	CD-ROM format
Sun Microsystems	Programming language for websites	Java
Rockwell and 3Com	56K modems	V90
Qualcomm	Digital cellular wireless communication	CDMA
Adobe Systems	Common file format for creating and viewing documents	Acrobat Portable Document Format
Bosch	Antilock braking systems	ABS and TCS (Traction Control System)
Symbian	Operating systems for mobile phones	Symbian OS

- Public (or *open*) standards are those that are available to all either free or for a nominal charge. Typically they do not involve any privately owned intellectual property or the IP owners make access free (e.g. Linux). Public standards are set by public bodies and industry associations. Thus, the GSM mobile phone standard was set by the European Telecom Standards Institute. Internet protocols – standards governing internet addressing and routing – are mostly public. They are governed by several international bodies, including the Internet Engineering Task Force.

- Private (*proprietary*) standards are those where the technologies and designs are owned by companies or individuals. If I own the technology that becomes a standard, I can embody the technology in a product that others buy (Microsoft Windows) or license the technology to others who wish to use it (Qualcomm's CDMA).

Standards can also be classified according to who sets them. *Mandatory standards* are set by government and have the force of law behind them. They include standards relating to automobile safety and construction specifications and to TV broadcasting. *De facto standards* emerge through voluntary adoption by producers and users. Table 11.4 gives examples.

A problem with de facto standards is that they may take a long time to emerge, resulting in duplication of investments and delayed development of the market. It was 40 years before a standard railroad gauge was agreed in the US.[17] One reason for the slow transition of wireless telecoms in the US from analog to digital technology was continuing competition between TDMA and CDMA standards. By contrast, Europe officially adopted GSM (a close relative of TDMA) in 1992.[18] Delayed emergence of a standard may kill the technology altogether. The failure of quadraphonic sound to displace stereophonic sound during the 1970s resulted from incompatible technical standards among manufacturers of audio equipment. The absence of a dominant standard discouraged record companies and consumers from investing in quadraphonic systems.[19]

Why Standards Appear: Network Externalities

Why do standards emerge in some product markets and not in others? Basically, standards emerge because suppliers and buyers want them. They want standards for those goods and services subject to *network externalities.*

A network externality exists whenever the value of a product to an individual customer depends on the number of other users of that product. The classic example of network externality is the telephone. Since there is little satisfaction to be gained from talking to oneself on the telephone, the value of a telephone to each user depends on the number of other users connected to the same telephone system. This is different from most products. When I pour myself a glass of Glenlivet after a couple of exhausting MBA classes, my enjoyment is independent of how many other people in the world are also drinking Glenlivet. Indeed, some products may have *negative* network externalities – the value of the product is less if many other people purchase the same product. If I spend $3,000 on an Armani silver lamé tuxedo and find that half my colleagues at the faculty Christmas party are wearing the same jacket, my satisfaction is lessened. Figure 11.5 compares such "exclusivity" products with "network externality" products.

Network externalities do not require everyone to use the same product or even the same technology, but rather that the different products are *compatible* with one another through some form of common interface. In the case of wireless telephone service, it doesn't matter (as far as network externalities are concerned) whether we purchase service from AT&T, Nextel, or T-Mobile – the key issue is that each supplier's system is compatible to allow connectivity. Similarly with railroads, if I am transporting coal from Wyoming to New Orleans, my choice of railroad company is not critical since I know that, unlike during the 1870s, every railroad company now uses a standard gauge and is required to give "common carrier" access to other companies' rolling stock.

Network externalities arise from several sources:

- *Products where users are linked to a network.* Telephones, railroad systems, and e-mail instant messaging groups are networks where users are linked together. Applications software, whether spreadsheet programs or video games, also link users – they can share files and play games interactively. User-level externalities may also arise through social identification. I watch *Big Brother* and the Hollywood Oscar presentations on TV not because I

FIGURE 11.5 Positive and negative network externalities

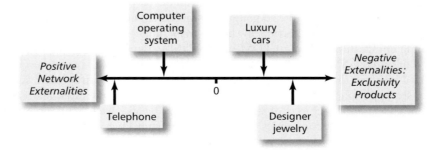

enjoy them, but in order to engage in conversation with my colleagues on these subjects.[20]

● *Availability of complementary products and services.* Where products are consumed as systems, the availability of complementary products and services depends on the number of customers for that system. The key problem for Apple Computer is that, because the Macintosh accounts for only 9% of the installed base of personal computers, fewer and fewer producers of applications software are writing Mac-based applications. I choose to drive a Ford Focus rather than a Ferrari Testarossa because I know that, should I break down 200 miles from Bismarck, North Dakota, spare parts and a repair service will be more readily available.

● *Economizing on switching costs.* By purchasing the product or system that is most widely used, there is less chance that I shall have to bear the costs of switching. By using Microsoft Office rather than Lotus SmartSuite, it is more likely that I will avoid the costs of retraining and file conversion when I become a visiting professor at another university.

The implication of network externalities is that they create *positive feedback.* The technology or system that has the largest installed base attracts the greatest proportion of new buyers because of the benefits of going with the market leader. Conversely, the more a technology is perceived to be a minority choice, the more will new and existing users defect to the market leader. This process is called *tipping*: once a market leader begins to emerge, the leader will progressively gain market share at the expense of rivals.[21] The result is a tendency toward a *winner-takes-all* market. The markets subject to significant network externalities tend to be dominated by a single supplier (Microsoft in the case of PC operating systems and office applications software, eBay in the case of internet auctions). Rival technologies may coexist for a time, but after one company appears to be gaining the upper hand, the market may then "tip" very quickly.

Once established, technical and design standards tend to be highly resilient. Standards are difficult to displace due to learning effects and collective lock-in. Learning effects cause the dominant technology and design to be continually improved and refined. A new technology, even though it may have the potential to overtake the existing standard, will initially be inferior. Even where the existing standard is inherently inferior, switching to a superior technology may not occur because of collective lock-in. The classic case is the QWERTY typewriter layout. Its 1873 design was based on the need to *slow* the speed of typing to prevent typewriter keys from jamming. Although the jamming problem was soon solved, the QWERTY layout has persisted, despite the patenting in 1932 of the more ergonomic Dvorak Simplified Keyboard (DSK).[22]

Winning Standards Wars

In markets subject to network externalities, control over standards is the basis of competitive advantage, and may be essential for survival. Apple Computer lost the standards war with IBM/Microsoft by the mid-1980s, since when it has been a marginal player in the computer industry. Other companies that lost standards wars with Microsoft – Lotus in spreadsheet software, Netscape in browsers, WordPerfect in word processing software – no longer exist as independent companies. What can we learn from these and other standards wars about designing a winning strategy in markets subject to network externalities?

The first key issue is to determine whether we are competing in a market that will converge around a single technical standard. This requires a careful analysis of the presence and sources of network externalities.

The second most important strategic issue in standards setting is recognition of the role of positive feedback: the technology that can establish early leadership will tend to attract new adopters. Building a "bigger bandwagon," according to Shapiro and Varian,[23] requires the following:

- *Before you go to war, assemble allies.* You'll need the support of consumers, suppliers of complements, even your competitors. Not even the strongest companies can afford to go it alone in a standards war.

- *Preempt the market* – enter early, achieve fast-cycle product development, make early deals with key customers, and adopt penetration pricing.

- *Manage expectations.* The key to managing positive feedback is to convince customers, suppliers, and the producers of complementary goods that you will emerge as the victor. These expectations become a self-fulfilling prophecy. The massive pre-launch promotion and publicity built up by Sony prior to the American and European launch of PlayStation 2 in October 2000 was an effort to convince consumers, retailers, and game developers that the product would be the blockbuster consumer electronics product of the new decade, thereby stymieing Sega and Nintendo's efforts to establish their rival systems.

The lesson that has emerged from the classic standards battles of the past is that in order to create initial leadership and maximize positive feedback effects, a company must share the value created by the technology with other parties (customers, competitors, complementors, and suppliers). If a company attempts to appropriate too great a share of the value created, it may well fail to build a big enough bandwagon to gain market leadership (see Strategy Capsule 11.3). Thus, most of the standards battles being waged currently involve broad alliances, where the owner makes the standard open and offers attractive licensing terms to complementors and would-be competitors. The current battle being fought between Sony and Toshiba for leadership in high-definition DVDs involves broad alliances: Toshiba has recruited Microsoft and Intel to its HD-DVD camp; Sony has enlisted Philips, Dell, and most Hollywood studios to back its Blu-ray format.[24]

Achieving compatibility with existing products is a critical issue in standards battles. Advantage typically goes to the competitor that adopts an *evolutionary strategy* (i.e., offers backward compatibility) rather than one that adopts a *revolutionary strategy*.[25] Microsoft Windows won the PC war against the Apple Macintosh for many reasons. Both companies offered an operating system with a graphical user interface. However, while Windows was designed for compatibility with the DOS operating system, the Apple Mac was incompatible both with DOS and the Apple II. Similarly, a key advantage of the Sony PlayStation 2 over the Sega Dreamcast and Nintendo Cube was its compatibility with the PlayStation 1.

What are the key resources needed to win a standards war? Shapiro and Varian emphasize the following:

- Control over an installed base of customers.

- Owning intellectual property rights in the new technology.

STRATEGY CAPSULE 11.3

Building a Bandwagon by Sharing Value: Lessons from VCRs and PCs

Profiting from standards requires two elements: first, setting the standard; second, retaining some proprietary interest in the standard in order to appropriate part of its value. There is a tradeoff between the two – the more value a company tries to appropriate, the greater the difficulty in building early support for its technology. Consider the standards wars in VCRs and PCs:

- In VCRs, Matsushita's VHS format won against Sony's Betamax format not because of the technical superiority of VHS, but because Matsushita did not insist on such tight ownership of its technology and was more effective in gaining acceptability in the market. The key here was Matsushita's encouragement of adoption through licensing of the VHS system to Sharp, Philips, GE, RCA, and other competitors.

- In personal computers, IBM was highly successful in setting the standard, partly because it did not restrict access to its technology. Its product specifications were openly available to "clone makers," and its suppliers (including Microsoft and Intel) were free to supply them with microprocessors and the MS-DOS operating system. IBM was remarkably successful at setting the standard, but failed to appropriate much value because it retained no significant proprietary interest in the standard – it was Intel and Microsoft that owned the key intellectual property. For Apple, the situation was the reverse. It kept tight control over its Macintosh operating system and product architecture, it earned high margins during the 1980s, but it forfeited the opportunity of setting the industry standard.

The tradeoff between market acceptance of a technology and appropriating the returns to a technology is shown below:

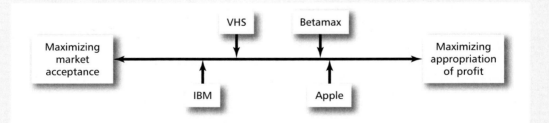

The innovator who enforces no ownership rights and gives away the innovation to anyone who wants it will probably maximize market penetration. On the other hand, the innovator who is most restrictive in enforcing ownership rights will maximize margins in the short run, but will probably have difficulty building a bandwagon big enough to establish market leadership. In recent battles over technical standards, the desire to gain market leadership has encouraged firms to be less and less restrictive over ownership in the interests of building their market bandwagon. Thus, in the battle for dominance of internet browser software, both Microsoft (Internet Explorer) and Netscape (Navigator) offered their products for free in the interests of wresting market leadership. When attacking an existing standard, there may be no alternative to giving the technology away: the only chance for Unix and Sun Microsystems' Java to establish themselves against Microsoft's Windows was by committing to an open standard.

Increasingly, companies are trying to reconcile market acceptance with value appropriation: Adobe gives away its Acrobat Reader to broaden the user base, but charges for the software needed to create pdf documents in Acrobat.

Where competition is weak, a company may be able to set the dominant standard while also appropriating most of the value: Nintendo in video games during the late 1980s and early 1990s is the classic example. However, once Nintendo met competition from Sega and Sony, its strategy backfired, as games developers and retailers welcomed competitors that offered a better deal.

Sources: *The World VCR Industry*, Case No. 9-387-098 (Boston: Harvard Business School, 1990); *Apple Computer – 1992*, Case No. 9-792-081 (Boston: Harvard Business School, 1994); *The Browser Wars, 1994–1998*, Case No. 9-798-094 (Boston: Harvard Business School, 1998); "Rivalry in Video Game Consoles," in R. M. Grant, *Cases to Accompany* Contemporary Strategy Analysis, 6th edn (Oxford: Blackwell Publishing, 2008).

- The ability to innovate in order to extend and adapt the initial technological advance.
- First-mover advantage.
- Strength in complements (e.g., Intel has preserved its standard in microprocessors by promoting standards in buses, chipsets, graphics controllers, and interfaces between motherboards and CPUs).
- Reputation and brand name.[26]

However, even with such advantages, standards wars are costly and risky. A prolonged standards war can rack up huge losses for all contenders, and may result in giving away so much value to partners and customers that the returns to the winner are meager. Microsoft won the browser war against Netscape, but only by offering its Internet Explorer for free. The key is to give away enough to ensure rapid market acceptance, while keeping hold of sufficient sources of value to make ownership of the winning standard valuable. Thus, Adobe achieved rapid customer acceptance for its Acrobat pdf software by making the Acrobat Reader freely available, while charging a remunerative price for the full version of the software.

Implementing Technology Strategies: Creating the Conditions for Innovation

As we have noted previously, strategy formulation cannot be separated from its implementation. Nowhere is this more evident than in technology-intensive businesses.

Our analysis so far has taught us about the potential for generating competitive advantage from innovation and about the design of technology-based strategies, but has said little about the conditions under which innovation is achieved. The danger is that strategic analysis can tell us a great deal about making money out of innovation, but this isn't much use if we cannot generate innovation in the first place. If the essence of innovation is creativity and one of the key features of creativity is its resistance to planning, it is evident that strategy formulation must pay careful attention to the organizational processes through which innovations emerge and are commercialized. Because the features of new products and processes are unknown when resources are committed to R&D and there is no predetermined relationship between R&D expenditure and the output of innovations, the productivity of R&D depends heavily on the organizational conditions that foster innovation. Hence, the most crucial challenge facing firms in emerging and technology-based industries is: how does the firm create conditions that are conducive to innovation?

To answer this question, we must return to the critical distinction between invention and innovation. Invention is dependent on creativity. Creativity is not simply a matter of individual brilliance; it depends on the organizational conditions that foster ideas and imagination at the individual and group levels. Similarly, innovation is not just a matter of acquiring the resources necessary for commercialization; innovation is a cooperative activity that requires interaction and collaboration between technology development, manufacturing, marketing, and various other functional departments within the firm.

Managing Creativity

The Conditions for Creativity Invention is an act of creativity requiring knowledge and imagination. The creativity that drives invention is typically an individual act that establishes a meaningful relationship between concepts or objects that had not previously been related. This reconceptualizing can be triggered by accidents: an apple falling on Isaac Newton's head or James Watt observing a kettle boiling. Creativity is associated with particular personality traits. Creative people tend to be curious, imaginative, adventurous, assertive, playful, self-confident, risk taking, reflective, and uninhibited.

Individual creativity also depends on the organizational environment in which they work – this is as true for the researchers and engineers at Amgen and Microsoft as it was for the painters and sculptors of the Florentine and Venetian schools. Few great works of art or outstanding inventions are the products of solitary geniuses. Creativity is stimulated by human interaction: the productivity of R&D laboratories depends critically on the communication networks that the engineers and scientists establish.[27] An important catalyst of interaction is *play*, which creates an environment of inquiry, liberates thought from conventional constraints, and provides the opportunity to establish new relationships by rearranging ideas and structures at a safe distance from reality. The essence of play is that it permits unconstrained forms of experimentation. Stefan Thomke argues that experimentation is the basis for innovation and that experimentation needs to be managed in order to maximize learning, speed discovery, and avoid costly mistakes. In almost all fields, the costs of experimentation have fallen substantially with developments in computer modeling and simulation that permit prototyping and market research to be undertaken speedily and virtually.[28]

The development of innovative ideas can be accelerated through conflict, criticism, and debate. Dorothy Leonard points to the merits of *creative abrasion* within innovative teams – fostering innovation through the interaction of different personalities and perspectives. Managers must resist the temptation to clone in favor of embracing diversity of cognitive and behavioral characteristics within work groups – creating what Leonard refers to as *"whole brain teams."* Managing creative groups – whether in research, product development, marketing, or quality management – requires that conflict is constructive rather than destructive. The role of the manager is to clarify goals, make operating guidelines explicit, and depersonalize conflict.[29]

Balancing Creativity and Commercial Direction A central challenge is balancing the creative freedom of individuals with the need for direction, discipline, and integration. Within media companies, the *Economist* notes: "The two cultures – of the ponytail and the suit – are a world apart, and combustible together."[30] Anita Roddick of Body Shop cultivated a culture of "benevolent anarchy – encouraging questioning of established ways and going in the opposite direction to everyone else." Yet this whirlwind of creativity can lead a company over the edge of chaos.[31] However, for most companies the dangers are in the opposite direction – reluctance to allow creative freedom for those in research, development, design and new business ventures. At Walt Disney, constant interference in creative processes by CEO Michael Eisner seems to be a key factor in Disney's wilting creative performance during 1998–2006. Conversely, the success of HBO in producing TV shows (such as *The Sopranos*, *The Wire*, and *Six Feet Under*) owes much to its ability to offer creative freedom to its content producers.

The most important discipline for ensuring that creativity is productive is to maintain linkage between creative processes and market need. Few important inventions have been the result of spontaneous creative activity by technologists; almost all have resulted from grappling with practical problems. James Watt's redesign of the steam engine was conceived while repairing an early Newcomen steam engine owned by Glasgow University. The basic inventions behind the Xerox copying process were the work of Chester Carlson, a patent attorney who became frustrated by the problems of accurately copying technical drawings. These observations reaffirm the notion that "necessity is the mother of invention," which explains why customers are such fertile sources of innovation – they are most acutely involved with matching existing products and services to their needs.[32] Involving customers in the innovation process is the first stage in the move towards *open innovation* – innovation processes that involve users, suppliers, and even competitors. The relocation of R&D from corporate research departments to operating businesses is motivated by the desire to link technology development more closely with the needs of the business. Innovating organizations not only have less defined internal structures, they are also likely to require the flow of knowledge and ideas between those in the organization and those outside. Open innovation is fostered by *creation nets* – networks of collaboration.

Organizing for Creativity Creativity requires management systems that are quite different from those appropriate to pursuing cost efficiency. In particular, creatively oriented people tend to be responsive to distinctive types of incentive. They desire to work in an egalitarian culture with enough space and resources to provide the opportunity to be spontaneous, experience freedom, and have fun in the performance of a task that, they feel, makes a difference to the strategic performance of the firm. Praise, recognition, and opportunities for education and professional growth are also more important than assuming managerial responsibilities.[33] Table 11.5 contrasts

SOURCE: BASED ON JAY K. GALBRAITH AND ROBERT K. KAZANJIAN, STRATEGY IMPLEMENTATION: STRUCTURE, SYSTEMS AND PROCESSES, 2ND EDN (ST. PAUL, MN: WEST, 1986).

TABLE 11.5 The characteristics of "operating" and "innovating" organizations

	Operating organization	Innovating organization
Structure	Bureaucratic. Specialization and division of labor. Hierarchical control. Defined organizational boundaries.	Flat organization without hierarchical control. Task-oriented project teams. Fuzzy organizational boundaries.
Processes	Emphasis on eliminating variation (e.g. six-sigma). Top–down control. Tight financial controls.	Emphasis on enhancing variation. Loose controls to foster idea generation. Flexible strategic planning and financial control.
Reward systems	Financial compensation, promotion up the hierarchy, power, and status symbols.	Autonomy, recognition, equity participation in new ventures.
People	Recruitment and selection based on the needs of the organization structure for specific skills: functional and staff specialists, general managers, and operatives.	Key need is for idea generators that combine required technical knowledge with creative personality traits. Managers must act as sponsors and orchestrators.

some characteristics of innovative organizations compared with those designed for operational efficiency.

From Invention to Innovation: The Challenge of Cross-functional Integration

The commercialization of new technology – in terms of developing and introducing new products and implementing new processes – requires linking creativity and technological expertise with capabilities in production, marketing, finance, distribution, and customer support. As we noted in Chapter 5, the challenge of new product development is that it draws upon every area of functional and technical expertise within the company. If the organizational requirements for innovation and "operation" are very different, the organizational challenge is to reconcile these two. If operating functions such as production and sales must be organized differently from technology and product development functions, there needs to be *differentiation* and *integration*.[34]

Achieving such integration is difficult. Tension between the operating and the innovating parts of organizations is inevitable. Innovation upsets established routines and threatens the status quo. The more stable the operating and administrative side of the organization, the greater the resistance to innovation. A classic example was the opposition by the US naval establishment to continuous-aim firing, a process that offered huge improvements in gunnery accuracy.[35]

In recent years, established corporations have striven to emulate the flexibility, creativity, and entrepreneurial spirit of technology-based startups and reconcile these traits with the quest for operational efficiency. Among the organizational innovations being introduced by large corporations to improve new product development and the exploitation of new technologies are the following:

- *Cross-functional product development teams.* Cross-functional product development teams have proven to be highly effective mechanisms for integrating the different functional capabilities required to develop a new product, and for developing communication and cooperation across functional divisions. Japanese companies in automobiles, electronics, and construction equipment have been the most prominent pioneers of product development teams. Autonomous product development teams allow specialists from different functional and technical departments the flexibility to share knowledge, learn, and develop innovative new products.[36] Clark and Fujimoto's study of new automobile development in Japan, the United States, and Europe provides fascinating insight into the organization of product development teams and the advantages derived from "overlapping" the different stages of product development rather than simply sequencing them, and from providing strong leadership through "heavyweight" product managers.[37]

- *Product champions* provide a means by which individual creativity and the desire to make a difference can be reconciled within organizational processes. The key is to permit the same individuals who are the creative forces behind an innovation or business idea also to be the leaders in commercializing those innovations. Companies that are consistently successful in innovation have the ability to capture and direct individuals' drive for achievement and success within their organizational processes; creating product champion roles is the most common means for achieving this. Given resistance to change within organizations and the need to forge cross-functional integration, leadership by committed individuals can help overcome vested interests in stability and functional separation. Schön's study of 15 major innovations concluded that: "the new idea either finds a champion or dies."[38] A British study of 43 matched pairs of successful and unsuccessful innovations similarly concluded that a key factor distinguishing successful innovation was the presence of a "business innovator" to exert entrepreneurial leadership.[39] 3M Corporation is exemplary in its use of product champions to develop new product ideas and grow them into new business units (see Strategy Capsule 11.4).

- *Buying innovation.* Ultimately, large corporations must recognize that small, technology-intensive startups have advantages in the early stages of the innovation process. Microsoft and Cisco Systems have become highly experienced in commercializing new areas of technology through acquiring small pioneers of innovation.

- *Incubators.* Large corporations also use technology-intensive startups as a means of developing their own innovations. During the 1990s, many large corporations established *corporate incubators* – business development units designed to provide infrastructure and venture capital funding for new business ideas, both from within and outside the corporation. Ford's Consumer Connect was created to identify and develop new ways to leverage the company's capabilities, consumer base, and purchasing power in the new economy. British Telecom set up Brightstar in 2001 to create new businesses that would exploit BT's portfolio of over 14,000 patents.[40]

STRATEGY CAPSULE 11.4

Innovation at 3M: The Role of the Product Champion

Start Little and Build

We don't look to the president, or the vice-president for R&D to say, all right, on Monday morning 3M is going to get into such-and-such a business. Rather, we prefer to see someone in one of our laboratories, or marketing or manufacturing units bring forward a new idea that he's been thinking about. Then, when he can convince people around him, including his supervisor, that he's got something interesting, we'll make him what we call a "project manager" with a small budget of money and talent, and let him run with it.

In short, we'd rather have the idea for a new business come from the bottom up than from the top down. Throughout all our 60 years of history here, that has been the mark of success. Did you develop a new business? The incentive? Money, of course. But that's not the key. The key . . . is becoming the general manager of a new business . . . having such a hot project that management just has to become involved whether it wants to or not. (Bob Adams, vice-president for R&D, 3M Corporation)

Scotchlite

Someone asked the question, "Why didn't 3M make glass beads, because glass beads were going to find increasing use on the highways?" . . . I had done a little working in the mineral department on trying to color glass beads we'd imported from Czechoslovakia and had learned a little about their reflecting properties. And, as a little extra-curricular activity, I'd been trying to make luminous house numbers – and maybe luminous signs as well – by developing luminous pigments.

Well, this question and my free-time lab project combined to stimulate me to search out

where glass beads were being used on the highway. We found a place where beads had been sprinkled on the highway and we saw that they did provide a more visible line at night . . . From there, it was only natural for us to conclude that, since we were a coating company, and probably knew more than anyone else about putting particles onto a web, we ought to be able to coat glass beads very accurately on a piece of paper.

So, that's what we did. The first reflective tape we made was simply a double-coated tape – glass beads sprinkled on one side and an adhesive on the other. We took some out here in St. Paul and, with the cooperation of the highway department, put some down. After the first frost came, and then a thaw, we found we didn't know as much about adhesives under all weather conditions as we thought . . .

We looked around inside the company for skills in related areas. We tapped knowledge that existed in our sandpaper business on how to make waterproof sandpaper. We drew on the expertise of our roofing people who knew something about exposure. We reached into our adhesive and tape division to see how we could make the tape stick to the highway better.

The resulting product became known as "Scotchlite." Its principal application was in reflective signs; only later did 3M develop the market for highway marking. The originator of the product, Harry Heltzer, interested the head of the New Products Division in the product, and he encouraged Heltzer to go out and sell it. Scotchlite was a success and Heltzer became the general manager of the division set up to produce and market it. Heltzer later went on to become 3M's president.

Source: "The Technical Strategy of 3M: Start More Little Businesses and More Little Businesses," *Innovation* no. 5 (1969).

Summary

In emerging industries and other industries where technology is the primary medium of competition, nurturing and exploiting innovation is the fundamental source of competitive advantage and the focus of strategy formulation. Does this mean that the principles of strategic management are fundamentally different in technology-based industries from other types of business environments? Many of the strategy issues we have discussed in this chapter are the same as those we covered in the previous chapters of the book. For example, the analysis of the determinants of the returns to innovation covered almost the same factors as our analysis of the returns to resources and capabilities: relevance to customer needs, barriers to imitation, and appropriability through well-established property rights.

At the same time, some aspects of strategic management in technology-based industries are distinctive. A common problem in technology-based industries is the speed of change and the difficulty of forecasting change. Conditions of Schumpeterian "creative destruction" (or, in Rich D'Aveni's terminology, *hypercompetition*) mean that traditional approaches to strategy formulation based on forecasting must be abandoned in favor of strategic management approaches that combine a clear sense of direction based on vision and mission, with the flexibility to respond to and take advantage of the unexpected.

Despite this turbulence and uncertainty, the principles of strategic analysis are critical in guiding the quest for competitive advantage in technology-intensive industries. Our analysis has been able to guide us on key issues such as:

● whether an innovation has the potential to confer sustainable competitive advantage;

● the relative merits of licensing, alliances, joint ventures, and internal development as alternative strategies for exploiting an innovation;

● the factors that determine the comparative advantages of being a leader or a follower in innovation.

This chapter also pointed to the central importance of strategy implementation in determining success. The key to successful innovation is not resource allocation decisions, but creating the structure, integration mechanisms, and organizational climate conducive to innovation. No other type of industry environment reveals so clearly the inseparability of strategy formulation and strategy implementation. Strategies aimed at the exploitation of innovation, choices of whether to be a leader or a follower, and the management of risk must take careful account of organizational characteristics.

Technology-based industries also reveal some of the dilemmas that are a critical feature of strategic management in complex organizations and complex business environments. For example, technology-based industries are unpredictable, yet some investments in technology have time horizons of a decade or more. Successful strategies must be responsive to changing market conditions, but successful strategies also require long-term commitment. The fundamental dilemma is that innovation is an unpredictable process that requires creating a nurturing organizational context, whereas strategy is about resource-allocation decisions. How can a company create the conditions for nurturing innovation while planning the course of its development? As John Scully of Apple has observed:

Management and creativity might even be considered antithetical states. While management demands consensus, control, certainty, and the status quo, creativity thrives on the opposite: instinct, uncertainty, freedom, and iconoclasm.[41]

Fortunately, the experiences of companies such as 3M, Sony, Merck, Cisco Systems, and Canon point to solutions to these dilemmas. The need for innovation to reconcile individual creativity with coordination points toward the advantages of cross-functional team-based approaches over the isolation of R&D in a separate "creative" environment. Moreover, the need to reconcile innovation with efficiency points toward the advantage of parallel organizational structures where, in addition to the "formal" structure geared to the needs of existing businesses and products, an informal structure exists, which is the source of new products and businesses. The role of top management in balancing creativity with order and innovation with efficiency becomes critical. The success of companies in both Japan and Silicon Valley in managing technology (especially compared with the poor innovation performance of many large, diversified US and British corporations) points to the importance of technological knowledge among senior managers.

The increasing pace of technological change and intensifying international competition suggests that the advanced, industrialized countries will be forced to rely increasingly on their technological capabilities as the basis for international competitiveness. Strategies for promoting innovation and managing technology will become more important in the future.

Self-Study Questions

1   Trevor Bayliss, a British inventor, submitted a patent application in November 1992 for a wind-up radio for use in Africa in areas where there was no electricity supply and people were too poor to afford batteries. He was excited by the prospects for radio broadcasts as a means of disseminating health education in areas of Africa devastated by AIDS. After appearances on British and South African TV, Bayliss attracted a number of entrepreneurs and companies interested in manufacturing and marketing his clockwork radio. However, Bayliss was concerned by the fact that his patent provided only limited protection for his invention: most of the main components – a clockwork generator and transistor radio – were long-established technologies. What advice would you offer Baylis as to how he can best protect and exploit his invention?

2   Table 11.1 shows that:

a)   Patents have been more effective in protecting product innovations in drugs and medical equipment than in food or electronic components;
b)   Patents are more effective in protecting product innovations than process innovations.

Can you suggest reasons why?

3   What lessons would you draw from the experiences of Dyson and Raisio (Strategy Capsule 11.1) as to the merits and pitfalls of licensing as a means by which individuals and small companies can exploit their inventions?

4   From the evidence presented in Table 11.3, what conclusions can you draw regarding the factors that determine whether leaders or followers win out in the markets for new products?

5   In the battle for dominance of the US satellite radio market, XM's lead was being rapidly eroded by Sirius following its signing of "shock jock" Howard Stern and new CEO Mel Kamazin. XM has deals with GM, VW, and Honda; Sirius with Ford, DaimlerChrysler, and BMW. XM carries Major League Baseball; Sirius the National Football League. XM has support from equipment manufacturers Delphi and Pioneer; Sirius with Kenwood. After holding a 3:1 advantage in subscribers during 2004, by the end of 2006, XM had about 8 million subscribers and Sirius 6.4 million. To what extent will satellite radio be a winner-take-all market? What recommendations would you offer XM for how it might gain market dominance?

Notes

1   "The Logic that Dares Not Speak its Name," *Economist* (April 16, 1994): 89–91.

2   R. D. Buzzell and B. T. Gale, *The PIMS Principles* (New York: Free Press, 1987): 274.

3   The excess of the benefit received by the consumer over the price they paid is called *consumer surplus* in the economics literature. See: D. Besanko, D. Dranove, and M. Shanley, *Economics of Strategy* (New York: Wiley, 1996): 442–3.

4   "Knowledge Monopolies: Patent Wars," *Economist* (April 8, 2000): 95–9.

5   The unit costs (and prices) of new products tend to decline rapidly. The ballpoint pen, invented by Ladislao Biro, is a classic example. At Christmas 1945, Biro pens sold at Gimbel's New York store for $12.50; by 1950, ballpoint pens were being sold for 15 cents. "Bic and the Heirs of Ball-Point Builder Are No Pen Pals," *Wall Street Journal* (May 27, 1988): 1, 27.

6   This section draws on: D. J. Teece, "Profiting from Technological Innovation: Implications for Integration, Collaboration, Licensing and Public Policy," in *The Competitive Challenge: Strategies for Industrial Innovation and Renewal* (Cambridge, MA: Ballinger, 1987): 190.

7   R. C. Levin, A. K. Klevorick, R. R. Nelson, and S. G. Winter, "Appropriating the Returns from Industrial Research and Development," *Brookings Papers on Economic Activity* 3 (1987).

8   P. Grindley and D. J. Teece, "Managing Intellectual Capital: Licensing and Cross-Licensing in Semiconductors and Electronics," *California Management Review* 39 (Winter 1997).

9   J. Jewkes, D. Sawyers, and R. Stillerman, *The Sources of Invention*, 2nd edn (London: Macmillan, 1969).

10   D. Hamberg, *Essays in the Economics of Research and Development* (New York: John Wiley, 1966).

11   D. Sull, "Strategy as Active Waiting," *Harvard Business Review* (September 2005): 120–9.

12   For example, data on penetration rates for electric toothbrushes and CD players were used to forecast the market demand for HD TVs in the United States (B. L. Bayus, "High-Definition Television: Assessing Demand Forecasts for the Next Generation Consumer Durable," *Management Science* 39 (1993): 1319–33).

13   See B. C. Twiss, *Managing Technological Innovation*, 2nd edn (New York: Longman, 1980).

14   E. Von Hippel, "Lead Users: A Source of Novel Product Concepts," *Management Science* 32 (July 1986).

15   In electronic instruments, customers' ideas initiated most of the successful new products introduced by manufacturers. See E. Von Hippel, "Users as Innovators," *Technology Review* 5 (1976): 212–39.

16   T. Peters, *Thriving on Chaos* (New York: Knopf, 1987): 259–66.

17   A. Friedlander, *The Growth of Railroads* (Arlington, VA: CNRI, 1995).

18   C. Shapiro and H. R. Varian, *Information Rules: A Strategic Guide to the Network Economy* (Boston: Harvard Business School Press, 1999): 264–7.

19   S. Postrel, "Competing Networks and Proprietary Standards: The Case of Quadraphonic Sound," *Journal of Industrial Economics* 24 (December 1990): 169–86.

20   S. J. Liebowitz and S. E. Margolis ("Network Externality: An Uncommon Tragedy," *Journal of Economic Perspectives* 8, Spring 1994: 133–50) refer to these user-to-user externalities as *direct externalities*.

21   M. Gladwell, *The Tipping Point* (Boston: Little Brown, 2000).

22   P. David, "Clio and the Economics of QWERTY," *American Economic Review* 75 (May 1985): 332–7; S. J. Gould, "The Panda's Thumb of Technology," *Natural History* 96, no. 1 (1986). For an alternative view see S. J. Liebowitz and S. Margolis, "The Fable of the Keys," *Journal of Law and Economics* 33 (1990): 1–26.

23   C. Shapiro and H. R. Varian, "The Art of Standards Wars," *California Management Review* 41 (Winter 1999): 8–32.

24   "Format Wars: Everyone Could End Up Losing," *Financial Times* (April 3, 2006).

25 Shapiro and Varian, "The Art of Standards Wars," ibid.: 15–16.

26 Ibid.: 16–18.

27 M. L. Tushman, "Managing Communication Networks in R&D Laboratories," *Sloan Management Review* (Winter 1979): 37–49.

28 S. Thomke, "Enlightened Experimentation: The New Imperative for Innovation," *Harvard Business Review* (February 2001): 66–75.

29 D. Leonard and S. Straus, "Putting Your Company's Whole Brain to Work," *Harvard Business Review* (July–August 1997): 111–21; D. Leonard and P. Swap, *When Sparks Fly: Igniting Creativity in Groups* (Boston: Harvard Business School Press, 1999).

30 "How to Manage a Dream Factory," *Economist* (January 16, 2003).

31 L. Grundy, J. Kickel, and C. Prather, "Building the Creative Organization," *Organizational Dynamics* (Spring 1994): 22–37.

32 E. Von Hippel, *The Sources of Innovation* (New York: Oxford University Press, 1988), provides strong evidence of the dominant role of users in the innovation process.

33 R. Florida and J. Goodnight, "Managing for Creativity," *Harvard Business Review* (July–August 2005).

34 P. Lawrence and S. Lorsch, *Organization and Environment: Managing Differentiation and Integration* (Cambridge, MA: Harvard University Press, 1967).

35 E. Morrison, "Gunfire at Sea: A Case Study of Innovation," in M. Tushman and W. L. Moore (eds), *Readings in the Management of Innovation* (Cambridge, MA: Ballinger, 1988): 165–78.

36 K. Imai, I. Nonaka, and H. Takeuchi, "Managing the New Product Development Process: How Japanese Companies Learn and Unlearn," in K. Clark, R. Hayes, and C. Lorenz (eds), *The Uneasy Alliance* (Boston: Harvard Business School Press, 1985).

37 K. Clark and T. Fujimoto, *Product Development Performance: Strategy, Organization, and Management in the World Auto Industry* (Boston: Harvard Business School Press, 1991).

38 D. A. Schön, "Champions for Radical New Inventions," *Harvard Business Review* (March–April, 1963): 84.

39 R. Rothwell et al., "SAPPHO Updated – Project SAPPHO Phase II," *Research Policy* 3 (1974): 258–91.

40 M. T. Hansen, H. W. Chesborough, N. Nohria, and D. N. Sull, "Networked Incubators: Hothouse of the New Economy," *Harvard Business Review* (September–October, 2000): 74–88; "How to Make the Most of a Brilliant Idea," *Financial Times* (December 6, 2000): 21.

41 J. Scully, *Odyssey* (Toronto: Fitzhenry and Whiteside, 1987): 184.

12

Competitive Advantage in Mature Industries

We are a true "penny profit" business. That means that it takes hard work and attention to detail to be financially successful – it is far from being a sure thing. Our store managers must do two things well: control costs and increase sales. Cost control cannot be done by compromising product quality, customer service, or restaurant cleanliness, but rather by consistent monitoring of the "vital signs" of the business through observation, reports, and analysis. Portion control is a critical part of our business. For example, each Filet-O-Fish sandwich receives 1 fluid ounce of tartar sauce and 0.5 ounces of cheese. Our raw materials are fabricated to exacting tolerances, and our managers check them on an ongoing basis. Our written specification for lettuce is over two typewritten pages long. Our French fries must meet standards for potato type, solid and moisture content, and distribution of strand lengths.

—EDWARD H. RENSI, PRESIDENT AND CHIEF OPERATING OFFICER, MCDONALD'S USA[1]

OUTLINE

Introduction and Objectives

Although technology-based industries grab the attention of both business journalists and strategy researchers, if importance is measured by share of GDP rather than share of press coverage, mature industries – food, energy, construction, vehicles, financial services, and restaurants – retain their preeminence, even in the advanced industrialized nations.

Despite their heterogeneity – they range from massage parlors to steel – mature industries present several similarities from a strategic perspective. The purpose of this chapter is to explore the characteristics of mature industries, the strategies through which competitive advantage can be established within them, and the implications of these strategies for structure, systems, and leadership style. As we shall see, maturity does not imply lack of opportunity. Companies such as Hennes & Mauritz (fashion clothing), Ryanair (airlines), Starbucks (coffee shops), and Nucor (steel) have prospered on the basis of innovative strategies. Coca-Cola, Exxon Mobil, and General Electric were founded in the 19th century, yet, over the past decade, have achieved combinations of profitability and growth that would make most high-tech companies envious. Nor does maturity mean lack of innovation: as we shall see, many mature industries have been transformed by new technologies and new strategies.

By the time you have completed this chapter, you will be able to:

● Recognize the principal strategic characteristics of mature industries.

● Identify key success factors within mature industries and formulate strategies directed toward their exploitation.

● Locate and analyze opportunities for strategic innovation in mature industries to establish competitive advantage.

● Design organizational structures and management systems that can effectively implement such strategies.

Competitive Advantage in Mature Industries

Our analysis of the industry life cycle (Chapter 10) suggests that maturity has two principal implications for competitive advantage: first, it tends to reduce the number of opportunities for establishing competitive advantage; second, it shifts these opportunities from differentiation-based factors to cost-based factors.

Diminishing opportunities for sustainable competitive advantage in mature industries stem from:

- Less scope for differentiation advantage resulting from increased buyer knowledge, product standardization, and less product innovation.
- Diffusion of process technology means that cost advantages based on superior processes or more advanced capital equipment methods are difficult to obtain and sustain. Once a cost advantage is established, it is vulnerable to exchange rate movements and the emergence of low-cost overseas competitors.
- A highly developed industry infrastructure together with the presence of powerful distributors makes it easier to attack established firms that occupy particular strategic niches.

Using different terminology, Warren Buffett – "The Sage of Omaha" – describes the same process of maturity leading to eroding competitive advantage as enterprises' transition from "franchises" into "businesses" (see Strategy Capsule 12.1).

This trend toward deteriorating industry profitability is a constant threat in mature industries. As rivalry encourages overinvestment in capacity, international competition increases, and differentiation is undermined by commoditization, attaining a competitive advantage becomes essential to achieving positive economic profits.

STRATEGY CAPSULE 12.1

The Transition of "Franchises" into "Businesses": The Media Sector

In assessing the profit prospects of a firm, Warren Buffett distinguishes "Franchises" from "Businesses":

> An economic franchise arises from a product or service that (1) is needed or desired; (2) is thought by customers to have no close substitute; and (3) is not subject to price regulation. Franchises earn high rates of return on capital . . . [and] can tolerate mismanagement . . . In contrast, "a business" earns exceptional profits only if it is a low-cost operator or if supply of its product or service is tight. And a business, unlike a franchise, can be killed by poor management.

Buffett identifies this erosion of competitive advantage within the media sector – newspapers, television, and magazines – "as retailing patterns change and entertainment choices proliferate." The problem is that as the businesses have transformed from "franchises" into "businesses," consumers "enjoy greatly broadened choices as to where to find them." Unfortunately, demand can't expand in response to the new supply: "500 million American eyeballs and a 24-hour day are all that's available. The result is that competition has intensified, markets have fragmented, and the media industry has lost some – though far from all – of its franchise strength."

Source: Letter to Shareholders, Annual Report of Berkshire Hathaway Inc., 1991.

Cost Advantage

If cost is the overwhelmingly important key success factor in most mature industries, what are the primary sources of low cost? Three cost drivers tend to be especially important:

- *Economies of scale.* In capital-intensive industries, or where advertising, distribution, or new product development is an important element of total cost, economies of scale are important sources of interfirm cost differences. The increased standardization that accompanies maturity greatly assists the exploitation of such scale economies. The significance of scale economies in mature industries is indicated by the fact that the association between ROI and market share is stronger in mature industries than in emerging industries.[2]

- *Low-cost inputs.* Where small competitors are successful in undercutting the prices of market leaders in mature industries, it is frequently through their access to low-cost inputs. Established firms can become locked into high salaries and benefits, inefficient working practices, and bloated overheads inherited from more prosperous times. New entrants into mature industries may gain cost advantages by acquiring plant and equipment at bargain-basement levels and by cutting labor costs. Valero Energy Corporation is the largest oil refiner in the United States: it acquired loss-making refineries from the majors at below-book prices then operated them with rigorous cost efficiency. A lower cost of capital can also be a key source of cost advantage. The acquisition of retailers, hotels, hospital groups, and chemical firms by private equity funds has been motivated in part by the attractions of substituting low-cost debt for high-cost equity.[3]

- *Low overheads.* During the early 1990s, some of the most profitable companies in mature industries tended to be those that had achieved the most substantial reductions in overhead costs. In discount retailing, Wal-Mart is famous for its parsimonious approach to overhead costs. Among the oil majors, Exxon is known for its rigorous control of overhead costs. Exxon's headquarters cost (relative to net worth) was estimated at less than one-quarter that of Mobil's.[4] When Exxon merged with Mobil, it was able to extract huge cost savings from Mobil. In newspaper and magazine publishing, newcomers such as EMAP in the UK and Media News Group in the US (run by "Lean Dean" Singleton) have acquired multiple titles then slashed overhead costs.

Because cost inefficiencies tend to become institutionalized within mature enterprises, cost reduction may require drastic interventions. *Corporate restructuring* – intensive periods of structural and strategic change – typically involves cost reduction through outsourcing, headcount reduction, and downsizing – especially at corporate headquarters.[5] Successful turnaround strategies typically involve aggressive cost cutting. Among mature US businesses, Hambrick and Schecter identified three successful approaches:

- *Asset and cost surgery* – aggressive cost reduction through reduction of excess capacity; halting of new investment in plant and equipment; and cutbacks in R&D, marketing expenditures, receivables, and inventories.

- *Selective product and market pruning* – refocusing on segments that were most profitable or where the firm possessed distinctive strength.

● *Piecemeal productivity moves* – adjustments to current market position rather than comprehensive refocusing or reorganizing, including reductions in marketing and R&D expenditures, higher capacity utilization, and increased employee productivity.[6]

Among British companies, cost reduction was also a key feature of turnaround strategies. Drastic upturns in performance (by so-called "sharpbender" companies) were typically the result of, first, changes in top management and, second, intensive efforts to reduce production costs.[7]

Segment and Customer Selection

Sluggish demand growth, lack of product differentiation, and international competition tend to depress the profitability of mature industries. Yet, even unattractive industries may offer attractive niche markets with strong growth of demand, few competitors, and abundant potential for differentiation. As a result, segment selection can be a key determinant of differences in the performance of companies within the same industry. Wal-Mart's profitability was boosted by locating its stores in small and medium-sized towns where it faced little competition. In the auto industry, there is a constant quest to escape competition by creating new market segments with "crossover" vehicles that span existing segments. Opportunities for establishing new segments can arise from the strategies of market leaders. The more that incumbents focus on the mass market, the more likely it is that new entrants can carve out new market niches by supplying underserved customer needs.[8]

The logic of segment focus implies further disaggregation of markets – down to the level of the individual customer. Information technology permits new approaches to *customer relationship management* (CRM), making it possible to analyze individual characteristics and preferences, identify individual customers' profit contribution to the firm, and organize marketing around individualized, integrated approaches to customers. In the same way that Las Vegas casinos have long recognized that the major part of their profits derives from a tiny minority of customers – the "high rollers" – so banks, supermarkets, credit card companies, and hotels increasingly use transactions data to identify their most attractive customers, and those that are a drag on profitability.

The next stage in this process is to go beyond customer selection to actively target more attractive customers and transform less valuable customers into more valuable customers. Alan Grant and Leonard Schlesinger point to the need for companies to optimize their *value exchange* – the relationship between the investment a company makes in a customer relationship and the return that investment generates.[9] For example:

● Credit card issuer Capital One has long been a leader in using data warehousing, experimentation, simulation, and sophisticated statistical modeling to adjust the terms and features of its credit card offers to the preferences and characteristics of individual customers. Capital One estimates the life-time profitability of each customer and analyzes the four key events in the credit card life cycle: acquiring the customer, stimulating the customer's card use, retaining the customer, and managing default.[10]

● Amazon.com uses information on customers' prior transactions and comparisons with other customers making similar purchases to generate individualized purchase suggestions.

The Quest for Differentiation

Cost leadership, we noted in Chapter 9, is difficult to sustain, particularly in the face of international competition. Hence, differentiating to attain some insulation from the rigors of price competition is particularly attractive in mature industries. The problem is that the trend toward commoditization narrows the scope for differentiation and reduces customer willingness to pay a premium for differentiation:

- In tires and domestic appliances, companies' investments in differentiation through product innovation, quality, and brand advertising reputation have generated disappointing returns. Vigorous competition, price-sensitive customers, and strong, aggressive retailers have limited the price premium that differentiation will support.

- Attempts by airlines to gain competitive advantage through offering more legroom, providing superior in-flight entertainment, and achieving superior punctuality have met little market response from consumers. The only effective differentiators appear to be frequent flier programs and services offered to first- and business-class travelers.

Standardization of the physical attributes of a product and convergence of consumer preferences constrains, but does not eliminate, opportunities for meaningful and profitable differentiation. Product standardization is frequently accompanied by increased differentiation of complementary services – financing terms, leasing arrangements, warranties, after-sales services, and the like. In consumer goods, maturity often means a shift from physical differentiation to image differentiation. Entrenched consumer loyalties to specific brands of cola or cigarettes are a tribute to the capacity of brand promotion over long periods of time to create distinct images among near-identical products.

The intensely competitive retail sector produces particularly interesting examples of differentiation strategies. The dismal profitability earned by many retail chains (Toys-R-Us, J. C. Penney, and Circuit City in the US; J. Sainsbury, Mothercare, and Kingfisher in the UK; Royal Ahold in the Netherlands) contrasts sharply with the sales growth and profitability of stores that have established clear differentiation through variety, style, and ambiance (Target, Lowe's, TJX, and Bed, Bath and Beyond in the US; Zara-Inditex from Spain; Hennes & Mauritz and IKEA from Sweden). A further lesson from highly competitive mature sectors such as retailing is that competitive advantage is difficult to sustain. Most of the outstandingly successful retailers of the previous decade – Toys-R-Us, Body Shop, and Marks & Spencer – have been displaced in the affections of consumers and investors by the rising stars of retail.

Innovation

We have characterized mature industries as industries where the pace of technical change is low. In many mature industries – steel, textiles, food processing, insurance, and hotels – R&D expenditure is below 1% of sales revenue, while in US manufacturing as a whole just three sectors – computers and electronics, pharmaceuticals, and aerospace – account for 65% of R&D spending.[11] In recent years, this conventional view of mature industries as lacking technological dynamism has come under attack. McGahan and Silverman show that, measured by patenting activity, mature industries are as innovative as emerging industries.[12] Certainly in mature products such as tires,

STRATEGY CAPSULE 12.2

Innovation in Mature Industries: Brassiere Technology

The first patent for a "breast-supporting device" was issued in the United States in 1864. However, the first patent relating to an undergarment named "brassiere" was issued to Mary Phelps Jacob in 1913. By 1940 over 550 US patents for brassieres and related breast supporters had been issued.

The technological quest for a better bra continued into the 21st century – the US Patent Office has issued over 200 patents relating to brassieres since January 2000. The design innovations of recent years include:

- Wonderbra (owned by Sara Lee) introduced a "variable cleavage" bra equipped with a system of pulleys.

- The Airotic bra designed by Gossard (also owned by Sara Lee) features "twin air bags as standard" – these are inflatable by a "unique G-pump system."

- Charnos's Bioform bra replaces underwiring with soft molded polypropylene around a

rigid ring – a design inspired by the Frisbee and engineered by Ove Arup, who also engineered London's Millennium Bridge (which had to be closed because of excessive wobbling).

- The Ultimo bra, designed by Scottish model Michelle Mone assisted by a team of German scientists, is equipped with silicone gel pads.

- A number of new brassieres use "spacer fabric" which comprises "two outer textile layers separated by a ventilated inner layer of spacer yarns, to allow heat and moisture to escape. Various properties can be added to the fabrics, including anti-microbial, anti-mildew, anti-static, flame-retardant, absorptive, water-repellent, and abrasion-resistant attributes . . ."

Sources: "Bra Wars," *Economist* (December 2, 2000): 112; salon.com (August 28, 2000); US Patent Database.

brassieres, and fishing rods, continuing technological development is indicated by a steady flow of new patents (see Strategy Capsule 12.2).

What is clear is that the pressure of competition and the limited opportunities for technology-based advantage create impetus for innovation in other areas of competitive strategy. The quest for new ways of doing business – "new game strategies" – was referred to in Chapter 6. In relation to the innovation cycles identified by Abernathy and Utterback (see Figure 10.2 in Chapter 10),[13] it is possible that there is a third phase of innovation – *strategic innovation* – which becomes most prominent once product and process innovation have begun to slacken. Because strategic innovation requires strategic initiatives that are new and unique, it is difficult to apply systematic, analytical approaches to their discovery and design. Value chain analysis can assist the identification of "new game strategies" that reconfigure the sequence of activities undertaken by the firm.

Strategic innovation may also result from redefining markets and market segments.[14] This may involve:

● *Embracing new customer groups.* Harley-Davidson has created a market for expensive motorcycles among the middle aged and Sony has extended video gaming from teenage boys to girls, adults and retirees. The most rapidly growing churches – e.g. Jehovah's Witnesses in Russia and Amway Christian Fellowship in America – tend to be those that recruit among underserved social and demographic groups.

● *Adding products and services that perform new but related functions.* In the US, Arco was an innovator in recreating the gas station as a convenience store. In book retailing, large stores such as Barnes and Noble as well as some small neighborhood bookstores have redefined book retailing by adding additional products and services. Many of these innovative forms of differentiation involve the creation of entirely new customer experiences – at restaurant chains such as Hard Rock Café and Planet Hollywood the food is a relatively minor contributor to the customer experience. Pine and Gilmore identify a progression of economic value that begins with commodities and leads through products and services before arriving at *experiences*. In the *experience economy*, companies go beyond providing a product or service that meets a clearly defined customer need and involve their customers in a process that engages them at the emotional, intellectual, even spiritual, level.[15]

Baden-Fuller and Stopford show that strategic innovation in mature businesses often results from the reconciliation of multiple (often opposing) performance goals. Their case analysis of successful mature companies concludes:

1 Maturity is a state of mind, not a state of the business; every enterprise has the potential for rejuvenation.

2 It is the firm that matters, not the industry. The industry sets a context, not a prison for the firm. Not only can the creative firm achieve success within a hostile industry environment, it can transform its industry environment (e.g. Honda in motorcycles).

3 Strategic innovation is the basis for competitive advantage in industries where the potential for competitive advantage seems limited. The essence of strategic innovation is reconciling alternatives: quality at low cost (Toyota), variety at low cost (Courtaulds), speed at low cost (Benetton), and so on.

4 Businesses should be selective in choosing their strategic territory. An island kingdom is more defensible than the Hapsburg Empire. The firm's market scope needs to be limited by its resources and capabilities.

5 The pursuit of strategic innovation requires an entrepreneurial organization with freedom to experiment and the capacity to learn.[16]

Rejuvenation represents as formidable a challenge to a mature enterprise as it does to an aging university professor. Indeed, change is likely to be even more difficult for organizations than for individuals. In Chapter 10, we noted the resistance to change caused by organizational inertia. Resistance to innovation and renewal arises not just from entrenched structures and systems but also from the propensity for managers to be trapped within their industry's conventional thinking about key success factors and business practices. Chapter 4 noted how established firms' responses to competitive threats may be limited by industry-wide systems of belief. J.-C. Spender refers to these common cognitive patterns as "industry recipes."[17] Studies of cognitive maps – the mental frameworks through which managers perceive and think about their environments and their companies – yield insights into why some firms are able to adapt better than others. A study of organizational renewal among railroad companies found that the ability of managers to learn in the form of changing their mental models of the business was critical to their capacity to renew themselves.[18]

The ability to break away from conventional wisdom and establish a unique positioning or novel form of differentiation may be critical in mature industries. Costas Markides identifies several examples of such contrarian thinking, including the following:

- Edward Jones, with 2,000 offices, mostly in the US but also in Canada and the UK, has rejected the brokerage industry's infatuation with economies of scale, product diversification, integration with investment banks, and e-commerce. Each office has just one investment adviser; there are no proprietary investment products; and no online investing. Edward Jones' strategy has been built on face-to-face relationships, motivating its office managers to develop their local business, and ambitious growth targets.[19]
- Enterprise Rent-A-Car has adopted a location strategy that is quite different from its major competitors Hertz and Avis. Rather than concentrate on serving the business traveler through locating at airports and downtown, Enterprise concentrates on suburban locations, where it caters primarily to the consumer market.[20]

How do companies break away from their traditional mindsets and achieve strategic innovation? According to Gary Hamel, the role of strategy should be to foster revolution through reorganizing the strategy-making process. This means breaking top management's monopoly over strategy formulation, bringing in younger people from further down the organization, and gaining involvement from those on the periphery of the organization.[21] Strategic innovation may be best thought of as a process that involves a sequence of managerial actions: "journeys of strategic renewal" and "trajectories of transformation."[22] Common to all these approaches is recognition that strategic innovation goes beyond rethinking strategies; it also requires new approaches to structuring and managing the mature business.

Strategy Implementation in Mature Industries: Structure, Systems, and Style

If the key to success in mature industries is achieving operational efficiency and reconciling this with innovation and customer responsiveness, achieving competitive advantage in mature businesses requires implementing structures, systems, and management styles that can mesh these multiple performance goals.

Efficiency through Bureaucracy

If maturity implies greater environmental stability, slower technological change, and an emphasis on cost efficiency, what types of organization and management approaches are called for? As we observed in Chapter 6, the conventional prescription for stable environments was "mechanistic" organizations characterized by centralization, well-defined roles, and predominantly vertical communication.[23] Henry Mintzberg describes this formalized type of organization dedicated to the pursuit of efficiency as the *machine bureaucracy*.[24] Efficiency is achieved through standardized routines, division of labor, and close management control based on bureaucratic principles. Division of labor extends to management as well as operatives – high levels of vertical and horizontal specialization are typical among managers. Vertical specialization is evident in the concentration of strategy formulation at the apex of the hierarchy, while middle and junior management supervise and administer through the application of standardized rules and procedures. Horizontal specialization takes the form of functional structures.

The machine bureaucracy as described by Mintzberg is a caricature of actual organizations – probably the closest approximations are found in government departments performing highly routine administrative duties (e.g., the Internal Revenue Service or departments of motor vehicle licensing). However, in most mature industries, the features of mechanistic organizations are evident in highly routinized operations and application of highly detailed rules and procedures. McDonald's may not be a typical bureaucracy, but it certainly operates with highly standardized and refined operating procedures that govern virtually every aspect of how it does business (see the quotation that introduces this chapter). The characteristics of mechanistic organization and principles of bureaucracy are prominent among the large enterprises found in most mature industries, whether we are looking at DaimlerChrysler, Exxon Mobil, or HSBC. The key features of these mature organizations are summarized in Table 12.1.

Beyond Bureaucracy

As was noted in Chapter 6, the past two decades have seen growing unpopularity of bureaucratic approaches to management, especially in mature industries. Factors contributing to this trend include:

- *Increased environmental turbulence.* Bureaucracy is conducive to efficiency in stable environments. However, the centralized, structured organization cannot readily adapt to change. Achieving flexibility to respond to external change requires greater decentralization, less specialization, and looser controls.

- *Increased emphasis on innovation.* The organizational structure, control systems, management style, and interpersonal relationships conducive to efficiency are likely to hinder innovation. As mature enterprises sought new opportunities for competitive advantage, so the disadvantages of formalized, efficiency-oriented organizations became increasingly apparent.

- *New process technology.* The efficiency advantages of bureaucratized organizations arise from the technical virtues of highly specialized, systematized production methods. The electronics revolution has changed the conditions for efficiency. Computer-integrated manufacturing processes permit cost efficiency with greater product variety, shorter runs, and greater flexibility. As automation displaces labor-intensive, assembly-line manufacturing techniques, there is less need for elaborate division of labor and greater need for job flexibility. Simultaneously, the electronic revolution in the office is displacing the administrative bureaucracy that control and information systems once required.

TABLE 12.1 Strategy implementation in mature industries: the conventional model

STRATEGY	Primary goal is cost advantage through economies of scale, capital-intensive production of standardized products/services. Strategy formulation primarily the realm of top managers; middle managers responsible for strategy implementation.
STRUCTURE	Functional departments (e.g., production, marketing, customer service, distribution). Distinction between line and staff. Clearly defined job roles with strong vertical reporting/delegation relationships.
CONTROLS	Performance targets are primarily quantitative and short term and are specified for all members of the organization. Performance is closely monitored by well-established, centralized management information systems and formalized reporting requirements. Financial controls through budgets and profit targets particularly important.
INCENTIVES	Incentives are based on achievement of individual targets and take the form of financial rewards and promotion up the hierarchy. Penalties exist for failure to attain quantitative targets, for failure to adhere to the rules, and for lack of conformity to company norms.
COMMUNICATION	Primarily vertical for the purposes of delegation and reporting. Lateral communication limited, often achieved through interdepartmental committees.
MANAGEMENT	Primary functions of top management: control and strategic decision making. Typical CEO: the administrator – who guides the organization through establishing and operating organizational systems and principles and building consensus (e.g., Alfred Sloan Jr. of General Motors); and the autocrat – whose primary role is decision making and who leads through aggressive use of power and sheer force of personality (Lee Iacocca of Chrysler and Al Dunlap of Sunbeam).

● *Alienation and conflict.* The dependence of bureaucracy on departmentalization, layering, and the control of some employees by others is conducive to alienation and conflict.

Companies in mature industries have undergone substantial adjustment over the past decade. Among large, long-established corporations management hierarchies have been pruned, decision making decentralized and accelerated, and more open communication and flexible collaboration fostered. The trend began in North America, spread to continental Europe, and is now evident in Japan and Korea. The changes are apparent in:

● Strategic decision processes that increase the role of business-level managers and reduce the role of corporate management; an emphasis on the strategy formulation process as more important than strategic plans per se.

- This shifting of decision-making power to the business level has been accompanied by shrinking corporate staffs.
- Less emphasis on economies of large-scale production and increased responsiveness to customer requirements together with greater flexibility in responding to changes in the marketplace.
- Increased emphasis on teamwork as a basis for organizing separate activities to improve interfunctional cooperation and responsiveness to external requirements.
- Wider use of profit incentives to motivate employees and less emphasis on controls and supervision.

Despite the changes, the primary emphasis on cost efficiency remains. However, the conditions for cost efficiency have changed. The most powerful force for organizational change in mature industries has been the inability of highly structured, centralized organizations to maintain their cost efficiency in an increasingly turbulent business environment. As we observed in Chapter 9, the requirements for dynamic efficiency are different from the requirements for static efficiency. Dynamic efficiency requires flexibility, which necessitates higher levels of autonomy and nonhierarchical coordination. A feature of the revitalization efforts of Jack Welch at General Electric, Carlos Ghosn at Nissan and Renault, Stuart Rose at Marks & Spencer, John Browne at British Petroleum, and Sandy Weill at Citigroup has been combining strong central direction with increased decision-making autonomy at the business level. By relying more on performance targets and less on approvals and committees, the old corporate empires have become more flexible and responsive while maintaining a strong focus on efficiency.

Strategies for Declining Industries

The transition from maturity to decline can be a result of technological substitution (typewriters, railroads), changes in consumer preferences (men's suits), demographic shifts (babyware in Italy), or foreign competition (cutlery in Sheffield, England). Shrinking market demand gives rise to acute strategic issues. Among the key features of declining industries are:

- Excess capacity.
- Lack of technical change (reflected in a lack of new product introduction and stability of process technology).
- A declining number of competitors, but some entry as new firms acquire the assets of exiting firms cheaply.
- High average age of both physical and human resources.
- Aggressive price competition.

Despite the inhospitable environment offered by declining industries, research by Kathryn Harrigan has uncovered declining industries where at least some participants earned surprisingly high profits. These included electronic vacuum tubes, cigars, and leather tanning. However, elsewhere – notably in prepared baby foods, rayon, and meat processing – decline was accompanied by aggressive price competition, company failures, and instability.[25]

What determines whether or not a declining industry becomes a competitive blood-bath? Two factors are critical: the balance between capacity and output, and the nature of the demand for the product.

Adjusting Capacity to Declining Demand

The smooth adjustment of industry capacity to declining demand is the key to stability and profitability during the decline phase. In industries where capacity exits from the industry in an orderly fashion, decline can occur without trauma. Where substantial excess capacity persists, as has occurred in the steel industries of America and Europe, in the bakery industry, in gold mining, and in long-haul bus transportation, the potential exists for destructive competition. The ease with which capacity adjusts to declining demand depends on the following factors:

- *The predictability of decline.* If decline can be forecast, it is more likely that firms can plan for it. The decline of traditional photography with the advent of digital imaging was anticipated and planned for. Conversely, the long-term decline of the US and Western European steel industries has been obscured by periodic cyclical upswings – most notably that of 2002–6. The more cyclical and volatile the demand, the more difficult it is for firms to perceive the trend of demand even after the onset of decline.

- *Barriers to exit.* Barriers to exit impede the exit of capacity from an industry. The major barriers are:
  - Durable and specialized assets. Just as capital requirements impose a barrier to entry into an industry, those same investments also discourage exit. The longer they last and the fewer the opportunities for using those assets in another industry, the more companies are tied to that particular industry.
  - Costs incurred in plant closure. Apart from the accounting costs of writing off assets, substantial cash costs may be incurred in redundancy payments to employees, compensation for broken contacts with customers and suppliers, dismantling the plant, and environmental clean-up.
  - Managerial commitment. In addition to financial considerations, firms may be reluctant to close plants for a variety of emotional and moral reasons. Resistance to plant closure and divestment arises from pride in company traditions and reputation, managers' unwillingness to accept failure, and loyalties to employees and the local community.

- *The strategies of the surviving firms.* Smooth exit of capacity ultimately depends on the decisions of the industry players. The sooner companies recognize and address the problem, the more likely it is that independent and collective action can achieve capacity reduction. In European gasoline retailing, for example, the problem of excess capacity was partially solved by bilateral exchanges of service stations among the major oil companies. Stronger firms in the industry can facilitate the exit of weaker firms by offering to acquire their plants and take over their after-sales service commitments. A key strategy among private equity firms has been initiating "roll-ups" in declining industries – consolidating multiple acquisitions.

The Nature of Demand

Where a market is segmented, the general pattern of decline can obscure the existence of pockets of demand that are not only comparatively resilient, but also price inelastic. For example, despite the obsolescence of vacuum tubes after the adoption of transistors, GTE Sylvania and General Electric earned excellent profits supplying vacuum tubes to the replacement and military markets.[26] In fountain pens, survivors in the quality pen segment such as Cross and Mont Blanc have achieved steady sales and high margins through appealing to high-income professionals and executives. Despite overall decline of the cigar market, quality cigars have benefited from strong demand and attractive margins.

Strategies for Declining Industries

Conventional strategy recommendations for declining industries are either to divest or to harvest, i.e., to generate the maximum cash flow from existing investments without reinvesting. However, these strategies assume that declining industries are inherently unprofitable. If profit potential exists, then other strategies may be attractive. Harrigan and Porter[27] identify four strategies that can profitably be pursued either individually or sequentially in declining industries.

- *Leadership*. By gaining leadership, a firm is well placed to outstay competitors and play a dominant role in the final stages of the industry's life cycle. Once leadership is attained, the firm is in a good position to switch to a harvest strategy and enjoy a strong profit stream from its market position. Establishing leadership can be done by acquiring competitors, but a cheaper way is to encourage competitors to exit (and then acquire their plants). Inducements to competitors to exit may include showing commitment to the industry, helping to lower their exit costs, releasing pessimistic forecasts of the industry's future, and raising the stakes – e.g., by supporting more stringent environmental controls that make it costly for them to stay in business.

- *Niche*. Identify a segment that is likely to maintain a stable demand and that other firms are unlikely to invade, then pursue a leadership strategy to establish dominance within the segment. The most attractive niches are those that offer the greatest prospects for stability and where demand is most inelastic.

- *Harvest*. By harvesting, a firm maximizes its cash flow from existing assets, while avoiding further investment. A harvesting strategy seeks to boost margins wherever possible through raising prices and cutting costs by rationalizing the number of models, number of channels, and number of customers. Note, however, that a harvest strategy can be difficult to implement. In the face of strong competition, harvesting may accelerate decline, particularly if employee morale is adversely affected by a strategy that offers no long-term future for the business.

- *Divest*. If the future looks bleak, the best strategy may be to divest the business in the early stages of decline before a consensus has developed as to the inevitability of decline. Once industry decline is well established, finding buyers may be extremely difficult.

FIGURE 12.1 Strategic alternatives for declining industries

COMPANY'S COMPETITIVE POSITION

		Strengths in remaining demand pockets	Lacks strength in remaining demand pockets
INDUSTRY STRUCTURE	Favorable to decline	LEADERSHIP or NICHE	HARVEST or DIVEST
	Unfavorable to decline	NICHE or HARVEST	DIVEST QUICKLY

Choosing the most appropriate strategy requires a careful assessment both of the profit potential of the industry and the competitive position of the firm. Harrigan and Porter pose four key questions:

● Can the structure of the industry support a hospitable, potentially profitable decline phase?
● What are the exit barriers that each significant competitor faces?
● Do your company strengths fit the remaining pockets of demand?
● What are your competitors' strengths in these pockets? How can their exit barriers be overcome?

Selecting an appropriate strategy requires matching the opportunities remaining in the industries to the company's competitive position. Figure 12.1 shows a simple framework for strategy choice.

Summary

Mature industries present challenging environments for the formulation and implementation of business strategies. Competition – price competition in particular – is usually strong and competitive advantage is often difficult to build and sustain: cost advantages are vulnerable to imitation, differentiation opportunities are limited by the trend to standardization. Stable positions of competitive advantage in mature industries are traditionally associated with cost advantage from economies of scale or experience, and differentiation advantage through brand loyalty.

Such strategies are typically implemented through hierarchical organizations, with high levels of specialization and formalization, and centralized decision making directed toward maximizing static efficiency.

Increased dynamism of mature industries resulting from international competition, economic turbulence, and greater pressure for innovation has had two consequences. First, the conditions for cost efficiency have changed. In a dynamic environment, cost efficiency is less dependent on scale, specialization, and rigid control, and more on rapid adjustment to change. Second, as competition has become more intense, companies (especially those in the advanced industrialized countries) have been forced to seek new sources of competitive advantage through innovation and differentiation. Reconciling the pursuit of scale economies with the need for responsiveness and flexibility, and the requirements of cost efficiency with the growing need for innovation and differentiation, poses complex strategic and organizational challenges. Some of the most successful companies in mature industries – Wal-Mart in retailing, BP in oil and gas, Nike in shoes and sportswear, and Coca-Cola in beverages – are companies that have achieved flexibility through dismantling bureaucratic structures and procedures, exploited new technology to combine variety and flexibility with efficiency, encouraged high levels of employee commitment, and relentlessly pursued financial targets. We return to some of these challenges and firms' responses to them in Chapter 17.

Self-Study Questions

1   The clothing manufacturers of northern Italy are facing rapid decline as retail chains and fashion houses increasingly outsource to China and other low-cost countries. What strategies would you recommend to small and medium-sized Italian garment manufacturers to assist them in surviving the onslaught of low-cost foreign competition?

2   Under Jacques Nasser, Ford's response to intensifying competition in the auto industry was to acquire a stable of luxury brands and forward integrate into car rental (Hertz), car repair (Kwik Fit), and financial services. Under the present CEO, Alan Mulally, Ford is moving in the opposite direction: divesting car rental, car repair, financial services, and some luxury brands (including Aston Martin and possibly Jaguar), and aggressively cutting costs and capacity. Given the characteristics of the industry and the company, examine the relative merits of each strategy and explain which strategy you would favor.

3   In both Europe and North America, established airlines are desperately cutting costs to compete with the increasing number of budget airlines. However, it is highly unlikely that these airlines will ever match the cost efficiency of Southwest, Jet Blue, or Ryanair. What opportunities are there for established airlines to improve their competitive position through differentiation strategies? Make specific proposals for how established airlines can differentiate their customer offerings more effectively.

4   Department stores (e.g. Federated Department Stores and Mays in the US, Selfridges and House of Fraser in the UK) face increasing competition from specialized chain retailers and discount stores. What innovative strategies might department stores adopt to revitalize their competitiveness?

Notes

1 E. H. Rensi, "Computers at McDonald's," in J. F. McLimore and L. Larwood (eds), *Strategies . . . Successes . . . Senior Executives Speak Out* (New York: Harper & Row, 1988): 159–60.

2 R. D. Buzzell and B. T. Gale, *The PIMS Principles* (New York: Free Press, 1987): 279.

3 "European Leveraged Buy-outs," *Economist* (August 10, 2006).

4 T. Copeland, T. Koller, and J. Murrin, *Valuation: Measuring and Managing the Value of Companies*, 3rd edn (New York: Wiley, 2000): 305.

5 R. Cibin and R. M. Grant, "Restructuring among the World's Leading Oil Companies," *British Journal of Management* 7 (December 1996): 283–308.

6 D. C. Hambrick and S. M. Schecter, "Turnaround Strategies for Mature Industrial-Product Business Units," *Academy of Management Journal* 26, no. 2 (1983): 231–48.

7 P. H. Grinyer, D. G. Mayes, and P. McKiernan, *Sharpbenders* (Oxford: Basil Blackwell, 1988).

8 G. R. Carroll and A. Swaminathan, "Why the Microbrewery Movement? Organizational Dynamics of Resource Partitioning in the American Brewing Industry," *American Journal of Sociology* 106 (2000): 715–62; C. Boone, G. R. Carroll, and A. van Witteloostuijn, "Resource Distributions and Market Partitioning: Dutch Daily Newspapers 1964–94," *American Sociological Review* 67 (2002): 408–31.

9 A. W. H. Grant and L. A. Schlesinger, "Realize Your Customer's Full Profit Potential," *Harvard Business Review* (September–October 1995): 59–72.

10 *Capital One Financial Corporation*, Harvard Business School Case No. 9-700-124 (2000).

11 National Science Foundation, *Research and Development in Industry: 2002* (www.nsf.gov).

12 A. M. McGahan and B. S. Silverman, "How Does Innovative Activity Change as Industries Mature?" *International Journal of Industrial Organization* 19, no. 7 (2001): 1141–60.

13 W. J. Abernathy and J. M. Utterback, "Patterns of Industrial Innovation," *Technology Review* (June/July 1978): 41–7.

14 D. Abell, *Managing with Dual Strategies* (New York: Free Press, 1993): 75–8.

15 B. J. Pine and J. Gilmore, "Welcome to the Experience Economy," *Harvard Business Review* (July–August 1998): 97–105.

16 C. Baden-Fuller and J. Stopford, *Rejuvenating the Mature Business* (Boston: HBS Press, 1994): especially Chapters 3 and 4.

17 J.-C. Spender, *Industry Recipes: The Nature and Sources of Managerial Judgment* (Oxford: Blackwell, 1989). On a similar theme, see also A. S. Huff, "Industry Influences on Strategy Reformulation," *Strategic Management Journal* 3 (1982): 119–31.

18 P. S. Barr, J. L. Stimpert, and A. S. Huff, "Cognitive Change, Strategic Action, and Organizational Renewal," *Strategic Management Journal* 13, Summer Special Issue (1992): 15–36.

19 "A Lesson in Small Town Economics," *Financial Times* (November 30, 2000): 16.

20 C. C. Markides, *All the Right Moves* (Boston: Harvard Business School Press, 1999).

21 G. Hamel, "Strategy as Revolution," *Harvard Business Review* 96 (July–August 1996): 69–82.

22 C. Baden-Fuller and J. Stopford, op. cit.; Henk Volberda, "Toward the Flexible Form: How to Remain Vital in Hypercompetitive Environments," *Organization Science* 7 (July–August 1996): 359–87; H. Volberda, C. Baden-Fuller, and F. van den Bosch, "Mastering Strategic Renewal," *Long Range Planning* 34 (April 2001): 159–78.

23 T. Burns and G. M. Stalker, *The Management of Innovation* (London: Tavistock Institute, 1961).

24 H. Mintzberg, *Structure in Fives: Designing Effective Organizations* (Englewood Cliffs, NJ: Prentice Hall, 1983): Chapter 9.

25 K. R. Harrigan, *Strategies for Declining Businesses* (Lexington, MA: D. C. Heath, 1980).

26 K. R. Harrigan, "Strategic Planning for Endgame," *Long Range Planning* 15 (1982): 45–8.

27 K. R. Harrigan and M. E. Porter, "End-Game Strategies for Declining Industries," *Harvard Business Review* (July–August 1983): 111–20.

V

CORPORATE STRATEGY

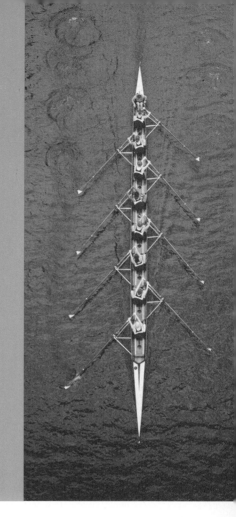

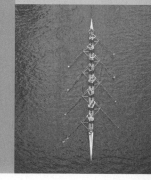

13

Vertical Integration and the Scope of the Firm

The idea of vertical integration is anathema to an increasing number of companies. Most of yesterday's highly integrated giants are working overtime at splitting into more manageable, more energetic units – i.e., de-integrating. Then they are turning around and re-integrating – not by acquisitions but via alliances with all sorts of partners of all shapes and sizes.

—TOM PETERS, LIBERATION MANAGEMENT

OUTLINE

Introduction and Objectives

Chapter 2 introduced the distinction between *corporate strategy* and *business strategy*. Corporate strategy is concerned primarily with the decisions over the *scope* of the firm's activities, including:

- *Product scope*. How specialized should the firm be in terms of the range of products it supplies? Coca-Cola (soft drinks), SAB-Miller (beer), Gap (fashion retailing), and Swiss Re (reinsurance) are specialized companies: they are engaged in a single industry sector. General Electric, Samsung, and Bertelsmann are diversified companies: each spans a number of different industries.

- *Geographical scope*. What is the optimal geographical spread of activities for the firm? In the restaurant business, Clyde's owns 12 restaurants in the Washington DC area, Popeye's Chicken and Biscuits operates throughout the US, McDonald's operates in 121 different countries.

- *Vertical scope*. What range of vertically linked activities should the firm encompass? Walt Disney Company is a vertically integrated company: it produces its own movies, distributes them itself to cinemas and through its own TV networks (ABC and Disney Channel), and uses the movies' characters in its retail stores and theme parks. Nike is much more vertically specialized: it engages in design and marketing but outsources most activities in its value chain, including manufacturing, distribution, and retailing.

Business strategy (also known as *competitive strategy*) is concerned with how a firm competes within a particular market. The distinction may be summarized as follows: corporate strategy is concerned with *where* a firm competes; business strategy is concerned with *how* a firm competes.[1] The major part of this book has been concerned with issues of business strategy. For the next four chapters, the emphasis is on corporate strategy: decisions that define the *scope of the firm.* I devote separate chapters to the different dimensions of scope – vertical scope (*vertical integration*), geographical scope (*multinationality*), and product scope (*diversification*). However, as we shall discover, the key underlying concepts for analyzing these different dimensions – economies of scope in resources and capabilities, transaction costs, and costs of corporate complexity – are common to all three.

In this chapter we begin by considering the overall scope of the firm. We then focus specifically on vertical integration. This takes us to the heart of the determinants of firm boundaries – in particular, the role of transaction costs. Moreover, vertical integration has been a central issue in corporate strategy in recent years as outsourcing, alliances, and e-commerce have caused companies to rethink which parts of their value chains they wish to include within their organizational boundaries.

By the time you have completed this chapter, you will be able to:

● Identify the relative efficiencies of firms and markets in organizing economic activity and apply the principles of *transaction cost economics* to explain why boundaries between firms and markets shift over time.

● Assess the relative advantages of vertical integration and outsourcing in organizing vertically related activities, understand the circumstances that influence these relative advantages, and advise a firm whether a particular activity should be undertaken internally or outsourced.

● Identify alternative ways of organizing vertical transactions – including spot market transactions, long-term contracts, franchise agreements, and alliances – and advise a firm on the most advantageous transaction mode given the characteristics and circumstances of the transaction.

Transaction Costs and the Scope of the Firm

In Chapter 6, we noted that firms came into existence because they were more efficient in organizing production than were market contracts between independent workers. Let us explore this issue and consider the determinants of firm boundaries.

Firms, Markets, and Transaction Costs

Although the capitalist economy is frequently referred to as a "market economy," in fact, it comprises two forms of economic organization. One is the *market mechanism*, where individuals and firms make independent decisions that are guided and coordinated by market prices. The other is the *administrative mechanism* of firms, where decisions over production, supply, and the purchases of inputs are made by managers and imposed through hierarchies. The market mechanism was characterized by Adam Smith, the 18th-century Scottish economist, as the "invisible hand" because its coordinating role does not require conscious planning. Alfred Chandler has referred to the administrative mechanism of company management as the "visible hand" because it is dependent on coordination through active planning.[2]

Why do institutions called "firms" exist in the first place? The firm is an organization that consists of a number of individuals bound by employment contracts with a central contracting authority. But firms are not essential for conducting complex economic activity. When I recently remodeled my basement, I contracted with a self-employed builder to undertake the work. He in turn subcontracted parts of the work to a plumber, an electrician, a joiner, a drywall installer, and a painter. Although the job involved the coordinated activity of several individuals, these self-employed

FIGURE 13.1 The scope of the firm: specialization versus integration

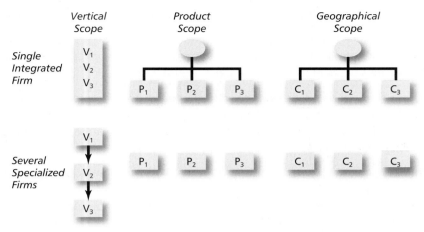

In the integrated firm there is an administrative interface between the different vertical units (V), product units (P), and country units (C). Where there is specialization, each unit is a separate firm linked by market interfaces.

specialists were not linked by employment relations but by market contracts ("$4,000 to install wiring, lights, and sockets").

What determines which activities are undertaken within a firm, or between individuals or firms coordinated by market contracts? Ronald Coase's answer was *relative cost*.[3] Markets are not costless: making a purchase or sale involves search costs, the costs of negotiating and drawing up a contract, the costs of monitoring to ensure that the other party's side of the contract is being fulfilled, and the enforcement costs of arbitration or litigation should a dispute arise. All these costs are types of *transaction costs*.[4] If the transaction costs associated with organizing across markets are greater than the *administrative costs* of organizing within firms, we can expect the coordination of productive activity to be internalized within firms.

This situation is illustrated in Figure 13.1. With regard to vertical scope, which is more efficient: three independent companies – one producing steel, the next rolling the steel into sheet, and the third producing steel cans – or having all three stages of production within a single company? In the case of geographical scope, which is more efficient: three independent companies producing cans in the US, UK, and Italy, or a single multinational company owning and operating the canmaking plants in all three countries? In the case of product scope, should metal cans, plastic packaging, and domestic appliances be produced by three separate companies, or are there efficiencies to be gained by merging all three into a single company?

The Shifting Boundary between Firms and Markets

The answers to these questions have changed over time. During the 19th and for most of the 20th century, companies grew in size and scope, absorbing transactions that had previously taken place across markets. As we observed in Chapter 6, companies that once were localized and specialized grew vertically, geographically, and across different industry sectors. This trend can be attributed to a fall in the administrative costs of the firm as compared with the transaction costs of markets. Two factors have greatly increased the efficiency of firms as organizing devices:

- *Technology*. The telegraph, telephone, and computer have played an important role in facilitating communications within firms and expanding the decision-making capacity of managers.

- *Management techniques*. Developments in the principles and techniques of management have greatly expanded the organizational and decision-making effectiveness of managers. Beginning with the dissemination of double-entry bookkeeping in the 19th century,[5] and the introduction of scientific management in the early 20th century,[6] the past six decades have seen rapid advances in all areas of management theory and methods.

Observing this growth in large corporations at the expense of markets, several leading economists of the late 1960s declared that the *market* economy had been replaced by a *corporate* economy. In 1969, J. K. Galbraith predicted that the inherent advantages of firms over markets in planning and resource allocation would result in increasing dominance of capitalist economies by a small number of giant corporations.[7]

During the 1980s and 1990s, these predictions were refuted by a sharp reversal of the trend toward increased corporate scope. Although large companies have continued to expand internationally, the dominant trends of the past 20 years have been "downsizing" and "refocusing," as large industrial companies reduced both their product scope through focusing on their core businesses, and their vertical scope through outsourcing. The result, as shown in Figure 13.2, was that the largest companies began to play a declining role in the US economy. These changes are associated with the more turbulent business environment that followed the oil shocks of 1973 and 1979, the end of fixed exchange rates (1972), the invention of the integrated circuit, and the upsurge of international competition. The implication seems to be that during periods of instability, the costs of administration within large, complex firms tend to rise as the need for flexibility and speed of response overwhelms traditional management systems.

Let us focus now on just one dimension of corporate scope: vertical integration. The question we will consider is this: is it better to be vertically integrated or vertically specialized? To answer this question, we shall draw in particular on Oliver Williamson's analysis of transaction costs, which forms the basis for a theory of economic organization that is particularly useful in designing vertical relationships.[8]

The Costs and Benefits of Vertical Integration

Strategies towards vertical integration have been subject to shifting fashions. For most of the 20th century, the prevailing wisdom was that vertical integration was generally beneficial because it allowed superior coordination and security. During the past 20 years there has been a profound change of opinion and the emphasis has shifted to the benefits of outsourcing in terms of flexibility and the ability to develop specialized capabilities in particular activities. Moreover, it has been noted that most of the coordination benefits associated with vertical integration can be achieved through interfirm collaboration.

However, as in other areas of management, fashion is fickle. In the media sector, vertical integration between content and distribution has become viewed as a critical

FIGURE 13.2 500 biggest US companies' share of total US private sector employment

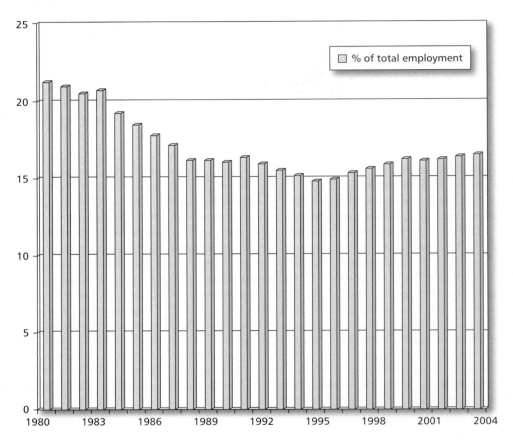

SOURCES: L. J. WHITE, "WHAT'S BEEN HAPPENING TO AGGREGATE CONCENTRATION IN THE U.S.? (AND SHOULD WE CARE?)," STERN SCHOOL OF BUSINESS, NEW YORK UNIVERSITY, 2001; FORBES 500 AND FORTUNE 1000 (VARIOUS YEARS).

advantage in the face of rapid technological change. The resulting wave of mergers between content producers and distributors (TV broadcasters, cable companies, and internet portals) has transformed the industry (see Strategy Capsule 13.1).

Our task is to go beyond fads and fashions to uncover the factors that determine whether vertical integration enhances or weakens performance.

Defining Vertical Integration

Vertical integration refers to a firm's ownership of vertically related activities. The greater the firm's ownership and control over successive stages of the value chain for its product, the greater its degree of vertical integration. The extent of vertical integration is indicated by the ratio of a firm's value added to its sales revenue. Highly integrated companies – such as the major oil companies that own and control their value chain from exploring for oil down to the retailing of gasoline – tend to have low expenditures on bought-in goods and services relative to their sales.

Vertical integration can be either *backward*, where the firm takes over ownership and control of producing its own components or other inputs, or *forward*, where the

STRATEGY CAPSULE 13.1

Vertical Integration in the Media Sector: Value Creating or Value Destroying?

Considerable vertical integration has occurred between content companies (film studios, music publishing, newspapers) and distribution companies (TV broadcasting, cable, satellite TV, telecom providers). News Corp. has expanded from newspapers into movie production (20th Century Fox), broadcast TV (Fox), satellite TV, and other sectors of the media business; Disney acquired TV broadcaster ABC; Viacom, formerly a cable company, acquired Paramount and Dreamworks; GE's NBC Universal combines studio production with cable and broadcast TV distribution; and AOL merged with Time Warner, a leading magazine, film, and music company. In 2004, Comcast, America's biggest cable operator, made a $54 billion hostile bid for Walt Disney Company.

Does vertical integration between media content and media distribution create or destroy value? Here are two contrasting views:

Steve Rosenbush, *Business Week*, February 11, 2004:

The economics of the TV-distribution business have been under siege for some time. That's why many of the business' smartest operators, like Liberty Media's John Malone and Viacom's Sumner Redstone, started shifting their investments into media years ago. Under Redstone, Viacom has been transformed from a cable operator into a media hothouse that includes everything from MTV to CBS. Buying Disney "shouldn't be a surprise. It's the logical next step," Comcast CEO Brian Roberts said at his Feb. 11 press conference announcing his bid for the Mouse House.

It isn't enough to be just a media company, either. Most content providers benefit from having a certain amount of distribution, which helps lower their costs. That's why, in the future, media and communications will be dominated by hybrids such as News Corp. which recently acquired satellite-TV operator DirecTV.

Comcast's Roberts has embraced this future. The question now is whether Disney CEO Michael Eisner – who spurned an offer for a friendly deal – can accept the same future. For decades, Disney and other programmers have held the balance of power in distribution deals. That's changing. The cable-TV business isn't just a collection of small family companies running regional outfits anymore. Comcast, which began life in Tupelo, Miss., in 1963, now has national reach. It has a greater market cap than Disney.

And it's competing with satellite-distribution companies like DirecTV that are also national in scope. Now that DirecTV is under Rupert Murdoch's control, it would be folly for Disney to pretend that it can still compete without a distribution partner of comparable stature. Comcast fits the bill.

John Kay, *Financial Times*, March 3, 2004

Media content needs delivery, and vice versa. And the same channels can often be used to disseminate text, images and music. This discovery was made at least 1,000 years ago by people who developed religious services, still among the most moving and spectacular multi-media displays.

But this old idea is frequently rediscovered by visionary chief executives, excitable consultants, and greedy investment bankers: the people who proclaimed the AOL–Time Warner deal a marriage made in heaven. And it was revealed with Damascene force to Jean-Marie Messier, a humble French water carrier.

But activities can converge without requiring that the companies that undertake them con-verge. The erstwhile maître du monde might have drawn a useful lesson from his experience at Compagnie Générale des Eaux before his apotheosis as chief executive of Vivendi Universal: sewers and the stuff that goes down them do not need common ownership.

firm takes over ownership and control of activities previously undertaken by its customers.

Vertical integration may also be *full* or *partial*:

- *Full integration* exists between two stages of production when all of the first stage's production is transferred to the second stage with no sales or purchases from third parties.
- *Partial integration* exists when stages of production are not internally self-sufficient. Among the oil and gas majors, "crude-rich" companies (such as Statoil) produce more oil than they refine and are net sellers of crude; "crude-poor" companies (such as Exxon Mobil) have to supplement their own production with purchases of crude to keep their refineries supplied.

Technical Economies from the Physical Integration of Processes

Analysis of the benefits of vertical integration has traditionally emphasized the *technical economies* of vertical integration: cost savings that arise from the physical integration of processes. Thus, most steel sheet is produced by integrated producers in plants that first produce steel, then roll hot steel into sheet. Linking the two stages of production at a single location reduces transportation and energy costs. Similar technical economies arise in pulp and paper production and from linking oil refining with petrochemical production.

However, although these considerations explain the need for the co-location of plants, they do not explain why vertical integration in terms of *common ownership* is necessary. Why can't steel and steel sheet production or pulp and paper production be undertaken by separate firms owning facilities that are physically integrated with one another? To answer this question, we must look beyond technical economies and consider the implications of linked processes for *transaction costs*.

The Sources of Transaction Costs in Vertical Exchanges

Consider the value chain for steel cans, which extends from mining iron ore to delivering cans to food processing companies (see Figure 13.3). Between the production of steel and steel strip, most production is vertically integrated. Between the production of steel strip and steel cans, there is very little vertical integration: can producers such as Crown Holdings and Ball Corporation are specialist packaging companies that purchase steel strip from steel companies on contracts.[9]

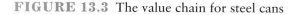

FIGURE 13.3 The value chain for steel cans

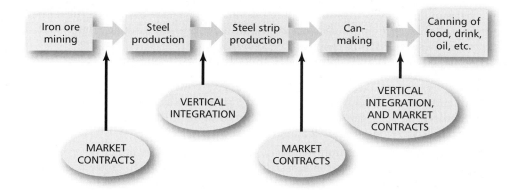

The predominance of market contracts between steel strip production and can pro-duction is the result of low transaction costs in the market for steel strip: there are many buyers and sellers, information is readily available, and the switching costs for buyers and suppliers are low. The same is true for many other commodity products: few jewelry companies own gold mines; few flour-milling companies own wheat farms.

To understand why vertical integration predominates across steel production and steel strip production, let us see what would happen if the two stages were owned by separate companies. Because there are technical economies from hot-rolling steel as soon as it is poured from the furnace, steel makers and strip producers must invest in integrated facilities. A competitive market between the two stages is impossible; each steel strip producer is tied to its adjacent steel producer. In other words, the market becomes a series of *bilateral monopolies*.

Why are these relationships between steel producers and strip producers prob-lematic? To begin with, where a single supplier negotiates with a single buyer, there is no equilibrium price: it all depends on relative bargaining power. Such bargaining is likely to be costly: the mutual dependency of the two parties is likely to give rise to *opportunism* and *strategic misrepresentation* as each company seeks to both enhance and exploit its bargaining power at the expense of the other. Hence, once we move from a competitive market situation to one where individual buyers and sellers are locked together in close bilateral relationships, the efficiencies of the market system are lost.

The culprits in this situation are *transaction-specific investments*. When a canmaker buys steel strip, neither the steel strip producer nor the canmaker needs to invest in equipment or technology that is specific to the needs of the other party. In the case of the steel producer and the steel roller, each company's plant is built to match the other party's plant. Once built, the plants have little value without the existence of the partner's complementary facilities. Once transaction-specific investments are significant then, even though there may be a number of suppliers and buyers in the market, it is no longer a competitive market: each seller is tied to a single buyer, which gives each the opportunity to "*hold up*" the other.

Hence, where a vertical relationship between companies requires one or both companies to make investments that are specific to the needs of the other party, a market contract will be inefficient due to the costs of negotiating and enforcing a contract, plus bargaining, monitoring, and dispute resolution. The basic case for vertical integration is that by bringing both sides of the transaction into a single administrative structure, these transaction costs may be avoided.

Empirical research gives considerable support to these arguments:

- Among automakers, specialized components are more likely to be manufactured in-house than commodity items such as tires and spark plugs.[10] Similarly, in aerospace, company-specific components are more likely to be produced in-house rather than purchased externally.[11]

- In the semiconductor industry, some companies specialize either in semiconductor design or in fabrication, while other companies are vertically integrated across both stages (e.g. Intel, ST Microelectronics). Which is more efficient? Again, it depends on the characteristics of the transaction between the designer and the fabricator. The more technically complex the integrated circuit and, hence, the greater the need for the designer and fabricator to engage in technical collaboration, the better the relative performance of integrated producers.[12]

If companies recognize that transaction-specific investments give rise to opportunism, why don't they write a contract that eliminates the potential for opportunism and misinterpretation by fully specifying prices, quality, and terms of supply? The problem is uncertainty about the future. When the steel producer and the steel sheet roller are agreeing to build their integrated plant, it is impossible to anticipate all the circumstances that might arise over the 30-year life of the plant. Hence contracts are inevitably incomplete.

Administrative Costs of Internalization

Just because there are transaction costs in intermediate markets does not mean that vertical integration is necessarily an efficient solution. Vertical integration avoids the costs of using the market, but internalizing the transactions means that there are now costs of administration. The efficiency of the internal administration of vertical relations depends on several factors.

Differences in Optimal Scale between Different Stages of Production

Suppose that Federal Express requires delivery vans that are designed and manufactured to meet its particular needs. To the extent that the van manufacturer must make transaction-specific investments, there is an incentive for Federal Express to avoid the ensuing transaction costs by building its own vehicles. Would this be an efficient solution? Almost certainly not: the transaction costs avoided by Federal Express are likely to be trivial compared with the inefficiencies incurred in manufacturing its own vans. Federal Express purchases over 40,000 trucks and vans each year, well below the 200,000 minimum efficient scale of an assembly plant. (Ford produced two million commercial vehicles in 2005.)

The same logic explains why specialist brewers such as Anchor Brewing of San Francisco or Adnams of Suffolk in the UK are not backward integrated into cans and bottles like Anheuser-Busch or SAB-Miller. Dedicated canmaking plants involve specific investments, creating problems of opportunism that vertical integration can avoid. However, small brewers simply do not possess the scale needed for scale efficiency in can manufacture.

Developing Distinctive Capabilities   A key advantage of a company that is specialized in a few activities is its ability to develop distinctive capabilities in those activities. Even large, technology-based companies such as Xerox, Kodak, and Philips cannot maintain IT capabilities that match those of IT services specialists such as EDS, IBM, and Accenture. The ability of these IT specialists to work with many different customers stimulates learning and innovation. If General Motors' IT department only serves the in-house needs of GM, this does not encourage the rapid development of its IT capabilities.

However, this assumes that capabilities in different vertical activities are independent of one another. Where one capability builds on capabilities in adjacent activities, vertical integration may help develop distinctive capabilities. Thus, IBM's half-century of success in mainframe computers owes much to its technological leadership in semiconductors and software. The efficiency of Wal-Mart's retailing operations depends critically on specialized IT and logistics from its in-house departments.

Managing Strategically Different Businesses   These problems of differences in optimal scale and developing distinctive capabilities may be viewed as part of a wider set of problems – that of managing vertically related businesses that are strategically very different. A major disadvantage to FedEx of owning a truck-manufacturing company is that the management systems and organizational capabilities required for truck manufacturing are very different from those required for express delivery. These considerations may explain the lack of vertical integration between manufacturing and retailing. Integrated design, manufacturing, and retailing companies such as Zara and Gucci are comparatively rare. Most of the world's leading retailers – Wal-Mart, Gap, Carrefour – do not manufacture. Not only do manufacturing and retailing require very different organizational capabilities, they also require different strategic planning systems, different approaches to control and human resource management, and different top management styles and skills.

Strategic dissimilarities between businesses have encouraged a number of companies to vertically de-integrate. Marriott's decision to split into two separate companies, Marriott International and Host Marriott, was influenced by the belief that *owning* hotels is a strategically different business from *operating* hotels. Similarly, Britain's major brewing companies have all de-integrated: Whitbread plc divested its breweries and specialized in pubs, restaurants, and hotels; Scottish & Newcastle sold off most of its pubs and hotels to become a specialist brewer.

The Incentive Problem   Vertical integration changes the incentives between vertically related businesses. Where a market interface exists between a buyer and a seller, profit incentives ensure that the buyer is motivated to secure the best possible deal and the seller is motivated to pursue efficiency and service in order to attract and retain the buyer. Thus, market contracts give rise to what are termed *high-powered incentives*. Under vertical integration there is an internal supplier–customer relationship that is governed by corporate management systems rather than market incentives. Performance incentives exist, but these are *low-powered incentives* – if Shell's tanker fleet is inefficient and unreliable, then employees will lose their bonuses and the head of shipping may be fired. However, these consequences tend to be slow and undramatic.

One approach to creating stronger performance incentives within vertically integrated companies is to open internal divisions to external competition. As we shall examine more fully in Chapter 16, many large corporations have created *shared service organizations* where internal suppliers of corporate services such as IT, training, and engineering compete with external suppliers of the same services to serve internal operating divisions.

Competitive Effects of Vertical Integration Monopolistic companies have used vertical integration as a means of extending their monopoly positions from one stage of the industry to another. The classic cases are Standard Oil, which used its power in transportation and refining to foreclose markets to independent oil producers; and Alcoa, which used its monopoly position in aluminum production to squeeze independent fabricators of aluminum products to advantage its own fabrication subsidiaries. Such cases are rare. As economists have shown, once a company monopolizes one vertical chain of an industry, there is no further monopoly profit to be extracted by extending that monopoly position to adjacent vertical stages of the industry. A greater concern is that vertical integration may make independent suppliers and customers less willing to do business with the vertically integrated company, because it is now perceived as a competitor rather than as a supplier or customer. After Disney's acquisition of ABC, other studios (e.g. Dreamworks) became less interested in collaborating with ABC in developing new TV programming.

Flexibility Both vertical integration and market transactions can claim advantage with regard to different types of flexibility. Where the required flexibility is rapid responsiveness to uncertain demand, there may be advantages in market transactions. The lack of vertical integration in the construction industry reflects, in part, the need for flexibility in adjusting both to cyclical patterns of demand and to the different requirements of each project. Vertical integration may also be disadvantageous in responding quickly to new product development opportunities that require new combinations of technical capabilities. Some of the most successful new electronic products of recent years – Apple's iPod, Microsoft's XBox, Dell's range of notebook computers – have been produced by contract manufacturers. Extensive outsourcing has been a key feature of fast-cycle product development throughout the electronics sector.

Yet, where system-wide flexibility is required, vertical integration may allow for speed and coordination in achieving simultaneous adjustment throughout the vertical chain. American Apparel is probably the fastest growing clothing *manufacturer* in the US with an internationally known brand – especially for T-shirts. Its tightly coordinated vertical integration from its Los Angeles design and manufacturing base to its 160 retail stores allows a super-fast design-to-distribution cycle. Vertical integration is also a central theme of brand identity. Figure 13.4 shows one of its advertisements.

Zara is another fashion clothing business that has cut cycle times and maximized market responsiveness through a vertically integrated strategy that challenges the industry's dominant model of contract manufacture (see Strategy Capsule 13.2).

Compounding Risk To the extent that vertical integration ties a company to its internal suppliers, vertical integration represents a compounding of risk insofar as problems at any one stage of production threaten production and profitability at all

FIGURE 13.4 An American Apparel advertisement

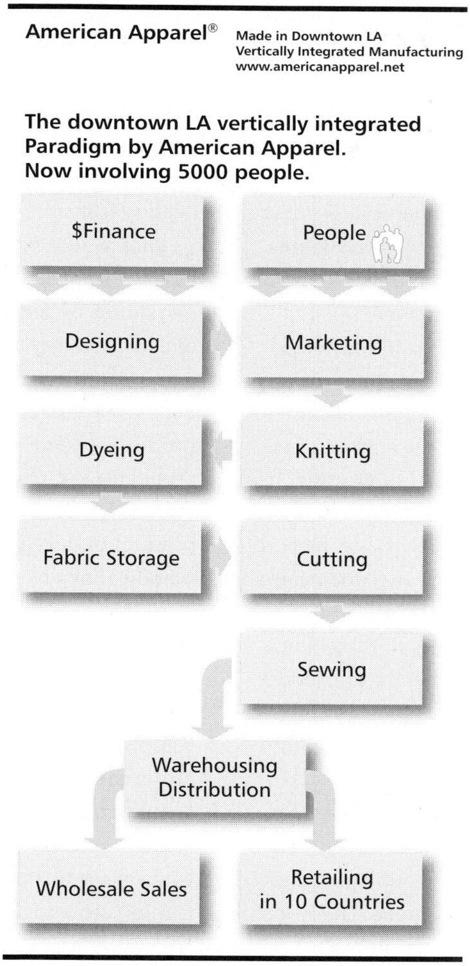
American Apparel®
Made in Downtown LA
Vertically Integrated Manufacturing
www.americanapparel.net
The downtown LA vertically integrated
Paradigm by American Apparel.
Now involving 5000 people.
$Finance
People
Designing
Marketing
Dyeing
Knitting
Fabric Storage
Cutting
Sewing
Warehousing
Distribution
Wholesale Sales
Retailing
in 10 Countries

© 2005 American Apparel Inc.

SOURCE: WWW.AMERICANAPPAREL.NET/PRESSCENTER/ADS/2005 VERTICAL.HTML

STRATEGY CAPSULE 13.2

Making Vertical Integration Work: Zara

Zara is the main division and brand of the Spanish clothing company, Inditex (Industria de Diseño Textil, S.A). Zara contributes 68% of Inditex's sales. Between 2000 and 2006, Inditex achieved sales growth of 30% a year, a net margin of 11%, and a return on average equity of 29% – well ahead of Gap, H&M, or Mango. By the end of 2006, Zara operated over 1,400 stores in 40 countries.

Zara's success is based on a business system that achieves a speed of response to market demand that is without precedent in the fast-moving fashion clothing sector. Zara's cycles of design, production, and distribution are substantially faster than any of its main competitors. For most fashion retailers there is a six-month lag between completing a new design and deliveries arriving at retail stores. Zara can take a new design from drawing board to retail store in as little as three weeks.

Products are designed at the Inditex headquarters in La Coruna on the northwest tip of Spain. Over 40,000 garments are designed annually with about one-quarter entering production. Designs are sketched, committed to the CAD system, then a sample is handmade by skilled workers located within the design facility. Working alongside the designers are "market specialists" who monitor sales and market trends in a particular country or region, and "buyers" who handle procurement and production planning. The three groups coordinate closely and jointly select which products go into production.

Close to half of Zara's products are manufactured within Zara's local network, which comprises Zara's own factories and subcontractors who undertake all sewing operations. The rest is outsourced to third-party manufacturers.

For its own production, 40% of fabric requirements are supplied by Comidex – a wholly owned subsidiary of Inditex. Most fabric is supplied undyed. Postponing dying until later in the production process allows colors to be changed at short notice.

Finished products are ironed, labeled (including tags with prices in local currencies), bagged in boxes or on hangers ready for retail display, then transferred by monorail to the La Coruna distribution center. Each retail store submits its orders twice a week and receives shipments twice a week. Orders are dispatched within eight hours of receipt and are delivered within 24 hours in Europe, 48 hours in the US, and 72 hours in Japan.

Zara owns and manages almost all its retail stores. This allows standardized layout and window displays and close communication and collaboration between store managers and headquarters.

Zara's tightly coordinated system allows quick response to market demand. At the beginning of each season only small numbers of each new item are produced and are placed in a few lead stores. According to market response, Zara then adjusts production. Typically, Zara's products spend no more than two weeks in a retail store. Product market specialists provide critical feedback that is used both to adjust production levels and to make design or color modifications to existing items.

The close, informal information networks within Zara are critical to product design. Although designers begin working on new designs some nine months before each new season, continuous adjustments to designs are made in response to new information on fashion trends and customer preferences. Designers and market specialists are encouraged to be alert to the new ranges released by the fashion houses of Milan, Paris, London, and New York; to the styles worn by trendsetters on TV, in popular music, and in the leading-edge clubs; and to feedback from store managers and other employees.

Zara's compressed product cycles have induced changes in customers' retail buying behavior. Zara customers make more frequent visits to their local stores than is typical for other fashion retailers. They also make faster purchase decisions in the knowledge that garments move quickly and are unlikely to be restocked.

Sources: Kasra Ferdows, Jose Machuca, and Michael Lewis, *Zara*, EECH Case Number 602-002-01, 2002; www.inditex.com

other stages. When union workers at a General Motors brake plant went on strike in 1998, GM's 24 US assembly plants were quickly brought to a halt. When technology or customer preferences are changing quickly it is especially likely that poor decisions at one stage have knock-on effects throughout the firm.

Assessing the Pros and Cons of Vertical Integration

Is vertical integration a beneficial strategy for a firm to pursue? As with most questions of strategy – it all depends. We have observed that there are costs and benefits associated with both vertical integration and with market contracts between firms. The value of our analysis is that we are in a position to determine the factors that will determine the relative advantages of the two approaches to managing vertical relationships. Table 13.1 summarizes some of the key criteria. Yet, even within the same industry, different companies can be successful with very different degrees of vertical integration. Thus in low-end fashion clothing, Zara is much more vertically integrated than either Hennes & Mauritz or Gap, while in designer clothing, Armani is more vertically integrated than Donna Karan. The key issue here is that, even when external circumstances are the same, the fact that different companies have different resources and capabilities and pursue different strategies means that they will make different decisions with regard to vertical integration.

Designing Vertical Relationships

Our discussion so far has compared vertical integration with arm's-length relationships between buyers and sellers. In practice, there are a variety of relationships through which buyers and sellers can interact and coordinate their interests. Figure 13.5 shows a number of different types of relationship between buyers and sellers. These relationships may be classified in relation to two characteristics. First, the extent to which the buyer and seller commit resources to the relationship: the arm's-length nature of

FIGURE 13.5 Different types of vertical relationship

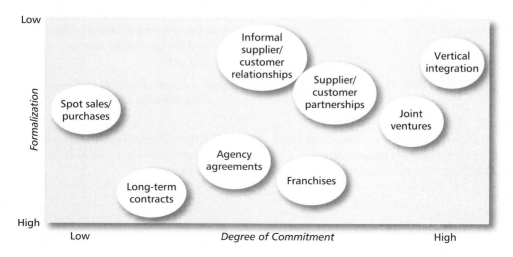

TABLE 13.1 Vertical integration (VI) versus outsourcing: some key considerations

Characteristics of the vertical relationship	Implication
How many firms are there in the vertically adjacent activity?	The fewer the number of firms, the greater are the transaction costs and bigger the advantages of VI
Do transaction-specific investments need to be made by either party?	Transaction-specific investments increase the advantages of VI
How evenly distributed is information between the vertical stages?	The greater are information asymmetries, the more likely is opportunistic behavior and the greater the advantages of VI
Are market transactions in intermediate products subject to taxes or regulations?	Taxes and regulations are a cost of market contracts that can be avoided by VI
How uncertain are the circumstances of the transactions over the period of the relationship?	The greater are uncertainties concerning costs, technologies, and demand, the greater the difficulty of writing contracts, and the greater the advantages of VI
Are two stages similar in terms of the optimal scale of operation?	The greater the dissimilarity, the greater the advantages of market contracts as compared with VI
Are the two stages strategically similar (e.g., similar key success factors, common resources/capabilities)?	The greater the strategic similarity, the greater the advantages of VI over outsourcing
How great is the need for continual investment in upgrading and extending capabilities within individual activities?	The greater the need to invest in capability development, the greater the advantages of outsourcing over VI
How great is the need for entrepreneurial flexibility and drive in the separate vertical activities?	The greater the need for entrepreneurship and flexibility, the greater the advantages of high-powered incentives provided by market contracts, and the greater the administrative disadvantages of VI
How uncertain is market demand?	The greater the unpredictability of demand, the greater the flexibility advantages of outsourcing.
Does vertical integration compound risk, exposing the entire value chain risks affecting individual stages?	The heavier the investment requirements and the greater the independent risks at each stage, the more risky is VI

spot contracts means that there is no significant commitment; vertical integration involves substantial investment. Second, the formalization of the relationship: long-term contracts and franchises typically involve complex written agreements; spot contracts may involve little or no documentation, but are bound by common law; collaborative agreements between buyers and sellers are by definition informal, while the formality of vertical integration is at the discretion of the firm's management.

Different Types of Vertical Relationship

Different types of vertical relationship offer different combinations of advantages and disadvantages. Consider for example the following:

- *Long-term contracts.* Market transactions can be either *spot contracts* – buying a cargo of crude oil on the Rotterdam petroleum market – or *long-term contracts* that involve a series of transactions over a period of time and specify the terms of sales and the responsibilities of each party. Spot transactions work well under competitive conditions (many buyers and sellers and a standard product) where there is no need for transaction-specific investments by either party. Where closer supplier–customer ties are needed – particularly when one or both parties need to make transaction-specific investments – then a longer term contract can help avoid opportunism and provide the security needed to make the necessary investment. However, long-term contracts introduce their own problems. In particular, they cannot anticipate all the possible circumstances that may arise during the life of the contract and run the risk either of being too restrictive or so loose that they give rise to opportunism and conflicting interpretation. The inflexibility problems of long-term contracts are particularly evident in IT outsourcing when the agreement may be for a period of 10 years or more.[13]

- *Vendor partnerships.* The greater the difficulties of specifying complete contracts for long-term supplier–customer deals, the more likely it is that vertical relationships will be based on trust and mutual understanding. Such relationships can provide the security needed for transaction-specific investments, the flexibility to meet changing circumstances, and the incentives to avoid opportunism. Such arrangements may be entirely *relational contracts* with no written contract at all. The model for vendor partnerships has been the close collaborative relationships that many Japanese companies have with their suppliers. During the late 1980s, Toyota and Nissan directly produced about 20 to 23% of the value of their cars, whereas Ford accounted for 50% of its production value and GM for about 70%. Yet, as Jeff Dyer has shown, the Japanese automakers have been remarkably successful in achieving close collaboration in technology, quality control, design, and scheduling of production and deliveries.[14]

- *Franchising.* A franchise is a contractual agreement between the owner of a trademark and a business system (the franchiser) that permits the franchisee to produce and market the franchiser's product or service in a specified area. Franchising brings together the brand, marketing capabilities, and business systems of the large corporation with the entrepreneurship and local knowledge of small firms. The franchising systems of companies such as McDonald's, Century 21 Real Estate, Hilton Hotels, and Seven-Eleven convenience stores facilitate the close coordination and investment in transaction-specific assets that vertical integration permits with the high-powered incentives, flexibility, and cooperation between strategically dissimilar businesses that market contracts make possible.

Choosing between Alternative Vertical Relationships

Designing vertical relationships is not just a "make or buy" choice. Between full vertical integration and spot market contracts, there is a broad spectrum of alternative organizational forms. Choosing the most suitable vertical relationship depends on the economic characteristics of the activities involved, legal and fiscal circumstances, and the strategies and resources of the firms involved. Even within the same industry, what is best for one company will not make sense for another company whose strategy and capabilities are different. While most food and beverage chains have expanded through franchising, Starbucks, anxious to replicate precisely its unique "Starbucks experience," directly owns and manages its retail outlets. While most banks have been outsourcing IT to companies such as IBM and EDS, US credit card group Capital One sees IT as a key source of competitive advantage: "IT is our central nervous system . . . if we outsourced tomorrow we might save a dollar or two on each account, but we would lose flexibility and value and service levels."[15]

In addition to the factors that we have already considered, the design of vertical relationships needs to take careful account of the following:

1 *Allocation of risk.* Any arrangement beyond a spot contract must cope with uncertainties over the course of the contract. A key feature of any contract is that its terms involve, often implicitly, an allocation of risks between the parties. How risk is shared is dependent partly on bargaining power and partly on efficiency considerations. In franchise agreements, the franchisee (as the weaker partner) bears most of the risk – it is the franchisee's capital that is at risk and the franchisee pays the franchiser a flat royalty based on sales revenues. In oil exploration, outsourcing agreements between the oil majors (such as Chevron, Exxon Mobil, and Eni) and drilling companies (such as Schlumberger and Halliburton) have moved from fixed-price contracts to risk-sharing agreements where the driller often takes an equity stake in the project.

2 *Incentive structures.* For a contract to minimize transaction costs it must provide an appropriate set of incentives to the parties. Thus, unless a contract for the supply of ready-mixed concrete to construction projects specifies the proportions of cement, sand, and gravel, there is an incentive to supply substandard concrete. However, achieving completeness in the specification of contracts also bears a cost. The $400 toilet seats supplied to the US Navy may reflect the costs of meeting specifications that filled many sheets of paper. Very often, the most effective incentive is the promise of future business. Hence, in privatizing public services – such as passenger rail services or local refuse collection – the key incentive for service quality is a fixed-term operating contract with regular performance reviews and the prospect of competition at contract renewal time. Toyota and Marks & Spencer's vendor partnerships depend on the incentive that satisfactory performance will lead to a long-term business relationship.

Recent Trends

The main feature of recent years has been a growing diversity of hybrid vertical relationships that have attempted to reconcile the flexibility and incentives of market transactions with the close collaboration provided by vertical integration. Although collaborative vertical relationships are viewed as a recent phenomenon – associated with Silicon Valley and Japanese supplier networks – closely linked value chains in which small, specialist enterprises collaborate are a long-time feature of craft industries in Europe, India, and elsewhere. These collaborative vertical relationships are evident in the industrial districts of northern Italy – notably in textiles,[16] packaging equipment,[17] and motorcycles.[18] The success of Japanese manufacturing companies with their close collaborative relationships with suppliers – including extensive knowledge sharing[19] – has exerted a powerful influence on American and European companies over the past two decades. There has been a massive shift from arm's-length supplier relationships to long-term collaboration with fewer suppliers. In many instances, competitive tendering and multiple sourcing have been replaced by single-supplier arrangements. Vendor relationships frequently involve supplier certification and quality management programs and technical collaboration.

The pace of outsourcing has been intensified by companies' enthusiasm for exploiting international cost differences. Large companies in North America and Western Europe are increasingly outsourcing manufacturing to China and services (including call centers and IT) to India. We shall return to these international dimensions of outsourcing in Chapter 14.[20]

The mutual dependence that results from close, long-term supplier–buyer relationships creates vulnerability for both parties. While trust may alleviate some of the risks of opportunism, companies can also reinforce their vertical relationships and discourage opportunism through equity stakes and profit sharing arrangements. For example: Commonwealth Bank of Australia took an equity stake in its IT supplier, EDS Australia; pharmaceutical companies often acquire equity stakes in the biotech companies that undertake much of their R&D; and, as already noted, oilfield services companies are increasingly equity partners in upstream projects.

However, in this world of closer vertical relationships, some trends have been in the opposite direction. The internet has radically reduced the transaction costs of markets – particularly in pruning search costs and facilitating electronic payments. The result has been a revival in arm's-length competitive contracting through business-to-business e-commerce hubs such as Covisint (auto parts), Elemica (chemicals), and Rock and Dirt (construction equipment).[21]

While the form of vertical relationships has changed, the trend towards increasing outsourcing has continued. The result is that most companies have specialized in fewer activities within their value chains. Outsourcing has extended from components to a wide range of business services including payroll, IT, training, and customer service and support. Increasingly, outsourcing involves not just individual components and services, but whole chunks of the value chain. In electronics, the design and manufacture of entire products are often outsourced to contract manufacturers such as Hon Hai Precision Industry Co., which makes Apple iPods, Nokia phones, and Sony's PlayStation.

The extent of outsourcing and vertical de-integration has given rise to a new organizational form: the *virtual corporation*, where the primary function of the company is coordinating the activities of a network of suppliers.[22] Such extreme levels of outsourcing reduce the strategic role of the company to that of a systems integrator. The critical issue is whether a company that outsources most functions can retain *architectural capabilities* needed to manage the *component capabilities* of the various partners and contractors. The risk is that the virtual corporation may degenerate into a "hollow corporation," where it loses the capability to evolve and adapt to changing circumstances.[23] If, as Prahalad and Hamel argue, core competences are embodied in "core products" then the more these core products are outsourced, the greater is the potential for the erosion of core competence.[24] Andre Prencipe's research into aero engines points to the complementarity between architectural capabilities and component capabilities. Thus, even when the aero engine manufacturers outsource key components, they typically maintain R&D into those component technologies.[25]

Summary

Deciding which parts of the value chain to engage in presents companies with one of their most difficult strategic decisions. The conventional analysis of vertical integration has looked simply at the efficiency of markets as compared with the efficiency of firms: if the cost of transacting through the market is greater than the cost of administering within the firm, then the company should vertically integrate across the stages. Transaction cost analysis does not, however, provide the complete answer. In the first place, vertical strategies are not simply make-or-buy choices – there is a wide variety of ways in which a company can structure vertical relationships. Secondly, the most critical long-run consideration is the development of organizational capability. If a company is to sustain competitive advantage, it must restrict itself to those activities where it possesses the capabilities that are superior to those of the other companies that perform those activities. If my company's data-processing capabilities are inferior to those of IBM and its logistics capabilities are inferior to those of Federal Express, I should consider outsourcing these activities. The most difficult issues arise where there are linkages between value chain activities. Even though a contract manufacturer may be able to manufacture my remote-controlled lawnmower more efficiently than I can internally, what would be the implications for my new product development capability if I no longer have in-house manufacturing?

Ultimately, vertical integration decisions revolve around two key questions. First, which activities will we undertake internally and which will we outsource? Second, how do we design our vertical arrangements with both external and internal suppliers and buyers? In the case of external relations, these may be conducted through spot contracts, long-term contracts, or some form of strategic alliance. Similar ranges of alternatives face the vertically integrated firm – including the option of arm's-length negotiated contracts. Both types of decision are critically dependent on the firm's competitive strategy and the capabilities it possesses. As we have already noted, the critical issue for the individual business is not to follow conventional wisdom but carefully to evaluate its strategic needs, its resources and capabilities at different stages in the value chain, the characteristics of the transactions involved, and the relative attractiveness of different stages of the value chain.

Self-Study Questions

1   The discussion of "The Shifting Boundary between Firms and Markets" argues that most of the developments in information and communication technology (e.g. telephone and computer) tended to lower the costs of administration within the firm relative to the transaction costs of markets. What about the internet? Has the impact of the internet been the same, or has the internet reduced the cost of market transactions to a greater extent than reducing the costs of internal administration?

2   Figure 13.2 notes that the large US companies account for a smaller percentage of total employment, a development which is attributed to greater specialization as a result of a more turbulent business environment. Explain why external turbulence encourages outsourcing and core business focusing.

3   In Strategy Capsule 13.1, Steve Rosenbush argues that integration between media content and media distribution companies (and, specifically, between Disney and Comcast) is strategically advantageous. John Kay suggests that there is little need for common ownerships between distribution channels and the content they carry. Explain the arguments of each. Who do you agree with?

4   Ford has narrowed its vertical scope by selling Hertz, its car rental subsidiary, and spinning off Visteon, its parts manufacturing subsidiary. Examine the pros and cons of Ford owning (a) a car rental company and (b) an auto parts manufacturer.

5   Zara manufactures close to half of the clothes sold in its retail stores and undertakes all of its own distribution from manufacturing plants to retail outlets. Gap outsources production and distribution. Should Zara outsource its manufacturing and distribution? Should Gap backward integrate into production and distribution?

Notes

1   In practice, determining the boundary between business strategy and corporate strategy is blurred. When Dell Computer expanded from PCs into servers, was this diversification or simply product line extension within the same business? It all depends on where we draw industry boundaries.

2   A. Chandler Jr., *The Visible Hand: The Managerial Revolution in American Business* (Cambridge: MIT Press, 1977).

3   R. H. Coase, "The Nature of the Firm," *Economica* 4 (1937): 386–405.

4   The term *interaction costs* has also been used to describe "the time and money expended whenever people and companies exchange goods, services or ideas." See J. Hagel and M. Singer, "Unbundling the Corporation," *Harvard Business Review* (March–April 1999): 133–44.

5   The invention of double-entry bookkeeping dates back to the 16th century. See L. Zan, "Accounting and Management Discourse in Proindustrial Settings: The Venice Arsenal at the Turn of the 16th Century," *Accounting and Business Research* 32 (2004): 145–75.

6   F. W. Taylor, *The Principles of Scientific Management* (Bulletin of the Taylor Society, 1916).

7   J. K. Galbraith, *The New Industrial State* (Harmondsworth: Penguin, 1969).

8   O. E. Williamson, *Markets and Hierarchies: Analysis and Antitrust Implications* (New York: Free Press, 1975); O. E. Williamson, *The Economic Institutions of Capitalism: Firms, Markets and Relational Contracting* (New York: Free Press, 1985). See also J. T. Macher and B. D. Richman, "Transaction Cost Economics: An Assessment of Empirical Research in the Social

Sciences," Working Paper, McDonough School of Business, Georgetown University (2006).

9   The situation is different in aluminum cans, where aluminum producers such as Alcoa and Pechiney and users such as Coca-Cola and Anheuser-Busch are major producers of beverage cans.

10 K. Monteverde and J. J. Teece, "Supplier Switching Costs and Vertical Integration in the Automobile Industry," *Bell Journal of Economics* 13 (Spring 1982): 206–13.

11 S. Masten, "The Organization of Production: Evidence from the Aerospace Industry," *Journal of Law and Economics* 27 (October 1984): 403–17.

12 J. T. Macher, "Technological Development and the Boundaries of the Firm: A Knowledge-based Examination in Semiconductor Manufacturing," *Management Science* 52 (2006): 826–43; K. Monteverde, "Technical Dialogue as an Incentive for Vertical Integration in the Semiconductor Industry," *Management Science* 41 (1995): 1624–38.

13 R. Johnston and P. R. Lawrence, "Beyond Vertical Integration: The Rise of Value Adding Partnerships," *Harvard Business Review* (July–August 1988): 94–101.

14 J. H. Dyer, "Effective Interfirm Collaboration: How Firms Minimize Transaction Costs and Maximize Transaction Value," *Strategic Management Journal* 18 (1997): 535–56; J. H. Dyer, "Specialized Supplier Networks as a Source of Competitive Advantage: Evidence from the Auto Industry," *Strategic Management Journal* 17 (1996): 271–92.

15 L. Willcocks and C. Sauer, "High Risks and Hidden Costs in IT Outsourcing," *Financial Times*, Mastering Risk (May 23, 2000): 3.

16 N. Owen and A. C. Jones, "A Comparative Study of the British and Italian Textile and Clothing Industries," Department of Trade and Industry (2003).

17 G. Lorenzoni and A. Lipparini, "The Leveraging of Interfirm Relationships as Distinctive Organizational Capabilities: A Longitudinal Study," *Strategic Management Journal* 20 (1999): 317–38.

18 G. Lorenzoni and A. Lipparini, "Organizing Around Strategic Relationships: Networks of Suppliers in the Italian Motorcycle Industry," in K. O. Cool et al. (eds), *Restructuring Strategy* (Oxford: Blackwell, 2005): 44–67.

19 J. H. Dyer and K. Nobeoka, "Creating and Managing a High-performance Knowledge-sharing Network: The Toyota Case," *Strategic Management Journal* 21 (2000): 345–68.

20 D. Farrell, "Smarter Outsourcing," *Harvard Business Review* (June 2006).

21 www.covisint.com; www.elemica.com; www.rockanddirt.com

22 "The Virtual Corporation," *Business Week* (February 8, 1993): 98–104; W. H. Davidow and M. S. Malone, *The Virtual Corporation* (New York: HarperCollins, 1992).

23 H. W. Chesborough and D. J. Teece, "When is Virtual Virtuous? Organizing for Innovation," *Harvard Business Review* (May–June 1996): 68–79.

24 C. K. Prahalad and Gary Hamel, "The Core Competences of the Corporation," *Harvard Business Review* (May–June 1990): 79–91.

25 S. Brusoni, A. Prencipe, and K. Pavitt, "Knowledge Specialization, Organizational Coupling and the Boundaries of the Firm: Why Do Firms Know More Than They Make?" *Administrative Science Quarterly* 46 (2001): 597–621.

14

Global Strategies and the Multinational Corporation

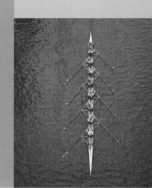

Globalization has changed us into a company that searches the world, not just to sell or to source, but to find intellectual capital – the world's best talent and greatest ideas.

—JACK WELCH, FORMER CHAIRMAN, GENERAL ELECTRIC

OUTLINE

Introduction and Objectives

Internationalization is the most important and pervasive force reshaping the competitive environment of business. It has opened national markets to new competitors and created new business opportunities for both large and small firms. Internationalization occurs through two mechanisms: trade and direct investment. The growth of world trade has consistently outstripped the growth of world output, increasing export/sales and import penetration ratios for all countries and all industries. For the United States, the share of imports in sales of manufactured goods rose from less than 4% in 1960 to over 30% in 2006. Trade in commercial services (transportation, communications, information, financial services, and the like) has grown even faster than merchandise trade. The scale of direct investment into the US is indicated by the fact that by 2006, the total stock of foreign direct investment by all companies was $11.7 trillion, compared with total US GDP of $12.8 trillion.[1]

The forces driving both trade and direct investment are, first, the quest to exploit market opportunities in other countries, and, second, the desire to exploit production opportunities by locating production activities wherever they can be conducted most efficiently. The resulting "globalization of business" has created vast flows of international transactions comprising payment for trade and services, flows of factor payments (interest, profits, and licensing fees), and flows of capital.

The implications for competition and industry structure are far reaching. During the 1960s, local companies dominated most domestic markets. Now the leaders in most industries are multinational players. Indeed overseas expansion is often viewed as a prerequisite for outstanding corporate success. For L'Oreal in cosmetics and toiletries, UBS and HSBC in banking, and McKinsey in consulting, international expansion has provided the foundation for profitability and growth. At the same time the risks too are great: for Saatchi & Saatchi in advertising, Daewoo in automobiles, and Marks & Spencer in retailing, overambitious internationalization marked the beginning of corporate decline.

For countries too, harnessing the forces of internationalization has been a prime determinant of relative economic performance. Within the European Union, Ireland's ability to take advantage of international trade and inward direct investment has resulted in real GDP per head increasing at an average annual rate of 7.6% during 1996–2006; Italy's increased a mere 1.3%.

This chapter examines the implications of the internationalization of the business environment for the formulation and implementation of company strategy. We will recognize that internationalization expands the market arena, bringing into competition firms with very different national resource bases, and making it possible for firms to access resources from outside their home country.

By the time you have completed this chapter, you will be able to:

● Use the tools of industry analysis to examine the impact of internationalization on industry structure and competition.

● Analyze the implications of a firm's national environment for its competitive advantage.

● Formulate strategies for exploiting overseas business opportunities, including overseas market entry strategies and overseas production strategies.

● Formulate international strategies that achieve an optimal balance between global integration and national differentiation.

● Design organizational structures and management systems appropriate to the pursuit of international strategies.

We begin by exploring the implications of international competition, first for industry analysis, and then for the analysis of competitive advantage.

Implications of International Competition for Industry Analysis

Patterns of Internationalization

Internationalization occurs through *trade* – the sale and shipment of goods and services from one country to another – and *direct investment* – building or acquiring productive assets in another country. On this basis we can identify different types of industry according to the extent and mode of their internationalization (see Figure 14.1):

● *Sheltered industries* are served exclusively by indigenous firms. They are sheltered from international competition by regulation, public ownership, barriers to trade, or because the goods and services they offer are more suited to small local operators than to large, multiunit corporations. Industries left in this category are primarily fragmented service industries (dry cleaning, hairdressing, auto repair, funeral services), some small-scale manufacturing (handicrafts, homebuilding), and industries producing products that are nontradable because they are perishable (fresh milk, bread) or difficult to move (four-poster beds, garden sheds).

● *Trading industries* are those where internationalization occurs primarily through imports and exports. If a product is transportable, not nationally differentiated, and subject to substantial scale economies, exporting from a single location is the most efficient means to exploit overseas markets, which would apply for example with commercial aircraft, shipbuilding, and defense

FIGURE 14.1 Patterns of industry internationalization

equipment. Trading industries also include products whose inputs are available only in a few locations: diamonds from South Africa, caviar from Iran and Azerbaijan.

- *Multidomestic industries* are those that internationalize through direct investment – either because trade is not feasible (as in the case of service industries such as banking, consulting, or hotels) or because products are nationally differentiated (e.g., frozen dinners, recorded music).

- *Global industries* are those in which both trade and direct investment are important. Most large-scale manufacturing industries tend to evolve towards global structures: in automobiles, consumer electronics, semiconductors, pharmaceuticals, and beer, levels of trade and direct investment are high.

By which route does internationalization typically occur? In the case of services and other nontradable products, there is no choice. The only way that Marriott, Starbucks, and Goldman Sachs can serve overseas markets is by creating subsidiaries (or acquiring companies) within these markets. In the case of manufacturing companies, internationalization typically begins with exports – typically to countries with the least "psychic distance" from the home country. Later a sales and distribution subsidiary is established in the overseas country. Eventually the company develops a more integrated overseas subsidiary that undertakes manufacturing and product development as well.[2]

Implications for Competition

For the most part, internationalization means more competition and lower industry profitability. In 1976, the US automobile market was dominated by GM, Ford, and

Chrysler with 84% of the market. By 2006 there were 11 companies with auto plants within the US; the former "Big Three" accounted for just 46% of auto sales; and the industry was suffering from excess capacity, intense price competition, and massive losses.

The impact of internationalization on competition and industry profitability can be analyzed within the context of Porter's five forces of competition framework. For the purposes of our analysis, let us take our unit of analysis as national markets where the relevant "industry" comprises the firms supplying that national market.

Competition from Potential Entrants

Barriers to entry into most national markets have fallen substantially. Tariff reductions, falling real costs of transportation, the removal of exchange controls, internationalization of standards, and convergence between customer preferences have made it much easier for producers in one country to supply customers in another. Many of the entry barriers that were effective against potential domestic entrants may be ineffective against potential entrants that are established producers in overseas countries.

Rivalry Among Existing Firms

Internationalization increases internal rivalry within industries in three ways:

- *Lowering Seller Concentration.* International trade typically means that more suppliers are competing for each national market. I have already noted how the dominance of the US automobile industry by domestic producers has been destroyed by international competition. By 2006, there were nine manufacturers with market shares greater than 2%. In other countries and in other industries, the impact of internationalization has been similar. The European motor scooter industry was once dominated by the Italian firms Piaggio (Vespa scooters) and Lambretta. There are now ever 20 manufacturers supplying the European market. In addition to the Italians (Piaggio, Aprilia, Benelli), there are Japanese firms (Honda, Yamaha, Suzuki), Americans (Baron), Taiwanese (Kymco), Chinese (BenZhou/Yiying, Baotian, Kaitong/Yiben), and many more. Even in industries where global consolidation has been rapid (e.g. paper, telecoms, oil, airlines, and aluminum), Ghemawat and Ghadar show that global concentration has declined as a result of national producers entering the global market.[3]

- *Increasing Diversity of Competitors.* The increasing international diversity of competitors implies differences in goals, strategies, and cost structures – all of which cause them to compete more vigorously while making cooperation more difficult.

- *Increasing Excess Capacity.* When internationalization occurs through direct investment, the result is likely to be increased capacity. To the extent that direct investment occurs through investment in new plants, industry capacity increases with no corresponding increase in market size. The automobile industry is a classic example of this – the investment by Japanese and Korean manufacturers in the US and Europe, and by US manufacturers in Latin America and Asia, added substantially to global excess capacity during the 1990s.

Increasing the Bargaining Power of Buyers A further implication of the internationalization of business is that large customers can exercise their buying power far more effectively. Global sourcing provides a key tool for cost reduction by manufacturers. The growth of internet-based markets for components and materials enhances the power of industrial buyers.

Analyzing Competitive Advantage in an International Context

The growth of international competition has been associated with some stunning reversals in the competitive positions of different companies. In 1986, US Steel was the world's biggest steel company; 20 years later, India-based Mittal Steel was global leader. In 1986, IBM and Apple were world market leaders in PCs. By 2006, IBM had exited the industry and Dell, HP, Lenovo, and Acer were the new leaders. In 1986, the world's biggest banks (by assets) were Deutsche Bank and Bank of Tokyo. By 2006, UBS and HSBC led the pack.

To understand how internationalization has shifted the basis of competition, we need to extend our framework for analyzing competitive advantage to include the influence of firms' national environments. Competitive advantage, we have noted, is achieved when a firm matches its internal strengths in resources and capabilities to the key success factors of the industry. International industries differ from domestic industries in their sources of competitive advantage. When firms are located in different countries, their potential for achieving competitive advantage depends not only on their internal stocks of resources and capabilities, but also on the conditions of their national environments – in particular, the resource availability within the countries where they do business. Figure 14.2 summarizes the implications of

FIGURE 14.2 Competitive advantage in an international context

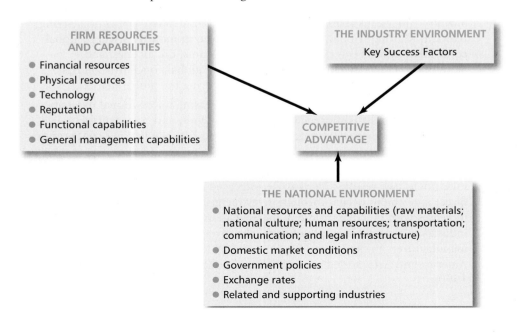

internationalization for our basic strategy model in terms of the impact both on industry conditions and firms' access to resources and capabilities.

National Influences on Competitiveness: Comparative Advantage

The role of national resource availability on international competitiveness is the subject of the *theory of comparative advantage*. The theory states that a country has a comparative advantage in those products that make intensive use of those resources available in abundance within that country. Thus, Bangladesh has an abundant supply of unskilled labor. The United States has an abundant supply of technological resources: trained scientists and engineers, research facilities, and universities. Bangladesh has a comparative advantage in products that make intensive use of unskilled labor, such as clothing, handicrafts, leather goods, and assembly of consumer electronic products. The United States has a comparative advantage in technology-intensive products, such as microprocessors, computer software, pharmaceuticals, medical diagnostic equipment, and management consulting services.

The term comparative advantage refers to the *relative* efficiencies of producing different products. So long as exchange rates are well behaved (they do not deviate far from their purchasing power parity levels), then comparative advantage translates into competitive advantage. Hence, comparative advantages are revealed in trade performance. Table 14.1 shows revealed comparative advantages for several product groups and several countries. Positive values show comparative advantage; negative values show comparative disadvantage.

Trade theory initially emphasized the role of natural resource endowments, labor supply, and capital stock in determining comparative advantage. More recently emphasis has shifted to the central role of knowledge (including technology, human skills, and management capability) and the resources needed to commercialize knowledge (capital markets, communications facilities, and a legal system).[4] The remarkable economic development of the "tiger economies" of South Korea, Taiwan, Hong Kong, Malaysia, and Singapore demonstrates how disadvantages in endowments of natural resources are far outweighed by the development of these home-grown resources.[5]

TABLE 14.1 Indexes of revealed comparative advantage for certain broad product categories

	USA	Canada	Germany	Italy	Japan
Food, drink, and tobacco	0.31	0.28	−0.36	−0.29	−0.85
Raw materials	0.43	0.51	−0.55	−0.30	−0.88
Oil and refined products	−0.64	0.34	−0.72	−0.74	−0.99
Chemicals	0.42	−0.16	0.20	−0.06	−0.58
Machinery and transportation equipment	0.12	−0.19	0.34	0.22	0.80
Other manufacturing	−0.68	−0.07	0.01	0.29	0.40

Note: Revealed comparative advantage for each product group is measured as: (Exports less Imports)/Domestic Production.

SOURCE: OECD.

FIGURE 14.3 Porter's national diamond framework

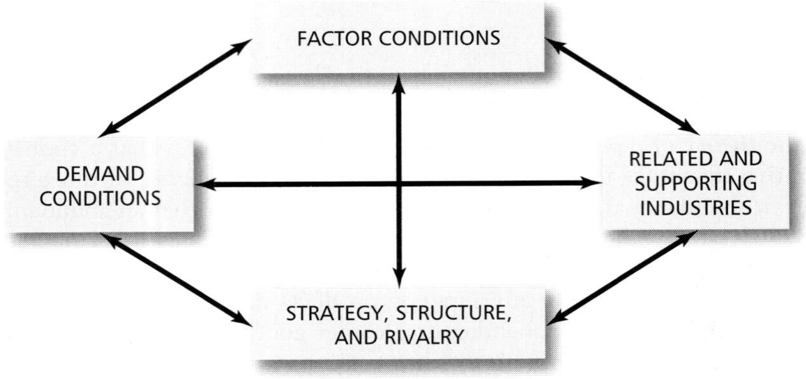

A large home market facilitates the development and exploitation of capital, technology, and infrastructure. Hence, in most capital- and technology-intensive industries, large countries (such as the US) are at an advantage over small countries.[6] A similar logic motivates the creation of free trade areas such as the European Union, Mercosur, and NAFTA.

Porter's National Diamond

Michael Porter has extended our understanding of comparative advantage by examining the dynamics through which specific industries in particular countries develop the resources and capabilities that confer international competitive advantage.[7] Porter's analysis is summarized in his national diamond framework (see Figure 14.3).[8]

Factor Conditions Whereas the conventional advantage of comparative analysis focuses on endowments of broad categories of resource, Porter's analysis emphasizes, first, "home-grown" resources and, second, the role of highly specialized resources. For example, in analyzing Hollywood's preeminence in film production, Porter points to the local concentration of skilled labor, including the roles of UCLA and USC schools of film. Also, resource constraints may encourage the development of substitute capabilities: in post-war Japan, raw material shortages spurred miniaturization and low-defect manufacturing; in Italy, restrictive labor laws have stimulated automation.

Related and Supporting Industries For many industries, a critical resource is the presence of related and supporting industries. One of the most striking of Porter's empirical findings is that national competitive strengths tend to be associated with "clusters" of industries. One such cluster is US strength in semiconductors, computers, and computer software. For each of these industries, critical resources are the other related industries. In Germany, a mutually supporting cluster exists around chemicals, synthetic dyes, textiles, and textile machinery.

Demand Conditions Demand conditions in the domestic market provide the primary driver of innovation and quality improvement. For example:

- The preeminence of Swiss watches may be attributed to the obsessive punctuality of the Swiss.

- The dominance of the world market for cameras by Japanese companies owes much to Japanese consumers' enthusiasm for amateur photography and their eager adoption of innovation in cameras.

- German companies' (Mercedes, BMW, Porsche) dominance of the high-performance segment of the world automobile industry, as compared with their much weaker position in mass-produced autos, may be linked to German motorists' love of quality engineering and their irrepressible urge to drive on autobahns at terrifying speeds.

Strategy, Structure, and Rivalry National competitive performance in particular sectors is inevitably related to the strategies and structures of firms in those industries. Porter puts particular emphasis on the role of intense domestic competition in driving innovation, efficiency, and the upgrading of competitive advantage. The success of the Japanese auto industry may reflect the presence of nine companies, all of which compete fiercely within the domestic market. The same can be said for cameras, consumer electronic products, and office machinery. Conversely, the weak position of European companies in many hi-tech industries may be a result of European governments' propensity to kill domestic competition by creating "national champions."

Consistency between Strategy and National Conditions

Establishing competitive advantage in global industries requires congruence between business strategy and the pattern of the country's comparative advantage. In audio equipment, it is sensible for Chinese producers, such as Dussun and Skyworth, to concentrate on the low end of the market and to supply western mass retailers under their own brands. For Bose, international competitiveness requires exploiting US strengths in basic research. For Danish consumer electronics maker Bang & Olufsen, international competitiveness requires exploiting European strengths in design and high-end marketing. Japanese producers such as Sony and Matsushita compete most effectively in the broad mid-market exploiting national strengths in consumer electronic technology.

The linkage between the firm's competitive advantage and its national environment also includes the relationship between firms' organizational capabilities and the national culture and social structure. Stimulated by Max Weber's analysis of the impact of religion on enterprise,[9] national culture has been shown to exert a powerful influence on management practices in general and on the capability profiles of firms in particular. The capabilities of Japanese companies in integrating diverse technologies into innovative new products (electronic musical instruments, color copying machines), and in quality enhancement through continuous improvement, owe much to Japanese traditions of assimilating outside ideas and cooperative social behavior. Similarly, the excellence of US firms in financial services and pioneering new industries through entrepreneurship may link with US traditions of individualism and quest for material wealth. We shall return to the implications of national cultures for strategic management later in this chapter.

Applying the Framework: International Location of Production

To examine how national resource conditions influence international strategies, we look at two types of strategic decision in international business: first, the decision of where to locate production activities and, second, the decision of how to enter a foreign market. Let us begin with the first of these.

So far, our discussion of the linkage between the competitive advantage of the firm and its national environment has assumed, implicitly, that each firm is based within its home country. In fact, an important motive for internationalization is to access the resources and capabilities available in other countries. Traditionally, multinational companies either concentrated production in their home country or located manufacturing plants to serve each of the countries where they marketed their products. Increasingly, decisions as to where to produce are being separated over decisions as to where to sell. For example, the biggest markets for Motorola's wireless handsets are the US and EU, yet handset manufacture is primarily in China, Singapore, Malaysia, and Brazil.

Determinants of Geographical Location

The decision of where to manufacture requires consideration of three sets of factors:

- *National resource availability*. Where key resources differ between countries in their availability or cost, then firms should manufacture in countries where resource supplies are favorable. For the oil industry this means exploring in Kazakhstan, offshore Angola, and the Gulf of Mexico. For Nike and Reebok, it means locating shoe assembly where labor costs are low: China, Thailand, India, and the Philippines. (Table 14.2 shows differences in employment costs

TABLE 14.2 Hourly compensation costs in US dollars for production workers in manufacturing

	1975	1985	1995	2000	2005
United States	6.36	13.01	17.19	19.76	23.17
Mexico	1.47	1.59	1.51	2.08	2.50
Australia	5.62	8.20	15.27	14.47	23.09
Japan	3.00	6.34	23.82	22.27	21.90
Korea	0.32	1.23	7.29	8.19	11.52
Taiwan	0.40	1.50	5.94	5.85	5.97
Sri Lanka	0.28	0.28	0.48	0.48	0.54
France	4.52	7.52	20.01	15.70	23.89
Germany (former West)	6.31	9.53	31.58	24.42	34.05
Italy	4.67	7.63	16.22	14.01	20.48
Spain	2.53	4.66	12.88	10.78	17.10
Sweden	7.18	9.66	21.44	20.14	28.42
Switzerland	6.09	9.66	29.30	21.24	30.26
United Kingdom	3.37	6.27	13.67	16.45	24.71

SOURCE: US DEPARTMENT OF LABOR, BUREAU OF LABOR STATISTICS.

between countries.) For semiconductor and computer companies, it means establishing R&D facilities in California's Silicon Valley where there is the world's greatest concentration of microelectronics expertise.[10]

● *Firm-specific competitive advantages.* For firms whose competitive advantage is based on internal resources and capabilities, optimal location depends on where those resources and capabilities are situated and how mobile they are. Wal-Mart has experienced difficulty recreating its capabilities outside of the US. Conversely, Toyota and Goldman Sachs have successfully transferred their operational capabilities to their overseas subsidiaries.

● *Tradability.* The ability to locate production away from markets depends on the transportability of the product. Production within the local market is favored when transportation costs are high, local customers have differentiated preferences, and governments create barriers to trade. Services – hairdressing, medicine, and banking – need to be produced in close proximity to the customer. However, even with some services, communications technology permits remote production.

Location and the Value Chain

The production of most goods and services comprises a vertical chain of activities where the input requirements of each stage vary considerably. Hence, different countries offer differential advantage at different stages of the value chain. Table 14.3 shows the pattern of international specialization within textiles and apparel. Similarly with consumer electronics: component production is research and capital intensive and is concentrated in the US, Japan, Korea, and Taiwan; assembly is labor intensive and is concentrated in China, Thailand, and Latin America.

In principle, a firm can identify the resources required by each stage of the value chain, then determine which country offers these resources at the lowest cost.[11] For example, Nike locates R&D and design in the US; the production of fabric, rubber, and plastic shoe components in Korea, Taiwan, and China; and assembly in India, China, the Philippines, and Indonesia.[12]

However, when companies are making decisions to shift certain activities outside their home country – a process referred to as *"offshoring"* – it is important to look beyond comparisons of current costs and consider the underlying resources and capabilities available in different locations. Cost advantages are vulnerable to exchange

TABLE 14.3 Comparative advantage in textiles and clothing by vertical stage

	Fiber production	Spun yarn	Textiles	Apparel
Hong Kong	−0.96	−0.81	−0.41	+0.75
Italy	−0.54	+0.18	+0.14	+0.72
Japan	−0.36	+0.48	+0.78	−0.48
USA	+0.96	+0.64	+0.22	−0.73

Notes:

1   Fiber production includes both natural and synthetic fibers.

2   Revealed comparative advantage is measured as (Exports − Imports) / (Exports + Imports).

SOURCE: UNITED NATIONS.

rate changes and wage inflation. Moreover, noncost aspects of operational performance may ultimately be more important:

> [W]estern companies are finding that offshoring locations such as China and India
> offer access to world-class skills. For example, Jim Breyer, managing partner of
> Accel Partners, a Silicon Valley venture capitalist, observed: "Taiwan and China
> have some of the world's best designers of wireless chips and wireless software."
> In certain types of precision manufacturing, including the processes that produce
> magnesium alloy casing for notebook computers, companies such as Waffer in
> Taiwan offer some of the most sophisticated technology in the world.
>
> Most of the leading Indian IT outsourcing companies operate at level 5 –
> the highest level of expertise – of the Capability Maturity Model (CMM), an
> international measure of technical skill, while most internal IT departments in
> western companies operate at level 2 or 3. Call centres, such as those operated by
> eTelecare – a Manila-based outsourcing provider – offer better average handling
> times and customer satisfaction relative to leading companies in the US.[13]

In the highly fragmented value chains of most electronic products, technology,
know-how, and speed are as important as cost in determining where different activities are located (see Table 14.4).

TABLE 14.4 Global production: the Hewlett Packard Pavilion 8000 laptop
computer

Component/Process	Provider and Location
Design	HP, California; also, HP design studios in Taiwan and China collaborate with third-party manufacturers
Assembly	Contracted to Quanta (Taiwan); assembled in China by Quanta and by third-party contractors
Microprocessor	Designed by Intel in California; manufactured at Intel plants in Oregon, New Mexico, and Israel
Graphics card	Designed by ATI Technologies in Canada; manufactured in Taiwan
Screen	Manufactured by LG Philips LCD Co. (a joint venture between LG of Korea and Philips of the Netherlands). Manufactured in South Korea
Hard disk drive	By Seagate. Designed in California; manufactured in Malaysia
Lithium ion battery	Manufactured by Sony in Japan
Logistics	Contracted to 40 third-party providers (some global, such as Federal Express, DHL, and TNT; others local)
Telephone sales and customer support	Contracted to third-party providers in Canada, UK, Ireland, and India

SOURCES: WWW.HP.COM; "THE LAPTOP TRAIL" WALL STREET JOURNAL (JUNE 9, 2005).

FIGURE 14.4 Determining the optimal location of value chain activities

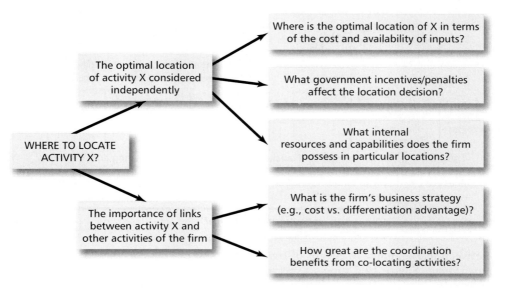

The benefits from fragmenting the value chain must be traded off against the added costs of coordinating globally dispersed activities. Transportation costs are one consideration. Another is increased inventory cost. Increased time can be the most costly consequence of dispersed activities. Just-in-time scheduling often necessitates that production activities are carried out in close proximity to one another. Although the labor cost of building an automobile in Mexico is only 20% of the labor cost in the US, this cost advantage of Mexican production is almost entirely offset by higher costs of components. The tradeoff between cost and time depends on the strategy of the company. Companies that compete on speed and reliability of delivery (e.g. Zara and Dell Computer) typically forsake the cost advantages of a globally dispersed value chain in favor of integrated operations with fast access to the final market.

Figure 14.4 summarizes the relevant criteria in location decisions.

Applying the Framework: Foreign Entry Strategies

Many of the considerations relevant to locating production activities also apply to choosing the mode of foreign market entry. A firm enters an overseas market because it believes that it will be profitable. This assumes not only that the overseas market is attractive – that its structure is conducive to profitability – but also that the firm can establish a competitive advantage vis-à-vis local producers and other multinational corporations (MNCs). We discussed the analysis of industry and market profitability in Chapters 3 and 4. Our focus here is on how the firm can best establish competitive advantage in a foreign market.

In exploiting an overseas market opportunity, a firm has a range of options with regard to mode of entry. These correspond closely to the firm's strategic alternatives with regard to exploiting innovation (see Chapter 11). The basic distinction is

FIGURE 14.5 Alternative modes of overseas market entry

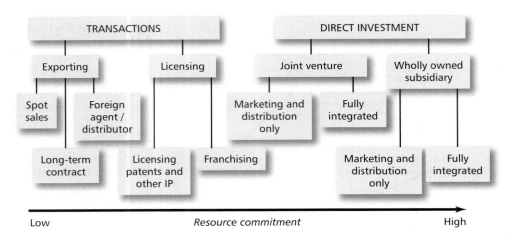

between market entry by means of *transactions* and market entry by means of *direct investment*. Figure 14.5 shows a spectrum of market entry options arranged according to the degree of commitment by the firm. Thus, at one extreme there is exporting through individual spot-market transactions; at the other, there is the establishment of a fully owned subsidiary that undertakes a full range of functions.

How does a firm weigh the merits of different market entry modes? Five key issues are relevant.

1. Is the firm's competitive advantage based on firm-specific or country-specific resources? If the firm's competitive advantage is country based, the firm must exploit an overseas market by exporting. Thus, to the extent that Hyundai's competitive advantage in the US car market is its low domestic cost base, it must produce in Korea and export to the United States. If Toyota's competitive advantage is company specific, then assuming that advantage is transferable within the company, Toyota can exploit the US market either by exports or by direct investment in US production facilities.[14]

2. Is the product tradable and what are the barriers to trade? If the product is not tradable because of transportation constraints or import restrictions, then accessing that market requires entry either by investing in overseas production facilities or by licensing the use of key resources to local companies within the overseas market.

3. Does the firm possess the full range of resources and capabilities for establishing a competitive advantage in the overseas market? Competing in an overseas market is likely to require that the firm acquires additional resources and capabilities, particularly those related to marketing and distributing in an unfamiliar market. Accessing such country-specific resources is most easily achieved by establishing a relationship with firms in the overseas market. The form of relationship depends, in part, on the resources and capabilities required. If a firm needs marketing and distribution, it might appoint a distributor or agent with exclusive territorial rights. If a wide range of manufacturing and marketing capabilities is needed, the firm might license its product and/or its technology to a local manufacturer. In technology-based industries, licensing technology to local companies is common. In marketing-intensive industries, firms with strong brands can license their trademarks to local companies. Alternatively, a joint venture might be sought with a local manufacturing company. US companies entered the Japanese market by joint ventures with local companies (e.g., Fuji–Xerox, Caterpillar–Mitsubishi). These combined the technology and brand names of the US partner with the market knowledge and manufacturing and distribution facilities of the Japanese firm.

4. Can the firm directly appropriate the returns to its resources?
Whether a firm licenses the use of its resources or chooses to exploit them directly (either through exporting or direct investment) depends partly on appropriability considerations. In chemicals and pharmaceuticals, the patents protecting product innovations tend to offer strong legal protection, in which case patent licenses to local producers can be an effective means of appropriating their returns. In computer software and computer equipment, the protection offered by patents and copyrights is looser, which encourages exporting rather than licensing as a means of exploiting overseas markets.

With all licensing arrangements, key considerations are the capabilities and reliability of the local licensee. This is particularly important in licensing brand names, where the licenser must carefully protect the brand's reputation. Thus, Cadbury-Schweppes licenses to Hershey the trademarks and product recipes for its Cadbury's range of chocolate bars for sale in the United States. This arrangement reflects the fact that Hershey has production and distribution facilities in the US that Cadbury cannot match, and that Cadbury views Hershey as a reliable business partner.

5. What transaction costs are involved?
A key issue that arises in the licensing of a firm's trademarks or technology concerns the transaction costs of negotiating, monitoring, and enforcing the terms of such agreements as compared with internationalization through a fully owned subsidiary. In expanding overseas, Starbucks owns and operates its coffee houses while McDonald's franchises its burger restaurants. McDonald's competitive advantage depends primarily upon the franchisee faithfully replicating the McDonald's system. This can be enforced effectively by means of franchise contracts. Starbucks believes that its success is achieved through creating the "Starbucks experience" which is as much about ambiance as it is about coffee. It is difficult to articulate the ingredients of this experience, let alone write it into a contract.

Issues of transaction costs are fundamental to the choices between alternative market entry modes. Barriers to exporting in the form of transport costs and tariffs are forms of transaction costs; other costs include exchange rate risk and information costs. Transaction cost analysis has been central to theories of the existence of multinational corporations. In the absence of transaction costs in the markets either for goods or for resources, companies exploit overseas markets either by exporting their goods and services or by selling the use of their resources to local firms in the overseas markets.[15] Thus, multinationals tend to predominate in industries where:

- firm-specific intangible resources such as brands and technology are important (transaction costs in licensing the use of these resources favor direct investment);

- exporting is subject to transaction costs (e.g., through tariffs or import restrictions);
- customer preferences are reasonably similar between countries.

International Alliances and Joint Ventures

During the past decade and a half, one of the most striking features of the development of international business has been the upsurge in the numbers of joint ventures and other forms of strategic alliance across national borders. For the Russian gas giant, Gazprom, alliances are the principal vehicle for Gazprom establishing a global presence. Gazprom is involved in pipeline alliances with Eni (Italy), CNPC (China), EON (Germany), PDVSA (Venezuela), and MOL (Hungary). It collaborates with Petrocanada and Sonotrach (Algeria) on liquefied natural gas. General Motors is another company that has used alliances to access markets, share technology, and exploit economies of size. Figure 14.6 shows GM's network of alliances with other automakers.

The traditional reason for cross-border alliances and joint ventures was the desire by multinational companies to access the market knowledge and distribution capabilities of a local company, together with the desire by local companies to access the technology, brands, and product development of the multinationals. Western banks entering China's booming credit card market have usually formed marketing alliances with local banks, often reinforced with an equity stake.[16] Host governments in China, India, and other emerging market countries often oblige foreign companies to take a local partner. In technology-based industries – computers, semiconductors, telecom

FIGURE 14.6 General Motors' alliances with competitors

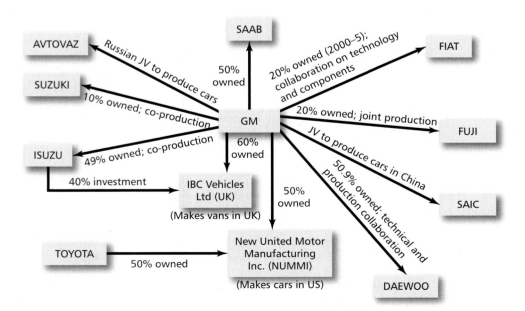

equipment, pharmaceuticals, and aerospace – the rapid growth of international collaboration reflects companies' desire to access other companies' different technological capabilities and to speed the global rollout of new products. In the energy sector, and other capital-intensive industries, joint ventures are important for sharing risks.

The success of cross-border joint ventures and other forms of international strategic alliance has been mixed. The Sony–Ericsson mobile phone joint venture, the Renault–Nissan alliance, and HP and Canon's collaboration in printers have been successes. BT and AT&T's Concert alliance, the GM–Fiat alliance, and Swissair's alliance network were all disasters. Joint ventures that share management responsibility are far more likely to fail than those with a dominant parent or with independent management.[17] The greatest problems arise between firms that are also competitors: reconciling cooperation with competition is a challenge for executives who lack the strategic insight or tolerance for ambiguity possessed by masters of diplomacy such as Bismarck or Metternich.

Disagreements over the sharing of the contributions to and returns from an alliance are a frequent source of friction. When each partner seeks to access the other's capabilities, "competition for competence" results.[18] In several of the alliances between Japanese and western firms, the Japanese partner was better at appropriating the benefits of the alliance.[19] However, in long-term partnerships there is the potential for the benefits to flow in both directions. When Xerox Corporation ran into problems during the 1990s, it was saved by technology, product designs, and management techniques from its Japanese joint venture Fuji–Xerox.[20]

The effective strategic management of international alliances, argue Hamel, Doz, and Prahalad, depends on a clear recognition that collaboration is competition in a different form.[21] They argue that how the alliance benefits are shared depends on three key factors:

- *The strategic intent of the partners*. The clearer a firm is about its strategic goals in entering an alliance, the more likely it is to achieve a positive result from the alliance. One of the problems of GM's network of alliances with foreign automakers was the lack of a coherent view of how each alliance fitted with GM's overall strategy.

- *Appropriability of the contribution*. The ability of each partner to capture and appropriate the skills of the other depends on the nature of each firm's skills and resources. Where skills and resources are tangible or explicit, they can easily be acquired. Where they are tacit and people embodied, they are more difficult to acquire. To avoid the unintended transfer of know-how to partners, Hamel et al. argue the need for a "gatekeeper" to monitor and administer contacts with strategic partners.

- *Receptivity of the company*. The more receptive a company is in terms of its ability to identify what it wants from the partner, to obtain the required knowledge or skills, and to assimilate and adapt them, the more it will gain from the partnership. In management terms, this requires the setting of performance goals for what the partnership is to achieve for the company and managing the relationship to ensure that the company is deriving maximum learning from the collaboration.[22] When a firm has a portfolio of alliances, a systematic approach to monitoring and performance evaluation is especially important.[23]

Multinational Strategies: Globalization vs. National Differentiation

So far, we have viewed international expansion, whether by export or by direct investment, as a means by which a company can exploit its competitive advantages not just in its home market but also in foreign markets. However, international scope may itself be a source of competitive advantage over geographically focused competitors. In this section, we explore whether, and under what conditions, firms that operate on an international basis are able to gain a competitive advantage over nationally focused firms. What is the potential for such "global strategies" to create competitive advantage? In what types of industry are they likely to be most effective? And how should they be designed and deployed in order to maximize their potential?

The Benefits of a Global Strategy

A global strategy is one that views the world as a single, if segmented, market. The late Ted Levitt argued that companies that compete on a national basis are highly vulnerable to companies that compete on a global basis.[24] The superiority of global strategies rests on two assumptions:

- *Globalization of customer preferences*. National and regional preferences are disappearing in the face of the homogenizing forces of technology, communication, and travel. "Everywhere everything gets more and more like everything else as the world's preference structure is relentlessly homogenized," observed Levitt. Nor is this trend restricted to technology-based products such as pharmaceuticals and computers; it is just as prevalent in branded consumer goods such as Corona beer, Adidas sportswear, and McDonald's hamburgers.
- *Scale economies*. Firms that produce for the world market can access scale economies in product development, manufacturing, and marketing that offer efficiency advantages that nationally based competitors cannot match. In pharmaceuticals, consumer electronics, and investment banking, few nationally focused firms have survived competition from global players.

Subsequent contributions to the analysis of global strategy point to benefits in addition to scale economies.[25] There are five major benefits from a global strategy:

Cost Benefits: Scale and Replication Levitt concentrated on the scale advantages of global operation. In most global industries, the most important source of scale economy is product development.

However, for most internationalizing firms, the major cost advantage from multinational operation derives from economies in the replication of knowledge-based assets – including organizational capabilities.[26] When a company has created a knowledge-based asset or product – whether a recipe, or a piece of software, or an organizational system – creating the original knowledge was costly but, once created, subsequent replication is typically cheap. Thus, once Disney has built Disneyland, Anaheim and Walt Disney World in Florida, a Disneyland theme park in Paris or Hong Kong can be built at a fraction of the cost. Similarly with McDonald's: its business system was built in the US over several decades. Once created, the incremental cost of replicating the system in another country is comparatively small.

Exploiting National Resources Efficiencies   Global strategy does not necessarily involve production in one location and then distributing globally. Global strategies also involve exploiting the efficiencies from locating different activities in different places. As we have seen, companies internationalize not just in search of market opportunities but also in search of resource opportunities. Traditionally this has meant a quest for raw materials and low-cost labor. Increasingly it means a quest for knowledge. For example, in the semiconductor industry, overseas subsidiaries are set up primarily to access knowledge in the host country rather than to exploit their existing knowledge.[27]

Serving Global Customers   In several industries – investment banking, audit services, advertising – the primary driver of globalization has been the need to service global customers. Thus, the internationalization of auto parts manufacturers has tended to follow the internationalization patterns of the auto assemblers.

Learning Benefits   If competitive advantage involves innovation and the constant deepening and widening of capabilities, then learning plays a central role in developing and sustaining competitive advantage. If learning involves communicating and interacting with one's proximate environment, then multinationals have the advantage of working within multiple national environments. The critical requirement is that the company possesses some form of global infrastructure for communication and knowledge transfer that permits new experiences, new ideas, and new practices to be transferred and integrated. A growing stream of research suggests that the most important advantage of multinationals over domestic companies is their ability to access knowledge in multiple locations, to synthesize that knowledge, and to transfer it efficiently across national borders.[28]

Competing Strategically   A major advantage of the Romans over the Gauls, Goths, and other barbarian tribes, was the Romans' ability to draw upon the military and economic resources of the Roman Empire to fight local wars. Similarly, multinational companies possess a key strategic advantage over their nationally focused competitors: multinationals can fight aggressive competitive battles in individual national markets using their cash flows from other national markets. At its most simple, this *cross-subsidization* of competitive initiatives in one market using profits from other markets involves *predatory pricing* – cutting prices to a level that drives competitors out of business. Such pricing practices are likely to contravene both the World Trade Organization's antidumping rules and national antitrust laws. More usually, cross-subsidization involves using cash flows from other markets to finance aggressive sales and marketing campaigns.[29] Thus, Japanese, Korean, and Taiwanese electronics firms financed their expansion in US markets with profits from their domestic businesses.[30]

Strategic competition between MNCs presents more complex opportunities for attack, retaliation, and containment.[31] The most effective response to competition in one's home market may be to retaliate in the foreign MNC's own home market. Fuji Film's incursion into Kodak's backyard was symbolized by Fuji's sponsorship of the 1984 Olympic Games in Los Angeles. Kodak responded by attacking Fuji in Japan.[32] To effectively exploit such opportunities for national leveraging, some overall global coordination of competitive strategies in individual national markets is required.

In industries that are dominated by MNCs – automobiles, semiconductors, and investment banking – conventional wisdom has been that companies should seek to position themselves in all three of the world's major industrial centers: North America, Europe, and Japan. Thus, in automobiles Daimler-Benz acquired Chrysler in the US and Mitsubishi in Japan. Ford and GM augmented their strong positions in the US and Europe with equity stakes in Japanese companies. McKinsey's Kenichi Ohmae argues the case for *triad power* – that the need to access technology, develop customer preferences, and scale economies requires global players to become true insiders within all of the world's big three: the US, Europe, and Japan.[33]

The Need for National Differentiation

For all the advantages of global strategy, the evidence of the past decade is that national differences in customer preferences continue to exert a powerful influence in most markets: products designed to meet the needs of the "global customer" tend to be unappealing to most consumers. Moreover, costs of national differentiation can be surprisingly low if common basic designs and common major components are used. Most auto firms have abandoned attempts to create global car models in favor of common platforms.[34] Flexible manufacturing systems have reduced the costs of customizing products to meet the preferences of particular customer groups.

Domestic appliances provide an interesting refutation of the globalization hypothesis. In washing machines, national preferences have shown remarkable resilience: French and US washing machines are primarily top loading, elsewhere in Europe they are mainly front loading; the Germans prefer higher spin speeds than the Italians; US machines feature agitators rather than revolving drums; and Japanese machines are small. In domestic appliances, the pioneers of globalization, such as Electrolux and Whirlpool, have been outperformed by some national and regional specialists.[35] Similarly in banking: most of the world's most profitable banks – US Bancorp, Bank of China, National Bank of Kuwait, and Anglo Irish Bank – are national rather than global players.

Apart from customer demand, several other factors encourage national differentiation:

- *Laws and government regulations.* Governments are the most important sources of obstacles to globalization. Legal and regulatory conditions create distinct national markets in financial services, pharmaceuticals and health services, alcoholic beverages, and telecommunications.

- *Distribution channels.* Differences between the distribution systems of different countries are among the biggest barriers to global marketing strategies. Procter & Gamble must adapt its marketing, promotion, and distribution of toiletries and household products to take account of the fact that, in the US, a few chains account for a major share of its US sales; in southern Europe, most sales are through small, independent retailers; while in Japan, P&G must sell through a multitiered hierarchy of distributors.

- *Presence of lead countries.* Countries differ in their levels of sophistication and acceptance of innovation on a product-by-product basis. For consumer electronics, Japan is the lead market; for computer hardware and software and financial services, the US is the lead market; for automobile technology and design, Europe tends to lead; for mobile telecommunications, South Korea has moved into the lead. These differences in market progressiveness encourage a sequential approach to global strategy in which products are introduced first in the lead market, followed by a global rollout. Sequential product launches allow firms to learn from experiences in the lead market and exploit that learning in subsequent country launches.

● *National cultures.* Underlying differences between countries in customer preferences and business methods are typically the result of differences in national cultures. Culture comprises assumptions, values, traditions, and behavioral norms. At its most general, culture may be described as a shared system of meaning within a group or society. Many of the problems of international expansion encountered by companies – from Wal-Mart in Germany and Korea, Disney with EuroDisneyland, and Marks & Spencer in Europe and North America – can be linked to problems of cultural adjustment. The need to adapt to local cultures may influence the mode of internationalization chosen. Franchising is an attractive international expansion strategy for service businesses because it utilizes the knowledge and cultural identity of local partners. In outsourcing production, customer support and administrative functions to Asia, most western companies have relied on contracts with local firms rather than face the cultural challenges of establishing their own overseas units. Strategy Capsule 14.1 examines differences in national cultures.

Reconciling Global Integration with National Differentiation

Choices about internationalization strategy have been viewed as a tradeoff between the benefits of global integration and those of national adaptation (see Figure 14.7).

FIGURE 14.7 Benefits of global integration versus national differentiation

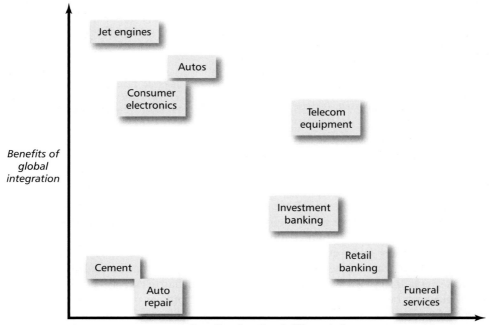

STRATEGY CAPSULE 14.1
How do National Cultures Differ?

Do people differ between countries with regard to beliefs, norms, and value systems? The answer from a series of research studies is "yes."

The best known study of national cultural differences is by Geert Hofstede. The principal dimensions of national values he identified were:

● *Power Distance* – the extent to which inequality, decision-making power in particular, is accepted within organizations and within society. Power distance was high in Malaysia, and most Latin American and Arab countries; low in Austria and Scandinavia.

● *Uncertainty Avoidance*. Preference for certainty and established norms was high in most southern European and Latin American countries; tolerance for uncertainty and ambiguity was high in Singapore, Sweden, UK, US, and India.

● *Individualism*. Concern for individual over group interests was highest in the US, UK, Canada, and Australia. Identification with groups and the collective interest was strongest in Latin America and Asia (especially Indonesia, Pakistan, Taiwan, and South Korea).

● *Masulinity/Femininity*. Hofstede identifies emphasis on work and material goals and demarcation of gender roles as "masculine"; emphasis on personal relationships rather than efficiency and belief in gender equality was viewed as "feminine." Japan, Austria, Venezuela, and Italy scored high on masculinity; Scandinavia and the Netherlands scored very low.

Other studies have used different measures for characterizing national cultures. Fons Trompenaars (another Dutchman) emphasizes "universalism" versus "particularism" in outlook (the US and Australia score highest on universalism); "neutral" versus "affective" relationships (Japan and UK are highest in terms of neutrality; Mexico and the Netherlands the most affective); and achievement orientation (Australia and US very high; Venezuela, Indonesia, and China very low).

Sources: G. Hofstede, *Culture's Consequences: International Differences in Work-related Values* (Thousand Oaks, CA: Sage, 1984); F. Trompenaars, *Riding the Waves of Culture* (London: Economist Books, 1993).

Industries where scale economies are huge and customer preferences homogeneous call for a global strategy (e.g. jet engines). Industries where national preferences are pronounced and where customization is not prohibitively expensive favor a "multi-domestic" strategy (e.g. retail banking). Indeed, if there are no significant benefits from global integration, then we may see these industries supplied almost entirely by locally specialized firms (as in funeral services and hairdressing). However, some industries may be low on most dimensions – cement and car repair services are fairly homogeneous worldwide, but also lack significant scale economies or other major benefits from global presence. Conversely, other industries offer substantial benefits from operating at global scale (telecommunications equipment, military hardware), but national preferences and standards may also necessitate considerable adaptation to the needs of specific national markets.

Reconciling conflicting forces for global efficiency and national differentiation represents one of the greatest strategic challenges facing MNCs. Achieving what Sony's former chairman described as "global localization"[36] involves standardizing product features and company activities where scale economies are substantial and differentiating where national preferences are strongest and where achieving them is not over-costly. Thus, a global car such as the Honda Civic (introduced in 1972 and sold in 110 countries of the world) now embodies considerable local adaptations – not just to meet national safety and environmental standards, but also to meet local preferences for leg room, seat specifications, accessories, color, and trim. McDonald's too makes considerable efforts to mesh global standardization with local adaptation (see Strategy Capsule 14.2).

STRATEGY CAPSULE 14.2
McDonald's Goes "Glocal"

For antiglobalization activists, McDonald's is a demon of globalization: it crushes national cuisines and small, traditional family businesses with the juggernaut of US fast-food corporate imperialism. In reality, McDonald's global strategy is a careful blend of global standardization and local adaptation.

McDonald's menus include a number of globally standardized items – the Big Mac and potato fries are international features – however, in most countries McDonald's menus feature an increasing number of locally developed items. These include:

● Australia – Roast Beef and BBQ Sauce Deli Sandwich; Chicken Tandoori Sandwich

● France – Croque McDo; McCroissant

● Hong Kong – Star-shaped Hash Browns; Rice Burgers; Plum Drink with Aloe Vera

● India – McVeggie Burger; McAloo Tikka Burger; Veg Pizza McPuff

● Saudi Arabia – McArabia Kofta; McArabia Chicken

● Switzerland – Shrimp Cocktail; Chickenburger Curry

● UK – Oat-So-Simple Porridge; Toasted Deli Sandwiches

● US – Tortilla Wraps; premium salad range.

There are differences too in restaurant decor, service offerings (internet access in the UK; home delivery in India), and market positioning (McDonald's tends to have a more up-market positioning outside the US). In Israel many McDonald's are kosher – they do not offer dairy products and are closed on Saturdays. In India neither beef nor pork is served. A key reason that almost all of McDonald's non-US outlets are franchised is to facilitate adaptation to national environments and access to local know-how.

Yet, the principal features of the McDonald's business system are identical throughout the world. McDonald's values and business principles are seen as universal and invariant. Its emphasis on families and children is intended to identify McDonald's with fun and family life wherever it does business. Community involvement and the Ronald McDonald children's charity are also worldwide. Corporate trademarks and brands are mostly globally uniform – including the golden arches logo and "I'm lovin' it" tag line. The business system itself – the franchising, the training of managers and franchisees through Hamburger University, restaurant operations, and supplier relations – is also highly standardized.

Traditionally, McDonald's international strategy was about adapting its US model to local conditions. Increasingly McDonald's is using local differentiation as a basis for worldwide adaptation and innovation through transferring new menu items and business concepts from one country to another. For example, the McCafe gourmet coffeehouses within McDonald's restaurants were first developed in Australia. By 2003, McCafes had become established in 30 countries, including the US. In responding to the growing tide of concern over nutrition and obesity in the developed world,

McDonald's has drawn upon country initiatives with regard to sandwiches, salads, and information labeling as a basis for global learning.

Whether or not McDonald's has the balance right between global standardization and local adaptation is open to debate. Simon Anholt, a British marketing expert, argues: "By putting local food on the menu, all you are doing is removing the logic of the brand, because this is an American brand. If McDonald's serves what you think is a poor imitation of your local cuisine, it's going to be an insult." But according to McDonald's CEO Jim Skinner: "We don't run our business from Oak Brook. We are a local business with a local face in each country we operate in." His chief marketing manager, Mary Dillon adds: "McDonald's is much more about local relevance than a global archetype. Globally we think of ourselves as the custodian of the brand, but it's all about local relevance."

Sources: www.mcdonalds.com; *McDonald's Localization Strategy: Brand Unification, Menu Diversification?* ICFAI Case Study 306-316-1 (2006).

Reconciling global efficiency with appealing to customer preferences in each country also means looking at the globalization/national differentiation tradeoff for individual products and individual function. In the banking industry, different products and services have different potential for globalization. Credit cards and basic savings products such as certificates of deposit tend to be globally standardized; checking accounts and mortgage lending are much more nationally differentiated. Some of the most successful international banks are those that have specialized in more global products and services – for example, Capital One and MBNA in credit cards; UBS in private banking for affluent individuals.

Different functions also have different positioning with regard to global integration and national differentiation. R&D, purchasing, IT, and manufacturing have strong globalization potential because of scale economies; sales, marketing, customer service, and human resource management tend to require much more national differentiation. These differences have important implications for how the MNC is organized.

Strategy and Organization within the Multinational Corporation

Managing business activities that cross national frontiers is complex. As a result, the success of international strategies depends critically on the effectiveness with which they are implemented. One of the greatest challenges facing the senior managers of MNCs is aligning organizational structures and management systems and their fit with the strategies being pursued.

The Evolution of Multinational Strategies and Structures

All companies are subject to organizational inertia. MNCs, because of their complexity, face particular difficulty in adapting quickly to external change. As a result, established MNCs are captives of their history: the strategy–structure configurations adopted by today's MNCs reflect the choices they made at the time of their international expansion. Radical changes in strategy and structure are difficult: once an international distribution of functions, operations, and decision-making authority has been determined, reorganization is slow, difficult, and costly – particularly when host governments become involved. Bartlett and Ghoshal argue that this "administrative heritage" of an MNC – its configuration of assets and capabilities, its distribution of managerial responsibilities, and its network of relationships – constrains its ability to build new strategic capabilities.[37]

Leadership in the internationalization of business has been held by companies from different countries at different times. Bartlett and Ghoshal identify three eras (see Figure 14.8). For the companies of each era, their management challenges today are still shaped by their historical experiences.

- *Early 20th century: Era of the European multinational.* European companies such as Unilever, Shell, ICI, and Philips were pioneers of multinational expansion. Because of the conditions at the time of internationalization –

SOURCE: C. A. BARTLETT AND S. GHOSHAL, *MANAGING ACROSS BORDERS: THE TRANSNATIONAL SOLUTION* (BOSTON: HARVARD BUSINESS SCHOOL PRESS, 1998). COPYRIGHT © 1989 BY THE HARVARD BUSINESS SCHOOL PUBLISHING CORPORATION, ALL RIGHTS RESERVED. REPRINTED BY PERMISSION OF HARVARD BUSINESS SCHOOL PUBLISHING.

FIGURE 14.8 The development of the multinational corporation: alternative parent–subsidiaries relations

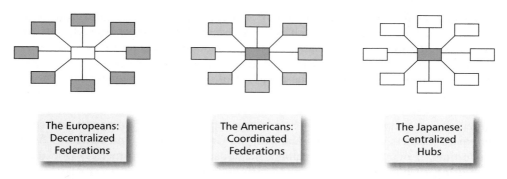

Note: The density of shading indicates the concentration of decision making.

poor transportation and communications, highly differentiated national markets – the companies created "multinational federations": each national subsidiary was operationally autonomous and undertook the full range of functions, including product development, manufacturing, and marketing.

- *Post-World War II: Era of the American multinational.* US economic dominance was the basis for the preeminence of US multinationals such as GM, Ford, IBM, Coca-Cola, Caterpillar, Gillette, and Procter & Gamble. While their overseas subsidiaries were allowed considerable autonomy, this was within the context of the dominant position of their US parent in terms of capital, new product and process technology, management capabilities, and management systems. US-based resources and capabilities were their primary competitive advantages in world markets.

- *The 1970s and 1980s: The Japanese challenge.* Japanese MNCs – Honda, Toyota, Matsushita, NEC, and YKK – pursued global strategies from centralized domestic bases. R&D and manufacturing were concentrated in Japan; overseas subsidiaries were responsible for sales and distribution. Globally standardized products manufactured in large-scale plants provided the basis for unrivalled cost and quality advantages. Over time, manufacturing and R&D were dispersed – initially because of trade protection by consumer countries and a rising value of the yen against other currencies.

The different administrative heritage of these different groups of MNCs continues to shape their organizational capabilities today. The strength of European multinationals is adaptation to the conditions and requirements of individual national markets. The strength of the US multinationals is their ability to transfer technology and proven new products from their domestic strongholds to their national subsidiaries. That of the Japanese MNCs is the efficiency of global production and new product development. Yet, these core capabilities are also core rigidities. The challenge for European MNCs has been to achieve greater integration of their sprawling international empires – for Shell and Philips this has involved reorganizations over a period of more than two decades. For US MNCs such as Ford and Procter & Gamble it has involved nurturing the ability to tap their foreign subsidiaries for technology, design, and new product ideas. For Japanese MNCs such as Nomura, Hitachi, and NEC the challenge is to become true insiders in the overseas countries where they do business.

Reconfiguring the MNC: The Transnational Corporation

Changing Organization Structure For North American and European-based MNCs, the principal structural changes of recent decades have been a shift from organization around national subsidiaries and regional groupings to the creation of worldwide product divisions. For most MNCs, country and regional organizations are retained, but primarily for the purposes of national compliance and customer relationships. Thus, Hewlett-Packard conducts its business through global product groups: Technology Solutions Group (comprising Enterprise Storage and Servers, Services, and Software), Personal Systems Group (its personal computer and entertainment business), and Imaging and Printing Group (printers and cameras). At the same time, it maintains three regional headquarters: for the Americas (located in Houston), for Europe, Middle East and Africa (located in Geneva), and for Asia Pacific (located in Singapore).

New Approaches to Reconciling Localization and Global Integration

However, the formal changes in structure are less important than the changes in responsibilities, decision powers, and modes of coordination within these structures. The fundamental challenge for MNCs has been reconciling the advantages of global integration with those of national differentiation. Escalating costs of research and new product development have made global strategies with global product platforms essential. At the same time, meeting consumer needs in each national market and responding swiftly to changing local circumstances requires greater decentralization. Accelerating technological change further exacerbates these contradictory forces: despite the cost and "critical mass" benefits of centralizing research and new product development, innovation occurs at multiple locations within the MNC and requires nurturing of creativity and initiative throughout the organization. "It's the corporate equivalent of being able to walk, chew gum, and whistle at the same time," notes Harvard's Chris Bartlett.

According to Bartlett, the simultaneous pursuit of responsiveness to national markets and global coordination requires, "a very different kind of internal management process than existed in the relatively simple multinational or global organizations. This is the *transnational organization*."[38] The distinguishing characteristic of the transnational is that it becomes an integrated network of distributed and interdependent resources and capabilities (see Figure 14.9). This necessitates that:

- Each national unit is a source of ideas, skills, and capabilities that can be harnessed for the benefit of the total organization.
- National units access global scale economies by designating them the company's world source for a particular product, component, or activity.
- The center must establish a new, highly complex managing role that coordinates relationships among units but does so in a highly flexible way. The key is to focus less on managing activities directly and more on creating an organizational context that is conducive to the coordination and resolution of differences. Creating the right organizational context involves "establishing clear corporate objectives, developing managers with broadly based perspectives and relationships, and fostering supportive organizational norms and values."[39]

FIGURE 14.9 The transnational corporation

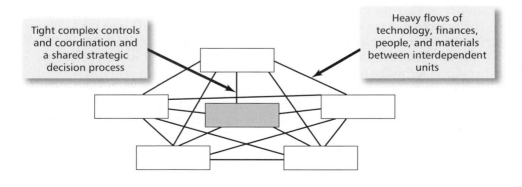

Balancing global integration and national differentiation requires that a company adapts to the differential requirements of different products, different functions, and different countries. Procter & Gamble adopts global standardization for some of its products (Pringles potato chips and high-end perfumes, for example); for others (hair coloring products and laundry detergent, for example) it allows significant national differentiation. Across countries, P&G organizes global product divisions to serve most of the industrialized world because of the similarities between their markets, while for emerging market countries (such as China and India) it operates through country subsidiaries in order to adapt to the distinctive features of these markets. Among functions, R&D is globally integrated while sales are organized by national units that are differentiated to meet local market characteristics.

The transnational firm is a concept and direction of development rather than a distinct organizational archetype. It involves convergence of the different strategy configurations of MNCs. Thus, companies such as Philips, Unilever, and Siemens have reassigned roles and responsibilities to achieve greater integration within their traditional "decentralized federations" of national subsidiaries. Japanese global corporations such as Toyota and Matsushita have drastically reduced the roles of their Japanese headquarters. American multinationals such as Citigroup and IBM are moving in two directions: reducing the role of their US bases while increasing integration among their different national subsidiaries.

MNCs are increasingly locating management control of their global product divisions outside their home countries. When Philips adopted a product division structure, it located responsibility for medical electronics in its US subsidiary and leadership in consumer electronics in Japan. Nexans, the world's biggest manufacturer of electric cables, has moved the head office of five of its 20 product divisions outside of France. For example, the head of ships' cables is based in South Korea – the world leader in shipbuilding.[40] Aligning structure, strategy, and national resources may even require shifting the corporate headquarters – HSBC moved from Hong Kong to London, Tetra Pak from Lund, Sweden to Lausanne, Switzerland.[41]

Organizing R&D and New Product Development Probably the greatest challenges facing the top managers of MNCs are organizing, fostering, and exploiting innovation and new product development. Innovation is stimulated by diversity and autonomy, while its exploitation and diffusion require critical mass and coordination. The traditional European decentralized model is conducive to local initiatives – but not to their global exploitation. Philips has an outstanding record of innovation in consumer electronics. In its TV business, its Canadian subsidiary developed its first color TV; its Australian subsidiary developed its first stereo sound TV, and its British subsidiary developed teletext TVs. However, lack of global integration has constrained its ability successfully to exploit its innovation on a global scale. During the 1980s and 1990s, Philips was on the losing side of a number of key standards battles: its V2000 VCR system lost out to Matsushita's VHS system and its digital audio tape lost out to other digital recording formats.

By assigning national subsidiaries global mandates it is possible for them to take advantage of local resources and develop distinctive capabilities while exploiting globally the results of their initiatives.[42] For example, P&G, recognizing Japanese obsessiveness over cleanliness, assigned increasing responsibility to its Japanese subsidiary for developing household cleaning products. Its "Swiffer" dust-collecting products were developed in Japan (using technology from Kao) then introduced into other markets. Where local units possess unique capabilities, they can be identified as *centers of excellence* as a means of assigning them specific responsibilities and signaling this leadership to the rest of the organization.[43]

Summary

Moving from a national to an international business environment represents a quantum leap in complexity. In an international environment, a firm's potential for competitive advantage is determined not just by its own resources and capabilities but also by the conditions of the national environment in which it operates, including input prices, exchange rates, and a host of other factors. The extent to which a firm is positioned in a single market or multiple national markets also influences its competitive position.

Our approach in this chapter is to simplify the complexities of international strategy by applying the same basic tools of strategy analysis that we developed in earlier chapters. For example, to determine whether a firm should enter an overseas market, our focus has been the profit implications of such an entry. This requires an analysis of (a) the attractiveness of the overseas market using the familiar tools of industry analysis, and (b) the potential of the firm to establish competitive advantage in that overseas market, which depends on the firm's ability to transfer its resources and capabilities to the new location and their effectiveness in conferring competitive advantage.

However, establishing the potential for a firm to create value from internationalization is only a beginning. Subsequent analysis needs to design an international strategy: do we enter an overseas market by exporting, licensing, or direct investment? If the latter, should we set up a wholly owned subsidiary or a joint venture? Once the strategy has been established, then a suitable organizational structure needs to be designed.

The fact that so many companies that have been outstandingly successful in their home market have failed so miserably in their overseas expansion demonstrates the complexity of international management. In some cases, the companies have failed to recognize that the resources and capabilities that underpinned their competitive advantages in their home market could not be readily transferred or replicated in overseas markets. In others, the problems were in designing the structures and systems that could effectively implement the international strategy.

As the lessons of success and failure from international business become recognized and distilled into better theories and analytical frameworks, so we advance our understanding of how to design and implement strategies for competing globally. We are at the stage where we recognize the issues and the key determinants of competitive advantage in an international environment. However, there is much that we do not fully understand. Designing strategies and organizational structures that can reconcile critical tradeoffs between global scale economies versus local differentiation, decentralized learning and innovation versus worldwide diffusion and replication, and localized flexibilities versus international standardization remain key challenges for senior managers.

Self-Study Questions

1   With reference to Figure 14.1, identify a "sheltered industry" (i.e. one that has been subject to little penetration either by imports or foreign direct investment). Explain why the industry has escaped internationalization. Explore whether there are opportunities for profitable internationalization within the industry and, if so, the strategy that would offer the best chance of success.

2   With reference to Table 14.1, what characteristics of national resources explain the different patterns of comparative advantage for the US and Japan?

3   According to Michael Porter's *Competitive Advantage of Nations*, some of the industries where British companies have an international advantage are: advertising, auction trading of antiques and artwork, distilled alcoholic beverages, hand tools, and chemical preparations for gardening and horticulture.

    Some of the industries where US companies have an international competitive advantage are: photo film, aircraft and helicopters, computer hardware and software, oilfield services, management consulting, cinema films and TV programs, healthcare products and services, and financial services.

    For either the UK or the US, use Porter's national diamond framework (Figure 14.3) to explain the observed pattern of international competitive advantage.

4   When Porsche decided to enter the SUV market with its luxury Cayenne model, it surprised the auto industry by locating its new assembly plant in Leipzig in eastern Germany. Many observers believed that Porsche should have located the plant either in central or eastern Europe where labor costs were very low, or (like Mercedes and BMW) in the US where it would be close to its major market. Using the criteria outlined in Figure 14.4, can you explain Porsche's decision?

5   British expatriates living in the US frequently ask friends and relatives visiting from the UK to bring with them bars of Cadbury's chocolate on the basis that the Cadbury's chocolate available in the US (manufactured under license by Hershey's) is inferior to "the real thing." Should Cadbury-Schweppes plc maintain its licensing agreement with Hershey or should it seek to supply the US market itself, either by export from the UK or by establishing manufacturing facilities in the US?

6   Has McDonald's got the balance right between global standardization and national differentiation (see Strategy Capsule 14.2)? Should it offer its franchisees in overseas countries greater initiative in introducing products that meet national preferences? Should it also allow greater flexibility for its overseas franchisees to adapt store layout, operating practices, and marketing? What aspects of the McDonald's system should McDonald's top management insist on keeping globally standardized?

Notes

1 US Statistical Abstract (www.census.gov).

2 This process was proposed by J. Johanson and J.-E. Vahlne, "The Internationalization Process of the Firm," *Journal of International Business Studies* 8 (1977): 23–32. See also L. Melin, "Internationalization as a Strategy Process," *Strategic Management Journal* 13 (1992 Special Issue): 99–118.

3 P. Ghemawat and F. Ghadar, "Global Integration ≠ Global Concentration," *Industrial and Corporate Change* 15 (2006): 595–624.

4 A key finding was that *human capital* (knowledge and skills) was more important than *physical capital* in explaining the pattern of US trade – the so-called *Leontief Paradox*. See W. W. Leontief, "Domestic Production and Foreign Trade," in R. Caves and H. Johnson (eds), *Readings in International Economics* (Homewood, IL: Irwin, 1968).

5 L. C. Thurow, *Building Wealth: The New Rules for Individuals, Companies and Nations* (New York: HarperCollins, 1999).

6 P. Krugman, "Increasing Returns, Monopolistic Competition, and International Trade," *Journal of International Economics* 9 (November 1979): 469–79.

7 M. E. Porter, *The Competitive Advantage of Nations* (New York: Free Press, 1990).

8 For a review of the Porter analysis, see R. M. Grant, "Porter's *Competitive Advantage of Nations*: An Assessment," *Strategic Management Journal* 12 (1991): 535–48.

9 M. Weber, *The Protestant Ethic and the Spirit of Capitalism* (London: Unwin University Books, 1930).

10 P. Almeida, "Knowledge Sourcing by Foreign Multinationals: Patent Citation Analysis in the US Semiconductor Industry," *Strategic Management Journal* 17 (December 1996): 155–65.

11 The linking of value-added chains to national comparative advantages is explained in B. Kogut, "Designing Global Strategies and Competitive Value-Added Chains," *Sloan Management Review* (Summer 1985): 15–38.

12 *Nike: International Context*, HBS Case Services Case No. 9-385-328 (Boston: Harvard Business School, 1985); and *Nike in China*, HBS Case Services Case No. 9-386-037 (Boston: Harvard Business School, 1985).

13 J. Hagel and J. S. Brown, "Thinking Global, Acting Local," *Financial Times* (August 9, 2005).

14 The role of firm-specific assets in explaining the multinational expansion is analyzed in R. Caves, "International Corporations: The Industrial Economics of Foreign Investment," *Economica* 38 (1971): 1–27.

15 The role of transactions cost is explained in D. J. Teece, "Transactions Cost Economics and Multinational Enterprise," *Journal of Economic Behavior and Organization* 7 (1986): 21–45. See also "Creatures of Imperfection," in "Multinationals: A Survey," *Economist* (March 27, 1993): 8–10.

16 D. von Emloh and Y. Wang, "Competing for China's Credit Card Market," *McKinsey Quarterly* (November 2005), www.mckinseyquarterly.com

17 J. P. Killing, "How to Make a Global Joint Venture Work," *Harvard Business Review* (May–June 1982): 120–7.

18 G. Hamel, "Competition for Competence and Inter-partner Learning within International Strategic Alliances," *Strategic Management Journal* 12 (1991): 83–103.

19 See R. Reich and E. Mankin, "Joint Ventures with Japan Give Away our Future," *Harvard Business Review* (March–April 1986).

20 *Xerox and Fuji Xerox*, Case No. 9-391-156 (Boston: Harvard Business School, 1992).

21 G. Hamel, Y. Doz, and C. K. Prahalad, "Collaborate with Your Competitors – and Win," *Harvard Business Review* (January–February 1989): 133–9.

22 Ibid.

23 J. Bamford and D. Ernst, "Managing an Alliance Portfolio," *McKinsey Quarterly* (2002, no. 3): 20–30.

24 T. Levitt, "The Globalization of Markets," *Harvard Business Review* (May–June 1983): 92–102.

25 G. S. Yip, *Total Global Strategy II* (Upper Saddle River, NJ: Prentice Hall, 2003); C. Baden-Fuller and J. Stopford, "Globalization Frustrated," *Strategic Management Journal* 12 (1991): 493–507; "Rough and Tumble Industry," *Financial Times* (July 2, 1997): 13.

26 S. G. Winter and G. Szulanski, "Replication as Strategy," *Organization Science* 12 (2001): 730–43.

27 P. Almeida, "Knowledge Sourcing by Foreign Multinationals: Patent Citation Analysis in the US Semiconductor Industry," *Strategic Management Journal* 17, Winter Special Issue (1996): 155–65. See the McDonald's individual country websites, e.g., www.mcdonalds.com (US), www.mcdonalds.co.uk (UK), www.mcdonalds.fr (France).

28 A. K. Gupta and P. Govindarajan, "Knowledge Flows within Multinational Corporations," *Strategic Management Journal* 21 (April 2000): 473–96; P. Almeida, J. Song, and R. M. Grant, "Are Firms Superior to Alliances and Markets? An Empirical Test of Cross-Border Knowledge Building," *Organization Science* 13 (March–April 2002): 147–61.

29 G. Hamel and C. K. Prahalad, "Do You Really Have a Global Strategy?" *Harvard Business Review* (July–August 1985): 139–48.

30 H. Simon and Y. Eriguchi, "Pricing Challenges for Japanese Companies in the 21st Century," *Journal of Professional Pricing* 14, no. 4 (2005), www.pricingsociety.com; B. Y. Aw, G. Batra, and M. J. Roberts, "Firm Heterogeneity and Export – Domestic Price Differentials: A Study of Taiwanese Electrical Products," *Journal of International Economics* 54 (2001): 149–69.

31 I. C. Macmillan, A. van Ritten, and R. G. McGrath, "Global Gamesmanship," *Harvard Business Review* (May 2003): 62–71.

32 R. C. Christopher, *Second to None: American Companies in Japan* (New York: Crown, 1986).

33 K. Ohmae, *Triad Power: The Coming Shape of Global Competition* (New York: Free Press, 1985).

34 The Ford Mondeo/Contour is a classic example of a global product that failed to appeal strongly to any national market. See M. J. Moi, "Ford Mondeo: A Model T World Car?" Idea Group (2001); C. Chandler, "Globalization: The Automotive Industry's Quest for a World Car" (http://globaledge.msu.edu/KnowledgeRoom/FeaturedInsights/0018.pdf).

35 C. Baden-Fuller and J. Stopford, "Globalization Frustrated," *Strategic Management Journal* 12 (1991): 493–507.

36 A. Morita, "Global Localization," in *Genryn* (Tokyo: Sony, 1996): Chapter 8.

37 C. A. Bartlett and S. Ghoshal, *Managing Across Borders: The Transnational Solution*, 2nd edn (Boston: Harvard Business School Press, 1998).

38 C. Bartlett, "Building and Managing the Transnational: The New Organizational Challenge," in Michael E. Porter (ed.), *Competition in Global Industries* (Boston: Harvard Business School Press, 1986): 377.

39 Ibid.: 388.

40 "The Country Prince Comes of Age," *Financial Times* (August 9, 2005).

41 J. Birkinshaw, P. Braunerhjelm, U. Holm, and S. Terjesen, "Why do some Multinational Corporations Relocate their Headquarters Overseas?" *Strategic Management Journal* 27 (2006): 681–700.

42 J. Birkinshaw, N. Hood, and S. Jonsson, "Building Firm-specific Advantages in Multinational Corporations: The Role of Subsidiary Initiative," *Strategic Management Journal* 19 (1998): 221–42.

43 T. S. Frost, J. M. Birkinshaw, and P. C. Ensign, "Centers of Excellence in Multinational Corporations," *Strategic Management Journal* 23 (2002): 997–1018.

15

Diversification Strategy

Telephones, hotels, insurance – it's all the same. If you know the numbers inside out, you know the company inside out.

—HAROLD SYDNEY GENEEN, CHAIRMAN OF ITT, 1959–78,
AND INSTIGATOR OF 275 COMPANY TAKEOVERS

For a company that has taken its original or main business as far as it can go, diversification as a means of channeling surplus resources should certainly be considered. For the company that has not yet developed its main business to the full potential, however, diversification is probably one of the riskiest strategic choices that can be made.

—KENICHI OHMAE, STRATEGY GURU AND FORMER HEAD OF
MCKINSEY & CO.'S TOKYO OFFICE

OUTLINE

393

Introduction and Objectives

Deciding "What business are we in?" is the starting point of strategy and the basis for defining the firm's identity. In their statements of vision and mission, some companies define their businesses broadly. Shell's objectives are "to engage efficiently, responsibly, and profitably in oil, oil products, gas, chemicals, and other selected businesses." Other companies define their businesses more narrowly: McDonald's vision is "to be the world's best quick-service restaurant chain"; Caterpillar will "be leader in providing the best value in machines, engines, and support services for companies dedicated to building the world's infrastructure and developing and transporting its resources."

A firm's business scope may change over time. Most companies have "refocused on core businesses" during the past 25 years. RJR Nabisco sold its interests in processed foods, Delmonte fruit, pet food, chewing gum, and cosmetics before emerging as Reynolds American, a specialized tobacco company. Some conglomerates – ITT, Hanson, Gulf & Western, Cendant, and Tyco – have broken up altogether.

Some companies have moved in the opposite direction. Microsoft, once a supplier of operating systems, expanded into application and networking software, information services, entertainment systems, and video games consoles. Other companies have totally transformed their businesses. Nokia, once a supplier of paper and rubber goods, emerged as the world's biggest manufacturer of mobile phones during the mid-1990s.

Diversification is a conundrum. It represents the biggest single source of value destruction ever perpetrated by CEOs and their strategy advisers at the expense of their unwitting shareholders. Yet, specialization restricts a firm's options and condemns it to the fortunes of its industry. Thus, because of its greater diversity across different soft drinks and convenience foods, PepsiCo has survived the downturn in the soda drinks market better than Coca-Cola.

Our goal in this chapter is to establish the basis on which companies can make corporate strategy decisions that create rather than destroy value. Is it better to be specialized or diversified? Is there an optimal degree of diversification? What types of diversification are most likely to create value?

In practice, we make these types of decision every day in our personal lives. If my car doesn't start in the morning, should I try to fix it myself or have it towed directly to the garage? There are two considerations. First, is repairing a car an attractive activity to undertake? If the garage charges $85 an hour, but I can earn $600 an hour consulting, then car repair is not attractive to me. Second, am I any good at car repair? If I am likely to take twice as long as a skilled mechanic, then I possess no competitive advantage in car repair.

Diversification decisions by firms involve the same two issues:

- How attractive is the industry to be entered?
- Can the firm establish a competitive advantage within the new industry?

These are the very same factors we identified in Chapter 1 (see Figure 1.4) as determining a firm's profit potential. Hence, no new analytic framework is needed for appraising diversification decisions: diversification may be justified either by the superior profit potential of the industry to be entered, or by the ability of the firm to create competitive advantage in the new industry. The first issue draws on the industry analysis developed in Chapter 3; the second draws on the analysis of competitive advantage developed in Chapters 5 and 7.

Our primary focus is on the latter question: under what conditions does operating multiple businesses assist a firm in gaining a competitive advantage in each? This leads into exploring linkages between different businesses within the diversified firm – a phenomenon often referred to as "synergy."

By the time you have completed this chapter, you will be able to:

● Appreciate the factors that have influenced diversification in the past and the recent trend toward "refocusing."

● Identify the conditions under which diversification creates value for shareholders and, in particular, to evaluate the potential for sharing and transferring resources and capabilities within the diversified firm.

● Determine the relative merits of diversification and strategic alliances in exploiting the linkages between different businesses.

● Recognize the organizational and managerial issues to which diversification gives rise and why diversification so often fails to realize its anticipated benefits.

Trends in Diversification over Time

As a background to our analysis of diversification decisions, let's begin by examining the factors that have influenced diversification strategies in the past.

The Era of Diversification, 1950–1980

In Chapter 13, we noted that diversification was a major aspect of the widening scope of the modern corporation during most of the 20th century. Between 1950 and 1980, diversification – the expansion of companies across different product markets – was an especially important source of corporate growth in all the advanced industrial nations.[1] The 1970s saw the height of the diversification boom, with the emergence of a new corporate form – the *conglomerate* – represented in the US by ITT, Textron, and Allied-Signal, and in the UK by Hanson, Slater-Walker, and BTR. (Table 15.1 shows how the diversification strategies of US and UK firms have changed over time.) These highly diversified enterprises were created from multiple, unrelated acquisitions. Their

TABLE 15.1 Changes in the diversification strategies of US and UK companies

	United States			United Kingdom		
	1949	1964	1974	1950	1970	1993
Single business	42%	22%	14%	24%	6%	5%
Dominant business	28%	32%	23%	50%	32%	10%
Related business	28%	37%	42%	27%	57%	62%
Unrelated business	4%	9%	21%	0%	6%	24%

SOURCES: R. P. RUMELT, "DIVERSIFICATION STRATEGY AND PROFITABILITY," *STRATEGIC MANAGEMENT JOURNAL* 3 (1982): 359–70; R. WHITTINGTON, M. MAYER, AND F. CURTO, "CHANDLERISM IN POST-WAR EUROPE: STRATEGIC AND STRUCTURAL CHANGE IN FRANCE, GERMANY AND THE UK, 1950–1993," *INDUSTRIAL AND CORPORATE CHANGE* 8 (1999): 519–50; D. CHANNON, *THE STRATEGY AND STRUCTURE OF BRITISH ENTERPRISE* (CAMBRIDGE: HARVARD UNIVERSITY PRESS, 1973).

existence reflected the naive view that senior management no longer needed industry-specific experience and, so long as managers adopted the new techniques of financial and strategic management, companies no longer needed to be constrained by industry boundaries.[2]

Refocusing, 1980–2006

After 1980, the diversification trend went into sharp reverse. Between 1980 and 1990, the average index of diversification for the Fortune 500 declined from 1.00 to 0.67.[3] Unprofitable "noncore" businesses were increasingly divested during the later 1980s, and a number of diversified companies fell prey to leveraged buyouts.[4] Although acquisition activity was extremely heavy during the 1980s – some $1.3 trillion in assets were acquired, including 113 members of the Fortune 500 – only 4.5% of acquisitions represented unrelated diversification.[5] Moreover, acquisitions by the Fortune 500 were outnumbered by dispositions. The refocusing trend was strongest in the US, but was also evident in Canada and Europe and, to a lesser extent, in Japan.[6]

This trend towards specialization was the result of three principal factors.

Emphasis on Shareholder Value   The overwhelmingly important factor driving the retreat from diversification and the refocusing around core businesses was the reordering of corporate goals from growth to profitability. Economic downturns and interest-rate spikes of the early 1980s and 1989–90 revealed the inadequate profitability of many large, diversified corporations. Increased pressure on incumbent management was exerted by institutional shareholders, including pension funds such as California's Public Employees Retirement system. One outcome of shareholder activism was increased CEO turnover.[7]

The surge in leveraged buyouts put further pressure on executives to boost shareholder returns. Where an incumbent management team had destroyed shareholder value, corporate raiders saw the opportunity to use debt financing to mount a takeover bid. Kohlberg Kravis Roberts' $31 billion takeover of the tobacco and food giant RJR Nabisco in 1989 demonstrated that even the largest US companies were not safe from acquisition.[8] The result was a rush by poorly performing corporate giants to restructure before leveraged buyout specialists did it for them. The tendency for the stock market to apply a "conglomerate discount" – to value diversified companies at market valuation of the whole as less than the sum of their parts – has added a further incentive for breakups.[9]

Turbulence and Transaction Costs In Chapter 13, we observed that the relative costs of organizing transactions within firms and across markets depend on the conditions in the external environment. Administrative hierarchies are very efficient in processing routine transactions, but in turbulent conditions the pressure of decision making on top management results in stress, inefficiency, and delay. As the business environment has become more volatile, specialized companies are more agile than large diversified corporations where strategic changes and investment proposals require approval at divisional and corporate levels. At the same time, external factor markets – capital markets especially – have become increasingly efficient. The tendency for some diversified companies to spin off their growth businesses has been influenced by the belief that these businesses could better exploit their growth opportunities by drawing directly on external markets for finance, human resources, and technology.

The refocusing trend has extended to Japan and South Korea. However, in the emerging countries of Asia and Latin America, large conglomerates continue to dominate their national economies: Tata Group and Reliance in India, Charoen Pokphand in Thailand, Astra in Indonesia, Sime Darby in Malaysia, Grupo Alfa and Grupo Carso in Mexico. One reason for the continued dominance of large conglomerates in emerging market countries may be higher transaction costs associated with their less sophisticated and less efficient markets for finance, information, and labor that offer diversified companies advantages over their specialized competitors.[10]

Trends in Management Thinking During the past decade there has been waning confidence in the ability of corporate headquarters to manage many different businesses, and greater emphasis on building competitive advantage by focusing on key strengths in resources and capabilities. If there are opportunities to deploy core resources and capabilities in new product markets, this is more likely to occur through collaborative arrangements with other companies rather than through diversification.

This is not to imply that ideas concerning synergies from operating in multiple product markets are dead. Indeed, recent years have seen continuing interest in economies of scope and the transferability of resources and capabilities across industry boundaries. The major change is that strategic analysis has become much more precise about the circumstances in which diversification can create value from multibusiness activity. Mere linkages between businesses are not enough: the key to creating value is the ability of the diversified firm to share resources and transfer capabilities more efficiently than alternative institutional arrangements. Moreover, it is essential that the benefits of these linkages are not outweighed by the additional management costs of exploiting them. Figure 15.1 summarizes some of the key developments in diversification strategy over the past 50 years.

Motives for Diversification

Diversification has been driven by three major goals: growth, risk reduction, and profitability. As we shall see, although growth and risk reduction have been prominent motives for diversification, they tend to be inconsistent with the creation of shareholder value.

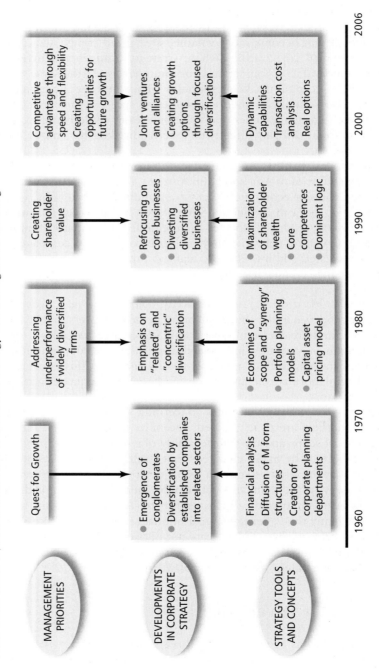

FIGURE 15.1 Diversification: the evolution of strategy and management thinking

Growth

In the absence of diversification firms are prisoners of their industry. For firms in stagnant or declining industries this is a daunting prospect – especially if the industry faces ultimate demise. However, the critical issue for top management is whether the pursuit of growth is consistent with quest for profitability. In principle, widening the firm's range of potential investment to include opportunities outside its existing industry should be entirely compatible with increasing profitability. Indeed, for companies such as 3M and Canon, deploying their capabilities in new product markets is a key source of value creation. However, the overall evidence is to the contrary. As we noted in Chapter 6 when discussing the *agency problem*, managers have incentives to pursue growth rather than profitability, one of the most serious consequences of which is the propensity to undertake unprofitable diversification. Companies in low-growth, cash flow-rich industries such as tobacco and oil have been especially susceptible to the temptations of diversification. During the 1980s, Philip Morris diversified into soft drinks (7-Up), beer (Miller), chewing gum (Clark), and food (Kraft, General Foods), while Exxon diversified into copper and coal mining, electric motors, and computers and office equipment. It is notable that when underperforming public companies are threatened by investor discontent or a corporate raider, they frequently resort to selling off diversified businesses.[11]

Risk Reduction

A second motive for diversification is the desire to spread risks. To isolate the effects of diversification on risk, consider the case of "pure" or "conglomerate" diversification, where separate businesses are brought under common ownership but the individual cash flows of the businesses remain unchanged. So long as the cash flows of the different businesses are imperfectly correlated, then the variance of the cash flow of the combined businesses is less than the average of that of the separate businesses. Hence, diversification reduces risk.

But does this risk reduction create value for shareholders? We must take account of the fact that investors hold diversified portfolios. If investors can hold diversified portfolios, what advantage can there be in companies diversifying for them? The only possible advantage could be if firms can diversify at lower cost than individual investors. In fact the reverse is true: the transaction costs to shareholders of diversifying their portfolios are far less than the transaction costs to firms diversifying through acquisition. Not only do acquiring firms incur the heavy costs of using investment banks and legal advisers, they must also pay an acquisition premium to gain control of an independent company.

The *capital asset pricing model* (CAPM) formalizes this argument. The theory states that the risk that is relevant to determining the price of a security is not the overall risk (variance) of the security's return, but *systematic risk*: that part of the variance of the return that is correlated with overall market returns. Systematic risk is measured by the security's *beta coefficient*. Corporate diversification does not reduce systematic risk: if three separate companies are brought under common ownership, in the absence of any other changes, the beta coefficient of the combined company is simply the weighted average of the beta coefficients of the constituent companies. Hence, the simple act of bringing different businesses under common ownership does not create shareholder value through risk reduction.[12]

Empirical studies are generally supportive of the absence of shareholder benefit from diversification that simply combines independent businesses. Studies of conglomerates in the United States have shown that their risk-adjusted returns to shareholders are typically no better than those offered by mutual funds or by matched portfolios of specialized companies.[13] Unrelated diversification may even fail to lower unsystematic risk.[14]

Hence, so long as securities markets are efficient, diversification whose sole purpose is to spread risk will not benefit shareholders. However, risk spreading through diversification may benefit other stakeholders. If cyclicality in the firm's profits is accompanied by cyclicality in employment, then so long as employees are transferable between the separate businesses of the firm, there may be benefits to employees from diversification's ability to smooth output fluctuations.

Special issues arise once we consider the risk of bankruptcy. For a marginally profitable firm, diversification can help avoid cyclical fluctuations of profits that can push it into insolvency. It has been shown, however, that diversification that reduces the risk of bankruptcy is beneficial to the holders of corporate debt rather than to equity holders. The reduction in risk that bondholders derive from diversification is the *coinsurance effect*.[15]

Are there circumstances where reductions in unsystematic risk can create shareholder value? If there are economies to the firm from financing investments internally rather than resorting to external capital markets, the stability in the firm's cash flow that results from diversification may reinforce independence from external capital markets. For Exxon Mobil, BP, and the other major oil companies one of the benefits of extending across upstream (exploration and production), downstream (refining and marketing), and chemicals is that the negative correlation of the returns from these businesses increases the overall stability of their cash flows. This in turn increases their capacity to undertake huge, risky investments in offshore oil production, transcontinental pipelines, and natural gas liquefaction. These benefits also explain why firms pursue hedging activities that only reduce unsystematic risk.[16]

Profitability

If we return to the assumption that corporate strategy should be directed toward the interests of shareholders, what are the implications for diversification strategy? We have already revisited our two sources of superior profitability: industry attractiveness and competitive advantage. For firms contemplating diversification, Michael Porter proposes three "essential tests" to be applied in deciding whether diversification will truly create shareholder value:

1 *The attractiveness test.* The industries chosen for diversification must be structurally attractive or capable of being made attractive.

2 *The cost-of-entry test.* The cost of entry must not capitalize all the future profits.

3 *The better-off test.* Either the new unit must gain competitive advantage from its link with the corporation, or vice versa.[17]

The Attractiveness and Cost-of-entry Tests A critical realization in Porter's "essential tests" is that industry attractiveness is insufficient on its own. Although diversification is a means by which the firm can access more attractive investment opportunities than are available in its own industry, it faces the problem of entering the new industry. The second test, *cost of entry*, recognizes that the attractiveness of an industry to a firm already established in an industry may be different from its attractiveness to a firm seeking to enter the industry. Pharmaceuticals, management consulting, and investment banking offer above-average profitability precisely because they are protected by barriers to entry. Firms seeking to enter these industries have a choice. They may enter by acquiring an established player, in which case not only does the market price of the target firm reflect the superior profit prospects of the industry, but the diversifying firm must also offer an acquisition premium of around 25 to 50% over the market price to gain control.[18] Alternatively, entry may occur through establishing a new corporate venture. In this case, the diversifying firm must directly confront the barriers to entry protecting that industry, which usually means low returns over a long period.[19]

The Better-off Test Porter's third criterion for successful diversification – *the better-off test* – addresses the basic issue of competitive advantage: if two businesses producing different products are brought together under the ownership and control of a single enterprise, is there any reason why they should become any more profitable? Combining different, but related, businesses can enhance the competitive advantages of the original business, the new business, or both. For example:

- Procter & Gamble's 2005 acquisition of Gillette was intended to boost the competitive position of both companies through combining the two companies' global marketing and distribution networks, transferring Gillette's new product development capabilities to P&G, and increasing both companies' bargaining power relative to retail giants such as Wal-Mart.
- Allianz's takeover of Dresdner Bank in 2001 to create the world's biggest bank-assurance company was to enable Allianz to sell its insurance products through Dresdner's retail bank network, to strengthen Dresdner's finance, and to allow the two companies to combine forces in creating pensions and investment products for Germany's aging baby-boomers.

Yet, although the potential for value creation from exploiting linkages between the different businesses may be considerable, the practical difficulties of exploiting such opportunities have made diversification a corporate minefield. Let us examine the issues systematically.

Competitive Advantage from Diversification

If the primary source of value creation from diversification is exploiting linkages between different businesses, what are the linkages and how are they exploited? As we shall see, the primary means by which diversification creates competitive advantage is through the sharing of resources and capabilities across different businesses. There is also the potential for diversification to enhance or exploit a firm's market power. However, since this possibility has interested antitrust authorities more than it has corporate managers, we will defer its discussion to an appendix to this chapter.

Economies of Scope

The most general argument concerning the benefits of diversification focuses on the presence of *economies of scope* in common resources:

Economies of scope exist whenever there are cost savings from using a resource in multiple activities carried out in combination rather than carrying out those activities independently.[20]

Economies of scope exist for similar reasons as *economies of scale*. The key difference is that the economies of scale relate to cost economies from increasing output for a single product; economies of scope are cost economies from increasing output across multiple products.[21] The nature of economies of scope varies between different types of resources and capabilities.

Tangible Resources   Tangible resources – such as distribution networks, information technology systems, sales forces, and research laboratories – offer economies of scope by eliminating duplication between businesses through creating a single shared facility. The greater the fixed costs of these items, the greater the associated economies of scope are likely to be. Entry by cable TV companies into telephone services, and telephone companies into cable TV, are motivated by the desire to spread the costs of networks and billing systems over as great a volume of business as possible. Similar considerations have encouraged British Gas, a former state-owned monopoly supplier of gas, to diversify into supplying electricity, fixed-line telephone services, mobile telephone services, broadband internet connections, home security systems, home insurance, and home appliance repair.

Economies of scope also arise from the centralized provision of administrative and support services by the corporate center to the different businesses of the corporation. Among diversified companies, accounting, legal services, government relations, and information technology tend to be centralized – often through *shared service organizations* that supply common administrative and technical services to the operating businesses. Similar economies arise from centralizing research activities in a corporate R&D lab. In aerospace, the ability of US companies such as Boeing and United Technologies to spread research expenditures over both military and civilian products has given these companies an advantage over overseas competitors with more limited access to large defense contracts.[22]

Economies of scope can also arise in finance. By combining an industrial company with a financial services company, General Electric lowers its cost of capital to both sides of the company.

Intangible Resources   Intangible resources such as brands, corporate reputation, and technology offer economies of scope from the ability to extend them to additional businesses at low marginal cost.[23] Exploiting a strong brand across additional products is called *brand extension*. Starbucks has extended its brand to ice cream, Starbucks bottled drinks, home espresso machines, and books.

Organizational Capabilities   Organizational capabilities can also be transferred within the diversified company. For example:

- LVMH is the world's biggest and most diversified supplier of branded luxury goods. Its distinctive capability is the management of luxury brands. This capability comprises market analysis, advertising, promotion, retail management, and quality assurance. These capabilities are deployed across Louis Vuitton (accessories and leather goods); Hennessey (cognac); Moet et Chandon, Dom Perignon, Veuve Clicquot, and Krug (champagne); Celine,

Givenchy, Kenzo, Dior, Guerlain, and Donna Karan (fashion clothing and perfumes); TAG Heuer and Chaumet (watches); Sephora and La Samaritaine (retailing); and some 25 other branded businesses.

● Sharp Corporation – originally established to manufacture metal products and the Ever Sharp Pencil – developed capabilities in the miniaturization of electronic products that it has deployed to develop and introduce a stream of innovative products, beginning with the world's first transistor calculator (1964), the first LCD pocket calculator (1973), LCD color TVs, PDAs, internet viewcams, ultraportable notebook computers, and 3G mobile telephones.

Some of the most important capabilities in influencing the performance of diversified corporations are *general management capabilities*. General Electric possesses strong technological and operational capabilities at business level and it is good at sharing these capabilities between businesses (e.g. turbine know-how between jet engines and electrical generating equipment). However, its core capabilities are in general management and these reside primarily at the corporate level. These include its ability to motivate and develop its managers, its outstanding strategic and financial management that reconciles decentralized decision making with strong centralized control, and its international management capability. Similar observations could be made about 3M. While 3M's capabilities in technical know-how, new product development, and international marketing reside within the individual businesses, it is the corporate management capabilities and the systems through which they are exercised that maintain, nourish, coordinate, and upgrade these competitive advantages.[24]

Economies from Internalizing Transactions

Although economies of scope provide cost savings from sharing and transferring resources and capabilities, does a firm have to diversify across these different businesses to exploit those economies? The answer is no. Economies of scope in resources and capabilities can be exploited simply by selling or licensing the use of the resource or capability to another company. In Chapter 11, we observed that a firm can exploit proprietary technology by licensing it to other firms. In Chapter 14, we noted how technology and trademarks are licensed across national frontiers as an alternative to direct investment. The same can be done to exploit resources across different industries. Starbucks' extension of its brand to other products has been achieved primarily through licensing: Pepsi produces and distributes Starbucks Frappaccino; Dreyer's produces Starbucks ice cream. Walt Disney exploits the enormous value of its trademarks, copyrights, and characters partly through diversification into theme parks, live theater, cruise ships, and hotels; and partly through licensing the use of these assets to producers of clothing, toys, music, comics, food, and drinks, as well as to the franchisees of Disney's retail stores. Disney's income from licensing fees and royalties was over $2 billion in 2005.

Even tangible resources can be shared across different businesses through market transactions. Airport and railroad station operators exploit economies of scope in their facilities not by diversifying into catering and retailing, but by leasing out space to specialist retailers and restaurants.

What determines whether economies of scope are better exploited internally within the firm through diversification, or externally through market contracts with independent companies? The key issue is relative efficiency: what are the transaction costs of market contracts, as compared with the administrative costs of a diversified enterprise? Transaction costs include the costs involved in drafting, negotiating, monitoring, and enforcing a contract. The costs of internalization consist of the management costs of establishing and coordinating the diversified business.[25]

Let's return to the Walt Disney Company. Why does Disney choose to license Donald Duck trademarks to a manufacturer of orange juice rather than set up its own orange juice company? Why does it own and operate its own Disneyland and Disney World theme parks rather than license its trademarks to independent theme park companies? And why, in the case of Tokyo Disneyland, did it choose a licensing arrangement with the Oriental Land Company, which owns and operates Tokyo Disneyland?

These issues are complex. Much depends on the characteristics of the resource or capabilities. Though the returns to patents and brand names can often be appropriated efficiently through licensing, complex general management capabilities may be near impossible to exploit through market contracts. There is little scope for 3M to deploy its new product development capabilities other than within its own business. Similarly, for Apple Computer, the only way for it to exploit its capabilities in innovation and user-friendly design outside its core computer business was for it to diversify into other areas of entertainment and consumer electronics. The more deeply embedded a firm's capabilities within the management systems and the culture of the organization, the greater the likelihood that these capabilities can only be deployed internally within the firm. In principle, Virgin could license its brand to other companies. In practice, the value of the Virgin brand depends critically on the dynamism of Virgin companies, the irreverence of the Virgin culture, and the personality of Richard Branson.

The Diversified Firm as an Internal Market

We see that economies of scope on their own do not provide an adequate rationale for diversification – they must be supported by the presence of transaction costs. However, the presence of transaction costs in any nonspecialized resource can offer efficiency gains from diversification, even where no economies of scope are present.

Internal Capital Markets   Consider the case of financial capital. The diversified firm represents an internal capital market: the corporate allocating capital between the different businesses through the capital expenditure budget. Which is more efficient, the internal capital markets of diversified companies or the external capital market? Diversified companies have two key advantages:

- By maintaining a balanced portfolio of cash-generating and cash-using businesses, diversified firms can avoid the costs of using the external capital market, including the margin between borrowing and lending rates and the heavy costs of issuing new debt and equity.
- Diversified companies have better access to information on the financial prospects of their different businesses than that typically available to external financiers.[26]

Against these advantages is the critical disadvantage that investment funds within the diversified company are not allocated solely on the basis of potential returns.

Corporate management is likely to be subject to goals other than shareholder value maximization and capital allocation tends to be a politicized process. How do these conflicting factors balance out? Despite inconsistent findings, the balance of the evidence is that diversified firms exhibit key weaknesses in their internal capital markets, including a tendency to cross-subsidize their poorly performing divisions, to waste resources in internal political competition for funding, and reluctance to transfer divisional cash flows to the divisions with the best prospects.[27] However, overall averages obscure sharp differences in the efficiency of capital allocation between different diversified companies. Makron Associated identified several conglomerates with exceptional performance in terms of ten-year shareholder returns. They included GE and Berkshire Hathaway of the US, Hutchison Wampoa of Hong Kong, Bouygues and Lagardere of France, Wesfarmers of Australia, ITC of India, and Carso of Mexico. The common characteristics of these companies were: "Strict financial discipline, rigorous analysis and valuation, a refusal to overpay for acquisitions, and a willingness to close or sell existing businesses."[28]

Internal Labor Markets Efficiencies also arise from the ability of diversified companies to transfer employees – especially managers and technical specialists – between their divisions, and to rely less on hiring and firing. As companies develop and encounter new circumstances, so different management skills are required. The costs associated with hiring include advertising, the time spent in interviewing and selection, and the costs of "head-hunting" agencies. The costs of dismissing employees can be very high where severance payments must be offered. A diversified corporation has a pool of employees and can respond to the specific needs of any one business through transfer from elsewhere within the corporation.

The broader set of opportunities available in the diversified corporation as a result of internal transfer may also result in attracting a higher caliber of employee. Graduating students compete intensely for entry-level positions with diversified corporations such as Canon, General Electric, Unilever, and Nestlé in the belief that these companies can offer richer career development than more specialized companies.

The informational advantages of diversified firms are especially important in relation to internal labor markets. A key problem of hiring from the external labor market is limited information. A resumé, references, and a day of interviews are a poor indicator of how an otherwise unknown person will perform in a specific job. The diversified firm that is engaged in transferring employees between business units and divisions has access to much more detailed information on the abilities, characteristics, and past performance of each of its employees. This informational advantage exists not only for individual employees but also for groups of individuals working together as teams. As a result, in diversifying into a new activity, the established firm is at an advantage over the new firm, which must assemble a team from scratch with poor information on individual capabilities and almost no information on how effective the group will be at working together.

Diversification and Performance

We have established that diversification has the potential to create value for shareholders where it exploits economies of scope and where transaction costs in the markets for resources make it inefficient to exploit these economies of scope through market contracts. Diversification that seeks to reduce risk or achieve growth is likely to destroy shareholder value. How do these predictions work in practice?

The Findings of Empirical Research

Empirical research into diversification has concentrated on two major issues: first, how do diversified firms perform relative to specialized firms and, second, does related diversification outperform unrelated diversification?

The Performance of Diversified and Specialized Firms Despite a large number of empirical studies over four decades, no consistent, systematic relationships have emerged between performance and the degree of diversification. However, there is some evidence that, beyond a certain point, high levels of diversification are associated with deteriorating profitability – possibly because of the problems of complexity that diversification creates. Among British companies, diversification was associated with increased profitability up to a point, after which further diversification was associated with declining profitability.[29] Other studies have also detected a curvilinear relationship between diversification and profitability.[30] Research by McKinsey & Company offers further evidence of the benefits of moderate diversification – "a strategic sweet spot between focus and broader diversification." Timing is the key, they note. Diversification makes sense when a company has exhausted growth opportunities in its existing markets and can match its existing capabilities to emerging external opportunities.[31] As with most studies seeking to link strategy to performance, a key problem is distinguishing *association* from *causation*. If diversified companies are generally more profitable than specialized firms, is it because diversification increases profitability or because profitable firms channel their cash flows into diversifying investments?

It is also likely that the performance effects of diversification depend on the mode of diversification. There is a mass of evidence pointing to the poor performance of mergers and acquisitions in general – for acquiring firms, the stock market returns to acquisition are unequivocally negative.[32] Among these, mergers and acquisitions involving companies in different industries appear to perform especially poorly.[33]

Some of the most powerful evidence concerning the relationship between diversification and performance relates to the refocusing initiatives by a large number of North American and European companies. The evidence, ranging from conglomerates such as ITT and Hanson, to the oil majors, tobacco companies, and engineering companies such as Daimler-Benz, is that narrowing business scope leads to increased profitability and higher stock market valuation. Markides provides systematic evidence of the performance gains to diversified companies from divesting non-core activities.[34] This may reflect a changing relationship between diversification and profitability over time: the growing turbulence of the business environment may have increased the costs of managing complex, diversified corporations. As already noted, the stock market's verdict on diversification has certainly shifted over time, with highly diversified firms having their earnings valued at a discount rather than a premium to the overall market and takeover announcements being greeted by share price reductions for bidding firms.[35] As a result, diversified companies have fallen prey to leveraged buyout specialists seeking to add value through dismembering these companies.

Related and Unrelated Diversification Given the importance of economies of scope in shared resources and capabilities, it seems likely that diversification into *related* industries should be more profitable than diversification into *unrelated* industries. Empirical research initially supported this prediction. Rumelt discovered that companies that diversified into businesses closely related to their core activities were significantly more profitable than those that pursued unrelated diversification.[36] By 1982, Tom Peters and Robert Waterman were able to conclude: "virtually every academic study has concluded that unchanneled diversification is a losing proposition."[37] This observation provided the basis for one of Peters and Waterman's "golden rules of excellence" – *Stick to the Knitting*:

> *Our principal finding is clear and simple. Organizations that do branch out but stick very close to their knitting outperform the others. The most successful are those diversified around a single skill, the coating and bonding technology at 3M for example. The second group in descending order, comprise those companies that branch out into related fields, the leap from electric power generation turbines to jet engines from GE for example. Least successful, as a general rule, are those companies that diversify into a wide variety of fields. Acquisitions especially among this group tend to wither on the vine.*[38]

However, other evidence shattered this consistent picture. The apparent superiority of related diversifiers could be explained by the impact of risk and industry influences.[39] Some studies even found unrelated diversification to be more profitable than related.[40]

The lack of clear performance differences between related and unrelated diversification is troubling. Three factors may help explain the confused picture. First, related diversification may offer greater potential benefits, but may also pose more difficult management problems for companies such that the potential benefits are not realized. I shall address this issue in Chapter 16. Second, the tendency for related diversification to outperform unrelated diversification might be the result of poorly performing firms rushing into unrelated diversification.[41] Third, the distinction between "related" and "unrelated" diversification is not always clear. Relatedness refers to common resources and capabilities, not similarities of products and technologies. Thus, champagne and luggage are not obviously related products: however, LVMH applies similar brand management capabilities to them. Let us consider this issue further.

The Meaning of Relatedness in Diversification

If relatedness refers to the potential for sharing and transferring resources and capabilities between businesses, there are no unambiguous criteria to determine whether two industries are related – it all depends on the company undertaking the diversification. Empirical studies have defined relatedness in terms of similarities between industries in technologies and markets. These similarities emphasize relatedness at the *operational* level – in manufacturing, marketing, and distribution – typically activities where economies from resource sharing are small and achieving them is costly in management terms. Conversely, some of the most important sources of value creation within the diversified firm are the ability to apply common general management capabilities, strategic management systems, and resource allocation processes to different businesses. Such economies depend on the existence of *strategic* rather than *operational* commonalities among the different businesses within the diversified corporation.[42]

TABLE 15.2 The determinants of strategic relatedness between businesses

Corporate Management Tasks	Determinants of Strategic Similarity
Resource allocation	Similar sizes of capital investment projects Similar time spans of investment projects Similar sources of risk Similar general management skills required for business unit managers
Strategy formulation	Similar key success factors Similar stages of the industry life cycle Similar competitive positions occupied by each business within its industry
Performance management and control	Targets defined in terms of similar performance variables Similar time horizons for performance targets

SOURCE: R. M. GRANT, "ON DOMINANT LOGIC, RELATEDNESS, AND THE LINK BETWEEN DIVERSITY AND PERFORMANCE," *STRATEGIC MANAGEMENT JOURNAL* 9 (1988): 641.

● Berkshire Hathaway is involved in insurance, candy stores, furniture, kitchen knives, jewelry, and footwear. Despite this diversity, all these businesses have been selected on the basis of their ability to benefit from the unique style of corporate management established by chairman Warren Buffett and CEO Charles Munger.

● Richard Branson's Virgin Group covers a huge array of businesses from airlines to bridal stores. Yet, they share certain strategic similarities: almost all are startup companies that benefit from Branson's entrepreneurial zeal and expertise; almost all sell to final consumers and are in sectors that offer opportunities for innovative approaches to differentiation.

The essence of such strategic-level linkages is the ability to apply similar strategies, resource allocation procedures, and control systems across the different businesses within the corporate portfolio.[43] Table 15.2 lists some of the strategic factors that determine similarities among businesses in relation to corporate management activities.

Unlike operational relatedness, where the benefits of exploiting economies of scope in joint inputs are comparatively easy to forecast, and even to quantify, relatedness at the strategic level may be much more difficult to appraise.

Diversification decisions are determined more by perceived relatedness than by actual relatedness. Prahalad and Bettis use the term *dominant logic* to refer to managers' cognition of the rationale that links their different business activities.[44] Certainly, a dominant logic in the form of a common view within the company as to its identity and rationale is a critical precondition for effective integration across different businesses. (This issue is discussed further in Chapter 16.) There is a danger, however, that dominant logic may not be underpinned by any true economic synergies. In the same way that Allegis Corporation attempted to diversify around serving the needs of the traveler, so General Mills diversified into toys, fashion clothing, specialty retailing, and restaurants on the basis of "understanding the needs and wants of the homemaker."

Summary

Diversification is like sex: its attractions are obvious, often irresistible. Yet, the experience is often disappointing. For top management it is a minefield. The diversification experiences of large corporations are littered with expensive mistakes: Exxon's attempt to build Exxon Office Systems as a rival to Xerox and IBM, Vivendi's diversification from water and environmental services into media, entertainment, and telecoms, AT&T's entry into computers with its acquisition of NCR. Despite so many costly failures, the urge to diversify continues to captivate senior managers. Part of the problem is the divergence between managerial and shareholder goals. While diversification has offered meager rewards to shareholders, it is the fastest route to building vast corporate empires. A further problem is hubris. A company's success in one line of business tends to result in the top management team becoming over-confident of its ability to achieve similar success in other businesses.

Nevertheless, if companies are to survive and prosper over the long term they must change, and this change inevitably involves redefining the businesses in which the company operates. Hewlett-Packard and IBM are among the longest-established companies in the fast-paced US electronics industry. The success and longevity of both have been based on their ability to adapt their product lines to changing market opportunities. While HP has shifted from measuring instruments to computers and printers, to cameras and other imaging products, IBM has moved from typewriters to computers to consulting services. New entrepreneurial startups will typically pioneer the development of new industries; at the same time the sophisticated organizational capabilities of large, long-established corporations offer the potential for these companies to create value in other industries when their core businesses are in decline. The histories of 3M, Canon, Samsung, and DuPont show that diversification is a central theme in the process by which large companies successfully evolve. In most examples of successful long-term evolution, diversification did not represent a discontinuity, it was typically a logical step in which existing resources and capabilities were deployed outside of the existing portfolio of businesses.

If companies are to use diversification as part of their long-term adaptation and avoid the many errors that corporate executives have made in the past, then better strategic analysis of diversification decisions is essential. The objectives of diversification need to be clear and explicit. Shareholder value creation has provided a demanding and illuminating criterion with which to appraise investment in new business opportunities. Rigorous analysis may also counter the tendency for diversification to be a diversion, a form of escapism resulting from the unwillingness of top management to come to terms with difficult competitive circumstances in the firm's core businesses.

The analytic tools at our disposal for evaluating diversification decisions have developed greatly in recent years. Twenty years ago, diversification decisions were based on vague concepts of synergy that involved the identification of linkages between different industries. More specific analysis of the nature and extent of economies of scope in resources and capabilities has given greater precision to our analysis of synergy. At the same time, we recognize that economies of scope are insufficient to ensure that diversification creates value. A critical issue is the optimal organizational form for exploiting these economies. The transaction costs of markets must be compared against the management costs of the diversified corporation. These management costs depend heavily on the top management capabilities and management systems of the particular company. This type of analysis has caused many companies to realize that economies of scope often can be exploited more efficiently and with less risk through collaborative relationships with other companies rather than through diversification.

Self-Study Questions

1   An ice cream manufacturer is proposing to acquire a soup manufacturer on the basis that, first, its sales and profits will be more seasonally balanced and, second, from year to year, sales and profits will be less affected by variations in weather. Will this risk spreading create value for shareholders? Under what circumstances could this acquisition create benefits for shareholders?

2   Tata Group is one of India's largest companies, employing 203,000 people in many different industries, including steel, motor vehicles, watches and jewelry, telecommunications, financial services, management consulting, food products, tea, chemicals and fertilizers, satellite TV, hotels, motor vehicles, energy, IT, and construction. Such diversity far exceeds that of any North American or western European company. What are the conditions in India that might make such broad-based diversification both feasible and profitable?

3   Giorgio Armani SpA is an Italian private company owned mainly by the Armani family. Most of its clothing and accessories are produced and marketed by the company (some are manufactured by outside contractors). For other products, notably fragrances, cosmetics, and eyewear, Armani licenses its brand names to other companies. Armani is considering expanding into athletic clothing, hotels, and bridal shops. Advise Armani on whether these new businesses should be developed in-house, by joint ventures, or by licensing the Armani brands to specialist companies already within these fields.

4   General Electric, Berkshire Hathaway, and Richard Branson's Virgin Group each comprise a wide range of different businesses that appear to have few close technical or customer linkages. Are these examples of unrelated diversification and do the corporate and ownership links within each of the groups result in the creation of any value? If so, what are the sources of this value creation?

Appendix: Does Diversification Confer Market Power?

The potential for diversification to enhance profitability by increasing a firm's market power and suppressing competition has been a continuing interest for antitrust authorities in the United States and Europe – and more recently in Japan and South Korea. It has been claimed that large diversified companies can exercise market power through four mechanisms:

- *Predatory pricing.* Just as global corporations derive strength from their ability to finance competitive battles in individual markets through cross-subsidization, so multibusiness companies can use their size and diversity to discipline or even drive out specialized competitors in particular product markets through predatory pricing – cutting prices to below the level of rivals' costs. In 2003, following up complaints from AOL, the European Commission fined France Telecom 10 million euros for the predatory pricing of ISP services by its subsidiary Wanadoo.[45]

- *Bundling.* A diversified firm can extend its monopoly in one market into a related market by bundling the two products together. The US Justice Department claimed Microsoft abused its monopoly power in PC operating systems by bundling its Explorer web browser with Windows, thereby squeezing Netscape from the browser market. The European Union made a similar case against Microsoft regarding its bundling of its media player with Windows.[46]

- *Reciprocal dealing.* A diversified company can leverage its market share across its businesses by reciprocal buying arrangements. These involve offers of the type: "I'll buy from you if you buy from me." A recent case involved Intel, which refused to supply microprocessors to Intergraph Corporation unless Intergraph licensed certain technology to Intel free of charge.[47] The potential for reciprocal dealing is greatest in those emerging market economies where a few large companies span many sectors.

- *Mutual forbearance.* Corwin Edwards argued that:

  > When one large conglomerate enterprise competes with another, the two are likely to encounter each other in a considerable number of markets. The multiplicity of their contacts may blunt the edge of their competition. A prospect of advantage in one market from vigorous competition may be weighed against the danger of retaliatory forays by the competitor in other markets. Each conglomerate may adopt a live-and-let-live policy designed to stabilize the whole structure of the competitive relationship.[48]

  Game theory shows that such *multimarket competition* is likely to inhibit aggressive action in any one market for fear of triggering more generalized warfare.[49] Empirical evidence suggests that such behavior is most likely among companies that meet in multiple geographical markets for the same product or service – the airline industry, for example.[50] Such tendencies may also exist where diversified companies meet in multiple product markets.[51]

Notes

1 A. D. Chandler Jr., *Strategy and Structure: Chapters in the History of the Industrial Enterprise* (Cambridge, MA: MIT Press, 1962); R. P. Rumelt, *Strategy, Structure and Economic Performance* (Cambridge, MA: Harvard University Press, 1974); H. Itami, T. Kagono, H. Yoshihara, and S. Sakuma, "Diversification Strategies and Economic Performance," *Japanese Economic Studies* 11, no. 1 (1982): 78–110.

2 M. Goold and K. Luchs, "Why Diversify? Four Decades of Management Thinking," *Academy of Management Executive* 7, no. 3 (August 1993): 7–25.

3 G. F. Davis, K. A. Diekman, and C. F. Tinsley, "The Decline and Fall of the Conglomerate Firm in the 1980s: A Study in the De-Institutionalization of an Organizational Form," *American Sociological Review* 49 (1994): 547–70.

4   For a discussion of restructuring of diversified companies, see R. E. Hoskisson and M. A. Hitt, *Downscoping: How to Tame the Diversified Firm* (New York: Oxford University Press, 1994).

5   A. Shleifer and R. W. Vishny, "The Takeover Wave of the 1980s," *Science* 248 (July–September 1990): 747–9.

6   L. G. Franko, "The Death of Diversification: The Focusing of the World's Industrial Firms, 1980–2000," *Business Horizons* (July–August 2004): 41–50.

7   During 2004 and 2005 CEO turnover reached an all-time high. See Booz Allen Hamilton, *CEO Succession 2005* (2006, www.boozallen.com/publications).

8   B. Burrough, *Barbarians at the Gate: The Fall of RJR Nabisco* (New York: Harper & Row, 1990).

9   L. Laeven and R. Levine, "Is there a Diversification Discount in Financial Conglomerates?" *Journal of Financial Economics* 82 (2006).

10 T. Khanna and K. Palepu, "Why Focused Strategies May Be Wrong for Emerging Markets," *Harvard Business Review* (July–August 1997): 41–51; D. Kim, D. Kandemir, and S. T. Cavusgil, "The Role of Family Conglomerates in Emerging Markets," *Thunderbird International Business Review* 46 (January 2004): 7–20.

11 D. A. Ravenscraft and F. M. Scherer, "Divisional Selloff: A Hazard Analysis," in *Mergers, Selloffs and Economic Efficiency* (Washington, DC: Brookings Institute, 1987); M. E. Porter, "From Competitive Advantage to Corporate Strategy," *Harvard Business Review* (May–June 1987): 43–59.

12 These principles are outlined in any standard corporate finance text. See, for example, R. A. Brealey, S. Myers, and F. Allen, *Principles of Corporate Finance*, 8th edn (McGraw-Hill, 2006): Chapter 8.

13 See, for example, H. Levy and M. Sarnat, "Diversification, Portfolio Analysis and the Uneasy Case for Conglomerate Mergers," *Journal of Finance* 25 (1970): 795–802; R. H. Mason and M. B. Goudzwaard, "Performance of Conglomerate Firms: A Portfolio Approach," *Journal of Finance* 31 (1976): 39–48; J. F. Weston, K. V. Smith, and R. E. Shrieves, "Conglomerate Performance Using the Capital Asset Pricing Model," *Review of Economics and Statistics* 54 (1972): 357–63.

14 M. Lubatkin and S. Chetterjee, "Extending Modern Portfolio Theory into the Domain of Corporate Strategy: Does It Apply?" *Academy of Management Journal* 37 (1994): 109–36.

15 L. W. Lee, "Coinsurance and the Conglomerate Merger," *Journal of Finance* 32 (1977): 1527–37.

16 S. M. Bartram, "Corporate Risk Management as a Lever for Shareholder Value Creation," *Financial Markets, Institutions and Instruments* 9 (2000): 279–324.

17 M. E. Porter, "From Competitive Advantage to Corporate Strategy," *Harvard Business Review* (May–June 1987): 46.

18 M. Hayward and D. C. Hambrick, "Explaining the Premiums Paid for Large Acquisitions," *Administrative Science Quarterly* 42 (1997): 103–27.

19 A study of 68 diversifying ventures by established companies found that, on average, breakeven was not attained until the seventh and eighth years of operation: R. Biggadike, "The Risky Business of Diversification," *Harvard Business Review* (May–June 1979).

20 The formal definition of economies of scope is in terms of "sub-additivity." Economies of scope exist in the production of goods $x_1, x_2, \ldots, x_n$, if $C(X) < \sum_i C_i(x_i)$

where: $X = \sum_i(x_i)$
$C(X)$ is the cost of producing all n goods within a single firm
$\sum_i C_i(x_i)$ is the cost of producing the goods in n specialized firms.

See W. J. Baumol, J. C. Panzar, and R. D. Willig, *Contestable Markets and the Theory of Industry Structure* (New York: Harcourt Brace Jovanovich, 1982): 71–2.

21 Economies of scope can arise in consumption as well as in production: customers may prefer to buy different products from the same supplier. See T. Cottrell and B. R. Nault, "Product Variety and Firm Survival in Microcomputer Software," *Strategic Management Journal* 25 (2004): 1005–26.

22 More generally, research intensity is strongly associated with diversification. For the US, see C. H. Berry, *Corporate Growth and Diversification* (Princeton: Princeton University Press, 1975); for the UK, see R. M. Grant, "Determinants of the Interindustry Pattern of Diversification by U.K. Manufacturing Companies," *Bulletin of Economic Research* 29 (1977): 84–95.

23 There is some evidence to the contrary. See H. Park, T. A. Kruse, K. Suzuki, and K. Park, "Long-term Performance Following Mergers of Japanese Companies: The Effect of Diversification and Affiliation," *Pacific Basin Finance Journal* 14 (2006); P. R. Nayyar, "Performance Effects of Information Asymmetry and Economies of Scope in Diversified Service Firms," *Academy of Management Journal* 36 (1993): 28–57.

24 The role of capabilities in diversification is discussed in C. C. Markides and P. J. Williamson, "Related Diversification, Core Competencies and Corporate Performance," *Strategic Management Journal* 15 (Special Issue, 1994): 149–65.

25 This issue is examined more fully in D. J. Teece, "Towards an Economic Theory of the Multiproduct Firm," *Journal of Economic Behavior and Organization* 3 (1982): 39–63.

26 J. P. Liebeskind, "Internal Capital Markets: Benefits, Costs and Organizational Arrangements," *Organization Science* 11 (2000): 58–76.

27 D. Scharfstein and J. Stein, "The Dark Side of Internal Capital Markets: Divisional Rent Seeking and Inefficient Investment," *Journal of Finance* 55 (2000): 2537–64; V. Maksimovic and G. Phillips, "Do Conglomerate Firms Allocate Resources Inefficiently Across Industries?" *Journal of Finance* 57 (2002): 721–67; R. Rajan,

H. Servaes, and L. Zingales, "The Cost of Diversity: The Diversification Discount and Inefficient Investment," *Journal of Finance* 55 (2000): 35–84.

28 C. Kaye and J. Yuwono, "Conglomerate Discount or Premium? How Some Diversified Companies Create Exceptional Value," Marakon Associates (2003).

29 R. M. Grant, A. P. Jammine, and H. Thomas, "Diversity, Diversification and Performance in British Manufacturing Industry," *Academy of Management Journal* 31 (1988): 771–801.

30 L. E. Palich, L. B. Cardinal, and C. C. Miller, "Curvilinearity in the Diversification-Performance Linkage: An Examination of over Three Decades of Research," *Strategic Management Journal* 22 (2000): 155–74.

31 N. Harper and S. P. Viguerie, "Are You Too Focused?" *McKinsey Quarterly* (2002 Special Edition): 29–37.

32 G. Andrade, M. Mitchell, and E. Stafford, "New Evidence and Perspectives on Mergers," *Journal of Economic Perspectives* 5, no. 3 (2001): 103–20.

33 J. D. Martin and A. Sayrak, "Corporate Diversification and Shareholder Value: A Survey of Recent Literature," *Journal of Corporate Finance* 9 (2003): 37–57.

34 C. C. Markides, "Consequences of Corporate Refocusing: Ex Ante Evidence," *Academy of Management Journal* 35 (1992): 398–412; C. C. Markides, "Diversification, Restructuring and Economic Performance," *Strategic Management Journal* 16 (1995): 101–18.

35 G. A. Jarrell, J. A. Brickly, and J. M. Netter, "The Market for Corporate Control: Empirical Evidence Since 1980," *Journal of Economic Perspectives* 2, no. 1 (Winter 1988): 49–68.

36 R. P. Rumelt, *Strategy, Structure and Economic Performance* (Cambridge, MA: Harvard University Press, 1974).

37 Tom Peters and Robert Waterman, *In Search of Excellence* (New York: Harper & Row, 1982): 294.

38 Ibid.

39 H. K. Christensen and C. A. Montgomery, "Corporate Economic Performance: Diversification Strategy versus Market Structure," *Strategic Management Journal* 2 (1981): 327–43; R. A. Bettis, "Performance Differences in Related and Unrelated Diversified Firms," *Strategic Management Journal* 2 (1981): 379–83.

40 See, for example, A. Michel and I. Shaked, "Does Business Diversification Affect Performance?" *Financial Management* 13, no. 4 (1984): 18–24; G. A. Luffman and R. Reed, *The Strategy and Performance of British Industry, 1970–80* (London: Macmillan, 1984).

41 C. Park, "The Effects of Prior Performance on the Choice between Related and Unrelated Acquisitions," *Journal of Management Studies* 39 (2002): 1003–19.

42 For a discussion of relatedness in diversification, see J. Robins and M. F. Wiersema, "A Resource-Based Approach to the Multibusiness Firm: Empirical Analysis of Portfolio Interrelationships and Corporate Financial Performance," *Strategic Management Journal* 16 (1995): 277–300; J. Robins and M. F. Wiersema, "The Measurement of Corporate Portfolio Strategy: Analysis of the Content Validity of Related Diversification Indexes," *Strategic Management Journal* 24 (2002): 39–59.

43 R. M. Grant, "On Dominant Logic, Relatedness, and the Link Between Diversity and Performance," *Strategic Management Journal* 9 (1988): 639–42.

44 C. K. Prahalad and R. A. Bettis, "The Dominant Logic: A New Linkage Between Diversity and Performance," *Strategic Management Journal* 7 (1986): 485–502.

45 "Wanadoo Fined €10m for Predatory Pricing," *Financial Times* (July 17, 2003).

46 "Microsoft on Trial," *Economist* (April 28, 2006) (www.economist.com).

47 E. D. Cavanagh, "Reciprocal Dealing: A Rebirth?" *St. Johns Law Review* 75 (2001): 633–47.

48 US Senate, Subcommittee on Antitrust and Monopoly Hearings, *Economic Concentration*, Part 1, Congress, 1st session (1965): 45.

49 B. D. Bernheim and M. D. Whinston, "Multimarket Contact and Collusive Behavior," *Rand Journal of Economics* 2 (1990): 1–26.

50 In the US airline industry, extensive multimarket contact resulted in a reluctance to compete on routes dominated by one or other of the airlines. See J. A. C. Baum and H. J. Korn, "Competitive Dynamics of Interfirm Rivalry," *Academy of Management Review* 39 (1996): 255–91.

51 S. Jayachandran, J. Gimeno, and P. R. Varadarajan, "The Theory of Multimarket Competition: A Synthesis and Implications for Marketing Strategy," *Journal of Marketing* 63 (July 1999): 49–66.

16

Managing the Multibusiness Corporation

Some have argued that single-product businesses have a focus that gives them an advantage over multibusiness companies like our own – and perhaps they would have, but only if we neglect our own overriding advantage: the ability to share the ideas that are the result of wide and rich input from a multitude of global sources.

GE businesses share technology, design, compensation and personnel evaluation systems, manufacturing practices, and customer and country knowledge. Gas Turbines shares manufacturing technology with Aircraft Engines; Motors and Transportation Systems work together on new propulsion systems; Lighting and Medical Systems collaborate to improve x-ray tube processes; and GE Capital provides innovative financing packages that help all our businesses around the globe. Supporting all this is a management system that fosters and rewards this sharing and teamwork, and, increasingly, a culture that makes it reflexive and natural at every level and corner of our Company.

—JACK WELCH, CHAIRMAN, GENERAL ELECTRIC COMPANY, 1981–2001

OUTLINE

Introduction and Objectives

In the last chapter, we concluded that the case for diversification rests ultimately on the ability of the diversified corporation to exploit sources of value from operating across multiple businesses more effectively than can specialized firms linked by markets. Chapters 13 and 14 arrived at the same conclusion in relation to vertical integration and multinational operations. Hence, multibusiness companies[1] – whether vertically integrated, multinational, or diversified across multiple products – face two critical issues. First, can value be created through the relationships between businesses that span different activities or different markets? Second, how should a company be structured and managed to exploit these sources of value? Chapters 13, 14, and 15 addressed the first question in relation to vertical, multinational, and multiproduct scope. This chapter addresses the second question.

To manage multiple activities in multiple markets, multibusiness corporations typically use *multidivisional structures* comprising several divisions or subsidiaries, coordinated by a corporate headquarters. We shall examine the structures, management systems, and leadership styles through which these – typically large, complex – corporations formulate and implement their strategies. As we will see, corporate strategy is not simply a matter of answering the question: "What businesses should we be in?" Some of the most difficult issues of corporate strategy concern the roles and activities of the corporate head office and the relationships between the businesses and the corporate center. These issues include: managing the business portfolio; resource allocation; strategic planning; controlling business unit performance; and coordinating across businesses.

By the time you have completed this chapter you will be able to:

● Recognize the principal organizational features of the multibusiness corporation.

● Apply the techniques of portfolio analysis to corporate strategy decisions.

● Analyze the potential for value creation through restructuring a multibusiness corporation.

● Understand how corporate headquarters manages its individual businesses through strategic planning and financial control and by managing linkages across businesses.

● Analyze the fit between a firm's corporate strategy, organization structure, management systems, and leadership style.

The Structure of the Multibusiness Company

Chapter 1 introduced the distinction between business strategy and corporate strategy and observed that, within the multibusiness company, corporate management takes primary responsibility for corporate strategy, and divisional management takes primary responsibility for business strategy. This corporate/divisional distinction is the basic feature of the multibusiness corporation. Whether we are referring to a multiproduct company (such as Viacom), a multinational company (such as SAB-Miller), or a vertically integrated corporation (such as Alcoa), almost all multibusiness companies are organized as multidivisional structures where business decisions are located at the business level and the corporate center exercises overall coordination and control. As we noted in Chapter 6, the emergence of the multidivisional structure during the early 20th century was one of the key innovations in the history of management since it facilitated the development of the large diversified, multinational corporations.

The allocation of decision making between corporate and divisional levels has shifted over time. The initial rationale for the multidivisional firm was the separation of strategic and operational decision making. During recent decades, more strategic decision making has been devolved to the divisional and business unit levels, while corporate headquarters have taken responsibility for corporate strategy and the management of overall corporate performance. Our primary focus is to analyze and understand the role of the corporate center in managing the multibusiness company.

The Theory of the M-form

Once Alfred Chandler had documented the origin and diffusion of the multidivisional form, it was left to Oliver Williamson to theorize about its rationale.[2] Williamson identified four key efficiency advantages of the divisionalized firm (or, in his terminology, the *M-form*):

1   *Adaptation to "bounded rationality."* If managers are limited in their cognitive, information-processing, and decision-making capabilities, the top management team cannot be responsible for all coordination and decision making within a complex organization. The M-form permits decision making to be dispersed.

2   *Allocation of decision making.* Decision-making responsibilities should be separated according to the frequency with which different types of decisions are made. The M-form allows high frequency decisions (e.g., operating decisions) to be made at divisional level and decisions that are made infrequently (e.g., strategic decisions) to be made at corporate level.

3   *Minimizing coordination costs.* In the functional organization, decisions concerning a particular product or business area must pass up to the top of the company where all the relevant information and expertise can be brought to bear. In the divisionalized firm, so long as close coordination between different business areas is not necessary, most decisions concerning a particular business can be made at the divisional level. This eases the information and decision-making burden on top management.

4   *Avoiding goal conflict.* In functional organizations, department heads emphasize functional goals over those of the organization as a whole. In multidivisional companies, divisional heads, as general managers, are more likely to pursue profit goals that are consistent with the goals of the company as a whole.

As a result, the multidivisional firm can help solve two key problems of large, managerially controlled corporations:

- *Allocation of resources.* Resource allocation within any administrative structure is a political process in which power, status, and influence can triumph over purely commercial considerations.[3] To the extent that the multidivisional company can create a competitive internal capital market in which capital is allocated according to financial and strategic criteria, it can avoid much of the politicization inherent in purely hierarchical systems. The multidivisional company can achieve this through operating an internal capital market where budgets are linked to past and projected divisional profitability, and individual projects are subject to a standardized appraisal and approval process.

- *Resolution of agency problems.* A related shortcoming of the modern corporation is that owners (shareholders) wish to maximize the value of the firm, while their agents (top managers) are more interested in salaries, security, and power. Given the limited power of shareholders to discipline and replace managers, and the tendency for top management to dominate the board of directors, the multidivisional form may act as a partial remedy to the agency problem. The rationale is as follows: by acting as an interface between the stockholders and the divisional managers, corporate management can enforce adherence to profit goals. With divisions designated as profit centers, financial performance can readily be monitored by the head office, and divisional managers can be held responsible for performance failures. So long as corporate management is focused on shareholder goals, the multidivisional structure can support a system for enforcing profit maximization at the divisional level. General Electric, Emerson Electric, and BP are prime examples of multidivisional companies where the corporate headquarters has been highly effective in creating profit-oriented systems and cultures.

Oliver Williamson explains these merits of the multidivisional corporation as follows:

> *The M-form conglomerate can be thought of as substituting an administrative interface between an operating division and the stockholders where a market interface had existed previously. Subject to the condition that the conglomerate does not diversify to excess, in the sense that it cannot competently evaluate and allocate funds among the diverse activities in which it is engaged, the substitution of internal organization can have beneficial effects in goal pursuit, monitoring, staffing, and resource allocation respects. The goal-pursuit advantage is that which accrues to M-form organizations in general: since the general management of an M-form conglomerate is disengaged from operating matters, a presumption that the general office favors profits over functional goals is warranted. Relatedly, the general office can be regarded as an agent of the stockholders whose purpose is to monitor the operations of the constituent parts. Monitoring benefits are realized in the degree to which internal monitors enjoy advantages over external monitors in access to information – which they arguably do. The differential ease with which the general office can change managers and reassign duties where performance failures or distortions are detected is responsible for the staffing advantage. Resource allocation benefits are realized because cash flows no longer return automatically to their origins but instead revert to the center, thereafter to be allocated among competing uses in accordance with prospective yields.*[4]

Can the corporate general office really be relied upon to act as an "agent of the stockholders"? Despite evidence that multidivisional structures are, in general, more effective for diversified firms than alternative structural forms,[5] some of the most notorious examples of chief executives operating their companies as personal fiefdoms are found among diversified, divisionalized corporations. Armand Hammer at Occidental Petroleum, Howard Hughes at Hughes Corporation, Ken Lay at Enron, Dennis Kozlowski at Tyco, and Jean-Marie Messier at Vivendi Universal all pursued empire building at the expense of shareholder return.[6] Corporate executives of diversified companies may be less emotionally committed to particular businesses, but this does not necessarily mean that they are more predisposed to shareholder return than to Napoleonic personal grandeur.

Problems of Divisionalized Firms

In principle, the divisionalized corporation reconciles the benefits of decentralization with those of coordination. As Henry Mintzberg points out, in practice, the multidivisional structure suffers from two important rigidities that limit decentralization and adaptability:[7]

- *Constraints on decentralization.* Although operational authority in the M-form firm is dispersed to the divisional level, the individual divisions often feature highly centralized power that is partly a reflection of the divisional president's personal accountability to the head office. In addition, the operational freedom of the divisional management exists only so long as the corporate head office is satisfied with divisional performance. Monthly financial reviews typically mean that variances in divisional performance precipitate speedy corporate intervention.

● *Standardization of divisional management.* In principle, the divisional form permits divisional management to be differentiated by their business needs. In practice, there are powerful forces for standardizing control systems and management styles which may inhibit individual divisions from achieving their potential. The imposition by Exxon of its standard financial control systems and hierarchical culture on its entrepreneurial IT subsidiary, Exxon Office Systems, was a key factor in the venture's eventual failure. The difficulties that many large, mature corporations experience with new business development often result from applying to new businesses the same management systems designed for existing businesses.[8]

The Role of Corporate Management

How does the corporate headquarters create value within the multibusiness corporation? If the multibusiness corporation is to be viable, then the additional profits generated by bringing several businesses under common ownership and control must exceed the costs of the corporate headquarters. To explore the potential for corporate management to add value, we must consider the role and functions of corporate managers.

So far we have identified corporate headquarters primarily with corporate strategy: determining the scope of the firm and allocating resources between its different parts. In fact, the responsibilities of corporate management also include administrative and leadership roles with regard to implementing corporate strategy, participating in divisional strategy formulation, coordinating the different divisions, and fostering overall cohesion, identity, and direction within the company. These functions extend beyond what is normally thought of as "corporate strategy." For this reason, Goold, Campbell, and Alexander refer to the role of the corporate headquarters in the multibusiness company as "corporate parenting."[9]

There are three main activities through which corporate management adds value to the multibusiness company:

● Managing the corporate portfolio, including acquisitions, divestments, and resource allocation.
● Exercising guidance and control over individual businesses, including influencing business strategy formulation and managing financial performance.
● Managing linkages among businesses by sharing and transferring resources and capabilities.

Let us consider each of these corporate management activities and establish the conditions under which they can create value.

Managing the Corporate Portfolio

The basic question of corporate strategy is: "What business are we in?" Hence, corporate strategy is concerned with the composition and balance of a company's portfolio of businesses. The key decisions relate to extensions of the portfolio (acquisitions, mergers, new ventures, and market entries), deletions from the portfolio (divestments), and changes in the balance of the portfolio through the allocation and reallocation of capital and other resources. While additions to and deletions from the corporate portfolio are typically major but infrequent strategic decisions, resource allocation among businesses is an ongoing strategic responsibility of corporate management. *Portfolio planning models* are useful techniques for appraising a firm's overall business portfolio and for formulating strategies for the individual businesses.

GE and the Development of Strategic Planning

Portfolio planning techniques were one outcome of the pioneering work in corporate strategy initiated by General Electric at the end of the 1960s.[10] Indeed, General Electric has been a leading source of corporate strategy concepts and innovations for more than half a century. GE has been among the top five members of *Fortune* magazine's "America's Most Admired Corporations" since the listings began.

At the end of the 1960s, GE comprised 46 divisions and over 190 businesses. To manage this sprawling industrial empire more effectively, GE launched a series of initiatives together with the Boston Consulting Group, McKinsey & Co., Arthur D. Little, and the Harvard Business School. The result was three innovations that would transform corporate strategy formulation in multibusiness companies:

- *Portfolio planning models* – two-dimensional, matrix-based frameworks to evaluate business unit performance, formulate business unit strategies, and assess the overall balance of the corporate portfolio.

- *The strategic business unit (SBU)* – the basic organizational unit for which it is meaningful to formulate a separate competitive strategy. Typically, an SBU is a business consisting of a number of closely related products and for which most costs are not shared with other businesses. McKinsey recommended the reorganization of GE into SBUs for formulating and monitoring business strategies.

- *The PIMS database* – an internal database comprising strategic, market, and performance data on individual business units. Using PIMS data, the impact on profitability of market structure and different strategic variables can be estimated.[11]

Portfolio Planning: The GE/McKinsey Matrix

The best-known products of GE's corporate planning initiatives of 1969–72 are the portfolio planning models developed by McKinsey, BCG, and A. D. Little. The basic idea was to represent the businesses of the diversified company within a simple graphical framework that could be used to guide strategy analysis in four areas:

1 *Allocating resources.* Portfolio analysis examines the position of a business unit in relation to the two primary sources of profitability: industry attractiveness and the competitive advantage of the firm. These indicate the attractiveness of the business for future investment.

2 *Formulating business unit strategy.* The current positioning of the business in relation to industry attractiveness and potential competitive advantage indicates the strategic approach that should be taken with regard to capital investment and can point to opportunities for repositioning the business.

3 *Analyzing portfolio balance.* The primary usefulness of a single diagrammatic representation of the company's different businesses is the ability of corporate management to take an overall view of the company. This permits planning the overall balance of:

- *cash flows*: by balancing cash-generating businesses against cash-absorbing businesses, the diversified company can achieve independence from external capital markets;
- *growth*: by balancing a mix of businesses in different stages of their life cycles, the diversified company can stabilize its growth rate and achieve continuity over time.

4 *Setting performance targets.* To the extent that positioning with regard to industry attractiveness and competitive position determine profit potential, portfolio-planning matrices can assist in setting performance targets for individual businesses.

The two axes of the GE/McKinsey matrix (see Figure 16.1) are the familiar sources of superior profitability for a firm: *industry attractiveness* and *competitive advantage*. Industry attractiveness combines the following factors: market size and growth rate; industry profitability (return on sales over three years); cyclicality; inflation recovery (ability to cover cost increases by higher productivity and increased prices); and importance of overseas markets (ratio of international to US sales). Business unit competitive advantage is computed on the basis of the following variables: market share; competitive position with regard to quality, technology, manufacturing, distribution, marketing, and cost; and return on sales relative to that of leading competitors.

Strategy recommendations are shown by three regions of Figure 16.1:

- Business units that rank high on both dimensions have excellent profit potential and should be *grown*.
- Those that rank low on both dimensions have poor prospects and should be *harvested* (managed to maximize cash flow with little new investment).
- In-between businesses are candidates for a *hold* strategy.

FIGURE 16.1 The GE/McKinsey portfolio planning matrix

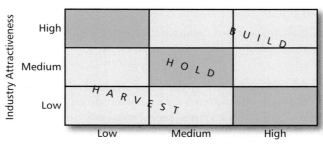

FIGURE 16.2 The BCG growth–share matrix

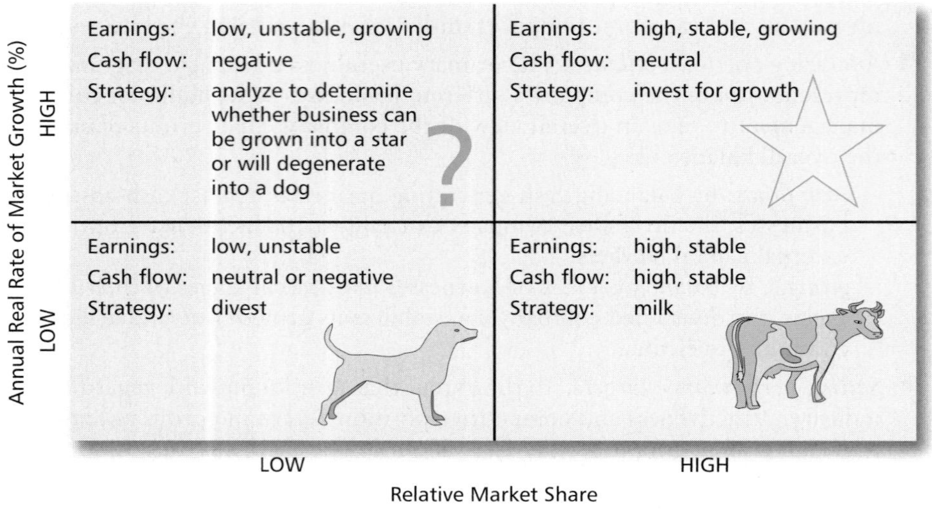

Portfolio Planning: BCG's Growth–Share Matrix

The Boston Consulting Group's matrix is similar: it also uses industry attractiveness and competitive position to compare the strategic positions of different businesses. However, unlike the McKinsey matrix, it uses single variables for each axis: industry attractiveness is measured by *rate of market growth*, competitive advantage by *relative market share* (the business unit's market share relative to that of its largest competitor).

The four quadrants of the BCG matrix predict patterns of profits and cash flow and offer strategy recommendations as to appropriate strategies. These are summarized in Figure 16.2.

The BCG growth–share matrix is even more elementary than the McKinsey matrix, yet, in providing a first-cut analysis, this simplicity is also a virtue:

- Because information on only two variables is required, the analysis can be prepared easily and quickly.
- It assists senior managers in cutting through the vast quantities of detailed information on individual businesses to reveal some key differences in their positioning.
- The analysis is versatile – it can be applied not only to business units, but also to analyzing the positioning and performance potential of different products, brands, distribution channels, and customers.
- It provides a useful point of departure for more detailed analysis and discussion of the competitive positions and strategies of individual business units.

The value of combining several elements of strategically useful information in a single graphical display is illustrated by the application of the BCG matrix to Time Warner (see Figure 16.3). This shows each business's positioning with regard to market growth and market share; it also indicates the relative size of each business and movements in its strategic position over time.

FIGURE 16.3 Applying the BCG matrix to Time Warner Inc.

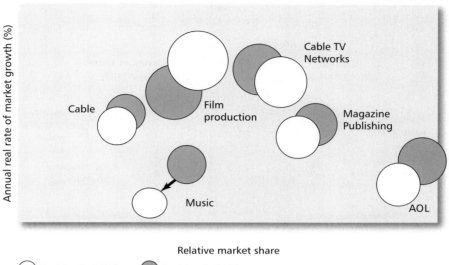

Since the 1980s, portfolio planning matrices (including those of BCG and McKinsey) have lost their popularity as analytic tools. Among their weaknesses are the following:

- Both are gross oversimplifications of the factors that determine industry attractiveness and competitive advantage. This is especially true of the BCG matrix, which uses just two variables: market share is a crude indicator of competitive advantage; market growth is a poor proxy for profit potential.

- The positioning of businesses within the matrix is highly susceptible to measurement choices. For example, relative market share in the BCG matrix depends critically on how markets are defined. Is BMW's North American auto business a "dog" because it holds about 2% of the total auto market, or a cash cow because BMW is market leader in the luxury car segment? Booz Allen Hamilton suggest that "dog" businesses may, in fact, offer attractive development opportunities.[12]

- The approach assumes that every business is completely independent. Where linkages exist between business units, viewing each as a standalone business inevitably leads to suboptimal strategy choices. As a standalone business, Disney's theatrical productions (such as *Lion King*) look like a dog. This ignores the fact that Disney's theatrical productions profitably exploit themes and characters developed for other media.

Value Creation Through Corporate Restructuring

During the past two decades, the major theme of corporate strategy has been re-focusing and divestment. As a result, the key issue for portfolio analysis is whether the market value of the company is greater *with* a particular business or *without* it (i.e., selling it to another owner or spinning it off as a separate entity).

FIGURE 16.4 The McKinsey restructuring pentagon

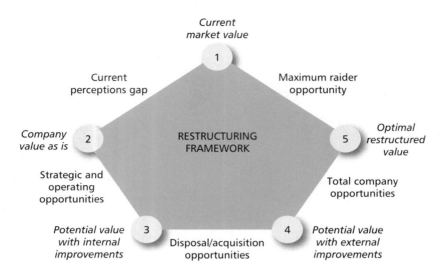

SOURCE: T. E. COPELAND, T. KOLLER, AND J. MURRIN, *VALUATION* (NEW YORK: WILEY, 1990), © 1990. REPRINTED BY PERMISSION OF JOHN WILEY & SONS, INC.

Applying the techniques of shareholder value analysis outlined in Chapter 2, McKinsey & Co. has proposed a systematic framework for increasing the market value of multibusiness companies through corporate restructuring.[13] McKinsey's *pentagon framework* consists of a five-stage process, illustrated in Figure 16.4. The five stages of the analysis are:

1 *The current market value of the company.* The starting point of the analysis is the current market value of the company, which comprises the value of equity plus the value of debt. (As we know from Chapter 2, this equals the net present value of the anticipated cash flow to the company.)

2 *The value of the company as is.* Even without any changes to strategy or operations, it may be possible to value simply by managing external perceptions of a company's future prospects. Over the past ten years, companies have devoted increasing attention to managing investor expectations by increasing the flow of information to shareholders and investment analysts and establishing departments of investor relations.

3 *The potential value of the company with internal improvements.* As we shall see in the next section, the corporate head office of a company has opportunities for increasing the overall value of the company by making strategic and operational improvements to individual businesses that increase their cash flows. Strategic opportunities include exploring growth opportunities such as investing in global expansion, repositioning a business in relation to customers and competitors, or strategic outsourcing. Operating improvements would include cost-cutting opportunities and taking advantage of the potential to raise prices.

4 *The potential value of the company with external improvements.* Once top management has determined the value of its constituent businesses and of the company as a whole, it is in a position to determine whether changes in the business portfolio will increase overall company value. The key issue is whether an individual business, even after strategic and operating

improvements have been made, could be sold for a price that is greater than its potential value to the company.

5 *The optimum restructured value of the company.* This is the maximum value of a company once all the potential gains from changing investor perceptions, making internal improvements, and taking advantage of external opportunities have been exploited. The difference between the maximum restructured value and the current market value represents the profit potential available to a corporate raider from taking advantage of the restructuring opportunities.

This type of analysis has been traditionally associated with leveraged buyout specialists and other corporate raiders. However, faced with the increasing threat of acquisitions, such analysis is increasingly being undertaken by corporate senior managers themselves. The restructuring measures undertaken by the oil majors during 1986–92 exemplify this process: increasing the value of existing businesses through cost cutting, while taking advantage of external opportunities for trading assets and selling businesses.[14]

Managing Individual Businesses

Despite the emphasis given to economies of scope and other types of linkage among the businesses within the multibusiness firm, some of the most important opportunities for corporate headquarters to create value arise from what Goold, Campbell, and Alexander call "standalone influence." This relates to the corporate parent's ability to:

> . . . *appoint the general manager of each business and influence management development and succession planning within the businesses. It can approve or reject budgets, strategic plans, and capital expenditure proposals and it can influence the shape and implementation of these plans and proposals. It can provide advice and policy guidance to the businesses. The parent also influences the businesses by the hints and pressures passed on through both formal and informal line management meetings and contacts, and, more indirectly, through the corporate culture.*[15]

There are two primary means by which the corporate headquarters can exert control over the different businesses of the corporation. It can control decisions, through requiring that particular categories of decision – typically those involving significant resource commitments – are referred upward for corporate approval. Thus, a company may require that all capital expenditure decisions involving a commitment of funds of over $20 million are approved by the executive committee. Alternatively, corporate headquarters may seek to control businesses through controlling performance targets, backed by incentives and penalties to motivate the attainment of these targets. The distinction is between *input* and *output* controls: the company can control the inputs into the process (i.e., the decisions) or it can control the outputs (the performance). Although most companies use a combination of input and output controls, there is an unavoidable tradeoff between the two: more of one implies less of the other. If a company exerts tight control over divisional decisions, it must accept the performance outcomes that arise from those decisions. If the company exerts rigorous controls relating to performance in terms of annual profit targets, it must give divisional managers the freedom to make the decisions necessary to achieve these targets. Corporate influence over business strategy formulation is primarily a form of "input control"; corporate financial control – especially the setting of performance targets – is a form of "output control."

The Strategic Planning System

In Chapter 1, I identified corporate strategy as being set at the corporate level and business strategy as set at the business level. In reality, business strategies are formulated jointly by corporate and divisional managers. In most diversified, divisionalized companies, business strategies are initiated by divisional managers and the role of corporate managers is to probe, appraise, amend, and approve divisional strategy proposals. The critical issue for corporate management is to create a strategy-making process that reconciles the decentralized decision making essential to fostering flexibility, responsiveness, and a sense of ownership at the business level, with the ability of the corporate level to bring to bear its knowledge, perspective, and responsibility for the shareholder interest. Achieving an optimal blend of business-level initiative and corporate-level guidance and discipline is a difficult challenge for the multibusiness corporation. Common to the success of General Electric, Exxon Mobil, Samsung, and Unilever is a system of strategic management that has managed this difficult tradeoff between business initiative and corporate control. Strategy Capsule 16.1 describes key elements of the strategic planning process at Exxon.

Rethinking the Strategic Planning System   For the past 25 years the strategic planning systems of large firms have been bombarded by criticism from academics and consultants. Two features of corporate strategic planning systems have attracted particular scorn:

- *Strategic planning systems don't make strategy*. Ever since Henry Mintzberg attacked the "rational design" school of strategy (see Chapter 1), strategic planning systems have been castigated as ineffective for formulating strategy. In particular, formalized strategic planning has been viewed as the enemy of flexibility, creativity, and entrepreneurship. Marakon consultants Mankins and Steele have observed that "strategic planning doesn't really influence most companies' strategy."[16] The principal reasons are its rigid annual cycle and its preoccupation with business unit plans – as a result "senior executives . . . make the decisions that really shape their companies' strategies . . . outside the planning process typically in an ad hoc fashion without rigorous analysis or productive debate." The approach they identify at companies such as Microsoft, Boeing, and Textron is what they call "continuous, decision-oriented planning" where the emphasis is, first, on analyzing the critical issues that face the company and, second, on decision making. The central feature of the process is that the top management team – the executive committee – becomes the key drivers of the strategy-making process.

- *Weak strategy execution*. A major theme of recent years has been the need for more effective strategy execution by large companies. This means a more effective linkage between strategic planning and operational management. Larry Bossidy and Ram Charan point to the key role of *milestones* that can ". . . bring reality to a strategic plan."[17] Thus, to keep Honeywell's strategy for cost cutting in its automotive business on track, managers developed short- and medium-term milestones for shifting production overseas. As was

STRATEGY CAPSULE 16.1
Strategic Planning at Exxon

Exxon (now Exxon Mobil) is the world's biggest company (in terms of revenue and market value) and is the most financially successful oil and gas major. Exxon's strategic planning system has successfully reconciled long-term strategic planning with rigorous, short-term financial control; and strong centralized direction with flexible, responsive, business-level decision making. Exxon's strategic planning process follows an annual cycle that is similar to the "generic" strategic planning process outlined in Chapter 6 (see Figure 6.6).

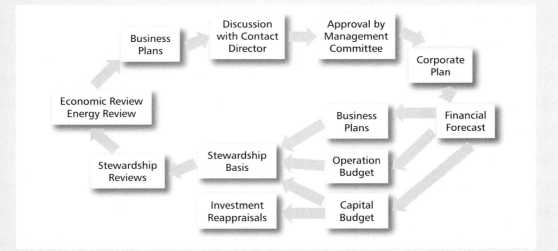

The principal stages of the planning cycle are as follows:

1 *Economic Review and Energy Review* are forecasts of the economy and energy markets prepared in spring by the Corporate Planning Department to provide a basis for strategic planning.

2 *Business Plans* are developed during the spring and summer by individual businesses and are aggregated and refined at the divisional level. Their time horizon is ten years for upstream, five years for downstream and chemicals. Prior to discussion, negotiation, and approval by the Management Committee, the plans are discussed with each division's Contact Director and evaluated by the Corporate Planning Department (during October).

3 *The Corporate Plan* results from the aggregation of individual business plans. The approved business and corporate plans then provide the basis for the financial and performance plans (formulated during November).

4 *The Financial Forecast* comprises forecasts of revenues, operating costs, capital expenditures, interest and other expenses, income, and cash flow for divisions and for the company as a whole over a two-year period.

5 *The Operating and Capital Budgets* are set for the upcoming year (the first year of the plans).

6 *The Stewardship Basis* comprises annual targets against which the next year's performance by each division will be judged. They include financial objectives, operating targets, safety and environmental objectives, and strategy mileposts.

7 *Stewardship Reviews*. In February of each year, each division's performance for the previous year is evaluated against its stewardship objectives. These reviews involve presentations by the divisional top management to the Management Committee.

8 *Investment Reappraisals* occur in August and September and involve the divisions reporting back on the outcomes of specific investment projects.

In addition to this annual strategic planning cycle, *Strategic Studies* are ad hoc projects by the Corporate Planning Department that address specific issues such as country and product studies and responses to major market, technological, and political changes.

Exxon's strategic management system features clearly defined corporate, divisional, and business unit responsibilities (with matching accountability). At the same time there is close communication and coordination between these levels. This takes place formally through the strategic planning and financial control system, and informally through ongoing communication between the Management Committee (composed of Exxon's executive board members) and the Divisional Presidents and their management teams. Each member of the Management Committee is "Contact Director" for two or three divisions. The dialog between the Divisional Presidents and the Contact Directors is a mechanism for knowledge sharing and initiating strategic changes that adds flexibility to the formal strategic planning process. The result is a system of strategy formulation and performance management that is simultaneously top–down and bottom–up.

Fundamental to Exxon's close integration of financial management with strategic planning is Exxon's emphasis on *stewardship* – a doctrine of managerial responsibility and accountability that makes each executive personally responsible to the corporation and its shareholders.

noted in Chapter 2, the *balanced scorecard* is another technique for translating strategy into specific functional and operational targets. Building on their balanced scorecard approach, Kaplan and Norton argue that *strategy maps* are used to plot the relationships between strategic actions and overall goals.[18] To ensure a close linkage between strategic planning and strategy implementation they recommend that companies establish an *office of strategy management*.[19] How does this differ from the familiar corporate planning department? The key, according to Kaplan and Norton, is that the office of strategy management is responsible not just for managing the annual strategic planning cycle but also for overseeing the execution of strategic plans, including: "communicating corporate strategy, ensuring that enterprise-level plans are translated into the plans of the various units and departments, executing strategic initiatives to deliver in the grand plan, and aligning employees' competency development plans and their personal goals and incentives with strategic objectives."[20]

Performance Control and the Budgeting Process

Most multidivisional companies operate a dual planning process: strategic planning concentrates on the medium and long term, financial planning controls short-term performance. Typically, the first year of the strategic plan includes the performance plan for the upcoming year in terms of an operating budget, a capital expenditure budget, and strategy targets relating to market share, output and employment levels, and specific strategic milestones. Annual performance plans are agreed between senior business-level and corporate-level managers. They are monitored on a monthly or quarterly basis, and are reviewed more extensively in meetings between business and corporate management after the end of each financial year.

The corporate head office is responsible for setting and monitoring performance targets for the individual divisions. Performance targets may be financial (return on invested capital, gross margin, growth of sales revenue), strategic (market share, rate of new product introduction, market penetration, quality), or operational (output, productivity). Performance targets are primarily annual, with less detailed performance targets set for up to five years ahead. Corporate emphasis is on annual targets which are monitored on a monthly and quarterly basis to detect deviations.

Performance targets are supported by incentives including financial returns (bonuses, enhanced authority, recognition) and sanctions. Some companies have combined demanding performance goals and powerful incentives to create an intensely motivating environment for divisional managers. At ITT, Geneen's obsession with highly detailed performance monitoring, ruthless interrogation of divisional executives, and generous rewards for success developed a highly motivated, strongly capable group of young, senior executives who were willing to work relentless long hours. They demanded as high a standard of performance from their subordinates as Geneen did of them.[21] Creating an intense, performance-driven culture requires unremitting focus on a few quantitative performance targets that can be monitored on a short-term basis. PepsiCo's obsession with monthly market share nourishes an intense, marketing-oriented culture. As CEO Indra Nooyi noted, "We are a very objective-driven company. We spend a lot of time up front setting objectives and our guys rise to the challenge of meeting those objectives. When they don't meet the objectives, we don't have to flog them because they do it themselves."[22] One executive put it more bluntly: "The place is full of guys with sparks coming out of their asses."[23] Even in businesses where interdependence is high and investment gestation periods are long, as in oil and gas, short- or medium-term performance targets can be highly effective. The key feature of BP's performance-oriented culture is a system of performance contracts in which each business unit general manager agrees a set of financial, strategic, and operational targets with the CEO.[24]

Linking individual incentives to company performance goals has proved to be more difficult than most advocates of performance management envisaged. Over time, top management compensation has become increasingly closely tied to company performance through performance-related bonuses and stock options. Moreover, performance bonuses and options packages have been extended down corporate hierarchies to increasing numbers of employees. In the UK, salary comprised 54% of total executive compensation as compared with bonuses 24%, and options and long-term incentive plans 22%.[25] However, financial incentives for executives seem to be poorly aligned with the goals of shareholders. The ability of top managers to design their own compensation schemes has resulted in massive growth in top management pay and in the manipulation of these schemes to the benefit of executives.[26] The stock market boom of the late 1990s created perverse incentives for executives to maximize short-term financial performance and even to manipulate financial statements.[27]

Balancing Strategic Planning and Financial Control

One implication of the tradeoff between *input control* (controlling decisions) and *output control* (controlling performance) is that companies must choose how far to emphasize strategic planning relative to financial planning as their primary control system. A study of British multibusiness companies by Michael Goold and Andrew Campbell found that their corporate management systems emphasized either strategic planning or financial control.[28] *Strategic planning* emphasized the longer term development of the businesses and was associated with substantial involvement by corporate headquarters in business-level planning. *Financial control* implied limited involvement by corporate management in business strategy formulation, which was the responsibility of divisional and business unit managers. The primary influence of headquarters was through short-term budgetary control and the establishment of ambitious financial targets that were rigorously monitored by headquarters. Table 16.1 summarizes key features of the two styles.

TABLE 16.1 Characteristics of different strategic management styles

	Strategic planning	Financial control
Business Strategy Formulation	Businesses and corporate HQ jointly formulate strategy. HQ coordinates strategies of businesses.	Strategy formulated at business unit level. Corporate HQ largely reactive, offering little coordination.
Controlling Performance	Primarily strategic goals with medium- to long-term horizon.	Financial budgets set annual targets for ROI and other financial variables with monthly and quarterly monitoring.
Advantages	Effective in managing (a) linkages among businesses, (b) innovation, (c) long-term competitive positioning.	Business unit autonomy encourages initiative, responsiveness, and the development of business leaders.
Disadvantages	Loss of divisional autonomy and initiative. Conducive to unitary strategic view. Resistance to abandoning failed strategy.	Short-term focus discourages innovation and long-term development. Limited sharing of resources and skills among businesses.
Style suited to:	Companies with a small number of closely related businesses. In sectors where technology and competition are important and projects are large and long term.	Companies with many businesses across a wide range of industries, and with limited linkages between them. Approach works best in mature, technologically stable sectors where investment projects are relatively small and short term.
UK Examples	BP, BOC, Cadbury-Schweppes, Lex Group, STC, United Biscuits.	Hanson, BTR, General Electric Company, Ferranti, Tarmac.

SOURCE: BASED ON M. GOOLD AND A. CAMPBELL, STRATEGIES AND STYLES (OXFORD: BLACKWELL, 1987).

Since Goold and Campbell's original study, it appears that financial control has become increasingly important – even in companies, such as BP, that fell into the strategic planning category. Thus, among the oil and gas majors, it was observed that strategic planning has become less concerned with strategic decision making and more focused on managing financial performance.[29]

Using PIMS in Strategy Formulation and Performance Appraisal

Some of the most sophisticated techniques for strategy development and performance appraisal have been those based on the PIMS (Profit Impact of Market Strategies) database. PIMS grew out of General Electric's internal database and was developed by the Strategic Planning Institute. It comprises information on over 5,000 business units that is used to estimate the impact of strategy and market structure on business-level profitability. Table 16.2 shows an estimated PIMS equation.

PIMS is used by multibusiness companies to assist in three areas of corporate management:

- *Setting performance targets for business units.* Using the regression coefficients in the PIMS profitability equations, it is possible to plug into the PIMS regression the actual levels of the strategic and industry variables for a particular business and thereby calculate its "Par ROI" – the level of ROI that would be expected for the business given its profile of strategic and industry characteristics if its performance were typical of the sample as a whole. "Par ROI" represents a benchmark that can be used to set profitability targets or to evaluate actual profitability.

- *Formulating business unit strategy.* Because the PIMS regression equations show the impact of different strategy variables on ROI, these estimates can indicate how a business can adjust its strategy to increase its profit performance.

- *Allocating investment funds between businesses.* Past profitability of business units is a poor indicator of the return on new investment. PIMS' "Strategic Attractiveness Scan" indicates investment attractiveness based on (a) estimated future real growth rate of the market, and (b) the "Par ROI" of the business. The analysis offers predictions as to the "strategic attractiveness" of investment in the business, and the cash flow that can be expected from it.

Managing Internal Linkages

As we saw in the previous chapter, the main opportunities for creating value in the multibusiness company arise from sharing resources and transferring capabilities among the different businesses within the company. This sharing occurs both through the centralization of common services at the corporate level and through direct linkages between the businesses.

Common Corporate Services

The simplest form of resource sharing in the multidivisional company is the centralized provision of common services and functions. These include corporate management

TABLE 16.2 The PIMS multiple regression equations: the impact of industry structure and business strategy on profitability

Profit Influences	Impact on:	
	ROI	ROS
Real market growth rate	0.18	0.04
Rate of price inflation	0.22	0.08
Purchase concentration	0.02	N.S.
Unionization (%)	−0.07	−0.03
Low purchase amount:		
low importance	6.06	1.63
high importance	5.42	2.10
High purchase amount:		
low importance	−6.96	−2.58
high importance	−3.84	−1.11
Exports–Imports (%)	0.06	0.05
Customized products	−2.44	−1.77
Market share	0.34	0.14
Relative quality	0.11	0.05
New products (%)	−0.12	−0.15
Marketing, percentage of sales	−0.52	−0.32
R&D, percentage of sales	−0.36	−0.22
Inventory, percentage of sales	−0.49	−0.09
Fixed capital intensity	−0.55	−0.10
Plant newness	0.07	0.05
Capital utilization	0.31	0.10
Employee productivity	0.13	0.06
Vertical integration	0.26	0.18
FIFO inventory valuation	1.30	0.62
R^2	0.39	0.31
F	58.3	45.1
Number of cases	2,314	2,314

Note: For example, if Real Market Growth Rate of a business was to increase by one percentage point, the equation predicts that its ROI (return on investment) would rise by 0.18% and ROS (return on sales) by 0.04%.

SOURCE: ROBERT D. BUZZELL AND BRADLEY T. GALE, *THE PIMS PRINCIPLES: LINKING STRATEGY TO PERFORMANCE* (NEW YORK: FREE PRESS, 1987): 274. © 1987 BY THE FREE PRESS. ALL RIGHTS RESERVED. REPRINTED BY PERMISSION OF THE FREE PRESS, A DIVISION OF SIMON & SCHUSTER, INC.

functions such as strategic planning, financial control, cash and risk management, internal audit, taxation, government relations, and shareholder relations. They also include services that are more efficiently provided on a centralized basis, such as research, engineering, human resources management, legal services, management development, purchasing, and any other administrative services subject to economies of scale or learning. By 2000, shared corporate services accounted for 43% of headquarters staff among large UK corporations.[30]

In practice, the benefits of centralized provision of common services tend to be smaller than many corporate managers anticipate. Centralized provision can avoid costs of duplication, but there is little incentive among headquarters staff and specialized corporate units to meet the needs of their business-level customers. The experience of many companies is that corporate staffs tend to grow under their own momentum with few obvious economies from central provision and few benefits of superior services.

As a result, many companies separated their corporate headquarters into two groups: a *corporate management unit* responsible for supporting the corporate management team in core support activities such as strategic planning, finance, and legal, and a *shared services organization* responsible for supplying common services such as research, engineering, training, and information technology to the businesses. Market incentives have been created for these shared service organizations by requiring them to supply services on an arm's-length basis to internal operating units, sometimes in competition with independent suppliers. For example:

- Amoco split its head office between a Corporate Roles group – comprising the Controller, Treasurer, Financial Operations, Corporate Planning, Corporate Secretary, and Quality Management – and a Shared Services Organization, including Human Resources, IT, Government Relations, Public and Government Affairs, Purchasing, Facilities and Services, Business Processing, Analytical Services, Environment-Health-Safety, Supply, Engineering and Construction, Tax, Auditing, and Legal Services. These 14 service groups initially had a three-year "monopoly" on supplying services to the business groups, after which the businesses were free to obtain services from inside or outside the Amoco group.
- Alcoa's Global Business Services was created in 2003. It offers financial accounting services; procurement; environment, health and safety services; people services; global credit; and information services. Its 1,900 employees are based in Pittsburgh, Monterrey (Mexico), Quebec (Canada), Szekesfehervar (Hungary), Booragoon (Australia), Sao Paulo (Brazil), and Bangalore (India). Its vision is to "deliver valuable services to Alcoa's business and resource units at a cost and quality better than competitive alternatives."[31]

Business Linkages and Porter's Corporate Strategy Types

Exploiting economies of scope doesn't necessarily mean centralizing resources at the corporate level. Resources and capabilities can also be shared between the businesses. Michael Porter has argued that the way in which a company manages these linkages determines its potential to create value for shareholders.[32] He identifies four corporate strategy types.

- *Portfolio management.* The most limited form of resource sharing is where the parent company simply acquires a portfolio of attractive, soundly managed companies, allows them to operate autonomously, and links them through an efficient internal capital market. The typical organizational structure for portfolio management is the *holding company* – a parent company that owns controlling stakes in a number of (typically unrelated) subsidiaries, but, beyond appointing the boards of the subsidiary companies, does not exert significant management control. Investor AB of Sweden (controlled by the

Wallenberg family), Koor Industries of Israel, and Berkshire Hathaway of the US (headed by legendary investor Warren Buffett) are leading examples. Value is created by acquiring companies at favorable prices, closely monitoring their financial performance, and operating an effective internal capital market.

- *Restructuring.* Conglomerates such as Tomkins, Tyco, and Textron create value by restructuring: acquiring poorly managed companies, then intervening to appoint new management, dispose of underperforming businesses, restructure liabilities, and cut costs. Recently, private equity groups such as Carlyle, KKR, Blackstone, and Texas Pacific in the US and Alchemy and Candover in the UK are performing the same restructuring role.[33]

- *Transferring skills.* Organizational capabilities can be transferred between business units. LVMH transfers brand management and distribution capabilities among its different luxury-brand businesses. Sharp transfers its optoelectronics and miniaturization capabilities across a number of consumer, electronic, and office equipment products. Creating value by sharing skills requires that the same capabilities are applicable to the different businesses, and also that mechanisms are established to transfer these skills through personnel exchange and best practice transfer.

- *Sharing activities.* Porter argues that the most important source of value arises from exploiting economies of scope in common resources and activities. For these economies to be realized, corporate management must play a key coordinating role, including involvement in formulating business unit strategies and intervention in operational matters to ensure that opportunities for sharing R&D, advertising, distribution systems, and service networks are fully exploited. Such sharing is facilitated by:
  - a strong sense of corporate identity;
  - a corporate mission that emphasizes the integration of business-level strategies;
  - an incentive for cooperation among businesses;
  - interbusiness task forces and other vehicles for cross-business cooperation.

The Corporate Role in Managing Linkages

The closer the linkages among businesses, the greater the opportunities for creating value from sharing resources and transferring capabilities, and the greater the need for corporate headquarters to coordinate across businesses. We noted earlier that the "financial control" style of management occurs mainly in conglomerates where the independence of each business limits the coordinating role of the head office to managing the budgetary process and establishing "framework conditions" for divisional planning.

In more closely related companies such as the vertically integrated oil companies, or companies with close market or technological links (such as IBM, Procter & Gamble, American Express, and Alcoa), corporate management uses a "strategic planning" style, which is likely to involve not only coordination of strategies but also operational coordination to exploit the economies of scope and transferable skills discussed in Chapter 15. Corporate involvement in interdivisional affairs has implications for the size of the corporate headquarters. Berkshire Hathaway, which has almost no linkages among its businesses, has a corporate staff of about 50. Hewlett-Packard, with about the same sales but much closer linkages between its divisions, has close to 3,000 employees at its Palo Alto head office. Goold and Campbell note that the companies that are closely involved with their businesses through *"value-added corporate parenting"* tend to have significant numbers of headquarters staff involved in developing key technical and functional capabilities. Thus, Pfizer and Corning have strong corporate R&D groups; Dow has a strong corporate manufacturing function; and Virgin's corporate team plays a key role in managing the Virgin brand.[34]

Opportunities for sharing and transferring resources and capabilities may require ad hoc organizational arrangements such as *cross-divisional task forces*. Such task forces might be formed for the introduction and dissemination of total quality management, to reengineer financial management practices, to promote fast-cycle new product development, to coordinate business development in China, and so on.

CEOs can use their authority to launch corporate-wide initiatives to encourage divisional managers to exploit interbusiness linkages and to take account of company-wide issues in their strategies and operating decisions. These initiatives provide a key mechanism for disseminating strategic changes, best practices, and management innovations.[35] At General Electric, Jack Welch was an especially effective exponent of corporate initiatives as a means of driving organizational change. These were built around communicable and compelling slogans such as "GE's growth engine," "boundarylessness," "six-sigma quality," and "destroy-your-business-dot-com."

Exploiting linkages between businesses requires careful management, and this imposes costs. Though Porter may be right that the *potential* for value creation increases as a company moves from a loose, "portfolio management" strategy toward the more integrated, "shared activity" strategy, it is not apparent that this potential is always realized. For example, most attempts at exploiting the potential for cross-selling across different businesses have yielded disappointing results, especially in financial services.[36] Lorsch and Allen shed light on the management implications of close linkages between businesses. They compared three conglomerates with three vertically integrated paper companies.[37] The coordination requirements of the paper companies resulted in greater involvement of head office staff in divisional operations, larger head office staffs, more complex planning and control devices, and lower responsiveness to change in the external environment. By contrast, the conglomerates made little attempt to exploit linkages even if they were present:

> The conglomerate firms we had studied seemed to be achieving appreciable degrees of financial and managerial synergy but little or no operating synergy. Some of the firms saw little immediate payoff in this operating synergy; others met with little success in attempting to achieve it.[38]

The success with which the corporate headquarters manages linkages between businesses depends on top management's understanding of the commonalities among its different businesses. As we noted in the last chapter, the underlying rationale of the diversified company has been called *dominant logic* by C. K. Prahalad and Richard Bettis.[39] They define dominant logic as "the way in which managers conceptualize the business and make critical resource allocation decisions." For a diversified business to be successful, they argue, there must be sufficient strategic similarity among the different businesses so that top management can administer the corporation with a single dominant logic.

Leading Change in the Multibusiness Corporation

Our conception of the role of management in the multibusiness corporation has shifted substantially in recent years. Two decades ago it was about the administration of large business empires. Today the focus is on value creation in an intensely competitive, fast-changing world. Corporate headquarters are concerned less with the problem of control and more with the problem of identifying and implementing the means for creating value within and between their individual businesses. The use of the term "parenting" to describe the corporate role, as opposed to the notion of "systems of corporate control," reflects this shift in thinking.

Changes in the management of multibusiness corporations have included decentralization of decision making from corporate to divisional levels, a shift from formal to informal coordination, and a more multidimensional role for the corporate headquarters. From being simply a control center, the corporate HQ acts as a service center, a guide to the future, and a knowledge hub.

Managing transition has been a key role for chief executives. The most celebrated of these "change masters" was Jack Welch, Chairman and CEO of General Electric from 1981 to 2001. Welch's style and the system he created has become a model for other large, multibusiness corporations – not just in North America, but in Europe and Asia too. Strategy Capsule 16.2 outlines Welch's style and methods.

As Welch has shown, managing large-scale organizational change is not simply about top–down decision making. A key component is fostering change processes at lower levels of the organization – GE's "Work-Out" is a prime example. A critical feature of organizational design is building structures and systems that permit adaptation.

STRATEGY CAPSULE 16.2

General Electric: Welch's Reinvention of Corporate Management

Jack Welch's 20 years as Chairman and CEO of General Electric began with an intensive period of restructuring, which transformed the composition of GE's business portfolio through acquisitions and disposals and extended the conglomerate's global reach. Toward the mid-1980s, Welch's attention shifted from the business portfolio to the structure, systems, and style of GE. Among the changes he initiated were the following.

1 *Delayering*. Welch's fundamental criticism of GE's management was that it was slow and

unresponsive. Welch eliminated GE's sector level of organization so that business heads reported directly to him. He pressured them to flatten their management pyramids. Overall, GE's layers of hierarchy were cut from nine or ten to four or five.

2 *Changing the Strategic Planning System*. During the 1970s, GE had developed a systematic and formalized approach to strategy formulation and appraisal. Welch believed that not only was the system slow and inefficient, it also stifled innovation and

opportunism. Welch replaced the staff-led, document-driven process with more personal, less formal, but very intensive face-to-face discussions. Instead of data-heavy documents, each business head was asked to produce a slim "play-book" that summarized key strategic issues and actions. Concise answers were required to questions about market dynamics, competitive activity, risks, and proposed GE business responses. These documents became the basis for a half-day review session where business heads and key executives met with the Office of the CEO in an open dialog on strategy and performance.[1]

3   *Redefining the Role of Headquarters*. The changes in the strategic planning system reflected broader changes in the role of the corporate headquarters. Welch viewed headquarters as interfering too much, generating too much paper, and failing to add value. His objective was to "turn their role 180 degrees from checker, inquisitor, and authority figure to faciliator, helper, and supporter" so that decisions could move more quickly:

> What we do here at headquarters . . . is to multiply the resources we have, the human resources, the financial resources, and the best practices . . . Our job is to help, it's to assist, it's to make these businesses stronger, to help them grow and be more powerful.[2]

4   *The Coordinating Role of Corporate*. A key role of corporate was facilitating coordination across GE's businesses. The Corporate Executive Council was reconstituted to include the leaders of GE's 13 businesses and several key corporate executives. It met two days each quarter to discuss common problems and issues. The Council became an important vehicle for

identifying and exploiting synergies. In 1990, Welch launched his concept of the "boundaryless company." This involved blurring internal divisions so that people could work together across functional and business boundaries. Welch aimed at "integrated diversity" – the ability to transfer the best ideas, most developed knowledge, and most valuable people freely and easily between businesses.

> Boundaryless behavior is the soul of today's GE . . . Simply put, people seem compelled to build layers and walls between themselves and others, and that human tendency tends to be magnified in large, old institutions like ours. These walls cramp people, inhibit creativity, waste time, restrict vision, smother dreams and, above all, slow things down . . . Boundaryless behavior shows up in the actions of a woman from our Appliances business in Hong Kong helping NBC with contacts needed to develop satellite television service in Asia . . . And finally, boundaryless behavior means exploiting one of the unmatchable advantages a multibusiness GE has over almost any other company in the world. Boundaryless behavior combines 12 huge global businesses – each number one or number two in its markets – into a vast laboratory whose principal product is new ideas, coupled with a common commitment to spread them throughout the Company.[3]

Notes:

1   *General Electric: Jack Welch's Second Wave (A)*, Case No. 9-391-248 (Boston: Harvard Business School, 1991).

2   Jack Welch, "GE Growth Engine," speech to employees (1988).

3   "Letter to Share Owners," General Electric Company 1993 Annual Report (Fairfield, CT, 1994): 2.

While CEOs cannot be the primary initiators of change, they need to be alert and responsive to signals. Intel's former CEO, Andy Grove, emphasizes the importance of CEOs identifying *strategic inflection points* – instances where seismic shifts in a firm's competitive environment require a fundamental redirection of strategy.[40] At Intel, such inflection points included the transition from DRAM chips to microprocessors, the decision to focus on its x86 series of microprocessors in favor of RISC architecture, and the decision to replace its faulty Pentium chips.[41]

Above all, CEOs need to be adept at managing contradiction and dilemma. For example:

- Companies must strive for efficiency, which requires rigorous financial controls; they must also be innovative and entrepreneurial, which requires autonomy and loose, flexible controls.

- Maximizing current performance requires strategies that exploit existing resources and capabilities across different markets; success for the future is dependent on the creation of new resources and capabilities and their deployment in new markets.

- Innovation, efficiency, and responsiveness require autonomy for business-level managers; yet the competitive advantage of the multibusiness corporation ultimately depends on integrating resources and capabilities across businesses. Is it possible for companies like Microsoft, Siemens, or Samsung to mesh the resource advantages of the giant corporation with the responsiveness and creativity of small enterprises?

Resolving these dilemmas requires that organizations operate in multiple modes simultaneously. In particular, they need to combine both decentralized flexibility and initiative *and* centralized purpose and integration. The transformation of IBM under Lou Gerstner offers some guidance as to how this can be achieved. Resisting Wall Street pressure to break up IBM, Gerstner was able to combine aggressive cuts in costs and jobs, entrepreneurship, and flexibility through decentralized decision making, and integration of technology and know-how by breaking down barriers both within IBM and between IBM and other companies.[42]

Flexible integration – whether it is sharing capabilities, harmonizing market initiatives in different countries, or collaborating to develop the new products and technologies required – cannot be hierarchically decreed: headquarters does not possess the necessary knowledge to be in the driver's seat. It must happen through horizontal collaboration among the businesses units. This requires that business-level general managers identify not only with their particular businesses, but also with the corporation as a whole. Fostering the necessary identity and direction within the multibusiness corporation is probably the most important task that the CEO must perform.

Creating this sense of identity is much more challenging for a company that spans several businesses than for one whose identity is determined by the products it offers (McDonald's or De Beers). It goes beyond "strategic relatedness" and "dominant logic" and embraces notions of vision and mission – concepts which were identified in Chapter 1 as lying at the foundations of companies' strategy formulation. In the previous chapter, I observed that the luxury goods giant LVMH deploys its core brand management capabilities across its different businesses. Its success in doing so depends critically upon establishing a corporate identity that forms a "cultural glue" between these disparate businesses:

The common cultural trunk is based on the permanent search for quality of the products and the management, human relations based on responsibility and initiative, and rewarding competences and services.[43]

Reconciliation and pursuit of multiple – often conflicting – performance goals requires differentiation and integration across the different levels of management. Bartlett and Ghoshal point to the need to redistribute management roles within the company.[44] They identify three central management processes: the *entrepreneurial process* (decisions about the opportunities to exploit and the allocation of resources), the *integration process* (how organizational capabilities are built and deployed), and the *renewal process* (the shaping of organizational purpose and the initiation of change). Conventionally, all three processes have been concentrated within the corporate HQ. Bartlett and Ghoshal propose a distribution of these functions between three levels of the firm: corporate ("top management"), the business and geographical sector coordinators ("middle management"), and the business units ("front-line management"). The critical features of the relationships between these management levels and between the individual organizational members form a social structure based on cooperation and learning. Figure 16.5 depicts their framework.

FIGURE 16.5 Management processes and levels of management

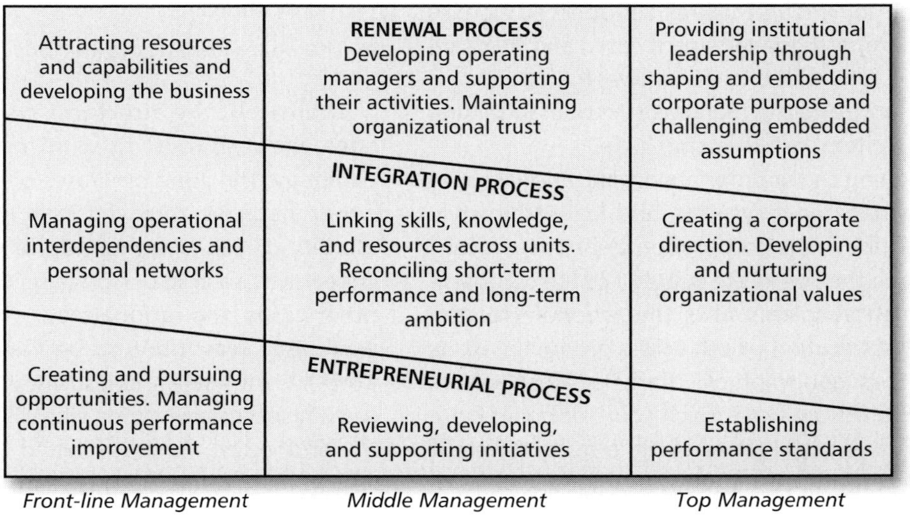

SOURCE: C. A. BARTLETT AND S. GHOSHAL, "BEYOND THE M-FORM: TOWARD A MANAGERIAL THEORY OF THE FIRM," *STRATEGIC MANAGEMENT JOURNAL* 14, WINTER SPECIAL ISSUE (1993): 38.

Front-line Management	Middle Management	Top Management
Attracting resources and capabilities and developing the business	**RENEWAL PROCESS** Developing operating managers and supporting their activities. Maintaining organizational trust	Providing institutional leadership through shaping and embedding corporate purpose and challenging embedded assumptions
Managing operational interdependencies and personal networks	**INTEGRATION PROCESS** Linking skills, knowledge, and resources across units. Reconciling short-term performance and long-term ambition	Creating a corporate direction. Developing and nurturing organizational values
Creating and pursuing opportunities. Managing continuous performance improvement	**ENTREPRENEURIAL PROCESS** Reviewing, developing, and supporting initiatives	Establishing performance standards

Summary

Formulating and implementing corporate strategy in the multibusiness company presents complex issues that challenge our tools of strategy analysis. We can classify firms in different strategic types but, ultimately, it is impossible to offer generic recommendations for how a multibusiness company should implement its corporate strategy: each firm possesses a unique portfolio of products and markets; each owns a unique set of resources and capabilities; each has developed a distinct administrative structure, management style, and corporate culture. Given these factors, it is hardly surprising that empirical research offers little clear guidance as to the correlates of superior performance – close relationships between businesses may or may not lead to higher profitability; sharing resources and capabilities offers economies but also imposes management costs; and there are no consistent relationships between a company's performance and the characteristics of its structure, control system, or leadership style.

Designing the appropriate organizational structure, management systems, and leadership style of a multibusiness corporation depends critically on *fit* with the corporate strategy of the company. Fundamental to this fit is the *rationale* for the firm. Diversification – both across product markets and across geographical markets – can create value in different ways. Each source of gain from diversification is likely to imply a quite different approach to managing the firm. For a conglomerate firm, value can be created through the strategic judgment of the CEO with regard to business prospects and company valuation, and the ability to operate a highly efficient internal capital market. Hence, organization and management systems should be oriented toward a clear separation of business levels on corporate decisions and a highly effective system for budgetary control and project evaluation. For a technology-based, diversified corporation, value is created through the transfer and integration of knowledge, ideas, and expertise. The company must be organized in order to facilitate the transfer and application of knowledge. Two sets of issues are critical:

- The characteristics of the resources and capabilities that are being exploited within the multibusiness corporation.
- The characteristics of the businesses.

Ultimately, the structure, systems, and management style must fit with the identity of the company. The conglomerates of the 1970s failed either because they did not establish a clear identity or because their identity was so closely linked with a single person (e.g., Geneen at ITT). In other cases, the rationale on which the identity was based was found to be flawed (e.g., Allegis Corp.). Conversely, multibusiness companies that sustain success over time establish clarity of identity and vision that is reflected in their strategy, structure, management systems, and leadership style. Moreover, they periodically revisit that identity and vision as their world changes.

Self-Study Questions

1   Williamson's "M-form" concept argues that the efficiency of the multidivisional firm is the result of (a) the separation of responsibilities between divisional and corporate management and (b) overcoming the "agency problem" of managers pursuing their own interests rather than those of shareholders. How effective are most multibusiness companies in achieving these advantages? Are there other performance advantages associated with multibusiness companies?

2   If you were VP of Strategic Planning for a large, multibusiness company, would you use portfolio planning techniques in your work? If so, for what purposes? If not, why not? Would your preference be to use the GE/McKinsey matrix or the BCG matrix?

3   Identify a poorly performing multibusiness company (examples might include Sony, Time Warner, Bombardier, Pearson, Matsushita, Fiat Group, or Tyco). Using the McKinsey pentagon framework, in which stage do you perceive the greatest opportunities for value creation through restructuring? (Use the company's website or Hoovers.com to access information on the company.)

4   For technology-based companies, building linkages across different businesses is critical to sustaining competitive advantage. Select a technology-based company that you are familiar with (possibilities might include Microsoft, HP, Apple Computer, Canon, Nortel Networks, or Finmeccanica), then identify how linkages between businesses are currently being exploited and identify opportunities for additional exploitation of cross-business linkages.

Notes

1   I use the term *multibusiness company* to refer to a company that comprises multiple business units. These may comprise different vertical activities, different geographical units, or different product sectors.

2   O. E. Williamson, *Markets and Hierarchies: Analysis and Antitrust Implications* (New York: Free Press, 1975); and O. E. Williamson, "The Modern Corporation: Origins, Evolution, Attributes," *Journal of Economic Literature* 19 (1981): 1537–68.

3   J. L. Bower, *Managing the Resource Allocation Process* (Boston: Harvard Business School Press, 1986).

4   Williamson, "The Modern Corporation," op. cit.

5   See, for example, P. Steer and J. Cable, "Internal Organization and Profit: An Empirical Analysis of Large UK Companies," *Journal of Industrial Economics* 21 (September 1978): 13–30; H. Armour and D. Teece, "Organizational Structure and Economic Performance: A Test of the Multidivisional Hypothesis," *Bell Journal of Economics* 9 (1978): 106–22; D. Teece, "Internal Organization and Economic Performance," *Journal of Industrial Economics* 30 (1981): 173–99.

6   E. J. Epstein, *Dossier: The Secret History of Armand Hammer* (New York: Carroll & Graf, 1999); B. Burrough, *Barbarians at the Gate: The Fall of RJR Nabisco* (New York: Harper & Row, 1990); J. Johnson and M. Orange, *The Man Who Tried to Buy the World* (Penguin, 2004).

7   H. Mintzberg, *Structure in Fives: Designing Effective Organizations* (Englewood Cliffs, NJ: Prentice Hall, 1983): Chapter 11.

8   J. Birkinshaw and A. Campbell, "Know the Limits of Corporate Venturing," FT Summer School, *Financial Times* (August 10, 2004).

9   M. Goold, A. Campbell, and M. Alexander, *Corporate-Level Strategy: Creating Value in the Multibusiness Company* (New York: Wiley, 1994).

10   *General Electric: Strategic Position – 1981*, Case No. 381–174 (Boston: Harvard Business School, 1981): 1.

11   The PIMS database is referred to in Chapter 3 and is discussed later in this chapter.

12   H. Quarls, T. Pernsteiner, and K. Rangan, "Love Your Dogs," Booz Allen Hamilton (March 15, 2005).

13 T. Copeland, T. Koller, and J. Murrin, *Valuation: Measuring and Managing the Value of Companies*, 3rd edn (New York: Wiley, 2000).

14 R. Cibin and R. M. Grant, "Restructuring Among the World's Largest Oil Companies," *British Journal of Management* 7 (December 1996): 411–28.

15 Goold, Campbell, and Alexander, op. cit.: 90.

16 M. C. Mankins and R. Steele, "Stop Making Plans; Start Making Decisions," *Harvard Business Review* (January 2006): 76–84.

17 L. Bossidy and R. Charan, *Execution: The Discipline of Getting Things Done* (New York: Crown Business, 2002): 197–201.

18 R. S. Kaplan and D. P. Norton, "Having Trouble With Your Strategy? Then Map It," *Harvard Business Review* (September–October 2000): 67–76.

19 R. S. Kaplan and D. P. Norton, "The Office of Strategy Management," *Harvard Business Review* (October 2005): 72–80.

20 Ibid.: 73.

21 Geneen's style of management is discussed in Chapter 3 of R. T. Pascale and A. G. Athos, *The Art of Japanese Management* (New York: Warner Books, 1982).

22 Tuck School of Business, CEO Speaker Series, September 23, 2002.

23 "Those Highflying PepsiCo Managers," *Fortune* (April 10, 1989): 79.

24 BP, "Performance Contracts" (www.bp.com/genericarticle?Id=25&contentId=2000476).

25 M. J. Conyon, S. I. Peck, L. E. Read, and G. V. Sadler, "The Structure of Executive Compensation Contracts: The UK Evidence," *Long Range Planning* 33 (August 2000): 478–503.

26 Option backdating was a particular problem. See "Nuclear Options," *Economist* (June 1, 2006).

27 See for example: P. Bolton, J. Scheinkman, and W. Xiong, "Pay for Short-term Performance: Executive Compensation in Speculative Markets," NBER Working Paper 12107 (March 2006); M. C. Jensen and K. J. Murphy, "Remuneration: Where We've Been, How We Got Here, What Are the Problems," ECGI-Finance Working Paper 44 (2004).

28 M. Goold and A. Campbell, *Strategies and Styles* (Oxford: Blackwell, 1987).

29 R. M. Grant, "Strategic Planning in a Turbulent Environment: Evidence from the Oil and Gas Majors," *Strategic Management Journal* 24 (2003): 491–518.

30 M. Goold, D. Pettifer, and D. Young, "Redesigning the Corporate Center," *European Mangement Review* 19, no. 1 (2001): 83–91.

31 IQPC, "Most Admired Shared Service Organizations, 2005" (www.iqpc.com).

32 M. E. Porter, "From Competitive Advantage to Corporate Strategy," *Harvard Business Review* (May–June 1987): 46.

33 "Going Private," *Business Week* (February 27, 2006).

34 M. Goold, D. Pettifer, and D. Young, op. cit.

35 J. Darragh and A. Campbell, "Why Corporate Initiatives Get Stuck," *Long Range Planning* 34 (January 2001): 33–52.

36 "Cross-selling's Elusive Charms," *Financial Times* (November 16, 1998): 21.

37 J. W. Lorsch and S. A. Allen III, *Managing Diversity and Interdependence: An Organizational Study of Multidivisional Firms* (Boston: Harvard Business School Press, 1973).

38 Ibid.: 168.

39 C. K. Prahalad and R. Bettis, "The Dominant Logic: A New Linkage Between Diversity and Performance," *Strategic Management Journal* 7 (1986): 485–502.

40 A. S. Grove, *Only the Paranoid Survive: How to Exploit the Crisis Points that Challenge Every Company* (New York: Bantam, 1999).

41 R. A. Burgelman and A. Grove, "Strategic Dissonance," *California Management Review* 38 (Winter 1996): 8–28.

42 L. V. Gerstner, *Who Says Elephants Can't Dance?* (New York: Harper Business, 2002).

43 *LVMH: Building Star Brands*, ICFAI Case MKTA016 (2004); R. Calori, "How Successful Companies Manage Diverse Businesses," *Long Range Planning* 21 (June 1988): 85.

44 C. A. Bartlett and S. Ghoshal, "Beyond the M-Form: Toward a Managerial Theory of the Firm," *Strategic Management Journal* 14, Winter Special Issue (1993): 23–46; C. A. Bartlett and S. Ghoshal, "The Myth of the General Manager: New Personal Competencies for New Management Roles," *California Management Review* 40 (Fall 1997): 92–116; "Beyond Structure to Process," *Harvard Business Review* (January–February 1995).

17

Current Trends in Strategic Management

In the half-century after the Second World War, the business corporation has brilliantly proved itself as an economic organization, i.e. a creator of wealth and jobs. In the next society, the biggest challenge for the large company – especially the multinational – will be its social legitimacy; its values, its mission, its vision.

—PETER DRUCKER[1]

Becoming a successful evolver will be a major challenge for most companies . . . For companies that do accept the challenge, the payoff promises to be considerable . . . Evolution will be the wave we ride to new levels of creativity and innovation rather than the tide that washes over us.

—ERIC BEINHOCKER[2]

OUTLINE

Introduction

Early indicators suggest that the 21st century may be at least as turbulent as its predecessor. At the time of writing, only seven years of the new century have elapsed, yet businesses have been buffeted by calamities on multiple fronts. These have included: the bursting of the dot.com and technology–media–telecom bubbles; a wave of corporate scandals that followed the collapse of Enron; the September 11, 2001 attacks in New York and Washington, followed by subsequent terrorist bombings in Bali, Madrid, and London; the invasions of Afghanistan, Iraq, and Lebanon; warnings of a world war between the West and Islam; the growing impact of China, India, and Russia on the world economy – including escalating commodity prices (Brent crude hit $76 a barrel in July 2006); and the threat that climate change may have reached "tipping point," triggering rapidly accelerating global warming.

These developments in the business environment have implications for business strategy at three levels. At the most general level, volatility and unpredictability of the technological, economic, and political environments have increased the importance of companies being flexible and responsive. Second, these developments have called for specific strategy responses from companies. For example, rapid industrialization in China and IT development in India has encouraged widespread outsourcing of manufacture to China and business services to India. The convergence of the markets for telecom, entertainment, computers, and consumer electronics requires that the firms in these sectors develop strategies for competing within a far broader market space. Finally, the new realities of the 21st century have triggered new thinking about the nature of strategy, the responsibilities of the corporation, and the role of management.

In this chapter we shall review the issues and ideas that are redirecting firm strategies and reshaping strategic analysis. We will begin by considering some of the major current trends in the external environment of business and consider their implications for strategic management. We will then go on to explore the ideas and theories influencing strategic thinking. Finally, we will consider how the structures, systems, and leadership of companies are adapting to these emerging imperatives.

Unlike the other chapters of this book, this chapter will not equip you with tools and frameworks that you can deploy directly in your own companies or in case analysis. My approach is exploratory. My goal is to introduce you to some of the ideas that are reshaping our thinking about business strategy and to stimulate your thinking about the kinds of strategies that are likely to be effective during this era of uncertainty and rapid change and the types of organization suited to implementing such strategies.

Trends in the External Environment of Business

The Third Industrial Revolution

The period of intense economic and technological change beginning in the latter part of the 1990s has been described as the "third industrial revolution." The first industrial revolution began in Britain at the end of the 18th century and involved the mechanization of production. The second industrial revolution began in the US at the end of the 19th century and saw the rise of the modern corporation and the introduction of telephones, automobiles, and electrical power. The third industrial revolution – also referred to as the "knowledge revolution" or the advent of the "New Economy" of the late 1990s – has been powered by digital technologies and new communications media – notably wireless telephony and the internet. It was fueled too by the worldwide trends towards privatization, deregulation, and free trade.

Despite the dot.com burst and telecom recession of 2000–3, the New Economy has proved not to be a mirage. At its root is the shift from an industrial to a knowledge economy, where software rather than hardware is the primary source of value. Stanford economists Brian Arthur and Paul Romer argue that economics of replication, network effects, and complementarities between different types of knowledge create increasing returns that permit unprecedented levels of productivity growth.[3] During the past decade, the rate of productivity growth of the US economy has exceeded that of any country in recorded history (see Figure 17.1).

FIGURE 17.1 US labor productivity: annual changes in nonfarm output per hour worked, 1990–2006

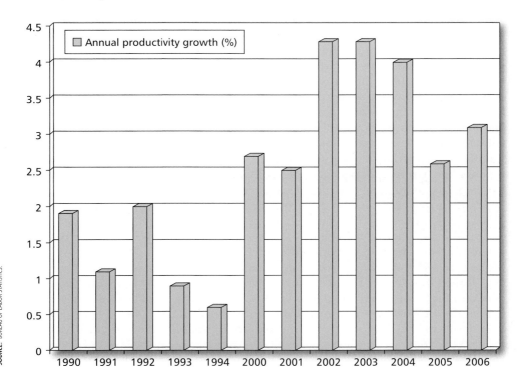

SOURCE: BUREAU OF LABOR STATISTICS.

The digitally driven knowledge revolution also creates what Brian Arthur calls the "casino of technology," where markets are transformed and established market leaders deposed.[4] The availability of the internet as a communication device and a global distribution channel allows new industries to be created and destroyed at unprecedented speed. Within the space of five years, two Scandinavian entrepreneurs, Niklas Zennstrom and Janus Friis, have triggered revolutions in two different industries. Their Kazaa file sharing system drove the recorded music industry towards a new business model, while their Skype VoIP internet telephony system threatens the world's fixed-line telecom industry.[5]

Digital technologies are also causing an intensification of competition within the industries that they have an impact on. Winner-take-all markets eliminate the potential for the cozy collusion that typified oligopoly markets – in video consoles, Sony and Microsoft are locked into unremitting rivalry. Equally important is the dissolution of industry barriers caused by digital convergence. Telecom operators, internet service providers, and cable TV companies compete to provide the same services.[6] In hand-held devices, Nokia, RIM (BlackBerry), Nintendo, and Apple are moving into closer competition.

Societal Pressures

Over the longer term, the values and expectations of society might be even more important than the imperatives of technology in shaping firms' strategies and the organizational systems through which they are implemented. The notion of "strategic fit" embraces not only a firm's economic environment but its social environment as well. Organizational ecologists have long emphasized that firm survival depends on social *legitimacy*.[7] This means that a firm's ability to prosper depends on its acceptability among consumers, the willingness of investors and financiers to fund it, support from government, and the willingness of its employees to apply their efforts and creativity in its service. This view of the business enterprise as a key social institution has encouraged a number of management thinkers – including Peter Drucker, Charles Handy, and Sumantra Ghoshal – to argue that firms must identify with the goals and aspirations of society and support their members in the quest for meaning in their lives.[8]

But what does this mean in practical terms? Which values should companies adopt? What social purposes should they identify with? The debate over the social responsibility of business – between those who view companies as agents of ethical and social values and those who view the sole social responsibility of business as making profit – shows little prospect of resolution. Most evidence, however, points to the wisdom of companies responding to the social concerns and pressures of the time.

At the current time, two trends are having an impact on the broader social conduct of business. In terms of ethics and values, the key drivers are the corporate scandals of 2000–3 and growing distaste over levels of executive compensation – especially when offered as retirement packages (Jack Welch at GE; Lee Raymond at Exxon Mobil), or when the CEOs' bonanza contrasts with meager shareholder returns (e.g. Robert Nardelli at Home Depot). Companies have adopted stricter codes of ethics for their executives and reined in abuses of stock options. Indeed, it is notable that levels of CEO compensation declined between 2001 and 2006.[9]

In terms of social responsibility, the key driver has been the increased environmental consciousness that has accompanied growing concerns over global warming. During 2006, "sustainable business" was embraced by some unlikely evangelists: Jeff

Immelt of General Electric, Lee Scott of Wal-Mart, and Rupert Murdoch of News International.[10]

Becoming a values-driven, socially responsible enterprise presents its own challenges. To begin with, does a company determine unilaterally the values that will govern its behavior, or does it seek to reflect those of the society in which it operates? Companies that embrace the values espoused by their founders are secure in their own sense of mission and can ensure a long-term consistency in their strategy and corporate identity (e.g. Walt Disney Company and Wal-Mart with respect to founders Walt Disney and Sam Walton). However, there is a risk that these values become out of step with those of the society as a whole or with the requirements for business effectiveness. Thus, Marks & Spencer's paternalism towards employees and suppliers became a source of rigidity rather than competitive advantage. Similarly, the principles on which Tom Watson had founded IBM had to be abandoned for IBM to survive in a networked world.

Alternatively, if the enterprise is to adapt to embrace the concerns and values of society, this is difficult if there is either a lack of social consensus or instability in social values. For most of the past half-century, there has been substantial consensus, in western societies at least, in relation to individual rights, equality of opportunity, and multiculturalism. Recent trends suggest a waning of the "liberal consensus" and increasing ideological and religious conflict in the areas of values and rights.

Decline of the Public Corporation

An alternative to adaptation to the demands of society and government is for firms to retreat into the greater anonymity provided by private ownership. Since 2000, the number of companies listed on the world's major stock exchanges has declined substantially. One reason has been the merger boom of recent years; another is the reversion of companies to private status, usually because of buyout by a private equity fund.

During 2006, Blackstone Group and Kohlberg Kravis Roberts, the world's biggest private equity firms, each launched buyout funds exceeding $14 billion, while the total value of private equity buyouts in the US and Europe rose from $265 billion in 2005 to $430 billion in 2006, accounting for about one-quarter of total M&A activity.[11] Major buyouts have included hospital chain HCA ($32 billion) and real estate giant Equity Office Properties ($39 billion). Recently private equity firms have extended their activities from mature industries to the technology sector. For example, a series of semiconductor businesses have recently been acquired, including Philips Semiconductor, Aligent, and Freescale Semiconductor.

At the same time, the incentives for going private have never been greater. The regulatory burden on public companies (notably the Sarbanes–Oxley Act in the US) increased substantially in the aftermath of the accounting scandals in the US (Enron, WorldCom) and in Europe (Parmalat, Royal Ahold, Vivendi Universal). At the same time, the pressures on executives and board members have increased substantially as a result of increased activism by institutional shareholders and various pressure groups. The number of US companies listed on the NYSE fell from 2,722 in 1998 to 2,289 in 2005.

Thus, while the challenges for business to respond to social pressures have increased, one response from the business community has been to retreat behind the greater anonymity afforded by private ownership. It is notable that, while the debate over levels of compensation for corporate executives continues to rage, many of the world's most sought-after executives are fleeing public corporations for private equity firms. Millard Dexler, former CEO of Gap and currently running J. Crew for the Texas Pacific Group, could make up to $300 million if J. Crew goes public. Private equity is also an increasing draw for MBA graduates. Stanford MBAs entering private equity during 2005 earned a median salary of $232,000.[12]

New Directions in Strategic Thinking

Beyond Downsizing and Shareholder Value

The early years of the 21st century have seen a shift in firms' strategy priorities in response to two key problems facing senior managers. First, the gains from cost cutting and corporate restructuring – the low-hanging fruit on the tree of profit – had been picked. Second, the unremitting quest for shareholder value had unforeseen and undesired consequences for many companies. Rather than maximize the flow of profits on which stock market valuation depended, many companies had focused excessively on short-term earnings, while others had gone further and had attempted to directly manage their stock market valuations through smoothing fluctuations in reported earnings and, in some cases, artificially manipulating financial statements.

The responses to these problems – in terms of strategic management – were twofold: first, a "back-to-basics" movement in which companies have refocused their strategies on the fundamental sources of profitability; second, an emphasis on accessing more complex and difficult-to-reach sources of competitive advantage.

Back to Basics   The bursting of the dot.com bubble and economic downturn of 2000–2 was followed by a wave of healthy skepticism over New Economy management alchemy and the power of radical new business models to deliver untold riches. In response, many companies have adopted a back-to-basics approach to strategy, which has seen them focus on the fundamentals of profitability. In essence, these mean deploying the tools of strategy analysis outlined in this book to probe and access the sources of profitability arising from deploying internal resources and capabilities to exploit opportunities in the external environment. Central to such a back-to-basics approach is avoiding management fads and strategy bandwagons in favor of unique, customized strategies that exploit idiosyncratic advantages.

A further aspect of this focus on the sources of profitability has been the old-fashioned quest for market power. Across a large number of market sectors, depressed profitability has triggered a scramble for consolidation through mergers and acquisitions. While business leaders sing the praises of entrepreneurship and the vibrant cut-and-thrust of "creative destruction," the strategic responses to the harsh realities of competition have often been defensive. In many industries, intense M&A activity has created a few global giants that are better able to manage excess capacity and limit pressure from buyers for lower prices. For example, the world cement industry has been transformed by mergers and acquisitions from a fragmented industry populated by local producers to one dominated by four global groups: Lafarge (France), Holcim (Switzerland), Cemex (Mexico), and Heidelberg (Germany). In aluminum, the leading groups – Alcoa (US), Rusal (Russia), Alcan (Canada), Norsk Hydro (Norway), and Pechiney (France) – form a global oligopoly.

The back-to-basics approach to strategy that has accompanied the disillusion with revolutionary new business models, financial engineering, internet economics, and management fads in general has encouraged greater attention to tailoring strategy to the specific circumstances of individual firms. Throughout this book I have emphasized the critical importance of *strategic fit*: strategy must be designed to meet the circumstances of the firm's competitive environment and its resources and capabilities.

Complementarity in Management Practices Recently, concern with strategic fit has received increased attention and stronger theoretical and empirical support from work on *complementarity* among the different management practices of a firm. Much of the research has been within the area of human resource management and has shown that firm performance depends on interaction among a wide range of human resource practices.[13] However, the general finding – that the adoption of any particular management practice will fail to improve performance unless every other complementary management practice is adjusted – is general to all areas of management. For example, a six-sigma quality management program is likely to be of little value unless it is accompanied by adjustments in incentives, recruitment policies, product strategy, and capital budgeting practices.

At one extreme, recognition of complementarities in management practices implies a retreat from rules and generalizations in formulating and implementing of strategy in favor of particularism: every firm is unique and must create a unique combination of strategic variables and management practices. In practice, the implications of complementarity are less stark. While every firm is unique, management choices tend to converge to a limited number of *configurations*. Thus, successful adaptation among large European companies was associated with a small number of configurations of organizational structure, processes, and boundaries.[14]

Seeking More Complex Sources of Competitive Advantage Focus on strategy fundamentals does not necessarily lead to simple strategies. In many industries, increasing pressure of competition and the entry of firms with unassailable cost advantages requires that established players access new sources of profitability. As we observed in Chapter 7, there are few competitive advantages that are sustainable over a significant period of time in today's dynamic business environment. Ultimately, the only sustainable competitive advantage is the ability to create new sources of competitive advantage. A key fear of companies that have maintained both profitability and market share over periods of many years is their capacity to build layers of competitive advantage – Toyota, Wal-Mart, 3M, Canon, Dell, and L'Oreal. These companies have meshed the diverse performance goals of cost efficiency, differentiation, innovation, responsiveness, and global learning. As we shall see, reconciling the different requirements of different performance dimensions imposes highly complex organizational challenges that are pushing companies to fundamental rethinking of the structures and management systems.

The need to adapt and upgrade existing capabilities and to add new capabilities places increased emphasis on the need for companies to develop *dynamic capabilities*. Dynamic capabilities allow a firm to adapt to external pressures and change. Zollo and Winter define a dynamic capability as: "a learned and stable pattern of collective activity through which the organization systematically generates and modifies its operating routines in pursuit of improved effectiveness."[15]

The Quest for a New Model of the Corporation Disillusion with the shareholder value model of the firm – in particular its encouragement to short-termism and untrammeled materialism – has stimulated the quest for an alternative model of the firm. Most observable alternatives are unappealing. Stakeholder models – certainly as represented by the German co-determination model or Japanese managerial capitalism – tend to display slow decision making and weak entrepreneurial vigor. Private capitalism – as represented by private equity funds – risks substituting one form of short-termism – the stock market's preoccupation with quarterly earnings – with another: the desire of private equity funds to "flip" companies to lock in a return.

Some of the most appealing approaches to rethinking the firm are those that abandon mechanistic, equilibrium ideas of the firm and embrace the basic reality of business: change and uncertainty. The implication – that firm performance is concerned with adaptability rather than optimization – suggests an evolutionary model of the firm. Thus, Peter Senge regards the firm as a *learning organization* – a social organism centered on a knowledge system.[16] Arie de Geus extends this concept of the firm as a living organism to examine the processes of adaptation among the world's longest-living companies (including Stora, a Swedish paper company founded in the 13th century, Japan's 400-year-old Sumitomo, 195-year-old DuPont, and Pilkington, the British glass maker founded in the 1820s).[17] De Geus observes that longevity is associated with *financial conservatism*, *sensitivity* to the external environment, and *cohesion* from a sense of identity infused through a strong corporate culture, yet with significant *tolerance* for individuality.

Moving beyond biological analogies to the elucidation of principles that relate strategy, structure, and management systems to organizational performance under conditions of complexity and unpredictability requires a major leap in the theoretical analysis that we deploy within strategic management. Fortunately, help is at hand. Let us examine two areas of theoretical advance: complexity and real options.

Complexity Theory

The weather, ant colonies, flocks of birds, human crowds, and seismic activity are all *complex systems* – open systems in which a large number of independent agents interact. Organizations are also complex systems. Complexity theory shows that complex systems display common and predictable patterns of adaptive behavior.

Some of the common features of complex adaptive systems are:

- *Unpredictability*. The behavior of complex adaptive systems cannot be predicted in any precise sense. There is no tendency to stable equilibria; cascades of change are constantly interacting and reshaping competitive landscapes. Exogenous changes are subject to a *power-law distribution* whereby small changes typically result in small consequences but may also trigger major movements. The typical example is dropping grains of sand onto a sand pile where small sand movements are interspersed by major landslides.[18]

- *Self-organization*. A key feature of biological and social systems is their capacity for self-organization. As with other living organisms – bee colonies and shoals of fish – companies have the capacity to self-organize, adapt to change, and create new structures and systems in the absence of formal authority. Computer simulations of synchronized behavior show that, with just a few simple rules, sophisticated patterns of coordination emerge at the system level. For human organizations there are three main requirements for self-organization:

- *Identity*. Organizations need to be founded on an intent that drives the sense-making process within the organization.
- *Information*. Information provides the medium through which an organization relates to its environment and through which the individuals within the organization know how to react to external changes.
- *Relationships*. Relationships are the pathways through which information is transformed into intelligent, coordinated action. The more access individuals have to one another, the greater the possibilities for organized activity. Responsiveness to a wide range of external circumstances necessitates every individual having a wide range of connections to other individuals, with the potential for unplanned connections.[19]

● *Inertia and chaos*. Evolutionary processes can produce three types of outcome: an orderly outcome where change is so limited that the system suffers inertia, disorder where changes produce chaotic outcomes, and an intermediate region where small changes that result in a power-law distribution result in small and large shifts and this achieves the most rapid evolutionary adaptation. These results point to the advantages of systems that evolve to the *edge of chaos* – they are capable of small, localized adaptations, but also have the potential to make larger leaps toward higher *fitness peaks* while avoiding tumbling off the fitness edge into chaos.[20]

The implications of these ideas for strategic management are radical and far-reaching. If business is a complex system, then it is inherently unpredictable – not only is it impossible to forecast the business environment, but managers cannot predict what the outcomes of their actions will be. The concept of the CEO as the peak decision maker and strategy architect is not only unrealistic, it is undesirable. Managers must rely on the self-organizing properties of their companies. The critical issues are how can they select the structures, systems, and management styles that will allow these self-organizing properties to generate the best outcomes? A key framework has been Kaufman's concept of a *fitness landscape*.[21] The challenge for managers is to design organizational systems that allow self-organization the best chance of attaining the highest level of performance ("*fitness*"). Drawing upon the contributions of Brown, Eisenhardt, McKelvey, and Levinthal, the following recommendations have been made as to how companies can best scale the performance peaks associated with locating at the edge of chaos:[22]

● *Establish simple rules*. If the complex coordinated behaviors of complex systems with no centralized authority (the flying formations of birds) can be simulated with a few simple rules, it seems feasible that such rules play a similar role in reconciling individual initiative and overall coordination within companies. Some companies do not plan strategy in any formal sense, but craft simple rules that can help locate the company where the opportunities are richest. These include rules of thumb in screening opportunities ("*boundary rules*"). Thus, Cisco's acquisitions strategy is guided by the rule that it will acquire companies with fewer than 75 employees of which 75%

are engineers. Second, rules can designate a common approach to how the company will exploit opportunities ("*how-to rules*"). Thus, Yahoo! has a few rules regarding the look and functionality of new web pages, but then gives freedom to developers to design new additions. Third, companies have rules to determine priorities in resource allocation ("*priority rules*"). Thus, Intel allocates manufacturing capacity according to each product's gross margin. It was this role that allowed it to evolve from a memory chip company to a microprocessor company even before such a transition had been determined by top management.[23] Many of Jack Welch's initiatives at GE fulfilled a similar role. Rather than offer specific direction to business-level chief executives, he introduced periodically key corporate initiatives: "Be number 1 or number 2 in your industry," "Six-sigma," "Destroy-your-business-dot-com." These stimulated and focused decentralized initiatives, but did not directly manage them.[24]

● *Establish conditions for both incremental and radical change*. If achieving the highest level of adaptive performance requires a combination of frequent small changes with occasional radical leaps, management systems can be designed to encourage these outcomes. Consider for example the reorientation of many companies' strategic planning systems from agreeing strategy inputs towards agreeing performance outputs. One of the merits of performance-based planning (at BP, for example) is that it provides strong incentives for cost reduction and continuous improvement, while establishing a framework where serious performance shortfalls trigger corporate intervention which will usually involve major strategic changes.

● *Accelerate evolution through flexible organizational structure*. Organizational structures tend to ossify over time as power centers build and interactions become institutionalized. Periodic large-scale corporate reorganizations are not enough: to exploit innovation and entrepreneurial initiative, flexibility in organizational structure is essential. Eisenhardt and Brown use the term "patching" to describe a process in which new organizational units are continually being created, merged, and redefined to foster initiative.[25] Achieving flexibility may require leaving structures only partially defined. This may be especially effective in assisting collaboration between different business units within a company. Rather than attempt to manage business unit linkages from the corporate level, it may be better for corporate to create a context within which businesses can co-evolve. The key elements of such a context are, first, linking rewards to individual business performance rather than to reward collaborative efforts; second, maintaining porous boundaries to each business such that a multiplicity of voluntary collaborations can thrive between individuals across the businesses. Walt Disney Company exemplifies co-evolution between different internal divisions. Disney's *Lion King* movie spawned videos, theme park attractions, a stage musical, and over 150 kinds of merchandise. These spinoffs were not planned by corporate strategists; they occurred through voluntary cooperation across Disney's different divisions.[26]

● *Use adaptive tension to position at the edge of chaos*. Given the tendency for too little tension to produce inertia and too much to create chaos, the challenge for top management is to create a level of adaptive tension that optimizes the pace of organizational change and innovation. Bill McKelvey shows how Jack Welch's management style may be interpreted from a complexity viewpoint as imposing a set of rules and powerful incentives that established levels of adaptive tension between the 1st and 2nd critical values. The rule of "Be number 1 or number 2 in your industry" combined with powerful incentives for individual managers established conditions highly conducive to rapid adaptation.[27]

Applications of complexity theory to strategy management promise to add analytic support to the argument of Mintzberg and others in favor of *emergent* rather than *planned* approaches to strategy making. Mintzberg's critique of the "planning" and "design" schools of strategy making was based on the argument that intuition and decentralized processes were better ways to make strategy than rational frameworks and systematic decision processes.[28] However, by establishing a body of theory that shows how self-organization and localized adaptation can take an organization toward the edge of chaos, complexity theory provides a sound intellectual basis for Mintzberg's intuition. Many of the changes that have taken place in the strategic planning systems of large companies in recent years – reduced formality, emphasis on performance goals, focus on direction rather than content – are consistent with the tenets of complexity theory.[29]

Real Options

We noted in Chapter 2 that there are two sources of value for individual projects or entire firms: cash flows and options. In recent years considerable progress has been made in developing principles and techniques for the valuation of real option values. Most of this analysis has been developed for valuing individual investment projects, though the same principles can be extended to valuing entire companies. However, despite these developments, our techniques of strategy analysis rest heavily upon the first component of firm value – cash flows to the firm. Thus, our analyses of industries and of resources and capabilities are primarily directed towards identifying the potential for profits.

As the business environment becomes increasingly volatile and unpredictable, the value of both projects and firms becomes increasingly dependent on option values. Under these circumstances, the principles of real option valuation become important not just to the appraisal of investment projects but also to the formulation of firm strategy. From an options viewpoint, strategy is concerned with creating and managing options.

Analysis of strategy in terms of option-creation has focused on particular types of strategic decisions – for example, R&D decisions,[30] acquisitions,[31] and alliance formation.[32] However, application of real options thinking to strategic analysis at a broader level has been limited to broad generalizations, such as the value of flexibility. If we are to take on board options thinking more widely, then we need to reconsider most of our core strategy models and strategy techniques. For example:

● Industry analysis has taken the view that decisions about industry attractiveness depend on profit potential. However, if industry structure becomes so unstable that forecasting industry profitability is no longer viable, it is likely that industry attractiveness will depend much more on option value. From an options perspective, an attractive industry is one that is rich in options – for example, an industry that produces a number of different products, is comprised of multiple segments, has many strategic groups, utilizes a diversity of alternative technologies and raw materials, and where internal mobility barriers tend to be low. Thus, consumer electronics, semiconductors, packaging, and investment banking would seem to be more attractive in terms of options than electricity or steel or car rental.

● An options approach also has major implications for the analysis of resources and capabilities. An attractive resource is one that offers opportunities for deployment in multiple businesses and to support alternative strategies. A Scottish island is likely to offer greater option value than a North Sea oilfield. Similarly with capabilities: highly specialized capabilities such as expertise in the design of petrochemical plants offers less option potential than expertise in the marketing of fast-moving consumer goods. The importance of dynamic capabilities is their ability to create new options. According to Eisenhardt and Martin, "Dynamic capabilities are the organizational and strategic routines by which firms achieve new resource combinations as markets emerge, collide, split, evolve, and die."[33]

Redesigning the Organization

As business environments become more complex, more competitive, and less predictable, survival requires that companies perform at a higher level with a broader repertoire of capabilities. Building multiple capabilities and achieving excellence across multiple performance dimensions requires managing dilemmas that cannot be resolved as simple tradeoffs. A company must produce at low cost, while also innovating; it must deploy the massed resources of a large corporation, while showing the entrepreneurial flair of a small startup; it must achieve high levels of reliability and consistency, while also being flexible. All of these dilemmas are aspects of the underlying conflict between achieving operational efficiency today, and adapting for tomorrow. Reconciling these conflicts within a single organization presents huge management challenges. We know how to devise structures and incentive systems that drive cost efficiency; we also know the organizational conditions conducive to innovation. But how on earth do we do both simultaneously?

Among the new developments in organizational design, two major trends may be discerned. The first is the design of organizations to facilitate the development and deployment of organizational capability. The second is the design of organizations to permit rapid adaptability.

Capability-based Structures

In Chapter 6, we noted that organizational design has been dominated by the requirements of cooperation rather than coordination. As a result, hierarchical structures have emphasized control and the need for unitary lines of command. Once we acknowledge that building outstanding capabilities is the primary goal of organizational design, then the emphasis shifts to the need to achieve effective coordination. If we accept that most enterprises need to deploy multiple capabilities and the coordination needs of different capabilities vary, it follows that our organizational structure must encompass different patterns of interaction. Hence, most business enterprises are unlikely to be successful with a unitary structure and will need to encompass multiple structures.

Beyond Unitary Structures   The principles of knowledge management offer one approach to understanding how different capabilities require different types of structure. Knowledge management distinguishes between activities directed toward building the firm's stock of knowledge and those directed toward deploying the existing stock of knowledge. James March refers to the former as *exploration* and the latter as *exploitation*.[34] The observation that exploratory capabilities (R&D and market research, for example) need to be organized differently from knowledge-exploiting capabilities (operations and finance, for example) is well known. A more difficult challenge is the fact that the same people undertake both exploratory and exploitation activities as part of their same jobs. Thus, a plant manager may be primarily engaged in knowledge exploitation, but when s/he is involved in training activities, new product development, and benchmarking studies, his/her emphasis is exploration.

The solution is the simultaneous deployment of different structures for different tasks.[35] Thus, the primary structure of the firm is established for the basic tasks of knowledge exploitation – purchasing, producing, selling, distributing. However, exploratory activities, such as new product development, typically require interacting with different people within a different type of collaborative relationship. Here, a multifunctional product development team is more conducive to developing and applying product development capability. Similarly, for identifying and transferring manufacturing best practices, an informal cooperative group comprising different plant managers is likely to be most effective.

Separate structures for pursuing the exploratory activities required for developing and adapting the organization have been described as *parallel learning structures*.[36] While operational tasks typically require high levels of specialization and coordination through rules and routines, activities oriented toward innovation and adaptation require lower levels of specialization and coordination through planning and mutual adjustment, both of which are likely to be communication intensive. For example, at 3M, the formal structure exists in terms of business units and divisions within which individuals have clearly defined job tasks. In addition, there is an informal structure for the purpose of new product development whereby individuals are permitted, indeed encouraged, to "bootleg" time, materials, and use of facilities to work on new product ideas. Promising new products that emerge from the informal structure are taken within the formal structure.

GE's "Work-Out" program was a classic example of a parallel structure effecting change within the formal structure. Work-Out sessions took the form of meetings held away from GE's offices, where the norms that governed the formal organization were suspended, and free interchange of ideas was encouraged. The outcome was a powerful device for initiating change within the formal structure.

Where the purpose of the new structures is to develop capabilities, they may be almost entirely informal. The appendix to Chapter 5 discussed informal knowledge-sharing networks called *communities of practice*.[37] Within the Royal Dutch Shell Group of companies, over 100 communities of practice have emerged. These have been merged into about 20 Global Networks that are focused around areas of technology such as the Wells Global Network and the Subsurface Knowledge Sharing Network, and around commercial activities such as Competitor Intelligence and Procurement. Communities of practice have emerged as important vehicles for capability development at organizations ranging from Hewlett-Packard to the World Bank.[38]

Team-based, Project-based, and Process-based Structures Creating structures that foster organizational capabilities may require different patterns of interaction than are typical of conventional structures. Increased reliance on teams reflects the recognition that routines require patterns of interaction that are spontaneous and poorly understood – hence, they cannot be "managed" in any directive sense. Flexible, team-based structures can achieve the kinds of adaptable integration that are the basis of dynamic capabilities, yet, beyond some very basic requirements of team structure, we know little about the dynamics of team interaction.[39]

More companies are organizing their activities less around functions and continuous operations and more around time-designated projects where a team is assigned to a specific project with a clearly defined outcome and a specified completion date. While construction companies and consulting firms have always been structured around projects, project-based organizations, featuring temporary cross-functional teams with specific objectives, are increasingly viewed as models achieving innovation, adaptability, and rapid learning in more traditional organizations. A radical experiment in project-based organization was initiated by Oticon A/S, the Danish manufacturer of hearing aids. CEO Lars Kolind abolished Oticon's formal organization and introduced a project-based company in which over 100 self-directed projects competed to attract employees. A ten-person top management team acted as project owners, but with few decision-making responsibilities other than to enforce basic rules such as "no paper-based communication."[40]

The desire to improve coordination across multiple, linked capabilities has encouraged companies to align their structures more closely with their internal *processes*. While business process reengineering directs attention to the microstructure of processes, interest in organizational capabilities has fostered a more integrated view of processes that focuses on how individual processes fit together in sequences and networks of complementary activities. For example, a company's order fulfillment process would span the whole chain of activities, from supplying information to potential customers, to customer selection and ordering, to manufacturing, through to distribution. Similarly, the customer relations process embraces the entirety of a company's interactions with its customers through marketing and after-sales services. In many cases, these macro processes extend beyond the company. Thus, supply-chain management involves linking internal logistics with those of suppliers and suppliers' suppliers. Volvo's reorganization of its "order fulfillment process" with the goal of a 14-day cycle between customer order and customer receipt of a customized automobile involved reorganizing and reintegrating the order process, the production planning process, supply chains, the distribution process, and dealer relations.[41]

Organizing for Adaptability

One of the implications we drew from our brief review of complexity theory was the idea that, in order to cope with a complex environment, an enterprise might have to resort to simple rules. A similar implication may be drawn in relation to internal organization. To the extent that organizations are required to perform tasks whose complexity and variety require structures and systems that we cannot design for the simple reason that we do not have the knowledge, then the optimal response may be to simplify the formal structure to allow the individuals within the organization to self-organize. Loosening the structure may be a critical step toward building the *ambidextrous organization* – one that can combine multiple capabilities and accommodate both gradual change, evolutionary change, and occasional revolutionary leaps.[42]

The paradox of simplicity is that reducing complexity at the formal level can foster greater variety and sophisticated coordination at the informal level. At GE, Jack Welch's emphasized the "3Ss" – "Speed, Simplicity, Self-confidence." This resulted in reformulating control systems around just a few performance indicators and using periodic corporate initiatives ("growth," "boundarylessness," and "six-sigma") to drive change. Yet, paradoxically, this paring down of formal systems permitted more complex patterns of coordination and collaboration within GE.[43] Welch's successor, Jeff Immelt, has also relied heavily on informal, cross-boundary collaboration for developing new growth initiatives.[44] In general, the greater the potential for reordering existing resources and capabilities in complex new combinations, the greater the potential for "consensus-based hierarchies" that emphasize horizontal communication over "authority-based hierarchies" that emphasize vertical communication.[45]

This focus on organizational context rather than organizational structure is a discernible trend across many companies. Thus, most companies have given more attention to organizational culture, values, and modes of behavior, while relying more upon coordination occurring voluntarily and spontaneously. Three concepts have proven practically useful in this: *identity*, *modularity*, and *networks*.

Identity To manage the organizational context includes influencing social and behavioral norms, but these depend on some shared cognition of what the organization is and an emotional attachment towards what the organization represents. These ideas are components of what has been termed *organizational identity* – a collective understanding of what is presumed core, distinctive, and enduring about the character of an organization.[46] A strong consensus around organizational identity provides a powerful focus for flexible, coordinated action, but to the extent that identity is rooted in a past that is no longer relevant to the present, identity can represent an impediment to strategic change. To this extent companies may need to manage their external image in order to achieve a change in identity. Thus, IBM's identity as a vertically integrated supplier of mainframe computers hampered its development as a supplier of PCs, peripherals, and IT services. Changing its identity required considerable investment in projecting images that allowed the reorientation of its identity.

Modularity If the essence of dynamic capability is in building over time strong capabilities in technologies and specific functions, and in reconfiguring these to meet the requirements of a changing environment, what kind of structure can achieve such a combination of continuity and flexibility? In Chapter 6, we examined the argument that hierarchical structures based on loosely coupled, semi-autonomous modules possessed considerable adaptation advantages over more tightly integrated structures. Such modular structures may be particularly useful in reconciling the need for close collaboration at the small-group level with the benefits of critical mass.[47] Thus, the key to Microsoft's success in designing huge software programs such as Windows NT, Internet Explorer, and Microsoft Office, which require the coordinated efforts of close to 500 software developers, is to modularize these programs using its "synch and stabilize" system.[48]

Networks A key feature of the changes in strategy, structure, and management systems has been less distinction between what happens within the firm and what happens outside it. Organization theory emphasizes the distinction between the organization and its environment, while economics distinguishes between markets and hierarchies as alternate organizational mechanisms. The growth of interfirm collaboration and the development of the "contingent workforce" – people who work for companies but who are not covered by long-term employment contracts – has blurred this distinction, and theory has recognized a continuum of organizational and contractual forms between spot markets at one extreme and unitary firms at the other. As "command and control" modes of management give way to less formal patterns of coordination, so internal relationships within the firm are less differentiated from external relationships. The immediate implication is that the boundaries of the firm are less distinct and more permeable. If cooperation across individuals and small enterprises can achieve the close coordination conventionally associated with corporations, the large, integrated company may disappear as the dominant organizational form in many industries. We have already noted how networks of small firms in the Italian clothing industry simultaneously achieve integration, flexibility, and innovation. The potential for networks of small firms to emulate the advantages of large corporations is evident in the Italian motorcycle industry, where small companies such as Aprilia, Italjet, and Ducati have used integrated networks of suppliers to compete with the dominant Japanese manufacturers through innovation, design, and proliferation of models.[49]

Internet technology plays a critical role in increasing the efficiency of communication and coordination within interfirm networks. Intranets that link together internal units of the enterprise with outside suppliers, customers, and partners have had a major influence in blurring corporate boundaries. At Cisco Systems, internet systems not only link customers and suppliers for the purposes of ordering and invoicing, but also provide common systems for managing technology and joint product development and extend budgeting and strategic planning systems to its partners.[50] The internet and intranets also allow the geographical expansion of networks. Some of the most remarkable and successful network forms are the open-source software communities that have created highly successful computer software such as Linux and Apache.

Interfirm networks facilitate the design and production of complex products that require a wide range of technical and commercial capabilities in sectors subject to rapid change. In automobiles, fashion clothing, aerospace, machine tools, and telecom equipment, networks allow each firm to specialize in a few capabilities while providing the close linkages needed to integrate these different capabilities. The flexibility of these linkages offers the potential for the capabilities resident within an interfirm network to be reconfigured in order to adapt quickly to external change.[51]

New Modes of Leadership

New organizational structures and strategic priorities point to new models of leadership. The era of restructuring and shareholder focus has been associated with "change-masters"[52] – highly visible, individualistic, often hard-driving management styles of CEOs such as Lee Iacocca at Chrysler, John Browne at BP, Michael Eisner at Disney, and Rupert Murdoch at News International. These leaders have been, first and foremost, strategic decision makers, charting the direction and redirection of their companies, and making key decisions over acquisitions, divestments, new products and cost cutting.

The responses that have been suggested to the problems of complex business environments in terms of both strategy formulation and organizational design imply a very different role for the chief executive than the "buck-stops-here" peak decision-making role traditionally associated with corporate leadership. The guidelines for strategy and organization design that we have discussed so far point to management leadership as directed more toward the creation and maintenance of the organizational environment rather than decision making per se.

If the foundation of strategy is a sense of organizational identity, then a key role of top management is to clarify and communicate that identity. James Collins and Jerry Porras, in their influential study of successful companies *Built to Last*, emphasize the critical and complementary roles of *core values*, *core purpose*, and an *envisioned future*.[53]

The role of values and purpose is not just to provide a foundation for strategy, but also to unify and inspire the efforts of organizational members. To this end, the purpose and values of the enterprise must be consistent with those of its employees. To the extent that our lives are a search for meaning, the satisfaction that our work offers will depend critically on the congruence between organizational purpose and our own aspirations. British Petroleum's 2000 rebranding included the theme "beyond petroleum," an attempt to communicate a more meaningful and resonant image to its stakeholders than the production of petroleum products. Ultimately, creating a common identity between the organization and those who work within it may require the organization to recognize the existence of human emotion and, ultimately, the human soul.[54]

What do these considerations imply about the job of the chief executive and the top management team? The emphasis has shifted away from "the CEO as decision maker" towards "the CEO leader of organizational culture, climate, identity, and processes responsible for clarifying shared vision; enriching the culture; aligning vision, strategy, organizational design, and human resources; and promoting understanding of events."

These roles are likely to require different types of management skills:

> *The balance has clearly shifted from attributes traditionally thought of as masculine (strong decision-making, leading the troops, driving strategy, waging competitive battle) to more feminine qualities (listening, relationship-building, and nurturing). The model today is not so much "take it on your shoulders" as it is to "create the environment that will enable others to carry part of the burden." The focus is on unlocking the organization's human asset potential.*[55]

Research into the psychological and demographic characteristics of successful leaders has identified few consistent or robust relationships – successful leaders come in all shapes, sizes, and personality types. However, a recent stream of research has pointed to the role of a set of personality attributes that have been referred to as *emotional intelligence*. These comprise:

- *Self-awareness* in terms of the ability to read and understand one's emotions and assess one's strengths and weaknesses, underlain by the confidence that stems from positive self-worth.
- *Self-management* in terms of control, integrity, conscientiousness, initiative, and achievement orientation.

- *Social awareness* in relation to sensing others' emotions (empathy), reading the organization (organizational awareness), and recognizing customers' needs (service orientation).
- *Social skills* in relation to influencing and inspiring others: communicating, collaborating, and building relationships with others; and managing change and conflict.[56]

In his more recent work, Goleman emphasizes the role of "social intelligence" in ability of individuals to operate effectively in organizational settings.[57]

Jim Collins' studies of companies that have achieved sustained success over long periods of time also claims to have identified some common characteristics of outstandingly successful companies. What he terms "Level 5 Leadership" involves a paradoxical combination of personal humility – often shyness – and intense resolve within the organization.[58] Transformational leaders such as Philip Morris's Joseph Cullman, Kimberley-Clark's Darwin Smith, and Nucor's Ken Iversen have combined these characteristics with a number of specific management practices:

- Giving priority to building the right team over creating the right strategy.
- Willingness to confront reality while maintaining faith in the future.
- Building organizational momentum.
- Possessing depth of knowledge concerning the fundamental economics of the business, what the company is best at, and how to ignite the passions of its people.
- Pioneering a few carefully selected technologies while maintaining skepticism over technology bandwagons.
- Maintaining discipline of thought, action, and people.

Summary

While the future remains unknowable, its roots are in the present and the past. From what we observe today, we can identify many of the key developments of the next few years. The trends that we discern in science and technology, economic development, government policies, social structure, demographics, and lifestyles will shape the business environment for the remainder of the decade. We have reviewed some of the sources of competitive advantage in the emerging business environment and the capabilities that companies will need to develop and deploy.

Some of the most critical, and difficult, issues concern the structures, systems, and styles needed to build and exercise these capabilities. The configurations that were so successful during the last two decades of the 20th century are unlikely to serve enterprises so well in this first decade of the new millennium.

Emerging theories of complexity, self-organization, knowledge management, and leadership can augment our existing standard tools of strategic management. Even more encouraging is the fact that experimentation and innovation at the coal-face of managerial practice offer lessons that are yielding solutions capable of wider application and the seeds of new principles and frameworks. AES's "honeycomb" structures, Sun Microsystems' networks of alliances, Kao Corporation's system of "biological self-control," Yahoo!'s strategy of "structured emergence," and Oticon's "spaghetti organization" suggest novel approaches to managing within complex, high-velocity environments.

Strategic management remains highly dependent on concepts and theories drawn from the basic disciplines of economics, sociology, psychology, biology, and systems theory. However, the encouraging feature of the past few years has been greater synthesis across these disciplines and between theory and practice. One indicator of progress is that strategic management is less obviously a net importer of ideas and findings from its contributing disciplines. In areas such as the analysis of competition, determinants of long-run profitability, organizational design, and the management of technology, it is strategic management scholars who are breaking new ground and influencing thinking in the underlying disciplines.

Formidable challenges lie ahead. As the opportunities for creating value from downsizing, refocusing, restructuring, and reengineering have become mined out, so managers have been forced to explore new territory seeking new sources of competitive advantage. In the aftermath of turn-of-the-century hype about the "new economy" and "new business models," it has become apparent that new sources of value are elusive. While our basic tools of strategy analysis – industry analysis and the analysis of resources and capabilities – remain valid and robust, it is clear that we shall need to continually develop our concepts and frameworks to meet the circumstances of tomorrow. The challenge is to apply what we know, recognize what we don't know, and engage in reflective observation to extend our domain of understanding.

Notes

1   P. Drucker, "The Next Society," *Economist* (November 3, 2001): survey section.

2   E. D. Beinhocker, "Strategy at the Edge of Chaos," *McKinsey Quarterly* (1997, no. 1): 24–39.

3   P. Romer, "The Soft Revolution," *Journal of Applied Corporate Finance* (Summer 1998); W. B. Arthur, "Increasing Returns and the New World of Business," *Harvard Business Review* (July–August 1996): 101–8.

4   W. B. Arthur (1996), op. cit.

5   "Catch Us if You Can," *Fortune* (February 9, 2004): 64–74; "The Skype Guys," *Time* (April 30, 2006).

6   "A Survey of Telecoms Convergence," *Economist* (October 14, 2006).

7   D. N. Barron, "Evolutionary Theory," in D. O. Faulkner and A. Campbell, *Oxford Handbook of Strategy*, vol. 1 (Oxford: Oxford University Press, 2003): 90–1.

8   S. Ghoshal, C. A. Bartlett, and P. Moran, "A New Manifesto for Management," *Sloan Management Review* (Spring 1999): 9–20.

9   "The Real CEO Pay Problem," *Fortune* (July 10, 2006).

10   "Sustainable Business," *Financial Times* (October 9, 2006): special section.

11   "Private Equity: the Uneasy Crown," *Economist* (February 8, 2007).

12   "Going Private," *Business Week* (February 27, 2006).

13   K. Laursen and N. J. Foss, "New Human Resource Management Practices, Complementarities and the Impact on Innovation Performance," *Cambridge Journal of Economics* 27 (2003): 243–63.

14   R. Whittington, A. Pettigrew, S. Peck, E. Fenton, and M. Conyon, "Change and Complementarities in the New Competitive Landscape," *Organization Science* 10 (1999): 583–600.

15   M. Zollo and S. G. Winter, "Deliberate Learning and the Evolution of Dynamic Capabilities," *Organization Science* 13 (2002): 339–51.

16   P. Senge, *The Fifth Discipline* (London: Century, 1996).

17   A. de Geus, *The Living Company* (Boston: Harvard Business School Press, 1997).

18   P. Bak, *How Nature Works: The Science of Self-organized Criticality* (New York: Copernicus, 1996).

19   M. J. Wheatley and M. Kellner Rogers, *A Simpler Way* (Berrett-Koehler, 1996).

20 For a review of the development of complexity theory and its applications to management, see P. Anderson, "Complexity Theory and Organizational Science," *Organization Science* 10 (1999): 216–32.

21 S. A. Kaufman, *The Origins of Order: Self Organization and Selection In Evolution* (New York: Oxford University Press, 1993).

22 S. L. Brown and K. M. Eisenhardt, *Competing on the Edge: Strategy as Structured Chaos* (Boston: Harvard Business School Press, 1998); W. McKelvey, "Energizing Order-creating Networks of Distributed Intelligence: Improving the Corporate Brain," *International Journal of Innovation Management* 5 (June 2001): 132–54; D. A. Levinthal, "Adaptation on a Rugged Landscape," *Management Science* 43 (1997): 934–50.

23 For discussion of the role of rules in strategy making, see K. M. Eisenhardt and D. Sull, "Strategy as Simple Rules," *Harvard Business Review* (January–February 2001): 107–16.

24 Bill McKelvey, "A Simple Rule Approach to CEO Leadership in the 21st Century" (Paper presented at the ISUFI Conference, Ostuni, Italy, September 11–13, 2003).

25 K. M. Eisenhardt and S. L. Brown, "Patching: Restitching Business Portfolios in Dynamic Markets," *Harvard Business Review* (May–June 1999): 72–84.

26 K. M. Eisenhardt and D. C. Galunic, "Coevolving: At Last, a Way to Make Synergies Work," *Harvard Business Review* (January–February 2000): 91–101.

27 Bill McKelvey, "A Simple Rule Approach to CEO Leadership," op. cit.

28 H. Mintzberg, *The Rise and Fall of Strategic Planning* (New York: Free Press, 1994); H. Mintzberg, B. Ahlstrand, and J. Lampel, *Strategy Safari: A Guided Tour through the Wilds of Strategic Management* (New York: Free Press, 1998).

29 R. M. Grant, "Strategic Planning In a Turbulent Environment: Evidence from the Oil Majors," *Strategic Management Journal* 24 (2003): 491–518.

30 R. G. McGrath, "A Real Option Logic for Initiating Technology Positioning Investment," *Academy of Management Review* 22 (1997): 974–96.

31 H. T. J. Smit, "Acquisition Strategies as Option Games," *Journal of Applied Corporate Finance* (2001): 79–89.

32 M. J. Leiblein and D. D. Miller, "An Empirical Examination of the Effect of Uncertainty and Firm Strategy on the Vertical Boundaries of the Firm," *Strategic Management Journal* 24 (2003): 839–60.

33 K. M. Eisenhardt and J. A. Martin, "Dynamic Capabilities: What are They?" *Strategic Management Journal* 21 (2000): 1105–21.

34 J. G. March, "Exploration and Exploitation in Organizational Learning," *Organization Science* 2 (1991): 71–8.

35 J. Ridderstråle, "Business Moves Beyond Bureaucracy," *Financial Times*, Mastering Management (November 6, 2000): 14–15.

36 G. Bushe and A. B. Shani, *Parallel Learning Structures* (Reading, MA: Addison-Wesley, 1991).

37 J. S. Brown and P. Duguid, "Organizational Learning and Communities of Practice," *Organizational Science* 2 (1991): 40–57.

38 E. C. Wenger and W. M. Snyder, "Communities of Practice: The Organizational Frontier," *Harvard Business Review* (January–February 2000).

39 J. R. Katzenbach and D. K. Smith, "The Discipline of Teams," *Harvard Business Review* (March–April 1993): 111–20.

40 For description and analysis of the Oticon experiment, see "This Organization Is Disorganization," *Fast Company* (April 1997): 77–83; and N. J. Foss, "Internal Disaggregation in Oticon: An Organizational Economics Interpretation of the Rise and Decline of the Spaghetti Organization" (Department of Industrial Economics and Strategy, Copenhagen Business School, October 2000).

41 S. Hertz, J. K. Johansson, and F. de Jager, "Customer-focused Cost Cutting: Process Management at Volvo," *Journal of Supply Chain Management* 6, no. 3 (2001): 128–41.

42 M. L. Tushman and C. A. O'Reilly III, "The Ambidextrous Organization: Managing Evolutionary and Revolutionary Change," *California Management Review* 38, no. 4 (Summer 1996): 8–30.

43 "Jack Welch and the General Electric Management System," in R. M. Grant, *Cases to Accompany Contemporary Strategy Analysis*, 6th edn (Oxford: Blackwell, 2008).

44 "Jeff Immelt at General Electric, 2001–2006," in R. M. Grant, *Cases to Accompany Contemporary Strategy Analysis*, ibid.

45 J. A. Nickerson and T. R. Zenger, "The Knowledge-based Theory of the Firm – A Problem-solving Perspective," *Organization Science* 15 (2004): 617–32.

46 D. A. Gioia, M. Schultz, and K. G. Corley, "Organizational Identity, Image and Adaptive Instability," *Academy of Management Review* 25 (2000): 63–81.

47 R. Sanchez and T. Mahoney, "Modularity, Flexibility and Knowledge Management in Product and Organization Design," *Strategic Management Journal* 17, Winter Special Issue (1996): 63–76; M. A. Schilling, "Toward a General Modular Systems Theory and its Application to Inter-firm Product Modularity," *Academy of Management Review* 25 (2000): 312–34.

48 M. A. Cusumano, "How Microsoft Makes Large Teams Work Like Small Teams," *Sloan Management Review* (Fall 1997): 9–20.

49 G. Lorenzoni and A. Lipparini, "Organizing around Strategic Relationships," in K. Cool, J. Henderson, and R. Abate (eds), *Restructuring Strategy* (Oxford: Blackwell Publishing, 2005).

50 P. J. Brews, "The Challenge of the Web-Enabled Business," *Financial Times*, Mastering Management (November 27, 2000): 4–7. See also D. Tapscott, D. Ticoll, and A. Lowry, *Digital Capital: Harnessing the Power of Business Webs* (Boston: Harvard Business School Press, 2000).

51 R. Gulati, N. Nohria, and A. Zaheer, "Strategic Networks," *Strategic Management Journal* 21 (2000): 203–15, reviews recent research into inter-firm networks.

52 R. M. Kanter, *The Change Masters* (New York: Simon & Schuster, 1983).

53 J. C. Collins and J. I. Porras, *Built to Last* (New York: Harper Business, 1996).

54 L. Grattan, *Living Strategy: Putting People at the Heart of Corporate Purpose* (London: Prentice Hall, 2000).

55 Ruth L. Williams and Joseph P. Cothrel, "Building Tomorrow's Leaders Today," *Strategy and Leadership* 26 (September–October 1997): 17–23.

56 D. Goleman, "What Makes a Leader?" *Harvard Business Review* (November–December 1998): 93–102.

57 D. Goleman, *Social Intelligence: The New Science of Human Relationships* (New York: Bantam Books, 2006).

58 J. Collins, "Level 5 Leadership: The Triumph of Humility and Fierce Resolve," *Harvard Business Review* (January 2001): 67–76.

INDEX